INTRODUCTION
TO CONTEMPORARY MUSIC

FOR

ERNEST AND RED HELLER

Braque, *Woman with Mandolin.*

INTRODUCTION TO CONTEMPORARY MUSIC

By

JOSEPH MACHLIS

PROFESSOR OF MUSIC
QUEENS COLLEGE OF THE CITY OF NEW YORK

HARLAXTON COLLEGE
UNIVERSITY OF EVANSVILLE
GRANTHAM, LINCS.

011443

LONDON: J. M. DENT & SON LTD.

CONTENTS

Part Two. THE EUROPEAN SCENE

I. LATE ROMANTICS

II. IMPRESSIONISM

Contents

III. THREE REPRESENTATIVE COMPOSERS

IV. AWAY FROM IMPRESSIONISM

Contents

Contents xvii

PREFACE

THIS BOOK attempts to lead the reader to an understanding and enjoyment of twentieth-century music. It surveys the broad panorama of the contemporary scene and tries to assess the forces that have shaped the musical climate we inhabit.

Musicians would generally agree as to the identity of the handful of composers who have played the decisive roles on the musical scene of our time. There would be far less agreement about the composers who occupy less commanding positions. Where those are concerned, no two musicians would see eye to eye about who should receive greater emphasis and who less. My aim has been to present the total picture: both the main trends and the subsidiary currents.

It would be pleasant to say that this work stands above geographical considerations. Such, however, is not the case. Books coming out of Paris or London devote considerable space to composers who are hardly known in the United States, but who are important in the musical life of their own country. By the same token, I have described at some length the doings of the American school. Some may feel that I have overemphasized our native music. Yet I believe that in a book written out of the American scene, this is as it should be.

I have discussed in detail only works that are available on records, as I consider it pointless for anyone to read about a piece of music unless he can hear it. This procedure offered no difficulty for the major figures, who are very well represented on records. In a few cases, it was a problem. For example, I originally included a discussion of Milhaud's First Symphony; but the piece was dropped from the record catalog just as I finished the book, and I had to substitute something else. The same thing happened with Dallapiccola's *Canti di Prigionia*.

Although no one can free himself entirely from his prejudices, I have tried not to inflict mine upon the reader. My goal, rather, is to explain what the composer set out to do and how he went about doing it—in other words, to prepare the reader for the music instead of making up his mind for him in advance.

I should like to acknowledge my indebtedness to Paul Henry Lang for his careful reading of the manuscript; to Jay Harrison for many exciting conversations on contemporary musical problems; and to Barbara Fried for her devoted editing of the copy. For innumerable kindnesses I am grateful to Barbara Greener, Music Librarian of Queens College, and her associate Anita Randolfi; and to Catherine K. Miller and the staff of the Music Branch of the New York Public Library. I am much obliged to Dr. Hans Heinsheimer of G. Schirmer, to Mr. George Marek of RCA Victor, to Mr. Goddard Lieberson of Columbia Records, to Mr. George Mendelssohn of Vox Records, to Mr. Kurt Stone of Associated Music Publishers and to Mr. Richard Wangerin of the Louisville Orchestra for making available to me the scores and recordings of some of the works discussed in this book; to Mr. Oliver Daniel of Broadcast Music, Inc., for supplying me with data concerning some of the composers; and to Mr. Maxwell Weaner for autographing the music examples.

JOSEPH MACHLIS

ACKNOWLEDGMENTS

The following acknowledgments are made for permission to reprint musical examples

Samuel Barber, Overture to *The School for Scandal*, Copyright by G. Schirmer, Inc. Reprinted by permission. *Medea's Meditation and Dance of Vengeance*, Copyright by G. Schirmer, Inc. Reprinted by permission. *Essay for Orchestra, No. 1*, Copyright by G. Schirmer, Inc. Reprinted by permission.

Béla Bartók, Fourth String Quartet, Copyright 1929 by Universal Editions, renewed 1956. Copyright and renewal assigned to Boosey & Hawkes, Inc. Used by permission. *Music for String Instruments, Percussion and Celesta*, Copyright 1937 by Universal Editions. Copyright assigned to Boosey & Hawkes, Inc. Used by permission. *Allegro Barbaro*, Copyright 1918 by Universal Editions. Copyright assigned to Boosey & Hawkes, Inc. Used by permission. Concerto for Orchestra, Copyright 1946 by Hawkes & Son (London) Ltd. Used by permission.

Alban Berg, *Wozzeck*, Copyright 1926, Renewed 1954 by Universal Edition A. G., Vienna. Violin Concerto, Copyright 1936 by Universal Edition A. G., Vienna.

Leonard Bernstein, *Jeremiah* Symphony, Copyright 1943 and 1945 by Harms, Inc.

Ernest Bloch, *Schelomo*, Copyright by G. Schirmer, Inc. Reprinted by permission. Benjamin Britten, *Peter Grimes*, Copyright 1945 by Boosey & Hawkes Ltd. Used by permission.

Carlos Chávez, *Sinfonía India*, Copyright 1950 by G. Schirmer, Inc.

Aaron Copland, Symphony No. 3, Copyright 1947 by Boosey & Hawkes Ltd. Used by permission. *Appalachian Spring*, Copyright 1945 by Hawkes & Son (London), Ltd. Used by permission.

Claude Debussy, *The Sunken Cathedral; Pelléas and Mélisande; Pagodes; La Fille aux cheveux de lin; Soirée dans Grenade; Ce qu'a vu le vent d'Ouest; General Lavine—Eccentric; Ibéria*. Permission for reprint granted by Durand et Cie, Paris, France, copyright owners; Elkan-Vogel Co., Inc., Philadelphia, Pennsylvania, agents.

Norman Dello Joio, *Variations, Chaconne and Finale*, copyright 1950 by Carl Fischer, Inc., New York.

Lukas Foss, *A Parable of Death*, copyright 1953 by Carl Fischer, Inc., New York.

George Gershwin, *An American in Paris*, Copyright 1929 by New World Music Corporation.

Charles Tomlinson Griffes, *The Pleasure Dome of Kubla Khan*, Copyright by G. Schirmer, Inc. Reprinted by permission.

The Rite of Spring, Copyright 1921 by Edition Russe de Musique. Copyright assigned to Boosey & Hawkes. Used by permission. *Symphony of Psalms*, Copyright by Edition Russe de Musique. Copyright assigned to Boosey & Hawkes. Revised version copyright 1948 by Boosey & Hawkes. Used by permission. *Agon*, Copyright 1957 by Boosey & Hawkes, Inc. Used by permission. *Threni*, Copyright 1958 by Boosey and Company, Ltd. Used by permission.

Randall Thompson, *The Testament of Freedom*, Copyright 1943 by Randall Thompson. Copyright assigned 1944 to E. C. Schirmer Company, Boston.

Virgil Thomson, *Louisiana Story*, Copyright 1948, 1949 by Virgil Thomson.

Heitor Villa-Lobos, *Bachianas Brasileiras*, Copyright 1947 by Associated Music Publishers, Inc., New York.

William Walton, *Belshazzar's Feast*, Copyright 1931 by Oxford University Press, London.

Anton Webern, Five Orchestral Pieces, Copyright 1923, renewed 1951 by Universal Edition A. G., Vienna. Symphony, Op. 21, Copyright 1929, renewed 1956 by Universal Edition A. G., Vienna. Cantata No. 1, Copyright 1957 by Universal Editions A. G., Vienna.

Part One

THE MATERIALS OF CONTEMPORARY MUSIC

"Music was chaste and modest so long as it was played on simpler instruments, but since it has come to be played in a variety of manners and confusedly, it has lost the mode of gravity and virtue and fallen almost to baseness."

Boethius (c. 480–524)

"Music was originally discreet, seemly, simple, masculine, and of good morals. Have not the moderns rendered it lascivious beyond measure?"

Jacob of Liège (c. 1425)

"They are so enamored of themselves as to think it within their power to corrupt, spoil, and ruin the good old rules handed down in former times by so many theorists and most excellent musicians, the very men from whom these moderns have learned to string together a few notes with little grace. For them it is enough to create a tumult of sounds, a confusion of absurdities, an assemblage of imperfections."

G. M. Artusi (1600)

"The Overture to Beethoven's opera *Fidelio* was performed recently, and all impartial musicians and music lovers were in complete agreement that never was anything written in music so incoherent, shrill, muddled and utterly shocking to the ear."

August von Kotzebue (1806)

"Serious music is a dead art. The vein which for three hundred years offered a seemingly inexhaustible yield of beautiful music has run out. What we know as modern music is the noise made by deluded speculators picking through the slagpile."

Henry Pleasants: *The Agony of Modern Music* (1955)

1

The Old and the New

"The modern and the old have always been."
Ferruccio Busoni

ONE THING in history never changes, and that is the element of change itself. True, men always resist the unfamiliar. But the dynamism of life forces them on to ever new perspectives and new solutions. The story of mankind is the story of a continual becoming, a ceaseless adventure whose frontiers ever widen.

What does change, from one age to the next, is the rate of change. Certain periods are comparatively stable. The force of tradition is strong, and acts to brake the new modes of thought that are struggling to be born. At other times society is in a state of flux. Horizons open up with breathtaking rapidity, and changes that in other epochs would be spread over many generations are telescoped into a single lifetime. Ours is such an era. Today the rate of change, both social and cultural, has been enormously accelerated. Life demands from us signal powers of adjustment if we are not to be left behind.

Music, one of the major manifestations of man's creative impulse, has changed constantly through the ages, as every living language must. Each generation of musicians inherits a tradition, an established body of usages and techniques which it enriches by its own efforts and passes on to the next generation. At three points in the history of music—as it happens, they were equally distant from each other—the forces of change were so much in the ascendant that the word *new* became a battle cry. Around the year 1300 progressive composers were referred to as *moderni* and their art designated as *ars nova*, "New Art." The breakthrough of this modernism produced new rhythmic and harmonic principles as well as basic reforms in notation. The year 1600 is another such landmark. The contemporaries of Monteverdi raised the banner of *le nuove musiche*, "The New Music"; expressive melody and the dramatic concept of opera challenged the tradition of religious choral music. Similarly, around 1900 there emerged the New Music, with an explosiveness that gave rise to many a bitter battle.

At the turn of the twentieth century the first signs of change revealed themselves in art before they appeared in the decaying social structure.

3

Europe was still living in traditional bourgeois comfort when revolutionary rumblings began to be heard in literature, painting, and music. The old order collapsed with the First World War, giving enormous impetus to the forces of change. During the decade of the war and in the 1920s the New Music made prodigious strides forward.

EVOLUTION OR REVOLUTION?

The new is born from the old and retains certain features of the old. In the heat of battle the new may seem like the ruthless destroyer of the old; but when the tumult subsides its innovations stand revealed as the inevitable continuation of the past. In the early years of this century audiences were persuaded that the art of music as they had known it was coming to an end, and responded accordingly. Perfectly respectable individuals in Paris and Vienna hissed and hooted, banged chairs, and engaged in fisticuffs with strangers. Less than half a century later, the works that caused these antics are enthroned as classics of the modern repertory. The men who wrote them are acknowledged masters; their disciples occupy key positions in our conservatories and colleges. The techniques and procedures once regarded as startling have become part of the accepted vocabulary of musical art. Although we like to think that human nature never changes, actually we are more adaptable than we suspect. Music that bewildered and jarred the listeners of fifty years ago is today heard by a rapidly growing public with every evidence of pleasure.

We are still too close to this great upheaval to be able to pass final judgment upon it. Yet, now that more than half our century is over, we can begin to view the New Music with some measure of perspective, and see that what at first appeared to be a violent revolution was in reality a necessary evolution. Significantly, the leaders of the modern movement disclaimed revolutionary intent. "I hold that it was error," Igor Stravinsky wrote, "to regard me as a revolutionary. If one only need break habit in order to be labeled a revolutionary, then every artist who has something to say and who in order to say it steps outside the bounds of established convention could be considered revolutionary." And Arnold Schoenberg to the same point: "I personally hate to be called a revolutionary, which I am not. What I did was neither revolution nor anarchy."

These statements attest to what every artist knows: that rules are not broken for the sheer joy of breaking them. For the artist, as for the philosopher, there is no absolute freedom, only freedom as "the recognition of necessity." The artist accepts the necessity of rules just as boys do when they play baseball, and for the same reason: to achieve freedom of action within a self-imposed frame. If he discards the inherited rules it is only because they have ceased to be meaningful—that is, fruitful—for him. He rejects them only so that he may impose other rules upon himself. In short, the rules change, but not the concept of rule, the eternal principle of law and order which is basic to the discipline of art.

When the New Music was first heard, people asked why composers could not go on writing like Tchaikovsky or Puccini. The answer is obvious. Art, as an integral part of life, has to change just as life itself changes. The melodies of Tchaikovsky and Puccini were part of the nineteenth-century world. Stravinsky, Schoenberg, Bartók, and their contemporaries no longer inhabited that world. They had perforce to move on, to discover melodies that would express the present as eloquently as those of the masters had expressed the past.

The last fifty years have witnessed a vast expansion of musical resources. New conceptions have enriched the language of music, and have had a great impact upon the artistic consciousness of our epoch. Contemporary music, so rich in its diversity of expression, so excitingly attuned to the spirit of the twentieth century, is the latest—consequently the most vivid—chapter in man's age-old attempt to impose his artistic intuitions upon the elusive stuff of sound: that majestic five thousand-year-old attempt to shape the sonorous material into forms possessing logic and continuity, expressive meaning and nourishing beauty.

WHAT IS MODERN?

We use the term *modern*, as we do baroque, classical, or romantic, to describe events of a certain period in time. Yet it would be wiser to avoid drawing hard and fast boundaries around the art of a period that is still in a state of flux. Besides, every generation has its own concept of what is modern. In general, we use *modern, new, twentieth-century,* and *contemporary* as though they were interchangeable. Yet are they? *Contemporary,* strictly speaking, is a chronological designation that refers to anything happening in our time. But not everything that is contemporary is modern. For example, Rachmaninov and Gretchaninov were contemporary with Stravinsky, Schoenberg, and Bartók. They all lived in the twentieth century; yet they most certainly differed in regard to the degree of modernity in their work.

Within the range of contemporary music are composers who are ultra-conservative and those who are ultra-radical, with all manner of middle-of-the-roaders between. It is neither necessary nor possible to find a label that will cover both Sibelius and Anton Webern, both Menotti and Karlheinz Stockhausen. In this book, therefore, we will use *contemporary* in its broadest sense as synonymous with twentieth-century music, taking as our point of departure the beginning of our century. *"New Music"* is a narrower term, and is used here to refer to the styles that emerged immediately before and after the First World War.

There was a time when books on modern music appealed to the reader to rid himself of his prejudices and to approach the subject with an open mind. Such exhortations are no longer necessary. We live in twentieth-century houses, we wear twentieth-century clothes, and we think twentieth-century ideas. Why then should we shut ourselves off from twentieth-century music? Only those who fear the present aspire to live in the long ago. They gaze so fixedly toward the past that, in the memorable phrase of H. G. Wells, they walk into the future backwards. Let us rather lay ourselves open to all music, savoring the best of the old along with the new. In the process we shall vastly enrich our understanding of both.

❧ 2 ❧

The Twilight of Romanticism

"The pull-away from romanticism was the most important interest of the early twentieth century."

Aaron Copland

CLASSIC VERSUS ROMANTIC

A WORK of art exists on two levels. On the one hand it embodies a deeply felt experience, a moment of rapturous awareness projected by a creative temperament. On the other, it embodies a way of shaping sensuous material—sounds, colors, blocks of marble, words—into artistic forms, according to techniques and procedures that derive from the nature of that material. In other words, a work of art possesses an expressive content and a formal content.

Form and content are indivisible parts of the whole. They can no more be separated than can body and mind. However, the emphasis may rest upon the one or the other. We call that attitude *classical* which seeks above all to safeguard the purity of form. We call that attitude *romantic* which concerns itself primarily with the expression of emotion.

The classicist exalts the values of order, lucidity, restraint. He seeks purity of style and harmonious proportion, striving to bring to perfection what already exists rather than to originate new forms. Achieving a certain measure of detachment from the art work, he expresses himself through symbols that have a universal validity. The romanticist, on the other hand, exalts the unique character of his personal reactions and strives always for the most direct expression of his emotions. He rebels against tradition, valuing passionate utterance above perfection of form. He sees the strangeness and wonder of life. His is an art of infinite yearning, rich in mood and atmosphere, picturesque detail, and striking color. Music for him is an enchantment of the senses, an outpouring of the heart.

Classic and romantic correspond to two fundamental impulses in man's nature: classicism to his love of traditional standards, his desire that emotion be purged and controlled within a form, romanticism to his longing for the unattainable, his need for ecstasy and intoxication. Both impulses have asserted themselves throughout the history of art. There have been times, however, when one markedly predominated over the other. One such era was the nineteenth century, which has come to be called the age of romanticism.

THE ROMANTIC MOVEMENT (c. 1820–1900)

The French Revolution signalized the birth of a new society which glorified the individual as never before. Freedom was its watchword: freedom of religion, freedom of enterprise, political and personal freedom. On the artistic front this need for untrammeled individualism took shape in the romantic movement. The romantic spirit pervaded the arts of poetry and painting, as is amply attested by the works of Keats and Shelley, Delacroix, Turner and their contemporaries. But it was in music that romanticism found its ideal expression: music, the art of elusive meanings and indefinable moods.

The nineteenth-century climate was hospitable to the belief that the prime function of music is to express emotion. The short lyric forms— art song and piano piece—came to the fore, incarnating all the youthful exuberance of the romantic movement. Schubert, Schumann, and

Mendelssohn, Chopin, Liszt, and Brahms carried this appealing genre to its finest flower, finding the romantic song and piano piece ideal for subjective lyricism and intimate communication with the listener.

At the same time the nineteenth century was drawn to the spectacular and the grandiose. Having inherited the symphony from Beethoven, the romantic composers transformed it into a vehicle for purple rhetoric and dramatic gesture—two elements dear to the age of Byron and Victor Hugo. Theirs was a music of sumptuous color and shattering climaxes, rich in poetic utterance, based upon the sonorous magic of the orchestra. Berlioz, Wagner, and Liszt were the leading proponents of what they boldly called "the Music of the Future." They perfected the genre of program music—that is to say, of music associated with specific literary or pictorial images—in which a poetic idea assumed a central position within the expressive scheme. In so doing they established music as a language of symbols, as the expression of literary-philosophical, world-encompassing ideas that must actuate all mankind. Program music was as basic to the nineteenth century as "pure" or absolute music was to the classically minded eighteenth. Why? Because to the romantic composer music was more than a manipulation of themes, harmonies, rhythms. To him, the sounds were inseparably allied with feelings about life and death, love and longing, God, nature, man defying his fate. To return to the terminology of the beginning of this chapter, the romantic musician valued the expressive content of music more than he did its purely formal content.

The central figure in the nineteenth-century ferment was Richard Wagner (1813–1883), whose grandiose dramas best exemplify the German penchant for attaching "deep" meanings to music. Nature and intuition are glorified in his operas, which hymn German forest and mountain, the Rhine, the ancient Teutonic myths of gods and heroes; which sing of love and passion with an abandon never before achieved; and in which, in *The Ring of the Nibelung*, the proceedings on stage are infused with all manner of political, moral and philosophical symbols. Wagner expressed the typically romantic desire for a "union of the arts." If music, poetry, and painting could produce such moving effects separately, how much greater would be their impact if they were combined. He was persuaded that only in his theater would all the arts find their mutual fulfillment: music, poetry, and drama, dance, painting (scenery), and sculpture (the plastic movements and poses of the actors). Through his use of *Leitmotive* or "leading motives"—compact themes which symbolize characters, emotions, ideas, and even objects in his dramas—he brought to its farthermost limits the romantic attempt to make music conjure up specific images and feelings. Wagner's harmonic procedures, we shall see, had decisive importance for those who came after him. *Tristan and Isolde* heralds the impending crises in romanticism, in harmonic language, and in the whole system of assumptions on which western music was based.

A classicist strain in romanticism was exemplified in the early part of the century by Mendelssohn, in the latter part by Brahms. These two composers were quite different from one another; and they differed even more from a musician like Verdi. Yet all three had in common a horror of philosophical disquisitions in music, and a desire to make their art function on a purely abstract level of expressivity. The most vociferous exponent of this classical point of view was the critic Eduard Hanslick (1825–1904). He is remembered today chiefly as the prototype of Beckmesser, Wagner's savage caricature of a hidebound pedant in *Die Meistersinger*. Actually, Hanslick was an able thinker who disliked Wagner's ideas rather than his music. He was irreconcilably opposed to the extramusical trend of the "Music of the Future." And he enthusiastically supported the attempts of his friend Brahms to lead music back to the purity of the absolute forms—to the symphony and sonata which the nineteenth century had inherited from the eighteenth.

The conflict between classical form and romantic content was thus basic to the romantic era. As the century wore on, the schism between these two esthetic attitudes widened steadily, irreparably.

THE END OF AN EPOCH

Increasing reliance upon extramusical elements—literary, pictorial, emotional—could not but weaken the sense of form and order in music. In the second half of the nineteenth century, structural values gave way in ever greater degree to autobiography, sensual intoxication, and "nature" pictures. Unbridled emotionalism came to be characteristic of a style that made more and more use of gargantuan orchestral forces and overexpanded forms. Harmony and orchestration were vastly developed at the expense of rhythm and structure. This emphasis upon emotion and self-expression ended in an exacerbated individualism. Traits appeared that invariably attend the twilight of a style: a tendency toward bombast and verbosity; a fondness for the theatrical and the grandiose; a sonorous apparatus and a wealth of effect in no way commensurate with the idea content. The irrepressible vitality that had carried music through the nineteenth century was depleted. It became apparent that the romantic impulse had exhausted itself.

The modern movement in art took shape as a violent reaction against everything the nineteenth century had stood for. Fernand Léger, *The Three Musicians*. (Collection Museum of Modern Art)

One of the first tasks of the New Music, consequently, was to shake off the burden of a tradition that was no longer fruitful. The twentieth century had to assert its independence much as an adolescent has to rebel against his parents. The revolt was twofold. Composers not only had to free themselves from the domination of their immediate predecessors, they also had to fight the romanticism within themselves. The

modern movement in art took shape as a violent reaction against everything that the nineteenth century had stood for. "The pull-away from
romanticism" was the crucial issue throughout the first part of our
century.

Out of this need came an irresistible swing toward a new classicism,
a powerful trend which was nothing less than a revolution in style
and taste.

·§ 3 §·

The Classical Heritage

"When a nation brings its innermost nature to consummate expression in arts and letters, we speak of its classic period."
Paul Henry Lang: *Music in Western Civilization*

THE CLASSICAL ERA (c. 1775–1825)

THE CLASSICAL period in music extended through the half century that
preceded the romantic. It reached its high point with the masters of
the Viennese school—Haydn, Mozart, Beethoven, and Schubert.

The classical era witnessed the American and French revolutions, as
well as the English movement for political reform. These countries
passed from absolute monarchy to a system based on political democracy
and capitalist technology. The art of the classical period reflects the
unique moment in history when the old order was dying and the new was
in process of being born; when the elegance of the aristocratic tradition
met the vigor and humanism of a rising middle-class culture. Out of
this climate emerged the grand form in both literature and music: the
novel and the symphony, both destined to be vehicles of communication with a larger audience than had ever existed before.

The eighteenth-century artist functioned under the system of aristocratic patronage. He was attached to the household of a nobleman; he
was employed by a municipal council or church; or he was commissioned to write a work for an opera house. In any case he produced
for immediate use and was in direct contact with his public. He was
a craftsman functioning in a handicraft society, creating beauty according to the accepted precepts of his time (although on occasion
he chose to transcend those precepts). His public consisted of con-

noisseurs who were familiar with his medium by virtue of their birth. For so fastidious an audience he could be as painstaking and as subtle as he pleased.

The concept of art as self-expression was clearly not part of this environment. The artist created because he had the gift, and because the world in which he lived was eager for his product. He was far less concerned than his romantic successor with problems of esthetics and artistic inspiration, or with the opinion of posterity. Indeed, posterity was largely a nineteenth-century invention. The eighteenth-century artist created for a public high above him in social rank, who were interested in his work rather than in him as an individual. To be personal in such circumstances would have been something of an impertinence. As a result, he was impelled to classical objectivity and reserve rather than to romantic revelation of self. The art of the classical era bears the imprint of the spacious palaces that were its setting. In this milieu, emotional restraint was a prerequisite of good manners; impeccable taste was prized above all.

Alien to this world, also, was the romantic concept of art as enchantment and dream. The classical era regarded music as a necessary adornment of gracious living. The eighteenth-century composer constructed a piece for people to sing or play, to dance to or listen to as an agreeable pastime; this accounts for the prevailing good humor of so many classical works, in contrast to the sense of the tragic that pervades the art of the romantic era. The classical composer took for granted the power of music to express emotion; he therefore did not feel it necessary constantly to emphasize this aspect of his art, as did the romantic. He directed his attention rather to craftsmanship, beauty of design, and purity of style. Ecstasy and intoxication were alike foreign to his intent. Consequently he never strove for the "strangeness and wonder" of the romantics. Instead, he achieved the ideal balance between the need for expression and the control of form. There resulted an urbane art that continues to appeal, in the words of John Burroughs, to "our sense of the finely carved, the highly wrought, the deftly planned."

The classical sonata-symphony was a spacious form allowing for the expansion and development of abstract musical ideas. The characters in this instrumental drama were neither Scheherazade nor the Sorcerer's Apprentice. What concerned the listener was the fate not of the lovers but of the themes. True, these themes had expressive content and mood. They might be vivacious or sorrowful, pathetic or humorous; yet they remained wholly within the domain of absolute music. The classical symphony steered clear of personal revelation, specific emotions, lit-

When the leaders of contemporary art repudiated their romantic heritage, they inevitably returned to the classical tradition. Pablo Picasso, *Three Women at the Spring*. (Collection Museum of Modern Art)

erary and pictorial associations. There is profound emotion in the late works of Haydn and Mozart, as in the volcanic symphonism of Beethoven; but this emotion is contained within the form, lifted from the subjective to the universal, from the temporary to the enduring, through the order and discipline of classical art.

The romantics tried to draw music closer to poetry and painting;

the classical masters conceived of music as an independent, self-contained art. Romantic music glorified folk song and dance; the music of the classical era issued from the culture of cities and the sophisticated circles of the court (even if the popular tone begins to assert itself, significantly, in the lively finales of Haydn). Nineteenth-century music was intensely nationalist in spirit; the music of the late eighteenth century spoke an inter-European language deriving from two international art forms—Italian opera and Viennese symphony. For the romanticist, color and harmony, melody and rhythm existed as values in themselves. The classicist subordinated all of these to the over-all unity of the form: form as the principle of law and order in art, born from the ideal mating of reason and emotion. It is this surpassing oneness of form and content that constitutes the truly classical element in late eighteenth-century music.

Nietzsche distinguished the classic from the romantic by two vivid symbols: he opposed Apollo, god of light and harmonious proportion, to Dionysus, god of wine and intoxication. The shift from the Dionysian principle to the Apollonian, as we shall see, became the first decisive gesture of the New Music.

✍ 4 ßↄ

Melody in Contemporary Music

"The melody is generally what the piece is about."
Aaron Copland

OF ALL the elements of music, melody stands first in the affections of the public. "It is the melody," observed Haydn a century and a half ago, "which is the charm of music, and it is that which is most difficult to produce." The statement still holds.

A melody is a succession of tones grasped by the mind as a significant pattern. Some modern theorists tell us that a melody simply is a succession of tones. What they mean is that if we hear any selection of tones often enough, we will impose on it a semblance of pattern. Be that as it may, to understand a melody means to grasp its underlying unity. In order to do this, we must perceive the relationship of the beginning to the middle, of the middle to the end. We must apprehend the tones not singly, but as part of the melodic line, just as we apprehend words in a sentence not separately, but in relation to the thought as a whole. Heard in this way, the melody takes on clarity, direction, meaning.

The melody in music is analogous to the line in drawing. It must have movement, tension, and variety. Amadeo Modigliani, *Woman, Head in Hand*. (Collection Museum of Modern Art)

MELODY IN THE CLASSIC-ROMANTIC ERA

Over the course of centuries, certain conventions were evolved in order to help the listener apprehend a melody. These devices, as might be supposed, are particularly prominent in folk music and popular songs. They are also to be found in abundance in the art music of the eighteenth and nineteenth centuries. Melody in the classic-romantic era was often based on a structure of four symmetrical phrases, each four measures in length, which were set off by regularly spaced cadences. (The cadence is the point of rest, the "breathing-place" in the melodic line.) As soon as the listener heard the first phrase, he knew that the other three would be of equal duration. The balanced phrases and cadences were like so many landmarks that kept him from being lost in the trackless wastes of sound. They set up expectancies that were sure to be fulfilled.

The structure was made even clearer to the ear by the use of repetition. Often, the second phrase was like the first; the third introduced an element of variety; and the fourth established the underlying unity by returning to the material of the first two phrases. (This A-A:B-A structure still prevails in our popular songs.) So too the melody emphasized a central tone that served as a point of departure and return. The fact that there was a keynote to which all the other tones gravitated imparted a clarity of direction to the melody, and gave the listener a sense of purposeful movement toward a goal. When the listener reached the final cadence he had a sense of tension released, action consummated: the melody had completed its journey. (For an example of symmetrical melody based on four-bar phrases, see Appendix I-a.)

Through symmetrical structure, repetition of phrases, and kindred devices the masters made themselves understood by a large public. From the time of Haydn and Mozart to that of Tchaikovsky, Brahms, and Dvořák, literally thousands of melodies in western music were oriented to four-bar phrase patterns. However, although a framework such as this begins by being a support, it ends by becoming a straitjacket. The artist finds it increasingly difficult to achieve significant expression within the conventional pattern. He begins to chafe under the restrictions of a form whose resources, he feels, have been exhausted. He is impelled to seek new modes of expression. At this point the revolt against tradition sets in.

The rebellion against the stereotypes of four-square melody began long before the twentieth century. At the height of the classical era Haydn and Mozart introduced asymmetries—phrases of three, five, or six measures—which lent their music the charm of the unforeseen. It remained for Wagner to cast off the shackles of symmetrical melody. He aspired to a melodic line that would sensitively reflect the emotions of his characters, and he could not reconcile this aim with slicing up a melody into neatly balanced phrases and cadences. To achieve the necessary intensity Wagner devised what he called "endless" or "infinite" melody—a melodic line, that is, which avoided stereotyped formations by evolving freely and continuously.

The public, naturally, was much upset at this. Singers maintained that Wagner's music was unsingable; audiences and critics alike insisted that it lacked melody. They meant that it lacked the familiar landmarks on which they had come to rely. When people had had time to become familiar with Wagner's idiom they discovered that it was not lacking in melody at all. In imposing his melodic image upon the nineteenth century, Wagner immeasurably expanded the accepted notion of what a melody could be.

Art music in Europe had employed freely unfolding melody before the classic-romantic era, from the sinuous traceries of Gregorian chant to the flowing arabesques of Bach. Western music thus had a rich store of melody that bore little or no trace of four-bar regularity, and Wagner was not inventing anything new when he espoused the cause of "endless" melody. He was merely reclaiming for music some of the freedom it had abdicated under the alluring symmetries of the classic-romantic era. Once he had done this, there could be no question of returning to symmetrical patterns.

THE NEW MELODY

Contemporary composers do not emulate either the formal beauty of classical melody or the lyric expansiveness of the romantics. They range far afield for models, from the plasticity of Gregorian chant, the subtle irregularities of medieval and renaissance music, to the luxuriance of Bach's melodic line. Or, looking beyond the orbit of European music, they aspire to capture for the west the freedom, the improvisational quality of oriental melody.

The contemporary composer is not inclined to shape his melody to standardized patterns of four or eight bars. He does not eke out a phrase to four or eight measures solely because the preceding phrase was that long. He states a thing once, rather than two or three times. By abandoning symmetry and repetition he hopes to achieve a vibrant, taut melody from which everything superfluous has been excised. His aim is a finely molded, sensitive line packed with thought and feeling, which will function at maximum intensity as it follows the rise and fall of the musical impulse. Such a melody makes greater demands upon us than did the old. It requires alertness of mind and unflagging attention on the part of the listener, for its clipped phrases do not yield their meaning readily.

If the contemporary composer does adhere to traditional patterns, he uses them with all the subtlety at his command. Cadences are slurred over, phrases do not rhyme; punctuation marks are not made too perceptible. Repetitions are compressed, departure and return are veiled. As a matter of fact, this condensation of thought is not limited to music. Compare, for example, the rolling sentences of Dickens or Thackeray with the sinewy prose of Hemingway or Steinbeck; or the impassioned rhetoric of Shelley with the terse, wiry utterance of contemporary poets. The melodies of Mozart, Schubert, Chopin, and Tchaikovsky were shaped to the curve of the human voice, even when written for instruments. This is why the instrumental themes of these masters can be converted, year after year, into popular song hits. Twentieth-century music, on the other hand, has detached instrumental melody from its vocal origins. The new melody is neither unvocal nor anti-vocal; it is simply not conceived in terms of what the voice can do. The themes of twentieth-century works contain wide leaps and jagged turns of phrase that are not to be negotiated vocally. Contemporary melody ranges through musical space, striding forward boldly along untrodden paths. Instinct with energy and force, its line is apt to be angular rather than curved.

In addition, contemporary melody does not unfold against a background of familiar chords and scales. It does not move in the rhythms that we have grown accustomed to. It does not gravitate to the central tone or keynote as obviously as it once did. In effect, it avoids many of the landmarks on which people rely to mark out a melody. This loss of conventional intelligibility, however, is made up for in strength and freshness of expression, and in the avoidance of all turns of phrase that had become stereotyped from overuse. In this fashion the melodic line has been revitalized and rendered capable of conveying new meanings —twentieth-century meanings.

It will be instructive to compare characteristic melodies from the eighteenth, nineteenth, and twentieth centuries. For example, in the famous opening theme of Mozart's G-minor Symphony, we notice at once the four-bar construction based on symmetrical phrases and rhyming cadences. The second phrase is an exact repetition of the first, pitched one tone lower; the two phrases constitute a clearcut question-and-answer formation. The melody moves stepwise, save for an upward leap in the center of each phrase; yet this is quite easy to sing, as the leap outlines a chord that has been established since the beginning.

More expansive in its gesture is the romantic theme from the opening movement of Tchaikovsky's *Pathétique* Symphony. The sweeping curve of this melody exemplifies the exuberant lyricism of the late nineteenth-century style. Here too we find symmetrical phrases and rhyming cadences. Of the four phrases shown here, the first, second, and fourth are alike, a clear A-A:B-A pattern. The range is wider than that of an eighteenth-century melody, the climax more impassioned. But the leaps in the first phrase outline a familiar chord, while the third or contrasting phrase moves stepwise.

The lyric theme from Samuel Barber's *School for Scandal* Overture is an example of contemporary melody that does not depart too far from traditional norms. The structure is based on two symmetrical four-measure phrases with rhyming cadences, answered by a longer phrase. The leaps are narrow, the melody is singable. After a few hearings of the work, we find ourselves humming along. Here is a twentieth-century tune that finds something fresh to say within the conventional pattern:

etc.

The case is different with the second theme in the opening movement of Shostakovich's First Symphony. This theme represents the lyrical element of the movement; yet the lyricism is instrumental in character, not vocal. The structure is asymmetrical; a phrase of five measures is answered by one of four:

The wide leaps outline a succession of unfamiliar chords. This angular line, heard in the crystalline tones of the flute, will not impress the listener at first hearing as being very much of a tune. Yet with repeated hearings the difficult skips lose their arbitrary character. Gradually the line takes on profile, engages the listener's fancy, and ultimately reveals itself—for all its wiriness—as a genuinely melodic idea.

The following fragment from Alban Berg's opera *Wozzeck* shows an even greater departure from traditional norms of melody. The zigzag leaps are not like those ordinarily associated with the voice. Small wonder that during the Twenties performers and listeners alike declared Berg's melody (even as their grandfathers had declared Wagner's) to be unsingable.

We must remember that twentieth-century music embraces many styles, ranging from the solidly conservative to extreme radicalism. For this reason any generalization about present-day melody must be accompanied by all sorts of qualifications. One fact, however, is indisputable. The twentieth century recognizes the primacy of melody even as did the eighteenth and nineteenth. When people accuse modern music of having abandoned melody, what they really mean is that it has abandoned the familiar landmarks on which they rely to recognize

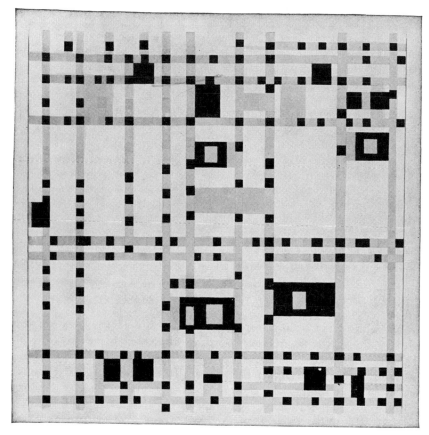

". . . the desire of our age for condensation of style and purity of expression, for athletic movement, economy, and architectonic unity." Piet Mondriaan, *Broadway Boogie Woogie*. (Collection Museum of Modern Art)

melody. Once we have learned to dispense with the punctuation marks of the good old days—just as we do when we read a telegram—we will be ready to respond to the exciting new conceptions of melody that have evolved in our time. We will find that, today as in the past, melody is a prime factor in musical expressiveness. For, as Igor Stravinsky has pointed out, "What survives every change of system is melody."

❦ 5 ❧

The New Harmony

"The evolution of the harmonic idiom has resulted from the fact that musicians of all generations have sought new means of expression. Harmony is a constant stream of evolution, a constantly changing vocabulary and syntax."

Roger Sessions

THE MELODY, in our music, is heard against a background of harmony. The chords that accompany the melody lend it color, clarify its direction and enhance its meaning. In effect, they define the musical space in which the melody has its being. Harmony is to music what perspective is to painting: the element of depth, the third dimension.

THE CLASSICAL SYSTEM OF HARMONY

It was the great achievement of the classical era to perfect a system of harmony in which each chord had its appointed place and function. This was the system of triadic harmony. The triad is the fundamental chord structure in western music. Hence Paul Hindemith's statement—one with which not all his colleagues might agree—"For as long as it exists, music will always take its point of departure from the triad and return to it." (The structure of the triad is explained in Appendix I-b.)

Melody constitutes the horizontal aspect of music, harmony the vertical. The melody unfolds its traceries above the chords that serve as supporting pillars. Throughout the classic-romantic period melody and harmony were interrelated in the closest possible way. Harmony, which started out as the support of melody, ended by shaping the melody and determining its curve. Indeed, many a tune of the classic-romantic era outlines a triad.

In the classical system, the triad on *do(do-mi-sol)* is the I chord or Tonic, the chord of rest. Around it are ranged the other triads, which are considered, in varying degrees, to be active or incomplete. The active triads seek to be completed or *resolved* in the rest chord. This seeking for resolution lends direction and purpose to the harmony; it establishes the point of departure and return. The triad on the fifth degree of the scale (*sol-ti-re*) is the Dominant or V chord, the chief representative

22

of the active principle. Dominant resolving to Tonic (V–I) is a basic formula in our music. We hear it affirmed again and again at the end of symphonies or overtures of the classic-romantic period. The IV chord (*fa-la-do*) is the Subdominant. This too is an active chord, although markedly less so than the Dominant. The progression IV–I makes a gentler cadence than V–I (the "Amen" at the end of hymns, for example). Classical harmony related all chords to the three basic functions—Tonic, Dominant, and Subdominant—allotting to each chord its place in a carefully graded hierarchy of values. It built these functions into a rational system that took on meaning for millions of listeners throughout the west. The ultimate triumph of Tonic over Dominant and Subdominant became the grand principle of classical form, a principle that reached its culmination in the symphony of Haydn, Mozart, and Beethoven.

ROMANTIC HARMONY

The romantic movement sprang from an age of revolution and social upheaval. Its music reflected the dynamism of this new age. Spurred on by the desire for passionate utterance, the romantic composers were increasingly drawn to the possibilities of dissonant harmony. Richard Wagner carried this tendency to its farthermost limits. In his music dramas Wagner consistently avoided the cadence—that is, the resolution. Through the imaginative use of dissonance he achieved extended structures marked by an accumulation of emotional tension greater than any that music had ever known before. In his work the active, dissonant harmony, seeking resolution in the chord of rest, came to symbolize one of the most powerful images of the romantic movement: the lonely questing man, whether the Dutchman or Lohengrin, Siegmund or Tristan, driven to find fulfillment in the all-womanly woman, Senta or Elsa, Sieglinde or Isolde.

Dissonance is the element that supplies dynamic tension, the forward impulsion that expends itself and comes to rest in consonance. There is a widespread notion that consonance is what is pleasant to the ear while dissonance is what is disagreeable. This distinction is much too vague to be useful. What is unpleasant to one ear may be agreeable to another. We will come closer the mark if we identify dissonance with the principle of activity and incompleteness, consonance with fulfillment and rest. "It cannot be too strongly emphasized," Walter Piston has written, "that the essential quality of dissonance is its sense of movement." And Stravinsky to the same point: "Dissonance is an element of transition, a complex or interval of tones which is not complete in itself and which must be resolved to the ear's satisfaction into a perfect consonance." Viewed thus, dissonance is seen to be the essential element of dynamism and tension without which music would be intolerably dull and static. The progression of dissonance to consonance mirrors the movement of life itself—its recurrent cycle of hunger and appeasement, desire and fulfillment.

We respond to one combination of sounds as dissonant and another as consonant for a number of reasons. A chord that strikes us as dissonant in one environment may sound much less so in another. Whether its tones are bunched together or spread out, whether it is played loud or soft, fast or slow, by an orchestra or on a piano; whether it occurs in a piece that is prevailingly dissonant or in one that on the whole is consonant—these and kindred factors affect how we will feel. Important, too, is the level of sophistication of the listener. One who listens regularly to music by Stravinsky and Bartók will have other standards of dissonance than one who limits himself to Beethoven and Brahms.

The history of music reflects a steady broadening of the harmonic sense, an ever greater tolerance of the human ear. In the course of this evolution, tone combinations which at first were regarded as dissonant came to be accepted, with time and familiarity, as consonant. The leader in this development has consistently been the composer. Striving to avoid the commonplace, he added a tone that did not properly belong to the chord, or held over a note from the old chord to the new, thereby creating a piquant effect to which, as time went on, people grew accustomed. This dissonance came to be treated with ever greater freedom, and gradually became a full-fledged member of the chord in which it had once been a stranger. Ultimately it lost its flavorsome quality, its character of dissonance, whereupon composers cast about for new combinations that would add zest and pungency to their music. "Every tone relationship that has been used too often," writes Arnold Schoenberg, "must finally be regarded as exhausted. It ceases to have power to convey a thought worthy of it. Therefore every composer is obliged to invent anew."

The history of the development of harmony, Schoenberg points out, is a record of dissonance rather than consonance, for dissonance is the dynamic element that leads the composer away from well trodden paths. By the same token, it is the element which in every age—whether Monteverdi's, Bach's, Wagner's, or our own—has acutely disturbed the adherents of the past. "Dissonances are more difficult to comprehend than consonance," Schoenberg observes. "Therefore the battle about them goes on throughout history."

This battle came to a head in the late nineteenth century. Wagner and his disciples assiduously explored the expressive powers of dissonance, and superimposed upon the classical system of harmony a network of relationships that completely changed the existing harmonic idiom. In so doing they enormously enriched the harmonic resources available to the composer, and set the stage for an exciting break with the past.

TWENTIETH-CENTURY HARMONY

The twentieth century inherited chord structures of three, four, and five tones. Carrying the traditional method of building chords one step farther, twentieth-century composers added another "story" to the chord, thus forming highly dissonant combinations of six and seven tones—for instance, chords based on steps 1–3–5–7–9–11 and 1–3–5–7–9–11–13 of the scale. The emergence of these complex "skyscraper" chords imparted a greater degree of tension to music than had ever existed before.

| Triad | 7th chord | 9th chord | chord of the 11th | chord of the 13th |

A chord of seven tones, such as the one shown above, hardly possesses the unity of the classical triad. It is composed of no less than three separate triads: the I chord (steps 1–3–5), the V chord (steps 5–7–9), and the II chord (steps 2–4–6 or 9–11–13). In this formation the Dominant chord is directly superimposed on the Tonic, so that Tonic and Dominant, the two poles of classical harmony, are brought together in a kind of montage. What our forebears were in the habit of hearing successively, we today are expected to hear—and grasp—simultaneously. Such a chord, which contains all seven steps of the major scale, not only adds spice to the traditional triad, but also increases the volume of sound, an effect much prized by composers. Here are two effective examples.

Bruckner   Milhaud

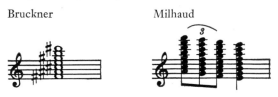

A seven-tone "skyscraper" is, in effect, a *polychord*. It is a block of sound that is heard on two or three planes. A succession of such chords creates several planes of harmony. One of the outstanding achievements of the new age is a kind of *polyharmony* in which the composer plays two or more streams of harmony against each other, exactly as in former times single strands of melody were combined. The interplay of the several independent streams adds a new dimension to the harmonic space. The following is a famous example of polyharmony from Stravinsky's *Petrushka*. The clash of the two harmonic currents produces a bright, virile sonority that typifies the twentieth-century revolt against the sweet sound of the romantic era:

No less significant was the appearance of new ways of building chords. Traditionally, these were formed by combining every other tone of the scale; that is to say, they were built in thirds. (See Appendix I-b for an explanation of intervals.) The third was associated with the music of the eighteenth and nineteenth centuries. To free themselves from the sound of the past, composers cast about for other methods of chord construction; they began to base chords on the interval of the fourth. This turning from *tertial* to *quartal* harmony constitutes one of the important differences between nineteenth- and twentieth-century music. Chords based on fourths have a pungency and freshness that are very much of the new age, as the following examples demonstrate.

Stravinsky

Scriabin

Schoenberg, *Chamber Symphony*, Opus 9.

Composers also based their harmonies on other intervals. Here is a chord of piled-up fifths from Stravinsky's *Rite of Spring*, and cluster chords based on seconds from Bartók's *Mikrokosmos*.

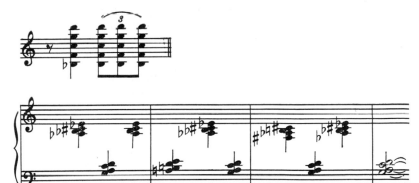

THE EMANCIPATION OF THE DISSONANCE

By the end of the nineteenth century many dissonances had become so familiar that the composer was ready to accept them as consonant. Twentieth-century music emancipated the dissonance—that is, freed it from the need to proceed to the resolving consonance. Now the com-

poser could either sidestep or entirely omit progressions that had become too standardized, excising what was not absolutely essential to his
thought. The new harmony, like the new melody, moved away from the
expansiveness of the classic-romantic style. It was marked by utmost
economy of means and condensation of thought: a taut, telegraphic
style that avoided the obvious and often derived its power from the
element of surprise.

Inevitably the contemporary composer has abandoned the time-
honored distinction between consonance and dissonance. To him the
consonance is not basically different from the dissonance; it is simply
less dissonant. As Schoenberg formulates it, "Dissonances are only the
more remote consonances." In other words, the distinction is relative
rather than absolute. A chord is no longer held to be consonant because
of its intrinsic character, but because it is less dissonant than the chords
that preceded it. Which means that a greater dissonance may be resolved
to a lesser as effectively as it once resolved to a consonance. Prokofiev,
for example, brings his Third Piano Concerto to a close on a chord that
formerly would have had no implication of finality, as it is not consonant. It serves here as a final cadence only because it is less dissonant
than what came before.

By abandoning the classical distinction between consonance and dissonance, contemporary music has changed the nature of the harmonic
cadence. Cadences are much less in evidence than they were formerly;
they are veiled, elided, subtilized. The old punctuation marks have disappeared. Often a modern work will unfold without a single complete
cadence in the course of it. This implies a much greater accumulation
of tension, and it means that the structure is less clearly articulated than
it used to be. The listener is expected to go for a much longer period
without "coming up for air"; in other words, to absorb a greater stretch
of music at a time.

Nineteenth-century music explored the possibilities of dissonant harmony for sensuous color, emotional expression, and sonorous enchant-

ment. The new harmony, on the other hand, exploited the dissonance as a percussive clang, a jabbing thrust of sound capable of engendering tension. Thus came into being the muscular harmonies of the New Music: those steely "hammered" chords that introduced a new tone into twentieth-century style. The following measures from Bartók's *Allegro Barbaro* offer a fine example of these percussive harmonies:

In a passage such as this the single chord is not conceived in relation to what comes before or after. It exists rather as a vertical entity, to be savored for its own color, resiliency and thrust. This emphasis upon the individual chord is one of the prime traits of twentieth-century harmony. Dissonance, emancipated from the restrictions imposed upon it by functional harmony, has become a value in itself.

MELODY AND HARMONY IN CONTEMPORARY MUSIC

In contemporary music, melody and harmony are no longer indivisible, as they were in the classic-romantic era. Twentieth-century melody sometimes moves irrespective of harmonic progressions, achieving a freedom undreamed of in former times. This melody is no longer conceived in relation to standard chord structures or bolstered by familiar harmonies. As often as not the skips in the melodic line imply harmonic groupings to which neither our ears nor our vocal cords are accustomed. If this absence of standardization allows for freshness and novelty, it also makes it more difficult for us to apprehend the melody— at any rate, until we have heard enough contemporary music to build up a body of memories and associations comparable to those which help us apprehend the traditional melodic patterns.

It is illuminating to compare the following three examples of melody-and-harmony from the eighteenth, nineteenth, and twentieth centuries. The first example, the opening measures of the *Turkish Rondo* from

Mozart's Piano Sonata in A, shows a clear-cut melody whose curve is shaped in direct relation to the triads in the accompaniment.

Second is a theme from the Love Duet in Act II of *Tristan and Isolde*. Wagner richly embellished the harmony; yet both the chords and the melody can be explained in terms of the triad and its derivatives.

Third is a passage from the *Concord* Piano Sonata of Charles Ives, in which we encounter dense chordal masses used with percussive effect.

The melody reveals the influence of unfamiliar chord patterns, and is far more independent of the harmony than in the other two examples.

Mysterious threads bind artistic expression to the world out of which it stems. Eighteenth-century classicism was interested above all in the resolution of dissonance to consonance—that is, in the restoration of law and order after momentary disturbance. Our era is interested in the dissonance rather than in the resolution. The greater amount of dissonance in contemporary music reflects the heightened tension and drive of contemporary life. Behind the new harmonic language is the wonderful capacity of the human ear to adapt to new conditions, to receive and assimilate ever more complicated sounds. Availing themselves of this capacity, contemporary composers have created tone combinations of unprecedented complexity capable of expressing the most subtle and elusive meanings. Twentieth-century harmony, infinitely venturesome in spirit, reveals to us the perspectives of an ever-expanding tonal universe.

6

New Conceptions of Tonality

"Tonality is a natural force, like gravity."
Paul Hindemith

THE TONES out of which music is fashioned take on coherence and unity if they are apprehended as a family or group; that is to say, if they are heard in relation to a central tone from which musical movement sets out and to which it ultimately returns. This central point is the *do*, the keynote or Tonic around which the other tones revolve and to which they gravitate. How basic this gravitation is may be gauged from Stravinsky's dictum, "All music is nothing more than a succession of impulses that converge towards a definite point of repose."

The sense of relatedness to a central tone is known as *tonality*. It has been the fundamental relationship in our music. As Roger Sessions has written, "Tonality should be understood as the principal means which the composers of the seventeenth, eighteenth and nineteenth centuries evolved of organizing musical sounds and giving them coherent shape."

A group of related tones with a common center or Tonic is known as a *key*. The tones of the key serve as basic material for a given composition. The key, that is, marks off an area in musical space within which musical growth and development take place.

We have said that dissonance implies movement, consonance represents the desire for rest. But movement and rest in relation to what? Tonality supplies the fixed center, the goal toward which this alternation of movement and rest is directed. By providing a framework for musical events, tonality becomes the first principle of musical architecture, a form-building element which unifies musical space and articulates musical structure. Tonality is no less potent in achieving variety. By moving from one key to another the composer creates a dramatic opposition between two tonal areas. He establishes his piece in the home key, then moves to a contrasting key—that is, he *modulates*. This modulation to a foreign area increases tension and gives a higher value to the ultimate triumph of the home key. "Modulation is like a change of scenery," says Schoenberg. The movement from home key to contrasting key and back came to be a fundamental pattern of musical structure, and may be described as Statement-Departure-Return. As a result of modulation, a movement of a sonata or symphony did exactly what its name implies—it moved! Out of the dramatic tension between the home key and the foreign emerged the impressive architecture of the classical symphony. "The development of tonality," Sessions observes, "was a necessary condition of the development of large design in music, since tonality alone carried with it the means of contrast."

THE MAJOR-MINOR SYSTEM

In western music the octave is divided into twelve equal parts. In other words, it contains twelve tones, which comprise what is known as the *chromatic scale*. A musical work, no matter how complex, is made up of these twelve tones and their duplication in the higher and lower octaves. From any degree of the chromatic scale to its neighbor is a distance of a half tone or semitone. Half tone and whole tone are the units of measurement in our musical system. The music of the Orient, on the other hand, uses smaller intervals, such as third and quarter tones.

The music of the classic-romantic era was based on two contrasting scales, the *major* and the *minor*. (Information on the major-minor system of scales and keys will be found in Appendix I-c.) The major and minor scales consist of seven tones selected out of the possible twelve. In other words, the classical system of harmony embodies the "seven-out-of-twelve" way of hearing music that prevailed throughout the eighteenth and nineteenth centuries. When seven tones are chosen to form a key, the other five tones remain foreign to that particular tonality. These extraneous tones are not entirely excluded from a composition in that key. They appear as embellishments of the melody and harmony, and they are used to form the unstable chords which lend spice to the harmony. They are particularly in evidence when the music is moving from the home key to foreign areas, that is, in passages of modulation. If music is to sound firmly rooted in a key, the seven tones that are directly related to the key center must prevail. If the five foreign tones are permitted too conspicuous a role, the magnetic pull to the Tonic is weakened, and the tonality becomes ambiguous. The term *diatonic* refers to movement according to the key—that is, according to the seven tones of the major or minor scale. The term *chromatic* refers to movement according to the twelve semitones of the octave. Diatonicism connotes the "seven-out-of-twelve" way of hearing music which strengthens the feeling of key. Chromaticism refers to those forces in music which tend to weaken or dissolve the sense of key.

TONALITY IN THE CLASSIC-ROMANTIC ERA

The classical system, with its twelve major and twelve minor keys, may be compared to a house with twenty-four rooms, the modulations being equivalent to corridors leading from one to the next. The classical composer clearly established the home key, then set out to the next-related area. For him the chief charm of modulation was "the getting there, and not the arrival itself." The home area, the contrasting area, and the corridor between were spaciously designed. Indeed, the forms of the classic era have a breadth that is the musical counterpart of the ample façades of eighteenth-century architecture and the stately periods of eighteenth-century prose. This amplitude of gesture reached its finest realization in the sonatas and string quartets, symphonies and concertos of Haydn, Mozart, and the younger Beethoven. Basic to the classical style, of course, was a manner of writing that neatly defined the various key areas: in other words, an emphasis on diatonic harmony.

Under the impetus of nineteenth-century romanticism, composers sought to whip up emotion and intensify all musical effects; they turned more and more to chromaticism. Besides, by then the system had become familiar, and listeners needed less time to grasp the tonality. Home key and foreign key were established with more concise gestures; the corridors between them steadily shrank. There came into being that restless wandering from key to key which fed the nineteenth-century need for emotional excitement. Modulation was ever more frequent, abrupt, daring. Each modulation led to new excursions. The result was that the distance from the home tonality steadily increased. It was in the music dramas of Wagner that the chromatic harmony of the romantic era received its most compelling expression. Wagner's harmonies—ambiguous, volatile, seductive—represented a new level of musical sensibility. His *Tristan and Isolde*, couched in a language of unprecedented expressivity, carried the chromatic idiom to the limit of its possibilities. The harmonic cadence—the element in music that defines and establishes tonality—was virtually suppressed in this epoch-making score, in favor of a continual scheme of modulation that built up extraordinary tension. Indeed, in the Prelude to the opera one no longer knows exactly what the tonality is. *Tristan*, the prime symbol of romantic yearning and unfulfillment, made it all too apparent that the classical system with its neatly defined key areas had begun to disintegrate.

For the better part of three hundred years the major and minor scales had supplied, in Alfredo Casella's phrase, "the tonal loom on which every melody was woven." Nineteenth-century composers began to feel that everything which could possibly be said within this framework had already been said, so that it became more and more difficult for them to achieve fresh expression within the confines of the major-minor system. Just as they turned against the symmetries of the four-measure phrase and the Dominant-Tonic cadence, so they had perforce to turn against the restrictions of the diatonic scale. In the final years of the nineteenth century the "seven-out-of-twelve" way of hearing music came to its natural end. The twentieth century was ready for a new way: twelve out of twelve.

THE EXPANSION OF TONALITY IN CONTEMPORARY MUSIC

In their desire to free music from what Béla Bartók called "the tyrannical rule of the major-minor keys," twentieth-century composers found their way to broader notions of tonality. One of the most fruitful of the new concepts involves the free use of twelve tones around a center. This retains the basic principle of traditional tonality, loyalty to the Tonic; but, by considering the five chromatic tones to be as much a part of the key as the seven diatonic ones, it immeasurably expands the borders of tonality. In other words, the chromatic scale of seven basic tones and five visitors has given way to a duodecuple scale of twelve equal members.

This expanded conception of tonality has not only done away with the distinction between diatonic and chromatic, but also wiped out the distinction between major and minor that was so potent a source of contrast in the classic-romantic era. The composers of the eighteenth and nineteenth centuries presented major-minor in succession; contemporary composers present them simultaneously. A piece today will be, let us say, in F major-minor, using all the twelve tones around the center F, instead of dividing them, as was done in the past, into two separate groups of seven. This serves to create an ambiguous tonality which is highly congenial to the taste of our time.

In general, the key is no longer so clearly defined an area in musical space as it used to be, and the shift from one key center to another is made with a dispatch that puts to shame the most exuberant modulations of the Wagner era. Transitional passages are dispensed with. One tonality is simply displaced by another, in a way that keeps both the music and the listener on the move. An excellent example is the popular theme from *Peter and the Wolf*. Prokofiev is extremely fond of this kind of displacement.

In similar fashion chords utterly foreign to the tonality are included, not even as modulations, but simply as an extension of the key to a new tonal plane. As a result, a passage will sound A major-ish, shall we say, rather than in A major. Composers such as Stravinsky and Hindemith were leaders in the attempt to broaden the traditional concept of loyalty to the Tonic and to free contemporary music from a frame of reference that had become restrictive. The following measures from the second movement of Hindemith's *Mathis der Maler* illustrate this expanded sense of tonality. The passage begins and ends in C major. But there is free chromatic inflection all along the way, and a cadence in G-sharp major in the middle.

In their turn away from the major-minor system, composers went back to procedures that had existed long before—to the music of the Middle Ages and Renaissance, and to the medieval scale patterns called the church modes.

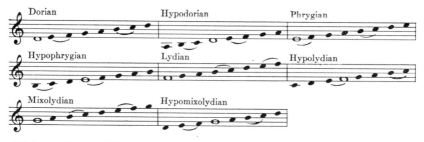

(Whole notes indicate final or central tones; slurs show the position of the semitones)

These modes served as the basis for European art music for a thousand years—from the Gregorian chants collated at the end of the sixth century to the masterpieces of Palestrina at the end of the sixteenth. The adjective *modal* describes the type of melody and harmony prevailing during this period, as distinguished from *tonal*, which refers to the major-minor harmony that supplanted the modes.

Based as they are on a white-note scale, the modes stand as far removed as possible from post-Wagnerian chromaticism. Their archaic sound was most attractive to a generation of musicians seeking to escape the overcharged sonorities of an outworn romanticism. The following passage from Vaughan Williams' *Pastoral* Symphony exemplifies the freshness and charm that modal flavoring brought to twentieth-century music.

Desirous of exploiting new harmonic resources, composers found inspiration in the exotic scales of China, India, Java, and other far eastern countries. They also turned to the ancient scales embodied in European folk music. And they began to experiment with the construction of new scales. Here are two examples—one devised by Béla Bartók, the other by Ferruccio Busoni.

However, of the new scales that came into use in the early twentieth century, only one attained wide currency, the whole-tone scale we will discuss in connection with Debussy.

POLYTONALITY

Tonality implies the supremacy of a single key and a single tone center. Composers in the past made the most out of the contrast between two keys heard in succession. Modern composers heighten the contrast by presenting them simultaneously.

The simultaneous use of two keys (*bitonality*) and of several (*polytonality*) came to the fore in the music of Stravinsky and Milhaud, whence it entered the vocabulary of the age. Toward the end of a polytonal piece, one key is generally permitted to assert itself over the others, and in this way an impression is restored of orderly progression toward a central point. Polytonality is used to bring out the different planes of the harmony. By putting two or more streams of chords in different keys the friction between them is immeasurably heightened. Piano music especially lends itself to this technique, right and left hands playing progressions of chords in different keys. Because the tension comes from the clash of keys, each stream of harmony must be rooted solidly in its own key. Polytonality, then, does not reject the principle of key. It merely extends this principle in a characteristically twentieth-century manner.

During the Twenties, Milhaud and his fellow experimenters were fond of combining three, four, or even five tonalities. However, it soon became apparent that most listeners are incapable of assimilating more than two keys at once with any degree of awareness. When three or more keys are combined, the music tends to blur into dissonant passages that belong to no key at all. As a result, in recent years composers have written far less music in the polytonal idiom. Bitonality, on the other hand, has remained a most effective procedure in contemporary music.

Following is a passage from Prokofiev's *Sarcasms* for piano, in which right and left hand play in different keys.

The great developments from the time of Bach and Handel to that of Mozart, from the time of Beethoven and Schubert to that of Wagner, had unfolded within the frame of the major-minor system. With the disintegration of this three-hundred-year-old structure, music entered upon a new phase. In effect, the twentieth century ushered in far-reaching changes in the basic relationships of the art of music.

Yet even so, the break with tradition is not as complete as many suppose. Schoenberg himself—who more than any other was instrumental in overthrowing the established order of tonality—declared, "There is still much good music to be written in C major."

⋞ 7 ⋟

Rhythm in Contemporary Music

"Rhythm and motion, not the element of feeling, are the foundations of musical art."

Igor Stravinsky

By RHYTHM we mean the principle of organization that regulates the flow of music in time. Since music is an art that exists solely in time, rhythm controls every aspect of a composition, from the minutest detail to the over-all unity of its architecture. Hence Roger Sessions's remark that "an adequate definition of rhythm comes close to defining music itself." The decisive role of rhythm in the musical process has always been recognized by composers. Hector Berlioz considered rhythmic pulsation "the very life-blood of the music." Hans von Bülow coined a famous phrase when he remarked, "In the beginning was rhythm." Contemporary musicians are no less explicit in acknowledging its importance. Sessions regards rhythm as the "primary fact" of music. Ernst Toch, speaking of rhythmic reiteration and contrast, states, "It is the interplay of these two elementary forces that builds and feeds the skeleton of music." And Aaron Copland calls rhythm "the most primitive element in music."

METRICAL RHYTHM AND FREE RHYTHM

We distinguish among several types of rhythmic organization in language. One kind of organization is metrical poetry, which utilizes an unmistakable pattern of syllables arranged in units of equal duration, marked by regular recurrence of accent—as in the following lines by Keats:

> Souls of Poets dead and gone,
> What Elysium have ye known,
> Happy field or mossy cavern
> Choicer than the Mermaid Tavern?

Free verse, in contrast, is less tightly organized than metrical poetry. Its speech rhythms are more supple, its accents more subtly placed. Still

40

more free in its flow is poetic prose, whose elastic rhythms—as in the prose of the Bible—are capable of a rich and varied music.

Musical rhythm, too, presents varying degrees of organization. At one extreme is the regular beat of a Sousa march or a folk dance, so obvious as to be unmistakable. At the other are the freely flowing arabesques of oriental song, or of Gregorian chant, or of operatic recitative. These are the musical equivalents of free-verse and poetic-prose rhythms. Their rhythmic impulse comes from speech rather than from the symmetries of the dance.

The trend in western music from 1600 to 1900 was steadily in the direction of tighter organization—that is to say, toward metrical rhythm. There were several reasons for this. To begin with, European music was influenced in ever greater degree by folk dance and folk song, both of which were allied to popular metrical poetry. Then again, as the various literatures of Europe developed highly organized metrical verse forms, these could not but affect the music to which they were set. A similar influence came from the Lutheran chorales, which used simple metrical patterns so that the congregation could keep together. As a result of these and kindred influences, western music steadily lost the plasticity of rhythm it had had during the Middle Ages and the Renaissance.

The movement toward standardized metrical rhythm reached its height in the classic-romantic era. Indeed, practically the entire output of the eighteenth and nineteenth centuries—an enormous amount of music—was written in two-four, three-four, four-four, and six-eight time—that is, two, three, four, or six beats to a measure, with a regularly recurring accent on the first beat. Such regular patterns set up expectancies whose fulfillment is a source of pleasure to the listener. People enjoy falling into step with the beat of a march or waltz. Metrical rhythm captures for music an image of the dance, a sense of physical well-being inherent in regular body movement. Besides, by using metrical rhythm, a composer is easily able to organize music in balanced phrases and cadences. Thus the standard meters went hand-in-hand with the four-bar structure of the classic-romantic style. (The basic meters are explained in Appendix I-d.)

"THE TYRANNY OF THE BARLINE"

The standardization of musical time into a few basic patterns had great advantages at a time when art music was winning a new mass public. It enabled composers to communicate their intentions more easily. It also helped large groups of performers to sing and play in time, thereby making feasible the huge choruses and orchestras that transformed music into a popular art.

All the same, composers chafed increasingly under "the tyranny of the barline"—the relentless recurrence of the accented ONE. As we have noticed in preceding chapters, what begins by being a support ends as a straitjacket. Musicians found the excessive standardization of meter increasingly hostile to artistic expression, and sought to free themselves from the trip-hammer obviousness of the accented beat.

These attempts began long before the twentieth century. Older masters, for instance, made liberal use of *syncopation*, a technique of shifting the accent to the off-beat, thereby upsetting—and enlivening— the normal pattern of accentuation. Composers also used more complex subsidiary rhythms within the measure. A characteristic subtlety was *cross rhythm*: shifting the accents within the measure so that a passage written in triple time briefly took on the character of duple time, or the other way around. Much favored too was the simultaneous use of two rhythmic patterns, such as "two against three" or "three against four." These devices figure prominently in the music of Chopin, Schumann, and Brahms.

A great impetus towards the freshening of rhythm came from the nationalist schools of the nineteenth century. Rhythms drawn from Polish, Hungarian, Bohemian, and Norwegian folk dance enlivened the standard patterns of the older musical cultures. The Russians played a leading role in this development. Musorgsky especially used rugged, uneven rhythms of great expressive power. In the final quarter of the century it became ever clearer that new conceptions of rhythm were in the making.

TWENTIETH-CENTURY RHYTHM

The revolt against the standard meters led twentieth-century composers to explore the possibilities of less symmetrical patterns. At the same time poets were turning from metrical to free verse. Both these developments reflect a general tendency in contemporary art to pull away from conventional symmetry in favor of the unexpected. As one critic expressed it, "We enjoy the irregular more than the regular when we understand it."

The revitalization of western rhythm was nourished by a number of sources. Composers felt obliged to try to capture the hectic rhythms of the life about them. Nineteenth-century rhythms were derived from

Contemporary music, like contemporary art, has rediscovered the charm of the irregular. Joan Miro, *Dutch Interior*. (Collection Museum of Modern Art)

peasant dances and bucolic scenes. Twentieth-century rhythms glorify the drive of modern city life, the pulsebeat of factory and machine. It is therefore natural for twentieth-century musicians to be preoccupied with that element of their art most closely associated with movement and physical activity. Also, the enormous popularity of

Russian ballet in the years after the First World War heightened the emphasis on rhythm. Nineteenth-century composers had concentrated on harmony and orchestral color, and had somewhat neglected rhythm. The New Music had to correct the imbalance.

In their desire to escape the obvious, composers began to draw inspiration from rhythmic conceptions outside European music. Especially fruitful was the interest in primitive art that arose in the opening years of the century. The pounding, hammering rhythms of Stravinsky and Bartók sent a breath of fresh air through European music. Not unrelated were the syncopations of jazz that became the rage in Europe and exerted a positive influence on contemporary music. The search for new rhythmic effects led composers far afield in time as well as space. They turned back to the free prose rhythms of Gregorian chant; they studied the supple rhythms of medieval motet and Renaissance madrigal, in which no single strong beat regularized the free interplay of the voices. Nationalism, too, made a vital contribution to the new rhythm. Vaughan Williams in England, Bartók in Hungary, and Charles Ives in the United States prized the rhythms of their cultures precisely for their "off-beat" qualities. From the interaction of all these forces came a new rhythm, tense and resilient, that electrified the world.

NEW RHYTHMIC DEVICES

The twentieth-century composer is apt to avoid four-bar rhythm. He regards it as too predictable, hence unadventurous. He prefers to challenge the ear with nonsymmetrical rhythms that keep the listener on his toes. This rejection of standard patterns has led composers to explore meters based on odd numbers: five beats to the measure $(3 + 2$ or $2 + 3)$; seven $(2 + 2 + 3, 4 + 3,$ or $2 + 3 + 2)$; nine $(5 + 4,$ or $4 + 5)$; also rhythms based on groups of eleven or thirteen beats. Within the measure small units of beats are subdivided in a great diversity of rhythmic patterns. In addition, the grouping of the bars into phrases is far more flexible than in earlier music. The result is that today rhythm is freer, more supple than ever before.

Often, in nineteenth-century music, an entire piece or movement is written in a single meter. Twentieth-century composers, striving for the suppleness of free-verse and prose rhythm, began to change from one meter to another with unprecedented rapidity and ease. In a word, they turned to *multirhythm*. The following passage from Stravinsky's *Rite of Spring* shows changes of meter with every measure. Rhythmic flexibility could hardly be carried any farther. Stravinsky had every right to remark, as he did, "It is for the conductor that I make things difficult."

This continual change of time generates an excitement that is most congenial to the modern temper. In a multirhythmic passage such as the one above, the unit of meter is no longer the measure—how can it be if it is changing constantly?—but the single beat. This becomes the nucleus of small rhythmic motives which combine in larger groups to produce an incisive, self-generating rhythm. The new motor rhythm is thus liberated from the bonds of conventional meter, to become a powerful expressive agent, a constructive force that keeps the sonorous material in a state of dynamic impulsion. In the passage just quoted from the *Rite of Spring*, the rhythmic patterns together with the dissonant harmony create a percussive rhythm highly characteristic of twentieth-century music. The tones are heard not as groups of tones, but rather as rhythmic blobs of sound. The violence that such a passage is capable of achieving must be heard to be believed.

It goes without saying that the barline has lost its former power as the arbiter of the musical flow. As a matter of fact, there are composers who dispense with it altogether. Others retain it, but mainly as a visual aid to the performer. In any case, through the use of multirhythms and similar devices, the old "tyranny of the barline" has been forever broken.

Occidental musicians marvel at the intricate patterns set up by African drummers who execute conflicting rhythms simultaneously. Similar effects abound in the music of the percussion orchestras of the far east. Contemporary composers have captured something of this intricacy, using conflicting rhythmic patterns that unfold at the same time: in a word, *polyrhythm*. An intriguing example is the following passage from the final movement of Charles Ives's *Three Places in New England* ("The Housatonic at Stockbridge"), where we find simultaneous groupings of two, three, five, six, seven, and eight notes to the beat.

Another device characteristic of contemporary rhythm is the *ostinato* (literally, "obstinate," that is, recurring over and over). Precedents for this device abound in the music of the seventeenth and early eighteenth centuries, in which a phrase in the bass would be repeated again and again (called *basso ostinato*) while above it the upper voices traced

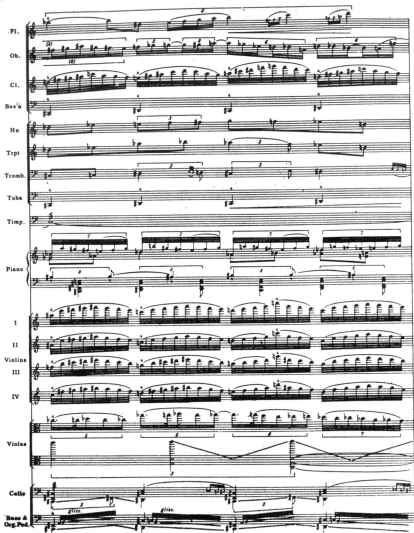

a set of variations. Twentieth-century musicians have adopted this procedure, basing the ostinato not on a melodic phrase but on a persistent
rhythmic pattern. The ostinato is unsurpassed as a means of building
up excitement. However, like all striking effects it must be used with
caution, as it easily degenerates into mannerism.

Twentieth-century rhythm, like melody and harmony, has abandoned
the landmarks on which the mass of music lovers depend. In much con-

temporary music (although by no means all!) the listener will miss the reassuring downbeat, the predictable accent that is so pleasant to nod, tap, and sway to, just as he will miss the symmetrical phrase-and-cadence structure based on four-bar rhythm. As he accustoms himself to do without those, he will discover a world of fresh and novel rhythms, impregnated with kinetic power and movement, and thoroughly attuned to the modern world. The emancipation of rhythm from the standard metrical patterns of the eighteenth and nineteenth centuries must be accounted one of the major achievements of the New Music. It has resulted in nothing less than a revitalization of the rhythmic sense of the West.

⊷ 8 ⊷

Texture in Contemporary Music

"Counterpoint is just as much subject to constant evolution and flux as are melody and harmony, with which it is indissolubly interwoven."

Ernst Toch

THE DICTIONARY defines *texture* as the arrangement or disposition of the threads of a woven fabric. Musicians have adopted the term, because it applies rather well to their art.

We distinguish three types of texture. First is *monophonic* or single-voice texture, in which the music is heard as a single strand of melody without harmonic background. All music up to a thousand years ago was monophonic; as is to this day the music of India and the Arabic world, China and Japan, Java and Bali. In Western music the great monument of the monophonic period is the fifteen-hundred-year-old liturgical music of the Catholic Church, Gregorian Chant, which was conceived as pure melody without reference to harmonic values.

Two or more melodic lines may be combined in a many-voiced or *polyphonic* texture. Polyphonic music is based on *counterpoint*, the art of combining several melody lines or "voices" in a unified musical fabric. The essence of contrapuntal style is the contrast between the independent voices, which are set off from each other by contrasts in rhythm and contour. These contrasts cause the music to unfold in several planes, creating an impression of depth and unflagging movement that can be attained in no other way.

In the third type of texture a single voice carries the melody line. The accompanying voices surrender their independence and coalesce in blocks of harmony, to become the chords that support and enrich the main part. This is *homophonic* or *chordal* texture. Here, as in monophonic music, the listener's attention is directed to a single line, but with a difference: the melody is not conceived as a self-sufficient entity, but is related to the harmonic background. Homophonic texture depends on the vertical tone-mass, the chord; while contrapuntal texture represents a concept of music based on the interplay of horizontal lines.

The three types of texture differ sharply, even graphically.

a) Monophonic—Gregorian Chant

Do - mi - ne De - us Rex coe - le - stis De - us Pa - ter om - ni - po - tens

b) Polyphonic—Chorus from Messiah

etc.

c) Homophonic—Chopin Waltz

p   *cresc.*   *mf etc.*

Although we draw a clear distinction between the harmonic and contrapuntal elements of music, they really represent two aspects of the same thing. In a contrapuntal work by Bach or Handel, the tones at any given point form a vertical block of sound—in other words, a chord. Conversely, suppose a vocal quartet is harmonizing a tune. We hear a single melody line with chords underneath—that is, homophonic texture. Yet each of the singers as he moves from one chord to the next follows his own horizontal line. Clearly the horizontal and the vertical, the contrapuntal and the harmonic elements, exist side by side in music. The difference is one of emphasis. We regard a texture as polyphonic when the conduct of the voices takes precedence over harmonic considerations. We regard a texture as homophonic when the relationship of the chords takes precedence over the counterpoint. (For information on basic procedures of counterpoint—imitation, canon, fugue—see Appendix I-g.)

Counterpoint exalts the structural and formal values of music. It has a special appeal for the intellectual musician, who sees in its abstraction and refinement of thought the purest, most exalted musical discourse. To fill a contrapuntal structure with feeling and poetry requires consummate mastery of technique, and poses problems that cannot fail to challenge the creative imagination.

TEXTURE IN THE MUSIC OF THE PAST

The late Middle Ages and Renaissance witnessed a magnificent flowering of polyphonic art in sacred and secular choral music, with which composers at that time were primarily concerned. This development continued throughout the Baroque era (1600–1750) and culminated in the music of the two giants of the late Baroque, Johann Sebastian Bach (1685–1750) and George Frideric Handel (1685–1759). These men brought to perfection a style of richly woven texture in which contrapuntal and harmonic elements were ideally mated, the counterpoint directed by harmony, the harmony animated by counterpoint. Their majestic fugues, both instrumental and choral, crown five centuries of polyphony and superbly reveal the capacities of counterpoint for the manipulation of purely musical means in a purely musical way.

In the period that followed, music turned from Baroque grandeur to the grace of the Rococo (c. 1725–1775). Richness of texture had been carried to the farthest development of which it was then capable. Composers consequently veered in the opposite direction and explored the possibilities of single-line melody against a simple chord background, presented in neatly balanced phrases rounded off by symmetrical cadences. Counterpoint and its "learned" devices were not congenial to the pleasure-loving Rococo, when music was designed above all to charm and entertain.

However, a new creative current soon asserted itself. The musicians of the latter eighteenth century developed a dynamic orchestral style based on the animated interplay of the different instrumental parts. Texture was reinstituted as a positive value in musical art—the light limpid texture we find in the works of the high classical period, the era of Haydn, Mozart, and the younger Beethoven. Once again the vertical and horizontal threads were interwoven in perfect balance—but with a difference. Bach and Handel were contrapuntists who used harmony to bind the flow of the voices. Haydn and Mozart were harmonists who utilized counterpoint to animate the movement of the chords.

The nineteenth century completed the swing from a horizontal to a vertical conception of music. Texture throughout the romantic era emphasized harmony and color rather than line. Composers were preoccupied above all with unlocking the magic power of the chord. This striving for luscious harmony impelled them to an ever richer orchestral sound. Texture grew thick and opaque. The mammoth orchestra favored by the disciples of Wagner—Richard Strauss, Mahler, and the youthful Schoenberg—brought the overelaborate textures of the postromantic era to a point beyond which no further progress was possible.

There is a healthy impulse in art to execute an about-face when an impasse has been reached. Contemporary music found a new direction.

TEXTURE IN THE TWENTIETH CENTURY

In pulling away from the emotional exuberance of the postromantic era, composers turned also against the sumptuous texture that was its ultimate manifestation. They had to lighten the texture, they felt, in order to give music once again a sense of unobstructed movement. The twentieth century thus saw a great revival of counterpoint, which represented a return to the esthetic ideals of the age of Bach, the last period when the horizontal-linear point of view had prevailed. Composers broke up the thick chordal fabric of the late romantic style; they shifted from opulent tone mass to pure line, from sensuous harmony and iridescent color to sinewy melody and transparency of texture. The "return to Bach" extended beyond the work of that master to the great contrapuntists of the fifteenth and sixteenth centuries. This new interest in linear thinking served the desire of the age for condensation of style and purity of expression, for athletic movement and architectonic unity; above all, for a point of view that concentrated upon compositional problems rather than upon the expression of personal feelings.

The interest in counterpoint did not exclude the lively exploration of new harmonic resources that we traced in an earlier chapter. The

two currents flowed side by side, each nourishing the other. We saw
that the "skyscraper" chords of contemporary music are really polychords which create several planes of harmony—what we referred to
as polyharmony. Composers now began to employ polyharmony in
the service of the new counterpoint, and combined independent successions of chords just as their predecessors used to combine single
lines of melody. It was as if each melodic strand of the old counterpoint
had been thickened out to become a composite stream of harmony.
In such music the contrapuntal interplay is no longer between lines of
single notes, but between moving blocks of harmony which are heard
on separate planes. The several streams of sound may approach one
another or separate, clash or coalesce, exactly as did the individual parts
in the older polyphony. The resulting sound is wholly of the twentieth
century. We quoted an example of this sonority from Stravinsky's
Petrushka on page 26. Here is another from Milhaud's Piano Sonata,
which the composer conceived on several harmonic planes.

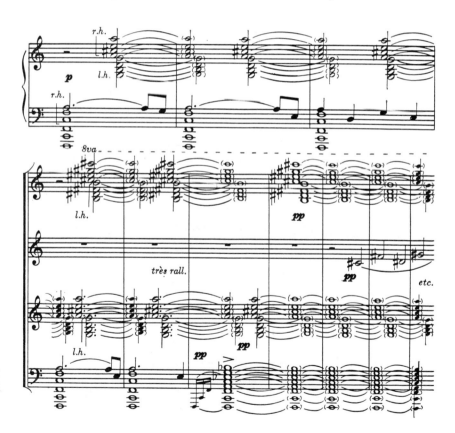

It should be added that polyrhythms also served the cause of the new linear texture. They reinforced the independence of the lines, contributing materially to achieving the contrast and inner tension which are the life blood of counterpoint.

DISSONANT COUNTERPOINT

Consonance unites, dissonance separates. The masters of polyphony in the past used consonant intervals—fifths, fourths, thirds, and sixths—at the decisive points of contact between the voices, so as to blend them into a unified texture. Contemporary composers, on the other hand, try to make the several lines stand out from one another. They use dissonances (seconds, sevenths, augmented and diminished intervals) to clarify the vertical sound and the disposition of the voices.

This purposeful kind of texture is known as *linear counterpoint*. The term is redundant, as all counterpoint is based on line and linear thinking. The adjective, however, emphasizes the fact that each line of this texture aspires to independence without trying to combine with the other voices. In recent years the more descriptive term *dissonant counterpoint* has come to denote the kind of texture in which dissonance energizes the movement and adds to the propulsive power of the lines. Here is an example from Hindemith, one of the masters of modern dissonant counterpoint.

The reconstitution of contrapuntal values must be regarded as one of the prime achievements of twentieth-century music. It has revealed to composers anew the expressive powers of melody and the constructive values of line. It has also restored the balance that was upset by nineteenth-century emphasis upon vertical elements at the expense of horizontal. Contemporary music has instituted counterpoint not as an accessory technique but as an integral part of the compositional process. As the English critic George Dyson put it, "Ours is an age of texture."

9

New Concepts in Orchestration

"We have had enough of this orchestral dappling and these thick sonorities. One is tired of being saturated with timbres and wants no more of all this overfeeding."

Igor Stravinsky

Unquestionably the most exciting instrument of our time is the orchestra. Orchestral sonority is a cardinal fact in our musical experience and is central to the shaping of our musical imagery. A little over two hundred years ago, Bach had at his disposal an orchestra of approximately twenty players. Towards the end of the eighteenth century, when Haydn and Mozart were writing their symphonies, the orchestra consisted of about thirty men. Our great orchestras today number upward of a hundred. To write for such an ensemble is no mean art.

In writing for an orchestra, the composer weaves the multicolored strands of sound into a variegated tapestry, blending and contrasting the different timbres, contracting and expanding the instrumental forces according to his dynamic purpose, and allocating themes to those instruments that will present them most effectively. He sees to it that the melody stands out clearly and vividly from the sonorous background. At the same time he contrives to make the accompanying lines interesting in their own right. He distributes the melodic, harmonic, and rhythmic material among the instrumental groups so as to secure the proper balance of tone and consistency of texture. Through the use of color he points up the design, sets off the main ideas from the subordinate, and welds the thousand and one details into an architectonic whole.

The orchestration, consequently, is associated most closely with his musical conception. As Walter Piston has observed, "The true art of orchestration is inseparable from the creative act of composing music." As a matter of fact, a composer's manner of orchestrating is as personal as is his shaping of the melody, harmony, or rhythm. (For background material on the orchestra and its instruments, see Appendix I-h.)

ORCHESTRATION IN THE CLASSIC-ROMANTIC ERA

The orchestra of Haydn and Mozart was capable of subtle nuances by which each timbre was made to stand out luminously. The eighteenth-century masters used their medium with surpassing economy. Color, for them, did not exist as an end in itself. It sprang from the nature of the thing said; it served the idea. Color highlighted form and structure, and contributed to achieving architectural unity.

For the romantic composers, color was an end in itself, and a perpetual source of wonder. Richard Strauss well understood this when he remarked that Hector Berlioz "was the first composer consistently to derive his inspiration from the nature of the instruments." In this regard the pioneering Frenchman was a true romantic. Until his time, as Aaron Copland pointed out, "composers used instruments in order to make them sound like themselves; the mixing of colors so as to produce a new result was his achievement."

It was Richard Wagner who created the sound image of the romantic orchestra which is most familiar to the world. His habit of blending and mixing colors continually, his technique of reinforcing (doubling) a single melody line with various instruments, and his addiction to sustained tones in the brass produced a rich massive texture that enchanted the audiences of the late nineteenth century. His was an opulent, multicolored cloud of sound in which the pure timbres of the individual instruments were either veiled or completely swallowed up; hence the frequent remark that Wagner's orchestra plays "with the pedal on." This technique was carried to its farthermost limits in the postromantic era, culminating in the orchestral virtuosity of Richard Strauss. Orchestration became an art that existed almost independently of composition. The composer displayed his sense of sound with the same mastery that former composers had shown in the field of thematic invention. The postromantic period saw the emergence of other brilliant orchestrators besides Strauss—Gustav Mahler, Maurice Ravel, Ottorino Respighi. But it happened in more than one work that the magnificence of the orchestral raiment far surpassed the quality of the musical ideas.

Between 1890 and 1910 the orchestra assumed formidable proportions. Strauss, in his score for *Elektra*, called for twelve trumpets, four trombones, eight horns, six to eight kettledrums. In Mahler's *Symphony of a Thousand* several choruses were deployed, in addition to mammoth orchestral forces. The texture of music began to assume a complexity beyond the capacity of the human ear to unravel. Despite the furious interplay of the instrumental lines, what emerged was a swollen, opaque stream of sound that brought to its ultimate development the vertical-harmonic—that is to say, the sheerly romantic—way of hearing music. The post-Wagnerian orchestra reached a point beyond which further advance was hardly possible.

Such an orchestral style, needless to say, could not appeal to a generation of musicians in revolt against the romantic esthetic. Debussy speaks of the "thick polychromatic putty" that Wagner spread over his scores. Stravinsky remarks that Wagner's orchestra "plays the organ." Copland describes the German master's orchestration as "an over-all neutral fatness of sound which has lost all differentiation and distinction." This change of taste went hand-in-hand with the simplification of texture described in the last chapter, and brought with it a lightening of the orchestral sound. Twentieth-century composers forced the postromantic orchestra to open its window, so to speak: to let in light and air.

THE NEW ORCHESTRATION

The turn from harmonic-vertical to contrapuntal thinking determined the new orchestral style. The nineteenth-century musician made his colors swim together; his twentieth-century counterpart aspires above all to make each instrument stand out clearly against the mass. Composers have turned back to classical ideals: clarity of line and transparency of texture. They have thinned out the swollen sound and reinstated the sharply defined colors of the eighteenth-century style. They no longer reinforce or double the melody line with a blend of instruments from various choirs; instead they emphasize individual timbres. As Stravinsky put it, "Doubling is not strengthening."

One may compare this change to a rejection of the rich composite colors of oil painting in favor of the naked lines of etching. The new orchestration reveals the interweaving of the melodic strands, the play of contrapuntal lines rather than the flow of harmonic masses. The result has been a reconstitution of true orchestral polyphony. There has been a return to the classical precept that color must function not as a source of enchantment but as a means of clarifying the structural design. The leaders of contemporary musical thought have emphasized again and again the need to free music from the seduction of romantic sonority. "We must outgrow the sentimental and superficial attachment to sound," wrote Paul Hindemith. Arnold Schoenberg maintained that "Lucidity is the first purpose of color in music. Perhaps the art of orchestration has become too popular, and interesting-sounding pieces are often produced for no better reason than that which dictates the making of typewriters and fountain pens in different colors." Stravinsky also warns against the "fundamental error" of regarding orchestration as "a source of enjoyment independent of the music. The time has surely come to put things in their proper place."

The desire to "decongest" the romantic sound brought in its wake a strong desire for a reduction of orchestral forces. From the monster ensemble of the 1890s, composers turned back to the smaller orchestra of the early nineteenth century. They revived the chamber orchestra of the eighteenth century—an ensemble of about twenty men in which each player functioned almost as a soloist. The adherents of the new classicism aspired to the radiant clarity of Mozart's orchestral texture, and to the *concertante* style of the age of Bach, in which single players or small groups opposed each other by their timbres instead of blending into a composite whole.

The lightening of orchestral texture is apparent in the widely spaced lines wherewith contemporary composers "ventilate" their scores. By eliminating all that is not essential they achieve a new sparseness in their scoring, setting down as few notes (where a Richard Strauss put down as many) as possible. It is instructive, in this regard, to compare a page from Strauss's *Till Eulenspiegel* with one from Stravinsky's *Orpheus* (pp. 58–59). Composers began to orchestrate in solid groups, opposing strings to woodwinds, woodwinds to brass, achieving thereby clean precise colors—what has well been called an enameled sound. Through the interplay and spacing of timbres they highlight the superposed successions of chords, enabling the listener to follow the several planes of harmony. Their modest linear scoring has taught the orchestra to play "without the pedal."

In effect, many contemporary composers brought into the orchestra the spirit of chamber music, and by so doing moved closer to what has always been the ideal of the string quartet and similar types of music: limpidity of texture, clarity of thought, refinement of expression, and subtlety of effect. As one writer expressed it, they have "chamberized" the orchestra. Composers today are not afraid to keep part of the orchestra silent if it suits their expressive purpose (unlike nineteenth-century composers, who felt that all the instruments had to play all the time). The pull away from Wagnerian opulence placed a new value upon a sober sound. Lack of brilliance, which the previous age would have regarded as a deficiency, now has come to be a virtue. "True sobriety," Stravinsky proclaimed, "is a great rarity, and most difficult of attainment." The string choir lost its traditional role as the heart of the orchestra, because its tone was felt to be too personal, too subjective. Composers began to favor the less expressive winds. Because of the distrust of overbrilliant sound, the darker instruments came into prominence; the lyrical violin was replaced in favor by the more reserved viola. Among the brass, the caressing horn was supplanted by the more incisive trumpet. All this, during the Twenties, was used as an antidote against the seductions of romantic sonority.

The exploration of percussive rhythm focused attention on the percussion instruments. These were emancipated from their hitherto subordinate position and brought into soloistic prominence. Indeed, percussion sound pervaded the entire orchestra. Composers were intrigued with the xylophone and glockenspiel, whose metallic, "objective" sonority accorded with the new esthetic. In addition, they began to model their sound upon instruments that had never been part of the orchestra. A case in point is Stravinsky's fondness for the accordion sound, or Schoenberg's for guitar and mandolin. The piano, which throughout the romantic era had been a solo instrument, was now included in the ensemble. Composers exploited its capacity for percussive rhythm, often treating it as a kind of xylophone in a mahogany box: a far cry, to say the least, from the instrument of Chopin and Liszt.

At the same time contemporary musicians continued the nineteenth-century attempt to open up new orchestral resources, using instruments in unusual ways, and exploring the expressive power of extreme registers and novel combinations. They exploited new effects—for example, the trombone glissando that Schoenberg employed so imaginatively. It can safely be said that musicians today are more adept in the art of orchestration than ever before. What with the prevalence of good orchestras, recordings, and radio, they have greater opportunities than did musicians of any earlier generation to hear orchestral music well played. As a result, many a young composer nowadays sets forth on his career with a mastery of orchestral technique it would have taken him half a lifetime to acquire a century ago.

Twentieth-century music is extremely dependent upon the orchestral

Strauss, Till Eulenspiegel

medium. We are able to get some idea of a classic or romantic symphony from a piano transcription; but this is hardly possible with modern works. Often a dissonance which sounds painfully harsh when a contemporary score is played on a piano has a luminous glow when it is heard in its proper spacing and timbre in the orchestra.

The advances in orchestral technique achieved during the nineteenth century made possible a new orchestral art. In restoring orchestral color to its function in classical times as the obedient handmaiden of form and idea, twentieth-century composers found a way to make the orchestra serve the esthetic goals of our time.

Stravinsky, *Orpheus*

⊰ 10 ⊱

New Conceptions of Form

"In music there is no form without logic, there is no logic without unity."

Arnold Schoenberg

WE HAVE traced fundamental patterns of organization in melody, harmony, tonality, rhythm and meter, texture and color. Out of the interplay of all these elements there emerges an impression of conscious choice and judicious arrangement, of coherence and continuity of thought: in a word, of artistic form. "Tonal elements," Stravinsky has written, "become music only by being organized." The over-all organization of these elements in musical time and space is what we mean by form.

A basic principle of musical form is repetition and contrast, which achieves both unity and variety. The one ministers to man's joy in the familiar and to his need for reassurance. The other satisfies his equally strong craving for the challenge of the unfamiliar. Repetition establishes a relationship between structural elements. Contrast sets off and vitalizes this relationship. The contrasting material brings with it a heightening of tension, which is resolved by the return of the familiar material. Hence Ernst Toch's fine phrase, "Form is the balance between tension and relaxation."

Form is the dwelling place of the idea, its visible shape and embodiment. In the highest art there exists the utmost unity between form and content, the two being as inseparable as are mind and body: *what* is said cannot be conceived as existing apart from *how* it is said. This becomes apparent when we try to retell the content of a poem, a novel, or play in our own words. We become aware that the content changes when it is removed from its form. The unity of form and content is especially strong in music, where the form is molded to the idea and the idea is shaped by the form. The form helps us grasp the inner content of a musical work. At the same time it can itself be a potent source of esthetic pleasure. "The principal function of form," declares Schoenberg, "is to advance our understanding. By producing comprehensibility, form produces beauty."

THE CLASSICAL FORMS

The principle of form which operates in all the arts manifests itself in music in a variety of traditional forms. It is important to remember that these are not so many ready-made molds into which the composer pours the stuff of his inspiration, so that it will harden and assume a shape approved by custom. The living forms of the masters grow organically from the material; the nature of the thing said dictates the treatment it receives. We can describe a sonata or fugue in a general way; but the fact remains that no two fugues of Bach, no two sonatas of Mozart are exactly alike. Each is a unique example of the adaptation of form to content. Each solves anew the subtle balancing of tension and relaxation, light and shade, feelingful content and structural logic.

"The form," Aaron Copland points out, "is a generalisation which has to be adapted to a particular situation."

In the Baroque and classical eras, the movement away from and back to the home key came to be the main gesture of musical form. The grand form of the classical era—the sonata—mobilized to the full the possibilities for unity and contrast, tension and resolution inherent in the major-minor system. Therewith the classical masters created an architectonic structure whose clarity of design, amplitude of gesture, and diversity of mood continue to command the admiration of the world. The classical sonata is an ideal tone-drama whose characters are the themes, and whose action is derived from purely musical elements without reference to literary or pictorial associations. The first movement is generally a spacious allegro. The second, as a rule, is a reflective slow movement. Third is a minuet or scherzo; and the cycle concludes with a lively finale. First, third, and fourth movements are usually in the home key, while the second is in a related key. The sonata cycle leaves the listener with the sense of a vast action resolved, an eventful journey brought to its conclusion. With its fusion of sensuous, emotional, and intellectual elements, of lyric contemplation and dramatic action, the sonata-symphony may justly claim to be one of the most compelling forms ever devised for the expressing of purely musical ideas in a purely musical way. There is every justification for Aaron Copland's comparing a great symphony to "a man-made Mississippi down which we irresistibly flow from the instant of our leave-taking to a long foreseen destination."

The characteristic movement of the cycle is the first, which is cast in *sonata form*. This is an epic-dramatic structure based on the opposition between the Tonic and the Dominant key—that is, between the home area and the related (but contrasting) area. The movement is in three sections: Exposition, Development, and Restatement (or Recapitulation). The Exposition sets forth two opposing ideas: a first theme (or theme-group) of strongly rhythmic character, which represents the home key; and a second theme (or theme-group) of lyrical character, which establishes the contrasting key. The Development hurls the opposing ideas into direct, violent conflict: themes are fragmented into their constituent motives, and tension is steadily built up through wandering farther afield, that is, through frequent modulation. In the Restatement the material is repeated more or less as we first heard it, but with one important change: nothing is allowed at this point to disturb the triumph of the home key. For which reason the second theme, originally heard in the foreign key, is shifted into the home key. In this way the Restatement reconciles the conflict posed in the Exposition. An ample *coda* or closing section rounds out the movement with a final affirmation of the home tonality. (For a detailed outline of sonata form and the other movements, see Appendix I-i.)

The four-movement cycle—whether as solo sonata, duo, trio, quartet or quintet, concerto, or symphony—satisfied the desire of the classical masters for an extended work that would derive its character from the nature of the instruments and its materials from the nature of music. Understandably this cycle had its greatest triumphs in the period when the major-minor system was at its peak: the age of Haydn, Mozart, Beethoven, and Schubert. The composers of the nineteenth century, for their part, adapted the classical form to romantic ends. They were concerned with picturesque detail, with mood, atmosphere, and color rather than the triumph of an over-all design. They loved expansive lyricism and rhetoric—so they distended the form and dissolved its outlines. Above all, in their preoccupation with chromatic harmony they veiled the boundaries of the key, and therewith undermined the contrast between Tonic and Dominant that was basic to the form. In their hands the symphony became a grandiose drama concerned with the triumph of faith over doubt, with man's struggle against fate, with the beauty of nature and the glory of one's native land. By the time César Franck, Bruckner, Tchaikovsky, Mahler, and Richard Strauss had done with it, the symphony had been taken a long way from its classical heritage; but it came to serve the expressive needs of the romantic period as effectively as it had met those of the classical age.

FORM IN CONTEMPORARY MUSIC

Contemporary composers have embraced the classical conception of form as a construction based on purely musical elements. They have restored form to its classical position as an absolute value in art, the symbol of purity and perfection of style. For the twentieth-century composer the purely musical elements of his art—line, harmony, rhythm, color—have as much appeal as had the literary or descriptive program for his romantic predecessor. He makes no distinction between the form and the emotion. Indeed, many musicians today affirm that form *is* emotion, and that the form of a piece is its meaning—the only meaning it can have. Even if this is an extreme statement of the formalist position— and one to which, assuredly, not all composers subscribe—it does express a significant current in present-day musical thought.

Considering the great changes that have taken place with respect to

The twentieth-century climate is hospitable to epigrammatic statement, to forms that are forthright, unpretentious, laconic. Maurice Utrillo, *Rue de Crimée*. (Collection: Alexander Jolas Gallery)

melody, harmony, rhythm, color, texture, and tonality, the changes in musical form have been considerably less spectacular. The traditional forms offer such ingenious solutions to the problem of unity and variety in music that they are not easily supplanted. The most important trend has been a moving away from the clear-cut symmetries of the classic-romantic era. The phrase is still the unit of musical architecture; but its beginning and end are no longer punched home to the ear. Repetition remains the basic principle of musical structure—but repetition disguised, varied, cropping up at irregular intervals and unexpected places. The whole conception of form based on clearly articulated formations of two, four, and eight measures has been drastically modified. This veiling of the structural outlines has resulted, naturally, in a certain loss of clarity and simplicity. But it has brought a corresponding gain of subtlety and freshness in expressive resources. "It is the barely perceptible irregularities that infuse life into artistic form," writes Ernst Toch. Contemporary music has rediscovered the charm of the irregular.

DYNAMIC SYMMETRY

The classical A-B-A pattern, with its outer sections balancing the middle part, is a clear adaptation to music of an architectural principle. In the classical view, eight measures of music in the first section had to be balanced by eight in the closing section. Contemporary esthetics has embraced a somewhat different position. When the A section of a three-part structure is repeated, the original statement is already removed from us in time. It has "shrunk" somewhat to our view, exactly as an object does that is removed from us in space. For this reason a shorter version of the A section, when it is repeated, will sound just as long to us as the original statement—especially since we already are familiar with the material. Contemporary composers consequently foreshorten the repetition, achieving the same effect of perspective in time as we are accustomed to in space. They have substituted dynamic symmetry for a symmetry based on exact repetition.

To the contemporary way of thinking, an intensification of style—a rise to more dramatic expression, more striking orchestral color, or more extreme dynamics—will cause six measures in the repetition, or five or four, to equal, psychologically, eight measures in the original version. What counts is not the number of measures, but the importance of the events taking place in them. In accord with this dynamic conception of form, contemporary composers are extremely reluctant to repeat themselves. They abridge the repetition, vary it, or entirely recast it. Their attitude in this regard is summed up by Schoenberg's admonition to students who brought him a piece with a section repeated: "Never do what a copyist can do!"

Our time avoids grandiloquence and verbosity, and rejects the over-extended forms of the post-Wagner period. The twentieth-century climate is hospitable to epigrammatic statement, to forms that are forthright and laconic. The emphasis is on nicety of detail, precision of thought, and simplicity of means.

THE TWENTIETH-CENTURY SONATA

At the beginning of our century the sonata form had apparently been rendered obsolete. It was overwhelmed on the one hand by Wagnerian music drama and the Straussian tone poem, on the other by the pictorial creations of Debussy and Ravel. The revival of classical canons of taste has restored the absolute forms to a central position in our musical life.

The classical sonata embodied the structural values inseparable from the major-minor system: contrasting key centers, clearcut harmonic cadences, sharply defined phrase structure, symmetrical sections, vertical texture, and the ultimate resolution of the Dominant harmony to the Tonic. But these are precisely the values that have either been abandoned or severely modified in the contemporary style. That the sonata has been able to accommodate itself to so changed an environment testifies to the extraordinary vitality of the grand form.

Contemporary harmony has expanded the sense of key; it is therefore evident that all musical forms based on tonality have had to be modified. We will not find in the modern sonata, whether for piano, string quartet or orchestra, the old Tonic-Dominant relationship, or a clearly molded bridge passage between the home key and the contrasting key. Transitional passages—the seams of musical fabric—are not favored today. Modulations are swift and abrupt, dispensing with the traditional connectives: one tonality is simply displaced by another. Key relationships, as might be expected, are extremely flexible and free. All the same, tonality still plays an important part in stabilizing harmonic areas and tonal masses. The present-day sonata has moved from the "seven-out-of-twelve" way of hearing music to the "twelve-out-of-twelve." But the form has retained, in a general way, the principle of contrasting key centers and the ultimate triumph of a Tonic.

The modern sonata structure is compact and firm in design. From what we have said about repetition in contemporary music, it is obvious that the Restatement is much curtailed. When the two themes return in this section they are often shifted to higher keys, for the purpose of intensification. A composer will sometimes bring back the second theme before the first, just as, when we return to a locality that we have left, familiar landmarks appear to us in reverse order. The repetition is often reduced to no more than a fleeting reference to the original statement. There is also a tendency to introduce new developments into the Restatement, to present the material in a new light so as to sustain the listener's interest. As a result, the Restatement plays a much more dynamic role than it formerly did.

The themes of the modern sonata are apt to be instrumental in character rather than vocal (as was the case during the romantic period). They are relatively short, precise, impregnated with movement and gesture, with motoric rhythm and propulsive force. They are building blocks in the fullest sense, lending themselves readily to developmental procedures and to contrapuntal combination. The distinction in style between Exposition and Development is observed far less today than in the classic-romantic era. Indeed, the modern sonata movement has largely given up the neatly sewn, three-section fabric of the classical pattern. Development has taken over the entire form, pervading Exposition and Restatement as well. As a result, the modern sonata form tends to be one continuous development from first note to last, a procedure that accords with the dynamic concept of form of our time. Often a movement unfolds without a full cadence from beginning to end, relinquishing clarity of punctuation in favor of uninterrupted momentum. More themes may be presented, and with less regularity than in the classical sonata. Connective passages may introduce new ideas that are immediately subjected to development. The arch of the form extends in a single span, with an unfaltering drive that steadily mounts in tension.

Equally significant are the changes in the cycle as a whole. Twentieth-century esthetics has come to grips with what was always a vulnerable spot in the sonata cycle. We all know that if we come too late to hear the first movement of a symphony, concerto, sonata, or string quartet, as like as not we have missed the most important part of the work. In many a work of the classic-romantic era the later movements hardly match the tension of the first. Contemporary musicians have tried to avoid the inevitable sense of anticlimax in one of three ways. First, by placing the most dramatic and spacious movement at the end of the cycle rather than at the beginning. (The late works of Beethoven already utilize this solution of the problem.) Second, by amalgamating the four movements into a single-movement form with contrasting sections; this retains the diversity of the classical cycle in condensed fashion. (The precedent here was established by Liszt.) Third, by reshuffling and interlocking the movements. The component sections of one movement are often lifted out of their context and linked with parts of another movement. In one sonata we may find a slow section interposed between Exposition and Development, while a scherzo-like section intervenes between Development and Restatement. In another, Exposition and Restatement may be separated to become the first and last parts of the cycle, providing a flexible frame for the intervening movements. The possibilities are manifold, and have been exploited very imaginatively by contemporary musicians.

It should be added, however, that present-day composers do not feel impelled to abandon the traditional scheme unless their expressive purpose demands it. The serious artist does not court innovation for its own sake. Many a work to be discussed in the following pages will be found to adhere to the Exposition-Development-Restatement pattern of the first movement, with the lyrical slow movement, the scherzo, and the finale following as in the old days.

The twentieth-century concept of form derives from the great tradition. Composers have taken from the old forms whatever could be of use to them, and have added new elements, thereby adapting the achievements of the past to the needs of the present. In our time, as formerly, they affirm the primacy of form in the musical tradition of the west: form as the supreme gesture of creative will and imagination; as the subjugation of all that is capricious and arbitrary to the discipline, the logic, the higher unity of art.

Part Two

THE EUROPEAN SCENE

"The secret of the tone must be always pursued anew."
Arnold Schoenberg

I. LATE ROMANTICS

"We are all of us children of our time—and can never leap
over its shadows."

Richard Strauss

✎§ 11 §✎

The Postromantic Generation

"Only when I experience intensely do I compose. Only when
I compose do I experience intensely."

Gustav Mahler

THE TRANSITION from the romantic era to the twentieth century was
effectuated by the generation of composers born in the 1860s and '70s.
These men came to artistic maturity at the turn of the century—that is
to say, in the twilight of romanticism. Their music constituted both
a continuation of the romantic heritage and a revolt against it. This
dualism added an inner strain to their art that on the one hand mili-
tated against its achieving perfection and on the other added to its
nostalgic charm. Essentially, these men were latecomers, writing under
the shadow of a greatness that could no longer be revived. But their
music is not merely retrospective: it sets forth new elements in which
one can clearly trace the shape of things to come.

A period of transition, being less stable than the noontide of an era,
is markedly less conducive to the production of enduring works. It
testifies to the vitality of the postromantic generation that so much of
their music continues to delight the public. For it was the unique mission of this group of composers not only to write the coda to the achievements of the preceding era, but also to lead music into the new age.

A characteristic figure of this generation was Gabriel Fauré (Pamiers,
Ariège, 1845–1924, Paris). Fauré is one of those composers who attain
an eminence in their native land they do not duplicate elsewhere. In
Fauré's case, this is partly due to the fact that he was basically a lyricist
who expressed himself best in the intimate forms of music—songs, piano
pieces, chamber music—whereas in our time the big public is reached
primarily through symphonies and operas. Moreover, his reticent charm,

his unpretentious and fastidious lyricism are traits least likely to impress the multitude.

Fauré's style exemplifies what he called "the eminently French qualities of taste, clarity, and sense of proportion." At a time when his countrymen were seduced by the grandiloquence of Wagner he hoped for a restoration of "our common sense, that is to say, the taste for clear thought, purity of form, and sobriety." Fauré is best known for his *Requiem* (1887). This music has an inner quietude of spirit that displays his characteristic trait of "intimate limpidity." His songs, of which he wrote almost a hundred, rank with the finest that France has produced. The nocturnes, barcarolles, and similar pieces for piano are imbued with personal lyricism. Fauré's chamber works achieve a graceful union of classical form and romantic content. Noteworthy in this category are two quartets for piano and strings (1879, 1886); two piano quintets (1906, 1921); and the string quartet he completed shortly before his death at the age of eighty. As head of the Paris Conservatoire for fifteen years, Fauré was in a position to impress his ideals upon French musical life. Among his pupils were Maurice Ravel and Nadia Boulanger.

In point of time Emmanuel Chabrier (Ambert, Puy de Dôme, 1841–1894, Paris) was contemporary with Tchaikovsky. If he deserves mention in a book on twentieth-century music it is because, while many composers were still exploring the depths of late-romantic subjectivity, this exuberant Frenchman emphasized humor and gayety in his works, thus pointing to a trend that became increasingly important in the new music and strongly influenced several key figures of the modern French school, especially Debussy, Ravel, and Satie. Chabrier is best known to the public for his tuneful orchestral rhapsody *España*. He also produced several operas; *Trois Valses romantiques* (1883) for two pianos; choral and piano music, and songs.

A typical figure of this generation was Sir Edward Elgar (Broadheath, near Worcester, 1857–1934, Worcester), the first important British composer in two hundred years—that is, since the death of Purcell. Elgar loved England, her past, her people, her countryside, and he responded to her need for a national artist much as Rudyard Kipling did. Perhaps he responded too eagerly. He became the musician laureate of the late Victorian and Edwardian eras; the mixture of idealism and imperialism prevalent during those years found perfect expression in his music. He was knighted by Edward VII, for whose accession he wrote the *Coronation Ode*. For years the first of his *Pomp and Cir-*

cumstance marches was the required accompaniment for newsreel glimpses of Britain's royal family. Elgar was a natural musician of great invention and spontaneity. "It is my idea," he said, "that music is in the air all around us, the world is full of it, and at any given time you simply take as much of it as you require." What he took was not always distinguished. But he shaped it lovingly into something that had enormous gusto and that shone with all the hues of the postromantic orchestra.

Elgar's music is full of sound and movement. It stems from an eclectic, late nineteenth-century style compounded of Brahms, Strauss, and even a little Verdi; but it bears the imprint of a thoroughly British personality. Having grown up in Worcester, Elgar knew at first hand the cathedral towns whose choir festivals are the backbone of musical life in provincial England. His oratorios met both the religious and musical needs of the time. Elgar's masterpiece in this category is *The Dream of Gerontius* (1900), a setting of the poem by Cardinal Newman. Elgar produced a varied repertoire of religious and secular cantatas, part songs, and chamber music; two symphonies (1908, 1909) which at one time enjoyed a phenomenal popularity; overtures and symphonic poems, among them *Froissart* (1890), *Cockaigne* Overture (In London Town, 1901), and *Falstaff* (1909); and a number of occasional pieces. Of his major works, the *Enigma Variations* (1899) and *Introduction and Allegro* for strings (1905) are still performed outside his homeland. The rest of his music is played chiefly in England, where Elgar is a veritable institution. "He might have been a great composer," his compatriot Cecil Gray said of him, "if he had not been such a perfect gentleman." Nonetheless Elgar served his country well. She will long remember him.

Although romanticism was not confined to any one country, its stronghold was in those lands that lay under the influence of the Austro-German musical tradition. We may therefore begin our detailed consideration of the late-romantic composers with the two most illustrious representatives of that tradition—Gustav Mahler and Richard Strauss.

◈ 12 ◈
Gustav Mahler (1860-1911)

"To write a symphony is, for me, to construct a world."

GUSTAV MAHLER continues to be one of the controversial figures in
modern music. For his admirers he is a major prophet whose troubled
spirit poured itself out in grandiose works. His detractors, on the other
hand, accuse him of banality, pose, and theatrical pathos. In other words,
he appeals only to a certain kind of sensibility—but does so very strongly.

Bettmann Archive

Gustav Mahler

HIS LIFE

Mahler was born and raised in Bohemia. His father, owner of a small
distillery, was not slow in recognizing the boy's talent. Piano lessons
began when Gustav was six. He was sent to Vienna and entered the

Conservatory at fifteen, the University three years later. Here he came under the influence of Anton Bruckner. Relations between master and disciple were so cordial that when he was eighteen the youth was entrusted with the task of preparing the piano arrangement of Bruckner's Third Symphony.

Together with other impecunious young musicians, he frequented the cafés where were discussed the advanced social and artistic theories of the day. He worshipped Wagner. He was persuaded for a time that mankind would be regenerated by means of a vegetarian diet. He gave piano lessons. He composed. His professional career began modestly enough when, at the age of twenty, he was engaged to conduct operettas at a third-rate summer theatre. A dynamic conductor who found his natural habitat in the opera house, Mahler soon achieved a reputation that brought him ever more important posts, until at twenty-eight he was director of the Royal Opera at Budapest. From Budapest Mahler went to Hamburg. Then, at thirty-seven, he was offered the most important musical position in the Austrian Empire—the directorship, with absolute powers, of the Vienna opera. His ten years there (1897–1907) made history. He brought to his duties a fiery temperament, unwavering devotion to ideals, and the inflexible will of the zealot. When he took over, Massenet was the chief drawing card. By the time his rule ended he had taught a frivolous public to revere Mozart, Beethoven, and Gluck, and made them listen to uncut versions of Wagner's operas.

When it was objected that his innovations flouted tradition, he retorted, "Tradition is laziness! In every performance the work must be born anew." Despite the prodigious outlay of energy entailed by his duties, during his Vienna period he produced five big symphonies—the Fourth to the Eighth. These were written down in rough draft during the summer months when the Opera was closed—he called himself *der Sommerkomponist*, the summer composer—and orchestrated during the winter, Mahler working at home every morning before he embarked on his duties as director. The conflict between his two careers, each pulling him in a different direction, could not but heighten the tensions within that turbulent temperament.

Shortly before he was appointed to Vienna, Mahler became a convert to Catholicism. This step was motivated in the first instance by the desire to smooth his way in a city where antisemitism was rampant. Beyond that, Mahler belonged to a generation of Jewish intellectuals who had lost identification with their religious heritage and who sought roots in the Austro-German culture of which they felt themselves to be a part. His was the inquiring intellect of the perpetual doubter; yet he yearned for the ecstasy of faith and the wholeness of soul that came with certainty. Alma Mahler tells in her *Reminiscences* how, during their courtship, when he played her his Fifth Symphony, she admired everything in the work save the triumphal chorale at the end, which she found unconvincing. " 'What about Bruckner!' he protested. 'He yes, but not you,' I said, and tried to make clear to him the radical difference between his nature and Bruckner's. I was touching here on a rift in his being which often brought him into serious conflict with himself." The man's need for roots involved also the artist's vision: hence his inordinate desire to ally his music with the Viennese tradition. "I am thrice homeless," he remarked. "As a Bohemian born in Austria. As an Austrian among Germans. And as a Jew throughout the world."

"Humanly I make every concession, artistically—none!" Such intransigence was bound to create powerful enemies. Mahler's final years in Vienna were embittered by the intrigues against him, which flourished despite the fact that he had transformed the Imperial Opera into the premier lyric theatre of Europe. The death of a little daughter left him griefstricken. A second disaster followed soon after: he was found to have a heart ailment. When he finally was forced to resign his post, the blow was not unexpected. Mahler, now almost forty-eight (he had only three more years to live), accepted an engagement at the Metropolitan Opera House. He hoped to earn enough to be able to retire at fifty, so that he finally might compose with the peace of mind that had never been granted him. His three years in New York were not free of the storms that his tempestuous personality inevitably provoked. In 1909 he assumed direction of the New York Philharmonic Orchestra. When the ladies of the Board made it plain to Alma that her husband had flouted their wishes, she expostulated, "But in Vienna the Emperor himself did not dare to interfere!"

His summers he spent in the countryside near Vienna. Here he composed his masterpiece, *Das Lied von der Erde* (The Song of the Earth). Although he thought of this as his ninth symphony, he was superstitious enough not to call it by that title, as neither Beethoven nor Schubert, Bruckner nor Dvořák had gone beyond their Ninth. His next symphony was therefore named the Ninth. Fate, however, was not to be cheated: he did not live to finish his Tenth. In the middle of a taxing concert season with the Philharmonic he fell ill with a streptococcus infection. It was decided to bring him to Paris, where a new serum treatment had been developed. Arrived in Paris, he took a turn for the worse. Thus he set forth on his last journey, back to the scene of his greatest triumphs—the enchanting, exasperating Vienna he both loved and detested. On his deathbed he conducted with one finger on the quilt, uttering a single word: "Mozart. . . ."

He was buried, as he had requested, beside his daughter at Grinzing. At last that unquiet heart was at rest.

HIS MUSIC

"The act of creation in me is so closely bound up with all my experience that when my mind and spirit are at rest I can compose nothing." In this identification of art with personal emotion Mahler was entirely the romantic. Music for him was vision, intoxication, fulfillment: "a mysterious language from beyond." The sounds were symbols of states of mind and soul. "What is best in music," he observed, "is not to be found in the notes." In his notes resound the great themes of an age that was drawing to its close: nature, poetry, and folklore, love of man and faith in God, the sorrow of human destiny and the loneliness of death. Mahler engaged in a gigantic effort to breathe vitality into the romantic world of thought and feeling that was in process of disintegration. This circumstance imparts to his music its fevered unrest, its nostalgia.

Mahler was the last in the illustrious line of Viennese symphonists that extended from Haydn, Mozart, Beethoven, and Schubert to Bruckner and Brahms. His tone imagery was permeated by the intimately jovial spirit of Austrian popular song and dance, and by the melodious folk tunes of his native Bohemia. He sought to assimilate these humble materials to the grand form of the past and to create a popular (in the best sense of the term) symphonic art for the modern age. In his desire to emulate the classical masters he sometimes ended by sounding like them. Yet even those who accuse him of being derivative will admit that he set the seal of his own personality upon everything he touched. He has his own sound. It is not to be mistaken for any other's.

Mahler was primarily a lyricist. The spirit of song permeates his art. He followed Schubert and Schumann in cultivating the song cycle. *Lieder eines fahrenden Gesellen* (Songs of a Wayfarer), composed in 1883, is a set of four songs suffused with Schubertian longing. Mahler wrote the texts himself, aroused by an image that appealed strongly to his imagination: the rejected lover wandering alone over the face of the earth. His next cycle was inspired by a famous collection of German folk poetry, *Des Knaben Wunderhorn* (The Youth's Magic Horn, 1888) which had been gathered in the early nineteenth century by the poets Achim von Arnim and Clemens Brentano. The moving *Kinder-totenlieder* (Songs on the Death of Children, 1902) is a cycle for voice and orchestra to the grief-laden poems of Rückert. The peak of his achievement in this direction is, of course, the cycle of six songs with orchestra that make up *Das Lied von der Erde*.

Song lyricism is the essential ingredient of Mahler's nine symphonies. (The Tenth, we saw, was left unfinished.) These works are monumental frescoes. The melody is long of line, with extravagant leaps which heighten its power to communicate. The harmony is rich and sur-charged with emotion. A favorite symbol is the funeral march, now as a solemn cortege, now as a lyrical meditation on life and death. The scherzos speak the Austrian popular dialect, running the gamut from earthy humor and peasant dance to the bizarre and the fantastic. Trum-pet and horn calls, an inevitable feature of the language of German romanticism, supply a sense of mystery and evoke the sound of nature; or, allied with rattling drums, conjure up the robust din of the town pipers and regimental bands that remain an indelible memory for any-one growing up in Germanic lands. Another important symbol is the chorale, used to create an atmosphere of religious faith. Hardly less im-portant are the motives derived from bird-calls, evoking the out-of-doors. Mahler increased the number of movements in the symphony to five or six, and tried to tighten the structure by bringing back in later movements the thematic material of earlier ones (cyclical structure). His feeling for drama caused him to make the last movement, rather than the first, the most important in the cycle, thereby avoiding any impression of anticlimax.

In his sense of color Mahler ranks with the great masters of the art of orchestration. He contrasts solo instruments in the manner of cham-ber music, achieving his color effects through clarity of line rather than massed sonorities. His predilection for pure (that is, unmixed) colors gave impetus to an important trend in twentieth-century music. He secures unusual effects by spacing the instrumental lines far apart and writing for the instruments in their extreme range: trumpets and bas-soons in high register, flutes in low. His strong rhythmic sense led him to write with great imagination for the percussion group, which he raised to solo importance. He calls for instruments not hitherto associated with the orchestra: guitar, mandolin, harmonium, piano, organ, cow-bells, hammer; a cornet in the Third Symphony, a tenor horn in the Seventh. He exploits unusual effects—additional instruments offstage to achieve a sense of distance, or a choir humming a wordless melody. His transparent "open-air" sound was not without influence. Composers as diverse as Schoenberg and Prokofiev, Honegger and Alban Berg, Shostakovich and Britten listened to him with profit.

It was in the matter of texture that Mahler made his most important contribution to contemporary technique. Basing his orchestral style on counterpoint, he caused two or more melodies to unfold simultaneously, each setting off the other. Through this songful polyphony he approached what was to become one of the most important types of new music—the chamber symphony. He was an innovator with respect to key: he would begin a movement—or a symphony!—in one key and end it in another. Characteristic is his dramatic juxtaposition of unrelated keys, as well as a Schubertian wavering between major and minor. Nevertheless, Mahler never abandoned the principle of tonality. He needed the key as a framework for his vast design. His refined and expressive chromaticism rests upon a firm foundation; he has been called "the last of the diatonic composers." Hand-in-hand with his loosening of the key structure went his expansion of symphonic form. He unfolds a large number of thematic groups, which are then subjected to a process of continuous variation, repetition, and development. He did overextend the symphonic form. The first movement of the Third Symphony and the finale of the Sixth are among the longest conceived by any composer.

The First Symphony (1888) is related both psychologically and thematically to *Lieder eines fahrenden Gesellen.* Similarly, the next three symphonies utilize material from the *Wunderhorn* songs, and call for voices in addition to the instruments. Of this group the best-known is the Second or *Resurrection* Symphony (1894), in which Mahler discourses of a theme that obsessed him—death and the life beyond. The finale is for huge orchestra and double chorus. Amidst the pealing of bells and the fanfares of the brass, the chorus intones Klopstock's *Ode to Immortality,* to which Mahler added his own lines: "Believe, my heart . . . I shall soar upwards, I shall die that I may live!" The Fifth (1902), Sixth (1904) and Seventh (1905) are purely instrumental works in which he forges his way to a concept of symphonic structure based on contrapuntal procedures. The middle period culminates in the Eighth or *Symphony of a Thousand* (1907), so called because of the vast array of performers required: an expanded orchestra with extra brass choir, eight solo voices, double chorus, boy's chorus, and organ. This work crowns the nineteenth century's predilection for the grandiose. The compositions of the final period breathe an inner serenity, a resignation that was new to Mahler. These include *Das Lied von der Erde* and the Ninth Symphony (1909).

Although he never wrote critical articles or formulated his esthetic creed, Mahler's letters are filled with observations that combine verbal felicity with keen insight. "In art as in life I am at the mercy of spontaneity. . . . Ugliness is an insult to God. . . . My music is, throughout and always, but a sound of nature. . . . Spitting on the floor won't make you Beethoven." After the completion of the Eighth Symphony he exulted, "I am the universe when it resounds." Asked to state the essence of his religious belief, he replied: "I am a musician. That tells everything!" In a letter to Bruno Walter: "Strange, when I hear music —even while I conduct—I can hear quite definite answers to all my questions and feel entirely clear and sure." And when his work met with incomprehension: "My time will come!"

DAS LIED VON DER ERDE
(THE SONG OF THE EARTH)

Mahler's most sustained piece followed the dark period when he was informed by his physician that he had a heart ailment. From initial despair he passed over to a heightened awareness of life. "I see everything in a new light. I thirst for life more than ever before and find the 'habit of existence' more sweet than it ever was." This mood spurred him to a work in which a fierce joy in the beauty of earthly things commingles with resignation.

He found his vehicle in Hans Bethge's translation—more accurately, reconstruction—of old Chinese poems. In their emphasis upon the transience of youth and happiness, these verses are similar in mood to those of FitzGerald's adaptation of the *Rubáiyát* of Omar Khayyám. The lyricist in Mahler responded to these fervid images of joy and despair, and the symphonist expanded the material in the orchestra. The piece was written in the South Tyrol in 1908. Mahler never heard it performed. *Das Lied von der Erde* had its premiere in Munich six months after his death, under the baton of Bruno Walter.

I. *Das Trinklied vom Jammer der Erde* (The Drinking Song of Earth's Sorrow).   For tenor and orchestra. (The complete text of *Das Lied von der Erde* and an English translation will be found in Appendix 4.)

> Now gleams the wine in the golden cup.
> But drink not yet—first will I sing you a song!
> Let the song of sorrow
> Resound with laughter in your soul. . . .

The impassioned opening establishes Mahler's favorite key of A minor. The movement is marked *Allegro pesante*. A leaping motive in the horns outlines the interval of a fourth which is basic to the work. (For an explanation of tempo terms, see Appendix I-e.)

Almost immediately the violins set forth the germinal theme that serves as the unifying principle of the several movements:

The principal motive (under the bracket) reappears in a number of metamorphoses: in longer note values (augmentation) or shorter (diminution); upside down (inversion) or backwards (retrograde). The motive creates the pentatonic atmosphere commonly associated with Chinese music, subtly underlining the exotic flavor of the piece.

The soloistic treatment of winds and strings sets off the lines with exemplary clarity. The music abounds in effects that Mahler loved: arpeggios on the harp; "fluttertonguing" on the flute, suggesting a sinister rattle; muted trumpets. "Dark is life, dark is death. . . ." The poignant refrain, with its fatalistic downward curve, returns thrice, each time a semitone higher, in a kind of intensification. The movement reaches its climax with a macabre image dear to the romantic imagination. "In the moonlight, in the churchyard, there gibbers a wild ghostly shape. . . ." The solo voice descends in an eerie slide over an octave, Mahler demanding from the singer a new kind of agility. In this passage we are well into the twentieth century, especially the Viennese section thereof.

"The time has come, comrades: drain your golden cups. . . ." The music fluctuates between major and minor, and closes with a last tumultuous outcropping of the germinal motive.

II. *Der Einsame im Herbst* (Autumn Loneliness). For contralto and orchestra.

> Autumn mists drift palely over the sea.
> Touched with frost, the grass stands rigid.
> It is as though an artist's hand had strewn
> Dust of jade on every leaf and blade. . . .

The movement is marked *Etwas schleichend—ermüdet* (somewhat lingering, listless.) Oboe, clarinet and violins trace delicate filaments that intertwine in an attenuated fabric. The opening melody on the oboe shows the interval of a fourth that figures so prominently in Mahler's tone imagery. Notice the transformations of the germ motive at *a* and *b:*

The turn to subjective feeling in the text is marked by exuberant leaps in the orchestral melody. The movement builds steadily to its emotional peak. There is a gentle subsiding, and a return to the dark D-minor tonality. This music is pale, disembodied, strangely poignant.

III. *Von der Jugend* (Of Youth). For tenor and orchestra. A dainty bit of *chinoiserie* that evokes a teahouse on the river where friends sit, drinking, conversing, or writing verses while their reflections ripple in the water below. The pentatonic patterns exhale a delicate exoticism.

IV. *Von der Schönheit* (Of Beauty). For contralto and orchestra. This movement is more amorous in character. Young maidens pick flowers by the river bank, their graceful movements bathed in sunlight. Suddenly there arrives a company of young gallants, to the sturdy strains of an Austrian regimental band. These gay blades hail from the Tyrol rather than Cathay; but love is stronger than geography, and the final measures, with their tenderly retrospective tones, are inescapably romantic.

V. *Der Trunkene im Frühling* (The Drunkard in Spring). For tenor and orchestra. The poet is awakened from his wine-drugged sleep by a bird in the tree. "I ask him if spring has come, for all is like a dream. He twitters, 'Yes—Spring is here!'" And the poet, contented, refills his cup. . . . The movement is an Allegro marked "Boldly, but not too fast." The colloquy between poet and bird is given with all the naïveté of which Mahler was sometimes capable: the enigmatic naïveté of the sophisticate. Notice the vaulting melodic line and the wide leaps, against shifting harmonies that play havoc with a tenor's intonation.

VI. *Der Abschied* (The Farewell). For contralto and orchestra. This movement, which takes about twenty-four minutes, is equivalent in length to a complete classical symphony. The opening chords establish an atmosphere of brooding. Dark colors are to the fore: oboe, contrabassoon, horn, gong, viola, and double bass, along with two harps.

> The sun sets behind the mountains.
> In every valley the shadows of evening descend . . .
> I tarry here and await my friend—
> I wait to bid him a last farewell.

The lyric line is of remarkable length. It unravels against a background of flickering sound set up by clarinets and harps—an effect characteristic of Mahler. "How I long for your presence, O my friend, to share with you the beauty of this evening. . . ." There is an ecstatic apostrophe to beauty: "O world intoxicated with eternal love and life!" A gong tolls, bringing us back to the tragic note—and the C-minor tonality—of the opening measures. A symphonic interlude unfolds in the manner of a bizarre march, charged with all the strangeness and wonder that Mahler inherited from the "satanism" of Berlioz and Liszt. The marchlike lamentation—fitting cortege for the dreams of a century—is woven out of a pregnant motive which is an inversion of the first three notes of the germinal theme.

The major mode breaks through momentarily as Mahler returns to the favorite image of his youth, the lonely wayfarer. "Where do I go? I go wandering in the mountains, seeking rest for my lonely heart!" The music reaches its destination, the key of C major. And now the shape of things is revealed. For C major is the relative key of A minor, in which the piece began. The vast design, for all its chromatic fluctuation, is seen to rest on a firm foundation of tonality. Celesta, mandolin, and harp impart a radiant lightness to the orchestral tissue as the voice repeats the last word, *ewig* (ever . . . ever . . .) until it is barely audible. The three tones of the germinal motive are reconciled in the final chord.

Mahler knew that in this Adagio he had reached the summit of his art. "What do you think?" he wrote Bruno Walter. "Is this to be endured at all? Will not people do away with themselves after hearing it?" The movement is regarded as Mahler's farewell to life. It is, even more, a tender leavetaking of that whole complex of thought and feeling which made up the sulphurous world of romanticism—that dying world which found in him so visionary a spokesman.

❧ 13 ❧
Richard Strauss (1864-1949)

"Hang it all! I cannot express it more simply."

HIS LIFE

THE MOST publicized composer of the early twentieth century was born in Munich. His father was a virtuoso horn player who belonged to the court orchestra. His mother was the daughter of Georg Pschorr, a successful brewer of Munich beer. In this solid middle-class environment, made familiar to American readers by the novels of Thomas Mann, a high value was placed on music and money. These remained Strauss's twin passions throughout his life.

Richard Strauss

The boy played the piano when he was four and composed his first pieces at the age of six. His father, a confirmed anti-Wagnerite, saw to it that he was brought up "in a strictly classical way." As a result, his early instrumental works show an allegiance to chamber music, concerto, and symphony. In conservative musical circles the gifted youth was hailed as the future successor to Brahms. But at the age of twenty-one Strauss, groping for a type of expression that would suit his temperament, found his way into the camp of program music. It became his aim "to develop the poetic, the expressive in music as exemplified in the works of Liszt, Wagner, and Berlioz."

The new orientation is apparent in the symphonic fantasy *Aus Italien* (From Italy). Strauss now found his metier—the writing of vividly descriptive tone poems. *Macbeth*, the first of the series (1886), was followed by *Don Juan* (1888), an extraordinary achievement for a young man of twenty-four. There followed the works that carried his name throughout the civilized world: *Tod und Verklärung* (Death and Transfiguration, 1889); *Till Eulenspiegel's lustige Streiche* (Till Eulenspiegel's Merry Pranks, 1895); *Also sprach Zarathustra* (Thus Spake Zarathustra, 1896); *Don Quixote* (1897); and *Ein Heldenleben* (A Hero's Life, an autobiographical symphonic poem, 1903). These works shocked the conservatives and secured Strauss's position as the *enfant terrible* of modern music—a role he thoroughly enjoyed.

In 1894 he married the singer Pauline de Ahna, daughter of a Bavarian general. A colorful personality, she devoted herself to presenting her husband's songs, often with him as accompanist. By this time he had made a great reputation as a conductor. He appeared all over Europe and in 1896 was summoned to the Berlin Opera. In 1904 Strauss and his wife visited the United States, where he conducted the world premiere of his *Sinfonia Domestica;* she performed his songs. Strauss, for the then fabulous fee of a thousand dollars per appearance, conducted two afternoon concerts in the auditorium of John Wanamaker's department store. The incident was seized upon by his detractors to point up his commercialism. His defense made very good sense: "True art ennobles any hall. And earning money in a decent way for wife and child is no disgrace—even for an artist!"

Strauss conquered the operatic stage with *Salome, Elektra*, and *Der Rosenkavalier* (The Knight of the Rose). The international triumph of the last opera, on the eve of the First World War, marked the summit of his career. Strauss was able to extract unprecedented fees for his scores; the publishing rights of *Elektra* brought him twenty-seven thousand dollars. To obtain the New York premiere of this work ahead of the Metropolitan Opera House, Oscar Hammerstein paid him ten thousand dollars and deposited an additional eighteen thousand in advance royalties. Such sums fifty years ago—and in the field of serious music—were something to talk about.

It was Strauss's ambition to become a millionaire, so that he would be free to devote himself to his art. He had achieved his goal by the time he was fifty. Unfortunately, in the thirty-five years that remained to him he created little that added to his reputation. His collaboration with Hugo von Hofmannsthal, the librettist of *Elektra* and *Rosenkava-lier*, continued until the latter's death in 1929. But the world out of which their art issued had come to an end in 1914. New winds were blowing. The one-time "bad boy of music" was now firmly entrenched as a con-servative. Strauss's later operas contain many passages of remarkable beauty; but they all speak, with various shades of refinement, the musical language of *Rosenkavalier*. To that degree they represent no fresh solution of problems, no real inner growth.

The coming to power of the Nazis in 1933 confronted Strauss with a crucial decision. He was a staunch social-democrat under the Weimar Republic, as he had been a staunch royalist under the Kaiser. The cos-mopolitan circles in which he traveled were not susceptible to Hitler's ideology. Hence the challenge to speak out against the Third Reich, or to leave Germany as Thomas Mann, Hindemith, and scores of artists and intellectuals were doing. On the other hand, the new Germany was courting famous men of art and letters. Strauss saw the road open to supreme power over German music. In 1933, when he was on the threshold of seventy, the former revolutionary artist was elevated to the official hierarchy as president of the *Reichsmusikkammer* (Reich Chamber of Music).

His conscience was uneasy, as was his reign. His opera *Die schweig-same Frau* was withdrawn by the Nazis because the author of the book, Stefan Zweig, like Strauss's earlier librettist, Hofmannsthal, was Jewish. Strauss resigned his post. The war's end found the eighty-one-year-old composer in a somewhat ambiguous position. He was permitted to re-turn to his sumptuous villa at Garmisch, in the Bavarian Alps. To his friends Strauss explained that he had remained in Nazi Germany because someone had to protect culture from Hitler's barbarians. Perhaps he even believed it.

There were speeches at the Bavarian Academy of Fine Arts on the occasion of his eighty-fifth birthday. He died shortly after.

HIS MUSIC

Strauss inherited the orchestra of Berlioz, Liszt, and Wagner at the moment when it was ready to be transformed into a mammoth virtuoso ensemble. He stood in the forefront of this development. His was a dazzling orchestral style in which all the instruments participated equally. Even those which up to that time had served mainly to support the rest—double bass, trombone, tuba, kettledrums—were thrust into soloistic prominence. For special effects he introduced a quartet of saxophones; machines to simulate wind, thunder, storm; in the *Alpine Symphony*, sixteen horns and cowbells. For the early twentieth century the Straussian orchestra came to represent the last word in musical invention and mastery. To the sober palette of the Germans he added Italian sensuousness and French verve. Strauss, significantly, was one of the first to abandon the traditional concept of writing within the character of the instruments. On the contrary, he forced the instruments beyond their limitations, composing "for the trombone as if it were a piccolo." He loved an intricate orchestral fabric. Page after page is strewn with notes, so that the ear is simply unable to unravel all that is going on. This Gothic abundance is an essential feature of his style. It produces an effect of inexhaustible fertility of ideas and psychic tension even when those are not actually present in the music.

His melodies are tense, nervous, rhythmically alive. When he is at his best, those leaping themes of his have immense vitality and sweep. At his less than best he does not escape banality. "I work very long on melodies," he said. "The important thing is not the beginning of the melody but its continuation, its development into a complete melodic form." He spoke the sumptuous language of post-Wagnerian harmony; but he was not averse to daring polytonal effects that pointed to the future. The secret of Strauss's art is its furious rhythm. A master of shock and surprise—in other words, of timing—he whipped the sound mass into unheard-of speed and mobility. Characteristic of his works is the tumultuous opening gesture which reveals not only his super-abundance of energy but also his constant need to dazzle and overwhelm.

The chief controversy aroused by Strauss's tone poems centered about what is today a dead issue—program music. Strauss brought to its farthermost limits the nineteenth-century fondness for story-and-picture music. His vivid imagination leaned toward action and movement. He desired music to be so graphic that it could depict a teaspoon in a glass—a curious aim, to say the least. His symphonic poems are a treasury of realistic sound effects—the clatter of pots and pans, the bleating of frightened sheep, the whirring of windmills—which today have been inherited by television drama and animated cartoon.

These works are no longer heard as often as they used to be; Strauss's influence today rests upon his operas. *Salome* we will discuss. *Elektra* (1909), on Hofmannsthal's version of the Greek tragedy, is a one-acter that moves relentlessly to its climax. In these two lyric tragedies Strauss explores the dark caverns of the soul, dealing respectively with lust and revenge at their psychopathic level. Therewith he gave impetus to the taste for the horrible that was to grow stronger in German lands after the First World War with the advent of expressionism. *Rosenkavalier* (1911), on the other hand, harks back nostalgically to the Vienna of Maria Theresa (even as *Arabella* evokes the Vienna of Emperor Franz Joseph). The score is perfumed eroticism. Its deliberate archaisms offer homage to Mozart and Johann Strauss. The aging Marschallin, the disreputable Baron Ochs, young Octavian and Sophie awakening to the wonder of love—they belong to that memorable company of operatic characters who come truly alive in music.

In *Ariadne auf Naxos* (Ariadne on Naxos, 1912), Strauss abandoned grand opera for the chamber variety, therewith foreshadowing an important trend. His later stage works include *Die Frau ohne Schatten* (The Woman without a Shadow, 1917); *Intermezzo* (1923); *Die ägyptische Helena* (Helen in Egypt, 1927); *Arabella* (1932); *Die schweigsame Frau* (The Silent Woman, 1935); *Friedenstag* (Day of Peace, 1936, forbidden by the Nazis after the outbreak of war); *Daphne* (1937); *Die Liebe der Danae* (The Loves of Danae, 1940); and *Capriccio* (1941). They seem at present to be enjoying something of a revival in Germany. American audiences were given an opportunity recently to view several of them—*Arabella, Die schweigsame Frau, Daphne*, and *Capriccio*. These reinforced the impression that Strauss's later operas represent no new development in his art.

As a writer of songs Strauss stands in the great lineage of the German romantic Lied. The finest among them, such as the Serenade, *Morgen* (Morning), *Ich schwebe* (I Soar) and *Traum durch die Dämmerung* (Dream through Twilight) represent a permanent contribution to the literature of this lyric genre. With the *Vier letzte Lieder* (Four Last Songs), written in 1948 when he was eighty-four, the master—in a mood of serene acceptance—bade a tender farewell to his art.

SALOME

DRAMA IN ONE ACT AFTER OSCAR WILDE'S PLAY

Salome (1905) displays to the full Strauss's powers as an operatic composer: his capacity for generating excitement, his vivid delineation of character, his sensuous vocal line, his powerful evocation of mood and atmosphere. Oscar Wilde's play may not be the greatest ever written, as we thought when we were in high school. But it makes a stunning libretto. The characters are sharply drawn, the issues clear, the climax overwhelming. The beautiful and perverse Princess of Judaea, inflamed to madness by her passion for the Prophet; her stepfather Herod, cruel and crafty, pursued by fears and hallucinations;

her mother Herodias, lascivious and vengeful; the handsome young captain Narraboth, who is hopelessly enamored of her; and Iokanaan the Prophet, unshakable in his faith—all are enveloped in a musical ambience whose spell is not easily forgotten.

The one-act drama unfolds on a terrace in the palace of Herod, Tetrarch of Judaea. The opera opens with the imperious gesture that is familiar to us from the Straussian tone poem. Narraboth, captain of the guard, gazes adoringly towards the banqueting hall. "How beautiful is the Princess Salome tonight!" The voice of Iokanaan is heard from the cistern, where he has been imprisoned for speaking out against the abominations of the Tetrarch's court. "After me shall come another who is greater than I. I am not worthy to unloose the latchet of his shoe. . . ." The elevated tone associated throughout the work with the Prophet is set forth at once by the serene (although highly chromaticised) C-major tonality, and by the sonority of sustained horns and trombones. Salome enters, and there is soon heard a sinuously chromatic theme in three-four time, capricious, willful, played by celesta and violins.

It is an idea capable of symphonic development, and returns in various guises throughout the action.

Iokanaan prophesies again, announcing the coming of the Son of Man. Salome, fascinated, demands to see him. The soldiers explain that Herod has strictly forbidden them to raise the cover of the well. Salome appeals to Narraboth, who is helpless against her blandishments. In deep anguish he orders that the Prophet be brought from the cistern.

Iokanaan's appearance is heralded by two characteristic motives. The first, solemn and exalted, is given out by the horns.

The second, suggesting the Prophet's denunciations, consists of a series of descending fourths intoned by trombones and cellos:

"Where is she who hath given herself to the young men of the Egyptians?" Salome knows whom he means. "It is of my mother that he speaks." Clarinets sound an eerie motive that returns throughout the opera to suggest her mad infatuation with the Prophet.

"I am amorous of thy body, Iokanaan! Thy body is white, like the lilies of the field that the mower hath never mowed." The vocal line takes on those wide leaps of well over an octave which were to figure ever more prominently in the melody structure of the Austro-German school.

"I will kiss thy mouth, Iokanaan," sings Salome, transported with desire. The Prophet shudders. "Never! daughter of Babylon! Daughter of Sodom—never!" The lovelorn Narraboth can bear his agony no longer. He plunges his sword into his heart and falls between Salome and the Prophet. Iokanaan bids Salome seek Him who is on a boat in the sea of Galilee, to bow at His feet and beg remission of her sins. But Salome is enamored of his lips. He curses her and returns to the cistern.

A change of atmosphere is needed to prepare for the entrance of the grotesque ruler and his evil queen. This is accomplished by a shrill passage on the E-flat clarinet. Herod is obsessed by his fancies. "The moon has a strange look tonight. She is like a mad woman. . . ." His vocal line—staccato, abrupt, querulous—at once establishes the character of the Tetrarch. He orders that the torches be lit, then steps in Narraboth's blood; persuaded that it is an evil omen, he commands the soldiers to remove the body.

The voice of Iokanaan is heard, prophesying the day of the coming of the Lord. Herodias demands that the Prophet be handed over to the Jews, who have been clamoring for him. Herod is reluctant, for he feels that Iokanaan is a man who has seen God. There follows an ensemble of five Jews, in which the music graphically mimics the acrimony

Louis Melancon

A scene from the Metropolitan Opera production of *Salome*.

of a theological disputation. Herod, inflamed with wine, gazes lustfully at his step-daughter and asks her to dance for him. Salome, who has been brooding over Iokanaan's rejection of her, at first refuses. When Herod promises her anything that she will request of him, the thought comes to her for which she has been remembered through the ages. "Whatsoever thou shalt ask of me, even to the half of my kingdom," Herod asserts. "You swear it, Tetrarch?" He swears by his life, his crown, his gods. "You have sworn an oath, Tetrarch!" Ominous trills are heard on the clarinets. Salome attires herself in seven veils and makes ready to execute the most famous dance in history.

The music of the dance is in turn savage and sensual, building to an impassioned climax based on Salome's motive. (Its main theme comes perilously close to sounding like a Viennese waltz, but Strauss no more seeks authenticity than did Verdi in *Aida* or Puccini in *Madame Butterfly*.) Herod is enchanted and asks Salome to name her reward. The weird trill on the clarinet is heard again. Salome, "rising, laughing," demands the head of Iokanaan on a silver charger. In vain the terrified Herod seeks to deflect her, offering her the choicest treasures of his kingdom. Salome is inflexible. "Give me the head of Iokanaan!" When all his offers are refused the Tetrarch, defeated, yields.

The Princess leans over the cistern. There is a terrible stillness as her bidding is done, punctuated by dry haunting *sforzandi* on the double basses. Herod hides his face in his cloak. Herodias smiles with delight and fans herself. The opera reaches its climax as Salome addresses the head on the silver charger, in as strange and affecting an apostrophe as was ever heard. "Ah! thou wouldst not suffer me to kiss thy mouth, Iokanaan. Well, I will kiss it now. I will bite it with my teeth as one bites a ripe fruit."

The sky grows dark, the moon disappears. The Tetrarch is overwhelmed with fear. Salome, oblivious of all, gratifies her obsession. "Ah! I have kissed thy mouth, Iokanaan. I have kissed thy mouth." The motive of Salome, luminous in its orchestral garb, rises to passionate exultation.

Herod can endure no more. "Kill that woman!" he cries. The soldiers rush forward and crush Salome beneath their shields. The curtain falls.

This is theater in the grand style. One can point to shortcomings; yet the opera has a boldness of conception and a sustaining of tension that bespeak a master. Salome, Herod, Herodias, Narraboth—each is driven by a magnificent obsession. And since it is in the nature of man to be driven, they rise from the shadows of their phantasmagoric world into the realm of what is humanly comprehensible and moving.

After having dominated the musical firmament for decades, Strauss's star at the moment is not in the ascendant. Yet other composers have gone through periods of eclipse, only to emerge the more brightly; and the same may happen to Richard Strauss. His art does not happen to accord with the temper of the mid-century. But let there be no mistaking: he was one of the great figures of our time.

◦§ 14 §◦

Jean Sibelius (1865-1957)

"When we see those granite rocks we know why we are able to treat the orchestra as we do."

JEAN SIBELIUS cut an important figure during the Twenties and Thirties —especially in England and the United States, where his cult was as widespread as in his native Finland. He never achieved comparable eminence in Paris or Berlin, Vienna or Rome. Sibelius appeared on the musical scene as a nationalist and nature poet in the postromantic tradition. His command of the large forms of orchestral music enabled him to conquer the big public.

HIS LIFE

Sibelius was born in the town of Tavestehus, of Finnish-Swedish stock. The son of a doctor, he grew up in an environment where music and art were much appreciated. At fifteen he was studying the violin, and soon made his first attempts at composition. In obedience to his family's wishes, he embarked upon the study of law at the University of Helsingfors. However, the impulse toward music soon blotted out all thought of a legal career. At twenty-one he left the University and thenceforth devoted himself to his art.

In 1889, when he was twenty-four, Sibelius went to Berlin, and the following winter to Vienna, the stronghold of the classical tradition. He studied with local celebrities; learned to admire Brahms and Bruckner without being influenced by either; and returned to Finland at a propitious moment. The repressions of the Czarist regime had released a torrent of patriotic sentiment among the Finnish population. Sibelius's career unfolded against a strong popular agitation for political and cultural independence. This mood he captured in his music. In his tone poems based on the legends of the national epic *Kalevala* (1895), as in the snarling defiance that hurls from the brasses in the opening measures of *Finlandia* (1899), his countrymen heard accents that corresponded to their deepest aspirations. In this surcharged climate he quickly assumed the position of national artist that he held throughout his career.

Sibelius benefited from the enlightened policy of the Scandinavian countries toward their creative artists. He was awarded an annual grant from the Finnish government, which made it possible for him to channel all his energies into composition. He paid a number of visits to the musical centers of Germany, Italy, France and England, making known his music. In 1913 he was invited to the United States, where he conducted a program of his works at the Norfolk festival in Connecticut. "I was quite astounded," he wrote, "at being so well known in America. I should never have believed it."

The composer had built a villa in the country north of Helsingfors, where he lived the retiring existence that accorded with his temperament. Here he and his wife raised a family of five daughters. Here too he wrote his major works, surrounded by the forests and fjords he loved so well. "It is true I am a dreamer and a poet of nature. I love the mysterious sounds of the fields and forest, waters and mountains. Nature has truly been the book of books for me." His fiftieth, sixtieth, and seventieth birthdays were occasions for public celebration throughout his homeland, when his countrymen gave touching evidence of their regard for "Finland's greatest son."

The laws governing artistic creativity are shrouded in mystery. With every incentive—fame, leisure, an eager public—to go on producing, Sibelius's muse fell silent when he was in his fifties. With the symphonic poem *Tapiola* and the incidental music to Shakespeare's *The Tempest*, both dating from the 1920s, his work was done. His ninetieth birthday in December, 1955 was observed with appropriate tributes to the grand old man of music. He died two years later.

HIS MUSIC

Sibelius functioned within the frame of the "poematic" symphonism of the late romantic era. His seven symphonies are impressive tone-canvases filled with the imagery of a far northern landscape and with expansive musings—now somber, now jubilantly affirmative—on man, nature, fate. Yet these works are not program music in the Straussian

sense. They evoke meanings, but they never describe. Sibelius's identification with his people was on that deep level which renders unnecessary
the quotation of folk tunes. "There is a mistaken impression among the
press abroad," he wrote, "that my themes are often folk melodies. So
far I have never used a theme that was not of my own invention." The
point is that many of his themes could have been popular tunes, and at
least one—the chorale from *Finlandia*—became one.

Sibelius had a natural affinity for the processes of musical logic and development that are inseparable from symphonic style. At the same time
he was a leader in the movement away from the grandiose expression
of such composers as Richard Strauss and Mahler. He moved steadily
toward sobriety of utterance, sparseness of texture, condensation of
form. In this search for stylistic purity we may recognize the stirrings of
that return to classical values (albeit within a postromantic frame) that
was to be one of the main preoccupations of the new era. He evolved
an effective technique of working not with elaborate themes that are
immediately recognizable as first or second subject, but with short motives—often no more than fragments—which take on significance
and are welded into organic unity as the music unfolds. This mosaic
style achieves a high degree of structural coherence and goes hand
in hand with an impressive capacity for sustaining tension and momentum.

The first two symphonies date from the turn of the century. They
are exuberantly romantic works that present no problem to the listener.
The Symphony No. 3 in C major is a sunny piece that marks the composer's progression toward greater concision. This trend culminates in
the brooding Fourth Symphony (1911). The Fifth (1915) is an expansive work, conceived in a broad accessible style. The Sixth (1923),
which the composer described as "wild and impassioned in character,"
never achieved the popularity of the others. Finally the Seventh (1924),
a work extravagantly admired by Sibelius devotees, which, Sibelius
wrote, has "joy of life and vitality, with appassionata passages." The
Sixth and Seventh he considered "more in the nature of professions of
faith than my other works."

Sibelius cultivated every form of music save opera. His huge output
includes symphonic poems, orchestral legends and suites; the once
widely played Violin Concerto (1903); works for string orchestra and
chamber music; cantatas and choral works; incidental music for plays;
and quantities of songs and piano pieces, good, bad, and indifferent. The
symphonies hold the central place in his output. Works like *En Saga*
(1892) and *Finlandia* are much heard at "Pop" concerts. *Valse Triste*

has established itself firmly in the repertory of radio music. In the concert life of the Scandinavian countries the works of Sibelius occupy the central place.

Sibelius's harmonic scheme is based on traditional elements, but he obtains novel effects through his individual way of spacing and connecting the chords. His melodies often revolve around a focal tone. This, together with their limited range and the repetition of significant fragments, gives them a primitive strength. His orchestral coloring is dark, being based on the use of instruments in their lower registers. Certain mannerisms are germane to his style, such as his addiction to passages in thirds on the flutes, or the sharp ejaculation of the brass in accented chords with sinister effect. Also, his use of rhetorical devices such as ostinato, insistent repetition of melodic motives, and slowly gathering crescendos. The use of these "hypnotic" effects has of course contributed heavily to his popularity with the masses. Sibelius's handling of form, in his later works, is marked by the excision of nonessentials. Transitional passages are suppressed in the interests of an elliptical style that proceeds directly from one idea to the next.

SYMPHONY NO. 2 IN D MAJOR, OPUS 43

The Second (1901) is the most popular of Sibelius's symphonies. It owes its pre-eminence to the freshness of its melodic material and to its sweeping outlines. The work exemplifies his method of creating a structure through synthesis: thematic fragments which at first seem to be unrelated are built up into larger units. The essence of symphonic writing, Sibelius held, lay in "the profound logic that creates an inner connection between all the motives."

I. *Allegretto.* The work opens on an idyllic pastoral note. Of the various ideas that make up the opening theme group, the first is most important. It establishes the home key of D major and sets the mood:

The contrasting theme group centers about an idea that is bold of gesture and full of tension. The melody structure is characteristic of Sibelius: a long-sustained note followed by a rhythmically active figure. This theme is introduced by woodwinds against a string accompaniment.

The buildup of the movement vividly evokes the nature sound, the suggestion of primeval forest and headlong mountain torrent so dear to the Finnish composer's imagery. Sibelius handles the pattern of Exposition—Development—Recapitulation with the utmost freedom. The development section leads into a majestic synthesis of the material. The Recapitulation introduces imaginative changes in the order and treatment of the themes.

II. *Andante.* The second movement opens with a songful theme announced by the bassoon against a pizzicato accompaniment in the cellos:

Sibelius follows Tchaikovsky's lead in introducing dramatic elements into what is essentially a lyrical movement. This Andante is not devoid of rhetorical gestures: the snarling of the brass in typical Sibelian fashion, the upward rushing scales, the wind instruments declaiming against a turbulent background of strings. All these are held together by the personal stamp of the composer's lyricism, which achieves consistency of style and mood.

III. *Vivacissimo.* Sibelius here adheres to tradition: his Scherzo is based on the tensions born of propulsive rhythm. The movement opens in the bright key of B-flat major and proceeds at a furious clip.

The middle section, the Trio, is marked *Lento e suave* (slow and suave). It is based on a melodic pattern whose first note is repeated nine times in a row, followed by the descending interval of a fifth that plays a germinal role in this symphony. An oboe solo creates the pastoral atmosphere traditionally associated with the trio; after which the Scherzo is repeated (A-B-A form). Following the celebrated example in Beethoven's Fifth Symphony, a transition built on a slowly gathering crescendo carries us without a break into the Finale. Embedded in this transitional passage, unobtrusively at first, is the motive that will take over at the psychological moment, that is, the opening of the Finale.

   IV. *Allegro moderato.*   The home key of D major is re-established by a broadly diatonic, proclamatory tune which is given the big treat-

ment, unfolding over a rhythmic ostinato on trombones and kettle-drums. A contrasting theme in F-sharp minor, marked *tranquillo*, does not make too much of an impression at its first appearance. Sibelius is saving his thunder for the reprise. The Development depends heavily on the cumulative power of simple reiteration. When the big tune returns, what with the joyous D-major tonality and the clatter of a thoroughly aroused orchestra, the effect is very grand. Now the second idea reappears, *tranquillo* as before, and is worked up into what is probably the longest drawn out crescendo in symphonic literature. The theme is repeated over and over in D minor, building up for the consummating moment when it shifts into D major. The climax is as obvious, shall we say, as the crucial moment when the hero of a play

swings from fear to courage or from hate to love—and, to those who are open to Sibelius's type of persuasion, as irresistible.

   Sibelius had a definite contribution to make in the first quarter of our century, when the public was finding its way to the new music. There was sufficient novelty in his work to attract those listeners who liked to think of themselves as advanced. At the same time there was enough of the old to reassure those who were not yet ready for the truly modern in art. Hence the enthusiasm of critics such as Cecil Gray in England and Olin Downes in this country, who were persuaded that Sibelius's symphonies represented "the highest point attained in this form since the death of Beethoven." We today see the Finnish master more realistically. His music came out of the last period in European culture that was capable of romantic idealism. It stands in the nineteenth-century tradition. By the same token, it has little relevance to the problems of contemporary musical thought. Withal it bears the imprint of a dedicated musician who in the course of a long, fruitful career won an honorable place for himself in the annals of his art.

⋖§ 15 §⋗

Alexander Scriabin (1872-1915)

"For the first time I found light in music; found this rapture, this soaring flight, this suffocation from Joy!"

ALEXANDER SCRIABIN has paid heavily for being a figure of the transition period. To his devotees of fifty years ago he appeared like the prophet of a new era. Today his orchestral compositions have almost vanished from the concert hall, while of his voluminous piano works only the short pieces are in evidence. Nevertheless, he represented the progressive trend in Russian music in the early years of our century, and played a not inconsiderable part in the ushering in of the New Music.

HIS LIFE

Scriabin, scion of an aristocratic family of Moscow, came out of the same milieu as his friend Sergei Rachmaninov; they were classmates at the Moscow Conservatory. He had the good fortune to attract the notice of the then Maecenas of Russian music, the publisher Belaiev. The latter helped to launch his career by organizing a concert tour on which Scriabin played his early piano works in Amsterdam, Brussels, Paris, and Berlin. In the next years Scriabin became a stormy petrel in the musical life of Moscow and St. Petersburg. The diehards were aghast at his harmonic daring and hissed his music. Yet the public as a whole did not long resist a composer whose art, no matter how unconventional in certain respects, stemmed from the romantic style.

Scriabin for several years was professor of piano at the Moscow Conservatory. In 1903, through the generosity of a wealthy woman who admired his talent, he was able to give up teaching. He took his wife and children abroad and gave concerts of his works, laying the basis for his European fame. In 1906 he appeared in a series of concerts in the United States, where he was warmly received.

In the next years Scriabin drew ever closer to theosophy, occultism, and the philosophy of the East. He saw the artist—that is, himself—as redeemer and prophet; his views combined mysticism with a delicate eroticism and longing for ecstasy, the whole tied together by faith in the essentially ideal nature of art. His music aimed to produce, as he put it, "a glimpse of higher spiritual planes." These ideas were embodied in two grandiose tone poems of a post-Wagnerian (also Lisztian) character: the *Poem of Ecstasy*, and *Prometheus—The Poem of Fire*. Scriabin intended the latter piece to be performed in conjunction with a "color organ" that was supposed to flash on a screen colors synchronized with the music. Nothing came of the idea (although it turned up several decades later, in modified form, in our motion picture temples).

Scriabin returned to Russia in 1910. He produced his last piano sonatas, and gathered round him a circle of disciples who shared his mystical ideas. He dreamed of writing a vast symphony for which all the peoples of the earth would unite in a great festival. This colossal Mystery would "mark the end of this stage of human consciousness." Based on a "mystic chord," his masterpiece was to be presented by two thousand white-robed performers as a semireligious rite in which music would unite with poetry, acting, dancing, colors, and perfumes. The Mystery remained one. Much as he talked about it, Scriabin never got around to writing it. His initial attempts at what he regarded as the consummation of his life's work were interrupted by the outbreak of the First World War. He gave a memorable series of concerts in aid of patriotic organizations, his delicate, overwrought pianism arousing his listeners to transports of enthusiasm. Shortly after one of these recitals he developed an abscess on the lip that resulted in blood poisoning. He died in April, 1915, a few months after his forty-third birthday.

HIS MUSIC

The mazurkas, nocturnes, impromptus, preludes, and études with which Scriabin began his career stemmed from the tradition of Chopin and Liszt. Within this idiom was asserted the personality of a sensitive miniaturist with a flair for the piano. Scriabin was unwilling to accept this status. He had, in his own eyes, to achieve the greatest. Consequently he was impelled to force his rather graceful intuitions into vast designs which he was then not capable of sustaining.

The force of his personality was such that he was able to impose his vision of himself not only upon his countrymen but also on people abroad. His music won a foothold in England, especially. The pronouncements upon Scriabin made by the leading British critics of a generation ago make curious reading today. His biographer, Eaglefield Hull, maintained that "the sonatas of Scriabin are destined in the future to occupy a niche of their own, together with the forty-eight Preludes of Bach, the thirty-two sonatas of Beethoven, and the piano works of Chopin." So serious a writer as W. J. Turner stated that Scriabin's works represented "the chief advance in musical consciousness since Beethoven's time." And Ernest Newman heard in Scriabin's music "the veritable wind of the cosmos itself."

It was in the field of harmony that Scriabin made his chief contribution. He was a leader in the attempt to found a new system of harmony on the higher overtones of the Chord of Nature (see Appendix I-j.). Guided by a refined sense of hearing and a bold imagination, he created chords that opened up new perspectives. His music in its unbridled chromaticism reached the outermost limits of the traditional key system, and pointed the way to a freer use of the twelve tones. He dispensed with key signatures; helped abolish the traditional distinction between major and minor; anticipated polytonal and atonal modes of thought. Also, he was one of those who led music away from chords based on the interval of a third to those based on the interval of a fourth, in other words, from triadic to quartal harmony; with the result that his music has a distinctly twentieth-century look. (See musical example on page 27.)

The conflict between highly romantic content and classical form comes to a crisis in Scriabin's large works. Among them are three symphonies (1900, 1901, 1905); the Piano Concerto (1899); *Poem of Ecstasy* (1908) and *Prometheus—The Poem of Fire* (1910); and ten piano sonatas. In these compositions the material is overextended, the structure tentative (although the Fifth Sonata, as performed by the Soviet pianist Sviatoslav Richter, had a demonic intensity that will be long remembered by those who heard it). Scriabin is at his best in the short song and dance pieces where formal elements do not confront him with problems. His piano pieces are lyric miniatures finely adapted to the keyboard. They move within a narrow range—dreams, fugitive visions, intensely personal moods, with occasional sallies into the pathos and satanism that link him to the nineteenth century.

Scriabin's best known orchestral composition, the *Poem of Ecstasy*, Opus 54, in C major, displays the fervid chromaticism of his harmony and his sumptuous orchestral writing. The work shows that the heritage of the Lisztian tone poem was still fruitful at the beginning of our century. With its *Allegro dramatico*, *Tragico*, *Tempestoso*, and its tumultuous progression from conflict to triumph, the *Poem of Ecstasy* stands in direct line of descent from *Les Préludes*. The main theme is an imperious trumpet call of a Lisztian cast, based on a rising sequence of fourths—the basic interval, that is, of Scriabin's melodic-harmonic

structure. The score is studded with directions such as *presque en délire* (almost deliriously) and *avec une volupté de plus en plus extatique*. These underline the caressing, voluptuous atmosphere that is of the essence in Scriabin's music. The material is overextended and is hardly weighty enough to support a piece of this length.

Scriabin is another of the composers who played an important part, in the first two decades of this century, in preparing the public for new conceptions. We shall never again view him with the enthusiasm he aroused among certain sections of the intelligentsia forty years ago. Yet one observes with interest that his music is currently enjoying a revival in his homeland; and he has devotees elsewhere. Now that we can see him in perspective, he takes his place as one of the picturesque figures in the transition from romanticism to the twentieth century.

৵৽ 16 ৵৽

Other Late Romantics

LEOŠ JANÁČEK (1854–1928)

LEOŠ JANÁČEK (born in Hukvaldy, Moravia; died in Moravian-Ostrau) is the representative figure of the modern Czech school. His country-men see him as the successor of Smetana and Dvořák. Janáček matured very slowly as an artist, and did not produce any significant music until he was in his forties. Indeed, it was not until he was past sixty that this retiring musician had anything more than a local reputation. He lived in the town of Brünn—now Brno—where his opera *Jenufa* (1894–1903) was given on and off for years without causing a stir. In 1916 *Jenufa* was presented in Prague and Vienna. The work created a sensation and disclosed the existence of a musician of European stature.

Janáček's art was nurtured by Slavonic folklore and nature mysticism. In his vocal music, which holds a place of honor in his output, he aspired to a plastic melody molded to the rhythms and natural inflections of speech. Janáček's musical language is of the postromantic period. His harmony is extremely mobile and expressive. In his later works he dispensed with key signatures. He had little interest in the traditional forms, preferring a mosaic structure based on the continual variation of a few basic motives. He has been compared to Musorgsky for his unconventionality of thought, his roughhewn and original harmonies, the compassion and love of humble folk that inform his art. In his operas Janáček emphasizes the orchestra, which wreathes the action in a flood of luminous sound. He avoids expansive lines in the vocal writing, as he does thematic development in the orchestra. The texture unfolds as a series of thematic nuclei which, because of the homogeneity of the style, combine in larger units and give a vivid musical characterization of the people on stage. The result is an extremely concentrated idiom marked by dramatic truth and sustained intensity.

Janáček's opera *Kata Kabanová* (1921), based on Ostrovsky's famous drama *The Storm*, ranks with *Jenufa* in dramatic power, as does *From the House of the Dead* (1928), which was inspired by Dostoicvski's portrayal of prison life in Siberia. The *Slavonic* Mass (1926) is an ample work that shows off to advantage Janáček's choral style. Now that several works of Janáček have been made available on records— the *Slavonic* Mass, Concertino for Piano and Chamber Orchestra (1925), *Diary of One Who Vanished* (1916), *From the House of the Dead*, Quartet No. 2 (1928), Sinfonietta (1926), and the symphonic poem *Taras Bulba* (1918)—the reader is in a position to acquaint himself with the art of a composer who commands extraordinary admiration throughout central Europe.

HUGO WOLF (1860–1903)

"Poetry is the true source of my music."

Hugo Wolf had nothing to protect him against the world but his genius. His career was short and tragic.

Wolf was born in the Austrian province of Styria. He entered the Vienna Conservatory when he was fifteen. The shy, withdrawn lad did not take kindly to academic restraints. His rebellion against the rules, both musical and otherwise, led to his being expelled from the institution two years later. From the age of seventeen he was cast upon his own resources. He taught himself from the scores of the masters, while he kept alive by doing odd jobs.

At twenty-four he managed to obtain a post as music critic on a Viennese journal. With all the ardor of the reformer he preached the gospel of his idols—Wagner, Bruckner and Berlioz. How intemperate he could be when his passions were aroused may be gathered from his pronouncement that "the art of composing without ideas has decidedly found its most worthy representative in Brahms." Wolf's critical articles added much to the liveliness of the musical scene in Vienna. But in the long run they harmed his career, for the influential figures whom he attacked—chiefly the anti-Wagner faction—never forgave him.

After some attempts at writing instrumental music Wolf found his true bent as a composer of songs. He came into his full powers when he was twenty-eight. His periods of creativity had about them the intensity of a seizure. He would work at white heat, turning out songs day after day, "hardly stopping to eat or sleep," until the flame of inspiration had burned itself out. Then he would sink into a mood of depression and lethargy until the next creative frenzy. Within a little over two years he produced almost two hundred lieder, the bulk of his output. Among them were fifty-three settings of poems by Edouard Mörike (1888); fifty-one settings of poems by Goethe (1889); forty-four settings from the *Spanish Song-book*, a collection of translations by Paul Heyse and Emanuel Geibel; and the first volume of twenty-two songs from the *Italian Song-book* by the same two poets. The list includes such masterpieces as *Anakreons Grab* (Anacreon's Grave), *Prometheus* and *Ganymed* (poems by Goethe); *Verborgenheit* (Secrecy) and *Um Mitternacht* (At Midnight), to the verses of Mörike; and the magnificent *Geh', Geliebter, geh' jetzt* (Go, my love, go now) from the *Spanish Songbook*.

Then—silence. The creative tension snapped, and for the better part of four years Wolf was unable to compose. He was thrown into the depths of despair. "I almost begin to doubt if the compositions that bear my name are really mine. Good God! what is the use of all this fame? What is the good of these great aims if only misery lies at the end? Heaven gives a man complete genius or no genius at all. Hell has given me everything by halves. I should like to hang myself."

In 1895 inspiration returned, breaking the grip of his melancholia. Within three months he composed his light opera *Der Corregidor* (The Governor General), on a libretto by Rosa Mayreder based on Alarcón's *The Three-Cornered Hat*. There followed the second volume of the *Italian Song-book* and the settings of three sonnets of Michelangelo. He was working "like a steam engine," he wrote, and was full of projects for the future. But the end was near. In his thirty-seventh year, as he was feverishly writing a second opera, his mind gave way. Wolf tried to drown himself, and was confined in an asylum near Vienna where he lingered on for several years, victim of a degeneration of the brain that caused general paralysis. He was released from this living death at the age of forty-three.

In the comparatively few years that he was vouchsafed as a composer, Wolf revealed himself as a master of psychological nuance, with an uncanny gift for capturing the essence of a poem. He introduced the methods of Wagnerian music drama into the domain of the lied. He exploited the leitmotiv in a technique of continuous expansion—his so-called symphonic style. He used "endless melody"—that is, a flowing melodic line free from symmetrical phrase structure—and achieved a plastic declamation for the voice that mirrored every nuance of the words. He developed the richly chromatic idiom of the post-Wagnerian era into a language pregnant with meaning, basing his idiom on the free use of dissonance as the chief dynamic factor in musical expression, and produced miniature tone dramas surcharged with feeling. One cannot speak of a piano accompaniment in his lieder; he himself called them "songs for voice and piano." The two parts are conceived as equally important entities within the whole. The piano part may proceed independently of the voice or, if the situation demands, in opposition to it. Out of the complex interplay between the two the drama is consummated, within a highly concentrated form.

"A man is not taken away," Wolf wrote, "before he has said all that he has to say." We have no way of knowing how true this was in his case. However, before his tragic career closed, he had struck the modern tone in his psychological awareness and his power of musical suggestion. He stands among the masters of the German lied.

MAX REGER (1873-1916)

Max Reger (born in Brand, Bavaria; died in Leipzig) fell heir to the difficulties inseparable from the lot of the latecomer. He sought to function within the classical German tradition at precisely the moment when its future direction was unclear. He drew sustenance at various times from Mozart and Beethoven, Liszt and Wagner, Hugo Wolf and Brahms. Most of all he was nourished by Bach. Yet, despite his allegiance to eighteenth-century forms, it is a mistake to regard Reger as an apostle of the new classicism. He preached the "return to Bach" from a strictly nineteenth-century point of view. He thickened the texture of Baroque polyphony and made it busy. To this he added contemplative lyricism of a Brahmsian cast, and a penchant for richly chromatic harmony that derived its impetus from Wagner. The result could hardly be termed classical in the twentieth-century sense.

Reger was one of the few musicians of the postromantic era for whom counterpoint was a natural means of expression. He rejected the romantic attitude that derived music from poetic inspiration or from the sights and sounds of nature. Music for him was abstract pattern-making. His importance springs from the fact that he held up an ideal of craftsmanship—of "writing" as such—which influenced a number of twentieth-century composers, notably Hindemith. He passed his outwardly uneventful life in such centers of German culture as Meiningen, where he was grand-ducal Kapellmeister for two years, and Jena, whose university atmosphere well suited his scholarly temperament. He held teaching appointments successively at Wiesbaden, Munich, and Leipzig. For a time he appeared in public as a pianist. He composed with inordinate facility and produced a prodigious amount of music in his short life. (He died of a heart attack at the age of forty-three.) His output includes more than two hundred and fifty songs, over a hundred and fifty piano pieces, a vast amount of organ and chamber music, besides a number of large choral and orchestral compositions. Like Bach and Brahms, the two masters for whom he had the closest affinity, he left the opera untouched.

Reger wrote too much. He possessed neither the capacity for self-criticism nor the faculty of curbing his luxuriant imagination. He cultivated eighteenth-century forms—prelude and fugue, toccata, chorale prelude, organ fantasy, suite; also the sonata for unaccompanied violin, in which difficult genre he achieved notable results. He was a master of variation technique and was especially stimulated when, borrowing a theme from another composer, he brought to bear upon it all his resources of craft and fancy. His orchestral works include the *Sinfonietta*, Opus 90; *Variationen und Fuge über ein lustiges Thema von J. A. Hiller* (Variations and Fugue on a Merry Theme by J. A. Hiller), Opus 100; *Symphonischer Prolog zu einer Tragödie* (Symphonic Prologue to a Tragedy), Opus 108; and *Eine Lustspielouvertüre*

(A Comedy Overture), Opus 120. These works, which date from the first decade of our century, show Reger's orchestral style at its most characteristic, as does the somewhat later composition *Variationen und Fuge über ein Thema von Mozart* (Variations and Fugue on a Theme by Mozart), Opus 132.

Reger's overwrought chromaticism and restless modulations place him squarely within the middle-European section of the postromantic era. He belongs to the class of composers who achieve a prominence in their native land which they never duplicate elsewhere. This is strikingly demonstrated by the fact that over twenty-five books on the man and his music have appeared in German, but not a single one in English. Although he has his devotees everywhere, Max Reger is a nonexportable composer. He springs out of the German past and speaks most eloquently to the German temperament.

OTHERS

Mention should be made of two other members of the Austro-German school. Hans Pfitzner (Moscow, 1869–1949, Salzburg) was a prolific composer who is best known for his opera *Palestrina* (1917). Franz Schreker (Monaco, 1878–1934, Berlin) wielded a strong influence on the musical life of Vienna and Berlin, and achieved his most substantial success with *Der ferne Klang* (The Distant Sound, 1903–09). Both men had a vogue during the Twenties, but their music never established itself outside the orbit of German musical culture.

We do not discuss the music of Giacomo Puccini (Lucca, 1858–1924, Brussels) because, although he was active in the postromantic era, he functioned within the tradition of Italian opera. The art of this sensitive and inventive musician had to remain within the limits of what was accessible to the big public. Yet many passages in his operas— especially in his last score, *Turandot*—show how keenly aware he was of the new currents of thought that swirled about him.

Spain, like England, had an illustrious musical past and then fell silent: she produced no composer of European stature in the eighteenth and nineteenth centuries. With Isaac Albéniz (Camprodón, 1860–1909, Cambo-Bains) and Enrique Granados (Lérida, 1867–1916, at sea) she resumed her place in the concert of nations. The picturesque piano pieces of these two composers are vivacious, colorful, and imbued with the spirit of the popular song and dance of their homeland. Much of their music is of the salon variety, but it served to spread the characteristic melody and rhythm of Spain throughout the world. Also, it

helped to create a musical climate out of which emerged the contemporary Spanish school.

The Russian composers of the postromantic generation followed the
traditions of their national school. Several gained only local reputations.
Others, like Anatol Liadov (St. Petersburg, 1855–1914, Novgorod) and
Anton Arensky (Novgorod, 1861–1906, Terijoki, Finland), won popularity abroad through some piano pieces of the salon variety. The songs
of Alexander Gretchaninov (Moscow, 1864–1956, New York) were
widely appreciated at one time, as were the symphonies and the Violin
Concerto of Alexander Glazunov (St. Petersburg, 1865–1936, Paris).
Only one other beside Scriabin cut a substantial figure on the international scene: Sergei Rachmaninov (Oneg, 1873–1943, Beverly Hills,
California). Although certain of his works have enjoyed a phenomenal
vogue with the public, Rachmaninov has no proper place in a book on
contemporary music. He was a traditionalist who moved within the
orbit of late nineteenth-century romanticism, following in the footsteps
of his idol Tchaikovsky. His piano style derived from Chopin and
Liszt. In his handling of the grand form, exemplified in his symphonies
and piano concertos, he leaned heavily on Tchaikovsky and Brahms.
The world out of which his art stemmed came to an end with the First
World War. One realizes with surprise that he was only nine years
older than Stravinsky; the two men seem to have lived in different
centuries—which, in a sense, they did. Rachmaninov's symphonies have
all but dropped from view. His piano works, on the other hand, live
on in the concert hall. The chances are that, mercilessly overplayed as
they are, they will continue to be with us for some time to come.

The Wagnerian influence was kept alive in France through a group
of composers who were disciples of César Franck. Chief among them
was Vincent d'Indy (Paris, 1851–1931, Paris), who exerted a vast influence on the course of French music in the postromantic era. D'Indy
was one of the founders and ultimately the director of the Schola
Cantorum, a private conservatory in Paris whose influence came to rival
that of the Conservatoire itself. As a composer he drew inspiration from
the distant past. Gregorian chant and the medieval modes were essential
ingredients of his style. Despite the influence of Wagner that hangs so
heavily over his operas, the clarity of his scoring stamps him a Frenchman.

D'Indy consistently sought to acclimate the German tradition to his
native land. For him this tradition included not only Wagnerian drama
but also the symphonism of Beethoven and the polyphony of Bach.
Yet in this amalgamation of styles he ran the risk of stifling his pure

lyric gift with German counterpoint. Time has not dealt kindly with his considerable output. The *Symphonie cévenole, sur un chant montagnard français* (Symphony on a French Mountain Air, 1887) and *Istar*, Symphonic Variations (1897), are still played outside France, but not much else. In his homeland, understandably, he fares much better.

Henri Duparc (Paris, 1848–1933, Mont-de-Marsan, Landes) was regarded by César Franck as the most gifted of his students. Duparc ranks with Fauré as one of the creators of the modern art song in France. He fell ill of a nervous affliction when he was thirty-seven and, despite his long life, composed nothing thereafter. His fame rests upon not many more than a handful of songs which are superb examples of intimate lyric art. Among them are *Extase, Invitation au voyage, Soupir* (A Sigh) and *Chanson triste* (A Song of Sadness).

Ernest Chausson (Paris, 1855–1899, Limay), like Duparc, was a pupil of Franck. His gifts unfolded slowly. He was independently wealthy, a highly cultivated and sensitive musician who seemed destined for a brilliant career when a bicycle accident cut short his life at the age of forty-four. He is known in this country for his *Poème* for violin and orchestra (1897); the Symphony in B-flat (1898); and his songs. His harmony and orchestration alike bear witness to the powerful influence exerted by Wagner upon the French musicians of Chausson's time.

Paul Dukas (Paris, 1865–1935, Paris) exemplifies a type of artist not rare in our century, who with a single work achieves an international success that he never again duplicates. To the world at large he is the composer of *L'Apprenti sorcier* (The Sorcerer's Apprentice, 1897). In France he is admired as well for his opera *Ariane et Barbe-Bleue* (Ariadne and Bluebeard, 1907), based on the play by Maurice Maeterlinck; his dance-poem *La Péri* (1912) and a number of instrumental compositions.

The French postromantics tried to create a national art without having freed themselves from subservience to the German tradition. Sooner or later there was bound to appear among them a musician who, to a public that revered Beethoven and Wagner, would dare to affirm the necessity of rejecting both the classical symphony and the romantic music drama. Appear in due time he did, in the person of a soft-spoken young man named Claude Debussy. Rarely have momentous tidings been delivered so gently—but firmly—as by the composer who opened wide the door to the twentieth century.

II. IMPRESSIONISM

"The century of aeroplanes deserves its own music. As there are no precedents, I must create anew."

Claude Debussy

~§ 17 §~

Impressionism

"In comparison with the pure dream, the unanalyzed impression, a definite or positive art is blasphemous."

Charles Baudelaire

THE ART of the nineteenth century aspired to that "embracing of the millions" which Beethoven hymned in the finale of his Ninth Symphony. The novels of Dickens, the paintings of Delacroix, the operas of Verdi are popular in the best sense. Such art exerts universal appeal and reinforces our common humanity.

In the twilight of an era, however, art tends to lose this directness of speech. The artist seeks greater refinement of style and reticence of feeling; with these, a select public that will respond to his subtleties. In the second half of the nineteenth century artists increasingly cultivated the unusual and the precious. On the one hand, this gesture constituted a revolt against the taste of the bourgeois. On the other, it embodied the desire to rid art of certain modes of expression that had lost their freshness. Paris was the center of the new style, which found its most compelling expression in the movement known as impressionism.

THE IMPRESSIONIST PAINTERS

It was in 1867 that the academic salons rejected a painting entitled *Impression: Sun Rising*, by Claude Monet (1840–1926), which the artist then exhibited under less conventional auspices. Before long *impressionism* was being applied as a term of derision to the painting of Monet and his comrades, such as Camille Pisarro (1830–1903), Edouard Manet (1832–83), Edgar Degas (1834–1917) and Auguste Renoir (1841–1919). The impressionist painters were desirous of discarding

The impressionist painter essayed to capture on canvas not the exact representation of things, but the artist's momentary impression of them, and to convey that with all spontaneity and freshness. Claude Monet, *Poplars at Giverny*. (Collection Museum of Modern Art)

everything in the romantic tradition that had hardened into academic formula. They essayed to capture on canvas not the exact representation of things, but the artist's momentary impression of them, and to convey that with all spontaneity and freshness. To this end they took painting out of the studio into the open air. They looked at nature with an "innocent eye." They saw the world in a continual state of flux, its outlines melting in a luminous haze. Nor did they mix their pigments on the palette, as had been the custom hitherto. Instead they juxtaposed bits of pure color on the canvas, leaving it to the eye of the beholder to do the mixing. The result was a fluidity of line and an iridescence of color such as had never been seen before.

The impressionists were repelled by the heroic themes of the romantic painters. The hero of their painting was not man, but light. They had an affinity for subject matter that the romantic painters would have been apt to dismiss as trivial: dancing girls, picnics, boating and café scenes, nudes, and still life; and, of course, nature—smiling and seductive, or veiled and mysterious. Their art is suffused with the magic of a city: Paris in all her allure supplies the setting for their shimmering oils and water colors. People laughed at first: whoever saw grass that's yellow and pink and blue? But the intrepid pioneers persisted and ultimately imposed their vision upon the world. By the end of the century impressionism had emerged as the leading school in European painting.

THE SYMBOLIST POETS

A similar revolt against traditional modes of expression took place in poetry, led by the symbolists, who aspired to the direct communication of poetic emotion without the intervention of intellectual elements. They used words for the sake of the music contained in them rather than for the meaning. They tried to impart the essence of poetic experience by presenting the symbol rather than stating the fact. As Verlaine's famous quatrain expressed it,

> For we desire above all—nuance,
> Not color but half-shades!
> Ah! nuance alone unites
> Dream with dream and flute with horn.

The French symbolists were strongly influenced by Edgar Allan Poe (1809–49), whose poetry was introduced into France by his admirer Charles Baudelaire (1821–67). The end-of-century saw the movement in full course with the rise of three important symbolist poets: Stéphane Mallarmé (1842–98); Paul Verlaine (1844–96); and Arthur Rimbaud (1856–91). Under their aegis, language achieved something of the elusiveness and subtlety of nuance that had hitherto belonged to music alone.

The symbolists, like the impressionist painters, turned away from the pathos of the romantic movement. They discarded the story element in poetry; they scorned the moral, whether expressed or implied. Rejecting the passionate humanism of Byron and Shelley, Hugo and Lamartine, they turned to nebulous suggestion and dreamlike evocation of mood. Theirs was an exquisite idiom nourished by art rather than by life, whose excessive refinement tended to replace objective reality by the private world of the poet. Symbolism was a hothouse flower that aptly represented the end of the century, with its longing for enchantment and escape.

The new esthetic doctrines could not but make a deep impression on such musicians as were sensitive to painting and poetry. In consequence,

Impressionism

Impressionism   113

the quest for subtilization of means and refinement of vocabulary soon passed over from painting and poetry to music.

IMPRESSIONISM IN MUSIC

Impressionism in music came as a French—or should one say Parisian? —gesture of revolt against the domination of German romanticism. For the emotional exuberance of Wagner and his followers Debussy sought to substitute an art that was delicate, subtle, and—to use a favorite word of his—discreet. A pictorial art that wove a web of sensuous allure and conjured up the evanescent loveliness of the world without rather than the searing conflicts of the world within.

When Debussy, as a young man, submitted his cantata *The Blessed Damozel* to the professors of the Paris Conservatoire, they stated in their report: "It is much to be desired that he beware of this vague impressionism which is one of the most dangerous enemies of artistic truth." Thus was transplanted to the realm of music a label that had already firmly established itself in art criticism. Debussy himself disliked the word and spoke acidly concerning "what some idiots call impressionism, a term that is altogether misused, especially by the critics." Despite him the name stuck, for it seemed to express what most people felt about his music. The impressionist painters, we saw, tried to capture the movement of color and light. But music is preeminently the art of movement. For this reason the favorite images of impressionist painting—the play of light on water, clouds, gardens in the rain, sunlight through the leaves—lent themselves readily to musical expression at the hands of a composer who "changed into music every impression his five senses received."

For Debussy, as for Monet and Verlaine, art was a sensuous rather than ethical or intellectual experience. The epic themes of German romanticism were foreign to his temperament. In the doctrine of art for art's sake he recognized the triumph of Latin *esprit* over the Teutonic love of "deep" meanings. "The French," he wrote, "forget too easily the qualities of clarity and elegance peculiar to themselves and allow themselves to be influenced by the tedious and ponderous Teuton." He counselled his countrymen to turn away from their German models and to rediscover the old masters of France. "Couperin and Rameau— these are true Frenchmen. French music aims above all to please." Debussy here upheld what was the age-old ideal of Gallic art: to charm, to entertain, and to serve—in his phrase—as a "fantasy of the senses."

THE REVOLT AGAINST GERMAN FORMS

The sonata-symphony, supreme achievement of German constructive genius, had never been altogether congenial to the Latin temperament. Already in the eighteenth century Fontenelle had inquired, "Sonata, what do you want of me?" Debussy's fervent desire to found a genuinely French art inevitably led him away from the grand form of Beethoven. He looked upon sonata form, with its exposition, development, and restatement of musical ideas, as an outmoded formula, "a legacy of clumsy, falsely interposed traditions." The working out of themes and motives he regarded as a species of dull "musical mathematics." It was this Gallic point of view that impelled him, at a concert, to whisper to a friend, "Let's go—he's beginning to develop!"

Even more incisive was his opposition to the Wagnerian music drama, which at that time held such powerful allure for the intellectuals of France. Debussy's hostility to Wagner is all the more significant in that, in his youth, he had fallen under the spell of the German master and had made, as he put it, "passionate pilgrimages to Bayreuth." He had to free himself from this domination if he was to find his own path, and he was persuaded that French music had to do the same. He aimed some of his choicest barbs at the *Ring of the Nibelung*. "The idea of spreading one drama over four evenings! Is this admissible, especially when in these four evenings you always hear the same thing? My God, how unbearable these people in skins and helmets become by the fourth night!"

From the grandiose architecture of symphony and music drama Debussy found his way to the short lyric forms that he used with such distinction—preludes, nocturnes, arabesques. In his hands these became chiseled miniatures whose moods were crystallized in such images as *Reflections in the Water, The Snow is Dancing, Sounds and Perfumes Turn in the Evening Air*. Significant is his use of names borrowed from the painters: *images, estampes* (engravings), *esquisses* (sketches). These pieces, impregnated with lyricism, reveal him as a true nature poet.

The question remains: was impressionism a revolt against the romantic tradition—as its adherents believed—or was it but the final manifestation of that tradition? There can be no question that Debussy raised the banner of revolt against certain aspects of the romantic heritage. Yet in a number of ways impressionism continued the basic trends of the romantic movement: in its allure, its addiction to beautiful sound, its rejection of classical conceptions of form, its love of lyricism. Romantic too was its emphasis on mood and atmosphere; its fondness for program music and poetic titles; its nature worship and imaginative tone painting; and—most romantic trait of all—its desire to draw music, painting, and poetry as closely together as possible. What the impressionists did, really, was to substitute a sophisticated French type of romanticism for the older German variety.

The impressionists had an affinity for subject matter that the romantic painters would have been apt to dismiss as trivial: dancing girls, picnics, boating and café scenes . . . Edgar Degas, *Rehearsal for the Ballet on Stage.* (Metropolitan Museum of Art)

In any case, the emergence of impressionism in music went hand in hand with the predominant position that French music assumed after the turn of the century. In 1905 Romain Rolland was able to write about "the sudden change which is being brought about in music. French art, quietly, is in the act of taking the place of German art."

❧ 18 ❧

Impressionist Methods

"Debussyism was not the work of Debussy alone but a traditionally logical stage of modern evolution."

Charles Koechlin

IMPRESSIONISM came to the fore at a time when composers were beginning to feel that they had exhausted the possibilities of the major-minor scale. Debussy's fastidious ear explored subtler harmonic relationships and impelled him to seek new sources of inspiration—specifically, those that lay outside the orbit of German music of the eighteenth and nineteenth centuries. He thus was led to develop his natural affinity with the exotic and the old.

MODAL INFLUENCES

The medieval modes could not but prove attractive to composers who were seeking to escape the tyranny of the major-minor sound. Consequently, modal harmony began to play an ever more prominent part in twentieth-century works. Debussy emphasized the primary intervals—octaves, fourths, and fifths—which he used in parallel motion. This style of writing somewhat resembled a medieval procedure known as *organum*, in which a melody was harmonized by another which ran parallel to it at a distance of a fifth or a fourth. (In four-part organum

Ninth-Century Organum

both parts were duplicated an octave higher.) The use of an organum-like style imparted to Debussy's music an archaic effect that was piquant in the highest degree. There is no denying the powerful austerity, the impression of old and remote things conveyed by a passage such as opens *La Cathédrale engloutie* (The Sunken Cathedral). The resemblance to medieval organum is apparent.

For centuries music had centered about the mellifluous intervals of
the third and sixth. Debussy's emphasis of the bare intervals of the
fourth and fifth was a departure of prime importance for his contemporaries and followers. Notice, in the above example, that the first
chord is sustained by the pedal, thereby creating a sonorous haze
against which the succeeding harmonies unfold. This use of a *pedal
point* or *organ point* was an effect prized throughout the classic-romantic era. The impressionists adopted the device and used it with great
imagination, deriving a multitude of striking effects from the clash of
the transient and the sustained harmony.

THE WHOLE-TONE SCALE

In the Exposition of 1889, held in Paris to celebrate the centenary of
the French Revolution, Debussy heard the musicians of the Far East
—Java, Bali, Indo-China. He was fascinated by the music of the native
orchestra, the gamelan, with its intricate interplay of percussive rhythms
and bewitching instrumental colors. Here was a new world of sonority
that could be drawn upon to invigorate the traditional patterns of the
west.

The music of the Far East makes use of certain scales that divide the
octave into equal parts, as does the *whole-tone scale* popularly associated
with Debussy. It should be added that he was by no means the first
to employ this scale—we find examples in the music of Glinka, Dar-
gomijsky, Rimsky-Korsakov, and Liszt; nor did he use it as often as
is generally supposed. He did, however, have a strong affinity for it.

The whole-tone scale divides the octave into six whole tones, as in
the sequence C, D, E, F-sharp, G-sharp, A-sharp, C.

This pattern lacks the half-tone distances that lend character and direction to the major scale. Hence its expressive scope is extremely limited. Yet its very fluidity made it an excellent vehicle for the elusive melodies and harmonies favored by impressionism. The following measures from the third act of *Pelléas et Mélisande* illustrate the special magic that Debussy was able to distill from the whole-tone scale.

THE PENTATONIC SCALE

Also favored by the impressionists was the pentatonic or five-note scale, which is sounded when the black keys of the piano are struck (or the tones C, D, F, G, A). Since this scale too, like the whole-tone pattern, omits the semitones of the major scale, it served the purpose of composers who were seeking a fresh sound.

The pentatonic scale is of very great antiquity and is found throughout the Far East as well as in various parts of Europe. It is popularly associated with Chinese music. Yet it is even more familiar to us through Scottish, Irish, and English folk tunes. *Auld Lang Syne*, for example, and *Comin' Through the Rye* are pentatonic melodies.

In his piano prelude *La Fille aux cheveux de lin* (The Girl with the Flaxen Hair), Debussy exploits the quiet charm of the pentatonic

scale to evoke the portrait of a Scottish lassie. In *Pagodes* (Pagodas) he uses themes based on the same scale to create an atmosphere of Chinese ritual music.

IMPRESSIONIST HARMONY

In the classical view, the individual chord was considered in terms of its role within the harmonic progression—that is, in relation to what preceded and followed. Impressionism, on the contrary, brought to the fore the twentieth-century tendency to regard the chord as an entity in its own right, a sonorous "thrill" that hit the ear and the nerves with a pungency all its own. What is more, if a single chord made a striking effect, the composer was apt to reinforce that effect by repeating the chord on various degrees of the scale, shifting it up or down without change. The individual chord was intended to arouse a sensation quite apart from any context, even as in symbolist poetry the picturesque word was removed from its normal environment. In effect, impressionism released the chord from its function in regard to the movement and goal of the music. Therewith the impressionists greatly loosened the forms that had been based on the classical—that is, the functional —concept of harmony.

In the following passage from Debussy's *Soirée dans Grenade* (Evening in Granada), the entire passage consists of a single chord structure which is duplicated on successive tones. We have here the "gliding"

chords that became an essential feature of the impressionist style. In a passage such as the above we may even question whether we are dealing with a series of chords at all. Rather we hear a succession of blobs of sound, just as in a melody we hear a succession of individual notes. The harmony here is really a thickening out of the melody; just as, in many an impressionist painting, the luminous haze is a thickening out of the single line.

PARALLEL MOTION

Harmonies, according to the classical tenet, resulted from the movement of the several voices. To maximize the tension of this movement, the lines were supposed to proceed as much as possible in *contrary* motion. Impressionism, on the other hand, by viewing the chord as a sonorous entity severed its relationship to the movement of the individual lines. Indeed, the very concept of shifting chords bodily up or down implies *parallel* rather than contrary motion; as is apparent from the last musical example. Parallel movement is a prime characteristic of impressionist music.

Classical harmony specifically forbade the parallel movement of certain intervals such as octaves and fifths, on the ground that this weakened the independent movement of the voice parts. To this day teachers of harmony go through their pupils' exercises hunting for the proscribed intervals. Debussy, contrariwise, used parallel fifths freely, therewith departing from the classic-romantic sound. The following example from a passage in *Chansons de Bilitis* creates an atmosphere of mystery and remoteness:

EXPANSION OF THE CONCEPT OF KEY

Once the chord became an independent entity, the pull to the Tonic naturally was weakened. The composer might even question its need to resolve at all. In the excerpt from *Soirée dans Grenade*, the first chord is a dissonance, which by classical standards would have to resolve to a consonance. Instead, it is duplicated in a succession of dissonances, none of which displays any move toward resolution. Debussy, like many of his contemporaries, greatly strengthened the twentieth-century drive toward the "emancipation of the dissonance." He helped to create a type of cadence in which the final chord takes on the function of a rest chord not because it is consonant, but because it is less dissonant than what preceded. A case in point is the dissonant chord which serves as final cadence at the end of *Ce qu'a vu le vent d'Ouest* (What the West Wind Saw), from the first book of Preludes.

The harmonic innovations inseparable from impressionism led to the formation of daring new tone combinations. Characteristic was the use of the five-tone combinations known as ninth chords. These played so prominent a part in *Pelléas* that the work came to be known as "the land of ninths." Here is a characteristic sequence of parallel ninth chords from *Pelléas*.

A characteristic of impressionist harmony is the use of what are known as "escaped" chords—harmonies, that is, which give the impression of having "escaped" to another key. Such chords are neither prepared for nor resolved in the conventional senses. They are simply permitted to "evaporate" while the original harmonies are sustained in the lower voices. The following example occurs at the opening of

Debussy's *General Lavine—Eccentric* from the second book of Preludes. C-major tonality is established in the first measure, against which is heard a series of triads alien to the tonality.

As a consequence of these usages, impressionist music floated in a borderland between keys, creating elusive effects that may be compared to the nebulous outlines of impressionist painting. Debussy and his followers contributed decisively to the twentieth-century expansion of the key sense. By the same token, they broke down the boundaries of the key as an area in harmonic space, and thereby gave impetus to the disintegration of the major-minor system.

OTHER ASPECTS OF IMPRESSIONIST MUSIC

The evanescent harmonies of the impressionist composers called for colors no less subtle. There was little room here for the heaven-storming climaxes of the romantic orchestra. Instead, we find a veiling of the orchestral sonority, against which the individual timbres stand out with delicate clarity. Impressionist orchestration shimmers with an impalpably pictorial quality. Flutes and clarinets are used in their dark lower register, violins in their luminous upper range. Trumpets and horns are discreetly muted, and the whole is enveloped in a silvery gossamer of harp, celesta and triangle, glockenspiel, muffled drum, and—at special moments—a cymbal brushed lightly with a drumstick. We saw that the impressionist painters, instead of mixing their pigments on the palette, juxtaposed specks of pure color on the canvas. The impressionist musicians similarly juxtaposed pure colors, leaving it to the ear of the hearer to do the mixing.

Instead of the broadly spun melodies of the romantic style, Debussy cultivated a melody composed of fragmentary phrases, each of which was often repeated. This mosaic-like structure makes for an intimacy of style that is very French. A corresponding modification occurred in rhythm. Debussy and his followers favored a stream of sound that veiled the beat and helped to free music from the "tyranny of the bar-line." This continuous flow from one measure to the next is most charac-teristic of impressionist music. As far as form went, impressionism moved away from the grand architecture of the classical heritage, seeking plastic forms that would capture something of the fluidity and charm of improvisation. The avoidance of clear-cut cadences made for an overlapping of phrases, periods, and sections. Structural landmarks as well as the classical pattern of tension-and-release were veiled in an uninterrupted flow of dreamlike sound.

It would be erroneous to suppose that the historic developments surveyed in this chapter owed their being exclusively to Debussy. The germs of impressionist procedures are already to be found in the music of Liszt, Musorgsky, Bizet and other composers. As the nineteenth century drew to its end, new conceptions of melody, harmony, rhythm, color, tonality, and form were in the air, and musicians everywhere sought ways to implement them. What Debussy did was to unite those in a personal style, to reinforce them with a well-reasoned esthetic doctrine, and to give them the shape in which they won acceptance throughout the world. He forced us, in Constant Lambert's fine phrase, "to listen less with our minds and more with our nerves." In so doing he set his seal upon an era.

≈§ 19 §≈
Claude Debussy (1862-1918)

"The music I desire must be supple enough to adapt itself to the lyrical effusions of the soul and the fantasy of dreams."

HIS LIFE

CLAUDE DEBUSSY was born in the town of St. Germain-en-Laye, near Paris. His father, who kept a china shop, wanted him to become a sailor, but the boy's musical talent brought him to the Paris Conservatory when he was eleven. In the next years Claude acquired a reputation as an iconoclast, scandalizing his fellow students and teachers with uncon-ventional harmonies that violated all the rules. "What rules do you observe, then?" one of his professors inquired. "None—only my own pleasure!" "That's all very well," came the reply, "provided you're a

genius." Before long, his teachers began to suspect that the daring
young rebel was.

At eighteen he was recommended as a pianist in the household of
Nadezhda von Meck, the patroness of Tchaikovsky. He played piano
duets with the wealthy widow, taught her children, and even proposed
—unsuccessfully—to one of her daughters. Madame described him in
one of her letters to Tchaikovsky as "Parisian from tip to toe, a typical
gamin, very witty and an excellent mimic." His imitations of Gounod
were "most amusing."

Bettmann Archive

Claude Debussy

When he was twenty-two his cantata, *L'Enfant prodigue* (The Prodigal Son), won the top award of the Conservatoire, the Prix de Rome.
The scholarship carried with it a protracted residence in the Italian capital at government expense. Debussy looked upon his stay in Rome as
a dreary exile: he could not be happy away from the boulevards and
cafés that constituted his world. He was required to submit a work each
year that would enable the authorities in Paris to judge of his progress.
Upon receipt of the first *envoi*, the professors of the Conservatoire
reported that "at present M. Debussy seems to be afflicted with a desire
to write music that is bizarre, incomprehensible and impossible to

execute." For his third and final piece he submitted what has remained the most successful of his early works, *La Damoiselle élue* (The Blessed Damozel), a lyric poem for solo voices, chorus, and orchestra based on the poem by Dante Gabriel Rossetti. It was this work that elicited the label *impressionism*, which henceforth was attached to Debussy's music.

With his return to Paris his apprenticeship was over. He frequented the salons where the *avant-garde* gathered; at the famous "Tuesday evenings" of Stéphane Mallarmé he met the leading impressionist painters and symbolist poets. Their influence bore rich fruit in 1894, when, at the age of thirty-two, he completed his first major orchestral work, the *Prélude à l'après-midi d'un faune* (Prelude to the Afternoon of a Faun), in which the Debussy style appears before us fully formed.

The Nineties constituted the most productive decade of Debussy's career. The culminating work of these years was the opera *Pelléas et Mélisande*. Based on the play by the Belgian symbolist Maurice Maeterlinck, *Pelléas* occupied the composer for the better part of ten years. Debussy continued to polish and revise the score up to the opening night, which took place at the Opéra-Comique on April 3, 1902. Public interest in this premiere was intensified by a bitter feud between the composer and his librettist. Maeterlinck had expected that the role of Mélisande would be created by his wife, Georgette Leblanc, but at the last moment the part was given to a young and practically unknown American—Mary Garden. Infuriated, Maeterlinck made the discovery which every poet does whose verses are set to music: that his creation had lost its independence. He had no ear for music, but he knew enough to suspect that his drama would never again stand on its own feet. In a letter to the press he announced that the operatic *Pelléas* was "a work which is now strange and hostile to me." His drama was "in the hands of the enemy"; he hoped for "its immediate and complete failure." The critics did attack the work as decadent and precious, but the originality and the quiet intensity of the score made a profound impression on the musical intelligentsia. The opera caught on, and soon established itself in the international repertory.

Until the success of *Pelléas*, Debussy had been pretty much the bohemian. His existence had been shared by the lovely Gabrielle Dupont —"Gaby of the green eyes"—for the better part of a decade. After her there was Rosalie Texier, a beautiful girl from Burgundy who had come to Paris to work as a dressmaker. Debussy married her in 1899, when he was in such straitened circumstances that he had to give a lesson in order to pay for the wedding breakfast. In 1904 he fell under the spell of Mme. Emma Bardac, wife of a Parisian banker. She was brilliant, worldly, an accomplished musician whose rendition of his songs gave the composer much pleasure. Swept by a consuming love, Debussy and Mme. Bardac eloped. Rosalie tried to kill herself, and was taken to the hospital with a bullet near her heart. After she recovered, a double divorce took place. Debussy was accused by certain of his friends of having been attracted to the glamorous Mme. Bardac because of her wealth. It might be closer the mark to say that she fulfilled the needs of this new phase of his career just as Rosalie had met those of the earlier period. Debussy's second marriage was idyllic. A daughter was born for whom, some years later, he wrote the suite for piano, *The Children's Corner*, and the ballet for children, *La Boîte à joujoux* (The Toy Box). To her mother were dedicated several of the most important works of his final years.

After *Pelléas*, Debussy was the acknowledged leader of the new movement in music, the center of a cult of worshipful disciples who copied his ideas and his mannerisms, and about whom the composer complained, "The Debussyites are killing me!" He appeared in the principal cities of Europe as a conductor of his works and wrote the articles that established his position as one of the wittiest critics of the century. His output slackened toward the end of his life. Although his energies were sapped by cancer, he continued to work with remarkable fortitude. The outbreak of war in 1914 confronted him with the dilemma of the artist amidst universal tragedy. "France," he felt, "can neither laugh nor weep while so many of our men heroically face death. What I am doing seems so wretchedly small and unimportant." Presently, however, he saw that, even as he had led the struggle of French music against German domination, so he must now contribute to the grimmer struggle between the two cultures in the only way he could —"by creating to the best of my ability a little of that beauty which the enemy is attacking with such fury." It was at this time of his country's peril that he assumed the proud title of *musicien français*.

The relentless advance of his malady brought the realization that his creative career was over. His last letters speak of his "life of waiting —my waiting-room existence, I might call it. For I am a poor traveler waiting for a train that will never come any more." He died in March 1918, during the bombardment of Paris. The funeral cortege passed through deserted streets while his beloved city was being ripped by the shells of the Big Berthas. It was only eight months before the victory of the nation whose art found in him so distinguished a spokesman.

HIS MUSIC

"I love music passionately," Debussy wrote, "and because I love it I try to free it from barren traditions that stifle it. It is a free art, gushing forth—an open-air art, an art boundless as the elements, the wind, the sky, the sea! It must never be shut in and become an academic art." This freedom from formula he strove to maintain throughout his life.

His chief orchestral works are firmly entrenched in the concert hall: the *Prelude to the Afternoon of a Faun,* a magical score; the three Nocturnes (1899)—*Nuages* (Clouds), *Fêtes* (Festivals) and *Sirènes* (Sirens), which show him in his most pictorial vein; *La Mer* (The Sea, 1905); and *Ibéria,* from his last period, which we shall consider in detail. His handling of the orchestra shows a truly French sensibility; his atmospheric writing for flute, clarinet, and oboe displays the traditional French mastery of the woodwinds. French, too, is his economy. There are no superfluous notes in his scores. The lines are widely spaced; the colors stand out in radiant purity. The sound mass is transparent and airy.

Debussy's piano music occupies in the twentieth-century repertory a position comparable to Chopin's in the nineteenth. He was one of the principal originators of the new piano style. With endless subtlety he exploited the resources of the instrument: the contrast of high and low registers, the blending of sonorities made possible by the pedals, the clash of overtones. From among the early works, the two Arabesques (1888) are still much played. Also *L'Îsle joyeuse* (The Happy Island, 1904) a luminous evocation of Watteau's make-believe world. The *Suite bergamasque* (1890) contains *Claire de Lune* (Moonlight), the most popular piece he ever wrote. *Soirée dans Grenade* (Evening in Granada, 1903) exploits the supple rhythm of the Habanera. *Jardins sous la pluie* (Gardens in the Rain, 1903) is an impressionistic tone painting, as is *Reflets dans l'eau* (Reflections in the Water, 1905). In *Hommage à Rameau* (1905), he pays his respects to the eighteenth-century French master. To his final period belong the two books of twelve Preludes each (1910–13), and the Etudes (1915), which he dedicated to the memory of Chopin. We should not be misled by the nebulous outlines of his piano pieces. These seemingly capricious forms bear the imprint of a craftsman who had sovereign command of compositional technique.

Debussy is one of the most important among those who, toward the end of the nineteenth century, established the French art song as a genre independent of the German romantic lied. Best known among the song sets are the *Cinq poèmes de Baudelaire* (Five Poems of Baudelaire, 1889); *Ariettes Oubliées* (Forgotten Little Tunes, 1888) and *Fêtes Galantes* (Courtly Festivals, 1892–1904), to poems of Verlaine; and *Chansons de Bilitis* (1897) to poems of Pierre Louÿs. Debussy's songs are poetic meditations. They demand a special sensitivity on the part of both singer and accompanist, not to mention the listener. Granted this, they are certain to weave their spell.

In chamber music, a field traditionally dominated by the Germans, Debussy achieved some important successes. His String Quartet in G minor, written when he was thirty-one (1893), is one of the most engaging in the recent literature. At the end of his career, when he was seeking greater clarity and firmness of structure, he returned to the sonata he had once derided. The three chamber sonatas—for cello and piano; for flute, viola and harp; and for violin and piano—belong to the years 1915–17. The critics who heard these works in the Twenties described them as indicating an ebbing of the composer's powers, and ever since then commentators have gone on repeating the statement. But one has only to listen to the Cello Sonata to feel oneself in the presence of a master. To the last years belongs also the music for Gabriele d'Annunzio's mystery play *Le Martyre de Saint Sébastien* (1911). This unjustly neglected work, with its austere medieval harmonies, possesses both spirituality and power.

Finally, *Pelléas et Mélisande*. This "old and sad tale of the woods," as Debussy called it, captures the ebb and flow of the interior life. It is a tale imbued with all the reticence and lyric charm at its creator's command. Mélisande of the golden hair (and the habit of saying everything twice); Pelléas, overwhelmed by the mystery of a love he never quite fathoms; Golaud, the husband, driven by jealousy to the murder of his half-brother; Arkel, the blind king of this twilight kingdom—they are the victims of a fate "they neither resent nor understand." Yet how compassionately they are conceived, and with what fullness of dimension. The music throughout is subservient to the drama. The orchestra provides a discreet framework and creates an atmosphere steeped in nature poetry. The setting of the text is masterly. Perhaps the real conflict of this strangely muted lyric drama is between the transience of human suffering and the eternal impassivity of nature. Listening to it, one understands Debussy's remark, "How much one must first find, how much one must suppress, in order to arrive at the naked flesh of the emotion!" One understands, too, Romain Rolland's description of him as "this great painter of dreams."

IBÉRIA

Ibéria (1908), the second of three *Images* for orchestra, ushered in the final decade of the composer's career. Those who know Debussy only from earlier scores such as the *Prelude to the Afternoon of a Faun* will notice at once the greater sharpness of outline and the brilliancy of color that characterize his later orchestral style. Also apparent are a tightening of structure and crystallization of idiom.

With *Ibéria* Debussy joined the line of French composers—Saint-Saëns, Bizet, Lalo, and Chabrier before him, Ravel after—who drew inspiration from Spain. Save for an afternoon spent in San Sebastian, near the border, Debussy never visited the country. For him, therefore, as for Bizet, Spain represented that unknown land of dreams which every artist carries in his heart.

The work is scored for full orchestra. The instruments are treated soloistically and retain their individual timbres throughout, with the luminosity of texture so characteristic of Debussy's style.

I. *Par les rues et par les chemins* (In the Streets and By-ways). The movement is marked *assez animé, dans un rythme alerte mais précis* (quite lively, in a rhythm that is tense but precise). The piece opens with a characteristic rhythm set forth by the woodwinds in alternation with pizzicato strings. Debussy is influenced here, as was Scarlatti in the eighteenth century, by the guitar sound that is indigenous to Spain. A plaintive melody emerges on the clarinet, marked "elegant and quite rhythmic." Its subtle syncopations and sinuous contours point to the Moorish element in the popular music of Spain.

The mood is festive, the setting meridional. The steady triple meter is alive with the gestures of the dance. Presently a contrasting idea emerges, *soutenu et très expressif* (sustained and very expressive). Presented by oboe and viola, this is a somber, long-breathed melody that moves languidly within a narrow range, with the frequent repetition of fragments characteristic of the folk style.

Exciting fanfares on the horns and trumpets introduce a slower section. The spirit of the Habanera enters the orchestra. The original idea returns in an abbreviated version. The movement dies away.

II. *Les parfums de la nuit* (Perfumes of the Night). The tempo indication is *Lent et rêveur* (slow and dreamy). Delicate pencillings of color in the opening measures make a characteristic sonority: flutes and oboes against muted violins in high register, a touch of xylophone, clarinet and bassoon silvered by celesta, against the subdued beat of a tambourine. A seductive melody emerges on the oboe, marked *expressif et pénétrant*.

Significantly, Debussy here departs from the purely harmonic writing of his earlier days. Horizontal strands of melody intertwine in a diaphanous counterpoint. This is a tender night song, yet the subjective element is always kept within the bounds of discretion. In the evocative power of its half-lights, this slow movement is indisputably one of Debussy's finest.

III. *Le matin d'un jour de fête* (The Morning of a Feast Day). The finale follows without a break. It is marked *Dans un rythme de marche lointaine, alerte et joyeuse* (in the rhythm of a distant march, tense and joyous), and is ushered in by a striking rhythm. A light-hearted dance tune is heard in the high register of the clarinet.

The music is vividly pictorial—even balletic—in its suggestion of movement. Those who know Debussy only in his twilight moods will be surprised at the percussive dissonance, incisive rhythm, and astringent sonorities that pervade this dance finale.

LA CATHÉDRALE ENGLOUTIE
(THE SUNKEN CATHEDRAL)

In *La Cathédrale engloutie* (1910), one of the twelve pieces in the first book of Preludes, Debussy's pictorial imagination allies itself with the floating sonorities of his favorite instrument. His point of departure was an old Breton legend, according to which the ancient cathedral of Ys rises out of the sea on certain mornings, its bells tolling, its priests intoning their prayers. Then the cathedral sinks back into the deep. Debussy's piano style lent itself admirably to the atmosphere of mystery and enchantment required for such a tale.

The composer's markings indicate the mood: *Profondément calme . . . dans une brume doucement sonore* (in a gently sonorous haze) . . . *doux et fluide* (gentle and fluid). We quoted the opening measures of *La Cathédrale engloutie* to suggest the resemblance between impressionist harmony and medieval organum (see Example, page 117). The sustained chords in the bass shown in that example act as organ points, creating a halo of sounds against which the parallel chords in the upper register unfold in a mystic procession. Debussy subtly exploits the overtones of the piano; the melody has a Gregorian flavor; the music evokes the sound of an organ in a cathedral, but heard as in a dream. Blocklike gliding chords, parallel fourths and fifths, added seconds and sevenths that give the harmony a percussive tang—all the features of the impressionist style are encountered here. Brief modulations to B major, E-flat major, subsequently to E, enliven the archaic modal harmony that prevails throughout the piece. The climax comes with bell-like harmonies in a clangorous fortissimo. (Dynamic terms are explained in Appendix

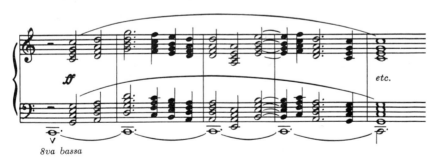

8va bassa

l-f.) Debussy intended this to be played *sonore sans dureté* (resounding without hardness). As the cathedral sinks beneath the waves the Gregorian motive is heard *expressif et concentré*. The bell-like motive returns against a rippling accompaniment in the bass, "floating and muffled, like an echo," as if the bells were still tolling under water. The opening chords return, but with added seconds, as the music dissolves in the mist out of which it came.

LA CHEVELURE
(TRESSES)

With the *Chansons de Bilitis* Debussy returned to the world of antiquity whence had issued the *Afternoon of a Faun:* the world of pagan hedonism and voluptuous delights. The three prose poems by Pierre Louÿs—*La flûte de Pan, La chevelure,* and *Le tombeau des naïades* (The Tomb of Naiads)—offered the composer an ideal frame for a lyric art both passionate and discreet.

In the second song of the set (1897) Pan speaks to Bilitis, telling her of a dream in which the pleasure of the senses commingled with the ecstasy of the soul:

Il m'a dit:
"Cette nuit, j'ai rêvé.
J'avais ta chevelure autour de mon cou.
J'avais tes cheveux comme un collier noir
autour de ma nuque et sur ma poitrine.

He told me:
"This night I dreamed.
I had your tresses round my neck.
I had your hair like a black necklace
Around my neck and across my chest.

"Je les caressais, et c'étaient les miens;
et nous étions liés pour toujours ainsi,
par la même chevelure, la bouche sur la bouche,
ainsi que deux lauriers n'ont souvent qu'une racine.

"I caressed your hair and it was mine;
And we were tied forever thus
By the same tresses, mouth against mouth,
Just as two laurels often have but one root.

"Et peu à peu, il m'a semblé,
tant nos membres étaient confondus,
que je devenais toi-même ou que tu entrais en moi
comme mon songe."

"And little by little it seemed to me
Our bodies were so entwined
That I became you and you entered into me
Like my dream."

Quand il eut achevé,
il mit doucement ses mains sur mes épaules,
et il me regarda d'un regard si tendre,
que je baissai les yeux avec un frisson.

When he had finished
He put his hands gently on my shoulders,
And he gave me such a tender look
That I lowered my eyes trembling with delight.

Languorous harmonies on the piano, containing clusters of seconds, create an atmosphere heavy with desire. The vocal line unfolds in a gentle recitative, marked *Très expressif et passionnément concentré.* A song of this kind, which spiritualizes the transports of erotic love, depends for its power upon the points of climax to which the voice builds ever so carefully. The first high point comes on the word *poitrine* (chest), followed by a gentle subsiding. The second climax surges up on the crest of a slightly higher wave, on the word *bouche* (mouth). The third and highest is on *moi*, in the phrase "and you entered into me as my dream."

Tenderness and passion, adoration and sensuality are wonderfully blended in this music. This is one of the great French art songs, over which hovers—like a delicate perfume—the quintessence of a civilization.

We today are so familiar with Debussy's language that it is difficult for us to realize how startlingly original it was in its own time. His music was without antecedents. Like Berlioz and Wagner before him, like Stravinsky and Schoenberg after, he stands among the great innovators in the history of his art.

◄§ 20 §►

Maurice Ravel (1875-1937)

"I did my work slowly, drop by drop. I tore it out of me by pieces."

THIRTEEN years the junior of Debussy, Maurice Ravel had to make his way in a milieu dominated by the older master. He imposed the stamp of his own classicist outlook on the impressionist idiom, and took his place alongside Debussy as a leader of the modern French school.

HIS LIFE

Ravel was born in Ciboure, near Saint-Jean-de-Luz, in the Basses-Pyrénées region at the southwestern tip of France. The family moved to Paris shortly after Maurice was born. His father, a mining engineer who had aspired to be a musician, was sympathetic to the son's artistic proclivities. Maurice entered the Conservatoire when he was fourteen. He remained there for sixteen years—an unusually long apprenticeship.

Ravel's career at the Conservatoire was enlivened by his repeated failure to win the Prix de Rome, the official prize that has been held by some of France's most distinguished composers—as well as by a number of nonentities. At his fourth attempt he was eliminated in the preliminary examination, even though his work had already begun to command respect in progressive musical circles. This high-handed action on the part of the professors caused a public scandal. The Director of the Conservatoire was forced to resign, and Gabriel Fauré—Ravel's teacher in composition—was appointed in his place. Ravel never forgot the affront. In later life he accepted honors from several foreign states, but refused the decoration of the Legion of Honor from a government that had withheld the Rome prize from a deserving young musician.

Bettmann Archive

Maurice Ravel

Ravel's artistic development was greatly stimulated by his friendship with a group of avant-garde poets, painters, and musicians who believed in his gifts long before those were recognized by the world at large. Youthful enthusiasts, they called themselves the "Apaches." "We had more or less the same tastes in art," wrote Léon-Paul Fargue, "which was lucky for people as hot-headed as we were because, as someone has said, you can't discuss things except with people of your own opinion. Ravel shared our preference, weakness or mania respectively for Chinese art, Mallarmé and Verlaine, Rimbaud, Cézanne and Van Gogh, Rameau and Chopin, Whistler and Valéry, the Russians and Debussy."

In this rarefied atmosphere the young composer found the necessary intellectual companionship, as had Debussy a decade earlier in the salon of Stéphane Mallarmé. He was affable and detached, presenting to the world a façade of urbanity that covered quivering sensibilities. His biographers are as reticent as was their subject in all that pertained to his personal life. He was enormously attached to his parents and brother; he made a loyal but possessive friend; in all other relationships, he was the suave man of the world. There is no evidence that he was capable of romantic love. Beneath his polished surface were limits beyond which he did not care to go.

Ravel's career followed the same course, more or less, as that of almost all the leaders of the modern movement in art. At first his music was hissed by the multitude and cried down by the critics. Only a few discerned the special quality of his work, but their number steadily grew. Ultimately the tide turned, and he found himself famous.

Ravel, like Debussy, was profoundly shaken by the outbreak of war in 1914. After making a vain attempt to join the air force, he became a driver in the motor transport corps and was sent to the Verdun sector. To his surprise, the horrors of war aroused no fear in him. On the contrary, they cast a terrible spell. "And yet I am a peaceful person," he wrote from the front. "I have never been brave. But there it is, I am eager for adventure. It has such a fascination that it becomes a necessity. What will I do, what will many others do, when the war is over?"

Having fallen seriously ill, he was discharged and returned to Paris just before the death of his mother. Her loss was a heavy blow. In a mood of severe depression he resumed his work with *Le Tombeau de Couperin*. (*Tombeau*, literally, a tomb, denotes a lyric form of the age of Louis XIV, offered as homage to a deceased person.) "In reality it is a tribute not so much to Couperin himself," he stated, "as to eighteenth-century French music in general." Grief is here transformed into six serenely graceful dance pieces, each dedicated to the memory of a fallen comrade.

In the years after the war Ravel came into his own. He was acknowledged to be the foremost composer of France and was much in demand to conduct his works throughout Europe. In 1928 he was invited to tour the United States. Before he would consider the offer he had to be assured of a steady supply of his favorite French wines and of French Caporals (he was a chain smoker). Ravel and America took to one another, although he tired first. "I am seeing magnificent cities, enchanting country," he wrote home, "but the triumphs are fatiguing. Besides, I was dying of hunger."

With the passing of the Twenties there began for the composer, as for the world about him, a period of depression. His over-refined, stylized art was not the kind that renews itself through deepening contact with life. Hence he found it increasingly difficult to compose. "I have failed in my life," he had written in a moment of depression. "I am not one of the great composers. All the great ones produced enormously. But I have written relatively very little, and with a great deal of hardship. And now I can not do any more, and it does not give me any pleasure." In these words we hear the self-induced impotence of an artist who ended as "a prisoner of perfection."

Toward the end of his life Ravel was tormented by restlessness and insomnia. He sought surcease in the hectic atmosphere of the Parisian nightclubs, where he would listen for hours to American jazz. As he approached sixty he fell victim to a rare brain disease that left his faculties unimpaired but attacked the centers of speech and motor co-ordination. It gradually became impossible for him to read notes, to remember tunes, or to write. Once, after a performance of *Daphnis et Chloé*, he began to weep, exclaiming: "I have still so much music in my head!" His companion tried to comfort him by pointing out that he had finished his work. "I have said nothing," he replied in anguish. "I have still everything to say."

So as not to watch himself "go piece by piece," as he put it, he decided to submit to a dangerous operation. This was performed toward the end of 1937. He never regained consciousness.

HIS MUSIC

Ravel's is an ultra-polished art. His delicate sense of proportion, his precision of line and ordered grace are in accord with everything we have come to associate with the French tradition. His emotions are controlled by his intellect. In this too he is one with the Gallic spirit. Art for him was created beauty, therefore compounded of artifice: the mirror that reflected his perception of reality, rather than reality itself. "Does it never occur to these people," he remarked, "that I am artificial by nature?" He had a horror of overstatement; he preferred irony and wit to the tragic gesture. Therefore he held on to the crystalline forms that constitute the element of control and "distance" in art. It was his one defense against his own emotions.

The critics of thirty years ago saw his music as a revolt against romantic subjectivity. They emphasized the constructional element in his work. Stravinsky called him a Swiss clockmaker. Ravel himself said,

"I make logarithms—it is for you to understand them." We today are in a position to judge more clearly. Ravel was a romantic at heart. Wistful sentiment and tenderness are everywhere present in his music, albeit at one remove, filtered through a supremely conscious artistry. For this reason he so ably represented the classical orientation, which in France has always been stronger than the romantic. All the same, his

Ravel stands to Debussy somewhat as Cézanne does to Monet. He was a post-impressionist. Paul Cézanne, *Mont Sainte-Victoire*. (Metropolitan Museum of Art)

pronouncements on music in his later years clearly reveal the romantic origins of his art. "Great music, I have always felt, must always come from the heart. Any music created by technique and brains alone is not worth the paper it is written on. A composer should feel intensely what he is composing."

Ravel stands to Debussy somewhat as Cézanne does to Monet. He was a post-impressionist. Like Cézanne, he feared that impressionism, with its emphasis upon the "fantasy of the senses," might degenerate into formlessness. His instinctive need for lucidity and clarity of organization impelled him to return—even as did the painter—to the classical conception of form.

Like Debussy, Ravel was drawn to the scales of medieval and exotic music. He too sought to expand the traditional concept of key. His imagination, like Debussy's, responded to pictorial and poetic titles as a stimulus to creation. (The literary element has always been prominent in French music.) Both men were attracted by the same aspects of nature: the play of water and light, clouds and fountains; the magic of daybreak and twilight; the wind in the trees. Both exploited exotic dance rhythms, especially those of Spain, and leaned toward the fantastic and the antique. Both were influenced by the pure, intimate style of the French harpsichordists: Ravel paid homage to Couperin even as Debussy did to Rameau. Both men admired the Russians, although Debussy responded to Musorgsky while Ravel leaned toward Rimsky-Korsakov and Borodin. Both were repelled by the rhetoric of the nineteenth century. Both felt an affinity for the symbolist poets, whose verses they set with exquisite taste and nuance. And both suffered from an overdeveloped critical sense that made it difficult for them to work in their later years.

The differences between the pair are no less striking than the similarities. The noontide brightness of Ravel's music contrasts with the twilight gentleness of Debussy's. Ravel's is the more driving rhythm. He is precise where Debussy is visionary. His humor is dryer, his harmony more incisive; the progressions are more cleanly outlined. His sense of key is firmer. He was not attracted to the whole-tone scale as was Debussy; he needed a more solid support for his structure. The voluptuous ambience of Debussy's music is absent from his. He is more daring with respect to dissonance, even as he is more conventional in the matter of form. Where Debussy was evocative and dreamlike, Ravel strove for the chiseled line. Thematic development was never the bugbear to him that it was to Debussy. Through his adherence to the classical form—in his Sonatina for Piano, his Trio, Quartet, and the two piano concertos—he achieved the distance he sought between the artistic impulse and its realization.

Ravel's melodies are broader in span than Debussy's, more direct. His orchestral brilliance derives in greater degree from the nineteenth century; he stands in the line of descent from Berlioz and Chabrier as well as Rimsky-Korsakov and Richard Strauss. Where Debussy aimed to "de-congest" sound, Ravel handled the postromantic orchestra with real virtuosity, with special emphasis on what has been called the "confectionary" department—harp glissandos, glockenspiel, celesta, and triangle. Ravel must be accounted one of the great orchestrators of modern times. Stravinsky called him "an epicure and connoisseur of instrumental jewelry." When his creative inspiration began to lag, he found it beguiling to exercise his skill on the music of other men, and orchestrated pieces by Chopin, Schumann, Musorgsky, Chabrier, Erik Satie, and Debussy.

Ravel ranks as one of the outstanding piano composers of the twentieth century. He extended the heritage of Liszt, even as Debussy was the spiritual heir of Chopin. His crisp piano style with its brilliant runs, its animation and fluency, owns kinship too with the eighteenth-century French harpsichordists. Among his early piano pieces, three attained enormous popularity: *Jeux d'eau*, which we will discuss; *Pavane pour une Infante défunte* (Pavane for a Dead Infanta, 1899); and the Sonatine (1905). The peak of his piano writing is found in *Gaspard de la nuit* (Gaspard of the Night, 1908), inspired by the fantastic verses of Aloysius Bertrand. The three tone poems of this set—*Ondine, Le Gibet* (The Gallows), *Scarbo*—show Ravel's pictorial imagination at its best.

The French song found in Ravel one of its masters. The witty *Histoires naturelles* (Stories from Nature, 1906), to Jules Renard's prose poems, aroused a storm of hostile criticism and established Ravel's reputation as an *enfant terrible*. The twentieth-century interest in chamber music with voice is exemplified by *Trois Poèmes de Stéphane Mallarmé* for voice, piano, two flutes, two clarinets, and string quartet (1913), and the sensuous *Chansons madécasses* (Songs of Madagascar, 1926). Ravel also cultivated the song with orchestra. *Shéhérazade* (1904), to the poems of his friend Tristan Klingsor, displays his exotic bent. *Deux Mélodies hébraïques* (Two Hebrew Melodies, 1914) was responsible in part for the widespread but erroneous belief that Ravel was Jewish.

It was through his orchestral works that Ravel won the international public. His first important composition in this medium was *Rapsodie espagnole* (Spanish Rhapsody, 1908). *Ma Mère l'Oye* (Mother Goose), originally written as a piano duet, was later orchestrated by the composer (1912). The five pieces of this set—*Pavane de la belle au bois dormant* (Pavane of the Sleeping Beauty); *Petit Poucet* (Hop o' my Thumb); *Laideronette, impératrice des pagodes* (Little Ugly One, Empress of the Pagodas); *Les Entretiens de la belle et la bête* (Conversations of Beauty and the Beast); and *Le Jardin féerique* (The Enchanted Garden)—are impregnated with that sense of wonder which is the attribute of children and artists alike. *Daphnis et Chloé* we will discuss. *La Valse*, a "choreographic poem" (1920), came out of the hectic period following the First World War. In this score Ravel deploys the surefire effects that have endeared him to the multitude. The same is true of *Boléro* (1928), which exploits the hypnotic power of relentless repetition, unflagging rhythm, steady crescendo, and brilliant orchestration.

Among his other works are the Piano Concerto in G (1931), which fully realizes the composer's dictum that a classical concerto "should be lighthearted and brilliant"; the dramatic Concerto for the Left Hand (1931), a masterly composition; *L'Heure espagnole* (The Spanish Hour, 1907), a delicious comic opera in one act concerning an elderly clock-maker and his faithless wife; and *L'Enfant et les sortilèges* (Dreams of a Naughty Boy, 1925), a one-act fantasy on a text by Colette. In the domain of chamber music there is the distinguished Trio for piano, violin, and cello (1914); the Introduction and Allegro for harp, string quartet, flute, and clarinet (1906), which is much slighter in substance; and the graceful String Quartet, written when Ravel was twenty-eight (1903) and dedicated to his teacher Gabriel Fauré. *Tzigane* (1924), a rhapsody for violin and piano (or orchestra), exploits the vein of capricious Gipsyism familiar to us from the Hungarian Rhapsodies of Liszt.

DAPHNIS AND CHLOÉ SUITE NO. 2

The second suite drawn from his ballet *Daphnis and Chloé* is generally accounted Ravel's masterpiece. The work, commissioned by Diaghilev for his Ballet Russe, was produced in Paris in 1912. The action is derived from a pastoral of the Greek poet Longus. Chloé, beloved of the shepherd Daphnis, is abducted by a band of pirates. Daphnis, prostrate with grief, arouses the sympathy of the god Pan. Daphnis dreams that the god will come to his aid. He awakes to find Chloé restored to him. The second suite contains three excerpts from the latter part of the ballet—Daybreak, Pantomime, and General Dance. The scoring is unusually rich and displays Ravel's mastery of orchestration.

I. *Daybreak.* "Nothing is heard but the murmur of rivulets. Daphnis lies stretched in front of the grotto of the nymphs. Day breaks gradually. The song of the birds is heard. Shepherds discover Daphnis

and awaken him. In anguish he looks about for Chloé. She appears, surrounded by shepherdesses. The two rush into each other's arms."

The music paints a morning mood. Woodwinds set up a flickering
sound in the upper register. A broadly arching theme emerges in the
lower strings. Harp glissandos, celesta, and a violin solo soaring above
the harmony create a characteristically Ravelian luminosity. At the
point in the action where the lovers embrace, a rapturous outburst
sweeps the orchestra. The brass enters, vividly suggesting an upsurge of
light.

II. *Pantomime.* "The old shepherd Lammon explains that Pan saved
Chloé in remembrance of the nymph Syrinx whom the god once loved.
Daphnis and Chloé mime the story of Pan and Syrinx. Chloé represents
the young nymph wandering through the fields. Daphnis represents
Pan who declares his love. The nymph repulses him. In despair he plucks
some reeds, fashions a flute, and plays a melancholy air."

A dialogue between oboe and flute sets the pastoral scene. The
famous flute solo—Pan's melancholy air—is heard against arpeggios in
the strings. This is a rhapsodic melody that Ravel marked "expressive

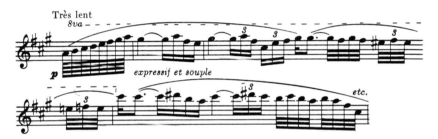

and supple," free in rhythm and unfolding in ornate traceries. There is
an echo of the first movement in a passage of characteristic harmony.
Typical of the many felicities of color is a spot where the flute sustains
a high trill while piccolo, harps, and violins outline the harmonic background and are answered by parallel chords on celesta and divided
strings—impressionism with a vengeance.

III. *General Dance.* "Before the altar of the nymphs Daphnis swears
his fidelity. Young girls enter dressed as bacchantes and shaking tam-
bourines. Daphnis and Chloé tenderly embrace. A group of young men
appear. Joyous tumult. A general dance."

The finale abounds in never failing effects. The frequent changes of
meter and the 5/4 time (three plus two) achieve a plasticity of rhythm

that is of the twentieth century. The movement is *Animé* (lively). There is an unabashed use of chromatic scales to whip up excitement. Behind the façade of Parisian sophistication lurk the shades of Rimsky-Korsakov and Borodin; the young blades of this Arcadia have gazed on Bagdad and the Polovetsian plains. Each fragment of melody is heard twice, a Debussy-like mannerism, and the "confectionary department" is much in evidence. The hectic climax is an example of Ravel's orchestral wizardry at its calculated best.

JEUX D'EAU
(FOUNTAINS)

"*Jeux d'eau*," wrote the composer, "is the original of all the novelties in pianism which people have noted in my work. This piece, inspired by the sound of water and the music of fountains, waterfalls and streams, is founded on two themes, in sonata form, but without being subjected to a classical tonal scheme." Carrying as its motto a line from Henri de Régnier—"A river god laughing at the waters that caress him"—*Jeux d'eau* (1901) was the first work in which Ravel's personality was fully revealed; he was twenty-six when he wrote it. Although it issues out of the piano style of Liszt, the piece is startlingly original and inaugurated a new piano technique. Coming as it did before any of Debussy's important piano compositions had been written, *Jeux d'eau* proves that Ravel was far less indebted to the older master than Debussy's admirers claimed.

The first theme displays Ravel's ornate piano style. The right hand plays extended arpeggios that exploit the upper register of the instrument, while the left presents atmospheric harmony, including parallel fifths.

The second subject is a typically Ravelian melody, which is given a special tang by the seconds in the right-hand accompaniment.

The classicist in Ravel impelled him to cast the work in the form of an exposition, development, and recapitulation. But the traditional scheme is followed very freely, in keeping with the fanciful subject of the piece; and the compact development section belongs to a sonatina rather than sonata movement. The visual image of water leaping, glistening in the sunlight, finds its musical realization in the stream of sixteenth and thirty-second notes that cascade across the keyboard. There are no mysterious shadows, as in Debussy's piano pieces; all is bright and airy. The hands interlock in intricate patterns. The middle section culminates in a dazzling glissando on the black keys. The first theme returns softly, marked Tempo I, followed by an extended passage in improvisational style that looks on paper like the cadenzas in the Hungarian Rhapsodies of Liszt, but sounds different. The second subject is repeated with a more intricate accompaniment, *Lento* and *espressivo molto*. Then the music dissolves in a spray of sixty-fourth notes, pianissimo.

Every pronounced trend in art engenders a reaction. Because of the enormous popularity of Ravel's music in the Twenties and Thirties, it is currently the fashion to deprecate his achievement. True, not all of his music is on the same high level: but whose is? It is important not to underestimate his achievement. Within the limits marked out for him by his temperament and outlook he explored a realm of sensibility all his own; and he did so with Gallic taste, wit, and imagination.

⤐ 21 ⤏
Frederick Delius (1862-1934)

"For me music is very simple. It is the expression of a poetic and emotional nature."

DELIUS's music evokes the English landscape and its seasons: the vernal freshness of spring, the shortlived rapture of summer, the sadness of autumn. His is a gentle lyricism compounded of dreams and longing, a passionate paean to the transience of all earthly things. His countrymen justly regard him as "the most poetic composer born in England."

HIS LIFE

Frederick Delius was born in Bradford, in Yorkshire. His father was a successful merchant who had emigrated from Germany and amassed a fortune in the wool business. Although a lover of music, he was horrified that any son of his should wish to devote his life to what he regarded as a pleasant pastime. The son, a handsome, strong-willed youth, was equally determined to escape his father's warehouse and to become a musician. Finally, after a violent family scene, it was decided that the young man should emigrate to Florida and run an orange grove. This plan appealed to his wanderlust and had the further advantage of removing him beyond the reach of parental authority. Accordingly, at twenty-one Delius found himself on an old Spanish plantation that his family bought for him, the Solano grove in Florida.

"In Florida, through sitting and gazing at Nature, I gradually learned the way in which I should eventually find myself. Hearing the Negroes singing in such romantic surroundings, it was then and there that I first felt the urge to express myself in music." He studied a while with Thomas F. Ward, a church organist who had come to Florida for his health; then asked his father for permission to go to Leipzig. When this was refused, he decided to achieve his goal through his own efforts. He persuaded his brother to take over the plantation and went to Jacksonville, where he taught music, sang in a church choir, and played the organ in a synagogue. Thence to Danville, Virginia, where he established himself as a teacher of violin, piano, harmony, and counterpoint. One of the high points of his stay there was his performance of the Mendelssohn Violin Concerto at the Roanoke Female College, "a finishing school for Young Women of the Baptist Denomination." His parents, alarmed at his long silence, were put in a more tractable mood. They finally discovered Delius's whereabouts and informed him that he would be allowed to go to Leipzig. In June, 1886, he sailed for home and proceeded to Germany.

He did not take kindly to the Leipzig tradition. "Learning kills instinct," he wrote in later life. "You can't teach a young musician how to compose any more than you can teach a plant how to grow, but you can guide him a little by putting a stick in here and a stick in there. Had it not been that there were great opportunities for hearing and talking music, and that I met Grieg, my studies at Leipzig were a waste of time." The friendship with Grieg had one important outcome. The Norwegian composer, when he visited London, met the elder Delius and interceded on behalf of the son. The wool merchant was still not convinced, but at least he refrained from cutting off the young man's allowance. Delius now settled in France, which was to be his home for the next forty-six years. Thenceforth he had as little as possible to do with his parents. Although they lived to see their son a widely admired composer, they refused to the end of their lives to hear a note of his music. It was their way of not having to acknowledge that they had been wrong.

During his years in Paris Delius associated with painters and writers rather than with musicians. His favorite cronies were two super-egoists like himself, August Strindberg and Paul Gauguin. In Paris too he met Jelka Rosen, a young painter of Danish-Jewish extraction who was singularly responsive to poetry and music. Although he found her a fascinating companion, he could not free himself from the spell of a young Negress to whom he had become passionately attached during his stay in Florida. With characteristic abruptness he decided to try to recapture the happiness he had known, and sailed for Florida. His search proved futile. He returned to France and shortly thereafter married Jelka. She made him an ideal wife—sympathetic, patient, and wholeheartedly devoted to the unfolding of his gifts.

In 1899 Jelka's mother presented the couple with a villa in Grez-sur-Loing, on the outskirts of the Fontainebleau forest. Here he lived for thirty-five years, leading a sheltered existence that revolved wholly around his work. The first decade-and-a-half of the new century was his most creative period. Delius was fortunate to find an ideal interpreter in Sir Thomas Beecham. The dynamic conductor undertook a crusade that attracted more and more followers until, in the Twenties, he succeeded in establishing Delius's music in the regard of the English public.

Tragedy struck during Delius's final years. On the threshold of sixty he fell victim to creeping paralysis and blindness; the last twelve years of his life were spent in an invalid's chair. After the initial access of despair there asserted itself an indomitable will to live. "So long as I can enjoy the taste of my food and drink, and hear the sound of my music, I want to live. Not being able to see does not bother me. I have my imagination. Besides, I have seen the best of the earth and done everything that is worth doing; I am content. I have had a wonderful life."

Having lost the use of his hands, Delius was able to resume composing when he found a devoted amanuensis in his disciple Eric Fenby, a young musician to whom he dictated his last works note by note. In his book, *Delius as I Knew Him*, Fenby left a moving portrait of the composer's last years. "There was nothing of the sickly, morbid, blind composer as known by popular fiction, but a man with a heart like a lion and a spirit as untamable as it was stern. Once you had crossed the threshold of that great door to the street you found yourself in another world—with its own laws, its own standards of right and wrong in all things, its own particular sense of beauty and its own music."

The highlight of those years was a six-day festival of Delius's works that Beecham organized and conducted in London in 1929. The ovations that greeted the composer both in Queens Hall and later as he was borne to his hotel could leave no doubt in his mind that he was at last recognized as one of England's major artists. He died in his seventy-second year at his home in Grez-sur-Loing. A year later his remains were brought to England and interred in the village churchyard at Limpsfield, in the south country—"the soft rich landscape of which his music speaks." Mrs. Delius died a few days later and was buried beside him.

HIS MUSIC

Delius was a sensitive nature poet, a mystic and dreamer whose art constitutes one of the final outcroppings of the romantic spirit. "As Beethoven is the morning and Wagner the high noon," wrote his biographer Peter Warlock, "so Delius is the sunset of that great period of music which is called Romantic." Thence springs the retrospective, the gently elegiac quality of his music—what has aptly been called his ecstatic melancholy.

Delius was primarily a harmonist. He was concerned with chordal texture rather than counterpoint. His rich chromatic harmony, with its iridescent hues and sensuous sweetness, achieved subtle nuances of mood and atmosphere. It goes without saying that the extended frame of the classical sonata-symphony was foreign to his nature. His mosaic-like structure is based on the "affectionate repetition" of short motives rather than on the dynamic development of themes. He evolved free flexible forms perfectly suited to his rhapsodic flights of fancy, and gave them poetic titles to suggest the mood and the scene. There resulted a music rich in pictorial suggestion and subjective emotion.

Delius consistently exalted the emotional aspect of music over the structural. "Music is an outburst of the soul. It is not experimental analysis, like chemistry. There is really only one quality for great music, and that is emotion." There is a certain resemblance between Delius's sensibility and that of Debussy. All the same, he evolved his style independently of the French master. He shares certain traits with Debussy, such as a fondness for modal scales and blocklike chords in parallel motion, for poetic landscape and twilight moods. He also shared Debussy's aversion to the complicated thematic work of the German symphony. In all this he is a true impressionist. Yet one has only to listen to his music to realize how greatly he differs from Debussy, particularly in his liking for a full orchestral sound, his virile handling of the brass, his frank emotionalism, and his subjective approach to nature. His music is suffused with rapture. It has the sensuous quality we associate with British poetry.

Delius inherited the choral tradition that has been the mainspring of English music since the days of the Tudor and Elizabethan composers. Works for chorus and orchestra occupy a prominent place in his output. "I am always at my best where there are words," he said. *Appalachia*, for soloists, chorus, and orchestra (1902), a fantasy on the Southern slave tune *Oh honey, I am coming down the river in the morning*, evokes the landscape he learned to love in his Florida days. *Sea Drift*, a setting of verses culled from Walt Whitman's *Leaves of Grass*, we will consider in detail. The same poet supplied the text for his last big choral work, *Songs of Farewell* (1932). *A Mass of Life*, for soloists, chorus and orchestra (1904–05), is based on a text drawn from Nietzsche's *Thus Spake Zarathustra*. Nietzsche's conception of the artist as hero and conqueror corresponded to all that was strong and intransigent in Delius's own nature. Of another stripe are the *Songs of Sunset*, to the poems of Ernest Dowson (which *Grove's Dictionary*, despite its concern for all things British, erroneously assigns to Arthur Symons).

Among the orchestral works are the nocturne *Paris: the Song of a Great City* (1899); *Brigg Fair*, an English Rhapsody in the form of variations on a popular tune (1907); two Dance Rhapsodies (1908, 1911); the fantasy *In a Summer Garden* (1908); and two pieces for small orchestra—*On Hearing the First Cuckoo in Spring* and *Summer Night on the River* (1912). The most effective of his operas is *A Village Romeo and Juliet* (1901), "a lyric drama in six pictures" on a libretto adapted by Jelka Delius from Gottfried Keller's novel. He also wrote concertos, piano and chamber music, and songs.

Delius was a limited artist who cultivated a highly personal idiom of a rather narrow range. He was interested in and capable of only certain kinds of expression. For this reason he has not the universality of a world figure. But for those who are responsive to his kind of sensibility, his music speaks eloquently of sweet, wistful things.

SEA DRIFT

Sea Drift (1904) is a large work for baritone solo, chorus, and orchestra, set to an excerpt from Walt Whitman's poem of that name. The piece had its first performance in Essen, Germany, in 1906.

The brief orchestral introduction opens with a characteristic harmony that becomes a formative element in the work. This motive, consisting of two descending fourths, is heard in the strings.

Chorus and soloist take turns in telling the tale of the "two feather'd guests from Alabama" who came "when the lilac-scent was in the air and Fifth-month grass was growing." The solo voice enters in the vein of contemplative lyricism that is so personal to this composer: "And every day the he-bird to and fro, near at hand, and every day the she-bird crouch'd on her nest. . . ." The reader has but to follow the music with Whitman's text (which is given in Appendix IV) to enter the special world of feeling that Delius has here created. The harmony has the Delian sweetness. There is a burst of light as the chorus takes over the narrative: "Shine! shine! shine! Pour down your warmth, great sun, while we bask, we two together!" The music evokes the surge of the sea. Yet this is not a seascape in the way, let us say, that Debussy's *La Mer* is. Here the sea is the setting—in its wildness and vastness perhaps the symbol—for that intensity of love and longing which is the composer's real theme.

The tonality shifts abruptly from the serene E major of the opening section. "Maybe kill'd, unknown to her mate," the she-bird vanishes, never to return. The mood of loss, of sorrowful longing, is sustained with remarkable consistency as the music builds to the climax, the chorus flowing behind and around the solo voice. "Loud! loud! loud! Loud I call to you, my love. . . ."

The sensuous sound subsides into an unaccompanied passage for chorus. We return to the motive of the opening, in the home key of E. An effective modulation to D♭ introduces one of the most poignant parts of the piece: "For somewhere I believe I heard my mate responding to me. . . ." The chorus comments mournfully, "O darkness, in vain, in vain!" and the solo voice echoes: "O I am very sick and sorrowful . . . O throbbing heart, and I singing uselessly, uselessly all the night."

The coda, in classical usage, was a structural feature intended to round out a work. Delius transforms the coda into a feeling, an atmosphere: a mood of gentle melancholy which has left grief and pain behind, having become resignation and remembrance: "O past! O happy life! O songs of joy in the air, in the woods, over fields. Loved! loved! loved! loved! loved! But my mate no more, no more with me! We two together no more." There is great tenderness in the final measures.

The creator of this poetic work was one of the lyric voices of the postromantic period. His influence has lessened in the world. For his countrymen, however, Frederick Delius remains a major prophet.

◄§ 22 §►

Other Impressionists

IMPRESSIONIST music achieved an enormous vogue in the first quarter of the twentieth century. A whole generation of musicians fell under its spell, among them such dissimilar figures as Paul Dukas and Albert Roussel; Isaac Albeniz and Manuel de Falla; Charles Martin Loeffler and Charles Griffes (whom we shall discuss when we come to the Americans). Echoes of its caressing harmonies are to be found in the music of Stravinsky, Schoenberg, and Bartók, Vaughan Williams, Puccini, and Sibelius. In addition, jazz arrangers and Hollywood composers came to be vastly intrigued with its devices, with the result that of all the idioms of twentieth-century music, the impressionist is the one most familiar to the public.

A characteristic figure among the non-French impressionists is Ottorino Respighi (Bologna, 1879–1936, Rome). Respighi produced three symphonic poems which scored international hits: *Le Fontane di Roma* (The Fountains of Rome, 1917); *I Pini di Roma* (The Pines of Rome, 1924); and *Feste romane* (Roman Festivals, 1929). Among his works were eight operas, three ballets, the one-act "mystery," *Maria Egiziaca* (Mary of Egypt, 1932); also a quantity of orchestral and chamber music, concertos, and a number of effective songs. Respighi was a facile composer with a talent for orchestration and a knack for writing music that was infallibly pleasant. He blended Debussyan impressionism with the sumptuous orchestral panoply of Richard Strauss, added a touch of the exotic which he had imbibed during a brief period of study with Rimsky-Korsakov, and projected the result with the expansive lyricism that was his birthright as an Italian. This novel combination of elements was destined for success, especially since the dazzling colors and surging rhetoric of his music were made to order for virtuoso conductors. He was, in consequence, one of the most frequently performed composers of the second quarter of the century. The chances are that time will not deal kindly with his works, except, perhaps, in his homeland. Elsewhere his vogue is on the wane.

That impressionism could be combined with national elements is demonstrated by the music of the Polish composer Karol Szymanowski (Timoshovka, Ukraine, 1882–1937, Lausanne, Switzerland), who brought to the idiom a Slavic intensity and rich chromaticism all his own. Szymanowski's *La Fontaine d'Aréthuse* (Fountain of Arethusa, 1915), for violin, shows his involvement with the Debussyan idiom. His experiments with atonal and polytonal effects broadened the expressive base of his idiom, as is clear from the Third Symphony (1916). While spending some time at a health resort in the Tatras region Szymanowski heard the ancient songs and dances of the Polish mountaineers. He was struck by the primitive power of the folk melodies, their irregular rhythms and modal turns of phrase. This new interest resulted in the ballet *Harnasie* (1926), and in mazurkas, Polish dances for piano, religious choral works, and songs. In these, as in abstract instrumental works like the *Symphonie Concertante* for piano and orchestra (1934), Szymanowski struck root in Polish soil and enriched his art by an imaginative use of folk melody. We should mention also his two violin concertos and the *Stabat Mater*. Szymanowski's best music reveals a poetic sensibility. For his countrymen he is a major figure.

Despite the many composers who were attracted to its dreamlike idiom, we are able, from our vantage point, to see that impressionism was largely a one-man movement. No one else of Debussy's stature found in it the complete artistic expression that he did. His procedures were so special, so easily recognized, that it grew to be practically impossible to write impressionistic music without sounding like him. The result was that composers were forced to seek other modes of expression.

By excluding pathos and the heroic element, impressionism narrowed the human appeal of music. It valued refinement above passion, elegance of form above profundity of thought. It exalted an immediate response to the sensuous allure of art above ethical values. In consequence, it was unable to muster the spiritual energy which alone elevates an artistic movement into a universal force. But on its own premises it created an enchanting art. It opened up to music a world of dream and fantasy. It cut away the excrescences of the grand style. It introduced harmonic procedures that were of crucial importance to the New Music. And it captured a moment of exquisite beauty in a twilight period of European culture.

III. THREE REPRESENTATIVE COMPOSERS

"There are only twelve tones. You must treat them carefully."
Paul Hindemith

✎§ 23 ≈

New Trends: The Flight from Romanticism

"Epochs which immediately precede our own are temporarily
farther away from us than others more remote in time."
Igor Stravinsky

IN REJECTING the nineteenth-century heritage, composers turned away
from the subjective and the grandiose; from pathos and heaven-storming
passion; from landscape painting and the quest for sensuous beauty.
The rising generation regarded the romantic agony as Wagnerian
histrionics. It considered itself to be made of sterner stuff. The New
Music aimed at nothing less than, as the distinguished critic Ortega y
Gasset wrote, "to root out private feelings from art, to purify it by
exemplary objectification." He considered this "conversion from the
subjective to the objective" to be the most important task of the time.

OBJECTIVISM

Twentieth-century artists tried to see the world not through the mist
of their own illusions but as it actually was. A spirit of detachment
began to pervade art. The New Music aspired to objectivity and directness.

Artists became aware that objects, whether in nature or in art, existed
independently of their personalities and feelings, and that a work of
art is not simply a projection of its creator's imagination—as the romanticists had assumed—but is a self-contained organism with a life
of its own. It became apparent that the laws which shape the work of
art are derived not from religion or philosophy or love, but solely from

the nature of the artist's material and the principles governing the formal organization of that material. The artist was supposed to set the mechanism going and to see that it reached its destination. He also, according to the new esthetic, was expected to keep his personal feelings from obtruding upon either the work or the spectator. He had to remain outside his creation, to respect its nature as pure art.

As a result, composers turned from the problem of expression to the

This emphasis on the structural aspect of art was not limited to music. A similar trend is to be observed in painting and sculpture, in the art of pure form that came to the fore with the constructivists and cubists. André Derain, *Three Trees*. (Collection Museum of Modern Art)

problem of formal organization. This emphasis on the structural aspect of art was not limited to music. A similar trend can be observed in painting and sculpture, in the cult of pure form that came to the fore with the constructivists and cubists. Under the impact of this movement, musicians abandoned the grandiose themes that had attracted them throughout the postromantic period. The new matter-of-factness demanded more sober subjects and quieter colors. The emphasis was on restraint and quietness of gesture in every department of musical expression. Once this point was reached, the stage was set for the neo-classic attitude which in the early 1920s won a dominant position in musical esthetics.

PRIMITIVISM

The end of romanticism mirrored the decline of an epoch—of the myriad impulses that had burst into flower with the French Revolution and had brought modern industrial society through its first phase. A great era in western culture was drawing to a close, its end marked by the First World War.

The spiritual exhaustion of European society at the opening of our century showed itself in an indefinable restlessness. Art sought to escape its over-refinement, to purify and renew itself in fresh streams of feeling. There was a desire everywhere to recapture the spontaneity and the freedom from inhibition that were supposed to characterize primitive life. The fine arts turned for inspiration to the magnificent abstraction of African sculpture. Concurrently, musicians discovered the dynamism of African rhythm.

Primitivism was a reaction from the over-refinement of such artists as Debussy and Ravel. Its adherents favored simple clear-cut tunes of folk character that revolved around a central note and moved within a narrow compass; massive harmonies based on blocklike chords moving in parallel formation with harshly percussive effect; and a strong impulsion to a tonal center. Much in evidence were ostinato rhythms repeated with an almost obsessive effect; and a rugged orchestration featuring massed sonorities which contrasted sharply with the coloristic subtleties of the impressionists.

Twentieth-century composers found inspiration not only in African music but also in the songs and dances of the borderlands of western culture—southeastern Europe, Asiatic Russia and the Near East. Out of the unspoiled, vigorous folk music of these regions came rhythms of an elemental power that tapped fresh sources of feeling and imagina-

The fine arts turned for inspiration to the magnificent abstraction of African sculpture. Fertility Symbol: Woman Standing (Museum of Primitive Art)

tion. Milestones in this development were such pieces as Bartók's *Allegro Barbaro* (1911) and Stravinsky's *Le Sacre du printemps* (The Rite of Spring, 1913).

URBANISM AND MACHINE MUSIC

The romantics had found an inexhaustible source of inspiration in nature. The New Music turned to the imagery of the city. The hectic pace of urban life engendered rhythms that were dynamically expressive of the new age.

With the mechanization of Western society came a widespread feeling that man had surrendered his soul to forces he neither understood nor controlled. The machine became a symbol of power, motion, energy; a symbol too of what was aptly called "the dehumanization of art." In the years after the First World War composers glorified the locomotive, the dynamo, and the turbine in their music. They regarded these as a welcome change from the birds, waterfalls, and twilights of the romantics, not realizing that they had merely exchanged one set of picturesque symbols for another.

The machine became a symbol of power, motion, energy; a symbol too of what was aptly called "the dehumanization of art." Charles Sheeler, *American Landscape*. (Collection Museum of Modern Art)

The new tendency produced such works as Honegger's *Pacific 231* (1924); John Alden Carpenter's *Skyscrapers* (1926); Antheil's *Ballet mécanique*, Prokofiev's *Pas d'acier* (Dance of Steel), Mossolov's *Iron Foundry*, and Carlos Chávez's *HP* (Horsepower), all dating from 1927.

The urban spirit found an especially fertile field in opera. The lyric stage for the first time in history witnessed scenes laid in hotel lobbies, bars, nightclubs, transatlantic liners, and city streets. Hindemith's opera *Neues vom Tage* (News of the Day, 1929) contains an aria sung by the heroine in the bathtub; the rhythmic clicking of typewriters and a business letter recited by the chorus. This was a far cry from the gods, kings, and duchesses of romantic opera.

The new symbols lent themselves to the spirit of objectivity prized by the Twenties. Even more important, they went hand-in-hand with a music in which movement and action, projected through kinetic rhythms, ursurped the place of honor formerly occupied by poetic emotion.

SPORTS AND BALLET

In the bitter years after the First World War, emphasis turned increasingly from spiritual values to the physical. Europe found surcease for its shattered nerves in the cult of the body. In ever greater degree sports and athletics became identified with tenacity, endurance, and the will to live.

Sportism became one of the subsidiary themes of the new urban spirit in music. Witness such works as Martinu's *Half-time* (1925), which sings the joys of football, and Honegger's *Skating Rink* (1922) and *Rugby* (1928). Highly significant was the continued popularity of the ballet, an art which glorifies the body both for its physical allure and its capacities as a precision machine. In the decade after the war the ballet widened its expressive scope and reached new heights of sophistication as an art form. Diaghilev with his Ballets Russes offered composers a platform that came to have prime importance for the new music. Almost every important composer of the day contributed to Diaghilev's repertory.

Under the influence of primitivism, machine music, sports, and ballet, the romantic soulfulness of the nineteenth century gave way to the physicality of the twentieth. Emotion was replaced by motion. The shift was well expressed in Stravinsky's dictum that "rhythm and motion, not the element of feeling, are the foundations of musical art."

HUMOR AND SATIRE

Romanticism had regarded music as inspired utterance: the composer was presumed to be a poet and prophet whose natural habitat was the noble and the sublime. Given such an attitude, it was inevitable that nineteenth-century composers were inclined to what Darius Milhaud has called *le sérieux à tout prix* (seriousness at all costs).

Twentieth-century composers increasingly turned to satire, irony, and humor. This tendency was given impetus by the fact that the new dissonant harmony lent itself admirably to cacophonously humorous effects. Erik Satie was a pioneer in this field with his whimsical parodies of the impressionist school. His Parisian disciples were determined not to let music take itself too seriously. They rejected all that smacked of what they contemptuously called "rhetoric." During the 1920s Satie's heirs essayed to revive what had been the ideal of French court music in the seventeenth and eighteenth centuries. They desired to write compositions which were charming, lucid, well-ordered; which would entertain and please.

Their efforts were matched by a wide variety of composers, among them Hindemith and Kurt Weill, Stravinsky and Prokofiev, Shostakovich and Walton. There came into being a witty music that made light of the idols of the past: one in which cleverness and spoofing held the place once pre-empted by pathos and passion. True, most of this music soon dropped out of sight. But the attitude behind it expressed a real need to bring music down to earth, and helped clear the air of much that had outlived its usefulness.

The general disillusion that came in the wake of the First World War impelled artists everywhere to avoid probing or revealing their emotions. The twentieth-century composer, unlike his nineteenth-century forebear, was not going to wear his heart on his sleeve. Introversion of any kind was indissolubly linked to the romantic ideals which, it was felt, had forever been done away with. By allying music with humor and satire, composers were able to give expression to the bitterness of their time. They felt it necessary to strip their art of the mystique in which both the romantics and the impressionists had enveloped it. In line with the new matter-of-factness, composers in the years after the war began to associate their music with deliberately prosaic themes. Milhaud, for example, set to music a *Catalogue of Agricultural Implements* (including the prices). Hindemith turned out music for a comic film called *Felix the Cat*. Such pieces, no matter how fugitive in nature, showed only too clearly that music was moving in a new direction.

THE INFLUENCE OF JAZZ

In the years after the First World War the jazz idiom began to claim the attention of serious musicians. The syncopations and polyrhythms of the jazz band could not but appeal to a generation that was finding its way to new rhythmic conceptions. Besides, the vogue of primitivism made Europeans particularly susceptible to the exotic. They were enchanted by a music whose ancestry went back to the African drums, which mirrored both the dynamic American temperament and the Negro's genius for rhythm. The kinetic rhythms of the dance band, instinct with the hectic pace of modern urban life, seemed to symbolize the restlessness and hunger for excitement of a war-weary world.

From the technical aspect, the chamber-music character of the jazz band was also appealing. A jazz band of the Twenties was an ensemble of soloists in which the "reeds" (saxophones and clarinets) and the "brasses" (trumpets, cornets, trombones) carried the melody over the steady throb of the "rhythm" (piano, string bass, banjo, or guitar, bolstered by drums and a variety of percussive instruments). The absence of string tone in many bands produced a sonority congenial to twentieth-century ears. Also in accord with contemporary taste was the ambiguity between major and minor typical of jazz music, the frequent poly-rhythms, the departure from regular four-bar phrase structure, and the "blue" intonation of certain intervals. After 1917, when a Negro jazz band scored a triumphant success abroad, a number of European musicians became interested in this novelty from America. Among the works that reflected the jazz influence were Erik Satie's ballet *Parade;* Stravinsky's *Ragtime for Eleven Instruments* and *Piano Rag;* Darius Milhaud's ballets *Le Boeuf sur le Toit* and *La Création du Monde;* Hindemith's *1922 Suite for Piano,* with two movements entitled "Shimmy" and "Ragtime"; Honegger's *Concertino* for piano and orchestra; and Ernst Krenek's opera *Jonny spielt auf!* (Johnny Plays!).

Once the jazz idiom and its procedures were absorbed into the language of contemporary music, the vogue passed. Composers turned elsewhere for source material. However, during the 1920s jazz played its part, along with the other influences we have described, in leading European music toward new objectives.

◄§ 24 §►

The New Classicism

"All order demands restraint. But one would be wrong to regard that as any impediment to liberty."

Igor Stravinsky

TWENTIETH-CENTURY CLASSICISM

WHEN twentieth-century composers turned to the classical ideal, they strove to recapture the spirit of an era when music had not yet begun to call on the other arts for heightened dramatic or pictorial effect; when the art had not yet become preoccupied with personal expression and psychological attitudes. By freeing music from elements alien to it, by building it out of elements derived solely from the nature of sound, they hoped to achieve what Stravinsky called "a wholesome return to the formal idea, the only basis of music." Only in this way, they were persuaded, could they retrieve for the art some of the wholeness that had been lost to it.

Classicism meant different things to different composers. To some it represented a return to the courtly style of the late eighteenth century —the age of Haydn and Mozart (the classical era proper). To others it meant turning for inspiration to the giants of the first half of the eighteenth century, when the late Baroque was in flower: Bach and Handel, Couperin, Vivaldi, and Scarlatti, in whose contrapuntal writing the new music found the unsurpassable model for linear texture. Others discovered a spiritual kinship with still earlier masters: Monteverdi, Lully, Purcell; Palestrina and Victoria; Marenzio and Gesualdo; the Tudor church composers and Elizabethan madrigalists; and the Flemish polyphonists of the fifteenth and sixteenth centuries. Classicism, in short, came loosely to denote everything that was untouched by the spirit of nineteenth-century romanticism.

The twentieth-century classicist did not attempt, as some people have supposed, to revive certain mannerisms associated with either the early or late eighteenth-century style. He sought rather to revive certain enduring principles of art that had been best understood in the Baroque and classical eras, but which had been either abandoned or obscured as the romantic tide swept over Europe. Naturally, there could be no "return to Bach" (or to another old master) in any real sense. The conditions that produce an art style are unique for that particular moment in history and cannot be duplicated by a later age. If the adherents of the New Classicism "returned" to preromantic music, they did so in a thoroughly twentieth-century manner.

We should draw a distinction between classicism as such, which attracted artists of diverse temperaments all over Europe, and the movement known as *neo-classicism*. This is a narrower term which came to be applied to the music written by Stravinsky, Hindemith, and other composers during the 1920s and '30s. The label is an unhappy one. Stravinsky never liked it, although it attached itself firmly to the works of his middle period. Historically it is inaccurate, as the neo-classicists were influenced by the contrapuntal writing of the early eighteenth century—the period of the late Baroque—rather than by the music of the late eighteenth century, the classical era proper. Indeed, *Neo-Baroque* would be a far more accurate description of the style. Be that as it may, neo-classicism emerged in the Twenties as a movement of prime importance for the New Music.

The changes in melody, harmony and rhythm, texture, orchestration, tonality, and form which we described in the first part of this book were so overwhelming that there had to follow a breathing spell during which composers could absorb the new acquisitions of their art. Neo-classicism made this period of consolidation possible. In doing so, it fulfilled a widely felt need for simplification, clarity, and order.

NEO-CLASSICISM: THE DOCTRINE

Since neo-classicism had its most articulate spokesman in Igor Stravinsky, it may be well to examine his utterances as an authoritative summary of neo-classic doctrine. Stravinsky, like many of his contemporaries, felt that the unbridled individualism of the romantic era could end only in the breakdown of artistic discipline. "Individual caprice and intellectual anarchy," he declared, "isolate the artist from his fellow artists and condemn him to appear as a monster in the eyes of the public, a monster of originality." Musicians, he maintained, must express not personal but universal truths. To do this they must impose on themselves the restraints of a universally valid style. This submission to discipline, he argued, not only does not encroach upon the artist's freedom but actually provides him with a frame within which to be free—a view, incidentally, that applies to art the Hegelian concept of freedom as "the recognition of necessity." As Stravinsky put it, "The more I limit my field of action and hem myself in with obstacles, the greater my freedom. The more restrictions I impose on myself, the more my mind is liberated from its shackles."

His own intuitions controlled by a lucid intelligence, Stravinsky consistently extols order and discipline above the emotional elements in art. "I cannot compose until I have decided what problem I must solve." But the problem is esthetic, not personal. "I evoke neither human joy nor human sadness," he wrote. "I move towards an ever greater abstraction." In this, of course, he was one with the other great classicist of our time, his friend Picasso. No less important was Stravinsky's attempt to re-establish the status of music as an autonomous art removed from the experiences of life. "The phenomenon of music is given to us with the sole purpose of establishing an order among things, including above all an order between man and time. To be realized, it needs only a construction. Once the construction is made and the order achieved, everything is said. It would be futile to look for or expect anything else from it." This view at one stroke rejects the symbolic meanings which composers from Beethoven to Mahler and Strauss associated with their music. Even more, Stravinsky's doctrine represents an effort on a grand scale to purge music of pictorial, literary, and ethical meanings, of the dreams and visions that had attached themselves to it not only during the romantic period but throughout the course of its history. Stravinsky's aim is to draw the listener's attention away from his own emotions and reveries, and to concentrate it on the tones instead. The emotion aroused by art, he insists, is of a special order that has "nothing in common with our ordinary sensations and our responses to the impressions of daily life."

It goes without saying that Stravinsky continued Debussy's revolt against the Wagnerian music drama, which he saw as the supreme embodiment of everything he disliked in German romanticism. Wagner's attempt to achieve a union of the arts he called "a terrible blow upon music itself." He inveighs against "the Art-Religion with its heroic hardware, its arsenal of warrior mysticism, and its vocabulary seasoned with an adulterated religiosity." Behind this blast is, of course, his profound hostility to the highly emotional conception of music which is at the core of Wagnerian art. "Most people like music because it gives them certain emotions such as joy, grief, sadness, an image of nature, a subject for daydreams or—still better—oblivion from 'everyday life.' They want a drug—'dope'. Music would not be worth much if it were reduced to such an end. When people have learned to love music for itself, when they listen with other ears, their enjoyment will be of a far higher and more potent order, and they will be able to judge it on a higher plane and to realize its intrinsic value."

From this position Stravinsky was driven to one of the most amazing statements ever to come from a musician. "I consider that music is by its very nature essentially powerless to *express* anything at all, whether a feeling, a state of mind, a psychological mood, a phenomenon of nature, and the like. *Expression* has never been an inherent property of music. That is by no means the purpose of its existence." The expressive power that we attribute to music he considers to be an illusion, a convention "which unconsciously or by force of habit we have come to confuse with its essential being." To rescue music from this illusion was to be the goal of his life.

That Stravinsky in the heat of polemics was impelled to overstate his case is understandable when we realize that the issue at stake was nothing less than a revolution in taste. Art cannot be separated from life to the degree that he desired. Nor would music have played the part it has in the history of civilization if it were only an objective manipulation of sonorous patterns. If, as he complains, "people will always insist upon looking in music for something that is not there," they do so for a very good reason. Only a trained musician can perceive the meaning of a musical work through its formal relationships—and in the case of certain complicated works even he will have to study the score. The music lover without technical training tends to attach emotional meanings to what he hears because only in this way can he relate the work to his own experience. It would in any case be difficult for the layman to distinguish between the organization of the "sonorous material" and the flow of feeling that this sets up in him.

Also, the masters of the past would hardly have agreed with the tenets of neo-classicism, if one may judge from their remarks about music. Only the social music of the late Baroque—the concerti grossi, suites, and harpsichord pieces—may be said to display that spirit of detachment which the twentieth century values so highly. In their great religious works, Bach, Handel and Vivaldi, like their contemporaries and predecessors, marshalled all the expressive resources of which the music of their time was capable. Inevitably each age recreates the past in its own image. The nineteenth century regarded Bach as a visionary and mystic. For the twentieth he became the model for many a passage of counterpoint that jogged along as amiably as ever did a piece of dinner music for an eighteenth-century princeling. What the neo-classicists took from Bach was his texture, not his passion.

As a matter of fact, Stravinsky adhered to his thesis less stringently than one might suppose. There is more emotion in his *Symphony of Psalms* than is dreamed of in his philosophy. True, his music of the early and middle Twenties exemplifies the artist's sheer delight in making patterns, in playing with the material. But in the later phase of his career he explicitly departs from his doctrine. Speaking of his *Symphony in Three Movements*, which was written during the Second World War, he says, "During the process of creation in this arduous time of sharp and shifting events, of despair and hope, of tension and at last cessation and relief, it may be said that all these repercussions have left traces in this symphony." Here, obviously, the separation between art and life is no longer upheld with the old finality.

Neo-classicism attracted artists as dissimilar as Schoenberg and Hindemith, Bartók and Milhaud, Honegger and Prokofiev, Aaron Copland and Roger Sessions. Sessions produced what has remained perhaps the best formulation of the neo-classic ideal. Writing in 1927, he declared: "Younger men are dreaming of an entirely different kind of music—a music which derives its power from forms beautiful and significant by virtue of inherent musical weight rather than intensity of utterance; a music whose impersonality and self-sufficiency preclude the exotic;

which takes its impulse from the realities of a passionate logic; which, in the authentic freshness of its moods, is the reverse of ironic and, in its very aloofness from the concrete preoccupations of life, strives rather to contribute form, design, a vision of order and harmony."

NEO-CLASSICISM: THE MUSIC

One of the prime achievements of the New Classicism was the revival of the absolute forms. Symphony, concerto, sonata and the various types of chamber music achieved a far greater importance than had been their lot in the first two decades of the century. Equally significant was the return to the forms of the preromantic era, such as the suite, divertimento, toccata, concerto grosso, fugue, passacaglia, and chaconne.

The music of the romantics had adhered to a melodic imagery based on the voice. The New Classicism, contrariwise, favored an instrumental melody that made use of wider intervals and a more extended range. Harmonically, neo-classicism moved away from the chromaticism of the post-Wagner era. Its music is based on the seven tones of the diatonic scale, although these are used much more freely than ever before. The term *pandiatonicism* is often used to indicate the new freedom with which the seven tones are combined harmonically and contrapuntally. Pandiatonicism offered a natural medium for the neo-classicists. In contrast to the multitude of sharps and flats in early twentieth-century music, pandiatonicism favored a sparing use of accidentals and showed a striking affinity for the key of C major. Indeed, it originated as a modern technique of playing the piano on the white keys. Hence the term "white music" that applies to many a page of neo-classic music, as in the following measures from Stravinsky's *Concerto for Piano and Wind Instruments* (1924):

To the full chordal texture of romantic and impressionist music, neo-classicism opposed a transparent linear texture. The neo-classic style found its characteristic expression in an agile dissonant counterpoint marked by clarity and freshness and propelled by lithe motor rhythms. In the matter of orchestral color, it need hardly be said, the neo-classicists veered away from the lush sonorities of the postromantic period toward sober, sharply defined colors that brought out the interplay of the several lines. Romanticism in music inevitably led to the use of harmony, rhythm, and color for their own sake; the New Classicism— and here perhaps was its most important contribution—ended this lawless independence of the separate elements. It restored these to their true function as parts of the whole, and rendered them strictly subservient to musical idea and design.

The neo-classic esthetic rejected the nineteenth-century concept of the Artist in favor of the older craftsman ideal. Stravinsky, significantly, has always disliked the term *artist*, which he considers pretentious and romantic. He prefers to regard himself as an artisan. In line with this attitude he welcomes a commission that imposes specific conditions and challenges the craftsman's ingenuity. "When I know how long a piece must take, then it excites me." He repudiates the romantic view of the artist as a being apart, creating out of his loneliness. The aim of art, he points out (in a sentence that might have been uttered by one of the art-craftsmen of centuries ago) is "to promote a communion, a union of man with his fellow men and with the Supreme Being."

The New Classicism attracted musicians of a certain taste and temperament—especially those who were fascinated by formal perfection and inclined to separate art from life. Its esthetic recalled a whole generation to the problems of the craft, focusing their attention on elegance of style and purity of taste. In exalting the *how* over the *what*, it led musicians to the classical virtues of order, discipline, balance, and proportion. At a moment when Western music was unable to proceed farther along the romantic path, the New Classicism pointed the way to an athletic musical style, Apollonian in its detachment and serenity, thus upholding the autonomy of music as a self-contained universe in which the artist could grapple with the problem of human freedom in its most abstract and ideal essence.

GEBRAUCHSMUSIK (WORKADAY MUSIC)

"It is to be regretted that in general so little relationship exists between the producers and the consumers of music."
Paul Hindemith

The changes in the musical language that occurred in the first two decades of our century could not but bewilder and alienate the mass of music lovers. There resulted an increasing distance between the composer and the majority of his public. Yet even while the leaders of musical advance—Stravinsky, Bartók, Schoenberg, and their compeers

—were formulating significant new concepts in style and expression, other forces were at work to effect some sort of rapprochement between "the producers and the consumers" of music.

One such influence, we shall see, emanated from Erik Satie and his disciples, who strove to create an "everyday" music. Another impetus in this direction came from Soviet Russia where the composer, functioning under the control of the state, had to solve the problem of reaching a great mass of listeners who were just discovering music. The fact that the works of the leading Soviet composers—Prokofiev, Shostakovich, Khatchaturian—achieved enormous popularity in the West could not fail to impress composers everywhere; and this reinforced the attempt to bring twentieth-century music closer to the average listener.

The climate that prevailed in Germany under the liberal Weimar Republic was especially favorable to "music for everyday living." Encouraged by the large publishing houses, composers sought to create a new public for contemporary music—amateurs, students, and the young. They began to cultivate a simple, practical music designed for use in the home and the community. *Gebrauchsmusik* (literally, "music for use"—that is, workaday music) emerged in a milieu of progressive youth movements, workers' choruses, and the strong desire to foster group activities. Its leading exponents were Paul Hindemith, Ernst Krenek, Kurt Weill, and Hanns Eisler. "The days of composing for the sake of composing are perhaps gone forever," wrote Hindemith in 1927. "A composer should write today only if he knows for what purpose he is writing." This view looked back to the craft practices of the preromantic era, when the composer was in the employ of a prince, a church or an opera house. It was precisely in this way, of course, that the operas of Monteverdi and Lully, the odes of Purcell and the cantatas of Bach came into being.

The trend towards Gebrauchsmusik produced Hindemith's "musical game for children," *Wir bauen eine Stadt* (We're Building a City, 1930); his Opus 45, "Music to Sing or Play—for amateurs or music lovers" (1928); his pieces for teaching young violinists the first position; and his music for community singing. Compositions such as these embodied the conviction of the younger generation of German composers that a healthy musical culture depended not on the much publicized virtuoso, but on a broad base of amateurs, young and old, who took part themselves in every phase of musical activity. This attitude, and the works that resulted from it, played a progressive role in the music of the Twenties and Thirties, and helped to bring about a rapprochement between modern composers and their public.

⤳ 25 ⤲
Igor Stravinsky (1882-)

"Music to me is a power which justifies things."

IT IS granted to certain artists to embody the profoundest impulses of their time and to affect its artistic life in the most powerful fashion. Such an artist is Igor Stravinsky, the Russian composer who for half a century has given impetus to the main currents in contemporary music.

HIS LIFE

Stravinsky was born in Oranienbaum, a summer resort not far from what was then St. Petersburg, where his parents lived. He grew up in a musical environment; his father was the leading bass at the Imperial

Bettmann Archive

Igor Stravinsky, a drawing by Picasso

Opera. Although he was taught to play the piano, his musical education was kept on the amateur level. His parents desired him to study law. He matriculated at the University of St. Petersburg and embarked on a legal career, meanwhile continuing his musical studies. At twenty he submitted his work to Rimsky-Korsakov, with whom he subsequently worked for three years.

Success came early to Stravinsky. His music attracted the notice of Serge Diaghilev, the legendary impresario of the Russian Ballet, who commissioned Stravinsky to write the music for *Le Oiseau de feu* (The Firebird), which was produced in 1910. Stravinsky was twenty-eight when he arrived in Paris to attend the rehearsals. Diaghilev pointed him out to the ballerina Tamara Karsavina with the words, "Mark him well —he is a man on the eve of fame."

The Firebird was followed, a year later, by *Petrushka*. Presented with Nijinsky and Karsavina in the leading roles, this production secured Stravinsky's position in the forefront of the modern movement in art. In the spring of 1913 was presented the third and most spectacular of the ballets Stravinsky wrote for Diaghilev, *Le Sacre du printemps* (The Rite of Spring). The opening night was one of the most scandalous in modern musical history; the revolutionary score touched off a near-riot. People hooted, screamed, slapped each other, and were persuaded that what they were hearing "constituted a blasphemous attempt to destroy music as an art." A year later the composer was vindicated when the *Sacre*, presented at a symphony concert under Pierre Monteux, was received with enthusiasm and established itself as one of the master-pieces of the new music.

The outbreak of war in 1914 brought to an end the whole way of life on which Diaghilev's sumptuous dance spectacles depended. Stravinsky, with his wife and children, took refuge in Switzerland, their home for the next six years. The difficulty of assembling large bodies of performers during the war worked hand-in-hand with his inner evolution as an artist: he moved away from the grand scale of the first three ballets to works more intimate in spirit and modest in dimension.

The Russian Revolution had severed Stravinsky's ties with his homeland. In 1920 he settled in France, where he remained until 1939. During these years Stravinsky concertized extensively throughout Europe, performing his own works as pianist and conductor. He also paid two visits to the United States. In 1939 he was invited to deliver the Charles Eliot Norton lectures at Harvard University. He was there when the Second World War broke out, and decided to live in this country. He settled in California, outside Los Angeles, and in 1945 became an American citizen. The observance of his eightieth birthday in June, 1962, showed that he was revered not only in his adopted country but throughout the world.

HIS MUSIC

Stravinsky throughout his career has refused to go on repeating himself. With inexhaustible avidity he has tackled new problems and pressed for new solutions. It has happened more than once that a phase of his career has seemed to move in the opposite direction from the one before. In retrospect, however, his various periods emerge as necessary stages in a continuous evolution toward greater purity of style and abstraction of thought.

Stravinsky issued out of the sound-world of the Russian national school. *The Firebird* displays all the shimmer of Rimsky-Korsakov's orchestra (to which are added the pastel tints of French impressionism). Here, as in the works that followed, Stravinsky worked within the frame of Russian folklore, drawing sustenance from popular song and dance. All the same, from the beginning he was aligned with those forces in Russian culture that were oriented toward the West—especially those that were receptive to Latin clarity and grace. He thus was free to move toward the universal values that underlie the classical outlook.

The mainspring of Stravinsky's art is rhythm. He was a leader in the revitalization of European rhythm. It is significant that his first great success was won in the field of ballet, where rhythm is allied to dynamic body movement and expressive gesture. His is a rhythm of unparalleled thrust and tension, supple, powerful, controlled. Units of seven, eleven, or thirteen beats, a continual shifting from one meter to another, the dislocation of the accent by means of intricate patterns of syncopation—these and kindred devices revolutionized the traditional concepts.

Stravinsky reacted strongly against the restless chromaticism of the postromantic era. He found the antidote in a harmonic language that is essentially diatonic. The key supplies him with the necessary framework; it delimits and defines the area of his activity. He achieves excitement by superposing harmonic planes—either melodies or streams of chords—in contrasting keys, obtaining pungent polytonal combinations. Yet no matter how complex the harmony may become, at the point of repose one key emerges triumphant over the rest, reaffirming the principle of law and order.

Stravinsky's subtle sense of sound places him among the master orchestrators. He turned away from the sonorous haze of the nineteenth-century orchestra and led the way to the *concertante* style of the eighteenth century, in which the instruments stand out soloistically against the mass. His writing is notable for its precision and economy. The nicety of his doublings, his individual way of spacing the harmonies, his use of unconventional registers, and his feeling for the character of the various instruments impart to his orchestration a clean, enameled lustre that is unmistakably his. There results a texture based on pure colors, so limpid that, as Diaghilev said, "One could see through it with one's ears."

Stravinsky sets great store on melody. "A return to the cult of melody," he has stated, "seems to me necessary and even urgent." In the works of his Russian period he was much given to those concise, fragmentary melodies, incisive and direct, that turn about themselves in such characteristic fashion. Later, in his neo-classic period, he developed the more flowing type of melodic line that is inseparable from a contrapuntal conception of music, finding his model in the self-generating arabesque of Bach. In respect to form, he adheres to the Baroque principle of continuous expansion rather than to the classical method of "working out" themes and motives, preferring the organic structure of the Baroque to the symmetrical sections of the classical style. His plastic conception of form has exerted a vast influence on the musicians of our time.

With *Petrushka* (1911), Stravinsky found his personal tone. Despite its Russianness, the ballet about the puppet who turns out to have a soul possesses universal appeal. Is not Petrushka, as the composer asks, "the immortal and unhappy hero of every fair in all countries?" The carnival scene with which the piece opens is dominated by the "big accordion" sound—a direct echo of the peasant instrument that held Stravinsky spellbound as a child. In *Petrushka* we encounter the laconic melodies, resilient rhythms and orchestral brightness that are the composer's very own. One of the most original scores of the century, this is the best loved of Stravinsky's works for the theater.

The *Rite of Spring* may be omitted here, as we shall discuss it later in detail. Also *L'Histoire du soldat* (The Soldier's Story). The works written after the First World War show the composer moving away from the Russian style of his first period toward the French-international orientation of his second. In the ballet *Pulcinella* (1919) he affirmed his kinship with the past. Scored for voice and small orchestra, the piece was based on themes drawn from several instrumental works ascribed to Giovanni Battista Pergolesi (1710–1736). At the same time his "passion for jazz," as he called it, gave rise to the *Ragtime for Eleven Instruments* (1918) and the *Piano-Rag Music* (1919). There followed the "burlesque tale" *Le Renard* (The Fox, 1922), for four vocalists, dancers, and chamber orchestra, based on a folk story that was put into dramatic form by Stravinsky himself. *Les Noces* (The Wedding, 1923) is a stylization of a Russian peasant wedding. Four singers and a chorus support the dancers, accompanied by four pianos and a diversified percussion group. This ballet-cantata, with its clear glacial sound and its percussive use of the piano, boasts one of Stravinsky's most powerful scores.

The neo-classical period was ushered in by the *Symphonies of Wind Instruments* (1920), dedicated to the memory of Debussy. The instrumental works that followed incarnate the principle of the old concerto grosso—the pitting against each other of contrasting tone masses. This "return to Bach" crystallized in the *Piano Sonata*, the Concerto for piano and wind orchestra, and the *Serenade in A*, all of which date from the years 1924–25. Stravinsky's writing for the piano derives from the crisp harpsichord style of the eighteenth century rather than from the singing Chopin style of the nineteenth.

His devotion to neo-classicism was hailed in certain quarters as conclusive proof that the romantic spirit finally was dead; but the master surprised his disciples by proclaiming his admiration for a number of nineteenth-century composers. He paid homage to Weber and Mendelssohn in the *Capriccio* (1929), a brilliant concert piece. The ballet *Le Baiser de la fée* (The Fairy's Kiss, 1922) was "inspired by the Muse of Tchaikovsky." A more successful score is that of the one-act opera buffa *Mavra* (1922), dedicated "to the memory of Pushkin, Glinka and Tchaikovsky." This genial little work is based on Pushkin's tale about the enterprising soldier who makes his way into his sweetheart's house by disguising himself as a maid-servant, only to be discovered in the act of shaving.

Stravinsky's classical period culminates in several major compositions. *Oedipus Rex* (1927) is an "opera-oratorio." The text is a translation into Latin of Cocteau's French adaptation of the Greek tragedy. Stravinsky's comment on his preference for the Latin is revealing. "What a joy it is to compose music to a language of convention, almost of ritual, the very nature of which imposes a lofty dignity! One no longer feels dominated by the phrase, the literal meaning of the words." From the shattering dramaticism of the opening chords, *Oedipus Rex* is an unforgettable experience in the theatre. The archaic Greek influence is manifest too in the ballet *Apollon Musagète* (Apollo, Leader of the Muses, 1928) which marked the beginning of his collaboration with the choreographer George Balanchine; *Perséphone* (1934), a choral dance drama on a text by André Gide; and the ballet *Orpheus* (1947), a severely classical work that ranks with the master's most distinguished creations.

The *Symphony of Psalms*, which many regard as the chief work of Stravinsky's maturity, we will discuss in detail. The *Symphony in C* (1940), a sunny piece of modest dimensions, pays tribute to the spirit of Haydn and Mozart. With the *Symphony in Three Movements* (1945), Stravinsky returns to bigness of form and gesture. The *Mass in G* (completed in 1948) is in the restrained, telegraphic style that he favored during his middle years. In 1950 there followed *The Rake's Progress*, an opera on a libretto by W. H. Auden and Chester Kallman, after Hogarth's celebrated series of paintings. Written as the composer was approaching seventy, this is a mellow, radiantly melodious score. Unfortunately, the opera does not quite come off in the theater, mainly because the libretto lacks dramatic tension.

Stravinsky, imperturbably pursuing his own growth as an artist, had still another surprise in store for his public. In the works written after he was seventy, he has shown himself increasingly receptive to the serial procedures of the twelve-tone style, to which in earlier years he was categorically opposed. The *Cantata on four poems by anonymous English poets of the 15th and 16th centuries*, for choir and chamber orchestra (1952), with its hidden canons and similar intricacies, justifies Stravinsky's remark that "counterpoint is my real home." The interest in formal abstraction is manifest in the Septet for piano, string, and wind instruments (1952); the *3 Songs from William Shakespeare* for mezzo-soprano, flute, clarinet, and viola (1954), and *In Memoriam Dylan Thomas* for tenor, string quartet, and four trombones (1954). The formalistic tendency flowers in the *Canticum sacrum ad honorem Sancti Marci nominis* (Sacred Song to Honor the Name of St. Mark, 1956) for tenor, baritone, chorus, and orchestra. The piece was written for St. Mark's Cathedral in Venice and received its premiere there in 1956. The *Canticum* shows the master's growing involvement with twelve-tone procedures as well as with the intricate canonic devices of sixteenth-century polyphony. There followed the ballet *Agon* (1957) and *Threni—id est Lamentationes Jeremiae Prophetae* (Threnodies: Lamentations of the Prophet Jeremiah, completed 1958). We will discuss these two examples of Stravinsky's late style in a subsequent chapter. (See pages 403–413.)

Stravinsky, then, has been a seminal influence for three generations of composers. In the decade of the First World War *Petrushka* and the *Sacre* revealed the power of "the displaced accent and the polytonal chord." He led the Twenties "back to Bach" and classicism. Now, as

Aaron Copland has said, "Because of Stravinsky all sorts of composers are experimenting with the tone-rows to which they hitherto were irreconcilably opposed." Stravinsky's detractors—he has them!—point to his changes of style as evidence of his lack of conviction and his opportunism; to which one can only reply that no opportunist ever executes an about-face while he is being successful, which is precisely what Stravinsky did. In his *Autobiography* he makes the following comment: "I have a very distinct feeling that in the course of the last fifteen years my written work has estranged me from the great mass of my listeners. They expected something different from me. Liking the music of *L'Oiseau de feu*, *Petrushka*, *Le Sacre*, and *Les Noces*, and being accustomed to the language of those works, they are astonished to hear me speaking in another idiom. . . . Their attitude certainly cannot make me deviate from my path. I shall assuredly not sacrifice my predilections and my aspirations to the demands of those who, in their blindness, do not realize that they are simply asking me to go backwards. It should be obvious that what they wish for has become obsolete for me, and that I could not follow them without doing violence to myself."

Stravinsky's aphorisms display a gift for trenchant expression. "We have a duty to music, namely, to invent it. . . . Instinct is infallible. If it leads us astray it is no longer instinct. . . . It is not simply inspiration that counts. It is the result of inspiration—that is, the composition." Speaking of his *Mass:* "The Credo is the longest movement. There is much to believe." When asked to define the difference between the *Rite of Spring* and the *Symphony of Psalms:* "The difference is twenty years." "How do you know when to end?" an admirer inquired. "Before I begin," was the craftsman's reply.

Granted a long span of life, Stravinsky was aided by that combination of inner and outer factors which makes for an international career. It was his historic role to incarnate a phase of the contemporary spirit. In upholding the Apollonian discipline in art, he revealed an era to itself. He is the representative musician of our time.

ᴖ 26 ᴖ

Three Works by Stravinsky

"In everyday life we choose our garments to fit the occasion, though our personality is the same whether we wear a dress suit or pajamas. The same applies to art. I garb my ideas in robes to fit the subject, but do not change my personality."

LE SACRE DU PRINTEMPS (THE RITE OF SPRING)

SCENES OF PAGAN RUSSIA

Le Sacre du printemps (1913) not only embodies the cult of primitivism that so startled its first-night audience; it also sets forth the lineaments of a new tonal language—the percussive use of dissonance, polyrhythms, polytonality. Stravinsky's granite-like orchestral sonority already possesses the "vibrating transparency," to use Erik Satie's fine phrase, which we associate with it. The work is scored for a large orchestra: 2 piccolos, 2 flutes, flute in G, 4 oboes, English horn, clarinet in E-flat, bass clarinet, 4 bassoons, double bassoon; 8 horns, 4 trumpets, trumpet in D, bass trumpet, 3 trombones, 2 tubas; 4 kettledrums, small kettledrums, bass drum, tambourine, cymbals, antique cymbals, triangle, guiro (a Latin American instrument consisting of a serrated gourd scraped with a wooden stick); and the usual complement of strings. Also, in certain passages, a second bass clarinet, second double bassoon, and 2 Wagner tubas.

PART I. *Adoration of the Earth.* The Introduction is intended to evoke the birth of Spring. A long-limbed melody is introduced by the bassoon, taking on a curious remoteness from the circumstance that it lies in the instrument's uppermost register.

174

The awakening of the earth is suggested in the orchestra. On stage, a group of young girls is discovered before the sacred mound, holding a long garland. The Sage appears and leads them toward the mound. The orchestra erupts into a climax, after which the bassoon melody returns.

Dance of the Adolescents.   Dissonant chords in the dark register of the strings exemplify Stravinsky's "elemental pounding"; their percussive quality is heightened by the use of polytonal harmonies. A physical excitement attends the dislocation of the accent, which is underlined by syncopated chords hurled out by eight horns. The ostinato—Stravinsky's favored rhythmic device—is repeated with hypnotic insistence. A theme emerges on the bassoons, moving within a narrow range around a central tone, with a suggestion of primitive power.

The main theme of the movement, a more endearing melody in folk style, is introduced by the horn. Stravinsky expands this idea by means of the repetition technique so characteristic of the Russian school.

Game of Abduction.   The youths and maidens on the stage form into two phalanxes which in turn approach and withdraw from one another. Fanfares on the woodwinds and brass remind us that the composer of these measures studied with the creator of *Scheherazade.*

Spring Dance.   A pastoral melody is played by the high clarinet in E-flat and the bass clarinet, against a sustained trill on the flutes. Modal harmonies create an archaic atmosphere. Four couples are left on stage. Each man lifts a girl on his back and with measured tread executes the Rounds of Spring. The movement is *sostenuto e pesante* (sustained and heavy), with blocklike harmonies propelled by ostinato rhythms.

Games of the Rival Cities—Entrance of the Sage—Dance of the Earth.   The peremptory beating of drums summons the braves of the rival tribes to a display of prowess. The main idea is presented by two muted trumpets. Notice that the third measure repeats the melodic curve of the two preceding ones, but with a rhythmic dislocation which causes the notes to fall on different beats within the measure:

The orchestration evokes a neolithic landscape. The score abounds in orchestral "finds," such as the braying sound produced by a simultaneous trill in trombones, horns, clarinets, oboes, and flutes over an ostinato in the double bass. The Entrance of the Sage touches off a powerful crescendo that rises over a persistent figure in the brass. An abrupt silence—a pianissimo chord in the strings as the dancers prostrate themselves in mystic adoration of the earth. Then they leap to their feet, and to music of the sheerest physicality perform the Dance of the Earth.

PART II. *The Sacrifice.* The Prelude, a "night piece," creates a brooding atmosphere. The Sage and the maidens sit motionless, staring into the fire in front of the sacred mound. They must choose the Elect One who will be sacrificed to ensure the fertility of the earth. A poignant melodic idea in Russian folk style, first presented by the muted violins in harmonics, pervades the movement.

The music is desolate, but there is nothing subjective about it. This desolation is of the soil, not the soul.

Mystic Circle of Young Girls. The theme of the preceding movement alternates with a melody presented by the alto flute, which stands

out against a dissonant background. The two themes are repeated in various registers with continual changes of color. The major-minor ambiguity goes hand in hand with the soft colors of the orchestration.

The Dance in Adoration of the Chosen Virgin has the Stravinskyan muscularity of rhythm. The eighth note is the metric unit, upon which are projected a series of uneven meters that change continually, sometimes with each bar. The piece develops into a frenzied dance.

Evocation of the Ancestors—Ritual Act of the Old Men. After a violent opening, the movement settles down to a kind of "Scythian blues." An English horn solo presents a sinuously chromatic figure against a background of primordial drums and pizzicato chords in the bass. The music carries a suggestion of swaying bodies and shuffling feet.

Sacrificial Dance of the Chosen Virgin. In this, the climactic number of the ballet, the elected maiden dances until she falls dead. The movement mounts in fury to the point where the Elect One has fulfilled the sacrifice. The men in wild excitement bear her body to the foot

of the mound. There is the scraping sound of the guiro, used here for the first time in European orchestral music; an ascending run on the flutes; and with a fortissimo growl in the orchestra this luminous score comes to an end.

Half a century has passed since *Le Sacre* was written. It is still an amazing work.

L'HISTOIRE DU SOLDAT (THE SOLDIER'S STORY)

L'Histoire du soldat (1918) was composed during one of the most difficult periods in Stravinsky's life. "The Communist Revolution, which had just triumphed in Russia, deprived me of the last resources which had still occasionally been reaching me from my country. I found myself, so to speak, face to face with nothing, in a foreign land and right in the middle of the war." Together with his friends, the conductor Ernest Ansermet and the writer C. F. Ramuz, he sought a way out of his predicament. "Ramuz and I got hold of the idea of creating a sort of little traveling theater, easy to transport from place to place and to show in even small localities." Thus Stravinsky came to the intimate chamber art that was to play so vital a role in the new music.

A collection of Russian folk tales provided the theme. "We were particularly drawn to the cycle of legends dealing with the adventures of the soldier who deserted and the Devil who inexorably comes to carry off his soul." In its final form the tale contained a musical image that could not but excite the composer. The Soldier barters his violin —symbol of his soul—for the allurements of the Devil. The theme of the violin—strangely haunting, fanciful, bittersweet—becomes the chief character in the unfolding of the tale:

Stravinsky chose an ensemble consisting of the most representative types, in treble and bass, of the different instrumental families. "For the strings, the violin and the double bass; for the woodwind, the clarinet —because it has the biggest compass—and the bassoon; for the brass, trumpet and trombone; and, finally, the percussion manipulated by only one musician." (Actually the score calls for a cornet—an instrument with a shorter tube than the trumpet, more agile and more incisive in tone.) The percussion includes drums of various sizes, with and without snares, as well as cymbals, tambourine, and triangle. This seven-piece band lends itself, needless to say, to the utmost individualization of timbre.

The action is presented by four characters. The Soldier and the Devil speak, dance, and act. The Narrator reads, comments in the manner of the Greek chorus, and at one climactic point leaps into the action to counsel the unfortunate hero. The Princess dances her role and mimes, but has no speaking part. Stravinsky and his librettist direct that the little orchestra be placed on one side of the stage. At the other end is a dais for the reader. The drama unfolds in the center.

The action opens as the Soldier, trudging to his native village, is accosted by the Devil. The Devil offers him a magic book that contains the secret of acquiring untold wealth, if the Soldier will surrender his fiddle in return. The Soldier accepts. The Devil also invites his victim for a three-day visit. Upon arriving at his village the Soldier discovers that the three days in reality were three years. There follows a series of adventures in which the Soldier regains his violin and wins the Princess. Ultimately, however, he falls into the Devil's clutches and is carried off. (Now that the work has been recorded in an English version, the reader can readily familiarize himself with Stravinsky's musico-dramatic intention.)

Strangely moving is the first number, the *Soldier's March*, with its arabesques tootled on clarinet and bassoon, the grotesque little tune that emerges on cornet and trombone, the staccato figures on the violin against the "oom-pah" of the double bass, and the rattle of the drums. The music to Scene I introduces the violin theme already quoted, which runs as a unifying thread throughout the piece. The music to Scene II (the Soldier's return to his village) is in the nature of a lyric interlude, in the course of which a dialogue between clarinet and bassoon unfolds against a background of string tone. In the third scene, where the Devil counsels the Soldier to concentrate on success, we hear again the violin theme with its curious mixture of irony and poignance.

Part II opens with a recapitulation of the *Soldier's March*. A long stretch of action and narration intervenes at this point, covering the Soldier's game of cards with the Devil, his recovery of his fiddle, and his determination to cure the Princess of her mysterious ailment. Upon his arrival at the palace we hear the pompous *Royal March*, a delicious bit of Stravinskyan burlesque. Cornet and trombone trace an agile melodic line against the steady beat of a four-four accompaniment. Three dances follow: the *Tango*, for violin, clarinet, and percussion; the sardonic *Waltz* in C major, which is related in mood to similar mock-serious moments in *Petrushka*; and the *Ragtime*, with slides on the trombone —a number that holds a nostalgic charm for all who remember the jazz of the Twenties. The *Devil's Dance* is properly frenetic. The Soldier and his Princess embrace to the sounds of the *Little Chorale*. The *Devil's Song* intervenes, unutterably malevolent. Then comes the *Great Chorale* —with a majestic distortion of *A Mighty Fortress Is Our God*—which is solemnly intoned by the brass against a dissonantal background. The *Triumphal March of the Devil* is climaxed by the solo passage for percussion, in changing meters of two, three, four, five, and six eighth-notes to the bar, which brings the work to a close.

In the bright clean sonorities of this score we find the aerated texture and objective outlook of the new classicist esthetic. Stravinsky here returns to the tradition of graceful entertainment music embodied in the eighteenth-century suite and divertimento. Yet, for all its cleverness, *L'Histoire* echoes the infinite disenchantment that pervaded the bitter years of the war. This profoundly human quality lifts *L'Histoire du soldat* into the realm of works that live beyond the time which produced them.

SYMPHONY OF PSALMS

The *Symphony of Psalms* (1930) was among the works commissioned by the Boston Symphony Orchestra to celebrate its fiftieth anniversary. "My idea was that my symphony should be a work with great contrapuntal development, and for that it was necessary to increase the media at my disposal. I finally decided on a choral and instrumental ensemble in which the two elements should be on an equal footing, neither of them outweighing the other." The result was one of Stravinsky's grandest works, written "for the glory of God" and dedicated to the Boston Symphony Orchestra.

The choice of instruments is unusual. The score omits clarinets and violins—whose seductive tone did not accord with the composer's intention—as well as violas. The woodwind section consists of five flutes (one doubling on the piccolo), four oboes, English horn, three bassoons, and a contrabassoon. The brass includes four horns, five trumpets, three trombones, and a tuba. Stravinsky also calls for two pianos, harp, kettledrums, bass drum, and the darker strings—cellos and double basses. The three movements are performed without a break. The first is the shortest. The slow movement is about twice, and the jubilant finale about three times, as long.

I

Psalmus XXXVIII (Vulgate) Verses 13–14	Psalm XXXIX (King James Version) Verses 12–13

Exaudi orationem meam, Domine,
    et depreciationem meam:
    auribus percipe lacrymas meas.
Ne sileas, quoniam advena ego apud te,
    et peregrinus, sicut omnes patres mei.
Remitte mihi,
    ut refrigerer priusque abeam,
    et amplius non ero.
	Hear my prayer, O Lord,
	    and give ear unto my cry;
	    hold not Thy peace at my tears.
	For I am a stranger with Thee,
	    and a sojourner, as all my fathers were.
	O spare me,
	    that I may recover strength,
	    before I go hence, and be no more.

The symphony opens with a prelude-like section in which flowing arabesques are traced by oboe and bassoon. These are punctuated by an urgent E-minor chord which, spread out across the orchestral gamut, asserts the principal tonality. The altos enter with a chant-like theme consisting of two adjacent notes—the interval of a minor second (semitone) that has structural significance throughout.

This idea alternates with the fuller sound of choral passages as the movement builds to its climactic point on the words *Remitte mihi* (O spare me) over a strong pedal point on E. The modal harmony creates an archaic atmosphere and leans towards the Phrygian (the mode that is sounded by playing the white keys on the piano from E to E). Tension is created by the fact that, although the music seems again and again to be climbing toward the key of C, that tonality will not be reached until the second movement. Toward the end, the semitonal theme is woven into the texture by the inner voices. The sonorous cadence on G serves to launch the slow movement.

II

Psalmus XXXIX (Vulgate) Verses 2, 3, and 4	Psalm XL (King James Version) Verses 1, 2, and 3

Expectans expectavi Dominum,
  et intendit mihi.
	I waited patiently for the Lord;
	  and he inclined to me,

Et exaudivit preces meas; et eduxit me de lacu miseriae,	and heard my cry. He brought me up also out of an horrible pit,
et de luto faecas.	out of the miry clay,

Et statuit supra petram pedes meos;
  et direxit gressus meos.
	and set my feet upon a rock,
	  and established my goings.

Et immisit in os meum canticum novum,
  carmen Deo nostro.
	And He hath put a new song in my mouth,
	  even praise unto our God;

Videbunt multi et timebunt:
  et sperabunt in Domino.
	and many shall see it, and fear,
	  and shall trust in the Lord.

The slow movement is in fugal style. The subject is announced by the oboe. Wide leaps impart to the melody its assertive character. The

orchestral fugue is in four voices. After a spacious exposition, the sopranos enter with the theme of the choral fugue. The interval of a falling fourth lends expressivity to the words *Expectans expectavi* (I waited patiently).

This theme is taken over by altos, tenors, and basses in turn, to be treated in strict fugal fashion, while the orchestra expatiates upon the opening theme. The movement consequently is in the nature of a double fugue, freely handled, and characterized by a purity of style worthy of its models, the fugues of Bach. The stretto comes on the words *Et statuit super petram pedes meos* (and set my feet upon a rock), with the theme entering in the different voices at an interval of half a bar. This is followed by a stretto in the orchestral fugue, the impression of mounting tension being underlined by dotted rhythms. In the final measures elements of the two fugal themes are combined in chorus and orchestra. The climax comes through understatement. In a sudden piano the chorus in unison sings *Et superabunt in Domino* (and shall trust in the Lord); while a high trumpet in quarter notes, buttressed by cellos and basses in eighths, remind us of the subject of the first fugue.

III

Psalmus CL (Vulgate)	Psalm CL (King James Version)
Alleluia.	Praise ye the Lord.
Laudate Dominum in sanctis ejus:	Praise God in His Sanctuary:
laudate eum in firmamento virtutis ejus.	praise Him in the firmament of His power.
Laudate eum in virtutibus ejus:	Praise Him for His mighty acts:
laudate eum secundum multitudinem magnitudinis ejus.	praise Him according to His excellent greatness.
Laudate eum in sono tubae:	Praise Him with the sound of the trumpet:
laudate eum in psalterio et cithara.	praise Him with the psaltery and the harp.
Laudate eum in tympano et choro:	Praise Him with the timbrel and dance:
laudate eum in chordis et organo.	praise Him with stringed instruments and organs.
Laudate eum in cymbalis bene sonantibus:	Praise Him upon the loud cymbals:
laudate eum in cymbalis jubilationis:	praise Him upon the high sounding cymbals.
omnis spiritus laudet Dominum.	Let everything that hath breath praise the Lord.
Alleluia.	Praise ye the Lord.

The solemn Alleluia serves as introduction. The modal harmony in the chorus is pitted against a C-major pedal point in the orchestra. The Allegro proper opens with Stravinskyan rhythms that project the spirit of the *Psalm* in dance-like measures. The music starts out in a bright C major, with the tonic chord repeated against a driving rhythmic ostinato in the bass, the whole set off by staccato interjections in the orchestra. As so often in Stravinsky's music, the syncopation is underlined by the device of shifting melodic-rhythmic patterns from one beat of the measure to another.

The altos enter on the *Laudate* with the two-note theme of the opening movement. But these notes are now a major instead of a minor second apart. The music gains steadily in power, its forward momentum reinforced by striking modulations. Presently there is a broadening into the slower tempo of the introduction. Then, *subito piano e ben cantabile* (suddenly soft and very songful), the peroration gets under way, on the words *Laudate eum in cymbalis bene sonantibus* (Praise Him upon the loud cymbals), in the key of E-flat. This serene coda, which takes up about one-third of the movement, unfolds over a four-note ostinato in the bass in three-four time, so that the bass pattern begins a beat later with each recurrence. The noble melody of the sopranos reaffirms the

semitone interval that has played a fertilizing role throughout the symphony; and the powerful E-flat major tonality rises at the very last to a cadence in C that evokes the Alleluia with which the movement opened.

For sheer grandeur of conception there is little in the output of the first half of our century to rival the closing pages of the *Symphony of Psalms*.

⋖§ 27 §⋗

Béla Bartók (1881-1945)

"I cannot conceive of music that expresses absolutely nothing."

IT WAS Béla Bartók's mission to reconcile the folk melodies and rhythms of his native land with the main currents in contemporary music. In so doing he revealed himself as the greatest composer Hungary has produced, and one of the towering figures in the music of the twentieth century.

HIS LIFE

Bartók was born in a district of Hungary that is now part of Romania. The sensitive, studious lad—he was rather frail in health—soon revealed a serious musical talent. When he was seventeen he was offered a scholarship at the Vienna Conservatory, but he decided instead to follow his friend Ernö Dohnányi to the Royal Academy of Music in Budapest. There young Bartók acquired a reputation as a brilliant pianist.

Bettmann Archive

Béla Bartók

He also came in contact with a strong nationalist movement that strove to shake off the domination of Austro-German culture. His first important work for orchestra was a symphonic poem on the life of the Hungarian patriot Louis Kossuth.

Bartók soon developed an absorbing interest in native folklore. He became aware that what passed for Hungarian folklore in the eyes of the world was either the Gypsy music that had been romanticized by Liszt or the popular tunes of the café musicians, which were overlaid with elements of Austro-German music. Impelled by what he later described as "an urge towards the unknown, a dim inkling that true folk music was to be found only among the peasant class," he undertook to collect the native songs before they died out. In company with his fellow composer Zoltán Kodály, and armed with the indispensable recording equipment, he set out on a series of investigations that took him to the remotest villages of the country. From these expeditions Bartók derived the basic element of his art. "Those days I spent in the villages among the peasants," he recalled later, "were the happiest of my life. In order really to feel the vitality of this music one must, so to speak, have lived it. And this is possible only when one comes to know it by direct contact with the peasants." He also explored the folk music of neighboring countries—Slovakia, Romania, Bulgaria, and what is now Yugoslavia—and subsequently extended his investigations to include Turkish and Arab folk song. Bartók later published a great deal on ethno-musicology and became one of the leading authorities in this field—a rare example of artistic creativity going hand-in-hand with a gift for scientific research.

His attainments as a pianist were recognized when, in 1907, he was appointed professor of piano at the Royal Academy in Budapest. His compositions, however, were much too advanced for a public accustomed to the standard German repertory. In 1911, along with Kodály and other young musicians, Bartók formed the New Hungarian Musical Society, which was dedicated to the goal of disseminating modern music. The project was defeated by the apathy of the public and the hostility of the critics. Bartók became so discouraged that for a time he gave up composing.

The tide turned when Hungary was declared independent of Austria. The resultant upsurge of national feeling created a favorable climate for Bartók's music. His ballet *The Wooden Prince* was presented with great success at the Budapest Opera, and was followed by his opera *Duke Bluebeard's Castle*. However, when Admiral Horthy came to power, Bartók's librettist—who had been active in the short-lived regime of Béla Kun—had to flee Hungary. The two works were dropped from the repertory. *The Miraculous Mandarin*, a ballet, was rejected by the authorities because of what they regarded as its immoral subject. Bartók undertook no further works for the stage.

In the ensuing years he was acclaimed throughout Europe as one of the leading figures of his generation. But he was less successful in his own country. Bartók was out of sympathy with the Horthy regime and did nothing to ingratiate himself with those who might have furthered his career. The alliance between Horthy and Nazi Germany confronted the composer with issues that he faced without flinching. His physical frailty had no counterpart on the moral plane. He spoke out against Hitler in a political climate where it was inexpedient to do so, protested the playing of his music on the Berlin radio, and lost no opportunity to make clear his abhorrence of Nazism. "In Hungary," Bartók wrote, "the 'civilized' Christian folk are almost entirely devoted to the Nazi system. I am really ashamed that I come from this class." To go into exile meant surrendering the official status he enjoyed in Hungary, and the economic security that went with it. But he would not compromise. "He who stays on when he could leave may be said to acquiesce tacitly in everything that is happening here." Bartók's friends, fearing for his safety, prevailed upon him to leave the country while there still was time. He arrived in the United States in 1940 and settled in New York City.

He embarked on a concert tour, playing two-piano music with his wife and onetime pupil, Ditta Pasztory-Bartók. He also received an honorary doctorate from Columbia University and an appointment there to do folklore research. (Bartók throughout his life refused to teach composition.) Despite this fair beginning, his life in America yielded little in the way of happiness. His retiring personality was not one to make an impact on the American public. He felt increasingly isolated in his new surroundings. His letters, some of them written in English, trace a mounting curve of discouragement. "Concerts are few and far between. If we had to live on those we would really be at the end of our tether. Our situation is getting daily worse and worse. I am rather pessimistic. I lost all confidence in people, in countries, in everything. Until now we had two free pianos, a baby grand and an upright. Just today I got the news the upright will be taken from us. So we will have no possibility to study two-piano works. And each month brings a similar blow. I am wondering and asking myself what next?" With the entry of the United States into the war, such income as Bartók still received from Hungary was cut off. "At Columbia," he wrote at the end of 1942, "I am 'dismissed' from Jan. 1 on. They seem to have no more money for me. Otherwise my career as a composer is as much as finished: the quasi boycott of my works by the leading orchestras continues; no performances either of old works or new ones. It is a shame —not for me, of course."

The onset of leukemia made it impossible for Bartók to appear in public any longer. Friends appealed for aid to ASCAP (American Society of Composers, Authors and Publishers). Funds were made available to provide the composer with proper care in nursing homes and to enable him to continue writing to the end. A series of commissions from various sources spurred him to the composition of his last works. They rank among his finest. When he realized that he was dying he worked feverishly to finish his Third Piano Concerto, in order to leave his wife the only inheritance within his power. The Viola Concerto was left unfinished, to be brought to completion from his sketches by his friend and disciple Tibor Serly. "The trouble is," he remarked to his doctor shortly before the end, "that I have to go with so much still to say." He died in the West Side Hospital in New York City.

The tale of the composer who dies in poverty only to be acclaimed after his death would seem to belong to the romantic past, to the legend of Mozart, Schubert, Musorgsky. Yet it happened in our time. Bartók had to die in order to make his success in the United States. Almost immediately there was an upsurge of interest in his music that soon assumed the proportions of a boom. As though impelled by a sense of guilt for their previous neglect of his works, conductors, performers, record companies, broadcasting stations, and even his publishers rushed to pay him the homage that might have brought him comfort had it come in time.

HIS MUSIC

Bartók set out from the world of Wagner and Liszt, Brahms and Richard Strauss. In the course of his development he assimilated and outgrew the devices of French impressionism. He was influenced by Stravinsky and Schoenberg, some of whose procedures he somewhat anticipated. Like them, he disclaimed the role of revolutionary. "In art there are only fast or slow developments. Essentially it is a matter of evolution, not revolution."

Despite the newness of his language he was bound by vital ties to the beauty and logic of form which are the essence of the classical heritage. "In my youth my ideal was not so much the art of Bach or Mozart as that of Beethoven." He espoused the Beethovenian vision of music as an embodiment of human experience. The quotation at the head of this chapter indicates an attitude altogether at variance with the formalist esthetic of Stravinsky. His art recaptures the heroic lyricism of an earlier age. In the introspective slow movements of his larger works is to be found the hymnic quality of the Beethovenian adagio.

The study of Hungarian folklore, he wrote, "was of decisive influence upon my work because it freed me from the tyrannical rule of the major and minor keys." The peasant tunes, based on old modes and pentatonic scales, were as liberating for Bartók as the sonorities and rhythms of the Balinese gamelan had been for Debussy. From the songs of southeastern Europe, he states, "we could learn how best to employ terseness of expression, to cultivate the utmost excision of all that is non-essential. And it was this very thing, after the excessive grandiloquence of the romantic period, that we thirsted to learn."

Bartók's idiom is concentrated, reticent, austere. The powerful melodic line is peculiarly his own. At times it loosens into freely flowing arabesques that suggest the rhapsodical improvisations of east European (and all eastern) music. Yet it can also be angular, taut. Characteristic are melodies which, like those of Stravinsky in his Russian period, move within a narrow range and circle about a single note. Bartók too is fond of repeating fragments on different beats of the measure, producing the primitive effect of a melody turned in upon itself. The influence of Hungarian folk melody is manifest in the abundance of intervals of the second, fourth, and seventh. The melody line often proceeds scalewise. Within the limits he imposes upon himself, Bartók achieves an astonishing diversity of effect.

Bartók loosened the old modes through a species of chromatic ornamentation. He also experimented in combining different modes (*polymodality*). Therefrom came his fondness for the simultaneous use of major and minor. Characteristic is his bold superimposing of independent streams of chords upon one another; his use of chords built in fourths instead of thirds; his addiction to cluster chords that take on a rude strength from the bunching together of the tones; and the use of parallel seconds, sevenths, and ninths which gives his music an extraordinary impact. He is a master of percussive dissonance. In the *Allegro barbaro* for piano, written in 1911, we find the hammer-blow treatment of astringent chords that reached its full vogue some years later with Stravinsky's *Rite of Spring*. (See musical example, page 29.) Although Schoenberg's thinking held a great attraction for him, Bartók never abandoned the concept of tonality. His frequent use of pedal points and of a drone bass—a feature of peasant instruments everywhere—binds together the harmony and emphasizes its tonal character. Given Bartók's free use of keys and modes, it would be difficult to describe a work of his as being in E major or minor. But we can say with assurance that it centers around E.

Bartók's is one of the great rhythmic imaginations of modern times. His pounding, stabbing rhythms are instinct with elemental force and tension. From the folk dances of southeastern Europe he developed a

rich store of asymmetrical formations. Typical is his fondness for repeated notes and for passages based on alternating patterns, such as triple
and duple, or a group of five beats and one of three—a procedure taken
from Bulgarian folk dance. Bartók, like Stravinsky, played a major role
in the revitalizing of Western rhythm, achieving a freshness and an erup-
tive force that were unheard of before his time.

Bartók was much preoccupied with formal unity and coherence,
which he attained through the cumulative development of themes and
motives. His music is imbued with the spirit of continuous variation; the
material is made to reveal new facets of its nature throughout. There
results a form that is thoroughly consonant with the twentieth-century
concept of dynamic symmetry, marked by a sense of relentless growth,
tension, and forward thrust.

Bartók's fugal texture is a masterly example of modern dissonant
counterpoint, and incarnates the urge of his era for abstraction of
thought, tightness of structure, and purity of diction. Counterpoint led
him, as it did Stravinsky, to simplification of style and compression. His
orchestration exemplifies the contemporary tendency to use color for
the projection of ideas rather than as an end in itself. He ranges from
brilliant mixtures to threads of pure color that bring out the interweaving melody lines; from a hard bright sheen to characteristically
Bartókian flickerings of color traced against a luminous haze. A somber
light permeates his slow movements, those brooding "night pieces"
which, to use Beethoven's famous phrase, are "more an expression of
feeling than tone painting." Bartók's personal way of handling such
familiar effects as glissandos, trills, tremolos, and harmonics; his arresting use of divided strings and of the percussion group—indeed, his
whole approach to sound—bespeaks a prodigious orchestral imagination.

A virtuoso pianist himself, Bartók typifies the twentieth-century
treatment of the piano as an instrument of percussive rhythm. The frequent cluster chords are hammered with the full weight of shoulder
and arm. The dissonant seconds are frequently played with one finger
—by the thumb or the fifth. (See examples on next page.)

Bartók was devoted to the miniature. The Bagatelles and Elegies
(1908), Burlesques and Sketches (1910), Hungarian Peasant Songs
(1906), and Romanian Dances (1910) are intimate genre pieces. There
are also several volumes of children's pieces. The most important piano
work of his later years is *Mikrokosmos* (1926–37), a collection of one
hundred and fifty-three pieces ranging from the simplest grade to virtu-

oso level. The Sonata for Two Pianos and Percussion (1938) is a remarkably original work which the composer later transcribed as the Concerto for Two Pianos and Orchestra.

The six string quartets (1910–39) rank among the major achievements of our century. In their breadth of vision and profound humanity these quartets are the legitimate progeny of Beethoven's. The two Sonatas for violin and piano (1921–22) stem from the period when Bartók stood closest to Viennese atonalism. The Sonata for unaccompanied violin (1944) is a tightly knit work in the difficult medium made famous by Bach. Bartók reached his creative peak in the final decade of his life. Turning to the chamber orchestra, he produced in 1936 the *Music for String Instruments, Percussion and Celesta*. Tonal opulence and warmth of expression characterize the *Concerto for Orchestra*. The master's final testament, the Third Piano Concerto (1945), is a work of vehemence and breadth. Its three movements are in turn dramatic, contemplative, and satanic. The last mood, a favorite with the romantics, constitutes a link between Bartók and his nineteenth-century compatriot Franz Liszt. The opera *Duke Bluebeard's Castle* (1911), the ballet *The Wooden Prince* (1914–16), and the ballet-pantomime *The Miraculous Mandarin* (1919) exemplify the modern trend toward concise dramatic works: each is in one act. *Bluebeard's Castle* aroused great interest when it was produced in New York in the fall of 1952, and proved to be full of grandly poetic sounds.

Bartók differs from Stravinsky in one respect. Each of the Russian master's works is homogeneous in style, no matter how much he may change from one work to the next. A piece by Bartók, contrariwise, is apt to incorporate diverse elements, these being held together by the sheer force of his personality. Bartók encompassed the various trends of his time, from polytonality to the atonal, from expressionism to the neo-classical, from folk song to the constructivist, from lyricism to the purely dynamic, from a rough primitivism to the intellectual, from racy humor and grotesquerie to the tragic; and—the ultimate step—from nationalism to the universal. And he reconciled all these with the high aim of a former time—to touch the heart.

Bartók's prime quality was an unflinching integrity that informed every act of the artist and the man. He was one of the great spirits of our time.

~§ 28 §~

Three Works by Bartók

"What is the best way for a composer to reap the full benefits of his studies in peasant music? It is to assimilate the idiom of peasant music so completely that he is able to forget all about it and use it as his musical mother tongue."

CONCERTO FOR ORCHESTRA

DURING his confinement in Doctors Hospital in New York in the summer of 1943 Bartók received a visit from Serge Koussevitzky. The conductor offered him a commission and first performance by the Boston Symphony Orchestra for any piece he would write. The incurably ill Bartók was immensely heartened by the knowledge that a major orchestra was waiting to perform the as yet unwritten score, and he was able to quit the hospital and go to Asheville, North Carolina, where he set to work. The Concerto for Orchestra was completed in 1943, the year before he died. "The general mood of the work," he wrote, "represents, apart from the jesting second movement, a gradual transition from the sternness of the first movement and the lugubrious death-song of the third to the life-assertion of the last."

Bartók called the work a concerto because of its tendency, as he put it, "to treat the single instruments in a *concertante* or soloistic manner."

The use of the term in this early eighteenth-century sense implies that the element of virtuosity prevails; but the virtuoso in this case is the entire orchestra. Of symphonic proportions, the piece exemplifies Bartók's mastery of the grand form, his highly personal use of folklore elements, and his wonderful sense of sound.

I. *Introduzione. Andante non troppo—Allegro vivace.* The spacious introduction prepares the listener for a big work. It opens with a solemn statement by cellos and basses against tremolos on upper strings and flute. The theme is based on the interval of a fourth (indicated by brackets) that was always prominent in Bartók's melodic writing.

The first theme of the Allegro is a robust, syncopated idea that ascends to a peak and as briskly descends. (Bartók was partial to this pattern.)

Here too the fourth plays a prominent role. A contrasting theme in folklore style consists mainly of two notes. The Development builds up tension through animated contrapuntal imitation. The Restatement, as is customary in twentieth-century works, is abbreviated. Noteworthy here is the quality of inevitable growth which is the essence of symphonic style.

II. *Giuoco delle coppie* (Game of Pairs). *Allegretto scherzando.* The title of this scherzo derives from the fact that the wind instruments are paired at specific intervals: bassoons in sixths, oboes in thirds, clarinets in sevenths, flutes in fifths, muted trumpets in seconds. This "jesting second movement," as Bartók called it, is a study in sonority. Bass drum and bassoons usher in music of a march-like nature that is replete with teasing ideas. One encounters here elements of the fantastic and the whimsical that Berlioz and Liszt exploited so effectively. The movement is a "chain" of five short sections, each featuring another pair of instruments. A chorale is intoned by the brass, after which the five sections are restated with more elaborate orchestration.

III. *Elegia. Andante non troppo.* This "lugubrious death song" is a rhapsodic outpouring of emotion. An oboe sings a lament against the flickerings of sound so characteristic of Bartók, which here are traced by clarinet, flute, and harp. The music rises to a tragic climax. This visionary movement stands in direct line of descent from the adagios of Beethoven.

IV. *Intermezzo interotto* (Interrupted Intermezzo). *Allegretto.* A plaintive little tune in folksong style is presented by the oboe and continued by the flute. The nonsymmetrical rhythm, an alternation of 2/4 and 5/8, imparts a wayward charm to the music. (This type of irregu-

larity, we saw, Bartók derived from Bulgarian dance rhythms.) The strings follow with a beautiful lyric theme. Suddenly the mood is broken by the jaunty strains of café music. The lyric theme returns on the muted strings, to round out a movement that is rich in both tenderness and caprice.

V. *Finale. Presto.* A few bars of introduction are marked *pesante* (heavily). The horns outline the germinal theme. This movement of "life-assertion" gets off to a whirlwind *perpetuum mobile* (perpetual motion) on the strings. The fugue that follows displays all the complex devices of counterpoint. But Bartók wears his learning lightly; there is nothing here to tax the ear. The exciting fugue subject is presented by the trumpet. Notice again the prominence of the interval of a fourth.

The folk tone as Bartók presents it here differs markedly from the romanticized treatment of peasant dances in the nineteenth century. The harmonies are acrid, the rhythms imbued with primitive strength. The movement rises steadily in emotional tension and ends on a note of affirmation.

In the Concerto for Orchestra Bartók followed the progression "through suffering to the stars" that constituted the epic theme of

Beethoven's symphony-dramas. Like those, it seeks to "embrace the millions." Bartók's attempt to reach out to the listener resulted in a work which, although it preserves intact the special quality of his art, has established itself in the affections of thousands of music lovers.

MUSIC FOR STRING INSTRUMENTS, PERCUSSION AND CELESTA

This piece (1936), a landmark in the twentieth-century cultivation of chamber-music textures, was written for Paul Sacher and the Basel Chamber Orchestra, which gave it its first performance. The unusual combination of instruments indicates the composer's intent to explore the sonorous possibilities of such an ensemble. Bartók's conception called for two string groups to frame the percussion. He carefully specified the arrangement of the players on the stage:

	Double Bass I		Double Bass II	
Cello I	Timpani		Bass Drum	Cello II
Viola I	Side Drums		Cymbals	Viola II
Violin II	Celesta		Xylophone	Violin IV
Violin I	Piano		Harp	Violin III

I. *Andante tranquillo.* The movement is based on a single crescendo that grows inexorably from *pp* to a *fortissimo* climax and then subsides. We hear a fugue based on an undulating chromatic theme that moves within the range of a fifth, from A to E, and includes all the semitones between. This subject is introduced by the muted violas. Each time the

subject enters it appears a fifth higher or lower, fanning out from the central tone A—first on E (a fifth above A), then on D (a fifth below A); on B (a fifth above E), G (a fifth below D), F-sharp (a fifth above B)—growing steadily in power until the climactic point is reached on E-flat. Thereupon the theme is inverted and the movement returns to the central A. Thus, the crescendo-decrescendo pattern is combined with ascending-descending motion. Since the entire movement is woven out

of the generating theme, this Andante achieves an extraordinary concentration of thought and consistency of texture.

II. *Allegro.* The main idea is a taut, imperious subject whose chromatic character relates it to the germinal theme of the preceding move-

ment. This Allegro is a closely-knit sonata form that draws its impetus
from the gestures of the dance. The Development section contains an
exciting passage in fugal style. In the Recapitulation, the main idea returns in Bartók's favorite alternation of 3 and 2 time, then settles into 3/8.
The two groups of strings are used antiphonally, in question-and-answer
formation.

III. *Adagio.* This "night piece" reveals Bartók's gift for evoking a
magical landscape through instrumental color. The eerie repetition of
the high F on the xylophone ushers in a rhapsodic cantillation on the
viola. The main theme of the movement is presented by celesta and
violin. Bartókian flickerings of sound—runs on the celesta mingled with
glissandos on harp and piano—provide a background for the free development of a chromatic idea born of the germinal theme. The climax
of the movement is based on a tense five-tone motive that is bandied
about among the instruments. This is the central point of the movement. The measures that follow it (at bar 49) are an exact replica—but
backwards—of those that came before.

IV. *Allegro molto.* The finale combines the passionate abandon of
Magyar folk dance with contrapuntal processes that are tossed off with
sheer virtuosity. The movement opens with plucked chords that conjure up the sound of folk instruments.

The central idea of this expanded rondo form outlines the Lydian
mode (see page 37). The rhythm is a Bulgarian dance pattern of 8/8
in groups of 2, 3, and 3:

The middle part of the rondo theme goes back to the sinuous contours
of the germinal theme. In the contrasting sections Bartók deploys his
propulsive rhythms, which at times take on a jazz-like animation, and his
powerful cluster chords on the piano. Each recurrence of the rondo

theme brings fresh variation. The movement builds up to a climax that leads to the triumphal return of the germinal theme, now purged of its

chromaticism. This diatonic version is presented with expanded intervals. The coda leads to a clangorous, affirmative cadence.

FOURTH STRING QUARTET

Bartók's Fourth Quartet (1928) rests on an architectonic conception that welds the five movements into an organic unity. The third or central movement is placed between two scherzos, which are related in thematic material, as are also the two outer movements. German theorists liken this kind of musical structure to an arch. The formal scheme of the Quartet is reinforced by the key relationships, even though these are treated very freely. The first and last movements center around C; the second around E (a major third above C); and the fourth around A-flat (a major third below C).

The musical tissue is fashioned out of motivic cells which lead into one another with that inevitableness which is the essence of classical form. The contrapuntal texture is closely woven, with an abundance of canonic and free imitation (although, interestingly, neither fugue nor fugato is present in the work). The writing throughout is of virtuoso calibre and makes the highest technical demands upon the players.

I. *Allegro.*   The first movement grows out of a compact germinal motive which pervades the entire work, generating rhythms and themes. Introduced by the cello in the seventh measure, this basic idea moves along the chromatic scale from B to D-flat, then down to B-flat:

Basic motive

We hear it almost immediately in inverted form:

Inversion

It is taken up by the viola in a diatonic version, its intervals expanded, and from then on undergoes a searching development. The music for the most part has a chromatic sound. The rhythmic patterns overlap, imparting to the movement its relentless drive. Notice the percussive effect of the cluster chords, the inexorable growth of the basic idea, the glissandos on all four instruments that make so striking a sonority, and the intensification that comes with the *Più mosso* (faster) at the end.

II. *Prestissimo.* The instruments play *con sordino* (with mutes). The germinal motive, now expanded to include the eight semitones from E to B, is introduced by viola and cello playing in octaves. This idea is

developed through variational procedures as the music slithers up and down the chromatic scale in a fleet *perpetuum mobile*. Its ghostly quality links it to the *scherzo fantastique* of the nineteenth century. A second motive emerges, consisting of a tone preceded by its upper and lower neighbors, which is presented in canonic imitation at the second. Ostinato rhythms, syncopation, and glissandos contribute to the effect of this movement, which vanishes as mysteriously as it began.

III. *Non troppo lento.* The brooding slow movement is the centerpiece of the work. The cello launches a long-breathed melody whose florid arabesques evoke the rapturous improvisation of Hungarian folk musicians on the *tárogató* (a woodwind instrument of the clarinet family). Much in evidence is the characteristic rhythm of Hungarian folk song, a sixteenth followed by a dotted eighth (♪♪.)—a pattern resembling the Scotch snap. The Bartókian flickerings of sound in the middle part suggest the "night music" that the master loved to write. The *tárogató* melody returns and is rounded off by a pianissimo allusion to the nocturnal music on the first violin.

IV. *Allegretto pizzicato.* Bartók desired, for the second scherzo, "a strong pizzicato, so that the string rebounds off the fingerboard." Both motives of the earlier scherzo return. The second is again treated in canonic imitation, this time at the ninth. Notice the violent dynamic contrasts between *ppp* and *ff*, and the folk quality of the plucked-string sound. For all its thematic relationship to the second movement, this scherzo has a quite different expressive content.

V. *Allegro molto.* Widely spaced fortissimo chords conjure up a rude peasant instrument of the drone-bass type. The ostinato rhythms have a primitive force, as have the open fifths of the accompaniment.

The germinal theme reappears in its diatonic form and is soon presented

in inversion, then with expanded intervals. The movement builds to a coda of immense power.

The Fourth String Quartet unites abstract thought and searching emotion within a convincing form. It is an extraordinary achievement in respect to imaginative handling of the string quartet medium, the achievement of organic unity through motivic coherence, sustained tension, and impassioned expressivity.

⇜ 29 ⇝

Paul Hindemith (1895-1963)

"One can still learn much from 'Papa' Haydn."

THE ARTIST endowed with a strong historic sense is impelled to affirm his kinship with the past. In the late nineteenth century it was Brahms who played this retrospective role. In our time it is Paul Hindemith who has found in his heritage the point of departure for his own work.

HIS LIFE

Hindemith was born in Hanau, a city near Frankfort, of a working-class family. His father being opposed to his choice of a musical career, the boy left home when he was eleven and made his way playing in dance bands, motion picture houses, cafés, and theaters. He managed to receive a sound musical training at the Conservatory of Frankfort and became concert master, ultimately conductor at the opera house of that city. A virtuoso on the viola, he played in the Amar Quartet, a group that won fame in the early 1920s for its performances of contemporary chamber music.

Hindemith was the most substantial figure among the composers who came into prominence in Germany in the years after the First World War. His music embodied the boldly experimental spirit that flourished

Paul Hindemith

under the Weimar Republic and was widely performed at the various festivals for contemporary music. It was at one of these that Richard Strauss, after hearing his more advanced compositions, remarked to the young man, "*You* don't have to write like that—you have talent!"

In 1927 Hindemith was made professor of composition at the Berlin Hochschule. Here, and at the *Volksmusikschule*—a project for the dissemination of musical knowledge among the masses—he put into practice his progressive theories of musical education. His aim was to produce versatile craftsmen in the sense of the eighteenth century, rather than the overspecialized virtuoso that had been brought into fashion by the nineteenth. He encouraged his students to learn to play a number of instruments, to perform each other's compositions, and to participate in a many-faceted musical experience based on group activity. In 1935 Hindemith found a more extensive laboratory for his theories when the Turkish government commissioned him to organize the musical activities of the country. He drew up the blueprint for a complete system of education, from elementary school level to teachers' training schools; founded symphony orchestras along the most advanced Western lines; and in the course of three visits to Turkey put the plan into effect.

Although the Nazi regime was eager to encourage artists of German blood, Hindemith was much too modern for a regime that recognized the Wagnerian as the proper path for contemporary German music. Propaganda Minister Goebbels accused him not only of "atrocious dissonance" but also of "cultural Bolshevism" and "spiritual non-Aryanism," and Hindemith's music was banned as being "unbearable to the Third Reich." The composer came to the United States shortly before the outbreak of the Second World War and joined the faculty of Yale University. Many young Americans came under his influence there and at the summer school of the Berkshire Music Center in Tanglewood, Massachusetts. In 1949 Hindemith was invited to deliver the Charles Eliot Norton lectures at Harvard University. He subsequently expanded these into a book, *A Composer's World*, which in lively fashion gives the essence of his artistic creed.

Hindemith exerted a strong influence on the American scene during the decade and a half he spent here. With the restoration of peace he felt the need of returning to the pattern of life in which he had his roots. In 1953 he went to live in Zurich. During the ensuing years he was ever more active as a conductor. In 1959 he came back to the United States for a series of concerts and conducted several of his recent works, the most important of which was the *Pittsburgh Symphony—1958*, written for that city's two-hundredth anniversary.

HIS MUSIC

Hindemith is German to the core. His heritage manifests itself in his love of florid counterpoint, his Gothic luxuriance of invention, and the ample curves of melody that revive the arabesque of Bach. German, too, is his love for the wind instruments, for which he writes with such mastery; his solid orchestral sound; his respect for workmanship; and his occasionally heavy-handed humor. "What I like about him," Francis Poulenc once remarked, "is that lyricism, at once heavy and agile, like mercury."

Like the masters of the German Baroque, Hindemith was rooted in the Reformation. His art was nurtured by the Lutheran chorales and the old song books; by the masters of sixteenth-century counterpoint; by the cantatas and fugues of Bach. For Hindemith, as for the medieval philosophers whom he likes to quote, the greatness of music lies in its moral significance. Sounds and forms, he maintains, "remain meaningless to us unless we include them in our own mental activity and use their fermenting quality to turn our soul towards everything noble, superhuman and ideal." Equally exalted is his conception of the composer's function. "A composer's horizon cannot be far-reaching enough; his desire to know, to comprehend, must incite, inspire, and drench every phase of his work. Storming the heavens with artistic wisdom and practical skill must be his least ambition."

Hindemith took his point of departure from the music of Brahms, Max Reger—who influenced him strongly—and Richard Strauss. From a harmonic conception of music he moved steadily to the contrapuntal art inherited from Bach and the polyphonists of the Renaissance. He played an important part in the development of dissonant counterpoint, which constitutes a basic element of his style. Hindemith's melody, rooted in the popular song of medieval Germany, emphasizes the fundamental intervals of a fourth and a fifth. Now ornate and discursive, now terse and muscular, it lends itself well to contrapuntal combination. It is personal but not subjective.

Hindemith's harmony is based on the free use of the twelve tones around a center. Certain daring combinations result from a counterpoint of chord against chord instead of note against note (polyharmony). He steadfastly adheres to the principle of tonality, which he regards as an immutable law. (Hence his opposition to the Schoenbergian school.) His use of simple triads as points of repose imparts to his music a serenity that is one of its outstanding traits. His harmony can be dry and dissonant; or, as in his later works, it may take on a mellow chromaticism. It often has a modal coloring, as is to be expected from a composer with so strong an affinity for old music.

In the matter of rhythm Hindemith is markedly less spectacular than either Stravinsky or Bartók. In his less inspired moments the counterpoint jogs along with a steady pulsation that reminds one of the music of the Baroque. But at his best, his emotion transforms itself into motion; he arouses himself to a rhythmic nervosity marked by diversified metrical patterns. There results a driving, motoric music that is entirely contemporaneous in spirit.

In respect to form Hindemith is a traditionalist. His models are the great contrapuntal forms of the Baroque: concerto grosso, passacaglia and chaconne, toccata and fugue. Also the balanced form of the classical sonata. He is partial to dance forms, and was one of the first Europeans to show an interest in jazz. His instrumental forms reveal qualities at the same time Hindemithian and German: clarity of design, spaciousness of architecture, and sturdiness of construction.

The neo-classic attitude pervades his handling of the orchestra (although he blends it with a somewhat romanticized Baroque). Color, he feels, should be subordinated to texture and form. In this, of course, he stands alongside Stravinsky, Schoenberg, and Bartók. By nature inclined to sobriety, he mistrusts the present-day emphasis on striking timbres. "Music as an agent of moral elevation seems to have lost its position. Sound and its effect on our auditory nerves apparently is the only factor considered essential. Symphony orchestras have degenerated into mere distributors of superrefined sounds, and the more sparkling and alluring the sounds appear, the higher is an orchestra's rating." This love of sensation, he warns, is inimical to true musical understanding. "It is the curse of virtuosity that it can beget nothing but virtuosity."

Hindemith has written an enormous quantity of music. Its quality, of necessity, is uneven. His best ranks with the best of our time. His less-than-best plays its part in the over-all scheme by preparing the way for something better. Chamber music occupies a central place in his output. The compositions entitled *Kammermusik*, for various combinations of instruments, are flanked by a long list of solo sonatas, duos, trios, quartets, quintets, and concertos. He has written copiously for his own instrument. Especially well known is *Der Schwanendreher* (The Swan-Catcher, 1935), a concerto for viola and small orchestra based on traditional folk songs. Also the *Trauermusik* (Funeral Music, 1936) for viola and strings.

His vocal works range from solo song to cantata and oratorio. In the first category the weightiest item is *Das Marienleben* (The Life of Mary, 1923; revised, 1948), a song cycle for soprano and piano to poems of Rainer Maria Rilke. Memorable too is *Die Junge Magd* (The Young Maid, 1922), a set of six somber songs for contralto accompanied by flute, clarinet, and string quartet. Of his choral works, mention should be made of his setting of Walt Whitman's *When Lilacs Last in the Dooryard Bloom'd* (1946).

Two of Hindemith's scores have won success as ballets—*Nobilissima Visione* (1937), and *The Four Temperaments*, a theme and four variations for piano and strings (1944). His most substantial achievement in the lyric theater is *Mathis der Maler* (Matthias the Painter, 1934). We will discuss the symphony he extracted from the score of this opera. A decade and a half later he embarked upon another opera centering about a famous personage, the astronomer Kepler: *Die Harmonie der Welt* (The Harmony of the Universe), from which he also derived a symphony (1951). But the later work did not make nearly the same impact on the musical world as did *Mathis*.

Hindemith's formative period fell in the decade following Germany's first defeat. In his youthful rebellion against romanticism he captured the nihilism of the Twenties. Sardonic humor and parody drove their way through his scores. His need to share in the life of his time brought him to the social viewpoint embodied in *Gebrauchsmusik*, the aims of which we described in an earlier section. At the same time his commitment to neo-classicism made itself felt in an emphasis upon linear writing and an objectivism that frequently verged on matter-of-factness. With the passing of the years he grew gentler. The harshness and the irony receded, the expressive element came to the fore. His poetic lyricism was allowed to assert itself in ever greater degree, ultimately bringing about a reconciliation with the romantic emotion which he began by rejecting. As he surrenders the modernism of his youth, a mystical strain creeps into his thinking; a retrospective tone envelops his later works in a gentle nostalgia. He himself has summed up this development: "Nothing is more wearisome or more futile than the most antiquated of all manias: the rage to be modern. With all the appreciation that one may reasonably bring to technical innovations, we should nevertheless minimize the word *new* in the term 'new art' and emphasize rather the word *art*."

In his first theoretical work, *Unterweisung im Tonsatz* (2 volumes, 1937, 1939; published in English as *The Craft of Musical Composition*, 1941), Hindemith made a comprehensive attempt to establish a modern theory of harmony. His teaching activities at Yale resulted in two books that have been widely used as texts—*A Concentrated Course in Traditional Harmony* (2 volumes, 1943, 1953), and *Elementary Training for Musicians* (1946). Like Stravinsky and Schoenberg, Hindemith has given much thought to the problems of contemporary music. The observations scattered through *A Composer's World* and other writings reveal a positive temperament and an incisive intellect. Almost every page yields characteristic utterances. "People who make music together cannot be enemies, at least not while the music lasts. . . . The proclamation of one's modernity is the most efficient cover for a bad technique, unclear formulations, and the lack of personality. . . . The reactions music evokes are not feelings but they are the images, memories of feelings. Dreams, memories, musical reactions—all three are made of the same stuff. . . . Genius seems to be the ability to retain the keenness of the first vision until its embodiment in the finished piece is achieved." Against the tendency to formalism in contemporary writing: "If music written on this basis has any message for others, it is the crassest order, 'You have to believe in my constructions,' in a time when we all are so terribly in need of some shiny little reflection of that other message, the one that Schiller and Beethoven gave to mankind: *Seid umschlungen, Millionen*—be embraced, ye millions." Finally: "If there is anything remaining in this world that is on the one side basically aristocratic and individualistic and on the other as brutal as the fights of wild animals, it is artistic creation."

SYMPHONY *MATHIS DER MALER* (MATHIS THE PAINTER)

The hero of Hindemith's opera is the painter Matthias Grünewald (1460–1528), whose art encompassed both the mysticism of the dying Middle Ages and the realism of the oncoming Renaissance. His masterpiece is the series of paintings for the altar at Isenheim executed for the Brothers of St. Anthony. These display an intensity of vision that places him in the company of Albrecht Dürer, Lucas Cranach, and Hieronymus Bosch.

The peasant revolts that marked the end of medieval serfdom and the beginnings of the Reformation confronted Mathis with a moral issue: How could the artist serenely pursue his work amid the suffering of his fellow men? Should he not rather abandon his art and join the struggle against oppression? Mathis leaves the service of his patron Cardinal Albrecht and casts his lot with the peasants. Also, in good operatic fashion, he falls in love with the peasant leader's daughter Regina. (The libretto, which was written by Hindemith, here comes to the assistance of history. Almost nothing is known of Grünewald's personal life.) Mathis soon becomes aware of the gulf that separates him from his companions in arms. When the peasants suffer defeat he flees with Regina, vainly seeking inner peace. In his disturbed state he relives in a kind of allegorical vision the subject of his grandest painting, the Temptation of St. Anthony. He doubts his genius, he questions the validity of art. Ultimately he passes through the crisis and comes to realize that only by creating beauty can he serve his fellow men. The final scene shows

Grünewald, *The Temptation of St. Anthony*, from the Isenheim Altar.

the aging artist, the turbulence of life and love far behind him, tran-
quilly awaiting his end.

This lofty theme, raising issues as pertinent to our century as to Grünewald's, offered Hindemith a congenial subject. Mathis embodies, in his
creator's view, "problems, wishes, and doubts which have occupied the
minds of all serious artists from remotest times. For whom are works of
art created? What is their purpose? How can the artist make himself

understood to his adversary?" The opera is pervaded by a contemplative lyricism bordering on the mystical. Its main elements derive from Gregorian chant, medieval modes, and the popular religious songs of the Reformation.

For his symphony (1934) Hindemith extracted three orchestral movements from the score, each named after another of Mathis's paintings. First is the Concert of Angels hymning the birth of Christ, which in the opera serves as overture. Second is The Entombment of Christ and the Lament of Mary. This music comes from an intermezzo in the last scene and accompanies Mathis's final withdrawal from life. Last is The Temptation of St. Anthony, a movement that accompanies the climax of the drama, the sixth scene.

Needless to say, we have here no symphony in the conventional sense. Nor is this program music of the descriptive variety. The work seeks rather to evoke in twentieth-century terms certain soul-states that went into the painting—and the beholding—of the Isenheim pictures.

I. *Concert of Angels. Ruhig bewegt* (moving quietly). The Introduction is based on modal harmonies. A religious folk song of the Middle Ages, *Es sungen drei Engel* (Three Angels Sang) is intoned by three trombones, creating an archaic atmosphere.

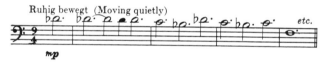

Wholly characteristic are the serene chords which establish points of repose within the forward movement.

The Allegro proper, in 2/2 time, is a tone poem of breadth and energy. The main theme, played by flutes and violins, bears the composer's personal stamp. Stepwise movement along the scales is enlivened by decisive intervals at the points of stress. The leap of a fifth (at x) is typical of Hindemith, as is the modal harmony.

The second theme is more placid. A true contrapuntist, Hindemith fashions this idea with a view ultimately to combine it with the first. Here too we find an upward leap of a fifth and a modal atmosphere.

The Development derives its excitement from the devices of imitative counterpoint. A heightening of temperature culminates in the return of the chorale on the trombones. Against it we hear an elaborate orchestral tissue woven out of the two main themes.

II. *The Entombment. Sehr langsam* (very slowly). Four-four. Muted violins answered by flutes set the elegiac tone. As in the first movement, Hindemith uses no key signature, indicating sharps or flats wherever he needs them. A broadly arching lament on the oboe unfolds against pizzicato chords on the strings. This is imitated by the flute. There is a mournful dialogue between both instruments. Tension is sustained through the persistent dotted rhythms, which serve as a unifying element. At the climax wind sonority is pitted against the strings, with superb use of trumpet tone. The music is withdrawn, inward. The serene major chord at the close achieves a Hindemithian effect of finality.

III. *The Temptation of St. Anthony.* In Grünewald's painting the Saint is tormented by noisome beasts. These become, in the scene that constitutes the emotional peak of the opera, the symbol of his own doubts and desires. The score bears the motto: "Where wert Thou, good Jesus, where wert Thou, wherefore didst Thou not give aid and heal my wounds?"

The rhapsodic declamation of the strings in unison is imbued with dramatic gesture. The movement proper, a frenetic Allegro in 9/8, opens with a broad characteristic melody. Tension mounts steadily.

There is brutal strength in the brass sound. A sustained trill on the violins, with a suggestion of the diabolical, ushers in a languorous episode in which the orchestra takes on a Straussian sensuousness. Clearly the holy man is sorely tried. The movement resumes with a furiously syncopated section in 2/4 that culminates in a fugato, out of which emerges the chorale *Lauda Sion Salvatorem* (In Praise of Zion that Shall Save Us). The massed brasses sing a hallelujah as Anthony-Mathis (and presumably Hindemith) achieve the faith that conquers anguish and banishes doubt. It is all very German, and very grand.

Hindemith's influence on the international scene reached its peak during the Forties. His music is considerably less in evidence at present. But this probably is only a temporary phenomenon. His contribution has been too substantial to be affected by the vagaries of fashion or the fluctuation of taste. In the art of the twentieth century Paul Hindemith has been a prime factor for order, stability, and the continuity of the great tradition.

IV. AWAY FROM IMPRESSIONISM

"Enough of clouds, waves, aquariums, nymphs, and perfumes of the night. We need a music that is down to earth—an every-day music."

Jean Cocteau

⋅≤§ 30 §⋅

Erik Satie (1866-1925)

"Am I French? But of course! Why would you want a man of my age not to be French? You surprise me. . . ."

ERIK SATIE was one of the first to see that impressionism, despite the significant innovations it had introduced, did not represent the path of the future. He reacted against the element of preciousness in the impressionist esthetic, as well as against the luscious complex harmonies cultivated by Debussy and his followers. In raising the slogan of a simple everyday music, Satie gave impetus to what became one of the most important currents in musical thinking in the years after the First World War.

HIS LIFE

Satie was born in the seaside town of Honfleur, on the Normandy coast. His father was a ship broker, his mother a London-born girl of Scottish parentage. The elder Satie subsequently established himself as a music publisher in Paris. Erik entered the Conservatoire when he was thirteen. From the beginning he manifested that deep-rooted hatred of convention which marked him the eternal rebel. The Conservatoire, citadel of tradition, he remembered to the end of his life as "that vast uncomfortable building" which was like "a jail devoid of any attractive features either inside or out." In characteristic fashion he described the opinion that his teachers held of his talent: "My harmony professor thought I had a gift for the piano, while my piano professor considered that I might be talented as a composer."

He was much preoccupied in early manhood with the Rosicrucian sect, which was oriented toward mystical ideas and medieval rites. Also, he officiated as pianist at a famous cabaret in Montmartre, *Le Chat Noir* (The Black Cat). At about this period he met Debussy. He was twenty-four, Debussy four years his senior, when they became friends. During a discussion with Debussy, Satie came forth with a phrase that became famous: "We ought to have our own music—if possible, without sauer-kraut!" He influenced the esthetic behind *Pelléas et Mélisande*. But when he saw the completed manuscript of Debussy's opera, he realized that there was nothing more for him to do in that direction. "I have to seek something else," he wrote to Jean Cocteau, "or I am lost." Dissatisfaction with his technical attainments led him, at the age of forty, to take an unusual step. He entered the Schola Cantorum to study counterpoint with Vincent d'Indy and Albert Roussel. "At your age," Debussy said to him, "one no longer changes one's skin." "If I fail," Satie retorted, "it means that I haven't got it in me to be a composer."

Some years before this Satie had left Montmartre and settled in the working-class suburb of Arcueil. "In this corner," he said, "one senses the mysterious presence of Our Lady of Lowliness." (He wrote a *Mass for the Poor*.) His early Catholic mysticism had long since been supplanted by Radical Socialism. At Arcueil he spent the rest of his life, known as an eccentric and fun-loving bachelor. Nightly he traversed Paris on foot in order to reach his haunts in Montmartre. "Young men," he wrote, "don't go to the cafés. Listen to the grave voice of one who spent much time in them—but who does not regret it!" He lived very humbly, in a single room. Satie was completely unworldly when it came to success or wealth. He handed over his works to the publishers for ridiculous prices. Dedicated to music and poverty, he was faithfully attended by both throughout his life.

Satie was drawn into the artistic ferment that centered about Serge Diaghilev's Russian Ballet; he collaborated with Cocteau, Picasso, and Picabia. In the years after the First World War he achieved a certain measure of fame. He became the champion of the new generation of musicians; specifically, he was the mentor of *Les Six*—a group of young composers that included Darius Milhaud, Arthur Honegger, and Francis Poulenc. So too, toward the end of his life, he guided the destinies of four young men—among them Roger Désormière and Henri Sauguet—who took the title of "École d'Arcueil" to show their admiration for the master who had made that suburb famous. A lingering illness carried him off at the age of fifty-nine. "He died as he had lived —without ever quite ceasing to smile."

HIS MUSIC

Satie is a controversial figure in the art of our time. His music never won a firm place in the repertory. Yet Ravel maintained that Satie had exerted the greatest influence upon him; while Darius Milhaud claims that each work of Satie's foretold the lines along which French music of the last half-century developed. There is no question that this sprightly Parisian exerted an influence on contemporary musical esthetics extending far beyond the actual performance of his works.

Satie was the apostle of simplicity. All that smacked of pretentiousness was foreign to his temperament. He strove for a forthright, unaffected music, as free from sentimentality as from the pathos of the grand style: a music stripped of nonessentials down to its "bare bones," as he put it. There could be no better statement of his esthetic doctrine than his description of the "new spirit" in music: "It teaches us to aim at an emotional simplicity and a firmness of utterance that enable sonorities and rhythms to assert themselves clearly, unequivocal in design and accent, and conceived in a spirit of humility and renunciation." It was this kind of impersonal music that the second quarter of the century desired.

During his mystical phase—the Rosicrucian period—Satie was attracted to Gregorian Chant and the medieval modes. He was thus one of the pioneers in the movement away from major-minor tonality. Like Debussy, Satie sought to lead French music away from the symphony of Beethoven and the music dramas of Wagner. Yet he was equally determined to avoid the vagueness and overrefinement of impressionism. The individual chord, for him, was never the column of magic that it was for Debussy. Always it was subservient to the needs of his chiseled melodic line. Satie's sober, sparse orchestration—"without sauce," as he called it—helped to usher in the style of writing that dominated the Twenties and Thirties. His years of activity in the cafés of Montmartre developed his flair for the robust, popular song style of French musical comedy which played a prominent role in his art. As Virgil Thomson has said, Satie realized that the wisest thing music in the twentieth century could do was to stop taking itself seriously. The unpretentious charm of Satie's works in the popular vein—such as the songs composed for the music-hall singer Paulette Darty—pointed out new fields for composers to cultivate. One has but to mention such works as Milhaud's *Le Boeuf sur le Toit*, Poulenc's *Mouvements Perpetuels* or Aaron Copland's *El Salón México* to realize how rich was the harvest.

Satie is best known to the public for his early piano pieces: the *Sarabandes* (1887), *Gymnopédies* (1887), and *Gnossiennes* (1890). Each set contains three dance pieces in the composer's characteristic manner. These works anticipate certain procedures that later became associated with the music of Debussy, notably the unconventional handling of unresolved chords of the ninth, the modal idiom, and the movement of the harmony in parallel, block-like formations. They also reveal Satie's fondness for unusual titles; *Gymnopédies* and *Gnossiennes* are words coined by himself to suggest that these sculpturesque dance forms were inspired by Greek antiquity. This music has a grave simplicity. It displays certain hallmarks of Satie's style: short symmetrical phrases repeated over and over; an airy melodic line, with an easy swing; limpid harmony, whose modal character is brought into focus at the cadences; lightness of texture; and establishment at the outset of a rhythmic pattern that persists throughout. In some of his piano music Satie omitted barlines as well as time and key signatures—a daring step in the 1890s.

The works written during and after his studies at the Schola Cantorum, from around 1905 until the eve of the First World War, foreshadow—in their emphasis on contrapuntal texture, economy, and sobriety of style—the neo-classic orientation that was to establish itself during the Twenties. In these pieces Satie continued to indulge his penchant for droll, mystifying titles. The list includes *Pièces froides* (Cold Pieces, 1897), with its *Airs à faire fuir* (Airs to Make One Flee); *Trois pièces en forme de poire* (Three Pieces in the Shape of a Pear, 1903); *Aperçus désagreables* (Disagreeable Impressions, 1908); *Croquis et agaceries d'un gros bonhomme de bois* (Sketches and Annoyances of a Wooden Man, 1913); and *Embryons desséchés* (Dried-up Embryos, 1913). According to Jean Cocteau, Satie's titles were meant "as a good-humored piece of ill-humor, maliciously directed against *Moons Descending on the Temple that Was* and *Sunken Cathedrals*."

Closely related to the humor of the titles were the admonitions to the performer, now whimsical, now nonsensical, that were strewn throughout the music. Here too we find a desire to parody the poetic directions of the impressionists. "Like a nightingale with toothache . . . sheepishly and coldly . . . light as an egg . . . with tenderness and fatality. . . ." Rollo Myers, in his perceptive biography of the composer, finds in these sallies "the bitterness of an essentially lonely man who is obliged to camouflage all his serious work in order to forestall the criticism he secretly fears."

Satie possessed a literary gift. His letters, like the essays he wrote throughout his career, abound in a personal brand of humor that ranges from mordant irony to inspired nonsense. A few examples will suffice to give the flavor of his wit. "Although our information is inaccurate, we do not guarantee it. . . . M. Ravel refuses the Legion of Honor, but all his music accepts it. . . . I came into a very young world in a very old time. . . . Before writing a work, I go round it several times accompanied by myself. . . . When I was young they said to me, 'You will see when you're fifty.' I am fifty, and I have seen nothing. . . . Last year I gave several lectures on 'Intelligence and the Appreciation of Music among Animals.' Today I am going to speak to you about 'Intelligence and the Appreciation of Music among Critics.' The subject is very similar. . . ."

The most significant work of Satie's late period is *Socrate*, a "symphonic drama in three parts" based on the Dialogues of Plato. This was completed in 1918. It is scored for four soprano soloists and chamber orchestra—flute, oboe, English horn, clarinet, bassoon, horn, trumpet, harp, kettledrums, and strings. For his text Satie drew upon Victor Cousin's translation of the *Symposium*, the *Phaedrus*, and *Phaedo*. This contemplative work embodies the neo-classic ideal of simplicity and economy of means. The melodic line has the archaic quality that Satie derived from Gregorian chant. The limpid orchestration brings out the lines of the polyphony. The consistent understatement and the absence of any desire to create an effect make for an inner quietude of spirit.

"Only a very remarkable personality," wrote the English critic, Wilfrid Mellers, "could attain to the degree of impersonality which makes this music, not one man's loneliness, but an aspect of the modern consciousness transformed into sound."

PARADE

The most important of Satie's works for the stage was written for Serge Diaghilev's *Ballets Russes*, on a scenario by Jean Cocteau, with décor and costumes by Picasso and choreography by Massine. *Parade* (1917) has well been called "a cubist manifesto." The cubist painters broke up the familiar objects of everyday life and reintegrated them in unusual contexts in order to achieve a fresh personal vision. In the same way, Satie's music juxtaposed seemingly incompatible elements and recombined them in a formal integration: snappy fragments of music-hall melody and a strict fugato, lyrical phrases and driving ostinato rhythms, simple diatonic harmonies and clangorous polytonal effects.

The inclusion in the score of a typewriter, steam whistle, rattle, and similar noisemakers was allied to the "shock-the-bourgeois" mentality of Paris during the second decade of our century. What reaches beyond the period is the freshness of montage achieved by Satie, with its combination of naiveté and sophistication, detachment and irony.

The cubist painters broke up familiar objects of everyday life and reintegrated them in unusual contexts in order to achieve a fresh personal vision. Juan Gris, *Guitar and Flowers*. (Collection Museum of Modern Art)

"The music-hall, the circus and American Negro bands," wrote Jean Cocteau, "fertilise an artist just as life does." All three elements are abundantly present in *Parade*. The action takes place outside a tent at a fair where three showmen try to attract the crowd by presenting excerpts from the performance that is soon to begin inside. (Such a series of sample tidbits is known in France as a *parade*.) The Sunday afternoon atmosphere is established at the beginning of Satie's brief overture by solemn chords intoned by the brass. There is a short fugato passage, then the music transports us to the fair. The Manager in Formal Attire is announced by strings and woodwinds over an ostinato figure, followed by a few measures of a pompous march. He presents his star attraction—the Chinese Conjurer, who proceeds to go through his tricks. This gives Satie an opportunity for a delicious bit of exoticism, gong and all, in Parisian music-hall style. Notice particularly his fluent contrapuntal writing.

The Manager from New York produces his performer, the Little American Girl. She goes through her turn, which includes an imitation of Charlie Chaplin, to a jazzy and frenetic passage based on two-step rhythm. It is at this point that the clicking of a typewriter is brought in to underline the American atmosphere. There follows the *Rag-time du paquebot* (Steamboat Ragtime), in which Satie tried to capture the spirit of American popular music of the 1915 vintage. (The melody duplicates almost verbatim that of Irving Berlin's *That Mysterious Rag*.)

The Manager on Horseback then presents his two acrobats to the strains of a carefree waltz. The three showmen and their artists make a frantic effort to attract customers. They try to explain to the crowd that the real show is to take place within. But they are unable to com-municate their message to those who refuse to understand. There is a fleeting reference to the fugato of the overture, and the ballet ends.

Satie's score is flavored with parody and with piquant sonorities; with "the sadness of the circus," as his disciple Georges Auric wrote, "and the nostalgia of the hurdy-gurdy that will never play Bach fugues." It is simple, almost factual in its down-to-earth way—and utterly unsentimental.

The music of this "forerunner of genius," as he has been called, was amazingly prophetic of much that came after. French music of the twentieth century owes much to Erik Satie.

⋖§ 31 §⋗

Les Six

> "I wish I knew what sort of music will be written by the children who are four-year-olds now."
>
> Erik Satie

JEAN COCTEAU shared Satie's views and outlined the new esthetic in a little work called *Le Coq et l'arlequin* (The Rooster and the Harlequin), in which he launched an uninhibited attack on the music of the nine-teenth century, "the kind one listens to with one's head in one's hands." Cocteau called for "music with a punch" and proclaimed the era of "the circus and the music-hall"—that is to say, an esthetic rid of ro-mantic *Weltschmerz*. So it was that Satie became the spiritual god-father and Cocteau the literary prophet of the younger generation of French musicians.

In January, 1920, the French critic Henri Collet published an article entitled "Five Russians, Six Frenchmen, and Erik Satie," in which he lauded a half-dozen of the up-and-coming composers, and said they were a coterie as important as the Russian "Five" had been in the mid-nineteenth century. The "Six"—Darius Milhaud, Louis Durey, Georges Auric, Arthur Honegger, Francis Poulenc, and Germaine Tailleferre —were certainly not the close-knit group, in terms of a common aim, that the "Mighty Five" had been. No matter. In a time given to artistic slogans and catchwords, *Les Six* caught on and attracted a vast amount of attention.

The emergence of these six composers marked the final phase in the emancipation of French music from German influence. They rebelled not only against the nineteenth century but also against Debussyan impressionism. Fervent devotees of American jazz and the Parisian music hall, they favored the bright, lean sonorities and the earthy approach to art that accorded with the temper of the time. They adored sophistication and wit by as much as they abhorred pathos and passion. Their irrepressible high spirits embodied an approach to music which—although it did not create much that was durable—was in its own time fresh and charming. And they helped to put Paris in the forefront of musical advance in the 1920s.

In one way they did resemble the Russian "Five": the differences among them in talent and temperament became increasingly apparent as the years wore on. Durey and Tailleferre, after a brief taste of fame, passed into obscurity. Auric is known outside France chiefly as a motion picture composer. Milhaud, Honegger, and Poulenc, on the other hand, soon outgrew the high jinks of their youth and became the leading figures of the contemporary French school.

⋉ 32 ⋊

Darius Milhaud (1892-)

"A composer should do everything with application, with all the resources of contemporary technique at his disposal. He can then hope that, after a life of hard work, he will see some works survive."

HIS LIFE

"I AM A Frenchman from Provence," Milhaud begins his *Autobiography*, "and by religion a Jew." This sentence points up the two poles of the composer's heritage. He came from a distinguished, well-to-do family that had lived in Aix-en-Provence for centuries. Growing up as he did in a cultured environment—both his parents were amateur musicians—his gift was accorded every opportunity to flower. Milhaud was seventeen when he entered the Paris Conservatoire. His major interest at this time was the violin. The exciting musical life of the metropolis opened up new horizons. With unerring instinct he found his way to whatever could nourish his talent: *Pelléas, Boris Godunov,* the Russian Ballet. By the same token, he was repelled by Wagner from the first. During the summer of 1911 he composed a Sonata for violin and piano, the first work he thought worth preserving. By the end of the following year Milhaud decided to abandon his career as a violinist in order to devote himself to composition.

Darius Milhaud

His strong literary inclinations drew him to the theater. He wrote a three-act opera on Francis Jammes' *La Brebis égarée* (The Lost Sheep). Shortly thereafter he met the poet Paul Claudel, who wrote the texts for a number of his operas, theater pieces, choral works, and songs. In the meantime the young composer was studying fugue in the class of the redoubtable Charles-Marie Widor. "That charming teacher would utter cries of alarm at every dissonance he came across in my works. As he listened he would exclaim: 'The worst of it is that you get used to them!' "

The war put an end to a carefree existence. Rejected for military service for medical reasons, Milhaud continued his musical activities in Paris. In 1916 Paul Claudel, who carried on his literary work together with a strenuous diplomatic career, was appointed Minister to Brazil and asked his young friend to accompany him as his secretary. For the next two years—from February, 1917, till the end of 1918—Milhaud was exposed to the sights and sounds of Rio de Janeiro, and came to love the rhythm and color of popular Brazilian song.

Back in Paris, Milhaud threw himself into the artistic life of the capital. He found himself in the midst of a brilliant circle that included such painters as Picasso, Braque, and Dufy, as well as a number of gifted writers: Cocteau, Lucien Daudet, Paul Morand, Apollinaire, Giraudoux, Blaise Cendrars, and Raymond Radiguet. "After dinner," he recalls, "we would visit the Fair of Montmartre or occasionally the Medrano Circus. We finished the evening at my house. Out of these meetings, in which a spirit of carefree gaiety reigned, many a fruitful collaboration was to be born. They also determined the character of several works strongly marked by the influence of the music hall."

The next fifteen years were spent mostly in Paris, with frequent journeys to the other musical centers of Europe. In the summer he generally returned to his ancestral home in Provence. He bore with fortitude attacks of crippling rheumatism, which eventually confined him for weeks at a time to a wheelchair. He was sustained in these trials by his wife, Madeleine, who was not only a devoted mate, but also a sensitive poet and actress who collaborated in a number of his dramatic works. After the collapse of France during the Second World War Milhaud, accompanied by his wife and young son, found a refuge in the United States. He arrived in 1940 and joined the faculty of Mills College at Oakland, California. A large number of young American musicians came under his influence during his stay there. The journey back to France in 1947, his reunion with his comrades, and his return to his native Provence were among the culminating experiences of a life that has been lived richly on every level.

Since 1947 Milhaud has divided his time between Paris, where he is professor of composition at the Conservatoire, and the United States, where on alternate years he teaches at one of several schools: Mills College, the Berkshire Music Center at Tanglewood, the Music Academy of the West at Santa Barbara, and the summer school at Aspen, Colorado.

HIS MUSIC

Milhaud is primarily a lyricist. His melodies are rooted in the soil of his native Provence. There is a simplicity and directness about them, a quietude of spirit and modesty of bearing that constitute the hallmark of his style.

Yet the pastoral songfulness we associate with such works as the *Suite provençale* (1936–37) or the opening movement of the First Symphony

reveals only one aspect of the composer's personality. No less characteristic is the undercurrent of nostalgia that informs so much of his music.
Still another side of him leans toward violence—the savage dissonances,
the clangorous masses of superimposed polytonal chords which resound
through his music for the dramas that Claudel adapted from Aeschylus:
Agamemnon (1913), *Les Choéphores* (1915) and *Les Euménides* (1922).
At the opposite pole are gay, strongly rhythmic works that conjure up
images of color and movement. Behind all these is so integrated a musical
personality that, no matter which of his many facets a particular piece
reveals, it is immediately recognizable as his.

From the point of view of harmonic language Milhaud is popularly
associated with polytonality, in the evolution of which he played an important role. His attempt to expand the language of contemporary
harmony by combining different tonalities was pursued with all the
logic of a keen, inquiring mind. Milhaud's polytonal writing serves to
set off the melodic lines against one another. It is, in effect, a poly-
melody. No matter how diligent his research in harmony and how
complex the results, he is too much the lyricist ever to forget the primacy
of melody. "The important thing," he maintains, "is the vital element
—the melody—which should be easily retained, hummed, and whistled
on the street. Without this fundamental element, all the technique in
the world can only be a dead letter."

Milhaud's orchestral writing has the French clarity of texture. He
has experimented widely with small groups of instruments treated in
chamber-music style. At the same time, he is capable of those massive
effects for full orchestra and chorus which since Berlioz have attracted
French composers to "the big machine." Milhaud's preoccupation with
the percussion group reflects the twentieth-century emphasis on rhythm.
He has always been fascinated by the rhythms of popular music: the
tangos, sambas, and maxixes he heard in Brazil, the pounding rhythms
of the music hall, the syncopations of jazz. He shares Stravinsky's fondness for the ostinato. In his approach to form Milhaud is very much
the Latin. He is given to neat, terse structures that go straight to the
point. The mosaic-like building up of small fragments into larger units
—a characteristic of French composers since the time of Couperin—
lends intimacy to his music and a special charm. The New Music, he
believes, must become a "simple, clear art renewing the tradition of
Mozart and Scarlatti." Despite this classical point of view, which was
especially strong in his younger years, Milhaud has moved steadily
toward the new romanticism. His lyricism, his pastoral gentleness, his
nostalgic charm are essentially romantic traits.

Milhaud is one of the most prolific composers of our time. A list of his works reaches well beyond the three-hundred mark, and embraces all branches and forms of music. Included are thirteen operas, three children's operas, thirteen ballets, incidental music for thirty-seven plays, music for twenty films, and twenty-eight choral works—cantatas, psalms, and settings of various poems. In this last category also are his settings of a number of Hebrew prayers. Among the orchestral works, mention may be made of the popular *Suite provençale*, five symphonies for small orchestra (1917–22) and eight symphonies for large (1939–58). Four piano concertos (1934–50); two violin concertos (1927, 1948); and a viola concerto dedicated to his friend Paul Hindemith (1929) stand out among the more than twenty works for solo instrument and orchestra. Milhaud has written a quantity of music for the radio, for military band and jazz band, for voice and orchestra. His chamber music includes eighteen string quartets, of which the fourteenth and fifteenth can also be played together as an octet. He has written over a hundred and fifty songs, among them the amusing *Catalogue de fleurs* (Flower Catalogue, 1920), a set of three songs to texts by Lucien Daudet; and the moving *Poèmes juifs* (Jewish Poems, 1916). There is a varied list of piano pieces, including two volumes of *Saudades do Brasil* (1921), a collection of atmospheric miniatures whose rhythms pungently evoke the landscape of his sojourn in Rio de Janeiro.

Milhaud's most important opera is *Cristophe Colomb*, in twenty-seven scenes (1928). Claudel's libretto gave him opportunity to experiment with novel musico-dramatic effects. The action includes allegory and symbolism; expressionist technique (as when Columbus talks with his second self); and the use of film. The Hellenic themes so popular in French literature are reflected in Milhaud's choice of operatic subjects. In this category are *Les Malheurs d'Orphée* (The Misfortunes of Orpheus, 1929); a one-act *Médée* (1938); and three little chamber operas, each lasting no more than eight minutes—*Europa, Ariadne,* and *Theseus* (1927). Of a different genre is *Le pauvre matelot* (The Poor Sailor, 1926) on a grimly realistic libretto by Cocteau. The full-length operas include also *Maximilien,* a lyric drama on the ill-fated Emperor of Mexico (1930); *Bolivar* (1943); and *David* (1953).

Given his passion for setting down notes on paper, it would be unrealistic to suppose that all of Milhaud's music is at the same high level. Much of his enormous output will undoubtedly fall into oblivion. Much already has. But the best will remain, because it came out of a genuinely musical impulse.

LA CRÉATION DU MONDE (THE CREATION OF THE WORLD)

In 1922 Milhaud visited the United States, appearing as pianist in his own works and giving lectures on the New Music. The high point of his stay in this country was a visit to Harlem. "The music I heard," he recalls in his *Autobiography*, "was absolutely different from anything I had ever heard before, and was a revelation to me. Against the beat of the drums the melodic lines crisscrossed in a breathless pattern of broken and twisted rhythms. This authentic music had its roots in the darkest corners of the Negro soul. Its effect on me was so overwhelming that I could not tear myself away. More than ever I was resolved to use jazz for a chamber work." The resultant piece was *La Création du monde*, a ballet depicting the creation of the world from the point of view of Negro folk legends, which was produced in 1923 with a scenario by Blaise Cendrars, choreography by the great Swedish choreographer Jean Borlin, and scenery and costumes by Fernand Léger.

"I made wholesale use of the jazz style," the composer points out, "to convey a purely classical feeling." He expanded the jazz ensemble to include two flutes, one oboe, two clarinets, bassoon, horn, two trumpets, trombone, piano, a diversified percussion group, two solo violins, saxophone, cello, and contrabass. He used this ensemble, as he puts it, "like a symphony concertante." Milhaud's evocation of the nostalgic blues, his simultaneous use of major and minor, and his intricate counterpoint—so close in spirit to the free dissonant counterpoint of Dixieland—are all highly characteristic. At times he captures the uninhibited improvisational quality of the jam session. Yet the jazz elements are infused with the elegance and wit of a sensibility that is wholly French. The theme of the ballet bears some resemblance to that of *Le Sacre du printemps*, but it is hardly necessary to point out that Milhaud's primitivism is infinitely gentler than Stravinsky's. Coming two years before Gershwin's *Rhapsody in Blue*, *La Création du monde* was a landmark in the music of the Twenties. It is one of the finest of Milhaud's earlier works.

Scene I. The curtain rises to show the chaos before creation; a shapeless mass of bodies fills the stage as three African deities—Nazme, Membere, and Nkwa—hold council and cast their spells. Scene II. The mass slowly begins to move; the darkness lifts. A tree appears; plants and animals come to life. Scene III. The animals join in a lively, heavily accented dance. Presently Man and Woman emerge from the tangled mass of bodies in the center of the stage, and gaze upon one another.

Scene IV. While the pair perform the Dance of Desire, other figures
disengage themselves from the mass and join in a dance that grows
wilder and wilder. The frenzy passes, the dancers disappear. Man and
Woman remain alone in an embrace. It is springtime. . . .

The score consists of an Overture and five sections played without
pause. The Overture, marked *Modéré*, establishes the mood of quiet
lyricism so characteristic of Milhaud. A serene melody is sung by the
saxophone; the sinuous accompaniment on the piano and strings features
the luscious thirds so dear to this composer. The movement is punctuated
by a syncopated figure in the trumpets. Slides on the trombone and
flatted sevenths create a jazz atmosphere. I. Against dry arpeggios on
the piano, the double bass introduces the theme of a jazz fugue, which is

presented in turn by trombone, saxophone, and trumpet, and then
developed in the orchestra. The movement mounts to a *fff* climax with
pungency and rhythmic bite. A sudden *pianissimo*, consisting of a descending scale in thirds on flutes and clarinets, leads into the next section. II. The melody of the Overture is now heard in the flute; the cello
recalls the theme of the fugue in augmentation. The oboe sings a blues
marked *très tendre*, which is related to the fugue theme. The accompaniment on the saxophone and strings makes a lovely sound. An animated
transition derives its special color from fluttertonguing on the flute.
III. The dance of the plants and animals, marked *vif* (lively), is executed
to a raffish tune in the violins which is worked up into a *fortissimo*, with

changes in instrumentation. The tempo slackens, the *fortissimo* subsides.
The theme of the blues returns as a counterpoint to the dance tune:
Man and Woman face one another. IV. Their Dance of Desire opens
with a clarinet melody in improvisational style, against a syncopated

accompaniment based on an ostinato rhythm played by the piano, saxophone, and strings. A new melody appears, containing triplet rhythms. The tranquil melody of the Overture returns in the oboe. Tension mounts as the clarinet theme returns, this time on the saxophone, and is combined with a motive from the fugue presented by the trumpet. The material undergoes free contrapuntal elaboration as the music builds to a *fff* climax. V. The concluding section, gently retrospective, is in the nature of an epilogue. The blues theme is played by the oboe, whence it passes to other instruments. There is a fleeting reminiscence of the opening theme. Fluttertonguing on flute, clarinet, and trumpet leads to a tranquil "blue" cadence.

La Création du monde was a work of startling originality in its time. Replete with charm and humor, the score has retained its freshness to an astonishing degree. The work, to borrow Aaron Copland's description, is "an authentic small masterpiece."

SCARAMOUCHE

Milhaud has followed the example of the old masters in reworking material he used in one piece to suit the character of another. He derived his two-piano suite *Scaramouche* (1937) from the incidental music he had written for Molière's *Le Médecin volant* and Supervielle's *Bolivar*. The important thing in such an adaptation is to infuse the music with the spirit of the new medium to which it has been transplanted. *Scaramouche* is conceived entirely in the spirit of two-piano music. (The composer recalls that the piece gave him more than the usual trouble.) The writing is thoroughly idiomatic, and is marked by that continual interchange of material between the players which constitutes the delight of two-piano music: a style based on "conversation between equals." *Scaramouche* is the kind of elegant salon music of which the French are undisputed masters. It is unpretentious, polished, tongue-in-cheek music, infused with the spirit of the cafés and boulevards: music that is witty, sophisticated, civilized. The title is used in a general sense, indicating the theatrical provenance of the suite: Scaramouche is a character out of the old comedy. Milhaud advised his publisher against taking the piece, feeling that no one would play it; but it turned out to be one of his most popular works.

I. *Vif* (lively), 4/4. The opening number exploits the capacities of the piano for percussive harmony, driving rhythms, and brilliant runs. The writing, of the motoric kind, is marked by deft syncopations. This Allegro is in a "C-majorish" tonality set off by flavorsome polytonal harmonies: a fine example of the "white music" dear to the neo-classicists. The middle section centers about F, then B-flat. The movement is tossed off with the airiness that is a prime requisite for this kind of music.

II. *Modéré*, 4/4. The second movement is cast in a vein of quiet lyricism, marked by the "intimate limpidity" so often encountered in French music. Milhaud's unassuming charm and songfulness appear to fine advantage in this Andante, which is in A-B-A form. As in the slow movements of the classical period, the emotion, though heartfelt, never goes beyond a certain point. The movement is in B-flat; the middle part, in a graceful 6/8, is in F. The reprise of the first section contains some enchanting modulations.

III. *Brazileira*, 2/2, in F. In this Samba, Milhaud conjures up happy memories of his sojourn in Brazil. A saucy melody unfolds over a

Mouvement de Samba

perpetual rhythm in the accompaniment. The movement is suffused with the coquetry and verve of Latin-American dance music. This finale, a tuneful music-hall number of irresistible gaiety, brings the suite to a brilliant conclusion.

Milhaud's music, urbane and distinguished, bears the imprint of a master craftsman. Its creator is a *musicien français* who traces his lineage from Couperin and Rameau, Berlioz, Chabrier, and Satie.

⋖ 33 ⋗

Arthur Honegger (1892-1955)

"The material of contemporary music is based on the scale of twelve chromatic tones, but used with the same freedom as the letters of the alphabet are used by the poet, or the colors of the spectrum by the painter."

ARTHUR HONEGGER had the good fortune to appear precisely when the time was ripe for what he had to offer. The works by which he is likely to be remembered crystallize certain significant trends in the art of the twentieth century.

HIS LIFE

Honegger was born in Le Havre of Swiss parents. His father was head of a successful importing house, his mother an amateur pianist of some attainments. Growing up in a solid bourgeois environment, the future composer did not fit the usual image of the sensitive young artist. He was an athlete who excelled at soccer, swimming, tennis, track, and had a passion for boats and machines.

The young musician spent his summers with his father's family in Zürich, where he steeped himself in the German classics. After two years at the Conservatory of Zürich he entered the Paris Conservatoire. Paris was a revelation to one who came from a musical milieu dominated by Bach, Mozart, Beethoven, and Wagner. Debussyism was in full flower. The young man met the two elder statesmen of the French school, d'Indy and Fauré. And there was his classmate, Darius Milhaud, who, he tells us, "worked and talked with an assurance, a gift of invention, an audacity that overwhelmed the timid little provincial. Our friendship left us, nonetheless, quite independent of each other. He became a fervent admirer of Satie; and I never cried 'Down with Wagner!' "

The outbreak of the First World War interrupted Honegger's studies. Although born in France, he was a Swiss national and was called up for service with the Swiss army. He spent his term of duty in the infantry, guarding the frontiers of his country. Returning to France in 1916, he resumed his composing and was caught up in the ferment that made Paris, in the postwar years, the artistic capital of the world.

Although he became one of *Les Six*, he was far less receptive to the doctrines of Cocteau and Satie than were his comrades. His Swiss-German background was not to be sloughed off that easily. His profession of faith, uttered in his early twenties, made it inevitable that he would be the first to break away from the group: "I do not follow the cult of the fair and the music-hall but, on the contrary, that of chamber music and symphony in their most serious and most austere aspect." In 1921 Honegger's oratorio *Le Roi David* (King David) won a sensational success, which was equalled three years later by that of *Pacific 231*, a symphonic poem glorifying the locomotive.

Honegger visited the United States in 1929, embarking on a concert tour that took him from New York to Boston, Chicago, San Francisco, and New Orleans. The "world-renowned composer," as he was referred to by the press, was accompanied by his wife, the pianist Andrée Vaurabourg, who played his *Concertino*. She shared as actively in his career as did Madeleine Milhaud in that of his friend. Although France was the center of his activities throughout the first period of his life, Honegger came to spend more and more time in his other homeland: Paris and Zürich remained the two poles of an unremittingly active career. During the last decade of his life he was professor of composition at the École Normale de Musique in Paris, where he was able to exert an influence on the younger generation of French musicians. He died in Paris in 1955, at the age of sixty-three.

HIS MUSIC

Honegger was eminently qualified to play the same role in the twentieth century as César Franck in the nineteenth—a mediator between French music and the German tradition. Both men felt a primary loyalty to French culture, tempered by a sense of allegiance to the German heritage. "I am," Honegger wrote, "what is known in the language of the passport as a 'double national',—that is to say, a mixture of French and Swiss. What do I owe Switzerland? Without doubt the Protestant tradition, a great difficulty in deceiving myself as to the value of what I do, a naïve sense of honesty, familiarity with the Bible. To France I owe all the rest: my intellectual awakening, my musical and spiritual affinity."

The German influence in Honegger's art manifested itself in his desire to achieve an architecture both solid and spacious. This led him away from the intimate, mosaic-like structure of the Parisian school. "I have perhaps an exaggerated tendency to seek polyphonic complexity. My great model is Johann Sebastian Bach." He set himself against the seeking after novelty that motivated a good deal of Parisian musical activity in the Twenties. The ties with tradition, he strongly felt, must be maintained. "Economy of means seems to me to be more difficult but also more useful than a too great eagerness to be daring. It is pointless to smash doors that one can open."

Honegger's is an elaborate texture in which the several melodic lines or superposed chords proceed with the utmost freedom, creating polytonal effects which at times take on a peculiarly incisive character. His conception of melody stems from the romantic tradition. "I have sought before all else the melodic line—ample, generous and flowing, and not the laborious juxtaposition of little fragments that fit together badly. The great spurt of melody is the touchstone of all successful works." He was addicted to massive harmonies. The athletic vigor of the man

transferred itself to the artist. Much of Honegger's music is monu-
mentally conceived, grandiose. It suggests the out-of-doors and lends
itself to performance in the open.

Honegger's attachment to a large canvas went hand-in-hand with
his fondness for sonata structure, intricate variation patterns, and extended thematic development. These derived from the German tradition, as did his view of music as an art of spiritual values that must
address itself to mankind. Honegger was much concerned with the
growing gap between the contemporary composer and the public, and
stood firmly with those who sought to remedy the evil. "My desire and
my ambition have always been to write music that would be accessible
to the great mass of listeners, yet sufficiently free from banality to interest the music lover. It is above all in those scores of mine which have
been amiably called 'large frescoes' that I pursued this double aim."
He succeeded in projecting the force of a manly temperament into
dramatic oratorios—one may call them choral operas—such as *King
David* and *Judith* (1926), which captured the heroic tone of the Han-
delian oratorio. The great mass of listeners who felt themselves left
behind by the music of the Twenties found in Honegger's works the
pathos and grandeur they had missed since the eclipse of romanticism.
This was the secret of his success. *King David*, first given at Mézières,
a little town in Switzerland, within a few years had reached Buenos
Aires, New York, Rome, Vienna, London, and Leningrad.

Although not quite as prolific as Milhaud, Honegger wrote much.
His catalogue includes more than a dozen operas and stage works of
various kinds. Among these are *Antigone*, on a libretto of Jean Cocteau
after Sophocles (1927); *Les Aventures du Roi Pausole* (The Adventures
of King Pausole, an operetta, 1930); *Jeanne d'Arc au bûcher* (Joan of
Arc at the Stake, a dramatic oratorio that remains one of his most widely
performed works, 1935); and *Charles le Téméraire* (Charles the Bold,
an opera in the grand manner, 1944). Of his twelve ballets, the best
known is *Skating Rink* (1921), which paid homage to the sports motif
so prominent in the Twenties. Honegger wrote incidental music for
more than twenty plays, among them André Gide's *Saül*, d'Annunzio's
Phaedra, Jean Giraudoux's *Sodom and Gomorrha*, and the *Oedipus*
of Sophocles. He produced about thirty film scores, including those of
Les Misérables, Mayerling, and *Harvest*.

Among the large choral works with orchestra are *Le Cantique des
cantiques* (Song of Songs, 1926); *La Danse des morts* (The Dance of
Death, on a text of Paul Claudel, 1938); and *Chant de Libération* (Song
of Liberation, which he wrote—in anticipation of that event—in 1942).

His orchestral works are varied in scope and form. *Pastorale d'Été* (Summer Pastorale, 1920), has always been a favorite. The place of honor in this category is held by his five symphonies (1930–51). The list also includes a number of compositions for solo instrument and orchestra. The best known is the *Concertino* for piano and orchestra (1923), the last movement of which reflects the influence of jazz. There is also a quantity of chamber music, piano pieces, and songs.

Despite his popularity in the Twenties and Thirties, Honegger could not help feeling toward the end of his life that the world had somehow slipped away from him. A vast disenchantment breathes from the pages of *Je suis compositeur* (I Am a Composer), a little book of reminiscences that appeared in 1951, when he was approaching sixty. "The métier of a composer," he wrote, "has the distinction of being the activity and the preoccupation of a man who exerts himself to produce a product that no one wants to use. I would compare it to the manufacture of Cronstadt hats, shoes with buttons, or Mystère corsets." In the same vein were the words of advice he addressed to his students at the École Normale: "Gentlemen, you absolutely wish to become composers? Have you reflected on what awaits you? If you write music no one will play it, and you will not be able to earn your living. If your father can support you, nothing prevents you from covering paper with black dots. You will find plenty of paper, but what you put down will have only a secondary importance for your fellows. They are not at all impatient to discover you and your sonata. Composing is not a profession. It is a mania, a gentle form of madness. . . ."

SYMPHONY NO. 5

"I have written four symphonies. I have enough," Honegger remarked during his last visit to the United States in 1947. "The work of serious composing is for young men. From time to time I write a little piece, perhaps." Ahead of him lay his fifth and finest symphony.

The piece was commissioned by the Koussevitzky Music Foundation and dedicated to the memory of Natalia Koussevitzky. The subtitle *Di tre re*, the composer explained, "is not an allusion to the three Magi or any other kings, but is used only to indicate that the note *re* (D) occurs three times to end each of the three movements." The Fifth Symphony (1950) is a work of maturity, stark, powerful, relentless: "a symphony of tragic import throughout," the composer called it.

I. *Grave.* The movement opens with a symphonic gesture of remarkable breadth. A majestic chorale is unfolded by the full orchestra

over stridently dissonant chords. Honegger here evokes the massive
sonority of the organ in the polytonal language of the twentieth century,
even as César Franck evoked it in the chromatic idiom of the nineteenth.

The second theme is a lyric idea presented first by bass clarinet, then
by English horn against delicate traceries in the orchestra. A crescendo
builds up over the even tread of the plucked cellos and basses and the
summons of the trumpet, gaining steadily in power and reaching a
shattering climax on the sustained trumpet note described by Honegger
as "an anguished cry that remains in suspense." The chorale returns
on divided strings against woodwind arabesques; then the melody passes
to the winds against figuration in the strings. The coda interpolates
snatches of the second theme among phrases of the first, and brings
the movement to an enigmatic close on a pizzicato D in the bass.

II. The Allegretto alternates lively sections in 3/8 time with two adagio episodes in 4/4, thus combining a Scherzo with a slow movement.
The Scherzo is sardonic rather than gay; the soloistic writing makes
for the utmost lightness of texture. Honegger's way of dividing a theme
among various instruments, assigning a few notes now to one, now to
another, creates a flicker of sound, with that touch of grotesquerie
which his generation inherited from Berlioz, Liszt, and Mahler. The
opening theme is played by a single violin in duet with a solo clarinet:

This plastic idea lends itself to the devices of counterpoint. It is presented almost immediately in contrary motion (inversion) and backward (retrograde).

The adagio section has a contrapuntal texture. Tuba and double basses carry one melodic line, muted trumpets another, while between them a muted trombone makes a sound not soon to be forgotten. The ensuing Allegretto presents the initial theme in canon with its inversion (bass clarinet and violas), and follows that with a canon between the retrograde of the theme and *its* inversion (bassoon and oboe). The second Adagio looks back to the opening chorale. Above it flutes and oboes present the Scherzo theme, so that the two moods are united. The coda leads inexorably to the second of the three pizzicato D's in the bass.

III. *Allegro marcato.* The finale fully merits Honegger's description of it as "violent in character." This music is about struggle, inner questioning, turbulent visions. An ostinato figure on the trumpets persists with inescapable urgency. The displaced accents of the chords in the strings contribute to the peremptory effect of the opening measures. Bassoons and horns drive home an imperious idea in which intervals of a fourth, seventh and ninth play a formative role.

There is a fleeting allusion to the chorale of the first movement. A march-like theme emerges on the brass, against a restless accompaniment of triplets in the strings. The materials presented in the Exposition of this very free sonata form are subjected to a development that accords with their dramatic character. Suddenly we hear a soaring tune in the horns, which assumes a dominant position in the middle part of the movement.

The Recapitulation telescopes the material: ideas first heard in succession are now presented simultaneously. There is an abrupt subsiding at the coda which, in the composer's words, is "suddenly hushed, as if terrified." The third mysterious D in the bass brings to a close this somber and intense work.

Much of Honegger's music has aged more rapidly than one would have guessed thirty years ago. But when he is at his best, as in his Fifth Symphony, he cuts an impressive figure. The piece must be accounted one of the high points of French symphonic writing in the mid-twentieth century.

⤳ 34 ⤶

Francis Poulec (1899-1963)

"I have sought neither to ridicule nor to mimic tradition, but to compose naturally as I felt impelled to."

FRANCIS POULENC is so completely the Frenchman that in order to express the Gallic spirit he need only be himself. It is precisely then that this Parisian achieves the clarity and elegance we have come to recognize as enduring traits of French art.

HIS LIFE AND MUSIC

Poulenc studied the piano with Ricardo Viñes, composition with Charles Koechlin. His precocious talent revealed itself in the *Rapsodie nègre* for piano, string quartet, flute, clarinet, and voice, which he wrote when he was eighteen. A year later there followed the *Mouvements perpétuels* for piano, in a vein of sophistication that he was to make particularly his own.

After a year in the army Poulenc resumed his musical career, and became one of the leading spirits of *Les Six*. Satie's influence is manifest in the unpretentious miniatures, imbued with humor and charm, that Poulenc produced at this time. The young composer's style was nurtured by the works of Chabrier, whose wit is so akin to his own; by the jeweled art of Ravel; and by Stravinsky. The spirit of the gamin that pervaded so much of Poulenc's music—a combination of insouciance and sheer hedonism—caused him to be hailed as "a musical clown of the first order." This, however, is only one side of the picture. In his vocal and piano music Poulenc is a lyricist possessed of the gift of fresh, spontaneous melody. Among the choral works are the *Litanies à la Vierge Noire de Rocomadour* (Litanies to the Black Virgin of Rocomadour, 1936); the Mass in G (1937); *Quatre Motets pour un temps de pénitence* (Four Motets for a Time of Penitence, 1939); *Exultate Deo* and *Salve Regina* (1941), and the *Stabat Mater* (1951). All these are for unaccompanied chorus, as is the cantata *Figure humaine*, on poems of Paul Éluard, a moving work inspired by France's sufferings during the German occupation.

Poulenc is the outstanding exponent of the art song on the present-day scene. He has written about one hundred and thirty songs. "I find myself able to compose music," he has stated, "only to poetry with which I feel total contact—a contact transcending mere admiration." Poulenc feels this contact mainly with contemporary poetry. He turns almost always to the same poets—Apollinaire, Éluard, Max Jacob, Louise de Vilmorin. "The reason is that I believe that one must translate into music not merely the literal meaning of the words but also everything that is written between the lines, if one is not to betray the poetry." His song cycles include *Le Bal masqué* (The Masked Ball, 1932), a "secular cantata" on the surrealist verses of Max Jacob; Éluard's *Telle Jour telle nuit* (Night is like Day, 1937); *Banalités*, on poems of Apollinaire (1940); *Chansons villageoises* (Village Songs, words by Fombeure, 1942); and the brilliantly executed *Le Travail du peintre* (The Painter's Work, 1957)—a set of seven impressions of contemporary painters by Éluard. Poulenc's songs place him in the tradition of Fauré, Duparc, Debussy, and Ravel.

His piano pieces constitute a twentieth-century brand of salon music. They are just right for what Anatole France called "the intimate conversations of five o'clock." His chamber music, characterized by the adroit writing for woodwinds for which French musicians have always been noted, is polished and witty. Mention should be made of the Sextet for flute, oboe, clarinet, bassoon, horn, and piano (1932), and the String Quartet (1946). Several among the larger instrumental works show the composer to good advantage: the *Concert champêtre* for harpsichord and orchestra (Rustic Concerto, 1928); the Concerto for two pianos (1932); and the Concerto for organ, strings, and percussion (1936).

Of Poulenc's ballets, the best known is *Les Biches* (The House Party, 1923). His "opera-burlesque," *Les Mamelles de Tirésias* (The Breasts of Tiresias, 1944) on a libretto by Guillaume Apollinaire, contains attractive music. But the humor grows tiresome, based as it is on a joke that is not really funny to begin with. The ways of talent are unpredictable. At the age of fifty-four the "apostle of the Parisian café-concert" undertook a tragic piece in the grand opera tradition. *Les Dialogues des Carmélites* (Dialogues of the Carmelites, 1953–55) is Poulenc's weightiest work. The play, by the Catholic poet Georges Bernanos, concerns a group of Carmelite nuns who refuse to disband during the French Revolution and suffer martyrdom. Here the composer was able to call upon his mastery in writing for women's voices. The *Ave Maria* in the last scene of the second act is in his finest vein, as is the *Salve Regina* sung in the final scene as the nuns mount the guillotine. The dramatic climaxes are projected through understatement. What fascinates the composer, clearly, is the drama of the inner life. The work received its premiere at La Scala, Milan, in January, 1957. Within a year it had been seen in Paris, Cologne, Geneva, London. The opera was introduced in the United States in 1957 by the San Francisco Opera Company and the NBC Opera Theater, in an English version by the present writer.

LA VOIX HUMAINE (THE HUMAN VOICE)
Lyric Tragedy in One Act

La Voix humaine (1958) is a *tour de force*—an opera with a single character. A woman sings a forty-five minute monologue into the telephone, bidding farewell to the lover who is abandoning her in order to marry another woman. Based on a play by Jean Cocteau (the English version is by the present writer), the work runs the gamut from tender recollection to unbearable anguish, mounting in an implacable line to the final outburst when, the conversation having come to its inevitable end, the woman falls on the bed sobbing "Je t'aime! Je t'aime!" The role offers remarkable opportunities to the actress who essays it. Berthe Bovy won success with it when the play was presented at the Comédie Française in 1932. Anna Magnani played the part in a film directed by Roberto Rossellini. The operatic version found its ideal interpreter in Denise Duval, who triumphed in *La Voix humaine* at the Paris Opéra-Comique and has sung it throughout Europe and in the United States.

The situation is an old one; the treatment is new. Poulenc faced difficult problems with such special material. Given the circumstances, the conversation between the abandoned mistress and her faithless lover has to be extremely volatile, moving abruptly from one thing to another, and, at the intense moments, verging on incoherence. Besides, the voice part is continually interrupted as the woman listens to what the man, presumably, is saying at the other end of the wire. To achieve lyric continuity in such a context is a feat, and one which Poulenc has brought off with real virtuosity. There is no room for lyric expansion. Anything approaching an aria would run hopelessly counter to the realistic tone of the whole. Nor, where the words are so important, must the orchestra ever be allowed to encroach upon the text. Poulenc's keen ear for prosody, his feeling for the feminine voice, his mastery of an orchestral

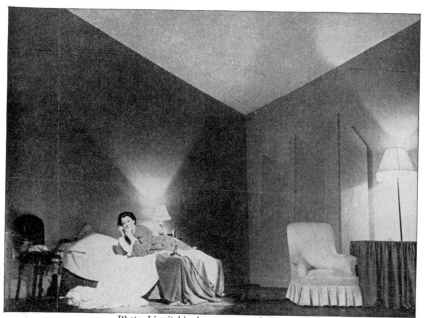

Photo Lipnitzki—by courtesy of S. A. des Disques Ricordi, Paris

The Paris Opéra-Comique production of *La Voix humaine.*

style as subtle as it is discreet stand him here in good stead. There results a work that is wholly French in its sensibility, Parisian in its setting and atmosphere, and thoroughly of our time in its dramatic-musical point of view.

Cocteau's play, for all the impression it gives of an overwrought woman rambling on in order to stave off the painful truth, is laid out in a number of sections that carefully reconstruct the relationship between the pair. Poulenc's score similarly is organized in a series of episodes—one in which the woman lovingly remembers little details of the affair; a second in which she confesses that she lied in telling the man she had been out to dinner when, as a matter of fact, she had been desperately sitting by the telephone waiting for it to ring; a third when she describes how forlorn their little dog is at his master's disappearance; a fourth when she tells of her attempt at suicide. All this on a party line where at any moment she can be (and occasionally is) cut off. Each episode has its own atmosphere. The vocal line, like a seismograph reflecting every nuance of tenderness and pain, of hope and despair in the woman's words, is couched in an understated, conversational recitative that sensitively follows the inflections of the language. All the more effective are the occasional surges of melody, generally entrusted to the orchestra, and the abrupt rise and fall of the woman's voice when her pretense of being brave collapses under the impact of her grief.

Poulenc's habit of immediately repeating fragments of melody or harmony produces that quality of intimacy germane to French composers from Couperin to Debussy. Yet so adroitly does he achieve a sense of continuity that the over-all effect is of an ample and sustained line. The emotional ambience of the work is suggested by the directions scattered throughout the score: *comme un cri* (like a cry) . . . *au comble de l'affolement* (utterly distracted) . . . *très agité* . . . *tendre et câlin* (tender and coaxing) . . . *coquette* . . . *hagarde* . . . *au comble de l'angoisse* (in the height of anguish) . . . *en s'efforçant de paraître calme* (forcing herself to appear calm) . . . *comme un être blessé* (like a wounded being) . . . *très sensuel et lyrique* . . . *au comble de la passion* . . . *très calme et voluptueux* . . . *dans une angoisse horrible*. . . . Two recurring fragments of melody achieve thematic significance. The first comes on the words *Souviens-toi du dimanche de Versailles* (You remember that Sunday in Versailles?):

The second, on the words *Oh! non, sûrement pas tout de suite* (Oh no! Certainly not right away).

Both are sweet and tender, and typically Poulenc. And both remind us once again that there's a bit of Massenet in every Frenchman.

La Voix humaine explores the secret places of the heart. It creates its own world of voluptuous tenderness, and in the hands of a great singing actress is a stunningly effective theater piece. Words and music tell us only too well that, although each love affair is different, the unhappy ones are all the same.

Poulenc began by being fashionable with the chic audience that desires above all to be amused. But the underlying honesty of his music, its melodic distinction and refinement, caused it to make its way with the larger public. He has the wisdom to attempt only what lies within his reach. The result is music with a style and a sound of its own. You will never mistake it for anyone else's.

V. CLASSICISTS

"Classical works are beautiful only by virtue of their subjugated romanticism."

André Gide

◄§ 35 §►

Ferruccio Busoni (1866-1924)

"Music was born free, and to win freedom is its destiny."

HIS LIFE AND MUSIC

IN FERRUCCIO BUSONI we encounter the cerebral composer—a type that, with the intellectualization of art in the twentieth century, has come to be ever more important. It was as a thinker as much as a composer that Busoni made an impact upon his time. He belongs to a rather special group of men who occupy an important position in the history of contemporary music even though their works never caught on with the big public.

Busoni was born at Empoli, in Tuscany, the son of two professional musicians. He came of German-Italian ancestry. To his Latin heritage he added the intellectuality of the German. He himself, though he made Berlin his home for the greater part of his career, considered himself an Italian. "What refreshes me," he declared, "is the Latin attitude to art, with its cool serenity and its insistence on outer form." All the same, one would hardly regard him as a countryman of Puccini and Mascagni.

Busoni at the turn of the century established his reputation as one of the great pianists of the age. Despite his triumphs in the capitals of Europe, he grew increasingly dissatisfied with the lot of the traveling virtuoso. His hyphenated existence as composer-pianist prevented him from devoting himself fully to either activity. As one follows the curve of his life one has the impression that he could not compose because he had to play concerts all the time. Upon closer observation, one begins to suspect that he played concerts all the time because he was not quite sure he could compose. It could not possibly have required so much to support a wife and two children.

239

Busoni lacked the spontaneous, almost naïve, capacity for expression which is at the core of the artist's nature—especially of the Italian artist's nature. "I reflect too much," he said. In his youth he leaned toward the grand manner of romanticism. As he matured he moved ever closer to the Mozartian ideal, seeking stylization in art, serenity and lightness. He came back to the Italian masters, and to the works that revived the spirit of classical comedy: Rossini's *Barber* and Verdi's *Falstaff*. "The German," he wrote, "is sober, sentimental and awkward—all that goes against art. The German is bourgeois; art is aristocratic. The Germans are becoming custodians of museums. Let us go forward and let us remain Italian."

Busoni's spiritual development, consequently, led him to a classical orientation. In this he anticipated the most important development in musical esthetics during the first quarter of the twentieth century. He moved away from the full rich scoring of Wagner to an orchestral idiom based on counterpoint. He wrote for the orchestra as though for an assemblage of solo players, therewith reviving the *concertante* ideal of the age of Bach. He foreshadowed the twentieth-century fondness for small and unusual combinations of instruments, and he cultivated the eighteenth-century forms: rondo, sarabande, gavotte, minuet, gigue; also the fugue and sonatina. He sought clarity of thought, sobriety of feeling, and lucidity of expression. For the grand rhetoric of the post-romantic era he substituted the spirit of comedy and harlequinade, the Latin ideal of brilliancy and grace.

So too he rebelled against the traditional scales which, he was persuaded, had lost their capacity to stimulate and to surprise. "We are tyrannized by Major and Minor—by that bifurcated garment!" He experimented with new scales, and came up with a hundred and thirteen possible ways of arranging whole and half steps within a seven-note series. (See Busoni scale, page 38.) Taking a leap into the future, he also advocated the use of microtones, that is, intervals smaller than the standard semitone of Western music.

As a composer, Busoni was most successful with works conceived in the antiromantic spirit of Harlequin. Those most likely to find favor are the two Symphonic Suites (1888, 1895); *Lustspielouvertüre* (Comedy Overture, 1897); Violin Concerto (1897); the Piano Concerto with choral finale for male voices (1904); *Rondo Arlecchinesco* for orchestra (1915); the operas *Arlecchino*, "a theatrical caprice" (1916), and *Turandot*, "a Chinese tale" after Carlo Gozzi (1917), for both of which he wrote the librettos; and the Concertino for clarinet and small orchestra (1919). Of his substantial output for piano the best-known works are *Fantasia contrappuntistica* (1910) and the six Sonatinas. He also wrote choral and chamber music, and songs. The last years of his life were devoted to his magnum opus, the opera *Doktor Faust*. Although it contains passages that mark the peak of Busoni's achievement as a composer, the work as a whole is uneven and lacking in theater sense. Left incomplete at his death, *Doktor Faust* was finished by Busoni's pupil, Philipp Jarnach. Busoni's artistic beliefs are brilliantly presented in his *Entwurf einer neuen Ästhetik der Tonkunst* (1907), which has been published in English as *Towards a New Esthetic of Music*.

"I feel myself to be a beginning. . . ." Busoni correctly estimated his position. His ideas took root because they met the needs of the age. The younger generation of central European composers learned much from his dexterous counterpoint, his light orchestral texture, the originality of certain of his effects. As is true of Erik Satie, Busoni's influence has reached well beyond the actual performance of his music.

◄§ 36 §►

Albert Roussel (1869-1937)

"I have always pursued the design of the construction and the rhythm. The search for form and its proper development have been my constant preoccupations."

AT A TIME when Debussy, Ravel, and Satie revealed anew the grace of Gallic art, Albert Roussel pointed the way to the discipline and logic inherent in the large-scale forms of absolute music. Therewith he effected a union between twentieth-century French music and the spirit of classical symphonism.

HIS LIFE

Roussel was born in Tourcoing, in French Flanders. He prepared for a naval career, and at the age of eighteen was accepted into naval college as a cadet. The next years were spent in arduous training, during which Roussel's sole musical activity was playing the piano when the future officers practiced their dancing.

Presently there asserted itself the urge to try his hand at composing. The young man acquired a treatise on harmony from which he attempted to teach himself the rudiments of the art. He wrote a *Fantaisie* for violin and piano. At twenty-three he had his first performance—an *Andante* for violin, viola, cello and organ. (Through ignorance he wrote the viola part in the wrong clef.) For a time Roussel tried to pursue a double career. He was promoted to the rank of lieutenant, was put in command of a torpedo boat, and made a trip to Cochin China. When he was twenty-five he reached the long-deferred decision: he resigned his commission, and was free to follow his true bent.

After some preliminary study, Roussel in 1896 entered the newly founded Schola Cantorum, of which Vincent d'Indy was the guiding genius. His active contact with d'Indy—as pupil, disciple, and ultimately professor at the Schola—extended over a period of eighteen years. The most important event of this period, in terms of its influence upon his future growth, was the extended trip that followed his marriage in 1908. Roussel and his bride visited the countries that he had seen, mainly from on board ship, during his years in the navy. Their tour included India, Ceylon, and Indochina. The contact with the music of the Far East strongly affected his thinking. The direct result of these impressions was a set of three *Évocations* for solo voices, chorus, and orchestra, and the opera *Pâdmâtavî*.

Work on *Pâdmâtavî* was interrupted in 1914 by the outbreak of war. Although in his mid-forties, the ex-naval officer became an ambulance driver in the Red Cross. Subsequently accepted into the army, he became a gunnery officer and saw active service at the Somme and Verdun. "I never would have believed," he wrote to his wife in 1916, "that I should have been able to endure as I have the fatiguing life I have led for seven months at the front. I have passed nights without sleep, days without food and, with it all, you will see that I still look well." He looked ahead confidently to the resumption of creative work. "I see in my music no trace of morbid or deliquescent influences. On the contrary, it seems to me that the general tone is for the most part healthy and strong. . . ."

Roussel's health ultimately did break down, however, and in 1918 he was invalided out of service. He resumed work on *Pâdmâvatî*, which was produced at the Paris Opera in 1923. Some years before, he had acquired a villa at Sainte-Marguérite-sur-Mer, outside the town of Varengeville, not far from Dieppe. Situated on the cliffs overlooking the sea, this country home afforded the composer the retired life that suited his temperament.

Roussel enjoyed great esteem among his colleagues. His integrity as man and artist, no less than his disinterested efforts on behalf of young

Albert Roussel

composers, won for him an affection as great as was the respect inspired
by his musical attainments. He was president of the French section of
the International Society for Contemporary Music. Nor was his reputation confined to his homeland. His Third Symphony was commissioned
for the fiftieth anniversary of the founding of the Boston Symphony
Orchestra. In connection with the performance of that work the composer, in 1930, paid a visit to the United States.

A heart attack led to his death in August, 1937. He was buried in the
cemetery overlooking the sea, near his favorite walk along the edge of
the cliff he called his "quarterdeck."

HIS MUSIC

Roussel started out as a composer of highly pictorial music. For a time
he was seduced, as he put it, by the allure of impressionism; but he
realized that it would only lead him to an impasse. He found his true
path by giving full play to his sense of form and construction—a sense
based on a solid contrapuntal technique. "What I want to realize," he
wrote, "is a music satisfying in itself, a music which seeks to eliminate
all picturesque and descriptive elements."

Paris in the Twenties considered both impressionism and the symphony outmoded. It was in this climate that Roussel espoused the cause
of a French neo-classicism oriented to the cultivation of the large forms
—symphony, concerto, sonata, suite, trio, quartet, and the like. He
had a varied ancestry within the French tradition. His melodic imagery
was nurtured by the old chansons; he responded to the charm of French
folksong. He was influenced by the eighteenth-century suite, with its
elegant pattern making, and by the decorative opera-ballets of Rameau.
The Baroque concerto grosso was congenial to his own rhythmic
vitality; while his years at the Schola Cantorum related him to the tradition of Franck and d'Indy. From Satie he learned to appreciate the delights of the café-concert and music-hall, whose spirit informs the saucy
tunes of his scherzos. His experience in the Orient sensitized him to
subtleties of melodic and rhythmic inflection unfamiliar in the West,
nor was he left untouched by the rhythmic innovations of his younger
contemporary, Stravinsky. All these influences were assimilated to an
idiom that was essentially lyrical, and that bore the imprint of a fastidious
musical personality.

Roussel's three "classical" symphonies stand as the centerpiece of his
output. The Second is sombre and intense (1921); the Third we will
discuss; and the Fourth (1934) combines lyricism with formal contra-

puntal devices. These works manifest the vigorous thought and carefully wrought detail characteristic of the composer. Closely related, in its classical orientation, is the Suite in F (1926), which is based on three eighteenth-century forms: Prelude, Sarabande, and Gigue. One should mention the Concerto for Small Orchestra (1927) and the Piano Concerto (1927), the latter a challenging piece even though Roussel had no real flair for the instrument. The classical line is manifest also in the Sinfonietta for Strings (1934) and the Cello Concertino (1936). Roussel wrote a considerable amount of chamber music. The Divertissement for piano, flute, oboe, bassoon, and horn is a prophetic work, considering that its date is 1906. The two Sonatas for violin and piano (1908, 1924), the Serenade for flute, violin, viola, cello, and harp (1925), and the String Quartet (1932) are valuable additions to the contemporary literature.

As a ballet composer Roussel is best known to the public through the concert suite derived from *Le Festin de l'araignée* (The Spider's Feast, 1912). Two later ballet scores are *Bacchus et Ariane* (1930) and *Aeneas* (1935). From the rest of Roussel's considerable output—stage works, songs, piano pieces, and choral music—one must single out his setting of Psalm XC for tenor solo, mixed chorus, and orchestra (1928).

SYMPHONY NO. 3 IN G MINOR, OPUS 42

"I force myself always to put out of my mind the memory of objects and forms susceptible to interpretation in musical sounds. I wish to make only music." Nowhere did Roussel give freer play to his purely musical impulses than in this sunny work (1930) that marks the high point of his commitment to the classical point of view.

I. *Allegro vivo.* The movement plunges directly into that continuous forward impulsion which gives Roussel's music its élan. The principal theme is announced by oboes, clarinets, and violins against an energetic accompaniment.

The second idea, bold of curve and ample in gesture, is introduced by a flute solo. The development section reaches its climax with the announcement of the five-note motto theme which runs through the symphony like a unifying thread. (This use of the same material in

different movements links the piece to the cyclical form espoused by
d'Indy and his master, César Franck.) The dynamic tension is sustained
throughout the Recapitulation, which restates the material in abbreviated form.

II. *Adagio.* The main idea of the slow movement derives from the
motto theme.

Roussel's ability to spin out a long melodic line is seen to excellent advantage in this Adagio, as is his command of flowing counterpoint.
The form is A-B-A. The middle part includes a syncopated Andante
into which there briefly intrudes the spirit of the dance hall—although
in stylized form. This is followed by an exhilarating fugato. The reprise
achieves a moving climax. The movement as a whole centers about E-
flat; yet here, as throughout the symphony, tonality is handled in extremely free fashion.

III. *Vivace.* The scherzo is a kind of rustic waltz which captures

the atmosphere of the country fair. As in the first movement, the
vitality of the music derives from unflagging rhythm. Notice the deft
tapering off at the end.

IV. *Allegro con spirito.* The gaiety of Roussel's finale has something in it of the circus and the music hall, yet it is stamped with refinement. The motto theme interrupts with a lyrical meditation for

solo violin, and reappears at the majestic climax of the movement, bringing the work to a close on a bright G-major cadence.

"It is really marvelous," observed Francis Poulenc of this symphony,
"to combine so much springtime and maturity." The composer of this
delightful work is one of the distinguished figures in modern French
music.

⌇ 37 ⌇

Other Classicists

BOHUSLAV MARTINU (1890–1959)

BOHUSLAV MARTINU was born in Politschka, a town in eastern Bohemia,
the son of a shoemaker. He entered the Prague Conservatory in his
teens, but did not take kindly to academic discipline and was twice expelled from that venerable institution. Martinu spent seventeen years
in Paris, where he studied with Albert Roussel. His music gradually
made its way and brought him a European reputation. The outbreak
of war made him decide to seek refuge in the United States, and he and
his wife left Paris hurriedly in June, 1940, with a single suitcase. During
his stay in the United States Martinu came to grips with the problems
of the symphony, a form he had not hitherto undertaken. His First
Symphony, commissioned by Serge Koussevitzky, was performed by
the Boston Symphony Orchestra in 1942, when the composer was fifty-
two years old. From this period dates the Violin Concerto commissioned by Mischa Elman (1943), as well as the Concerto for two pianos
written for Pierre Luboshutz and Genia Nemenoff (1943). At the end
of the war Martinu was offered a professorship in composition at the
Prague Conservatory, and returned to his native land after an absence
of twenty-three years.

Martinu belonged to the spontaneous type of musician we associate
with Bohemia. He produced a vast amount of music in all the forms and
genres of his art: ten operas, ten ballets, and several choral works; a
varied list of orchestral compositions, among which the six symphonies
are the most important; much chamber music, including five string
quartets; piano pieces; and songs.

Martinu was the most prominent among a new generation of Czech
musicians who looked for inspiration to Paris instead of Vienna. The

neo-classic influence is manifest in such works as the Partita for strings (1931), the Sinfonia for two orchestras (1932) and the Piano Concerto (1935). This classical outlook, as time went on, was tempered with the romantic streak that was at the core of his nature. He turned to Czech song and dance, and found himself as an artist by asserting the relationship between music and the life of the emotions. In works such as the Double Concerto for two string orchestras, piano, and kettledrums (1940), which was written after the betrayal of his country at Munich, he echoed the mood of a tragic time. Out of the same current of feeling came the *Mass at Camp* for baritone, male chorus, wind, and percussion (1939), and the *Memorial to Lidice* (1943).

Martinu succeeded in amalgamating Czech musical traditions with contemporary western trends. His clean compact writing abounds in spontaneous melody and kinetic rhythms. He consistently upheld the primacy of expression over technique. In this, as in his carefully wrought music, he was a worthy representative of one of the most musical nations in Europe.

ALFREDO CASELLA (1883–1947)

The Italian school had the difficult task of creating a base for modern instrumental music in a land where Verdi and Puccini reigned supreme. A leader in this development was Alfredo Casella (born in Turin, died in Rome). Advocating a "return to the pure classicism of our ancestors," Casella attempted to lead Italian music away from the nineteenth century; away, too, from the Beethovenian symphony, whose processes of thematic development he considered alien to the Italian tradition, and from impressionism, which he thought had exhausted its force. Casella spent almost twenty years of his life in Paris, where he studied with Fauré. He also came under the influence of Stravinsky, about whom he later wrote a book. He returned to his homeland in 1915.

It was not easy for Casella to find his true path. He leaned for a time toward a picturesque nationalism based on folk material, and was briefly under the influence of Schoenberg. He ultimately found his way to a style based on a lucid contrapuntal texture for which his models were the masters of the late Baroque, especially Bach, Vivaldi, and Scarlatti. This neo-classic orientation, for which he became the chief spokesman in Italy, is apparent in the works of his maturity: the Partita for piano and orchestra (1924), based on old instrumental forms such as the passacaglia, *gagliarda* and *giga*; the *Concerto Romano* of 1926; and *Scarlattiana* for piano and orchestra (1927). Casella's output includes operas; ballets, of which the best known is *La Giara* (The Jar, 1924), a "choreographic comedy" after Pirandello; choral and orchestral works, concertos, chamber music, piano pieces, and songs. He wrote a theoretical work, translated into English as *The Evolution of Music through the History of the Perfect Cadence,* which reveals the wide culture and trenchant thinking that made Casella a leader of musical modernism in Italy.

GIAN FRANCESCO MALIPIERO (1882–)

Gian Francesco Malipiero (born in Venice) ably seconded the efforts of his friend Casella to revive the traditions of the Italian Baroque. His monumental edition of the complete works of Claudio Monteverdi, in sixteen volumes, was a labor of love that left an indelible mark upon his own music. Equally significant is his edition of the complete works of Antonio Vivaldi. Malipiero moved away from the thematic development and recapitulation that is the basic technique of German symphonism, adopting instead the Baroque interplay of contrapuntal lines within a continuous texture. His dislike of thematic development inclines him, both in his instrumental and vocal music, toward the short forms. Malipiero's melody has absorbed elements both from sixteenth-century Italian song and Gregorian chant. His fondness for setting old texts goes hand-in-hand with his affinity for modal harmony and a certain archaic atmosphere. He strongly opposes what he considers the false sentimentality of late-nineteenth century Italian opera, especially Puccini. His models are the operatic masters of the seventeenth and eighteenth centuries—Cavalli, Cesti, Monteverdi—and the *commedia dell'arte.*

Malipiero's huge output includes over twenty operas, eleven symphonies, a dozen choral works of ample dimension, four ballets, four piano concertos, seven string quartets, piano music, and songs. From this list one may single out his first string quartet, *Rispetti e Strambotti* (Ditties and Roundelays, 1920); the opera *La favola del figlio cambiato* (Fable of the Changed Son, 1933), on Pirandello's text; two operas based on Shakespeare—*Giulio Cesare* (1935) and *Antonio e Cleopatra* (1938); and a *Missa Pro Mortuis* to mark the passing of his friend, Gabriele d'Annunzio (1938).

VITTORIO RIETI (1898–)

Vittorio Rieti represents that segment of modern Italian music which is oriented toward French neo-classicism. His long residence in Paris, which has been his home as much as Rome, has imparted to his music a cosmopolitan character. Rieti was born in Alexandria, Egypt, of Italian parents. He studied briefly with Respighi, came under the influence of Casella, and learned more from the scores of Stravinsky than from any teacher. He came to maturity as an artist through his collaboration with Diaghilev, who produced his ballet *Barabau* in London in 1925 and *Le Bal* at Monte Carlo in 1929. Rieti's harmonic language is strongly tonal in that at any given moment it is directly related to a center; but the center is constantly shifting, so that an attractive tension is set up between the stability of the various sections and the unstable tonality of the whole. His orchestral coloring is vivid, the texture light; his rhythms have a balletic impulsion.

Rieti's copious output includes operas, ballets, choral works, orchestral and chamber music, concertos, piano pieces, and some extremely effective songs. The *Second Avenue Waltzes* for two pianos (1944), Fifth Symphony (1945), Third String Quartet (1953), and Quintet for Woodwinds (1958) show the elegance of his instrumental writing. The Partita for harpsichord, flute, oboe, and string quartet (1945), which has been recorded, combines Rieti's Italian lyricism with the formal procedures of French neo-classicism. The one-act opera *Don Perlimplin* (1949), on a poetic drama by Federico García Lorca, unites elements of *commedia dell'arte* with those of romantic opera. A one-acter, *The Pet Shop* (1959), is by turns humorous, whimsical and tender, although the libretto comes nowhere near the music in wit and fancy.

Rieti settled in the United States in 1939 and became an American citizen some years later. His refined art avoids all that smacks of the rhetorical, seeking to charm rather than to impress. Behind it stands a composer who is irresistibly drawn to whatever is subtle and urbane.

WILLEM PIJPER (1894–1947)

Willem Pijper (born in Zeist, near Utrecht, died in Leidschendam) is the chief figure among modern Dutch composers. His parents intended him to become a church organist; his own desire was to be a pianist. At the Utrecht Music School, which he entered at the age of seventeen, he changed to theory and composition. His early works show the influence of Debussy; his First Symphony (1917) was written under the shadow of Mahler. From these beginnings Pijper developed a personal style based upon a firmly classical alignment. This approach is evident in a series of large instrumental works of an abstract nature that show Pijper's affinity for polymodal and polytonal—more accurately, bitonal—writing and polyrhythmic movement. His music is based on triadic harmonies which he often combined in two independent streams, from whose interplay he derived incisive dissonantal combinations. Pijper also experimented with a synthetic scale consisting of an alternation of semitones and whole tones: C, D-flat, E-flat, E-natural, F-sharp, G, A, B-flat. In the buildup of his music he favored a technique based upon the expansion of germinal motives or fragments into larger theme groups, resulting in formal clarity and logic.

Pijper's progress toward simplification of style and directness of thought may be traced in his Second and Third Symphonies (1921, 1926); the Piano Concerto (1926), Cello Concerto (1936), and Violin Concerto (1938); as well as in two sonatas for violin and piano and two for cello and piano. The chamber music includes five string quartets (1914–46, the last unfinished); a Sextet for wind instruments and piano (1923); and a Quintet for flute, oboe, clarinet, bassoon, and horn (1929). In his chamber music, as in his orchestral and choral writing, Pijper shows a predilection for an elaborate contrapuntal texture with emphasis on canonic imitation and similar devices. He made a study of the folk songs of his country, and based several of his choral works on the ancient ballads of Holland. Characteristic of this preoccupation are two major choral works, *Heer Halewijn* (1920) and *Heer Danielken* (1925), both for unaccompanied eight-part chorus. The first also supplied the material for his opera—he called it a "symphonic drama"—*Halewijn* (1934). His second opera, *Merlijn* (1939–46), based on the legendary magician of the ancient Celtic tales, was left unfinished at the time of his death.

As head of the Rotterdam Conservatory Pijper trained a large number of pupils and strongly influenced the younger generation of Dutch composers.

MARCEL POOT (1901–)

Marcel Poot, who was born at Vilvorde, near Brussels, is the best known among contemporary Belgian composers. He was educated at the Brussels Conservatory and continued his studies at the Royal Flemish Conservatory of Antwerp. In 1925 he founded, in association with seven other young composers, a group known as *Synthétistes*, dedicated to the propagation of musical modernism. Poot's musical personality is marked by a rhythmic vivacity and a rare ability to treat humorous subjects. These manifested themselves in the first work in which he found his style, a set of three symphonic sketches entitled *Charlot*, which were inspired by Charlie Chaplin's films (1926). Poot's classicism derives from the Stravinskyan canon. He does not eschew emotional expression, but spices it with a kind of "scherzo-ness," as Prokofiev called it, which is somewhat related in mood to the impish, ironic quality that the Russian master favored in his early years. This love of gaiety informs such works as the *Ouverture joyeuse* (1934). Poot's rejection of romantic grandiloquence goes hand in hand with his desire for concision of form and sobriety of color.

Poot's technique expresses itself in clear-cut designs based in the main on a strongly tonal idiom. His passing involvement with jazz produced the *Jazz Music* of 1930. A prolific composer, Poot has written operas, oratorios, an operetta, two ballets; a variety of orchestral works, including two symphonies (1935, 1951); chamber music; and works for various instruments. Poot plays a leading part in the musical life of his country. He is director of the Brussels Conservatory; a member of the music committee of the Ministry of Public Education; president of the Royal Flemish Academy; an adviser to the Belgian Broadcasting Company; and president of *Sabam*, the Belgian association of composers.

BORIS BLACHER (1903–)

Boris Blacher was born in Newchwang, China, of Estonian-German parentage. He went to Berlin at the age of nineteen, and after completing his studies in composition followed courses in musicology at Berlin University. Blacher fell upon hard times during the Nazi regime. His uncompromising modernism was unacceptable to the then arbiters of German musical taste, and his works were proscribed as "degenerate." After the Second World War Blacher's music quickly took its rightful place on the contemporary scene. In 1948 he was appointed professor of composition at the Hochschule für Musik in West Berlin, and in 1953 succeeded Werner Egk as director of the school.

Blacher's is an idiom of striking originality, based upon free atonal counterpoint. His adherence to the neo-classic esthetic manifests itself in his fondness for terseness and directness of expression. His orchestral writing is bright, vivid, and thinned out according to a careful selection of instruments. The result is a lightness and transparency which is at the opposite pole from the fat sound of German postromanticism. The rhythmic subtlety of Blacher's music derives from a technique of "variable meters" that are worked out according to definite mathematical progressions. The meter changes from bar to bar according to a pre-existent series which applies to rhythm the tone-row principle of twelve-tone music. (See Ch. 53.) Yet Blacher does not transform this technique into a system, leaving himself free to vary it according to his needs. His penchant for satire and irony goes hand in hand with a suppleness and volatility that are not often found in German music. The classical strain is further apparent in Blacher's predilection for eighteenth-century forms, drawn either from the late Baroque, as in the *Concertante Music* (1937) and Partita for string orchestra and percussion (1945), or from the high classical period, as in the Divertimento for wind orchestra (1935) and Divertimento for trumpet, trombone, and piano (1944).

Blacher's operas include *Fürstin Tarakanowa* (Countess Tarakanova, 1941); a one-act chamber opera, *Die Flut* (The Deluge, 1946); *Das preussisches Märchen* (Prussian Fairytale, 1952), an opera-ballet; and *Abstract Opera No. 1*, for three soloists, two reciters, chorus, and orchestra (1951). Blacher has written several ballets, among them *Hamlet* (1950) and *Lysistrata* (1951). He has cultivated successfully a type of dramatic work intermediate between opera and oratorio, examples of which are *Romeo und Julia*, a "scenic oratorio" after Shakespeare, for soprano, tenor, small chorus, and chamber orchestra, and *Der Grossinquisitor* (The Grand Inquisitor), a "dramatic oratorio" after Dostoievsky, for baritone, chorus, and orchestra. Among his important instrumental works are the *Variations on a Theme by Paganini*, for orchestra (1947); two piano concertos (1948, 1952); *Ornaments*, based on "variable meters"; and three string quartets (1941–49). These, together with his stage works, establish his position as one of the outstanding representatives of the modern movement in Germany today.

OTHER CLASSICISTS

Alan Bush (London, 1900–) has moved, especially since the war, from the complexities of his earlier works to a more accessible idiom. His Marxist convictions have impelled him to seek a means of communicating with the mass of music lovers, and have also been responsible for the political programs he attaches to certain of his works. Bush has developed a "thematic" technique in which, as he explains, every note must be thematically significant. Therewith he strives to attain through serial procedures the same kind of formal integration as does the twelve-tone composer, although within a tonal frame and on the basis of triadic harmony. His attempts to simplify his language have led him from a rather severe style based on counterpoint to an ever greater emphasis on the sensuous aspects of harmony. This development has gone hand in hand with a progression from cosmopolitanism to an increased re-

liance on distinctly national elements. A sense of drama shapes his large
works. Among his principal compositions are *Dialectic* for string quartet
(1929); Piano Concerto, with baritone solo and men's chorus in the
last movement (1937); *The Winter Journey*, for soprano, baritone,
chorus, string quintet, and harp (1946); Violin Concerto (1948); Symphony No. 2, *Nottingham* (1949); and the opera *Wat Tyler* (1950),
which was first performed in Germany.

Lennox Berkeley (Boar's Hill, near Oxford, 1903–) studied in Paris
with Nadia Boulanger, from whom he imbibed the Stravinskyan esthetic
that strongly influenced his thinking. His commitment to neo-classic
ideals manifests itself in the transparency of his texture, the delicacy
of his orchestration, and his addiction to gently dissonant counterpoint of a diatonic nature. In his earlier works he was inclined to a
certain looseness of form. He has moved closer to the classical concept
of form, striving for terse, lucid structures in which the melodic element plays an important part. Berkeley's graceful writing inclines towards the miniature; hence his affinity for the short forms. His comic
chamber opera *The Dinner Engagement*, presented at the Aldeburgh
Festival in 1954, is a more fully realized work than is his grand opera,
Nelson (1951). The *Stabat Mater* for six solo voices and chamber orchestra (1940) shows Berkeley's lyricism and his sensitive ear for tone
colors. His orchestral works include the Serenade for Strings (1939),
Symphony No. 1 (1940), Divertimento in B-flat (1943), and the lyrical
Nocturne (1945). Berkeley has also written theater and film music,
concertos, chamber music, works for various instruments, a quantity
of piano music, and songs.

The music of Michael Tippett (London, 1905–) proceeds from a
forceful personality. It is intelligent, technically expert, and marked
by contrapuntal originality. Its emotional content is apt to be controlled,
in the larger works, by preoccupations of a severely intellectual order.
Tippett's complex rhythms owe as much to the suppleness of the English
madrigal as to either Stravinsky or Bartók. His is a polyphonic conception based on melodic line, but the melodic writing is highly ornamented. Tippett does not share the twentieth-century aversion to literal
repetition. As a result, his forms have a simplicity of outline that contrasts with their abstract content. Chief among Tippett's choral pieces
is *A Child of our Time*, an oratorio for solo voices, chorus, and orchestra
on his own text (1941). His opera *The Midsummer Marriage* (1951)
is based on his own libretto. Tippett's instrumental output, from the
Concerto for double string orchestra (1939) to the Symphony No. 1
(1945), shows a steady growth toward concentration of thought and

a rather austere type of expression. He has written three string quartets (1935–46); a *Fantasy on a Theme by Handel* for piano and orchestra (1941); and a variety of works for piano, for organ, and for voice.

Alan Rawsthorne (Haslingden, Lancashire, 1905–) represents that section of the New Classicism which finds inspiration in the Baroque rather than in the classical era proper. He is more at home with the continuous expansion techniques of the age of Bach than with the balanced sections and tonal contrasts of the sonata of Mozart and Haydn. The variation procedures and the concerto grosso of the seventeenth and early eighteenth centuries have strongly influenced his idiom, which is marked by consistency of texture and nervous intensity of expression. His music is fluent and readily communicates its emotional content. It fluctuates restlessly from one key to the next; the resultant tonal instability, if anything, heightens its appeal. Rawsthorne is unique among the English composers of his generation in that he devotes himself almost exclusively to instrumental music. His harmonic language is expressively chromatic, and is projected by means of a lively figuration that shows his natural affinity for instrumental writing. Rawsthorne's direct kind of eloquence has given his works a currency in his homeland not frequently achieved by contemporary music. He is widely known for the *Symphonic Studies* (1938), two piano concertos (1943, 1951), and the Violin Concerto of 1947. He has also written a symphony (1950), several overtures, chamber music, pieces for various instruments, music for films and radio productions, songs, and *A Canticle of Man* for baritone, chorus, flute, and strings (1953).

Gottfried von Einem (1918–) was born in Switzerland; his father was the Austrian military attaché at Berne. He grew up in Germany; was imprisoned by the Gestapo for four months when he was twenty; studied with Boris Blacher, who helped him further by writing librettos for his operas; and was strongly influenced by such composers as Stravinsky, Milhaud, and Prokofiev. Einem was also attracted to jazz, especially to the music of George Gershwin and Duke Ellington. He made his name when his opera *Dantons Tod* (Danton's Death), based on the drama by Georg Büchner, was produced at the Salzburg Festival in 1947. Einem's second opera, *Der Prozess* (The Trial, 1953), is based on Kafka's chilling story of a man who is accused and convicted, yet never discovers of what. With its angular vocal line, which is of the expressionistic persuasion, its strong component of jazz, and its dexterous counterpoint, *The Trial* looks back to the operas that were being written in Berlin in the Twenties. The work has a profile, and succeeds in conjuring up the hallucinatory atmosphere of Kafka's story. Einem has

also written a variety of compositions reflecting his neo-classic approach
to the absolute forms of instrumental music. Among these are the
Capriccio for Orchestra, Concerto for Orchestra, *Orchestermusik*, Serenade for Double String Orchestra, Piano Concerto Opus 20, Symphonic Scenes, Opus 22, and—for the Louisville Symphony—*Meditations for Orchestra* (1954), which is more romantic in tone.

Jacques Ibert (Paris, 1890–1962) is a facile composer who combines
impressionist and neo-classic techniques. He is best known for *Escales*
(Ports of Call, 1922), a set of three symphonic sketches; the *Concertino
da camera* for alto saxophone and small orchestra (1934); and the amusing *Angélique* (1927), the most successful of his six operas. He has also
written ballets; incidental, radio, and film music; choral, orchestral, and
chamber works; piano pieces; and songs. From 1937 to 1955 Ibert was
director of the French Academy in Rome.

Jean Françaix (Le Mans, 1912–) studied composition with Nadia
Boulanger. The Concertino for piano and orchestra, written when he
was twenty, shows his neo-classic bent. Among his works are the Trio
for violin, viola and cello (1933); String Quartet, and Quintet for violin,
viola, cello, flute, and harp (1934); Quartet for saxophones (1935);
and Divertissement for bassoon and string quintet (1942).

Igor Markevitch (Kiev, 1912–) is one of the younger composers
who came out of the Diaghilev circle. A pupil of Nadia Boulanger,
he bases his style on dissonant counterpoint within a strongly tonal
frame, as in his Sinfonietta (1928), Concerto Grosso (1929), and Partita
for piano and orchestra (1936). In a more romantic style are a huge
cantata based on *Paradise Lost* (1936), and *Lorenzo the Magnificent*
(1941), a cantata for soprano and orchestra. Markevitch has achieved
a reputation as a conductor both in Europe and America.

VI. NATIONALISTS

"Every composer cannot expect to have a worldwide message, but he may reasonably expect to have a special message for his own people. Is it not reasonable to suppose that those who share our life, our history, our customs, our climate, even our food, should have some secret to impart to us which the foreign composer, though he be perhaps more imaginative, more powerful, more technically equipped, is not able to give us? This is the secret of the national composer, the secret to which he only has the key."

Ralph Vaughan Williams

⋅§ 38 §⋅

The New Nationalism

"A genuine peasant melody of our land is a musical example of perfected art. I consider it quite as much of a masterpiece—in miniature—as a Bach fugue or Mozart sonata is a masterpiece in the larger forms."

Béla Bartók

NATIONALISM in music was a powerful current within nineteenth-century romanticism. National tensions on the Continent—the pride of the conquering nations, and the struggles for freedom of the subjugated ones—gave rise to emotions that found ready expression in music. The German war of liberation against Napoleon inspired Carl Maria von Weber and created a receptive atmosphere for his opera *Der Freischütz*. Poland's struggle for freedom from Czarist rule aroused the national poet in Chopin; Franz Liszt explored the Gypsy idiom of his native Hungary. A united Italy seeking independence from Austria found her national artist in Verdi. Wagner reached the zenith of his career in the newly constituted German Empire, which viewed his epic dramas, based on Teutonic legends, as a monument to national pride. Smetana and Dvořák in Bohemia, Grieg in Norway, the Russian national school—these marked the emancipation of the "younger" nations (musically speaking) from the yoke of the three older musical cultures, Italy, Germany, and France. Musical nationalism retained its vigor into the twentieth century. In the postromantic era national composers appeared in Finland, Hungary, England, Spain, Poland, Czechoslovakia, and Romania, to be joined a little later by national schools in the United States and Latin America.

Nineteenth-century nationalism added a variety of idioms to the language of European music. It exploited the picturesque aspects of local color, and fed the romantic predilection for mood and atmosphere. By associating music with love of country, nationalism aligned the art with the great social and political movements of the age, so that composers were able to give expression to the deepest aspirations of millions of people. The romantic composers idealized the life of the folk. They heard peasant tunes through a poetic haze of myth and legend. If these tunes departed from the major-minor scale or from accepted metrical patterns, the composer "corrected" the irregularities. In general, the romantics regarded the folk song as workable material to be embedded —like some piquant flavoring—in orchestral movement molded to the formulas of classical symphonism.

Twentieth-century nationalism, understandably, took a different turn. The new nationalists brought recording equipment into the field, and—as we saw with Bartók—mastered the techniques of scientific research. They took special care not to violate the essential character of the folk tunes. "It was not a question," Bartók wrote, "of merely taking unique melodies in any which way and then incorporating them, or parts of them, in our works, there to develop them according to the traditional formulas. What we had to do was to divine the spirit of this unknown music and to make this spirit, so difficult to describe in words, the basis of our own works."

Twentieth-century interest in folk song went hand in hand with the upsurge of interest in old music. Many of the authentic peasant tunes had originated long before the major-minor system. They had much to offer a generation of musicians who were striving to escape the nineteenth-century sound. Instead of smoothing out the ancient songs to make them fit the rules of major-minor harmony and regular meter, contemporary composers treasured precisely those characteristics of the melodic line that departed from standard patterns. They gloried in the freshness of this material, deriving from the old tunes all manner of novel harmonies, asymmetrical rhythms, new conceptions of melody and form.

We should distinguish between the *nationalist* composer, who deliberately emphasizes national characteristics in his art, and the *national* composer, who may embody them in his work without having to make any special effort because they form the basic layer of his thinking and feeling. The national composer is apt to be the more universal, hence the more accessible to the world at large. The nationalist composer may be more picturesque, but he is more limited in his appeal. Tchaikovsky is a national composer; Rimsky-Korsakov, one would be inclined to say, is a nationalist. Bartók is a national composer; Kodály is a nationalist. Sometimes, of course, an artist may move from one level to the other. Sibelius, for example, in his early tone poems emphasized picturesque local color and legendry in the manner of the nationalist composer. In his later symphonies he was a national composer, subjecting his material to a process of stylization in abstract works that brought to the fore the universal aspects of his art. A similar development may be observed in nationalists like Vaughan Williams and Manuel de Falla.

Nationalism in music has certainly not been as important a force in the twentieth century as it was in the romantic era. Yet it was still sufficiently powerful to create schools, to inspire composers, and to produce works that enjoy wide popularity in our time.

⤛§ 39 §⤜

Manuel de Falla (1876-1946)

"Our music must be based on the natural music of our people. In our dance and our rhythm we possess the strongest of traditions that no one can obliterate."

THE MUSICAL renascence in Spain at the end of the nineteenth century followed lines similar to those we have traced in England and Hungary. On the one hand, there was a revival of interest in the sixteenth-century masters, such as Tomas Luís de Victoria, Morales, and Cabezón. On the other there was a turning to authentic folk music based on modes that antedated the major-minor. Prime mover of the renascence was Felipe Pedrell (1841–1922). As a composer Pedrell is all but forgotten. But his teachings fell on fertile ground; he raised a generation of composers. Albéniz and Granados profited from his pioneering. His most distinguished pupil was Manuel de Falla, who became the leading figure of the modern Spanish school.

HIS LIFE

Falla was born in Cadiz of a family of merchants. His esthetic goals were shaped by his three years of study with Pedrell. Falla's career got under way in 1905 when his opera *La Vida breve* (Life is Short) won first prize in a competition held by the Academy of Fine Arts at Madrid. That year he also won a prize for his piano playing.

Despite this success, his hopes for a production of *La Vida breve* were not fulfilled. Falla's thoughts turned increasingly to Paris, at that time the Mecca of all progressive musicians. It was not until 1907 that he was able to realize his ambition. "Without Paris," he later wrote, "I would have remained buried in Madrid, submerged and forgotten, dragging out an obscure existence, living miserably by giving a few lessons, with the prize certificate framed as a family memento and the score of my opera in a cupboard." Instead, he was catapulted into the mainstream of European music. He was befriended by Debussy and Ravel. More important, his opera made an impression on Paul Dukas, who set about getting it produced. *La Vida breve* was given first at Nice in 1913, and toward the end of that year was produced in Paris at the Opéra-Comique. It scored a resounding success and established Falla's reputation.

The outbreak of hostilities in 1914 made it necessary for him to return to his homeland. He was soon acknowledged as the leading musician of Spain and enjoyed something of the status of a national artist. After seven years in Madrid, Falla moved to Granada, where he found a quieter mode of life which suited his retiring disposition. The years of civil war were a time of intense anguish for the sensitive, deeply religious composer; he had strong ties on both sides. After Franco's victory, the new regime was eager to honor him, and in 1938 he was named president of the Institute of Spain. But Falla found it difficult to accommodate himself to the new order. When an opportunity arose to conduct an orchestra in Buenos Aires, he eagerly accepted the invitation.

He left Spain in 1939 and spent the last seven years of his life in voluntary exile in Argentina. He lived in the town of Alta Gracia, in the heart of the "New Andalusia" which could never mean as much to him as the old. There he died in November, 1946.

HIS MUSIC

Falla's was not a sustained kind of creativity. Although he was granted the Biblical span of three score and ten, his fame rests on half a dozen works, almost all of them—with the exception of *La Vida breve*—composed between 1915 and 1925. Falla was an exacting artist who set high standards for himself; but these standards apparently became so inhibiting that after he passed his fiftieth year the creative impulse no longer asserted itself with anything of the old certainty.

Falla belonged to that group of nationalist composers who feel that their imagination is constrained by the use of existing folk tunes. Hence his slogan, "Truth without authenticity." To him this meant that he was free to create the artistic truth as he saw it, without limiting himself to what was externally authentic but not of his own coinage. We will find no authentic folk tunes in his works. Yet his music is unfailingly true to the image we have of Spain.

Falla was not primarily an operatic composer. His temperament was lyric rather than dramatic. Nevertheless *La Vida breve* abounds in lovely sounds that evoke the landscape of his native Andalusia. The Andalusian style (which most people identify as "Spanish") is continued in the one-act ballet *El Amor brujo*, which we will discuss. In 1915 Falla completed his three "symphonic impressions," *Noches en los jardines de España* (Nights in the Gardens of Spain), for piano and orchestra, in which the Spanish idiom is combined with French impressionism. His so-called Andalusian period came to an end with the ballet *El Sombrero de tres picos* (The Three-Cornered Hat, 1919), a humorous work based on Alarcón's *The Magistrate and the Miller's Wife*. (Hugo Wolf used the same story for his opera *Der Corregidor*.)

The national element is less prominent in Falla's last works; yet they are none the less characteristic of the composer and his heritage. *El Retablo de Maese Pedro* (Master Pedro's Puppet-Show, 1919), an opera for marionettes and singers based on an incident in *Don Quixote*, recreates the era of Cervantes. The Concerto for harpsichord—or piano—and flute, oboe, clarinet, violin, and cello (1926) evokes, in the solo part, the classical keyboard style of Domenico Scarlatti (who spent the major part of his career in Spain). This is one of Falla's most distinguished works. The Spanish idiom is here refined and stylized, and in the process is lifted above the realm of the picturesquely local.

EL AMOR BRUJO
(BEWITCHED BY LOVE)

In *El Amor brujo* (1915)—which has also been variously translated as *Love the Magician* and *The Specter's Bride*—Falla conjures up the rapturous melodic line of the Andalusian Gypsies, with its oriental coloring and fanciful ornamentation. The action revolves about the theme of exorcism that is to be found in the folklore of all countries. The beautiful Candelas has been in love with a dissolute Gypsy who, now that he is dead, returns to haunt her. She is loved by the handsome Carmelo. Spellbound by the ghost of her former sweetheart, she is unable to grant Carmelo the kiss of love which alone can release her. Carmelo, knowing the habits of his dead rival, decides to trick him. He persuades Lucia, a friend of Candelas, to flirt with the specter, who immediately is smitten with her. Carmelo is thus able to convince Candelas that his love for her is greater than that of the dead man. As day dawns the bells of the village chime; Candelas and her swain exchange the kiss of love. The ghost is forever exorcised.

The music opens with the impassioned motto theme that runs through the score.

The next number, *In the Cave*, shows Falla's imaginative use of woodwinds and brass to evoke a sinister atmosphere. A rhapsodic solo on the oboe introduces the *Song of Injured Love*, which projects the emotional intensity we associate with flamenco singing. Note the guitar sound that pervades the orchestral accompaniment. Some properly ghostly measures suggest the coming of the specter. The *Dance of Terror* that follows, with its insistent rhythm and its repeated-note figure on the muted trumpet, is in Falla's most characteristic vein.

There is an interlude; then the clock strikes twelve. Candelas tries to drive away the evil spirit to the strains of one of the most popular—and frenetic—pieces of twentieth-century music, the *Ritual Fire Dance*, which mobilizes the hypnotic effect of repetition, gradual crescendo, and ostinato rhythm. The motto theme reappears, followed by an ornate cantilena shared by flute and oboe. The *Song of the Will-o'-the-Wisp* is in Andalusian folk style. The orchestra then plays one of Falla's most alluring melodies, in a supple 7/8 meter compounded of alternating groups of 3 and 4. In the *Dance of the Game of Love*, the voice traces a sinuous melody in syncopated rhythm against a guitar-like accompaniment. Finally, the morning bells ring out the glad tidings that love conquers all.

Throughout the Twenties Falla was one of the best known among modern composers; one of the very few who were able to live on their royalties and performance fees without having to seek other means of livelihood. Now that the public has begun to catch up with contemporary music, interest has turned to those who have come more directly to grips with twentieth-century problems. Nonetheless, Falla's colorful rhythm and evocative melodies continue to delight a worldwide audience. And in Spanish lands Manuel de Falla—like Delius in England and Sibelius in Finland—is regarded as a major figure.

✑ 40 ཉ
Ernest Bloch (1880-1959)

"I am a Jew. I aspire to write Jewish music because it is the only way in which I can produce music of vitality—if I can do such a thing at all."

ERNEST BLOCH found his personal style through mystical identification with the Hebraic spirit. His response to his heritage was on the deepest psychic level. "It is the Jewish soul that interests me, the complex glowing agitated soul that I feel vibrating throughout the Bible: the freshness and naivete of the Patriarchs, the violence of the books of the Prophets, the Jew's savage love of justice, the despair of Ecclesiastes, the sorrow and immensity of the Book of Job, the sensuality of the Song of Songs. It is all this that I strive to hear in myself and to translate in my music—the sacred emotion of the race that slumbers deep in our soul."

HIS LIFE

Bloch was born in Geneva, the son of a dealer in clocks. He began his studies with Jaques-Dalcroze in Geneva, and subsequently entered the Conservatoire at Brussels where he worked with the celebrated violinist Ysaÿe. After further study in Germany he produced his first major composition, a symphony, at the age of twenty-two. The young musician hopefully made his way to Paris. Unable to obtain a hearing, he fell prey to discouragement, returned to Switzerland and entered his father's business. He continued, however, to compose at night; and in this way he wrote his opera *Macbeth*. The manuscript, submitted to the Opéra-Comique in Paris, was accepted. *Macbeth* was produced in 1910. The work, which was extremely advanced for its time, made so profound an impression on Romain Rolland that he journeyed to Geneva expressly to meet Bloch, and became a zealous propagandist for the younger man's art.

In 1916 Bloch came to the United States as conductor for the dancer Maud Allen and her company. This venture came to grief, leaving him stranded, but his presence did not long go unnoticed. He was invited to conduct his *Trois Poèmes juifs* (Three Jewish Poems) with the Boston Symphony Orchestra. He settled in New York and taught for a time at the Mannes School of Music. In 1919 he won the Elizabeth Sprague Coolidge Award with his *Suite for Viola and Orchestra*. Performances and prizes came to him in profusion during the next decade, which marked the peak of his vogue with the public.

In 1920 Bloch was appointed director of the Cleveland Institute of Music. His advanced ideas about teaching and his unreadiness to compromise with boards of directors made his administration a stormy one. In 1925 he was forced to resign. Bloch then became director of the San Francisco Conservatory, where he remained till 1930. Among his students were Roger Sessions, Douglas Moore, Bernard Rogers, Randall Thompson, Frederick Jacobi, Quincy Porter, Ernst Bacon, Theodore Chanler, Mark Brunswick, Ray Green, and George Antheil. The highlight of this decade, as far as his fame was concerned, came in 1927 when his "epic rhapsody" *America*—a gesture of homage to his adopted country—won a three thousand dollar prize offered by the magazine *Musical America*, and was launched simultaneously by the New York Philharmonic, Boston, Chicago, Philadelphia, and San Francisco Symphony Orchestras.

A ten-year grant from a wealthy music lover from San Francisco made it possible for Bloch to give up teaching and devote himself to composition. For three years he lived in retirement in Switzerland. He later visited Italy, where his music was received as warmly as it had been in the United States. *Macbeth*, after more than twenty-five years of neglect, finally came into its own; the opera was revived in Naples and scored a huge success. History, however, intervened to cheat the composer of his belated triumph. In 1938 Mussolini promulgated the antisemitic decrees of his German ally, and the work could no longer be performed.

Bloch returned to the United States at the end of that year. After a lifetime of wandering he found the haven he needed at Agate Beach, a secluded spot in Oregon overlooking the Pacific Ocean, where he spent the last years of his life.

HIS MUSIC

Bloch faced a rather special problem as a nationalist composer. There was no body of indigenous folk music that he could use as source material, since the popular melodies of the Jews were permeated with the idioms of the countries they had lived in. Bloch did, however, have an authentic national inheritance in the cantillation of the synagogue, which is of great antiquity. This florid, monophonic chant has remained free of the influences to which the Jews were subject in the course of their wanderings, for it is sung according to signs written into the sacred texts. The synagogal cantillation, then, with its rapturous Oriental melismas—those ornate passages in the style of improvisation, which figure so prominently in Oriental song—served Bloch as a point of departure and gave him the image he sought to recreate in his music.

Bloch's goal, like Manuel de Falla's, was "truth without authenticity"; that is to say, the creation of a poetic image in convincing musical terms rather than the quotation of actual folk songs. "It is not my purpose or my desire," Bloch stated, "to attempt a 'reconstruction' of Jewish music, or to base my work on melodies more or less authentic. I am not an archaeologist." He rejected the consciously picturesque use of national elements in favor of the kind of nationalism that wells up from the artist's unconscious, coloring his whole outlook on life and binding him to his spiritual heritage with a thousand ineluctable threads. "I have but listened to an inner voice, deep, secret, insistent, ardent, a voice which seemed to come from far beyond myself."

Given in equal degree to sensuous abandon and mystic exaltation, Bloch saw himself as a kind of messianic personality. Yet the Biblical vision represented only one side of Bloch's art. He was also a modern European and a sophisticate, member of an uprooted generation in whom intellect warred with unruly emotion. When he succeeded in imposing order upon the conflicting elements in his style—the German, French, and Swiss, the Hebraic, romantic, and neo-classic—he produced works that stand high among the achievements of our time: the First String Quartet (1916), the Suite for viola and piano (1919), the Sonata for violin and piano No. 1 (1920), and—probably his most sustained work—the noble Quintet for piano and strings (1923). In all these, rhapsodic content is submitted to the discipline of classical form. On the other hand, when his psychic tension lagged, this highly individual artist lapsed into commonplace, as in *America* (1926) and in the "symphonic fresco," *Helvetia*, a tribute to his native land (1928). Ultimately the inner struggle became greater than even so strong a personality could maintain. In his mid-fifties, when he should have been at the height of his powers (and when, ironically, he had achieved the leisure of which every artist dreams), there was a marked slackening of his creative energy. Bloch continued to work into his seventies. Yet with the exception of the *Sacred Service* (1933), the works on which his fame rests were almost all written between his thirtieth and forty-fifth years.

Bloch's compositions stand in direct line of descent from nineteenth-century romanticism. They combine the grand rhetoric of Liszt's Rhapsodies with the imperious gesture, dynamic rhythm, and sumptuous orchestration of the Straussian tone poem, fused by "the passion and the violence" he believed to be the essential characteristics of his nature. Not for him the doctrine promulgated by the Stravinskyites that music is a play of abstract sounding forms. Music to him was an expression of passionate emotion, a vision of splendor, a symbol. His highly charged idiom helped to create a receptive audience for modern music at a time when Stravinsky, Schoenberg, and Bartók were still too advanced for the generality of concert goers. However, as the neo-classic esthetic swept across the Twenties, Bloch could not help feeling that the public which had once hailed him was now worshipping at other altars. A certain disenchantment resulted, which played its part in the slackening of his powers. Bloch was a romantic artist lost in an antiromantic world.

Bloch's "Jewish Cycle" includes his most widely played work, *Schelomo* (Solomon, 1916); the *Israel* Symphony (1912–16); *Trois Poèmes juifs* (1913); Psalms 114 and 137 for soprano and orchestra, and Psalm 22 for baritone and orchestra (1914); *Baal Schem*, on Jewish legends, for violin and piano (1923, subsequently arranged for orchestra); and *Voice in the Wilderness* for cello and chamber orchestra (1936). We mentioned that several of Bloch's works lie outside the sphere of the specifically national. The best known of these is the Concerto Grosso for strings with piano obbligato, which Bloch wrote in 1925 as a model for his students in the neo-classic style. To this category belong also several of the later works, such as the Violin Concerto (1938), *Suite Symphonique* (1945), and String Quartet No. 2 (1946). In his non-programmatic compositions we see the tone poet refining the picturesque national elements in his idiom, sublimating them in order to achieve greater abstraction and universality of style.

SCHELOMO (SOLOMON)

HEBRAIC RHAPSODY FOR VIOLONCELLO AND FULL ORCHESTRA

Bloch's musical portrayal of King Solomon (1916) evokes a Biblical landscape now harsh and austere, now lush and opulent; an antique region wreathed in the splendor that attaches to a land one has never seen. This image is projected with all the exuberance of a temperament whose natural utterance inclined to the impassioned and the grandiose. The music conjures up the image of Solomon in all his glory—king and warrior, poet and lover, sage and prophet; the builder of the Temple, the sensualist of the *Song of Songs*, the keen wit of the Proverbs, finally the disenchanted Preacher proclaiming that all is vanity.

The rhapsody is a congenial form for Bloch. It lends itself to his favorite method of fashioning a work out of fully developed melodic forms that flower into one another (as opposed to the tightly knit development of themes and motives which constitutes the classical method of the symphony). *Schelomo* ranges over a variety of moods, from brooding introversion to rhetorical flourishes, that are woven into a unity through consistency of tone and texture. The piece is conceived in terms of a twofold contrast—between the dark singing tone of the cello and the full orchestral sound; and that between the high and low registers of the solo instrument. The dotted-note rhythm that dominates the first part of the work, like the repeated-note figure that comes to the fore in its second half, serves to propel a species of "endless melody" which, in its nervous expressivity, suggests Oriental cantillation. The wide leaps, sinuous arabesques and supple rhythms of the cello part are

set against a background abounding in pageantry and exaltation. One feels the absence of a firmly welded architecture; yet formal restraint would hardly accord with the rapturous mood of the piece.

Bloch's kind of music is not in fashion at the moment. But fashions change more quickly than we suspect. His eclipse may prove to be as temporary as the eclipse that overtook Tchaikovsky and Mendelssohn a quarter-century ago. If he seems at the moment to be cut off from the mainstream of contemporary musical thought, it is quite likely that, as his distinguished pupil Roger Sessions prophesies, "the adjustments of history will restore to him his true place among the artists who have spoken most commandingly the language of conscious emotion."

⊰ 41 ⊱
Other Nationalists

SINCE BARTÓK's death Zoltán Kodály has been the acknowledged leader of the Hungarian national school. He was born in 1882 in the town of Kecskemet and received his training at the Royal Academy of Music in Budapest, where Béla Bartók was one of his classmates. In 1906 he began his momentous collaboration with Bartók, with whom he journeyed to outlying villages to study folk music. A visit to Paris in the following year brought him into contact with the music of Debussy. He returned home to join the faculty of the Academy of Music in Budapest, where he has taught for the greater part of his career. Kodály's idiom is markedly less radical than that of Bartók. It avoids the percussive dissonance and primitive rhythms that played so important a part in Bartók's art. Kodály's music is strongly tonal. Tinged with romantic and impressionist elements, it is written in a strongly national idiom that is forthright, vigorous, and pleasing.

Kodály's great success came in 1923 with the *Psalmus Hungaricus*, a setting of Psalm LV for tenor, chorus, children's voices, and orchestra, which conquered the public in the same spectacular fashion as did Honegger's *King David*. Three years later he completed *Háry János*, a play with music centering about the exploits of a retired old soldier of exuberant imagination, one of those quixotic, lovable characters who abound in the peasant lore of eastern Europe. The suite that Kodály fashioned from this work spread his name throughout the world. Kodály's catalogue of works includes music for the theater; church music, in which field his most impressive achievement is the *Budavári Te Deum* (1936); a large amount of choral music, a medium for which he has a particular affinity; a variety of orchestral compositions, among them the *Dances of Galanta* (1934), *Variations on a Hungarian Folk-*

song (1939), and *Concerto for Orchestra* (1941); a substantial number of chamber works, including two string quartets (1908, 1917); piano music, organ works, and songs. Kodály today is the elder statesman of Hungary's cultural life. His compatriots have recognized his achievements by electing him to the National Assembly and to the presidency of the National Arts Council of Hungary.

In the twentieth-century concert of nations, Georges Enesco (Liveni, Romania, 1881–1955, Paris) was the accredited representative of Romania. He received a solid grounding at the Vienna Conservatory, then went to Paris where he studied with Massenet and Fauré. He was primarily a concert violinist; but in his compositions he went beyond the sphere of his chosen instrument. Piano music, chamber music, songs, and three symphonies are included in his output. Enesco's imagination was captured by the Gypsy fiddlers of his homeland, whose melodies shaped the imagery of his two *Rumanian Rhapsodies* (1901, 1902). These vastly successful pieces, which have passed into the repertory of the "pop" concert, are tuneful and full of dash. More serious in character is the opera *Oedipus*, after the drama of Sophocles, which was produced at the Paris Opera in 1936; but this work failed to win the acceptance accorded his less ambitious compositions. In his later years Enesco became interested in teaching. Yehudi Menuhin is one of several distinguished violinists who owe much to his guidance.

The older generation of Russian composers had the task of bridging the transition from Czarist to Soviet Russia. Chief among them was Reinhold Glière (Kiev, 1875–1956, Moscow), a pupil of Arensky, Taneyev, and Ippolitov-Ivanov. Trained in the romantic style that characterized the Moscow school at the turn of the century, Glière found his way to a colorful manner of expression based on the folk idioms of the Asiatic national groups within the Soviet Union. An extremely prolific composer, he turned out operas, ballets—one of which, *The Red Poppy* (1927), carried his name all over the world—symphonies, symphonic poems, and overtures; chamber music; about two hundred songs; and a like number of piano pieces. His most impressive achievement is his Third Symphony, *Ilya Murometz* (1911), which evokes the epic of a legendary Russian hero. As professor at the Moscow Conservatory he helped train two generations of Soviet composers, among them Miaskovsky, Prokofiev, and Khatchaturian.

Nikolai Miaskovsky (Novogeorgievsk, near Warsaw, 1881–1950, Moscow) is one of those composers who achieve fame within the borders of their homelands without ever winning comparable eminence elsewhere. He was the most prolific symphonist of the first half of the twentieth century, with twenty-seven symphonies (1908–50) to his credit. He also wrote choral and orchestral pieces, nine string quartets, piano music, and songs. Miaskovsky taught at the Moscow Conservatory and influenced several among the younger Soviet composers.

≈§ 42 ß»

The Russians

"Can the true artist stand aloof from life and confine his art within the narrow bounds of subjective emotion? Or should he be where he is needed most, where his words, his music, his chisel can help the people live a better, finer life?"

Sergei Prokofiev

THE SOVIET VIEW

THE RUSSIAN attempt to bridge the gap between contemporary composers and their listeners differs, in one fundamental respect, from similar attempts in our society. With us the decision is left to the individual. In the Soviet Union, on the other hand, the matter is considered to be a concern of the State. The notion that the individual artist creates as a form of self-expression is as alien to the Communist view as the notion that the individual entrepreneur is free to invest in and develop his own business. Art is held to be created for the nation as a whole. It is supposed to reflect Marxist ideology and to educate the public in the Communist way of life.

The musicians of the West, accustomed to complete freedom of choice in all matters pertaining to their art, would find it well-nigh impossible to function within such a frame. Yet the leaders of the Soviet school not only have added a number of significant works to the present-day repertory, but have won immense popularity precisely in the two countries which are farthest removed from the political ideology of their homeland—the United States and England.

The question arises: may we accept their music as a sincere expression of their artistic convictions, or are their works written to please the commissars? It must be remembered that the composers who found it impossible to accept the Soviet regime—Rachmaninov, Stravinsky, Glazunov—left Russia and pursued their careers in exile. On the other hand, musicians like Shostakovich and Khatchaturian, Tikhon Khrennikov and Dmitri Kabalevsky grew up under the Soviet regime. They are products of Soviet education and culture. They have received enormous admiration from their countrymen, honors and rewards from their government. As Virgil Thomson pointed out in a perceptive analysis, "Soviet music is the kind of music it is because the Soviet composers have formally and long ago decided to write it that way, because the Communist party accepts it that way, and because the people apparently take it. Russians mostly, I imagine, believe in their government and country. Certainly these great, official public figures do. They could not, in so severe and censored a period, have become national composers by mere chicanery."

The Soviet composer has to write music that will communicate its meaning to a large circle of listeners. This can be quite a problem. On the other hand, he is sustained in his task by the knowledge that he is needed, and that his music will be published, performed, discussed and listened to eagerly by his compatriots.

SOCIALIST REALISM

The esthetic path officially approved by the Soviet government is known as *socialist realism*. This theory of art stresses the connection between music and the imagery of life, and tends to link musical expression with a strongly emotional content. As Shostakovich explains it, "Bringing into being a work that must be permeated with great ideas and great passions, that must convey through its sounds tragic suspense as well as deep optimism and must reaffirm the beauty and dignity of man—this is the difficult and complicated task demanded by realism."

The emphasis upon art as socially significant communication rather than individual self-expression has its roots in the intellectual climate of nineteenth-century Russia. One has but to read Tolstoi's *What is Art?* to realize how far he stood from the doctrine of art for art's sake that was beginning to conquer the Western world. Musorgsky's letters reveal the same preoccupation. "Art is a means of communicating with mankind," declared this most Russian of composers. "Let us look life boldly in the eye!" Dostoievsky's creed was similar: "My function is to portray the soul of man in all its profundity." And even earlier, Glinka had maintained that "It is the people who create, we composers only arrange."

A similar continuity is to be observed in the music itself. The present generation of Soviet composers studied at the conservatories of Moscow and Leningrad with the pupils and heirs of Rimsky-Korsakov, Musorgsky, Tchaikovsky, and Anton Rubinstein. Despite the great changes that separate them from the Russia of the Czars they have retained the chief characteristics of their forebears: brilliant orchestral coloring; a flair for exciting rhythms; a fondness for direct forms based on repetition and sequence, rather than on the intricacies of thematic-motivic development so dear to the German mind; an exuberant use of folk and popular elements; and exploitation of exotic themes drawn from Asiatic Russia.

If socialist realism is the proper path for the Soviet artist to follow, all that he must not do is summed up under the label of *bourgeois formalism*. This, in Soviet parlance, is always a term of reproach. It implies "an excessive observance of form," or "obedience to stock formulas." Formalists are those who "sacrifice the *substance* of the musical thought for the sake of its *form*." They use their technical skill and mastery "for the sole purpose of disguising the fact that they, for the moment, have no worthy musical thought to express." Soviet opposition to bourgeois formalism is aimed equally at Stravinskyan neo-classicism and the twelve-tone school of Arnold Schoenberg. Both, with their emphasis on abstract technical procedures, are considered to reject the emotional imagery that relates music to life. Both are regarded as representing all that the Soviet composer is supposed to avoid.

THE COMPOSER AND THE GOVERNMENT

If the members of the contemporary Russian school would dutifully follow the path of socialist realism and avoid that of bourgeois formalism, there would be no problem. Soviet composers, however, are like composers everywhere. They are vitally interested in exploring the technical resources of their art. They cannot remain altogether oblivious of the experiments of their Western colleagues. As a result, despite every wish on their part to serve the regime, some of them inevitably come into conflict with the authorities.

As a matter of fact, there was a brief period in the Twenties when modernism in art—in music, poetry, and painting—was made welcome in the Soviet Union. It was not until the Thirties that a wall was erected to shut out foreign influences. This rejection was made manifest in 1936 when *Pravda*, official organ of the Communist Party, launched a scathing attack on Shostakovich's opera *Lady Macbeth of Mzensk*. "The listener is from the very first bewildered by a stream of deliberately discordant sounds. Fragments of melody, beginnings of a musical phrase appear on the surface, are drowned, then emerge again to disappear once again in the roar. To follow this 'music' is difficult; to get anything out of it, impossible. The composer apparently does not set himself the task of listening to the desires and expectations of the Soviet public. He scrambles sounds to make them interesting to formalist esthetes who have lost all good taste."

The problem was in abeyance during the period of the Second World War, when Soviet composers duly expressed in their music their love of country and their joy in its victory. Shortly afterward, however, they again aroused the ire of the government because of their susceptibility to the influence of the West. In January, 1948, they were summoned to a conference by the Central Committee of the Communist Party, at which they were taken to task by Andrei Zhdanov, one of the leading Soviet theoreticians on art, philosophy, and music. In his address to the composers Zhdanov exhorted them to emulate the classical masters, who were able "to obtain unity of brilliant artistic form with profound content, to combine great mastery with simplicity and comprehensibility." He urged them to base their works upon folk song, to concentrate on operatic and program music, admonishing them not to allow their interest in rhythm to tempt them away from the primacy of melody. "The government," he stated, "has given many of you, including those who erred along formalistic lines, Stalin prizes. In doing so, we did not believe that your work was free of shortcomings, but we were patient, expecting our composers to find the strength to choose the proper road. We want you to overcome as quickly as possible the lag from which you are suffering, and to develop into a glorious cohort of Soviet composers who will be the pride of the entire Soviet people."

The government point of view was embodied in the Decree of 1948, which criticized Shostakovich, Prokofiev, and others for their formalist tendencies. It accused them of having "torn themselves away from the ideals and artistic tastes of the Soviet people" and took them to task for having "cloistered themselves in a narrow circle of specialists and musical epicures." The Decree goes on to combat the notion that the artist creates for posterity and must therefore leave his contemporaries behind. "In our country, composers are given unlimited opportunities. They have a listening audience such as no composer ever knew in the past. It would be unforgivable not to take advantage of all these opportunities, and not to direct one's creative efforts along the correct realistic path."

Despite all this, the problem was not solved. Soviet composers continued to be alternately praised and blamed by the government until the end of the Stalin era, when a more permissive attitude came into being. The new orientation is apparent in an editorial in *Pravda* in November 1953, which warned against the dangers of uniformity: "One of the most terrible evils for art is leveling, trimming everything according to one pattern, even if it is the best pattern. Such an approach to creative work obliterates all individuality, gives rise to clichés, imitations, deters the development of creative thought, deprives art of the joy of searching. That is why it is so important sometimes to support an artist in his daring . . . to respect the artist's right to independence, courage, and experimentation." The new line of thought culminated in the statement of the Central Committee of the Communist Party of May 1958, which was elucidated in a lengthy article in *Pravda*. The government admitted that the criticisms launched in 1948 against its leading composers had been "unfounded and unjust," and blamed these on "Stalin's subjective attitude to art." The *Pravda* editorial went on to state that "in questions of literature and art it is necessary to be high-principled, considerate and attentive to artists, and helpful in supporting their creative initiative."

It is against this background that we must understand the music of the Soviet school.

⌘ 43 ⌘

Sergei Prokofiev (1891-1953)

"The cardinal virtue (or, if you like, vice) of my life has always been the search for originality. I hate imitation. I hate hackneyed methods. I do not want to wear anyone else's mask. I want always to be myself."

SERGEI PROKOFIEV was one of those fortunate artists who achieve popularity with the mass public and at the same time retain the admiration of musicians. The brilliance and versatility of his gifts won him a place among the foremost composers of our time.

Sovfoto

Sergei Prokofiev

HIS LIFE

Prokofiev composed his first piece, a *Hindu Gallop*, when he was five-and-a-half. He entered the St. Petersburg Conservatory at the age of thirteen, arriving for the entrance examination armed with the manuscripts of four operas, two sonatas, a symphony, and a number of piano pieces. Rimsky-Korsakov, who was one of the examiners, exclaimed "Here is a pupil after my own heart."

At nineteen Prokofiev made his first public appearance in St. Petersburg. He played a group of his piano pieces, among them the *Suggestion diabolique*. The dynamism of this music revealed at once a distinctive personal style. The works that followed—particularly the Second Piano Concerto, the Second Piano Sonata, and the *Sarcasms* for piano— established Prokofiev as the *enfant terrible* of Russian music. He rather enjoyed the role. In May, 1914, he completed his course at the Conservatory. Over the opposition of Alexander Glazunov, the conservative director of the school, he was awarded the first prize in piano playing.

Exempt from military service, Prokofiev during the war years composed with unflagging productivity. The Revolution of 1917 caught him unawares, since politics was outside his sphere of interest. As the conditions of life grew ever more difficult, he began to think seriously of emigrating to the United States, where he would be able to work in peace. The *Classical Symphony* was given its premiere in Petrograd in April, 1918, and made a strong impression on the new People's Commissar of Education, Anatole Lunacharsky. When Maxim Gorky introduced Prokofiev to Lunacharsky, the composer spoke of his desire to go to America. The Commissar replied, "You are a revolutionary in music, we are revolutionaries in life. We ought to work together. But if you wish to go, I shall place no obstacles in your way." In May, 1918, Prokofiev set out for Vladivostok. He gave two concerts in Tokyo and one in Yokohama; in September he arrived in New York.

His first recital in Aeolian Hall drew praise for his playing and invective for his music. The critics spoke of "a carnival of cacophony," "Russian chaos in music," "Bolshevism in art." Prokofiev fared better in Chicago, where his *Scythian Suite* met with success. More important, the head of the Chicago Opera Company, Cleofonte Campanini, decided to produce his new opera, *The Love for Three Oranges,* as soon as Prokofiev had finished the score. Campanini's sudden death caused the production to be postponed. "This put me in a most awkward position. I had been engaged on the opera for almost a year and had completely neglected my concerts." Prokofiev tried to retrieve his position by giving recitals; but he was doomed to fail. Audiences at that time were avid for foreign pianists who played Beethoven, Chopin, and the rest. A modern composer performing his own works was definitely not a drawing card. It became clear to him that the conquest of the new world was not going to be as easy as he had imagined. "I wandered through the enormous park in the center of New York and, looking up at the skyscrapers that bordered it, thought with cold fury of the marvelous American orchestras that cared nothing for my music, of the critics who balked so violently at anything new, of the managers who arranged long tours for artists playing the same old hackneyed programs fifty times over." There was nothing for it but to admit defeat and try Paris.

Things looked up immediately he reached the French capital. Diaghilev produced his ballet *Chout* (The Buffoon), which had a resounding success. In the meantime Mary Garden had assumed the direction of the Chicago Opera Company, and decided to honor the contract with Prokofiev. *The Love for Three Oranges* received its premiere in Chicago on December 30, 1921, with Prokofiev conducting, and was warmly received. In New York, on the other hand, the opera met with hostility. "The production cost 130,000 dollars," one critic quipped, "which is 43,000 dollars per orange. But the opera fell so flat that its repetition would spell financial ruin." New York made amends a quarter century later, when *The Love for Three Oranges* became one of the most popular works in the City Center repertory.

For the next ten years Prokofiev made Paris his headquarters, with frequent journeys to the musical centers of Europe and the United States to perform his music. Yet the sense of being uprooted grew within him. An encounter with Maxim Gorky in Naples could not but sharpen his longing for his native land. He continued for another few years, composing and touring; but his return to Russia presented itself to him more and more as an inescapable necessity. To his devoted friend Serge Moreux he wrote, "I've got to live myself back into the atmosphere of my native soil. I've got to see real winters again, and Spring that bursts into being from one moment to the next. I've got to hear the Russian language echoing in my ears. I've got to talk to people who are of my own flesh and blood, so that they can give me back something I lack here—their songs, my songs. Here I'm becoming enervated. I risk dying of academicism. Yes, my friend—I'm going back!"

The sixteen years of wandering between 1918 and 1934 were followed by nineteen years spent for the most part in his homeland. During this period he consolidated his position as the leading composer of the Soviet school. As one who had voluntarily rejoined the Soviets when he might have made a career abroad, he was sought out by the regime, laden with honors and financial rewards. In 1943 he received the Stalin Prize for his Seventh Piano Sonata. The following year he was given the Order of the Red Banner of Labor for outstanding services in the development of Soviet music.

At the same time, of all the Soviet composers he was the one who, due to his long residence abroad, was most closely associated with the Western influences which the regime considered inimical to socialist art. What was worse, he had worked in close collaboration with Diaghilev, whom the Soviet press described as "the degenerate, blackguard, anti-Russian lackey of the Western bourgeoisie," and had been friendly with such "servile and corrupt musical businessmen as Stravinsky." As a result, when the Central Committee of the Communist Party in 1948 accused the leading Soviet composers of bourgeois formalism, Prokofiev was one of the principal targets of criticism.

The government showed its displeasure with its recalcitrant composers by ordering the works of Prokofiev to be removed from the repertory, along with those of Shostakovich, Khatchaturian, and

Miaskovsky. However, as these men happened to be the Big Four of Soviet music, the prohibition could not very well be maintained. After a few months Prokofiev's works—first his ballets, then his symphonies —began to be performed again. His next compositions, the Sixth Symphony and the opera *A Tale of a Real Man,* on a subject drawn from contemporary Soviet life, were attacked in the official press as being formalistic. *Izvestia* called the opera an example of "impractical, ivory-tower workmanship"; *Pravda* doubted whether one could expect anything "to satisfy the needs of the great Soviet people" from a composer whose work was penetrated to the core by "Western formalist decay." Prokofiev, who had sincerely tried to meet the requirements of social-ist-realist art, was taken aback by the severity of the criticism. His answer was the Seventh Symphony, which received its premiere in Moscow in October, 1952. This work of his ripest maturity quickly established itself, both within the Soviet Union and abroad, as one of his finest.

He died five months later, at the age of sixty-two. His death came one day after that of Josef Stalin. The Soviet Government withheld the news for forty-eight hours, presumably so that the one event would not overshadow the other.

HIS MUSIC

Prokofiev appeared at a twilight moment in the history of Russian music, when the mysticism of Scriabin and the introverted romanti-cism of Rachmaninov dominated the scene. Into this atmosphere his youthful works—audacious, earthy, gloriously alive—came like a burst of fresh air. The wholesome athleticism of his music—what Russian critics called its "football" quality—went hand in hand with a rare knack of capturing in music the vivid gesture, the mocking grimace; he epitomized the revolt against romanticism.

In his middle or "Western" period Prokofiev came under the in-fluence of Diaghilev and tried to function within the Stravinskyan esthetic of abstract art which dominated the Parisian scene. But the constructivist approach, natural to Stravinsky, was not at all suited to Prokofiev's particular gifts. After the failure of his Fourth Symphony in Paris, Prokofiev found his path by moving toward the romanticism that he had so long repressed in himself. "Music," he wrote, "has definitely reached and passed the greatest degree of dissonance and of complexity that it is practicable for it to attain. Therefore I think the desire which I and many of my fellow composers feel, to achieve a more simple and melodic expression, is the inevitable direction for the musical art of the future."

Hence it need not be concluded that Prokofiev wrote as he did in his final years because of his return to Soviet Russia. We may be closer the mark in supposing that it was the other way around. He returned to Soviet Russia because he felt that he would find there a favorable environment for the kind of music he wanted to write. The point has been well taken by the British critic Gerald Abraham: "Why should Prokofiev, who was continuing a brilliant career outside Russia, have voluntarily returned to a land where he knew certain limitations would be imposed on his work, unless he felt that these limitations would be unimportant? The truth is, I think, that he had already been tending in this direction for some time." The melodic appeal of his music, his fondness for Russian themes, his mastery of operatic and choral writing, his avoidance of introversion, and his prevailing optimism were precisely the traits that accorded with the dominant trends in Soviet art.

Prokofiev himself has provided us with an analysis of the elements of his style. "The first is classical, originating in my early infancy when I heard my mother play Beethoven sonatas. It assumes a neo-classical aspect in my sonatas or concertos, or imitates the classical style of the eighteenth century." In the *Classical Symphony* (1917), composed "as Haydn might have written it had he lived in our day," Prokofiev came as close as anyone in the twentieth century to recapturing the gayety of Haydn's effortless Allegros. The second element in his style he identified as the search for innovation. "At first this consisted in the quest for an individual harmonic language, but was later transformed into a medium for the expression of strong emotions." This strain is manifest in such early works as *Sarcasms* (1912); *Visions fugitives* (1917) for piano; and the *Scythian Suite* (1914) with its deliberate primitivism.

"The third is the element of the toccata, or motor element, probably influenced by Schumann's *Toccata*, which impressed me greatly at one time." The toccata is associated with a strong rhythmic drive, generally of the "perpetual motion" type that is so much to the fore in the music of our century. "The fourth element is lyrical. Since my lyricism has for a long time been denied appreciation, it has grown but slowly. But at later stages I paid more and more attention to lyrical expression." This element understandably dominated the final phase of his work.

"I should like to limit myself to these four elements, and to regard the fifth, that of the grotesque which some critics try to foist on me, as merely a variation of the others. In application to my music, I should like to replace the word grotesque by 'Scherzo-ness' or by the three words giving its gradations: *jest, laughter, mockery*." Prokofiev stood in the forefront of those who attempted to broaden musical expression to include the comic and the mischievous. In his later years the grotesquerie mellowed into a compassionate humor.

The bold thrust of his melody, with its wide leaps and unexpected turns of phrase, is no less characteristic of his style than are his athletic, march-like rhythms. His orchestration possesses all the brilliance of the earlier Russian masters. His harmonic language is remarkably varied and expressive. It can be pungently dissonant, but is essentially diatonic. Typical are the sudden changes of key that add excitement to his scores. Also his fondness for the bright C major, as striking a preference as, say, that of Mendelssohn for E minor. His compositional method was based on the clear-cut definition of key. Although there are atonal passages in his works, these are used, as he said, "mainly for the sake of contrast, in order to bring tonal passages to the fore." To fashion a work without tonality was, to him, "like building on sand." In his devotion to the large forms Prokofiev was a traditionalist. His classicism derived from Scarlatti, Haydn, and Mozart rather than, as in the case of Stravinsky, from Bach. "I want nothing better, nothing more flexible or more complete than the sonata form, which contains everything necessary to my structural purpose."

Both because of the nature of his gifts and of the esthetic philosophy that he embraced, Prokofiev became one of the most popular of all twentieth-century composers. A greater number of his works have established themselves as "classics" than those of almost any other of his contemporaries save Stravinsky. Among them we find *Lieutenant Kije* (1934), a suite arranged from his music for the film; *Peter and the Wolf* (1936), a "symphonic fairy-tale for young and old," in which each of the characters, animal and human, is represented by a distinctive instrumental color and theme; *Alexander Nevsky* (1938), a cantata arranged from the music for the celebrated Eisenstein film; the ballets *Romeo and Juliet* (1935) and *Cinderella* (1944); the *Scythian Suite;* and the *Classical Symphony*. The two Violin Concertos (1914, 1935) have found favor with music lovers the world over, as has the Third Piano Concerto, which we will discuss. The ten piano sonatas (1909–53, the last left incomplete) are a contribution of prime importance to the modern repertory for the instrument. Especially popular with pianists are the sets of short pieces, such as the *Sarcasms* and

Visions fugitives. Prokofiev, himself a virtuoso, wrote for the piano with profound insight; his powerful rhetoric helped to create the twentieth-century piano style.

In his later symphonies Prokofiev sought to recapture the heroic affirmation of the Beethovenian symphony. This is especially true of the Fifth (1944), dedicated "to the spirit of Man," and the last, the Seventh (1953). Of his operas, two in particular found favor outside his homeland: *The Love for Three Oranges* (1919), and *The Duenna* (1941), a sprightly work based on Sheridan's comedy. *The Flaming*

A scene from the NBC television production of *War and Peace:* General Kutuzov and his staff. (NBC)

Angel (1925) aroused much interest when it was produced at the Spoleto Festival in the summer of 1959. Prokofiev's major effort in the lyric theater is *War and Peace* (1941–42), on a libretto that he and his wife, the poet Mira Mendelssohn, fashioned from Tolstoi's epic novel. The work was introduced to this country through a television performance by the N. B. C. Opera Theater in January, 1957, in an English version by the present writer. The attempt to make an opera out of Tolstoi's mighty panorama of Russian society confronted the composer with almost insuperable difficulties. In addition, his decision to hew as closely as possible to Tolstoi's prose forced him into a meandering kind of arioso-recitative that bears little evidence of his melodic gift, and makes the work seem diffuse. Yet the opera is conceived in the grand tradition. Among its highlights are the moonlit scene during which Prince Andrei is first attracted to Natasha; Natasha's first ball in St. Petersburg; the heroic war scenes centering about Marshal Kutuzov; and the affecting scene of Andrei's death.

PIANO CONCERTO NO. 3

The elements that Prokofiev enumerated as basic to his style are abundantly present in his most celebrated work for the piano (completed in 1921).

I. *Andante—Allegro.* "The first movement," Prokofiev wrote, "opens with a short introduction. The theme is announced by an unaccompanied clarinet and is continued by the violins for a few bars.

Soon the tempo changes to Allegro, the strings having a passage in sixteenths, which leads to the statement of the principal subject by the piano." This driving theme exemplifies—as does the entire work —Prokofiev's skill in achieving rhythmic diversity within the traditional meters.

"Discussion of this theme is carried on in a lively manner, both the piano and the orchestra having a good deal to say on the matter." Prokofiev exploits the contrast between piano and orchestral sonority with great élan. "A passage in chords for the piano alone leads to the more expressive second subject, heard in the oboe with a pizzicato accompaniment."

"This is taken up by the piano and developed at some length, eventually giving way to a bravura passage in triplets. At the climax of this section the tempo reverts to Andante and the orchestra gives out the first theme, fortissimo. The piano joins in, and the theme is subjected to an impressively broad treatment." The Allegro returns, the two main ideas are treated with great brilliance, and the movement ends with an exciting crescendo.

II. *Andantino.*   The second movement consists of a theme with five variations. The theme, strongly Russian in character, is announced by the orchestra.

"In the first variation," the composer explained, "the piano treats the opening of the theme in quasi-sentimental fashion, and resolves into a chain of trills as the orchestra repeats the closing phrase. The tempo changes to Allegro for the second and third variations, and the piano has brilliant figures, while snatches of the theme are introduced here and there in the orchestra. In Variation Four the tempo is once again Andante, and the piano and orchestra discourse on the theme in a quiet and meditative fashion. Variation Five is energetic (*Allegro giusto*) and leads without pause into a restatement of the theme by the orchestra, with delicate chordal embroidery in the piano." This embroidery is colored by a spectral chromaticism that embodies the composer's love of the fantastic.

III. *Allegro ma non troppo.*   The Finale displays the gradations that Prokofiev assigned to "scherzo-ness"—jest, laughter, mockery. Also present is that spirit of grotesquerie so vital to his expression. The mood is established at the outset by the staccato theme for bassoons and pizzicato strings:

This is interrupted by what Prokofiev called the blustering entry of the piano, played chordal textures of great propulsive force. "The orchestra holds its own with the opening theme and there is a good deal of argument, with frequent differences of opinion as regards key." The solo part carries the first theme to a climax.

The melodist in Prokofiev is represented by the second theme, in his finest vein of lyricism, introduced by the woodwinds. "The piano replies with a theme that is more in keeping with the caustic humor of the work." Then the lyric theme is developed in the grand manner. An exciting coda brings the work to a close on a dazzling C-major cadence. (See musical example, page 28.)

Despite his difficulties with the doctrine of socialist realism, Prokofiev appears to have remained faithful to the esthetic he espoused upon his return to Russia. A year before his death he wrote the following lines, which may be taken as a final affirmation of his creed: "When I was in the United States and England I often heard discussions on the subject of whom music ought to serve, for whom a composer ought to write, and to whom his music should be addressed. In my view the composer, just as the poet, the sculptor or the painter, is in duty bound to serve man, the people. He must beautify human life and defend it. He must be a citizen first and foremost, so that his art may consciously extol human life and lead man to a radiant future. Such, as I see it, is the immutable goal of art."

⊰ 44 ⊱

Dmitri Shostakovich (1906–)

"I consider that every artist who isolates himself from the world is doomed. I find it incredible that an artist should wish to shut himself away from the people, who in the last analysis form his audience. I always try to make myself as widely understood as possible; and if I don't succeed, I consider it my own fault."

DMITRI SHOSTAKOVICH belongs to the first generation of artists who grew up under the Soviet regime. He is entirely a product of Soviet training, and may be regarded as the representative artist of the new order in Russia.

HIS LIFE

He was born and raised in what was then St. Petersburg. His parents and relatives were close to the revolutionary underground, and for them the overthrow of the monarchy in 1917 signalized the dawn of a new era. Dmitri made his way to school through streets crowded with fiercely debating soldiers and civilians. "I met the October Revolution on the street," he later remarked. Among the lad's first efforts at composition were a *Hymn to Liberty* and a *Funeral March for the Victims of the Revolution.*

Guillumette

Dimitri Shostakovich

His youth came in a bitter time. Civil war, inflation, and famine shook the social order to its foundations. The death of his father left the family exposed to privation. It was his mother who, in the face of almost insurmountable difficulties, made it possible for the boy to continue at the St. Petersburg Conservatory, where he studied with Alexander Glazunov and Maximilian Steinberg, the two favored disciples of Rimsky-Korsakov.

The severe conditions under which he grew up took their toll. For a time he was threatened with tuberculosis. At the lowest point in his fortunes he earned a few rubles by playing the piano in a movie house. Fortunately he did not have to wait long for success. His First Symphony, written as a graduation exercise when he was not yet nineteen, made an extraordinary impression and blazoned his name throughout the musical world.

Shostakovich began his career at a propitious moment. The defection to the West of such major figures as Rachmaninov and Stravinsky, who subsequently were joined by Glazunov himself, left a void which it became almost a matter of national honor to fill. Of the musicians of the rising generation, Shostakovich was clearly the most gifted. His star rose rapidly.

Shostakovich's Second Symphony (1927) commemorated the October Revolution. The Third was the *First of May* Symphony (1931). Each was "a proletarian tract in tones," as the composer later expressed it. Neither was successful. This phase of Shostakovich's career culminated in the four-act opera *Lady Macbeth of Mzensk*. Produced in Leningrad and Moscow in 1934, the work scored an immediate hit with the Russian public. The following year *Lady Macbeth* was presented with great éclat at the Metropolitan Opera House as well as in Cleveland and Philadelphia. The sensational theme of the opera—the heroine kills both her husband and her father-in-law for the sake of her lover—and the ultra-realistic handling of the material attracted a great amount of attention, with the result that Shostakovich at thirty was one of the best-known among contemporary composers.

For two years *Lady Macbeth* ran in Leningrad to packed houses. Then, in January 1936, *Pravda*, official organ of the Soviet government, printed its scathing attack upon the opera. We quoted a paragraph in our discussion of the Soviet musical scene. The article went on to state: "The author of *Lady Macbeth* was forced to borrow from jazz its nervous, convulsive and spasmodic music in order to lend 'passion' to his characters. While our music critics swear by the name of socialist realism, the stage serves us, in Shostakovich's work, the coarsest kind of naturalism. The music quacks, grunts and growls, and suffocates itself in order to express the amorous scenes as naturalistically as possible. And 'love' is smeared all over the opera in the most vulgar manner."

The article made it clear that the government did not call into question either Shostakovich's talent or his ability "to depict simple and strong emotions in music." What was questioned was only the use to which he put his talent. Nor could it escape the attention of his countrymen that a *Pravda* editorial—a space customarily reserved for political matters of the gravest import—had been turned over to the doings of a thirty-year-old musician. To be singled out so, even in a negative way, could not but add to Shostakovich's fame.

As for the composer himself, he went through a period of stern self-examination; he was too deeply committed to the Soviet view to question the directives of the rulers of his country. His Fourth Sym-

phony (1936), a gloomy and introspective work, was already in rehearsal. He withdrew it. A year later, he was reinstated when the
Leningrad Philharmonic presented his Fifth Symphony (1937). Across
the score was written, "Creative reply of a Soviet artist to just criticism." The work was a triumphal success. *Pravda* praised the "grandiose vistas of the tragically tense Fifth Symphony, with its philosophical
seeking." Shostakovich's personal victory was followed by a greater
one when, in 1940, his Piano Quintet was awarded the Stalin Prize of
a hundred thousand rubles, probably the largest sum ever paid for a
chamber music work.

The Nazi invasion of Russia released a surge of patriotism in the
composer. "I volunteered for service at the front, and received the
reply: 'You will be called when required.' So I went back to my
duties at the Leningrad Conservatory." (He was professor of composition at his alma mater.) His Seventh or *Leningrad* Symphony (1941)
was inspired by the militant spirit of his native city when it was besieged by the Germans, and at this critical moment Shostakovich inevitably assumed the role of poet laureate. "He rested his ear against
the heart of his country," wrote the novelist Alexei Tolstoi, "and
heard its mighty song." The Seventh Symphony marked the high tide
of Shostakovich's popularity in the United States. It was introduced
by Arturo Toscanini in a much heralded broadcast in the summer of
1942, and was subsequently played throughout the country. A writer
in *Life Magazine* facetiously pointed out that it was almost unpatriotic,
even for Americans, not to like the piece.

When *Pravda* launched its attack on formalism in 1948, Shostakovich
was again one of the principal targets. His reply to the charges showed
that even when he himself was assailed, he remained an unofficial
spokesman for the government's "stern but paternal solicitude for us
Soviet artists." "Work—arduous, creative, joyous work on new compositions that will find their path to the heart of the Soviet people—
this will be a fitting response to the Resolution of the Central Committee."

A year later, in March, 1949, he was sent to the United States as
delegate to the Cultural and Scientific Conference for World Peace.
Had he come five years earlier he would have been acclaimed and
feted. Now, however, the cold war was in full swing. He was not
allowed to travel outside of New York City; his visa was limited to
the duration of the conference. After a stay of ten days, during which
one caught a glimpse of him at a concert of the New York Philhar-

monic, he took his leave. His second visit, in November, 1959, was a much happier one.

In the past decade Shostakovich has added steadily to a list whose opus numbers have passed well beyond the hundred-mark. However, his later works show a falling off of creative vigor and originality. In 1956, on the occasion of his fiftieth birthday, he was awarded the Order of Lenin.

HIS MUSIC

If the art of Prokofiev is based on vocal melody, that of Shostakovich derives from the language of the instruments. His themes stride over a wide range; he writes for the orchestra with real flair. Certain devices are pushed to the length of mannerism: the use of instruments in their extreme registers, mischievous leaps from low to high, the "hollow" ring of widely separated orchestral lines, unison and octave passages; glissandos on the strings, unexpected contrasts of sound, long melodies traced by a single woodwind, and rhythmic patterns repeated relentlessly. Purple passages abound in his works; but his music always "sounds," and his effects are surefire.

Shostakovich handles the large forms of instrumental music with great assurance. He has the capacity for sustaining and developing a musical line which marks the born symphonist. His way of foreshortening the recapitulation section is in line with present-day musical esthetics, as is his transparent orchestration. Contemporary too is his fondness for linear texture and his contrapuntal technique.

Shostakovich is given to black-and-white contrasts of mood. On the one hand, impudent satire, mocking gayety, and a humor verging on the boisterous; on the other, a lyric strain that is meditative and impregnated with sentiment. His orchestral cantilena can be diffuse, and sometimes lacks distinction. At its best, however, it achieves power, unfolding in a broad recitative that builds up into impassioned climaxes. His resilient rhythms bound along with gusto. His pungent harmonies lean toward the chromatic, as might be expected in a style that shows the influence of César Franck and Mahler. Indeed, Mahler's music holds such attraction for him that his Moscow colleagues used to say he suffered from an attack of Mahleria. Withal, Shostakovich's music rests on a firm diatonic base. He is one of the few who still conceive a piece as being in A major or E minor.

His model is Beethoven, whom he regards as the orator of an epoch no less turbulent than his own. "Only Beethoven," he writes, "was a forerunner of the revolutionary movement." The epic quality of Beethoven's art is exemplary for him. "I see our epoch," he states, "as heroic, spirited, and joyous." The Beethovenian concept of victory through struggle is basic to his thinking. "Good music lifts and heartens people for work and effort. It may be tragic but it must be strong."

Shostakovich's First Symphony (1925), a work bursting with creative vigor, is a wonderful piece for a youth of nineteen to have written. The Fifth we will examine in detail. The Sixth (1939) exemplifies the composer's attempt to condense and simplify his style; it has never achieved the popularity of its predecessor. The seventh or *Leningrad* Symphony is an uneven work, and too long; but it captures the immediacy of the stirring events that inspired it. The Eighth (1946) displays the winding melodies in which Shostakovich recreates the arabesque of Bach. It is the outpouring of a sensitive spirit still tormented by memories of the war. The Ninth (1945), on the other hand, is a happy work, classical in its simplicity and its espousal of the chamber music ideal. In the Tenth (1953) Shostakovich adopts the emotional tone of the late nineteenth-century symphony to depict his own drive for inner harmony. The Eleventh (1957) is a programmatic work of heroic cast, dedicated to the Russian Revolution of 1905.

In the Concerto for piano, trumpet, and strings (1933) the composer pays homage to the neo-classic spirit. The dry toccata-like passages show Shostakovich's predilection for grotesquerie. The Violin Concerto (1955) is a work of the composer's maturity, projecting the moods of struggle and aspiration that have occupied him in recent years. The Piano Concerto of 1957 is a decidedly weak work. Shostakovich's six string quartets (1938–56) show his serious approach to the problem of contemporary chamber music. The later quartets are preoccupied with the same moods of inner struggle as figure in the Tenth Symphony. The Quintet for piano and strings (1940) displays the composer's ingenuity in handling what has always been a difficult combination, and is a most satisfying work. Shostakovich has written a quantity of film and ballet music, as well as incidental music for plays; but these, because of the themes they handle, are hardly for export. One little item, the Polka from *The Age of Gold* (1930), has been much played. The *Twenty-Four Preludes* (1933) for piano show his idiomatic writing for the instrument, and are full of ideas. He has also written songs and choral pieces; but these are the least important part of his output.

SYMPHONY NO. 5, OPUS 47

Shostakovich's attempt to recapture the epic tone of Beethovenian symphonism is most successfully realized in his Fifth Symphony (1937). "The theme of my symphony," he wrote, "is the stabilization of a personality. In the center of this composition, which is conceived lyrically from beginning to end, I saw a man with all his experiences. The finale resolves the tragically tense impulses of the earlier movements into optimism and the joy of living."

I. *Moderato.* The opening subject is announced in antiphonal imitation between low and high strings. It is a tense, lofty idea that establishes the D-minor tonality of the work. The widely striding intervals of the first phrase are balanced by stepwise movement in the second.

From this idea grows another which is sung by the first violins. The movement unfolds in flowing lines, embodying the singing polyphony that Shostakovich took over from Mahler. Mahlerian too is the elevated pathos that pervades this broadly conceived sonata form. The writing exploits the warmly emotional tone of the strings, which is pitted against the cooler timbres of the woodwinds. The second theme, introduced by first violins against chords on the harp and strings, is a soaring melody marked by expressive leaps, which is subsequently

taken over by the cellos. The Development is characterized by a steady quickening of tempo and an ever greater reliance on the brass. The themes are manipulated chiefly by means of imitative procedures and rhythmic transformation (diminution, augmentation), with a relentless build-up of tension. Dramatic use is made of trumpet fanfares and dotted-note patterns, against the tumultuous kind of figuration in the strings that Tchaikovsky used so effectively. Thematic transformation results in a resolute march, *poco sostenuto*. The opening motive is again presented antiphonally, but this time in a rapid tempo. The Recapitulation is ushered in by an overpowering proclamation of this motive, *largamente, fff*, by woodwinds, horns and strings in unison. The second theme, now transposed into D major, is presented in canonic imitation by solo flute and horn. The coda has a gently retrospective quality. A solo violin soars above the orchestra, silvered by the tones of the celesta, as the movement dies away.

    II. *Allegretto.* The Scherzo evokes that spirit of the Austrian Ländler so prominent in Mahler's symphonies. The element of grotesquerie, a favorite mood with Shostakovich in his younger years, is established at the outset. Tonality is handled very freely, the music rotating between A minor and C major. The main theme, redolent of the "scherzo fantastique" of the romantic period, is in C minor.

The movement is an A-B-A form (actually a Scherzo and two Trios), with repetition of sections and an over-all symmetry that goes hand in hand with the popular character of the material. At least one of the melodies verges on the deliberately banal. When the main theme returns, *da capo*, it is shifted up a half tone to C-sharp minor, for intensification. The movement as a whole gives an effect of freshness, earthiness, and rhythmic élan.

    III. *Largo.* The centerpiece of the symphony is the slow movement in F-sharp minor, which unfolds in great arcs of self-propelling, songful counterpoint. This is in the great tradition of the romantic Adagio, introspective, "tragically tense," as the composer called it,

and is suffused with personal lyricism. The test of such a movement is
its capacity to sustain tension. Shostakovich succeeds—this is incomparably the most fully realized of his Adagios—because of his ability
to shape purely lyrical material into large, continuous structures.

In even greater degree than the first movement, the Largo is based
on the emotive power of string tone, which is pitted against the woodwinds. The brass is silent throughout. The tracing of a single line by
a solo woodwind against a curtain of string sound—a practice that
Sibelius taught those who listened to him—comes off effectively in the
middle of the movement. The massively sonorous climax that Shostakovich achieves without recourse to trumpets, horns, or trombones
must be accounted a real feat of orchestration. One has a sense throughout the movement that he previsioned every combination of timbres
with the utmost vividness. The pianissimo F-sharp major chord at the
close makes for an effect of utter serenity.

IV. *Allegro non troppo.* Massed trumpets, trombones, and tuba
present the theme of a "satanic" march against the beating of the

kettledrums. The key is D minor. The music is dark in color, full of
propulsive energy and tension, and with a touch of the bizarre. The
movement is a rondo; the references to the earlier movements make
the symphony an example of cyclical form. The progression from
tumult and strife to triumphal fulfillment hinges on the shift from
minor to major—a time-honored device that can be carried off only
if it is managed without self-consciousness, which is precisely how
Shostakovich does it. He handles the classical procedures of thematic-
motivic development, as he does the palette of the romantic orchestra,
with all the customary exuberance of the Russian school. This finale
is rooted in the surging rhetoric of Tchaikovsky's symphonies. It is a
heritage that Shostakovich comes by honestly and uses well. The
grandiose coda in D major brings the symphony to its end on a note
of heroic affirmation.

The problem of the individual in a collective society has formed the
central drama of Shostakovich's life. He has moved along a difficult
path, sustained in equal degree by passionate conviction and a big
talent. We shall never know what direction Shostakovich's gift would
have taken had it been exercised in a society different from his own.

There is no conditional in history. Given the time and place in which he appeared, his role was cut out for him. In fulfilling it, he became a leader in the attempt to adapt the language of contemporary music to the emotional needs of the common man.

৺§ 45 ৡ৵

Other Soviet Composers

ARAM Khatchaturian (Tbilisi, Georgia, 1903–) is an Armenian who stands far closer to the romantic heritage than does either Prokofiev or Shostakovich. His use of folklore material accords, on the one hand, with the Soviet desire to build a melodious music accessible to the masses, and on the other, with the government's attempt to draw into the sphere of art the songs and dances of the national minorities within its borders. Khatchaturian is basically a folk singer who has learned to adapt to his ends the ample instrumental forms of the classical tradition. These he uses in conventional fashion. He is given to rhapsodic improvisation and to the broadly spun arabesques of Oriental song. His forms are diffuse and marked by an abundance of material that militates against organic growth and structure. But his music is packed with color and excitement. His First Symphony (1934) is much appreciated by his countrymen. He is known abroad for his Piano Concerto (1936), which derives from the bravura style of Liszt; the expansive Violin Concerto (1940); and the ballet *Gayane* (Happiness, 1942). One number from *Gayane*—the Saber Dance—caught on in the United States and for a season was played so relentlessly that one hoped never to hear it again. Another widely played work is the Concerto for Cello and Orchestra (1950). Like most of his colleagues, Khatchaturian has turned out incidental music for the theater, film music, choral and chamber works, and piano pieces.

Khatchaturian plays an important part in the musical life of his country. He is professor at the Moscow Conservatory and also active as a conductor. He feels that within the frame in which Soviet composers function, each must find his individual way. "Socialist realism in art," he wrote in 1954, "cannot tolerate leveling, dull uniformity, and clichés. It presupposes the free expression of creative individuals who, in different ways, always truthfully and excitingly solve great artistic tasks. Let there be in our family of composers rich and varied creative personalities. And let them freely and daringly compete in creating the art of our day."

Dmitri Kabalevsky (St. Petersburg, 1904–), a pupil of Miaskovsky, comes out of the tradition of Musorgsky and Borodin, Tchaikovsky and Scriabin. Kabalevsky is best known in the West for the overture to his opera *Colas Breugnon* (1937), based on Romain Rolland's novel, and for *The Comedians*, a suite for small orchestra (1940). His writing is strongly rhythmic and tonal. He has produced operas, ballets, incidental and film music, and patriotic choral works; four symphonies; a number of concertos, including three for the piano; chamber music, piano pieces, and songs.

Tikhon Khrennikov (Elets, 1913–) holds several official positions and is thus a powerful figure in Soviet music. His reputation was established by his Opus 1, a piano concerto, when he was twenty. His war songs enjoyed wide popularity. Khrennikov's list of works includes three operas, the most impressive of which is *Mother* (1957); ballets, and incidental and film music; two symphonies; and piano pieces.

⤜§ 46 §⤛

Ralph Vaughan Williams (1872-1958)

"The art of music above all other arts is the expression of the soul of a nation. The composer must love the tunes of his country and they must become an integral part of him."

ENGLAND, as we noted in our discussion of Elgar, produced no major composer for two hundred years. The rise of a native school in the postromantic period consequently fulfilled a deep need in that music-loving nation. The English renascence was heralded by an awakening of interest in native song and dance. The folksong revival centered about the work of Cecil Sharp and his disciples, who went into the villages and hamlets and took down the traditional tunes from the lips of folk singers. This movement toward a national music was strengthened by the revival of interest in the masters of Tudor church music, in the Elizabethan madrigalists, and in the art of Purcell. Out of this ferment came a generation of composers. The most important figure among them was Ralph Vaughan Williams, who succeeded Elgar as the representative of English music on the international scene.

HIS LIFE

Ralph Vaughan Williams was born in Down Ampney, Gloucestershire, the son of a well-to-do clergyman. He was sent to Charterhouse when he was fifteen, and three years later entered the Royal College of Music. There he studied with the elder statesmen of the English renascence, Sir Charles Hubert Parry and Sir Charles Villiers Stanford.

Bettmann Archive

Ralph Vaughan Williams

At twenty, Vaughan Williams entered Trinity College, Cambridge, where he took both a musical and general degree. There followed a short stay abroad during which he studied in Berlin with Max Bruch, a composer in the romantic tradition. He then returned to Cambridge; and in 1901 received his doctorate in music, the most respectable appendage a British musician can have. A decisive influence at this time was Vaughan Williams's involvement with the folksong revival. He worked along the lines laid down by Cecil Sharp, going into the villages of Norfolk to collect traditional melodies. In 1904 he undertook to edit the music of a hymn-book, and enriched the hymnology with some simple tunes of his own. "Two years of close association with some of the best (as well as some of the worst) tunes in the world was a better musical education than any amount of sonatas and fugues."

Despite this activity, in 1908—he was then thirty-six—Vaughan Williams came to the conclusion that he was "lumpy and stodgy, had come to a dead-end, and that a little French polish" would do him good. He decided to study with Ravel, his junior by three years, and went to Paris for that purpose. There could hardly have been a stranger choice of master for the bluff, homespun Englishman than the elegant Parisian. "When I had shown him some of my work he said that, for my first lesson, I had better *écrire un petit menuet dans le style de Mozart*. I saw at once that it was time to act promptly, so I said in my best French, 'Look here, I have given up my time, my work, my friends and my career to come here and learn from you, and I am *not* going to write a *petit menuet dans le style de Mozart.*' After that we became great friends and I learned much from him."

The outbreak of war in 1914 relegated music to a secondary place in the composer's life. Although he was forty-two, he enlisted, was commissioned as a lieutenant in the Royal Garrison Artillery, and saw combat duty in France throughout 1918. The war over, he resumed his career. He became professor of composition at the Royal College of Music, in which post he helped train many gifted musicians of the new generation. He was the most active of the so-called "folksong school of composers," and for many years directed the Leith Hill Musical Festival held annually at Dorking in Surrey, where he made his home. After Cecil Sharp's death in 1933 he guided the destinies of the English Folk-Song Society. He received an honorary Doctorate of Music from Oxford University in 1919; and he visited the United States in 1922 in order to conduct his *Pastoral Symphony* at the Norfolk Festival in Connecticut. On a second American visit, in 1932, he delivered a course of lectures at Bryn Mawr College. (These were later collected in a book entitled *National Music*.) In 1935 Vaughan Williams, having refused official honors on earlier occasions, accepted the Order of Merit. These are the external landmarks of an intense inner life whence issued a steady stream of works, vocal and instrumental, in all genres. In the last years of his life Vaughan Williams was the unofficial composer laureate of his native land. This aspect of his career was underlined when the Credo and Sanctus of his Mass in G minor were performed in Westminster Abbey at the coronation of Queen Elizabeth II.

In 1954, when he was in his eighty-third year, Vaughan Williams came for the third time to the United States to deliver the series of lectures at Cornell University subsequently published as *The Making of Music*. He was widely hailed as one of the masters of our time, and his major works were performed throughout the nation. He completed his Ninth Symphony at the age of eighty-five, and died a year later.

HIS MUSIC

Vaughan Williams stood at the farthest possible remove from the "art for art's sake" doctrine of an esthete like Delius. Basic to his view was the desire to bring art into the most direct relationship to life. "The composer," he wrote, "must not shut himself up and think about art: he must live with his fellows and make his art an expression of the whole life of the community." But life is not lived in the abstract. It is experienced in a certain place and shared with a certain group of people. Hence Vaughan Williams took his stand as an advocate of national music. "Art, like charity, should begin at home. It is because Palestrina and Verdi are essentially Italian and because Bach, Beethoven and Wagner are essentially German that their message transcends their frontiers. The greatest artist belongs inevitably to his country as much as the humblest singer in a remote village."

In the ancient tunes of the peasantry Vaughan Williams found the living expression of the English spirit. Having assimilated the character of popular melody to his personal thinking, he wrote music that sounded national whether he quoted actual folk songs or not. As a matter of fact there are fewer quotations of folk song in Vaughan Williams's music than is commonly supposed. What is decisive in his art is the fact that in the English folk song revival he found his spiritual habitat. "This revival," he wrote, "gave a point to our imagination; far from fettering us, it freed us from foreign influences which weighed on us." He suggests how a composer in England can draw inspiration from his environment. "Have we not all about us forms of musical expression which we can take and purify and raise to the level of great art? For instance, the lilt of a chorus at a music-hall joining in a popular song, the children dancing to a barrel organ, the rousing fervor of a Salvation Army hymn, St. Paul's and a great choir singing in one of its festivals, the Welshmen striking up one of their own hymns whenever they win a goal at the international football match, the cries of the street pedlars, the factory girls singing their sentimental songs. Have all these nothing to say to us? We must cultivate a sense of musical citizenship: why should not the musician be the servant of the State and build national monuments like the painter, the writer or the architect?"

He was devoted to all manifestations of the English spirit. His numerous settings of hymns and carols exemplify his dictum that the traditional tunes must be treated "with love." Basic ingredients of his style derive from the Elizabethan madrigalists and the polyphonists of the Tudor era. His homage to the golden age of English music took shape in one of his most successful works, the *Fantasia on a Theme by Tallis* (1910). Even more, it shows itself in his flair for choral music. "A massive, broad, bare choral style like his," one of the leading British critics wrote, "has not been heard among English musicians since Purcell."

The English language powerfully affected Vaughan Williams's vocal line. He ranged wide in his choice of poets, from Chaucer, Shakespeare and Milton to Coleridge, Shelley, Tennyson and Hardy. His democratic leanings found a sympathetic echo in Walt Whitman, whose poetry he set in *Towards the Unknown Region*, a cantata for chorus and orchestra (1905), and *A Sea Symphony*, for soprano, baritone, chorus and orchestra (1910). The Bible was an abiding influence, as was Bunyan. *Flos Campi* (Flower of the Field, 1925), for viola solo, wordless chorus, and small orchestra, bears mottoes from *The Song of Solomon*. The cantata *Sancta Civitas* (Holy City, 1926) is based on Biblical texts. *Job*, "a masque for dancing" (1930), was inspired by William Blake's illustrations for the Book of Job. Most important in this category is his symbolic opera or "morality" *The Pilgrim's Progress* (1949), on a text by his wife, the poet Ursula Wood, after Bunyan. These, like his religious works, are imbued with the spirit of English Protestantism. True, his finest piece of church music, the Mass in G minor (1922), uses the text of the Roman Catholic rite. But the spiritual provenance of this music is the Anglican service.

Vaughan Williams's response to the English landscape is projected in the *London* (1914) and *Pastoral* (1922) symphonies; his "symphonic impression" *In the Fen Country* (1904); *The Lark Ascending*, a romance for violin and orchestra based on a poem of George Meredith (1914); and the song cycle *On Wenlock Edge*, for tenor, string quartet, and piano, to lyrics drawn from A. E. Housman's *A Shropshire Lad* (1909). Of his nine symphonies, the most dramatic is the Fourth in F minor (1935), a somber, uncompromising work of great impact. Vaughan Williams's operas are not for export; they speak to the English mind. *Hugh the Drover*, a ballad opera (1914), is in the tradition of those nationalist works which glorify the life and virtues of the folk. *Sir John in Love* (1929), based on Shakespeare's *Merry Wives of Windsor*, suffers from inevitable comparison with one of the most luminous of all operas, Verdi's *Falstaff*. If any stage work of Vaughan Williams ever succeeds in establishing itself outside his homeland it will probably be *Riders to the Sea* (1937), on Synge's powerful one-act play about Irish fishermen; the work shows Vaughan Williams's expressive declamation and his ability to sustain a mood.

Vaughan Williams was primarily a melodist. His love of folk tunes was part of an essentially melodic approach to music. He shied away from chromatic harmony. His natural expression was diatonic, with strong leanings—encouraged by his interest in old music—toward modal harmony and counterpoint. Characteristic is his great fondness for the flatted seventh step, an effect found in folk tunes based on old scales, and for modal cadences. Common chords figure prominently in his writing, and he also liked to use strings of triads in parallel motion. In his later works he adopted daring harmonic procedures, building up simple chord formations into complex dissonances of great expressivity. His preoccupation with the Elizabethan madrigal liberated him from the four-square rhythms of the classic-romantic period; his rhythmic flexibility is especially noticeable in his sudden shifts from duple to triple patterns. He favored old forms—the passacaglia, fugue, and concerto grosso; also the Elizabethan fantasia, with its flowing counterpoint. Like Sibelius, whom he very much admired—he dedicated his Fifth Symphony to the Finnish master—Vaughan Williams held the attention of the world largely because of his command of the grand form. His nine symphonies are ample of gesture and noble in tone.

Vaughan Williams's huge output runs the gamut of his art. His music is fresh, cool, wholesome. It has strength and lyricism, yet the emotion is held in check by natural reticence. It retains a certain roughness and directness of manner despite the composer's long years of schooling; these traits were part of his personality. His honesty in all that regarded his art was as engaging as the humility with which he spoke of his achievements. As when he wrote, "I have struggled all my life to conquer amateurish technique and now that perhaps I have mastered it, it seems too late to make any use of it." One is reminded of Haydn's touching remark: "I have only just learned in my old age how to use the wind instruments, and now that I understand them I must leave the world."

A LONDON SYMPHONY

This work (1914; revised 1920) is the second and most popular of Vaughan Williams's symphonies. Apprehensive lest it be taken for a descriptive program piece, the composer emphasized that it could stand on its own as music. "Hearers," he wrote, "may if they like localize the various movements and themes, but it is hoped that this is not a necessary part of the work." The symphony is scored for an orchestra of the usual size, with cornets added to trumpets and the percussion group augmented by jingles and glockenspiel.

I. *Lento—Allegro Risoluto.* The mysterious introduction suggests the city awakening. (To some it has suggested the London fog.) Cellos and double basses state the germinal motive *ppp.* This consists of two ascending fourths, an interval that is prominent in Vaughan Williams's

melodic writing. A pentatonic melody defines the locale, as do the modal harmonies throughout the work. Harp and clarinets evoke the chimes of "Big Ben." The Allegro proper opens with a vigorous theme group that suggests the bustle of the city and establishes the home key of G minor. The dynamic first idea shows the parallel triads and triplet

rhythm so characteristic of Vaughan Williams's music. The remaining themes of this group reinforce the suggestion of big-city hubbub.

The contrasting theme group presents several arresting ideas. A suave melody of ambiguous tonality is sung by strings and woodwinds. A bold fanfare-like motive in B-flat is hurled out fortissimo by woodwinds and brass. An irresistibly jaunty tune conjures up memories of cockney humor:

With such a wealth of material to choose from, the composer has no difficulty in shaping an exciting development section. This culminates in a pianissimo passage rich in the manly lyricism so dear to the English heart. In accordance with twentieth-century practice, the Recapitulation presents the material in abbreviated form, the themes being combined contrapuntally.

II. *Lento*. The slow movement, in A-B-A form, evokes the quiet of London's "grey skies and secluded by-ways." Parallel chords on muted strings usher in the main idea, a lyric theme on the English horn

which owes its charm to its modal cast. The buildup of the movement is not dissimilar, technically, to Sibelius's way of meshing fragments into a continuous whole. In the middle part Vaughan Williams introduces the street cry of the London lavender vendors, which goes very well with his own material. There is a restrained climax, after which the material of the first part is restated in curtailed form.

III. *Allegro vivace*. The subtitle *Nocturne* indicates that this animated Scherzo is intended to suggest the city at night. The first idea, in D minor, sets the mood. It is a perky tune in folk-dance style introduced by the clarinets.

With the modulation to B-flat modal-minor, several subsidiary ideas enter, notably one on the horns that becomes the subject of a brief fugato. A few measures which sound startlingly like a mouth organ usher in a gay street tune in C major. The shift from 6/8 to 9/8 imparts suppleness to the movement, as does the alternation of two- and three-bar phrase lengths. In the coda, a short solo for harp and clarinets suggests the striking of a distant clock. The hour is late; the crowd melts away, as does the music.

IV. *Andante con moto—Maestoso alla marcia*. A dramatic introduction leads into a solemn modal tune in the style of a ceremonial march:

This is repeated with fuller orchestration against a countermelody. Tension builds to a hard-hitting Allegro, after which the march returns. There is a fleeting reference to the main idea of the first movement. The harp again evokes Big Ben; the chimes strike not the half-hour as before, but the three-quarters. The Epilogue brings back the four-note motive from which the work grew, heard against tremolos in the strings and woodwinds. The symphony dissolves in the misty stillness out of which it came, on a G-major cadence.

One senses the manly personality and the warm heart behind this music. "He looks like a farmer," Stephen Williams wrote of him. "A big, heavy, lumbering figure, usually dressed in rough tweeds, who looks as though he is on his way to judge the shorthorns at an agricultural fair." Vaughan Williams in extraordinary fashion met the needs of his time and place. He was, as one of his compatriots called him, "the most English of English composers."

47

Benjamin Britten (1913-)

"I believe that it is possible and desirable to develop a kind of British opera that will explore the vital native qualities of the English voice and language."

Benjamin Britten is a musician of great invention, technical mastery, and charm. He is undoubtedly the most important English composer of his generation.

HIS LIFE

Britten was born in Lowestoft, in Suffolk, the son of musical parents. By the time he was fourteen the boy had produced ten piano sonatas, six string quartets, three suites for piano, an oratorio, and dozens of songs. After several years of study with the composer Frank Bridge, he won a scholarship to the Royal College of Music, where he soon distinguished himself both in piano and composition.

Bettmann Archive

Benjamin Britten

He had his first public performance shortly after his nineteenth birthday, when the *Phantasy for String Quintet* and some part-songs were presented at a concert of contemporary music. His Sinfonietta for chamber orchestra was heard a few weeks later. His schooling over, Britten went to work for the G. P. O. Film Unit, a politically progressive group that produced documentary films. "The company I was working for had very little money. I had to write scores not for large orchestras but for six or seven instruments, and to make these instruments make all the effects that each film demanded." He could not have served a more valuable apprenticeship.

His work for the films, radio, and theater brought him into contact with the forward-looking young poets of the day—Auden, Isherwood, Spender, C. Day Lewis, and Louis MacNeice. These writers were affected by the political ferment of the times—this was the period of the Spanish Civil War—and they played an important part in Britten's intellectual development. On the musical front he scored his first big success with *Variations on a Theme of Frank Bridge* for string orchestra.

The European situation continued to deteriorate, and early in 1939 Auden left for the United States, having decided that only there would he find the proper conditions for his work. Britten decided to follow his friend's example. He left England in the summer of 1939, and settled in New York. The American sojourn saw the production of a number of major works: the Violin Concerto (1939); *Les Illuminations* (1939), a song cycle in which with rare felicity he caught the bitterness of Rimbaud's poems; *Diversions on a Theme* for piano and orchestra (1940), and *Sinfonia da Requiem* (1940). By this time England was taking the punishment of the *Luftwaffe* raids. Britten, although a pacifist, felt more and more that his rightful place was in his homeland. While in California he read a British magazine in which his attention was caught by the opening line of an article by E. M. Forster: "To think of Crabbe is to think of England." This reference to the poet of his native Suffolk, who was born two centuries before at Aldeburgh, not far from his own birthplace, filled him with homesickness. His decision was taken forthwith.

It was no easy matter to cross the Atlantic in the fall of 1941. He waited in New York for almost six months before he could obtain passage. The delay made it possible for him to hear his *Sinfonia da Requiem* conducted by Serge Koussevitzky in Boston. The conductor, struck by the dramatic quality of Britten's music, offered him a commission for an opera. Thus Britten was able to go ahead with a project that already had taken shape in his mind—the writing of an opera based on material from George Crabbe's poem *The Borough*. In March, 1942, he returned to England.

Exempted from active service as a conscientious objector, Britten was permitted to aid the war effort in his own way. He appeared as a pianist all over England and continued to compose. A number of new works were completed during the war, among them *Peter Grimes*, on a libretto by Montague Slater based on Crabbe's poem. The work received its premiere in June, 1945, was presented in practically all the opera houses of the world, and established Britten as an international figure.

In 1947 he settled in Aldeburgh, in a house overlooking the sea. The village immortalized by Crabbe has become the center of his activities, which include frequent appearances as conductor and pianist both in England and abroad. Britten was instrumental in organizing the Alde-

burgh Festival, which has been held every summer since 1948. His involvement with the scene of his labors was well described by the
composer when, in the summer of 1951, he was made an Honorary
Freeman of the Borough of Lowestoft: "Suffolk, the birthplace and
inspiration of Constable and Gainsborough, the loveliest of English
painters; the home of Crabbe, that most English of poets; Suffolk, with
its rolling, intimate countryside; its heavenly Gothic churches, big and
small; its marshes, with those wild seabirds; its grand ports and little
fishing villages. I am firmly rooted in this glorious country. And I
proved this to myself when I once tried to live somewhere else."

HIS MUSIC

Britten is essentially a lyricist. Whether he happens to be writing for
voices or instruments, his art draws its imagery and its melodic line
from that most personal of instruments, the human voice. It follows
that the grand forms of instrumental music—the sonata and symphony
—attract Britten far less than they do the majority of his contemporaries. Much more to his taste is the theme and variations which, because it is less architectonic than the sonata, permits the shorter flights
of fancy that appeal to the lyricist. Hence his devotion to the passacaglia. He also has assiduously cultivated the three forms in which
a series of numbers adds up to a large-scale work: the suite, the song
cycle, and the opera.

Britten is devoted to the classical view of the artist as a master craftsman. For him, as for Stravinsky, each composition represents a particular problem that must be solved. He enjoys working on a commission, and readily shapes his inspiration to conditions imposed from
without. The classicist in Britten demands a certain distance between
the raw emotion and its sublimation into art. Hence his addiction to
formal procedures such as the canon and fugue. His operas display
a number of devices for creating distance between the action and the
audience: the male and female chorus in the *Rape of Lucretia;* or the
framework in *Billy Budd,* whereby Captain Vere in his old age reflects
upon the tragedy of Billy.

Like every artist of classical persuasion, Britten is keenly aware of
his heritage. The art of the Elizabethan madrigalists, of the Tudor
church composers, and of Purcell is a living reality to him. "One of
my chief aims," he writes in his preface to *Peter Grimes,* "is to try
and restore to the musical setting of the English language a brilliance,
freedom, and vitality that have been curiously rare since the death of

Purcell." Even as Purcell did in the seventeenth century, Britten assimilated important influences emanating from the Continent and adapted them to the English taste. He responded to the rhythmic élan of the early Stravinsky (he does not care for the Russian's later works); to the orchestral lyricism of Mahler, who influenced him profoundly; and to the operatic expressionism of Alban Berg.

Britten is too sophisticated a musician to build successfully on folk materials. The national element in his music is of a subtler order; it resides rather in the imponderable atmosphere that surrounds his works. His melody takes its shape from the rhythms and inflections of English speech. His choice of texts reveals a discriminating literary taste that ranges over the whole of English literature, from George Withers and Francis Quarles to Hilaire Belloc and W. H. Auden; from Ben Johnson and Donne to Blake, Keats, and Tennyson. Those of his operas which are set in his native Suffolk—*Peter Grimes, Albert Herring, The Little Sweep*—reveal the landscape of East Anglia, its way of life, its soul.

Britten has the imagination of the musical dramatist. He is adept at the delineation of character through music, at suggesting a mood or an atmosphere with a few telling strokes. He exemplifies the present trend back to the classical conception of opera. "I am especially interested," he writes, "in the general architectural and formal problems of opera." He therefore rejected the Wagnerian concept of "endless melody" in favor of the classical practice of separate numbers which, as he says, "crystallize and hold the emotion of a dramatic situation at chosen moments." Nor does he always set the text in accordance with the natural inflections of the words, adhering rather to the doctrine that it is permissible to distort the prosody in the interest of heightened expression.

Peter Grimes announced to the world that a musical dramatist of stature had arrived upon the scene. This impression was in no way belied by *The Rape of Lucretia* (1946), even though Britten's second opera, on a libretto by Ronald Coleman, has none of the earthy vitality of the first. Instead, it is a highly stylized treatment of the Roman story, and shows true elegance in its classical restraint. *Albert Herring* (1947) represents Britten's solitary venture into the field of comic opera. The libretto by Eric Crozier was freely adapted from a story by Maupassant. Audiences throughout England were delighted, by all accounts, with the tale of Lady Billows's search for a virtuous May King. But this kind of humor is definitely not for Americans. In 1948 Britten came forth with a new version of *The Beggar's Opera*. The following year he wrote *The Little Sweep*, a poignant children's opera which, together with its prologue, is known as *Let's Make an Opera*, and allows for audience participation. This work too achieved a success in Europe not duplicated in the United States. It is excellent material for young people at a summer camp. On Broadway it lasted three nights.

The case is different with *Billy Budd* (1952), the libretto of which was adapted by E. M. Forster and Eric Crozier from Melville's famous story. The symbols of good and evil implicit in the tale of the ill-fated sailor inspired the composer to a somber work that is powerful musically no less than dramatically. This was followed by *Gloriana* (1953), an opera about Elizabeth and Essex, written in honor of the coronation of her namesake, which received its premiere in the presence of the Queen. Certainly no Englishman present on that occasion could fail to be moved. All the same, *Gloriana* is strictly for home consumption. *The Turn of the Screw*, which was presented at the Venice Festival of 1954, shows Britten's customary resourcefulness when it comes to lyric drama. Yet the opera suffers from the fact that Henry James's celebrated tale is an adventure in the realm of the imagination, and gains very little from being either staged or sung. *Noye's Fludde*, a one-acter for children (1958), was followed by *A Midsummer Night's Dream*, which was given its premiere at the Aldeburgh Festival of 1960.

Britten's operas are an outgrowth of the music-festival movement, which offers the contemporary composer a much more hospitable platform than does the traditional opera house. He has found a congenial medium in chamber opera, a genre whose small cast and modest orchestra allow subtleties that would be lost in the larger frame of grand opera. Here Britten's classical economy of means, transparency of texture, and flair for supple rhythms show to their best advantage, as does his predilection for harmonic directness and a light, radiant sound.

To the works we have mentioned may be added *A Boy was Born* (1933), a set of variations for unaccompanied mixed chorus; *Our Hunting Fathers* (1936), a "symphonic cycle" for high voice and orchestra, on old poems assembled by Auden; *A Ceremony of Carols* (1942), a cycle for treble voices and harp; the lovely *Serenade* for tenor solo, horn, and string orchestra (1953); the *Spring Symphony* for soloists, chorus, and orchestra—a cycle of lyric poems in praise of spring by twelve English poets (1949); and the *Five Flower Songs*, for unaccompanied mixed chorus (1950). The Piano Concerto in D major (1938, revised 1945) is a brilliant virtuoso piece. The *Young Person's Guide to the Orchestra*, a set of variations and fugue on a theme by

Purcell (1946), is both entertaining and instructive. *The Prince of Pagodas* (1957) is one of the showpieces of the Royal Ballet. It is too long (except for balletomanes), and the scenario seems like a hodge-podge of all the fairy-tale ballets that have ever been. But the score has some enchanting moments.

PETER GRIMES

OPERA IN THREE ACTS AND A PROLOGUE

"In writing *Peter Grimes* [1945], I wanted to express my awareness of the perpetual struggle of men and women whose livelihood depends on the sea." Around this struggle revolves the daily life of the Borough, a fishing village in Suffolk. The time is 1830. Locale and atmosphere are of prime importance in the opera.

Louis Melancon

A scene from the Metropolitan Opera production of *Peter Grimes*.

Writers on music like to say that the real hero of *Boris Godunov* is the Russian people, as embodied in the chorus. It is even truer that the real hero of *Peter Grimes* is the Borough. Both the composer and his librettist have taken extraordinary care to build up the various characters that inhabit Crabbe's village. The balance between the protagonist and his environment is heavily weighted in favor of the latter. For example, the first act takes up a hundred and forty pages in the vocal score, of which less than twenty are devoted to Peter.

The theme that underlies most of Britten's operas—"the persecution and betrayal of innocence"—is here presented through a powerful symbol: the lonely individual ranged against a hostile society. The drama, projected through the figure of the misunderstood fisherman who hardens into a misanthrope, mounts in a relentless line to Peter's suicide. Grimes, in the original poem, is a sadistic ruffian. In Britten's opera he takes on dimension and humanity. He yearns for love, but his pride prevents him from accepting it when Ellen offers it to him. He dreams of happiness, but the fatal conflict within his nature drives him to destroy whatever happiness he might have hoped to attain. Doomed from the start, his futile attempts to escape his fate mark him for the tragic figure he is.

The arias, for the most part, are brief. They are built into larger musical structures through the use of several devices that have done duty on the operatic stage for generations: a storm brewing, dramatic dialogue while people sing in church, action unfolding while a dance is in progress, and the like. The solo passages are interjected into extended pieces for chorus that root the opera solidly in the English choral tradition, and these in turn are linked by orchestral interludes. Britten has poured a wealth of musical invention into the score, although one feels occasionally that the choral scenes have been expanded at the expense of Peter and Ellen. (The recording of the opera conducted by Britten himself affords the best possible introduction to his music.)

The Prologue takes place in a room inside the Moot Hall, arranged for a coroner's inquest. Peter is questioned about the death of his apprentice at sea. He tells how, having made a huge catch, he steered for London; but the wind blew the boat off its course, they ran out of drinking water, and the boy died. Peter is exonerated; but it is evident that his fellow villagers do not regard him as innocent. The wide leaps in the vocal line establish the expressionist utterance that the composers of Britten's generation learned from Alban Berg's *Wozzeck*. The village types—the pompous lawyer Swallow, the officious Hobson, the excitable Boles, the incorrigible Auntie, the meddling Mrs. Sedley, and Ellen Orford, the widowed schoolmistress who loves and understands Peter—are vividly characterized from the start.

The interludes not only link the scenes, but play a unifying role: they refer back to what has already passed, or anticipate what is to follow. Interlude I, *Dawn*, marked *Lento e tranquillo*, is an atmospheric genre piece in 2/2 time that portrays the break of day on a cold gray morning in the village, and subsequently serves as background for the opening chorus in Scene 1. The main idea of this little tone poem is a plaintive tune in high register that unfolds in delicate traceries on flutes and violins, in A modal-minor.

The first scene of Act I shows the Borough beach and street. "The people sing quietly to themselves as they move about their work, folding and cleaning nets, baiting lines, mending sails." The librettist opens the opera with a quotation from Crabbe's poem: "Oh, hang at open doors the net, the cork, / While squalid seadames at their mending work. / Welcome the hour when, fishing through the tide, / The weary husband throws his freight aside." In the course of a characteristic chorus several worthies engage our attention: Balstrode, who except for Ellen is Peter's only friend; Auntie, mistress of the village pub, the Boar, whose main attraction is her two "nieces"; Swallow, and the Rector, and Mrs. Sedley. Ned Keene, "apothecary and quack," informs Peter that he has found a new apprentice for him at the workhouse. When Hobson the carter refuses to fetch the lad, Ellen—to the surprise of the crowd—volunteers to go along and bring him back. Her arioso, "Let him among you without fault cast the first stone," introduces a note of tenderness and charity where both have been lacking. The approaching storm is heralded in a spirited fugue for soloists and chorus. (The use of well-defined musical types and forms underlines the classical conception of opera that found favor in the second quarter of the century.) The villagers take refuge in their houses or in the Boar.

Peter stays behind with Balstrode, who wonders why his friend does not leave the Borough and seek his fortune elsewhere. "I am native," Peter retorts, "rooted here." "Rooted by what?" "By familiar fields, marsh and sand, ordinary streets, prevailing wind." In the ensuing scene, Peter reveals his inmost thoughts: the bitter memory of the day his apprentice died; his hopes of gaining wealth and respect and of marrying Ellen. Hobson suggests that he ask Ellen now; but Peter will not have her marry him because she feels sorry for him. Balstrode goes into the Boar. Peter, left alone, dreams of his future happiness in a moving arioso whose opening interval, a major ninth, is associated with him throughout the opera. (See the example on next page.)

Interlude II, *The Storm*, is a *Presto con fuoco* in 2/2 that rages loudly and picturesquely, with expert use of snarling trombones and trumpets moving in parallel fifths, and angry horns answering in

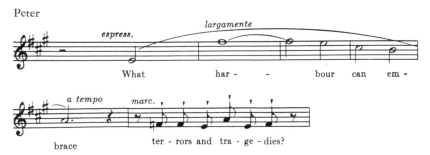

octaves. The storm music boils over into the second scene of Act I, which takes place inside the Boar that evening, and erupts whenever someone enters the tavern. This scene, like the first, is based on the chorus. An extended ensemble serves further to build up the characters of the play—easy-going Auntie and her two frivolous "nieces"; virtuous Mrs. Sedley who, quite unaccustomed to such surroundings, has come against her better judgment to obtain some sleeping pills from the apothecary; Boles, the Methodist fisherman, who in his drunken moments forgets religious scruples in order to pursue one of the nieces; and the rest.

The entrance of Peter throws a pall on the carousers. They shrink back from him. In an arioso of great breadth, he sings of the stars that guide our fate: "Now the Great Bear and Pleiades, where earth moves, are drawing up the clouds of human grief." The others think he is either mad or drunk. There is a tense moment when the drunken Boles is about to bring down a bottle on Peter's head, but Balstrode averts a conflict and bids them strike up a song. The extended round that follows, *Old Joe has Gone Fishing*, in 7/4, is related thematically to Peter's motive. Peter's entry for a moment upsets the round, as he slightly distorts each of the three tunes of which it is composed—an effective way of informing us that he does not fit in. Then the round overwhelms him and sweeps on its merry course. The scene ends with the return of Ellen and the carter who bring with them Peter's new apprentice. Ellen says to the boy, "Peter will take you home." As Peter leads the boy into the storm the rest cry maliciously, "Home! do you call that home!"

Interlude III, *Sunday morning*, is an *Allegro spiritoso* in 2/2 that evokes "a fine sunny morning, with church bells ringing." The opening measures of this sonorous tone painting, in a bright A major, show how potent was the influence of Musorgsky on Britten's generation. The pealing churchbells of this East Anglian village are descendants of

those that ring out in the Kremlin for Boris's coronation. The interlude
continues into the first scene of Act II, coloring Ellen's opening line,
"Glitter of waves and glitter of sunlight. . . ." The organ sounds from
the church as she sits down on a breakwater, the boy quietly playing
by her side. She tries in vain to make him talk (he does not say a word
throughout the opera), and wonders what his life was like. The scene
between them unfolds against the singing of the congregation in
church. She notices that the boy's coat is torn, then discovers that his
neck is bruised. "It's begun!" she cries in horror.

Peter appears. He has spied a shoal of fish and is eager to get his
boat out, even though it is Sunday. Ellen tries to dissuade him in a
scene of mounting tension that is skillfully integrated with the service
in the church. "What peace will your hard profits buy?" Ellen asks.
Peter's reply is thematically related to his vision of the future in Act
I: "Buy us a home, buy us respect, and buy us freedom from pain."
Defiance and tenderness struggle within him. Yet when Ellen says,
"Peter, we've failed, we've failed!" his need to destroy the thing he
loves overpowers him. He strikes her, cries out in agony, "So be it—

and God have mercy upon me!" and rushes out, driving the boy
fiercely in front of him. Ellen goes the other way, weeping.

Auntie, Ned Keene and Boles, who have been watching the scene,
sing a trio whose principal phrase, *Grimes is at his exercise!*, derives
from Peter's outcry after he had struck Ellen. She returns to collect
her things and defends Peter against the mutterings of the crowd. But
the villagers, convinced that Peter will cause the death of his new
apprentice as he did of the last, work themselves into a fury. The
Rector orders Hobson to fetch his drum and summon the Borough to
Grimes's hut. The men march off behind Hobson, the Rector, and
Swallow; the women follow. Ellen, Auntie, and the two nieces remain
behind. In a pensive quartet they muse upon the strange ways of men.

Interlude IV is a Passacaglia in 4/4 marked *Andante moderato*. The
theme is a seven-note motive related to Peter's phrase, "So be it—and
God have mercy upon me!", and to the phrase "Grimes is at his exercise!" in the preceding chorus. The tonality is not clearly defined, being based on the free use of twelve tones around F:

A passacaglia depends for its effectiveness, first, on the use of a distinctive idea for the repeated phrase in the bass; second, on the composer's imagination in envisioning what can be put above it. Britten's Passacaglia is as remarkable for the wealth of musical fantasy displayed as for the dramatic rightness of the piece. The theme, announced pizzicato by cellos and basses—an infallibly dramatic symbol this, whether of the beating heart or the approaching footfall—becomes an image of impending catastrophe; while over it there gradually pile up terrifying masses of sound. The final measures—solo violin in the upper register against celesta and sustained harmonics on violas, cellos, and basses—make a sound to be remembered.

The second scene of Act II takes place in Peter's hut, an upturned boat beside the cliff overlooking the sea. Peter and his new apprentice arrive. Peter, in a towering rage, throws the boy's boots and oilskin at him. The lad is crying with fear. Peter looks out over the sea, exulting at the prospect of making a good catch. He dreams of his future happiness with Ellen; but the mood is interrupted by memories of the apprentice who died. "I can see him—he is there! His eyes are on me as they were that evil day." Hobson's drum is heard in the distance, coming toward the hut. Peter is roused from his thoughts and catches sight of the procession drawing near. He accuses the boy of having talked about him to the villagers. Defiant, he determines to make for his boat, and orders the boy to take nets and tackle down the steep path that leads to the sea. The villagers reach the hut as Peter makes for the back door. The boy has started down the cliff. Overcome by panic, he loses his hold and with a scream falls to his death. Some moments later the Rector, Swallow, Keene, and the other men come into the empty hut. They find nothing amiss and sheepishly withdraw—all except Balstrode, who looks round the hut, sees the boy's Sunday clothes, hesitates, finally goes up to the cliff door, looks out, and climbs down the path.

Interlude V, *Moonlight*, an Andante in 2/2 in E-flat, serves as an atmospheric prelude to the first scene of Act III, which shows the moonlit street of the village and the beach a few nights later. A dance is in progress in the Moot Hall; the band can be heard playing a Barn Dance. Against a background of movement and gaiety, Mrs. Sedley tries to relay to Ned Keene her suspicions that the new apprentice has been the victim of foul play. Ellen and Balstrode walk up slowly from the beach. Balstrode informs her that Peter's boat has come in, but Peter himself seems to have disappeared. Ellen reveals that she has found the boy's jersey on the beach, the one she had embroidered with an anchor on the chest. There follows her poignant arioso in B minor, in 5/8 time, "Embroidery in childhood was a luxury of idleness. . . . Now my broidery affords the clue whose meaning we avoid."

Mrs. Sedley, who has overheard this conversation, goes to the door of the Boar, calls Swallow, and tells him that a crime has been committed. The dancers and drinkers crowd out of the Moot Hall and Boar and congregate on the green. In a lively chorus, based on the transformed version of one of the dance tunes previously heard, they decide to form a posse to hunt Peter down.

Interlude VI, a Lento in 4/4, is a brief, intense fantasy piece that suggests Peter's torment as grief and remorse unhinge his mind. There are fleeting reminiscences of his earlier music—his dream of success and wealth, his vision of happiness with Ellen, the terrible moment outside the church when he lost his temper with her, and similar references to the past. The final scene shows the street some hours later, in a thick fog. The cries of the men searching for Peter can be heard. He comes in, exhausted, crazed by his suffering. In the incoherent monologue that follows he calls upon Ellen, realizes that there is no hope for him, and is driven to frenzy at hearing the villagers incessantly calling his name. Ellen and Balstrode find him. Peter calms himself, and resigns himself to his fate. For the last time he returns to the dream that was doomed to fail: "What harbor shelters peace away from tidal waves, away from storms. . . ." Balstrode advises Peter to sail out beyond sight of land. "Then sink the boat. D'you hear? Sink her. Goodbye, Peter." He helps Peter push out the boat. Then he returns, takes Ellen by the arm and leads her away.

Dawn comes, and the Borough slowly comes to life. We hear again the music of the first Interlude and the opening chorus of Act I. The librettist again quotes Crabbe: "To those who pass, the Borough sounds betray / The cold beginning of another day, / And houses sleeping by the waterside / Wake to the measured ripple of the tide." Calmly the life of the Borough flows on.

In *Peter Grimes* Britten has produced a genuinely national work. The opera is suffused with the sights and sounds of an English village. Its vocal lines are shaped by the rhythms and inflections of English speech. And its music springs from what one of Britten's countrymen has well called "an unusually compassionate and English heart."

VII. THE NEW ROMANTICS

"The abundance of technical means allows the heart to expand freely."

Olivier Messiaen

❧ 48 ❧

Toward a New Romanticism

"The composer of today without some trace of romanticism in his heart must be lacking in something fundamentally human."
Arnold Schoenberg

WE HAVE traced the revolt against romanticism as one of the first gestures of self-assertion of the twentieth century. Yet the romantic heritage, too powerful to be shaken off entirely, persisted. On the one hand it attracted those composers who were too conservative by temperament to want to break entirely with the past. These men continued within the nineteenth-century tradition, striving to bring the inheritance of the past into line with the needs of the present. On the other hand, the new romanticism attracted a number of composers who, having gone through the hectic experiments of the New Music, found themselves ready for a certain measure of reconciliation with the inheritance they formerly had rejected. Once the breakaway had been effected, it was no longer necessary to proffer such determined resistance to the past. Thus, several composers who had led the neo-classic movement in the earlier part of their career showed a mellowing of spirit as they grew older. Bartók's *Concerto for Orchestra*, Hindemith's *Mathis der Maler*, and Prokofiev's *Romeo and Juliet* are among the works that exemplify this trend.

The political and economic upheavals which swept the world in the second quarter of the century created a hunger for the romantic qualities of enchantment and solace. The Second World War was a traumatic event that impelled many composers to place their art at the service of intensely emotional expression. Then again, the very strength with which the New Classicism had asserted itself was bound to set off a reaction in the opposite direction. The result was that, as the mid-century approached, the stage was set for a resurgence of romantic attitudes. There was a revival of programmatic music with a poetic or dramatic content; a return to the cult of melody; and a reaffirmation of the primacy of music as the language of the heart.

The New Romanticism absorbed the heady innovations of the first decades of the century. It was tempered by the classical trend of the Twenties, and obeyed the imperatives that shaped musical thought and feeling in the Thirties. In short, it added fresh elements to the romantic heritage. Twentieth-century romanticism was only one strand within the diversified language of contemporary music; but it attracted adherents representing a variety of temperaments and points of view.

The older members of this group continued, by and large, in the footsteps of the late romantic generation. A typical figure was Ernö (Ernst von) Dohnányi, who was born in Poszony (Pressburg), Hungary, in 1877. He achieved a reputation as a concert pianist at the turn of the century and was professor of piano at the Berlin Hochschule from 1908 to 1915, when he went to live in Budapest. In the next thirty years Dohnányi was the great man of Hungarian musical life, completely overshadowing both Bartók and Kodály. He was director of the Conservatory, conductor of the Budapest Philharmonic, director of the Hungarian Radio, and president of the Hungarian Academy. Dohnányi's music represented the final upsurge of Hungarian romanticism. His compositions, facile in a Brahmsian way, posed no problems and won a following in central Europe. Best known among them is the *Variations on a Nursery Song* for piano and orchestra (1913). Dohnányi left Hungary after the Second World War. In 1949 he settled in the United States, and became professor of piano and composition at Florida State College in Tallahassee. He died in 1960.

Ildebrando Pizzetti (Parma, 1880–) belongs to the category of composers who achieve a formidable reputation in their own country without reaching comparable eminence on the international scene. He is of the generation of Italians who grew up under the spell of Gabriele d'Annunzio. The fiery poet, in his characteristically grandiloquent manner, named him "Ildebrando of Parma" and honored him with his friendship. Pizzetti's opera *Fedra* (1915) was based on a libretto by d'Annunzio. His other operas for the most part are based on his own librettos. The most successful are *Debora e Jaele* (1921), on the Biblical story; *Fra Gherardo* (1927); and *Assassinio nella cattedrale* (1958), after T. S. Eliot's *Murder in the Cathedral*. He is also known to his countrymen as a composer of choral, orchestral, and chamber music, violin and piano pieces, and songs. Pizzetti succeeded Respighi as professor of composition at the Santa Cecilia Academy in Rome, and was director of the Academy from 1948 to 1951.

The most eminent of Pizzetti's pupils is Mario Castelnuovo-Tedesco (Florence, 1895–), scion of an old Spanish-Jewish family that settled in Italy at the time of the Inquisition. Castelnuovo-Tedesco absorbed his master's skill in choral music. He has also written song and piano pieces. Among his orchestral works may be mentioned the Hebrew Rhapsody *Dances of King David;* seven overtures to Shakespeare's plays, from *The Taming of the Shrew* (1931) to *King John* (1942); and a suite, *The Birthday of the Infanta* (1944), after Oscar Wilde's fairy tale. Of his operas, the most successful is *La Mandragola* (The Mandrake, 1926), after Machiavelli's famous comedy. His love of English poetry impelled him to set all the songs of Shakespeare's plays, a project that occupied him for five years.

Castelnuovo-Tedesco was forced to leave Italy in 1939, after Mussolini promulgated his racial laws. He took refuge in the United States and settled at Beverly Hills in California, where he still resides. A facile, agreeable composer, Castelnuovo-Tedesco is one of those who achieved popularity a quarter-century ago because they were working in a postromantic idiom accessible to the public. Their avoidance of contemporary problems has told heavily against them. The time has passed them by.

The English are well represented in this group. John Ireland (Bowden, 1879–1962, Washington, England) evolved a personal style in which postromantic and impressionist elements were combined with the modal and pentatonic patterns of English folk song. His varied output includes church music, choral works, part songs, orchestral pieces, works for piano and orchestra, chamber music, pieces for various instruments, piano works, and songs. Sir Arnold Bax (London, 1883–1953, Cork, Ireland) was a proponent of Celtic romanticism, to which he added impressionist elements and a richly chromatic harmony. His seven symphonies occupy the central place in a large output that includes symphonic poems and orchestral works, vocal and chamber music, sonatas for various instruments, and settings of folk songs. Sir Arthur Bliss (London, 1891–) shows a leaning toward classicism in his chamber music. The romantic element is to the fore in his theater and film music, his choral works, his orchestral pieces with programmatic connotations, and his songs. His fiendishly difficult Piano Concerto (1938) at moments sounds like Rachmaninov. Arthur Benjamin (Sydney, Australia, 1893–) has written three operas: *The Devil Take Her* (1931); *Prima Donna* (1933); and *A Tale of Two Cities* (1950), after Dickens's novel. Also ballet, choral, orchestral, and chamber music; pieces for various instruments; piano music, and songs. He is a facile composer who works in a traditional idiom.

Several composers in this group came out of the Austro-German tradition. Ernst Toch (Vienna, 1887–) is a prolific composer. He has written four operas, of which the most successful is *The Princess and the Pea* (1927). After Germany passed to Hitlerism, Toch settled in the United States. He lived for a time in New York City, then moved to Hollywood. As a film composer Toch is best known for *The Private Life of Don Juan* (1934); *Peter Ibbetson* (1935); and *On Such a Night* (1937). Several of his works have achieved popularity: *Big Ben*, a set of variations on the Westminster Chimes (1934); *Pinocchio, a Merry Overture* (1936), after Collodi's famous story; and the Quintet for Piano and Strings (1938). He has written much chamber music, including nine string quartets; a considerable amount of piano music; and four symphonies (1950, 1952, 1955, 1957). The Third won the Pulitzer Prize. Toch's book, *The Shaping Forces in Music* (1948), reveals a musical outlook rooted in the Viennese tradition.

Paul Pisk (Vienna, 1893–) studied with Franz Schreker and Schoenberg. He has written about a hundred works of all types, in which he combines the idiom of Viennese postromanticism with classical and Baroque forms. Pisk's music was frequently heard at the central European music festivals in the years between the two wars. He came to the United States in 1936 and was professor of music at the University of Redlands in California from 1937 until 1948, when he became director of the school of music there. In 1951 he joined the faculty of the University of Texas in Austin. He has produced a variety of works during his residence in this country, among them a *Requiem*, for baritone and orchestra (1942); *Toccata by Galuppi*, for narrator and chamber orchestra (1947); the ballet *American Suite* (1948); and *Baroque Chamber Concerto* for violin and orchestra (1953).

Karol Rathaus (Tarnopol, Poland, 1895–1954, New York City) studied in Vienna with Franz Schreker. In 1920 Rathaus followed his teacher to Berlin, where he soon established his own reputation. He taught at the Hochschule from 1925 until the coming of Hitler; lived in London for several years; and emigrated to the United States in 1938. After a short stay in Hollywood, he returned east and became the first professor of composition at Queens College of the City of New York, a post he occupied until his death. Rathaus's music is compounded of three main elements. The song and dance patterns of his native Poland are embodied in mazurkas and similar genre pieces.

From the spiritual climate of east European Jewry stems a strain of brooding mysticism that asserts itself in ecstatic dance moods and lyricism of a rhapsodic cast. These two elements are assimilated to the tradition of Austro-German postromanticism, which lies behind his sumptuous orchestral sound, his chromatic harmony, closely woven texture, and discursive handling of the classical forms. An accomplished pianist himself, Rathaus wrote four idiomatic sonatas for the instrument. His Fourth String Quartet, Opus 59, reveals his chamber-music style at its best. The Third Symphony (1942) and a number of large choral works stand out in a varied list that includes songs, ballets, operas, film music, and music for the theater. The works written in the United States include a Piano Concerto (1942); *Polonaise symphonique* (1944); *Twenty-third Psalm* for chorus and orchestra (1945); a chorus for women's voices and French horn based on *Iphigenia in Aulis* by Euripides (1947); *Vision dramatique* for orchestra (1948); and *Diapason*, a cantata for baritone solo, mixed chorus, and orchestra, on texts of Dryden and Milton (1952).

Marcel Mihalovici (1898–) was born in Bucharest, but spent the greater part of his career in Paris. His taste and outlook were formed by Vincent d'Indy, from whom he derived his solidity of construction, his fondness for variation technique, and his command of the processes of thematic development. Mihalovici's music, based on the free use of the twelve tones, shows what one may call *atonicity*—the absence of a Tonic, rather than the absence of tonality. His works include the *Toccata* for piano and orchestra (1939), *Variations libres pour piano* (Free Variations for Piano, 1941); and an opera, *Phèdre* (1948).

⊸§ 49 §⊸
Carl Orff (1895-)

"Melody and speech belong together. I reject the idea of a pure music."

THE TWELVE years of Nazi rule, which bound composers to a post-Wagnerian ideology, were a period of retrogression for German music. In that time Germany lost the commanding position she had occupied in the modern movement throughout the Twenties. However, since the Second World War several German composers have succeeded in winning an international reputation. Significantly, the most widely known among them—Carl Orff—is a thoroughgoing conservative.

HIS LIFE AND MUSIC

Orff was born in Munich, where he has spent the greater part of his career. He was active in the progressive school movement in the late Twenties, and was much influenced in his work as a teacher by the principles of Jaques-Dalcroze. Orff's *Schulwerk—Elementare Musik-übung* (School Work—Elementary Exercise in Music), a didactic work written between 1930 and 1933, epitomizes his theories as an educator. It was aimed especially at beginners and amateurs, and was scored for various combinations, with emphasis on recorders and percussion instruments. The work bears some relation to the then current practices of *Gebrauchsmusik*. Nor is it surprising that Orff, born in the same year as Hindemith, should have moved in the same direction —although along his own path.

Orff took his point of departure from the clear-cut melody, simple harmonic structure, and vigorous rhythm of Bavarian popular song. His music derives its emotional appeal from the *Gemütlichkeit* of the Munich *Bierstube*, from the glow that envelops the heart after enough steins have been emptied in a low-ceilinged, smoke-filled room. He is of the twentieth century in that he regards rhythm as the form-building element in music (as distinct from the nineteenth-century musicians, who found that element in harmony). His rhythm draws its strength from the simple patterns of folk tune and peasant dance: patterns which he at times repeats with a ferocity bordering on obsession. Orff's melodies are born of this rhythmic impulse. He avoids harmonic complexity and the intellectual attitudes inherent in contrapuntal writing. The themes are repeated without any attempt at variation; for contrast, they are shifted to other keys. As one would expect, Orff's writing is strongly tonal, despite an occasional admixture of clashing polytonal chords. In the absence of thematic and contrapuntal elaboration, the impression is one of an almost primitive simplicity and forthrightness.

Orff's desire to reach the public goes hand in hand with his affinity for the theater, which by its very nature appeals to a mass audience. It has been his intention to rid the lyric drama of the intellectual preoccupations that have been attached to it in recent years; to find his way to a type of lyric drama that will have immediate impact and wide appeal. A theater based almost exclusively on rhythmic dynamism is apt to be very exciting; and that, at its best, Orff's theater certainly is. Moments of comedy in his operas alternate with lyrical passages; the music supports and illumines the action without ever embarking on any expansion of its own. And always there is the rhythm, relentless and irresistible, to keep the action moving and the tension high. Orff functions at his best where he can work in broad simple outlines, without getting himself involved in psychological complexities. For this reason he is attracted to texts drawn from ancient and medieval literature, to fairy tales and legends. "I am often asked," he states, "why I nearly always select old material, fairy tales and legends for my stage works. I do not look upon them as old, but rather as valid material. The time element disappears, and only the spiritual power remains. I write for the theater in order to convey a spiritual attitude."

Orff's two best known theater works, *Der Mond* (The Moon, 1937–38, revised 1941) and *Die Kluge* (The Wise Woman, 1942), are based on Grimm fairy tales. They have Orffian rhythm and tunefulness in abundance. Among his other works are *Carmina Burana*, which we will discuss; *Catulli Carmina* (Songs of Catullus, a "scenic cantata," 1942); *Die Bernauerin* (The Bernauer Woman, 1944–45), an opera in the style of a dramatic ballad, which, like *Der Mond* and *Die Kluge*, is on his own libretto; *Antigonae*, on Hölderlin's adaptation of the Sophoclean tragedy (1947–48); and *Trionfo di Afrodite* for soloists, large and small chorus, and orchestra (1951).

For those who are seriously concerned with contemporary musical problems, Orff represents the most reactionary tendencies on the present-day scene. They regard his archaism, his deliberate naïveté and Bavarian folkishness with the same distaste as a modern poet might feel for the primitive rhymes of the librettos that Orff writes. By the same token, the big public finds his music accessible, fresh, and enormously appealing.

CARMINA BURANA

Orff calls his most celebrated work (1936) a "dramatic cantata." It can be given in a stage version, with dancing and pantomime, and has been so presented. Actually, it is a concert piece for solo singers, chorus, and orchestra. The choral forces are in three groups—a large chorus, a small one, and a boys' chorus. The supporting body is an orchestra of the usual size augmented by two pianos, five kettledrums, and a large percussion group.

The text is drawn from the famous thirteenth-century collection of Goliard songs and poems that was discovered in the ancient Bavarian monastery of Benediktbeuren in 1803. Hence the name *Carmina Burana* (Songs of Beuren). These *cantiones profanae,* or secular songs, were written in a mixture of medieval Latin, low German, and French by wandering students, minstrels, vagabond poets, and runaway monks— the rascals, artists, dreamers, and bohemians who stood outside the pale of respectable society. Their poems hymn nature and love, the joys of

A scene from the New York City Center production of *Carmina Burana.*

the tavern and the free life; yet they contain also an undercurrent of protest against the cruel fate of those who do not fit in. From this extraordinary document of the late middle ages Orff selected twenty-four lyrics, in which earthy humor and mockery mingle with moods of rebellion, bittersweet joy, longing, and sorrow.

The melodies are of a folk-like simplicity. They are borne aloft by driving rhythms, with frequent use of ostinato figures. The setting of the Latin meters is accomplished with great dexterity. There is no thematic development. The music consists of clear-cut stanzas which are repeated, often with a crescendo.

The piece is divided into three sections—*In the Spring, In the*

Tavern, and *The Court of Love*, preceded by an invocation to Fortune, Empress of the World, which is repeated at the end.

Introduction: 1. "O Fortune, variable as the moon. . . ." The chorus opens on a note of impassioned protest. Its ostinato rhythm is repeated insistently, building to the intense emotion of the closing lines: "Weep with me, all of you, for fate crushes the brave." 2. "I lament fortune's blows. . . ." The second poem continues the mood of the first. But the Latin meter is different, which engenders a different effect in the musical rhythm. This choral song displays some striking asymmetries in the metrical distribution of the phrase.

I. *In the Spring.* 3. "The bright face of spring shows itself to the world. . . ." The third number, for small chorus, opens with the intriguing sonority of high woodwinds against two pianos. Orff here evokes the medieval atmosphere of monophonic melody, achieving the sense of remoteness and the supple prose rhythms we associate with Gregorian chant. 4. "The sun, pure and fine, tempers all; a new world is opened by the face of April." An appealing song for baritone, each stanza of which is introduced by four strokes on glockenspiel and piccolo. 5. "Behold the spring, welcome and long awaited. . . ." A melodious chorus in the gregarious *Sängerverein* tradition, supported by a luminous orchestra. The first word of each stanza is given special treatment in long notes; even as, in medieval manuscripts, the first word of a chapter is ornamented. 6. *On the lawn:* a dance in which the orchestral sonority conjures up folk instruments of the mandoline and accordion type. The rhythm has a Stravinskyan suppleness, the meter alternating between four and three time, and in certain passages changing with each measure. 7. "The noble wood is filled with buds and leaves. Where is my love?" Based on the contrast between large and small chorus, this number is notable for the melodious writing for women's voices, the harmonization of the melody in thirds, and a melodic line built on triads. The first stanza is in Latin, the second repeats the thought in German. 8. "Shopkeeper, give me color to paint my cheeks, so that the young men will not resist my charm." The folk tone is continued in this German song for sopranos and chorus. The orchestral interludes suggest a hurdy-gurdy. 9. A round dance. First the orchestra, then the large and small choruses make sweet sounds in the Bavarian—or should one say Orffian?—manner. The interludes evoke the sound of guitars. 10. "Were the world all mine, from the sea to the Rhine, I would gladly forsake it all if the Queen of England were in my arms." The vision of so exalted a personage calls for trumpets.

II. *In the Tavern.* 11. "In rage and bitterness I talk to myself . . . I am like a leaf that the wind plays with." A rousing song for baritone. The text is compounded of bravado and bitterness; the refrain has a march-like resilience. 12. "The roasted cygnet sings: 'Once I dwelt in the lake, once I was a beautiful swan. O miserable me! Now I am roasted black!' " An "ironic lament" for tenor, sung in falsetto against the eerie rasp of muted trombones, with a syncopated refrain by the chorus. 13. "I am the Abbot of Cucany, and I spend my time with drinkers . . . Whoever meets me in the tavern over dice, by the end of the day has lost his shirt." A drunken parody of Gregorian chant for baritone solo, with the male chorus supplying a mocking refrain. 14. "When we are in the tavern, we don't care who has died . . . The mistress drinks, the master drinks, the soldier and the clergyman. This one drinks and that one drinks, the servant and the maid. . . ." A gay drinking song for male chorus, whose rhythmic patter brings the second part of the work to a rousing conclusion.

III. *The Court of Love.* 15. "The God of Love flies everywhere and is smitten with desire. . . ." The pure sound of boys' voices makes a vivid contrast with the soprano's lament: "If a girl lacks a man she misses all delight." 16. "Day and night and all the world against me. . . ." The lover's complaint, for baritone solo, mingles Latin with old French. 17. "There stood a maid in a red tunic. When it was touched, the tunic rustled." A bit of folklore. 18. "My heart is filled with sighing. . . ." The baritone sings a kind of waltz song in Latin, and is consoled by the chorus in German. 19. "When a boy and a girl are alone together, happy is their union. . . ." For three tenors, baritone, and two basses, and written with a keen ear for the possible contrasts among the male voices. 20. "Come, come, do not let me die. . . ." A double chorus whose deft antiphonal writing is propelled by driving ostinato rhythms. 21. "My mind is torn between opposites: between love's desire and chastity. . . ." An appealing bit for the soprano voice, which is treated with affectionate understanding.

22. "Pleasant is the season, o maidens; now rejoice, you lads!" Another number in the popular manner, for soprano, baritone, chorus, and boys' chorus, based on contrasts of timbre and register. 23. "Sweetest boy, I give myself completely to you!" A rhapsodic bit of writing for coloratura soprano. 24. "Hail to thee, most beautiful. . . ." A majestic chorus in praise of love. 25. "O Fortune, variable as the moon. . . ." The opening number returns, to enclose the work in a somber frame.

The composer of this dynamic piece is a personality with a view and an approach of his own. His music does not wear well with those who respond to the intellectual aspects of music. But to those who hear it for the first time *Carmina Burana* is apt to bring an excitement all its own. One can understand why it has become one of the hits of the mid-century.

⊸§ 50 §⊷
William Walton (1902-)

"I seriously advise all sensitive composers to die at the age of thirty-seven. I know I've gone through the first halcyon period, and am just about ripe for my critical damnation." [1939]

WILLIAM WALTON is the most striking figure of the generation of English musicians who came to maturity in the decade after the First World War. He has moved slowly but steadily from the exuberant cleverness of his youthful works to the unashamed romanticism of his later ones. In so doing he has found his true bent, and managed to win for himself a substantial place in the musical life of our time.

HIS LIFE AND MUSIC

Walton was born in Oldham, the son of a music teacher. At the age of ten he entered the choir school attached to Oxford Cathedral. A brilliant student, he was only sixteen when he matriculated at Christ Church College. His friendship with the Sitwells—Sacheverell, Osbert, and Edith—exerted an important influence upon his intellectual development. Edith Sitwell's poetry provided the text for his first important work, *Façade*, written when he was twenty. He set the poem as a rhythmic recitation against an accompaniment played by six instruments: flute-piccolo, clarinet-bass clarinet, saxophone, trumpet, percussion, and cello. *Façade*, with its music hall gaiety and jazz rhythms, captured the spirit of the time and brought Walton speedy fame. There followed in 1925 his "comedy overture," *Portsmouth Point*, a vigorous evocation of ships and sailors inspired by an old print of the caricaturist Thomas Rowlandson.

After the high jinks of his youth and a period of commitment to neo-classicism (he was known for a time as the English Hindemith), Walton took his stand as one of the principal proponents of the new romanticism. This orientation is set forth in the Viola Concerto (1929), in which he explored the expressive possibilities of an instrument which the nineteenth century had neglected in favor of the more brilliant violin. The work received its first performance in 1929, with Walton conducting and Paul Hindemith playing the solo part.

Considering the reputation he enjoys with the public, Walton has written surprisingly little. He is known outside England by a handful of works: the Viola Concerto; *Belshazzar's Feast*, which we will discuss; and the Violin Concerto he wrote for Jascha Heifetz (1939) which is an amply designed piece compounded of soaring lyricism and technical fireworks. Walton's Symphony is vastly admired in his homeland, but has never duplicated its success elsewhere. Written when Sibelius was at the height of his fame, the work reflects the strong influence that the Finnish master exerted on English musicians.

Walton is very much appreciated as a film composer. He wrote an outstanding score for Bernard Shaw's *Major Barbara* (1941). Admirable too were his scores for Lawrence Olivier's *Henry V* (1944) and *Hamlet* (1947), the first of which especially abounded in the bright virile sounds that stir the British heart. His opera *Troilus and Cressida* (1954) appears to have hit off the British taste, but is a shade too well-bred for the American stage. The libretto by Christopher Hassall (based on Chaucer's version of the love story) is extremely literary. The characters are a gentlemanly lot, but they remain curiously remote. And the music, much as one respects its finely woven textures, is unable to bring them to life.

Walton's style at its best is characterized by sensuous lyricism, spontaneity, and charm of sentiment. His ability to spin out a long melodic line is one that musicians regard with respect. Walton's music is tonal, generously spiced with dissonance. His harmonic idiom, based on the free use of the twelve tones around a center, is overlaid with chromaticism. He favors the major-minor ambiguity that has attracted so many contemporary composers. He feels at home in the large instrumental forms. In line with present-day musical esthetics, he shows great ingenuity in condensing and freshening the material when it returns in the final section of the classical sonata form.

As regards rhythm, Walton belongs to the generation that was deeply influenced by Stravinsky. He also had a passing interest in jazz. From these two sources derive the changes of meter, the syncopations, and the percussive-rhythm effects that energize his music. Walton is fond of vivid orchestration; but he also courts sobriety. Like Sibelius, he is fond of scoring a long, slow melody for a single woodwind, also of pitting horns against trumpets in stentorian contrast. Despite the clarity of his orchestral texture, Walton is not a contrapuntal composer. Richness of harmony means more to him than linear texture. In this he is the romantic.

Walton is a fortunate artist: he is a prophet with honor in his own country. The English admire his music and make much of him at every opportunity.

BELSHAZZAR'S FEAST

Filled with the tumult and vitality of youth—Walton was twenty-nine when he wrote it—*Belshazzar's Feast* (1931) adapts the English oratorio tradition to the requirements of twentieth-century style. Based on massive choral writing—"perhaps the only compositional technique that English composers are heir to," as the British critic Peter Heyworth observed—it is a concentrated piece which in thirty-five minutes of music presents a series of vivid choral frescoes. The text, by Sir Osbert Sitwell, drawn from the Psalms and the Book of Daniel, moves swiftly to the incident that constitutes the dramatic climax—the handwriting on the wall and the subsequent destruction of Babylon. The Narrator is a baritone whose florid recitatives not only introduce the choral episodes but also evoke the savage intensity of the Biblical tale. Yet this is no drama of individuals. The emphasis, as in many of Handel's oratorios, is on the crowd. The action is presented through the collective view, through voices massed in sorrow, gaiety, or exultation. The chorus at times comments on the action, at times participates. It has no fixed identity. In the first section of the work it speaks for the Jews, in the second for the Babylonians, in the third again for the Jews.

Walton's setting of the text is molded to the natural inflections of the English language. The orchestration matches the choral writing in vividness and dramatic suggestion. The score calls for a full-sized orchestra augmented by piano, organ, and—in the manner of Berlioz—

by two extra brass bands, each consisting of 3 trumpets, 3 trombones and tuba.

I. A trumpet call on a single repeated note ushers in the opening passage for unaccompanied tenors and basses: "Thus spake Isaiah: 'Thy sons that thou shalt beget, they shall be taken away and be eunuchs in the palace of the King of Babylon. . . .'" An expressive phrase in the cellos and basses leads into the most lyrical part of the work, a setting of Psalm 137: "By the waters of Babylon there we sat down; yea, we wept and hanged our harps upon the willows. . . ." Walton shows the temperament of the true choral composer: his musical imagery takes wing from the words. Notice, for example, the billowing figure on the word *waters*, and the change of harmony that highlights the word *Babylon*. The music gathers momentum as the captive Jews sing of their tribulations. Finally, "If I forget thee, O Jerusalem, let my right hand forget her cunning. . . ." The destruction of Babylon is prophesied, the opening lines return, as does the expressive phrase on the cellos and basses, rounding off the first part into a self-contained whole.

II. The solo baritone, in a passage of flowing recitative marked *robusto*, describes the magnificence of the city. The chorus takes over the narrative. "In Babylon Belshazzar the King made a great feast to a thousand of his lords. . . ." Angular rhythms, riotous color in the orchestra—particularly the metallic sound of the xylophone—and clangorous dissonances suggest the barbaric splendor of the scene. Tension mounts steadily to the point where the King and his court worship their idols. The god of gold is praised to the accompaniment of an energetic march full of pomp and circumstance. Glockenspiel and triangle join in praise of the god of silver; gong and anvil are mustered in praise of the god of iron; xylophone and woodblock pay tribute to the god of wood. Cymbal and slapstick hail the god of stone; and the two extra brass bands join in to praise the god of that useful metal.

The semi-chorus continues the story from the standpoint of the Jews. "After they had praised their strange gods . . . false gods who can neither see nor hear, called they for the timbrel and the pleasant harp, to extol the glory of their King." As the Babylonians hail Belshazzar, the music broadens into a majestic passage that brings the second part to a stirring close.

III. The Narrator resumes: "And in that same hour as they feasted, came forth fingers of a man's hand, and the King saw the part of the hand that wrote." An ominous sound accompanies the handwriting on the wall: chords on flutes, bassoons, and two solo cellos against an ostinato on bassoons, double basses, and the lowest register of the piano; a tremolo on divided cellos *sul ponticello* (the spectral effect obtained by bowing close to the bridge); tympani, castanets, gong, tenor drum, cymbals, and harp. It is a dramatic moment.

"In that night was Belshazzar the King slain"—the word is shouted in terror by the chorus—"and his Kingdom divided." There follows a wild hymn of thanksgiving, *allegro giocoso.* "Then sing aloud to God our strength: Make a joyful noise unto the God of Jacob. . . ." Exultation abates as the half-chorus paints the woe of the fallen enemy. "While the Kings of the earth lament, and the merchants of the earth weep, wail and rend the raiment. . . ." An unaccompanied passage for double choir prepares for the re-entry of the orchestra in full force and the triumphal peroration: "Then sing aloud to God our strength. . . . For Babylon the Great is fallen. Alleluia!"

The creator of this broadly designed work is now Sir William Walton. The title accords well with a virile music that is rooted in tradition and British to the core.

◄§ 51 §►

Olivier Messiaen (1908-)

"It is a glistening music we seek, giving to the aural sense voluptuously refined pleasures. At the same time this music should be able to express noble sentiments."

HIS LIFE AND MUSIC

OLIVIER MESSIAEN was born in Avignon of Flemish and Provençal stock. His father, Pierre Messiaen, was a professor of literature and translator of Shakespeare; his mother was the poetess Cécile Sauvage. Messiaen began to compose at eight, entered the Paris Conservatory when he was eleven, and won most of the prizes offered by that venerable institution. In 1931 he was appointed organist at the Church of the Trinity in Paris, a post he still holds. Some years later he and several other young composers organized *La jeune France*, a group that reaffirmed the human and spiritual values of music. Thus, in the very citadel of neo-classicism, Messiaen became a leader of the new romanticism.

Messiaen taught at the École Normale and the Schola Cantorum from 1936 until the outbreak of war in 1939. He was called into the army, was captured by the Germans, and was interned in a prison camp in Silesia. After his repatriation he was appointed professor of harmony at the Paris Conservatoire, and in the years after the war emerged as a decisive influence on the younger generation.

The French have always been partial to instrumental music of a literary-descriptive order. This tendency has been given new vitality by Messiaen, whose deeply religious nature impells him to place his art, as he says, "at the service of the dogmas of Catholic theology." Among his orchestral works are *Le Banquet eucharistique* (1928); *Simple Chant d'une âme* (The Simple Song of a Soul, 1930); and the *Hymne au Saint Sacrement* (Hymn to the Holy Sacrament, 1932). If neo-classicism favored compression, the new romanticism is given to expansiveness. Messiaen's *Quatuor pour la fin du temps* (Quartet for the End of Time, for violin, clarinet, cello and piano, 1941), written during his wartime imprisonment, lasts a full hour. *Vingt Regards sur l'enfant Jésus* (Twenty Glances at the Infant Jesus, 1944), for piano, takes two and a half hours to perform in its entirety. Messiaen harks back to César Franck and Vincent d'Indy in his use of motto themes, which recur as unifying elements throughout the different movements of a work.

In his two-volume treatise, *Technique de mon langage musical* (The Technique of My Musical Language, 1944), Messiaen identifies the sources of his style. There is the medieval element, manifest in his partiality for Gregorian chant and the old modes. The Oriental strain derives from Hindu music, with its flexible and minute rhythms. The impressionist influence comes from *Pelléas et Mélisande*. To these is added a mystical sense of oneness with nature, embodied in his careful study of bird songs. Messiaen's attempt to introduce into Western music the rhythmic subtleties of the Far East, particularly the asymmetrical rhythms of Hindu music, has led him to innovations that have not been without their influence upon the younger French composers, particularly his pupil Pierre Boulez. He bases his conception upon unequal time values, rhythmic augmentation and diminution, what he calls reversible and nonreversible rhythms (that is to say, rhythmic series which exist as patterns apart from the pitches), rhythmic counterpoints and canons. Messiaen's strongly polyphonic idiom, with its frequent use of pedal point and *basso ostinato*, derives from the imagery of the organ. An accomplished organist himself, he is one of the few contemporary composers who have made an important contribution to the literature of that instrument. To listen to the massive sonorities of a Messiaen organ piece slash their way through the resonant space of a church is a memorable experience.

Messiaen, like a number of his compatriots, has been attracted to and used new instruments, such as the electrophonic *ondes Martenot* (Martenot waves), and the vibraphone—a percussion instrument played like the marimba with little hammers, with metal bars and an electrically actuated valve which gives each note a sustained vibrato. His vivid color sense draws him to unusual combinations of instruments. In his *Trois Petites Liturgies de la Présence Divine* (Three Little Liturgies of the Divine Presence, 1944), a soprano choir is accompanied by celesta, vibraphone, maracas, Chinese cymbals, gongs, piano, *ondes Martenot*, and strings. The Hindu influence dominates Messiaen's *Turangalîla-Symphony* (1948). The title of this enormous work in ten movements is the Hindu word for love song. The composer's description gives a good idea of his expressive intent: "The three keyboard instruments, glockenspiel, celesta and vibraphone, have a special part similar to that of an East Indian *gamelan* as used in the islands of the Sonde (Java and Bali). The percussion, amply furnished, performs true rhythmic counterpoints. In addition an *ondes Martenot* dominates the orchestra with its expressive voice. Finally, a part for piano solo, which is extremely difficult, is designed to make the orchestra shine with brilliance, with chord clusters and bird songs, almost transforming the *Turangalîla*-Symphony into a concerto for piano and orchestra."

Messiaen's novel style, incisive personality, and strongly held views have caused a stir in our time. Almost single-handedly he broke the long-standing association of Paris with neo-classicism, which in itself was a major coup.

↭ 52 ↮

Other Romantic Composers

ANDRÉ JOLIVET (Paris, 1905–) studied with Edgar Varèse and was strongly influenced by Schoenberg and Alban Berg. He was active alongside Messiaen in *La jeune France*. His personal brand of religiosity led him not to Catholic mysticism, as was the case with Messiaen, but to a more primitive kind of faith that considers the universe to be an emanation of invisible psychic forces. Jolivet's conception of music as a kind of magical incantation is implicit in certain of his orchestral works: for instance, the prelude entitled *Cosmogonie* (1938); the *Cinq Danses rituelles* (Five Ritual Dances, 1939); *Suite delphique* (Delphic Suite, 1942) for wind, *ondes Martenot*, harp, and percussion; and the symphonic poem *Psyché* (1946), in which he tries to picture the struggle of the soul to free itself from material bonds. As was also true of Messiaen, Jolivet's return to instrumental music with evocative titles represents an about-face in musical esthetics as decisive as any that has taken place in our century. The circle is now complete: from post-romantic program music to neo-classic abstraction in the first quarter of the century; from abstraction back to programmatic romanticism in the second. Jolivet has experimented with polytonality and asymmetrical rhythms; but the subjective lyricism of his music makes for an accessible idiom. He is musical director at the Comédie Française and has written widely for the theater. His works include the comic opera *Dolores* (1942); two ballets; choral and chamber music; piano pieces; and songs.

Henry Barraud (Bordeaux, 1900–) does not adhere to the Parisian esthetic. His affinity for Berlioz, about whom he has written a book, inclines him to the monumental rather than the charming. He prefers, he states, "inward and lyric music." Barraud adheres to tonality; uses modal scales; borrows from folklore; and values a theme for its melodic rather than its contrapuntal potential. Most important among his works are the oratorio *Le Mystère des Saints Innocents* (The Mystery of the Holy Innocents, 1947), on a text by Péguy; and the opera *Numances*, on a dramatic poem by Salvador de Madariaga, which was presented at the Paris Opera in 1955. As musical director of the French radio network (*Radiodiffusion Française*), Barraud plays an important part in the cultural life of his country.

Henri Sauguet (Bordeaux, 1901–) is a disciple of Erik Satie. He achieved success with his ballets *La Chatte* (The Cat), produced by Diaghilev in 1927, and *Les Forains* (The Travelers, 1945), which has become one of the hits of Roland Petit's company. Sauguet wrote the incidental music for Giraudoux's *The Mad Woman of Chaillot*. He has been influenced by the Satiean esthetic of a simple, unpretentious music, melodious, graceful, and pleasing in character. His works in the lighter vein exemplify the Parisian outlook on life and art. The romantic element is more prominent in his weightier compositions, such as *La Chartreuse de Parme* (The Charterhouse of Parma, 1927–36), a grand opera based on Stendhal's novel—the most important of his five operas—and the *Symphonie expiatoire* (1946), dedicated "to the innocent victims of the war." Besides his operas and ballets Sauguet has written much incidental, film, and radio music; church music; choral and orchestral works; two piano concertos; vocal and instrumental chamber music; pieces for a variety of instruments, piano and organ music, and a large number of songs.

Manuel Rosenthal (Paris, 1904–) was a pupil of Ravel at the Conservatoire. His most important composition is the oratorio *St. Francis of Assisi* (1946), on a text by Roland-Manuel, which is scored for large choral and orchestral forces, including vibraphone and *ondes Martenot*.

Werner Egk (1901–) is a Bavarian. He began his career by writing a number of works for the radio, among them a genial setting of La Fontaine's fable about the fox and the crow. His first opera, *Die Zaubergeige* (The Magic Fiddle, 1935), had a huge success in Germany, mainly because of the popular kind of melody that abounds in the score. *Peer Gynt* (1938), on a libretto by the composer after Ibsen's poetic drama, is a more sophisticated opera, and displays Egk's effective orchestral style. Egk is a neo-romantic. Like Orff, he has avoided the problems of contrapuntal writing and the formal abstraction we associate with the neo-classic school. His music for the theater comes out of the world of Richard Strauss. The influence of Stravinsky and of the Parisian school makes itself felt in the piquancy of his rhythms and in his keen sense of instrumental color. His earlier music adhered strictly to the principle of tonality, but lately he has moved toward a polytonal idiom. His strong point is his tunefulness, which has won him a wide following in his native land. His list of compositions includes four operas besides those mentioned: *Columbus* (1941); *Circe*

(1948), on a libretto by the composer after Calderón; *Irische Legende* (Irish Legend, 1955), after Yeats; and *Der Revisor* (The Inspector-General, 1957), after Gogol's famous comedy, in which the orchestration and the humor are on the heavy side. He has also written ballets, choral and orchestral works, vocal music, and a piano sonata.

VIII. TWELVE-TONE COMPOSERS

"I believe composition with twelve tones is not the end of an old period but the beginning of a new one."

Arnold Schoenberg

◄§ 53 §►

The Twelve-Tone School

"If it is art it is not for all, and if it is for all it is not art."

Arnold Schoenberg

OF ALL the idioms of twentieth-century music, that of the twelve-tone school is likely to pose the greatest problem for the layman. Twelve-tone composers are the first to explain that they do not address themselves to the big public. The nature of their idiom makes it mandatory for them to reject the Beethovenian dream of "embracing the millions." "There are relatively few people," Schoenberg wrote, "who are capable of understanding, purely musically, what music has to say. Such trained listeners have probably never been very numerous, but that does not prevent the artist from creating only for them. Great art presupposes the alert mind of the educated listener." Neither he nor his two chief disciples—Alban Berg and Anton Webern—regarded the difficulty of their art as a drawback. On the contrary, they accepted it as an inevitable characteristic of their language.

When an artist relinquishes the hope of communicating with the audience of his own time, he is driven to pin his hope on the future. He invokes posterity. Schoenberg had no doubt as to the outcome. "In a few decades audiences will recognize the *tonality* of this music today called *atonal*. . . . Tonal is what is understood today. Atonal is what will be understood in the future." And in the same vein: "This is the essence of genius—that it is in the future. This is why the genius is nothing to the present"—a statement not quite borne out by the careers of geniuses like Sophocles, Michelangelo, Shakespeare, and

Beethoven. René Leibowitz, one of the chief theoreticians of the twelve-tone school, expresses the same faith in posterity. In discussing Webern's music, he states, "After all, a masterpiece is in no hurry. It transcends time. It can be misunderstood or ignored—all this is quite unimportant, and the time will come when its beauty will be revealed without any outside assistance."

EXPRESSIONISM

"There is only one greatest goal," wrote Arnold Schoenberg, "towards which the artist strives: to express himself." Expressionism was the German answer to French impressionism. Where the Latin genius delighted in luminous impressions received from the outer world, the Germanic dug down to the hidden regions of the soul. Where Parisian artists cultivated a refined, highly pictorial nature poetry, those within the middle European orbit rejected the reality about them in order to fasten their gaze on the landscape within. In Vienna, where Sigmund Freud developed the theories of psychoanalysis, artists tried to capture for art the shadowy terrain of the unconscious. *Expressionismus* set up inner experience as the only reality. Through the symbolism of dreams and the glorification of the irrational, it aspired to release the primordial impulses that intellectual man too long had suppressed.

As with impressionism, the impetus for the expressionist movement came from painting and poetry. Schoenberg was influenced by the painters Wassily Kandinsky and Oscar Kokoschka, Paul Klee and Franz Marc, by the poets Stefan George and Richard Dehmel—even as Debussy had been influenced by Monet and Manet, Mallarmé and Verlaine. The distorted images on the canvases of the expressionist painters issued from the realm of the unconscious: hallucinated visions that defied the traditional notion of beauty in order to express more powerfully the artist's inner self. In similar fashion, musical expressionism rejected what had hitherto been accepted as beautiful; this rejection produced new conceptions of melody, harmony and tonality, rhythm, color, and form.

Within a twentieth-century framework, expressionism retained certain attitudes inherited from the nineteenth century. It took over the romantic love for overwhelming effect and high-pitched emotion, for the strange, the macabre, and the grotesque. Expressionism, actually, may be viewed as the last gesture of a dying romanticism. Its search for the most powerful means of communication presents certain elements of the romantic style in their most exacerbated form. Expression-

The images on the canvases of the expressionist painters issue from the realm of the unconscious: hallucinated visions that defied the traditional notion of beauty in order to express more powerfully the artist's inner self. Wassily Kandinsky, *Composition No. 4, 1914.* (Collection Museum of Modern Art)

ism is familiar to the public through the painting of Kandinsky and Klee, Franz Marc and Kokoschka; the writing of Franz Kafka; the dancing of Mary Wigman (whose esthetic was acclimated in the United States by the art of Martha Graham); the stylized acting of Conrad Veidt; and through such epoch-making films as *The Cabinet of Dr. Caligari* and Fritz Lang's *M.* Expressionist tendencies were already apparent in European opera in Strauss's *Salome* and *Elektra,* and reached their full tide in the theater works of Schoenberg and his

disciple Alban Berg. Within the orbit of our own culture, expressionistic elements are to be discerned in the work of such dissimilar artists
as James Joyce, William Faulkner, and Tennessee Williams.

Expressionism was the suppressed, the agonized, romanticism of an
antiromantic age. Its violence was the violence of a world overwhelmed, one that turned to the unconscious and the irrational in its
flight from a reality no longer to be controlled or understood. The
musical language of expressionism took its point of departure from the
ultrachromatic idiom of *Tristan and Isolde*. It favored a hyperexpressive harmonic language linked to inordinately wide leaps in the melody
and to the use of instruments in their extreme registers. Previous composers had always set texts in accordance with the natural inflections
of the language; expressionist composers deliberately distorted the
normal accentuation of words, just as expressionist actors distorted the
normal pattern of gesture, in order to secure a heightening of tension,
a reality transcending the real. Expressionism allied music to "strong"
plots replete with violence and unusual behavior, the best example of
which is the hallucinatory atmosphere surrounding Wozzeck, the hero
of Berg's expressionist opera. Most important of all, expressionism
aspired to maximum intensity all the time, an unflagging, unrelenting
intensity; hence it had to reject those elements—such as the consonance
in music—which represented a slackening of tension. In its preoccupation with states of soul, expressionism sought ever more powerful
means of communicating emotion, and soon reached the boundaries of
what was possible within the tonal system. Expressionist music was
inevitably impelled to push on to atonality.

ATONALITY

Tonality in European music, we saw, was based on the principle that
seven of the twelve tones belong to a key, while five lie outside it. The
whole development of chromatic harmony in the nineteenth century
tended to obliterate the distinction between these two groups. Wagner
had pushed chromaticism as far as possible while still remaining within
the boundaries of the key. Schoenberg took the next step. The time
had come, he argued, to do away with the distinction between the
seven diatonic tones and the five chromatic ones. The twelve tones,
he maintained, must be treated as equals. They must be regarded as
being freely related to each other rather than to a central tone. By
giving them equal importance, Schoenberg hoped to make it possible
to exploit fully all the resources of the chromatic scale.

To do away with the Tonic means abandoning a principle as funda-mental to the musical universe as gravity is to the physical. (How fundamental becomes apparent if we sing the *do-re-mi-fa* scale and stop on *ti*, resisting the almost physical compulsion to continue to *do*.) Schoenberg maintained that the major-minor system had not existed for more than three centuries, so there was no reason to suppose it could not be superseded. "Tonality is not an eternal law of music," he declared, "but simply a means toward the achievement of musical form." The time had come to seek new means.

The music of Schoenberg and his school has been described by the label *atonality*. He disliked the term as much as Debussy did *impres-sionism*. "I regard the expression *atonal* as meaningless. *Atonal* can only signify something that does not correspond to the nature of tone. A piece of music will necessarily always be tonal in so far as a relation exists from tone to tone." He suggested that his innovations be de-scribed as *pantonal*, as they aimed at "the synthesis of all tonalities"—the relationship of all tones to one another. But *atonality* took root, for to most people it summed up the cardinal point of Schoenberg's teaching—his rejection of tonality.

The concept of key, it will be recalled, depends on the distinction between consonance and dissonance: the dissonant chord constitutes the element of tension which finds resolution in the ultimate conso-nance, the Tonic. But the consonance, according to Schoenberg, had become so hackneyed, so obvious, that it could no longer play a fruit-ful role in art. Other contemporary composers, faced with the same problem, sought to inject vitality into consonances by adding tones that had hitherto been considered foreign to them. Schoenberg went them one better by discarding consonance altogether. Dissonance now became the norm: his music moves from one level of dissonance to another. He justified this procedure on the grounds that consonance and dissonance are different not in kind, but only in degree. "Dissonant tones," he maintained, "appear later among the overtones, for which reason the ear is less acquainted with them. Dissonances are only the remote consonances." There could thus be no "foreign" or chromatic tones. "The alleged tones believed to be foreign to harmony do not exist. They are merely tones foreign to our accepted harmonic system."

By eliminating the consonance Schoenberg moved toward a music that functions always at maximum tension. This circumstance imparts to it its furious restlessness, what Schoenberg's biographer Dika Newlin has called "its well-nigh hysterical emotionality." Dissonance resolving

to consonance is symbolically an optimistic act, affirming the triumph
of rest over tension, of order over chaos. Atonal music appeared, significantly, at a moment in European culture when belief in that triumph was sorely shaken. It is music that lends itself to moods of convulsive intensity. Inevitably it established itself as the language of German expressionism.

Tonality had supplied the framework within which the great forms
of classical music unfolded their spacious dimensions. The absence of
this framework forced Schoenberg, after he rejected the concept of
key, to limit himself to short pieces and songs. He felt the need of a
unifying principle that would take the place of tonality and enable
him to develop large-scale forms. This he found in the technique he
evolved in the years after the First World War. He named it "the
method of composing with twelve tones."

THE TWELVE-TONE METHOD

"I was always occupied," Schoenberg declared, "with the desire to
base the structure of my music *consciously* on a unifying idea." The
twelve-tone technique made it possible for him to achieve coherence
and unity in a musical composition without recourse to traditional
procedures such as tonal organization, harmonic relationships, expansion and development of themes, and the articulation of symmetrical
phrases. According to Schoenberg's method, every composition is
based on an arbitrary arrangement of the twelve chromatic tones which
is called a *tone row*—or, as he terms it, a basic set. This row or set is
the unifying idea which is the basis of that particular composition,
and serves as the source of all the musical events that take place in it.
The term *serial technique* is often used in this connection, an allusion
to the series of twelve tones. European writers prefer the expression
dodecaphonic, which is the Greek equivalent of *twelve-tone*.

The twelve-tone set differs from a scale in one important respect.
A scale is a traditional pattern which serves as the basic series for
hundreds of composers and thousands of compositions. It soon becomes
familiar to the listener; any departure from the pattern is at once perceptible to the ear. The tone row, on the other hand, is the basic series
of a particular composition, constituting a unique configuration of the
twelve tones not to be found in any other piece. Since the twelve
tones of the row are regarded as equally important, no one of them
is allowed to appear more than once in the series lest it take on the

prominence of a Tonic. (The tone may be repeated immediately, but this is regarded as an extension, not a new appearance.) When the basic set has unfolded it is repeated, with the twelve tones always in the same order. The row may be turned upside down (inversion); it may be presented backward (retrograde); or upside down and backward (retrograde of the inversion). Each of these four versions—the original row and its three variants—may begin on any one of the twelve tones of the scale, giving forty-eight possibilities. The movement from one level to a higher or lower is loosely analogous to the passing from one key to another (modulation) in the old tonal architecture. The tone row, in fine, pervades the entire fabric of the composition, engendering not only the melody but the contrapuntal lines that unfold against it; also the harmony, since segments of the row may appear in vertical formation as chords. Thus, the unifying idea creates all the other ideas within a piece.

The twelve-tone method represents Schoenberg's concept of "perpetual variation," according to which the maximum diversity of musical forms is derived from a minimum of material. It is a kind of variation technique, perhaps the most highly integrated that ever was. "The main advantage of this method of composing with twelve tones," Schoenberg declared, "is its unifying effect. I believe that when Richard Wagner introduced his Leitmotive—for the same purpose as that for which I introduced my Basic Set—he may have said, 'Let there be unity!'" As the possible combinations of twelve tones in forty-eight positions have been calculated to add up to almost half a billion, dodecaphonic composers have a long way to go before they exhaust the possibilities of the system.

The basic set, of course, establishes not only a series of pitches but —even more important—a series of interval relationships. The persistence of this series of intervals in the melodies, harmonies, and counterpoints of an extended composition cannot but result in the closest possible relationship among these three dimensions of the musical tissue. The old distinction between melody and accompaniment is thereby done away with, the result being a texture of unparalleled homogeneity. Twelve-tone music, in short, seeks the utmost variety within the most stringent unity.

The following example shows the four versions of the basic set of Schoenberg's Wind Quintet, Opus 26. O stands for the original form, R for retrograde, I for inversion, and RI for the retrograde of the inversion. E-flat in the original version is the equivalent of D-sharp in the inversion.

All this, you will object, is quite arbitrary. To which your Schoen-bergian will retort that all art is arbitrary. Precisely its artifice makes it art. Musical composition has always had its rules of the game. If they seem to be more in evidence here, it is only because the system is new and its procedures are unfamiliar. The only valid criterion is: are Schoenberg's rules such as to enable a creative musician to express his thoughts, his feelings, and his time? Schoenberg's followers answer with an emphatic yes.

Dodecaphonic melody differs from the traditional kind in one important respect. Melody as we have come to know it springs out of what the voice can do. Therefore it generally lies in one register. But in twelve-tone music the octaves are regarded as interchangeable. The seven *C's* of the diapason are no longer regarded as so many individual tones, but rather as representatives of the "pitch class" *C*. The same holds for the *D's*, the *E's* and the rest. From the dodecaphonic point of view, consequently, music no longer consists of the eighty-eight tones that make up the piano keyboard. Rather, only the twelve basic tones exist, no matter in which octave they happen to appear.

This octave equivalence destroys the conventional relationships we have attached to tones, giving them a new kind of meaning. The successive notes of a melody may appear in different octaves—even in vocal music—which produces the enormous leaps and zigzag melody line so characteristic of dodecaphonic music. In addition, the gravi-

Webern: Opus 29

Hel - le   stei - gen,   bald   im Him -   mel

tational pull attaching to tones in the traditional harmonic system is weakened or wholly destroyed. For example, the strongest drive in tonal music is that of the leading tone to the Tonic (*ti* to *do;* for example, *B* ascending to *C*). This drive is circumvented in twelve-tone music if the *B* ascends a ninth to the *C* of the octave above, or descends a seventh to the *C* below. As a matter of fact, intervals of the seventh and ninth are extremely prominent in twelve-tone music, as are augmented and diminished intervals. The major, minor, and perfect intervals are too fraught with tonal implications to be admitted freely into the dodecaphonic realm.

Twelve-tone thinking is essentially contrapuntal thinking. It represents a horizontal-linear conception of music, with emphasis on melodic line rather than on the harmonic mass. This conception is implemented by the devices of counterpoint: canonic and fugal imitation; augmentation and diminution (the duplication of a motive in longer or shorter note values); inversion; and crab canon or *cancrizans* (the imitation of a motive backward). The twelve-tone method eliminates the repetitions and sequences, the balanced phrases and cadences of the older style. The dynamic of this music requires that no thought ever be repeated or duplicated save in some new form. Let us recall Schoenberg's advice to his students: "Never do what a copyist can do instead." His esthetic calls for a terse language of telegraphic compression which says "the most important things in the most concentrated manner in every fraction of the time."

The tone row is not to be regarded as the theme of the piece. By the time a dodecaphonic composer has presented it in inverted and retrograde forms, and derived from it all his melodies, harmonies, and contrapuntal lines, in constantly varied rhythms, the row will have lost its identity as far as the ordinary ear is concerned. You will hardly be able to follow its peregrinations as you can follow the course of a theme in a symphony. Actually, the tone row is what you do *not* hear (or if you do, it is mainly at the beginning of the piece, where the row is generally presented in its basic form). However, since the row determines the choice and succession of the intervals, it inevitably shapes the over-all sound. More important, it pervades the thinking of the composer, providing him with the framework for his piece, even if that framework is no more visible to the beholder than is the steel skeleton that holds up a building.

Twelve-tone music, clearly, unites two contradictory elements. On the one hand it embodies an intensely expressive content based on an ultrachromatic idiom. On the other, it follows strict forms and objective procedures. It is almost as if Schoenberg had united in his art the two opposites in the German character: its love of the hyperemotional and the irrational, and its equally strong love of logic and order. One may detect here a good example of overcompensation. Precisely because the idiom is so supercharged with feeling and the sound is so volatile, the sonorous flow is chained within successions of notes calculated to the minutest detail, controlled by as rigorous a set of formal devices as ever artist imposed upon himself. The first masters of the style display all the logic of this rigidly organized system; yet over their music brood the troubled visions that agonized the consciousness of Europe in the aftermath of the First World War.

The Schoenbergian method resembles Stravinskyan neo-classicism in several ways: both emphasize the abstract nature of music, and both focus attention on an elaborate scheme of structural devices. Both represent a phase in which the enjoyment of music has become increasingly intellectual, and in which emotional factors are subjected to an elaborate formalism. Both too return to the kind of thematic-motivic work to which the impressionists and post-impressionists were so bitterly opposed.

To Schoenberg's adherents, twelve-tone music is a concept of truth and beauty to which they are dedicated with an almost religious fervor. All the same, many musicians have great difficulty in forming a connection with it, as they suddenly find themselves in a realm where all the landmarks of music as they know it have been swept away. Some, like Hindemith, oppose the twelve-tone style because it repudiates what they regard as the immutable law of any organized musical art—gravitation to the Tonic. Others reject it because it is completely unrelated to folk and popular song; and because its jagged melody lines, with their enormous leaps, are antivocal. They maintain that the formal procedures of twelve-tone music bear no relation to what the ear can hear, that dissonance unrelieved by consonance becomes monotonous, and that twelve-tone music moves within an extremely narrow expressive range.

Despite these strictures, the devotees of the twelve-tone method have gained tremendous influence in the past few years. If their music does not reach the big public (any more than does *Finnegans Wake*), it does challenge the musical intelligentsia, and it is exerting a fruitful influence even on those composers who do not accept its ideology *in toto*. For it opens up exciting new ways of utilizing the resources of the twelve-tone scale. Today dodecaphonic thinking represents the most advanced line of thought in musical esthetics, and has emerged as a profoundly significant movement on the contemporary scene.

◦§ 54 §◦
Arnold Schoenberg (1874-1951)

"I am a conservative who was forced to become a radical."

It is significant that, like Stravinsky, the other great innovator of twentieth-century music disclaims revolutionary intent. The reader may recall Schoenberg's remark on this point: "I personally hate to be called a revolutionist, which I am not. What I did was neither revolution nor anarchy." Quite the contrary; his disciples regard him as having carried to its logical culmination the thousand-year-old tradition of European polyphony.

HIS LIFE

Arnold Schoenberg was born in Vienna. He began to study the violin at the age of eight, and soon afterward made his initial attempts at composing. Having decided to devote his life to music, he left school while he was in his teens. The early death of his father left him in

Arnold Schoenberg
344

straitened circumstances. For a time he earned his living by working in a bank, and meanwhile continued to compose, working entirely by himself. Presently he became acquainted with a young musician two years older than himself, Alexander von Zemlinsky, who for a few months gave him lessons in counterpoint. This was the only musical instruction he ever had.

Through Zemlinsky young Schoenberg was introduced to the advanced musical circles of Vienna, which at that time were under the spell of *Tristan* and *Parsifal*. In 1899, when he was twenty-five, Schoenberg wrote the string sextet *Verklärte Nacht* (Transfigured Night). The following year several of Schoenberg's songs were performed in Vienna and precipitated a scene. "And ever since that day," he once remarked with a smile, "the scandal has never ceased."

It was at this time that Schoenberg began a large-scale work for voices and orchestra, the *Gurrelieder*. For the huge forces, choral and instrumental, required for this cantata he needed music paper double the ordinary size. Work on the *Gurrelieder* was interrupted by material worries. To earn a livelihood, Schoenberg turned to orchestrating popular operettas. In 1901, after his marriage to Zemlinsky's sister, he moved to Berlin and obtained a post in a theater, conducting operettas and music-hall songs. He even wrote a cabaret song, but it was too difficult to be performed. Schoenberg's early music already displayed certain traits of his later style. A publisher to whom he brought a quartet observed, "You must think that if the second theme is a retrograde inversion of the first theme, that automatically makes it good!"

Upon his return to Vienna Schoenberg became active as a teacher and soon gathered about him a band of disciples, of whom the most gifted were Alban Berg and Anton von Webern. Also among their number were the pianists Eduard Steuermann and Rudolf Serkin. The devotion of these advanced young musicians sustained Schoenberg in the fierce battle for recognition that lay ahead. At this time too he came under the influence of the abstract painter Wassily von Kandinsky, and began to paint. An exhibition of his pictures in 1910 revealed a striking talent and a starkly expressionist style.

An important adherent was Gustav Mahler, who exercised considerable influence upon Schoenberg's development. When Schoenberg's Chamber Symphony Opus 9 was first presented and the audience responded by whistling and banging their seats, Mahler sprang up in his box to command silence. He recognized the creator in Schoenberg. But he knew too that the younger man—they were separated by fourteen years—belonged to a future in which he himself had no part. To his wife Alma he confided, "I do not understand his work. But then he is young and may well be right. I am old, and perhaps I do not have the ear for his music."

Despite the hostility of the public, Schoenberg's music and doctrines slowly made their way. The tide turned in 1913 with the first performance of the *Gurrelieder*, which was received with wild enthusiasm by the Viennese. In this long-delayed moment of triumph Schoenberg was unable to forget the years of rejection that had been inflicted on him by his native city. Called to the stage again and again, he bowed to the conductor Franz Schreker and to the orchestra, but would not acknowledge the ovation tendered him by the public. "For years those people who greeted me with cheers tonight refused to recognize me. Why should I thank them for appreciating me now?"

With each new work Schoenberg moved closer to the point where he would have to reach out beyond the tonal system. "I already feel," he wrote in 1909, "the opposition that I shall have to overcome. I suspect that even those who have believed in me until now will not be willing to see the necessity of this development. It is not lack of invention or of technical skill that has urged me in this direction. I am following an inner compulsion that is stronger than education, and am obeying a law that is natural to me, therefore more powerful than my artistic training."

The war years interrupted Schoenberg's creative activity. Although he was past forty, he was called up for military service in the Vienna garrison. He had reached a critical point in his development. There followed a silence of seven years, between 1915 and 1923, during which he clarified his position in his own mind and prepared for as bold a step as any artist has ever taken—the rejection of tonality. True, there already had been stirrings in this direction before him. But it was he who set the seal of his personality upon this development, and who played the crucial role in creating a new grammar and syntax of musical speech.

The goal once set, Schoenberg pursued it with that tenacity of purpose without which no prophet can prevail. His "method of composing with twelve tones" caused great bewilderment in the musical world. All the same, he was now firmly established as a leader of contemporary musical thought. His fiftieth birthday was marked by a performance of his *Friede auf Erden* (Peace on Earth, 1907) by the chorus of the Vienna Opera, an address by the burgomaster of the city, and a "birthday book" of appreciative articles by his disciples and by leading figures in the world of art. The following year he was appointed to succeed Ferruccio Busoni as professor of composition at the Berlin Academy of Arts. The uniquely favorable attitude of the Weimar Republic toward experimental art had made it possible for one of the most iconoclastic musicians in history to carry on his work from the vantage point of an official post.

This period in Schoenberg's life ended with the coming to power of Hitler in 1933. Like many Austrian-Jewish intellectuals of his generation, Schoenberg had been converted to Catholicism. After leaving Germany he found it spiritually necessary to return to the Hebrew faith. He arrived in the United States in the fall of 1933. After a short period of teaching in Boston, he joined the faculty of the University of Southern California, and shortly afterward was appointed professor of composition at the University of California in Los Angeles. In 1940 he became an American citizen. He taught until his retirement at the age of seventy, and continued his musical activities till his death six years later. A seeker after truth until the end, to no one more than to himself could be applied the injunction he had written in the text of his cantata *Die Jacobsleiter* (Jacob's Ladder, 1913): "One must go on without asking what lies before or behind."

HIS MUSIC

Schoenberg stemmed out of the Viennese past. He took his point of departure from the final quartets of Beethoven, the lyricism of Hugo Wolf, the richly wrought piano writing of Brahms, and the orchestral sonority of Bruckner and Mahler—behind whom, of course, loomed the un-Viennese figure of Wagner.

Given this background, Schoenberg may be regarded as the antipodal figure to Stravinsky. Stravinsky rejects the concept of art as personal expression; Schoenberg adheres to it with romantic fervor. "I write what I feel in my heart—and what finally comes on paper is what first coursed through every fibre of my body. A work of art can achieve no finer effect than when it transmits to the beholder the emotions that raged in the creator, in such a way that they rage and storm also in him." Stravinsky rigidly separates art from the experiences of life; Schoenberg upholds their connection. "What else can I do than express the original word, which to me is a human thought, a human word, a human aspiration." Stravinsky is spokesman for the classic view of life; Schoenberg as steadfastly upholds the opposite. "I warn you of the danger lurking in the die-hard reaction against romanticism. The old romanticism is dead; long live the new!" Stravinsky recoils in distaste from any attempt to attach metaphysical meanings to music; for Schoenberg, the mystical approach is most congenial. "My personal feeling is that music conveys a prophetic message revealing a higher form of life towards which mankind evolves. There is only one content which all great men wish to express: the longing of mankind for its future form, for an immortal soul, for dissolution into the universe."

The paradox at the root of Schoenberg's thinking lies in the fact that the emotional, visionary elements in his personality were allied with a strong taste for abstract speculation and intellectual control. He had the true German reverence for the Idea. Music to him was "not another amusement but a presentation of musical ideas." For all his passion, he was an intellectual. "It is really only in the mental realm—where musical thought must be rich in variety—that an artistic expression is possible." His aim above all was "to join ideas with ideas." Here then is the strange duality at the heart of Schoenberg's music: a hyperexpressive content descended from the turbulently chromatic idiom of *Tristan*, controlled by as rigidly intellectual a system of formal procedures as artist ever devised.

Basic to Schoenberg's teaching was the search for organic unity. "It is with a work of art as with every perfect organism. It is so homogeneous in its constitution that it discloses in every detail its truest and inmost being." In this respect art may learn from nature. "In an apple tree's blossoms, even in the bud, the whole future apple is present in all its details. . . . The most important capacity of a composer is to cast a glance into the most remote future of his themes or motives. He has to be able to know beforehand the consequences which derive from the problems existing in his material and to organize everything accordingly. The theme consists not of a few notes but of the musical destinies of those notes."

Schoenberg's first period may be described as one of post-Wagnerian romanticism; he still used key signatures and remained within the boundaries of tonality. The best known work of this period is *Verklärte Nacht*, Opus 4. *Pelleas und Melisande*, Opus 5, after Maeterlinck's symbolist play, was written in 1902, the year in which Debussy's opera on the same subject was first produced. Lasting almost an hour, this fervid symphonic poem exploits to the full the expressive possibilities of the mammoth orchestra of the Strauss-Mahler period. The post-romantic orchestral style is carried to its farthermost limits in the *Gurrelieder*, a work that occupied Schoenberg intermittently from

1900 until 1911. This gigantic cantata, on a cycle of lyrics by the Danish poet Jens Peter Jacobsen, centers about the tragic love of King Waldemar IV of Denmark and the beautiful Tove, who is subsequently poisoned by Waldemar's jealous queen. The work, cast in a hyper-emotional post-*Tristan* idiom, calls for an orchestra of about a hundred and forty players; five soloists; and four choruses—three male choirs singing in four parts and a mixed choir in eight parts: all in all, almost four hundred performers.

During these years Schoenberg also produced works along quite different lines. The songs of Opus 2 and 3 set forth the vein of lyricism in Schoenberg's art. The *Eight Songs* of Opus 6 (1905) already display the dislocation of the vocal line through the use of wide intervals which became one of the hallmarks of his school. The First String Quartet in D minor, Opus 7 (1904–05) embodies the preoccupation with chamber-music style that came to have an ever greater influence on Schoenberg's orchestral writing. This tendency comes to the fore in the First Chamber Symphony for fifteen instruments, Opus 9 (1906), in which the polyphonic cast of Schoenberg's thought made necessary the utmost individualization of the instrumental lines. The tonal period ends with the String Quartet No. 2 in F-sharp minor, Opus 10 (1907–08), the last work in which Schoenberg used a key signature. He introduced a voice in the final movement which sings—significantly —Stefan George's *Ich fühle Luft von anderen Planeten* (I feel the air of other spheres).

Schoenberg's second period, the atonal-expressionist, gets under way with the *Three Piano Pieces* Opus 11 (1909), in which he abolishes the distinction between consonance and dissonance, and also the sense of a home key. He is moving from a harmonic-vertical mode of thought to a contrapuntal-horizontal one; from romantic subjectivity to an objective, classical orientation in which lyric emotion is controlled by thematic logic, and in which formal procedures such as canonic imitation play an ever more important role. During this period too Schoenberg turns to the utmost condensation of utterance. His output centers about the short lyric forms—piano and orchestral pieces, and songs. On the one hand he was reacting against the overextended forms of the Mahler-Strauss period as well as his own *Pelleas* and *Gurrelieder*. On the other, the new atonal idiom was so concentrated and intense, its future direction as yet so uncertain, that he could best work out its structural problems in abbreviated forms.

The fifteen songs to Stefan George's expressionist poems *Das Buch der hängenden Gärten*, Opus 15 (1908) show the increasing complexity of Schoenberg's vocal writing. The voice is no longer supported by the accompaniment but must negotiate the zigzag vocal line on its own, sustained only by the singer's stout heart and (a prerequisite!) absolute pitch. To this phase of Schoenberg's career belong two expressionist works for the theater—they can hardly be called operas. *Erwartung* (Expectancy, 1909), on a libretto by Marie Pappenheim, is a "monodrama": it has a single character, requires a huge orchestra, and is about half an hour in length. The action, which runs the gamut from tenderness to jealous rage, concerns a woman who wanders through a wood at night seeking the lover who has abandoned her for another. She relives the relationship in memory and finally stumbles upon the dead man's body. *Die glückliche Hand* (The Lucky Hand, 1913) has a libretto by Schoenberg himself. The action is extremely symbolic, revolving around such matters as the quest for happiness and the struggle between man's higher and lower impulses. In one scene Schoenberg the painter-composer calls for a crescendo in both sound and color, from red through brown, green and blue-gray to purple, red, orange, yellow, finally white: the Viennese-expressionist counterpart of Scriabin's attempt to correlate sound and color.

The *Five Orchestral Pieces*, Opus 16, constitute one of the high points of this period. Another is *Pierrot Lunaire* (Pierrot of the Moon, Opus 21, 1912), for female reciter and five instruments—flute, clarinet, violin, cello, and piano (with three alternating instruments—piccolo, bass clarinet, viola). The work is written in free rhythms and unequal measures—what Anton Webern called "the prose of music." It introduces an eerily expressive kind of declamation midway between song and speech, known as *Sprechstimme* (speaking voice). This was the first composition to carry Schoenberg's name beyond his immediate circle. Its moonstruck hero, a Pierrot far removed from his Russian counterpart Petrushka, remains one of the most striking creations of German expressionism.

The atonal-expressionist phase of Schoenberg's career ended with the *Four Songs* for voice and orchestra, Opus 22 (1914). Schoenberg's third period, that of the twelve-tone method, was ushered in—after the long silence we referred to—by the *Five Piano Pieces* of Opus 23 (1923). In the last of the set the new technique is revealed in all its features. It should not be supposed that Schoenberg completely changed his musical language when he adopted the twelve-tone method. The serial manner of writing merely enabled him to organize the intuitions that had been present in his earlier works, to systematize the aims toward which he had been moving for years. There is much less difference in sound between the pre-twelve-tone works and those that followed than one might imagine. Seen in retrospect, the third period stemmed naturally out of the second; the evolution was as continuous as it was inevitable.

The twelve-tone method is in evidence in the Serenade for seven instruments and bass voice, Opus 24 (1923). The third and fourth movements, the *Variationen* and *Sonett*, are based on tone rows. The classical objectivity that informs this phase of Schoenberg's work is manifest in a work such as the *Suite for Piano*, Opus 25 (1924). The constructive logic of the twelve-tone method made it possible for him to undertake longer works than those written in his atonal period, and to reconcile the new technique with the classical sonata form. This rapprochement is effected in the Quintet for flute, oboe, clarinet, bassoon, and horn, Opus 26 (1924); and the String Quartet No. 3, Opus 30 (1926), in which the serial technique is used in a somewhat freer manner. To this period also belong the one-act opera *Von Heute auf Morgen* (From Today till Tomorrow, 1929); *Begleitungsmusik zu einer Lichtspielszene* (Accompaniment to a Film Scene, 1930), in which Schoenberg used the twelve-tone idiom to project moods of anxiety and fear; and the *Variations for Orchestra*, Opus 31 (1927–28), one of his most powerful works.

The fourth and last period of Schoenberg's career—the American phase—brought to light several interesting tendencies in the evolution of his art. On the one hand he carried the twelve-tone technique to further stages of refinement. On the other, he modified his doctrine sufficiently to allow tonal elements to coexist with the twelve-tone style, and on occasion even returned to the major scale and to key signatures. He was far less doctrinaire in this matter than many of his disciples. "In the last few years," he wrote, "I have been questioned as to whether certain of my compositions are 'pure' twelve-tone, or twelve-tone at all. The fact is I do not know. I am still more a composer than a theorist. When I compose I try to forget all theories and I continue composing only after having freed my mind of them. It seems to me urgent to warn my friends against orthodoxy. Composing with twelve tones is not nearly as forbidding and exclusive a method as is popularly believed." In this connection he used to say that the use of the twelve-tone technique was "a family affair": it involved the composer but not the listener, who had to be moved by a piece of music rather than to concern himself with its formal intricacies.

In the category of tonal works we find the Suite for String Orchestra in G major (1934), intended for the use of students; also the *Kol*

Nidre for speaker, chorus, and orchestra, Opus 39 (1939), an impressive setting of the ancient Hebrew prayer; the *Variations on a Recitative for Organ,* Opus 40 (1940); and the Theme and Variations for Orchestra in G minor, Opus 43B—a rescoring of an earlier work intended for the use of student groups, Variations for Band, Opus 43A (1943). Several among the late works present the twelve-tone style in a manner markedly more accessible than earlier pieces, often with tonal implications. Among these are the brilliant Piano Concerto (1942); the *Ode to Napoleon* (1944), a setting of Byron's poem for string orchestra, piano, and rhythmic narration; and the cantata *A Survivor from Warsaw* (1948), for narrator, men's chorus, and orchestra, with a text in English by Schoenberg himself—the composer's tribute to the Jews who perished in the Nazi death camps.

The strict use of twelve-tone technique is represented by such compositions as the lyrical String Quartet No. 4, Opus 37 (1936), his last work in this medium; the String Trio, Opus 45 (1946), one of his profoundest works; and the *Fantasy for Violin and Piano,* written in 1949 when the composer was seventy-five. Also the Violin Concerto, Opus 36 (1936), which is in Schoenberg's most uncompromising manner. He said of it: "I am delighted to add another *unplayable* work to the repertoire. I want the Concerto to be difficult and I want the little finger to become longer. I can wait." Mention should be made too of the Biblical opera *Moses and Aaron,* a most stirring work. The first two acts were finished by 1932, but the work was interrupted by his emigration to the United States; he never went back to it.

Schoenberg was a tireless propagandist for his ideas, a role for which his verbal gifts and his passion for polemics eminently fitted him. From his *Treatise on Harmony* (1911), which begins with the famous "This book I have learned from my pupils"—he dedicated the work to the memory of Gustav Mahler—essays and articles flowed from his pen, conveying his views in a trenchant, aphoristic style which, late in life, he transferred from German to English. The following observations are characteristic: "Genius learns only from itself, talent chiefly from others. . . . One must believe in the infallibility of one's fantasy and the truth of one's inspiration. . . . Creation to an artist should be as natural and inescapable as the growth of apples to an apple tree. . . . The twelve tones will not invent for you. When you find that something you have written is very complicated, you should at once be doubtful of its genuineness." (It cannot be said that he always adhered to this maxim.) "No art has been so hindered in its development by teachers as music, since nobody watches more closely over his property than the man who knows that, strictly speaking, it does not belong to him. . . . It is said of many an author that he has indeed technique, but no invention. That is wrong: either he also lacks technique or he also has invention. . . . Mannerism is originality in subordinate matters. . . . An apostle who does not glow preaches heresy. . . . The laws of nature manifested in a man of genius are but the laws of the future."

His belief in the ineluctable necessity and the rightness of his doctrines sustained him and gave him the strength to effectuate his revolution. His doctrine has focused attention on basic compositional problems and has profoundly affected the course of musical thought in the twentieth century. Now, as during his lifetime, Arnold Schoenberg continues to be—as the critic Paul Rosenfeld once called him—"the great troubling presence of modern music."

◄§ 55 §►

Four Works by Schoenberg

"Time is a great conqueror. He will bring understanding to my works."

VERKLÄRTE NACHT (TRANSFIGURED NIGHT), OPUS 4

THIS early work (1899) relates the origins of Schoenberg's art to Wagnerian chromaticism. It stands in direct line of descent from *Tristan*. Originally written for string sextet, the piece was later arranged by Schoenberg for string orchestra. *Verklärte Nacht* brought the spirit of program music into the "pure" realm of chamber music, for it was inspired by a poem of Richard Dehmel. This tells of two who wander through a moonlit grove. The woman confesses that she is with child by another man. Now that she has found love, she is tormented by guilt. The man bids her cast away despair. He will raise the child as his own, for their love has made him even as a child. Through his forgiveness he is transfigured. They embrace in the moon-drenched night.

The music is steeped in nature poetry. The chromatic harmonies, restless modulations, and impassioned climaxes make for an utterly romantic tone poem. Schoenberg exploits the possibilities of the medium, the piercing sweetness of the strings in their high register, the dark resonance of the low, and the rich palette of colors between. The material is overextended, an interesting circumstance in view of his later striving for the utmost concision of speech. Although the piece derives its emotional ambience from Wagner, its sensibility is wholly Viennese. Certain turns of the harmony remind one of Franz Liszt, a composer who is never mentioned as having exerted an influence on Schoenberg. *Verklärte Nacht* became something of a hit as the score for Antony Tudor's ballet *Pillar of Fire*, bringing Schoenberg a measure of the popular approval from which he turned away in his later works.

The opening melody, a descending motive in D minor played by violas and cellos, evokes a brooding landscape.

Certain devices dear to the romantic imagination are much in evidence: the tremolo in dark lower register, a solo violin soaring high above the harmony, imitation between one instrument and another in a manner suggesting tender dialogue. The work unfolds through a continuous flowering of themes and motives, presenting an admirable unity of texture. The seven lines—two groups each of violins, violas, and cellos, supported by double bass—unite in a finely spun fabric. The sound has the nervosity, the light and luminous quality characteristic of Schoenberg's later works. Despite its sensuous harmony, his music even at this early stage leans toward counterpoint. After much restless wandering and building up of tension, the piece reaches its resolution in a Lisztian cadence in D major.

Verklärte Nacht is a sweet, tender work. It reveals the vast technical adroitness with which Schoenberg began his career, and forcefully refutes the oft-repeated contention that the master turned to the iron-clad logic of his twelve-tone method because he lacked the lyric gift.

FIVE PIECES FOR ORCHESTRA, OPUS 16

The *Five Pieces for Orchestra* (1909) constitute one of the key works of Schoenberg's second period, when his language became atonal. The use of short lyric forms, we saw, was characteristic of the years when he was stabilizing the new idiom. The expressionist esthetic underlying his music at that time led him to connect the Five Orchestral Pieces with specific emotions and moods; he therefore gave them descriptive titles. Yet he felt uneasy about their being regarded as program music, and soon discarded the titles. Forty years later—in 1949 —he revised the *Five Pieces,* rescoring them for an orchestra of the usual size instead of the huge ensemble required in the original version. At this time, significantly, he restored the titles, thereby underlining the relationship of this music to certain moods and images.

Schoenberg's style, as we encounter it here, is based on a pointillisme that uses the full orchestra for the tracing of evanescent sonorities. We find the soloistic writing for instruments, the epigrammatic structure, the perpetual variation of thematic elements in an intricate polyphonic texture, the fluctuating rhythms liberated from traditional meters; the rarefied—one might say "pulverized"—writing that was to reach its ultimate expression in the music of Webern; and the restless movement from one level to another of unresolved tension.

I. Vorgefühle (see p. 356)

I. *Vorgefühle* (Premonitions). *Molto Allegro.* The first piece shows how well the atonal idiom lends itself to the expression of fear and anxiety. This music evokes a hallucinatory world where agony of soul reigns unrelieved. The basic theme is an ascending motive that is announced at the outset by muted cellos, against descending parallel fifths on clarinets. (H̅ indicates *Hauptstimme*, the principal voice.) This theme reappears throughout the piece in manifold guises, with changes of rhythm (augmentation and diminution) and variation in the size of its intervals. The climb to the final note underlines the continuous sense of climax. Schoenberg exploits striking instrumental effects, such as the frightening rasp of muted horn and trombone, and fluttertonguing on the muted trumpet. He intrigues the ear with unwonted contrasts of high and low registers, achieves a remarkable luminosity of texture, and keeps the sound mass in a state of dynamic impulsion.

II. *Vergangenes* (The Past). *Andante.* A lyrical meditation, intensely romantic in character. The opening harmonies are composites of colors as well as tones: each note of the chord is played by a different instrument.

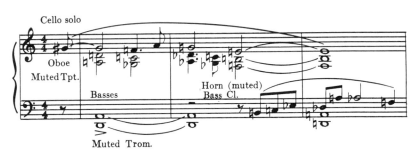

The bare look of the notes on the page shows the line of descent from the fervidly chromatic idiom of *Tristan.* The introductory motive on the cello sets the mood for a music that seems to be suspended in time.

A new section is ushered in by an expressive idea on the muted viola, which emerges as the principal theme of the piece. There enters a hopping figure on the bassoon, against a flowing ostinato on the celesta, which becomes a countersubject for the principal idea. The climax is a whisper: sixteenth-note figures derived from the bassoon motive build up—to a *ppp!* The chief motive dominates the closing pages. The final sounds are extremely rarefied: a splash of color on the celesta, harmonics on strings and harp, against sustained harmonies in woodwinds and muted brass.

III. *Sommermorgen an einen See: Farben* (Summer Morning by a Lake: Colors). *Moderato.* Schoenberg originally called this study in sonority *Der wechselnde Akkord* (The Changing Chord). The piece sprang out of a conversation he had with Mahler, in which he argued that it should be possible to create a melody by sounding a single tone on the different instruments: in other words, the Schoenbergian concept of *Klangfarbenmelodie* (tone-color melody). Mahler disagreed. In the writing, Schoenberg expanded his original notion. The harmonies in the piece do change, but so imperceptibly that the ear is led to concentrate on the continual shifting of color.

When he wrote the piece Schoenberg was much interested in painting. Hence the musical conception connected itself in his mind with a visual image—the shimmer of the morning sun on the calm surface of a lake. The harmonic current flows so slowly that it seems hardly to move, gleaming gently as the various colors play upon it. The opening measure illustrates Schoenberg's method in this essay in pure orchestration. The first chord is played by two flutes, clarinet, bassoon, and viola. It is then repeated, with a subtle change of color, by English horn, bassoon, muted horn, trumpet, and double bass.

IV. *Peripetie. Molto Allegro.* The Greek word *peripetia* signifies a sudden crisis or reversal in the events of a drama. We are back in the brooding atmosphere of the first piece. Woodwinds and brass by turns trace impetuous figures. The music shows the rhythmic flexibility, fragmentation of texture, and wide leaps in the melody so characteristic of Schoenberg. He makes dramatic use of the muted brass playing fortissimo. Tension mounts to the end.

V. *Das obligate Rezitativ* (The Obligatory Recitative). *Allegretto.* The last of the set is in a vein of impassioned lyricism. The short breathless phrases communicate intense emotion. Schoenberg here achieves his desire to create a melody that perpetually renews itself, never weakening its tension through repetition. He was increasingly aware of the problem that his intricate polyphonic textures posed to conductor, performer, and student. In *Das obligate Rezitativ* he used for the first time a system of signs to distinguish the principal voice from the other contrapuntal lines—a practice he retained in all his later scores and in his revisions of earlier works.

VARIATIONS FOR ORCHESTRA, OPUS 31

Schoenberg's Opus 31 (1928), the first twelve-tone work for orchestra, signalizes the master's return to orchestral writing after a decade and a half. Having achieved a continuous texture in the short forms, he was ready to apply his method to a more ample structure. For this attempt, significantly, he chose variations rather than symphony. This accorded with his goal of "perpetual variation," whereas the symphony —with its contrasting key areas—he naturally regarded as the citadel of tonal thinking.

The work calls for a large orchestra that includes mandoline, harp, celesta, and a full percussion section. The ensemble is handled for the most part in the manner of a chamber orchestra, with the tutti passages standing out, by sheer weight, against soloistic and concertante textures. The large orchestra was made necessary by Schoenberg's technique of fragmenting the contrapuntal lines and distributing them among various instruments. Besides, he needed a full orchestra to support the spacious architecture of the *Variations*.

The following example gives the tone row on which *Variations for Orchestra* is based. The original version of the row is labelled O, the backward or retrograde form R, the inversion I, and the retrograde of the inversion RI.

Introduktion. Mässig, ruhig (moderate, calm), 2/2. Schoenberg's conception that every passage in a work should have its own structural function is well exemplified in the opening portion of the work. The mysterious pianissimo of the opening tremolos, fraught with expectancy, is in the nature of a preparation. Toward the end of the introduction the trombone introduces the motive *B-A-C-H* (in German musical nomenclature *H* is B-flat), which plays a unifying role in the piece. Significantly this motive is never transposed, but always appears in its original form. The intervals of the basic series are gradually presented; but it accords with the introductory character of this passage that the clear-cut statement of the theme is postponed until the next section.

Thema. Molto moderato, 3/4. The vagueness is dispelled. The theme, composed of four distinct phrases, is set forth by the cellos. In the

fourth phrase it is taken over by the violins, while the cellos play a
counterpoint. The melody is harmonized by chords in the horns,
woodwinds, and double basses.

The theme is based on the original row; its transposition begins on
G, a major sixth or ten semitones up. The following example, which
gives the four orders of the transposed row, is therefore marked O-10,
R-10, I-10, and RI-10. (For convenience, the row is transposed a minor
third down instead of a major sixth up. See next page.)

Phrase A of the theme presents the original form of the row (O),
phrase B the transposed inversion in retrograde order (RI-10); phrase
C the original version in retrograde (R); phrase D the transposed inversion (I-10). The theme thus presents the four basic forms of the
row. At the same time these four phrases set forth motives X, Y, and Z,
which take on structural significance throughout the work. The three
motives reappear in the fourth phrase; but this time X is inverted, Y is
transformed, Z is inverted, and its two final tones are prolonged. The
theme as a whole, consequently, might be regarded as a kind of A-B-A
form (or, since the last phrase is a variant of the first, an A-B-A'). A
comparison of the theme with the row makes clear the Schoenbergian
concept of octave equivalence. The pitch is the crucial fact, regardless
of whether it occurs in a higher or lower octave. Also, spelling does
not matter: G-flat equals F-sharp, F-flat is equivalent to E, and so on.

Now let us consider the harmony. Motive X, consisting of five tones,
is harmonized by a five-tone chord; motive Y, consisting of four tones,
by a four-tone chord; motive Z, consisting of three tones, by a three-
tone chord. This concordance between melody and harmony persists
throughout the theme. The twelve tones in the bass that harmonize
phrase A spell out the transposed version of the row, that is, I-10:
G, Db (C#), B, D, C, G# (Ab) and so on. The eleven tones in the
bass that harmonize phrase B spell out the backward version of the
original row (R): C, B, Ab (G#), G, Db (C#), D, A, F, Eb (D#),
Gb (F#), Bb. The tone E, clearly, is omitted because at measure 43

it is prominent in the soprano. The twelve bass tones that harmonize phrase C spell out, backwards, the inverted form of the transposed row; that is, RI-10. The eleven bass tones that harmonize phrase D spell out the original row, the twelfth tone E being omitted because at this point—measure 51—it is emphasized in the soprano. There results the following symmetrical arrangement:

	Phrase A	Phrase B	Phrase C	Phrase D
Melody:	O	RI-10	R	I-10
Harmony:	I-10	R	RI-10	O

It becomes clear that the harmony is the vertical arrangement of the row even as the melody is the horizontal arrangement thereof. Melody and harmony, the horizontal and vertical dimensions, are both projections of the same entity.

It would take us beyond the confines of our chapter to continue this detailed analysis of the *Variations*. (René Leibowitz, in his book *Introduction à la musique de douze sons*, has devoted over a hundred pages to analyzing this work alone.) Enough has been said to give the reader an insight into the way Schoenberg derives all his material— melodic, harmonic, contrapuntal—from the original row. The diversity of the thematic-motivic material that he fashions in this manner, matched by the diversity of the rhythms and orchestral colors in which they are garbed, bespeaks a prodigious mastery of the compositional process in general and of the twelve-tone technique in particular.

Variation I. *Moderato*, 3/4. Oboes, violins, then horns, harp, violas, and cellos set up a light nervous movement in which sixteenth notes predominate. The theme unfolds in the bass against a counterpoint composed largely of thirds and sixths. The prevalence of these intervals contributes to the gentle atmosphere that envelops this variation.

Variation II, marked *Langsam* (slow), in 9/8 time, introduces a complex polyphonic tissue articulated by eighteen instruments used soloistically. The texture is based on a triple canon between cello and bassoon, bass clarinet and flute, muted violin and oboe. The last two present the theme against the contrapuntal intricacies of the other instruments, intricacies which involve all four versions of the row and canonic imitation in contrary motion.

In the next five variations the theme is relegated to a subordinate position, emphasis being placed on new countersubjects and fresh rhythmic structures. Variation III, marked *Mässig* (moderate), in 3/4, is presented as an orchestral tutti. The virile tone is implemented by energetic rhythms and the prominence of the brass. The theme is in the horns. In Variation IV, a *Walzertempo* (waltz-time), the theme is presented by harp, celesta and mandoline as an accompaniment to new contrapuntal lines. The instrumental writing is light and mobile, in the nature of a chamber orchestra. Variation V, *Bewegt* (agitated), in 3/4, opens with a grandiose tutti. The theme is mostly in the bass, in the cello part. Schoenberg dissolves it in the orchestral tissue so as to focus our interest on other matters.

Variation VI, an *Andante* in 4/8, returns to the concertante style. Three solo cellos, a viola, and a double bass are pitted against the mass, and are joined by the full string section. The dissolution of the theme proceeds, it being almost wholly confined to the first cello and the middle register. Variation VII, marked *Langsam* (slow), in 4/4 time, expounds several new ideas in a richly polyphonic texture. The theme, presented by piccolo, glockenspiel, and solo violin, *ppp*, dissolves into a series of isolated points; yet it occupies a more important position than in the preceding variation. Schoenberg, in effect, is preparing to bring it back into the limelight.

Variation VIII, marked *Sehr rasch* (very lively), in 2/2, involves the entire orchestra. The theme dominates the musical discourse. The variation unfolds as a kind of free canon in contrary motion between the theme and a counterpoint against a rhythmic ostinato in eighth notes punctuated by chords. Variation IX is marked bilingually: *L'istesso tempo; aber etwas langsamer* (same tempo, but somewhat slower). This variation has a more complex structure than those that preceded. The different parts of the theme are superposed upon one another, so that what has been heard in succession is now presented simultaneously. The theme, introduced by the piccolo, is imitated in contrary motion by the clarinets.

The Finale opens with a recitative that evokes the same air of gentleness which characterized the Introduction. The first section, marked *Mässig schnell* (fairly fast), introduces the B-A-C-H motive with pianissimo fluttertonguing on the flutes. The *Grazioso* that follows, first in 2/4, then 3/4, presents new aspects of the theme and new countersubjects. An accelerando leads into the *Presto*, which combines the B-A-C-H motive with the theme; a canon in contrary motion on the B-A-C-H motive is played by two trumpets. The climax of the movement is reached in the *Pesante* (heavy); this interrupts the Presto and presents the B-A-C-H motive as a kind of motto theme. An extraordinary Adagio of six measures—one of the most beautiful passages, in regard to sonority, that Schoenberg ever wrote—leads back into the Presto that completes the work. The final chord appropriately unites all twelve tones of the chromatic scale.

PIANO CONCERTO, OPUS 42

The Piano Concerto (1942) belongs to Schoenberg's final period. The relaxation of strict dodecaphonic procedure that manifested itself during his American sojourn is reflected in this work. Although the writing is dodecaphonic, we find a vaguely tonal atmosphere.

Schoenberg retains some of the traditional features of the piano concerto in his Opus 42. There are three movements—really four, as the last is subdivided into two sections. The instrument's technical resources are fully exploited. The work boasts two cadenzas. Yet pyrotechnical display for its own sake is sedulously avoided. Piano and orchestra are integrated in a symphonic whole, with a constant interchange of ideas between them. The writing for the piano, as so often with Schoenberg, bears, in its rich texture and sweeping use of the keyboard, some resemblance to the piano style of Brahms. Indeed, the look of the notes on the page—the spread of the left-hand part, the double notes and full chords in the right—would remind one of that master, were it not for the accidentals and for the fact that this, really, is another language.

The piece has a high emotional content. The continual shifting from quiet lyricism to impassioned utterance suggests its romantic provenance. The orchestral writing fully justifies Virgil Thomson's description of the Concerto as "chamber music for a hundred players." There is no attempt at the grand gesture in this rather intimate work, written when the master was approaching seventy.

I. *Andante*, 3/8. The tone row with which the Concerto opens

pervades all three movements. The piano announces the row in a quietly lyrical mood. Notice that in this presentation Schoenberg departs from strict twelve-tone procedure, since he repeats several notes before all twelve have been heard:

The row is immediately heard in an inversion of the retrograde, trans-posed; then a retrograde version on the original pitch; and then a transposed inversion. These four forms constitute a thirty-nine measure statement of the theme. The meditative mood is continued as the violins take over the row and carry it to the high register against the figuration of the piano.

The first five tones of the row (under the bracket) serve as a motive that pervades the work. Schoenberg called it the *Kopfmotiv* or "head-motive" and used it as a structural element in the Concerto. The cus-tomary fragmentation of texture associated with the dodecaphonic style gives way, in this work, to a continuity of line and movement closer to traditional norms. The orchestral writing musters his favorite devices, such as harmonics on the strings, trills in the extreme registers, and fluttertonguing on the muted brass. The transformations of the row are carried out with extreme ingenuity, yet an ingenuity wedded to imagination. Writing such as this could be done only by one who envisioned the possibilities of the twelve-tone idiom in the way that, let us say, Keats envisioned the possibilities of the sonnet.

II. *Molto Allegro.* The second movement is in 2/2 time, with ex-cursions to 3/2, 3/4, and 6/4. The opening measures present an ani-mated interchange among xylophone, brass, and piano. The frequent changes of meter and tempo impart rhythmic flexibility to the move-ment. A stringendo passage builds up to the climax. Tension subsides in a transitional passage that leads into the third movement.

III. *Adagio*, 3/2. One of the most lyrical movements that Schoenberg ever wrote, this Adagio opens with an expressive duet between oboe and bassoon which is a transposition of the basic row, accompanied by its inversion in the trombones and violas. The opening passage for orchestra leads into a piano cadenza requiring agile fingers. Another evocative passage for the orchestra introduces delicate figuration on the piano against a subtle background of winds and strings. A brief cadenza for the piano ushers in the last movement.

IV. *Giocoso* (moderato), 2/2. The finale is a lively movement in rondo style. The opening phrase is an inverted version of the first six notes of the piano theme, while the next six notes present the second half of the row arranged backward.

A vigorous orchestral passage in triplet rhythm is followed by an animated exchange with the piano. The movement mounts in tension until the coda, which is taken at an increased speed. The "head-motive"

appears in a new guise, and in the furious final measures is combined, in the piano part, with its inversion.

The Piano Concerto is a mellow work of the master's maturity. It embodies Schoenberg's majestic attempt to unite the emotional, intellectual, and technical aspects of his art in a single embracing synthesis.

∽§ 56 §∾
Alban Berg (1885-1935)

"Not a measure in this music of ours—no matter how complicated its harmonic, rhythmic, and contrapuntal texture—but has been subjected to the sharpest control of the outer and the inner ear, and for the meaning of which, in itself and in its place in the whole, we do not take the artistic responsibility."

IT WAS the unique achievement of Alban Berg to humanize the abstract procedures of the Schoenbergian technique, and to reconcile them with the expression of feeling. Upon a new and difficult idiom he imprinted the stamp of a lyric imagination of the first order.

AMP

Alban Berg

HIS LIFE

Berg was born in Vienna. He came of a well-to-do family and grew up in an environment that fostered his artistic proclivities. The urge to write music asserted itself during his adolescence. At nineteen he made the acquaintance of Arnold Schoenberg, who was sufficiently impressed with the youth's manuscripts to accept him as a pupil.

During his six years with Schoenberg he acquired the consummate mastery of technique that characterizes his later work. Schoenberg was not only an exacting master, but also a devoted friend and mentor who shaped Berg's whole outlook on art; in a sense, Schoenberg filled a void that had been left by the early death of Berg's father. The young musician was shy and introverted, a dreamer who did not find it easy to pass from intention to deed. Schoenberg's forceful nature supplied the necessary antidote to the uncertainties of the artist and the man.

Berg's letters give evidence of the strong ties that bound him to his teacher. In 1910—he was then twenty-five—he wrote to his friend Webern: "How despondent you must be again, far away from all these divine experiences, having to forgo the walks with Schoenberg and miss the meaning, the gestures and cadence of his talk. Twice a week I wait for him at the Karlsplatz, before teaching begins at the Conservatory, and for the fifteen to thirty minutes' walk amidst the hubbub of the city, which is drowned out by the 'roar' of his words. But to tell you about all this is only to increase your suffering and sense of deprivation." Only a talent of the first order could outgrow such a hold. Of the fairly large group of students that surrounded Schoenberg in Vienna, only two—Berg and Webern—emerged as creative personalities in their own right.

Berg's Piano Sonata Opus 1, the early songs of Opus 2, and String Quartet Opus 3 were presented at concerts of Schoenberg's pupils and elicited a certain amount of appreciation among the musical intelligentsia; but they did not yet indicate his true stature. The outbreak of war in 1914 hurled him into a period of depression. "The urge 'to be in it'," he wrote to Schoenberg, "the feeling of helplessness at being unable to serve my country, prevented any concentration on work." A few months later he was called up for military service, despite his uncertain health (he suffered from asthma and attacks of nervous debility). He was presently transferred to the War Ministry in Vienna. Already *Wozzeck* occupied his thoughts; but he could not begin writing the music until the war was over. He then worked assiduously at the opera and completed it in 1921. Three excerpts were performed in Frankfort in 1924. In December, 1925, *Wozzeck* was presented at the Berlin State Opera. At one stroke Berg was lifted from comparative obscurity to international fame.

In the decade that remained to him he produced only a handful of works; but each was a significant contribution to his total output. During these years he was active as a teacher. He also wrote about music, propagandizing tirelessly on behalf of Schoenberg and his school. Although after *Wozzeck* he was admired all over the world, he remained a prophet without honor in his own country. In a letter to Webern concerning his nomination to the Prussian Academy of Arts in 1930, he writes ironically: "It pleased me very much, especially on account of Vienna, that is, of Austria, which—as is well known—has virtually overloaded us for years with honors and appointments."

With the coming to power of Hitler, the works of Schoenberg and his school were banned in Germany as alien to the spirit of the Third Reich. The resulting loss of income was a source of worry to Berg, as was, to a far greater degree, the rapid Nazification of Austria. Schoenberg's enforced emigration to the United States in the fall of that year was a bitter blow, especially as the master could not readily accept the fact that both Berg and Webern were remaining behind.

Exhausted and ailing after the completion of the Violin Concerto, Berg went to the country for a short rest before resuming work on his opera *Lulu*. An insect bite brought on an abscess that caused infection. Upon his return to Vienna he was stricken with blood poisoning. He was taken to the hospital and given a transfusion. On catching sight of the donor, a typical young Viennese, he remarked jokingly, "Let's hope I don't become a composer of operettas." During the final delirium his mind was occupied with *Lulu;* he went through the motions of conducting the music, exhorting the orchestra to play more firmly. He died on Christmas Eve, 1935, seven weeks before his fifty-first birthday.

HIS MUSIC

Berg's art issued from the world of German romanticism—the world of Schumann, Brahms, Wagner, Richard Strauss, and Mahler. The romantic streak in his temperament bound him to this heritage even after he had embraced the dodecaphonic style. His tendency to incorporate tonal elements into the twelve-tone language makes him the most accessible of the composers of Schoenberg's school, consequently the one with the widest public.

Berg's was the imagination of the musical dramatist. For him the musical gesture was bound up with character and action, mood and atmosphere. The natural outlet for this kind of imagination is, of course, the opera house. Yet even in his abstract instrumental works, the shaping of the material into self-contained forms took on psychological overtones. In the *Lyric Suite,* for example, the titles of the various movements clearly indicate the composer's relationship to romantic tone-poetry: I. *Allegro gioviale.* II. *Andante amoroso.* III.

Allegro misterioso; trio estatico. IV. *Adagio appassionato.* V. *Presto delirando.* VI. *Largo desolato.*

Where Berg showed himself the true Schoenbergian was in his penchant for intricate contrapuntal structures, his mastery of the principles of perpetual variation, and the extreme condensation of his forms. Like his teacher, he leaned toward the formal patterns of the past—fugue and invention, passacaglia, variations, sonata, and suite. (Interestingly, the symphony for full orchestra is absent both from his and Schoenberg's output.) His use of the classical molds indicates how clearly he felt the need for a firm structural framework to compensate for the loss of the unifying power of tonality.

Like so many of his contemporaries, Berg favored the interval of the fourth as a constructive element in melody and harmony. He used the seventh as a prime source of melodic and harmonic tension. He was master of an imaginative orchestral palette, which he employed with classical economy and precision. We find in his works the rarefied sonorities of the dodecaphonic school, and all the devices native to it —the evanescent glissandos, trills, fluttertonguings, harmonics, and muted passages. Characteristic was his exploitation of what he called "constructive rhythm," in which a rhythmic pattern was allotted the same decisive role in the unfolding of a movement as would ordinarily be given a distinctive melodic figure. These and kindred devices were synthesized into an extremely personal style marked by lyric feeling and dramatic élan.

The list of his published works begins with the Piano Sonata Opus 1 (1907–09), a highly charged work in a post-Wagnerian idiom. The four songs of Opus 2 (1909) reveal the composer in a period of transition from Mahlerian romanticism to the expressionist tendencies of his later years. In the last of the four, the young composer abandons key signatures. The String Quartet Opus 3, in two movements (1910), shows the ambiguity of key that was native to Berg's thinking. Opus 4 consists of *Five Songs* for voice and orchestra (1910), on picture-postcard (literally) texts by the Viennese poet Peter Altenberg. These texts were pithy utterances that Altenberg was in the habit of dashing off to his friends. In this work Berg profited from the experiments of Schoenberg and Webern in new orchestral sonorities and in the unconventional handling of the voice. The last piece of the set, a Passacaglia, contains a twelve-tone row. Berg wrote it years before Schoenberg formalized the dodecaphonic technique. The set of four pieces for clarinet and piano, Opus 5—the first of the works Berg dedicated to his teacher—was written in 1913. In his striving for the utmost condensation of material Berg was influenced by the short piano pieces of Schoenberg. The *Three Orchestral Pieces*, Opus 6 (1913–14), consisting of a *Prelude*, *Round*, and *March*, date from a period of severe inner crisis when Berg was seeking his way as an artist. They show affinity with Mahler rather than with Schoenberg, to whom they were dedicated. With the third piece of this set we find ourselves in the atmosphere of *Wozzeck*.

We shall discuss Berg's masterpiece in detail. This milestone in operatic literature was followed by the *Chamber Concerto* for piano, violin, and thirteen wind instruments, which was completed in 1925 and dedicated to Schoenberg on the latter's fiftieth birthday. The work is notable for its use of contrapuntal procedures associated with the twelve-tone school: strict canonic imitation, inversion, and retrograde motion. It displays, too, Berg's love of musical anagrams; the basic theme consists of all the letters in the names Arnold Schoenberg, Anton Webern, and Alban Berg that have musical equivalents. (In German usage, *S* and *H* are respectively E-flat and B-flat.)

Berg's most widely known work, after *Wozzeck*, is the *Lyric Suite*, written in 1925–26. The first and last movements follow strictly "the method of composing with twelve tones." The slow movement contains an allusion to the Prelude of *Tristan and Isolde*. Originally written for string quartet, the *Lyric Suite* achieved such popularity that in 1928 the composer arranged the three middle movements for string orchestra.

Berg spent the last seven years of his life on the opera *Lulu*. The work is based on a twelve-tone row. The composer fashioned the libretto himself from two dramas by Frank Wedekind—*Earth Spirit* (1893) and *Pandora's Box* (1901). Lulu is the eternal type of *femme fatale* "who destroys everyone because she is destroyed by everyone." Berg's opera is strong stuff as a libretto. Murder, blackmail, sexual perversion and imprisonment enter into a tale that takes us from Berlin to a gambling den in Paris, and to the final degradation of the aging heroine on the streets of London. The choice of such a subject for an opera accorded with the social and intellectual climate that prevailed in central Europe in the Twenties. Berg was in the midst of orchestrating *Lulu* when he interrupted the task to write the Violin Concerto. The opera remained unfinished at his death. However, the sketches he left behind would make it possible to complete the work according to his intentions. *Lulu* has been recorded, and in years to come may very well take its place alongside *Wozzeck* as one of the challenging works of the modern lyric theater.

   Alban Berg is today one of the most widely admired masters of the twelve-tone school. His premature death robbed contemporary music of a major figure.

⇜ 57 ⇝

Two Works by Berg

> "When I decided to write an opera, my only intention was to give to the theater what belongs to the theater. The music was to be so formed that at each moment it would fulfill its duty of serving the action."

WOZZECK

OPERA IN THREE ACTS

IN 1914 Berg saw the play which impelled him to the composition of *Wozzeck*. He finished the draft of the libretto by the summer of 1917. Most of the music was written from 1918 to 1920 and orchestrated the following year. The vocal score was published in 1923 with the financial help of Alma Mahler, to whom *Wozzeck* was dedicated.

   The author of the play, Georg Büchner (1813–1837), belonged to the generation of intellectuals who were stifled by the political repressions of Metternich's Europe. His socialist leanings brought him into conflict with the authorities. After his death at twenty-four, the manuscript of *Danton's Tod* (The Death of Danton) and the unfinished *Woyzeck* (this was the original spelling) were found among his papers. In the stolid infantryman Wozzeck he created an archetype of "the insulted and the injured" of the earth. Though it issued from the heart of the romantic era, Büchner's stark drama is surprisingly contemporary in thought and feeling. Above all—as Berg, with the intuition of genius, immediately recognized—the play was ideally suited to the emotional atmosphere of the expressionist theater and the atonal music of the twentieth century.

   Berg's libretto tightened the original play. He shaped the material into three acts, each containing five scenes. These are linked by brief orchestral interludes whose motivic facture serves to round off what has preceded as well as to introduce what follows. As a result, Berg's "opera of protest and compassion" has astonishing unity of texture and mood.

THE DRAMA

Act I, Scene 1: Wozzeck is shaving the sadistic Captain, who twits the soldier on his stupidity, his lack of moral sense, and the illegitimate child he has had with Marie. Wozzeck tries to defend himself. Scene 2:

Louis Melancon

Wozzeck, Scene 2, from the Metropolitan Opera production.

Wozzeck and his friend Andres are cutting branches in a thicket. Wozzeck is frightened at the silence, and insists that the place is haunted. Scene 3: Marie, her child in her arms, stands at the window of her room as a military band approaches. She admires the handsome Drum Major. She slams the window shut when her neighbor Margaret taunts her, and sings a lullaby to the little boy. Wozzeck stops by, still pursued by the phantoms of his morbid fancy. Scene 4: The Doctor's study. The Doctor, a coldly scientific gentleman, uses Wozzeck for his experiments, to which Wozzeck submits because he needs the money. The doctor regards Wozzeck as an obsessional case and is delighted when the soldier's distracted remarks seem to bear out his theories on the relationship of diet to mental disorder. Scene 5: The street outside Marie's dwelling. Marie flirts with the Drum Major. She makes a show of resisting him, but not for long. They disappear within.

Act II, Scene 1: Marie admires the earrings the Drum Major has given her. Wozzeck appears, and questions her about the earrings. She insists she found them. He gives her some money and leaves. Marie is overwhelmed by guilt. Scene 2: The Captain meets the Doctor. The latter, commenting on the Captain's thick neck and bloated features, considers the possibility of his suffering apoplexy. When Wozzeck passes by they torment him with sly remarks about the Drum Major. Scene 3: Wozzeck, beside himself with jealousy, threatens Marie. Scene 4: The garden of an inn. Marie dances with the Drum Major while Wozzeck, brooding, watches them from a bench by the door. Scene 5: The guard room in the barracks, where the soldiers are sleeping. Wozzeck awakes with a moan. The Drum Major arrives, very drunk, and boasts of his new conquest. He offers a drink to Wozzeck, who refuses. The two men fight. Wozzeck is thrown to the ground. The Drum Major leaves, triumphant. Wozzeck picks himself up and sits staring before him.

Act III, Scene 1: Marie, alone with her child, reads the Bible by candlelight and begs God to forgive her sinful behavior. Scene 2: Marie and Wozzeck walk along a forest path by a pond. She wishes to return to the town, but he makes her sit down beside him. The moon rises, blood-red. Wozzeck draws his knife and plunges it into Marie's throat. Scene 3: A tavern. Wozzeck dances with Margaret, who notices blood on his hand. Wozzeck tries to explain by saying he has cut himself. When Margaret persists in her questioning, he rushes out in a fury. Scene 4: The pond by moonlight. Wozzeck is obsessed by the notion that the knife will betray him. He comes upon Marie's body, finds the knife, and throws it into the pond. He fears that he has not thrown it far enough and rushes into the water. Crazed by his guilt, he wades farther and farther until he drowns. The Doctor and the Captain enter. The Doctor thinks he has heard a groan, but is not certain. The Captain insists that they leave. Scene 5: Bright morning in front of Marie's house. Children are playing. Marie's little boy rides a hobbyhorse. Other children rush in with news of the murder, but Marie's son does not understand. They run off. The child continues to ride and sing. Then, noticing that he has been left alone, he rides off after the others.

THE MUSIC

Berg's chief problem was one of structure: how to weld the opera into a unity. "How could I hope to achieve, without the well-tried resources of tonality and its possibilities of formal organization, the same compelling musical unity? Unity not only in the short scenes but in the formal design of whole acts and, indeed, in the over-all structure of the opera?" The answer to this question led Berg, like many another opera composer of the twentieth century, away from the loose Wagnerian recitative to closed musical forms. But because the atonal idiom in which he was working was so much more volatile than the traditional idiom, the musical organization had to be all the tighter.

The first act is the Exposition of the theme: "Wozzeck in relation to his environment." The music here takes the form of five character pieces. The opening scene between Wozzeck and the Captain, in which the dialogue ranges over a number of topics only to return to its starting point, is cast in the form of a classical suite: prelude, pavane, cadenza, gigue, and gavotte, with the prelude repeated in retrograde motion. Scene 2, where Wozzeck and Andres are in the fields outside the town, is a Rhapsody on three atonal harmonies. To these Berg attaches functions comparable to those of Tonic, Dominant, and Subdominant (I, V and IV) in classical harmony. Scene 3, in Marie's room, consists of a military march, Marie's lullaby, and a short *scena* between her and Wozzeck. Scene 4, between Wozzeck and the Doctor, is a passacaglia: twenty-one variations on a twelve-tone theme. How better express the Doctor's *idée fixe*—the connection between nutrition and insanity—than by a theme and variations? Scene 5, where Marie yields to the Drum Major, is an *andante affettuoso* in rondo form. The rondo theme, suggesting the physical attraction that the Major has for Marie, returns again and again to direct the action.

Act II is the Development of the theme: "Wozzeck becomes more and more convinced of Marie's infidelity." The five scenes of this act present the core of the tragedy; therefore their musical investiture takes the most organic form in music: a symphony in five movements. Scene 1, where Wozzeck catches sight of the earrings and becomes suspicious, is in first-movement or sonata form (Exposition, Development, Recapitulation). Scene 2, in which the Captain and the Doctor deride Wozzeck, is an Invention and Fugue on three subjects. Scene 3, in which Wozzeck accuses Marie of being unfaithful, is the slow movement—a Largo for chamber orchestra. The dance at the Inn is the Scherzo. The scene in the barracks is a *rondo marziale*.

Act III is the catastrophe and epilogue: "Wozzeck murders Marie

and atones by suicide." The music consists of six Inventions. Scene 1
—Marie reading the Bible—is an Invention on a theme. Scene 2—the
murder—is an Invention on a single note. Scene 3—Wozzeck at the
tavern—is an Invention on a rhythm. Scene 4—Wozzeck's death—is
an Invention on a chord. The orchestral interlude that follows is an
Invention on a key. Scene 5—the children at play—is an Invention on
a persistent movement in triplets (*perpetuum mobile*).

Yet, despite the care with which he worked out the structural details, Berg felt that they were important only for the writing of the
opera, not for the listening. He ended a lecture on *Wozzeck* by begging the audience "to forget all theory and musical esthetics" when
they attended the performance. Berg regarded it as his particular
achievement that "no one in the audience, no matter how aware he
may be of the musical forms contained in the framework of the opera,
of the precision and logic with which it has been worked out, no one,
from the moment the curtain parts until it closes for the last time, pays
any attention to the various fugues, inventions, suites, sonata movements, variations and passacaglias about which so much has been written. No one gives heed to anything but the vast social implications of
the work which by far transcend the personal destiny of Wozzeck."
What comes across the footlights is the blazing emotion behind the
notes, the intensity of Berg's vision.

The vocal line sensitively portrays characters and situations. The
writing ranges through a variety of vocal styles. On the one hand,
out-and-out melody and the free vocal declamation that has been
basic to the German lyric theater since Wagner. On the other, the
Sprechstimme that Berg took over from Schoenberg—the rhythmic
declamation, midway between speech and song, of *Pierrot Lunaire*.
Berg also makes effective use of spoken passages synchronized with
the music. Harmonically, the greater part of the opera lies within the
domain of atonality. Berg anticipates certain procedures of the twelve-
tone system; he also looks back to the tonal tradition and casts a
number of passages in major and minor keys. He uses diatonic and
nondiatonic scales as well as serial rows to unify the work. Also
leitmotifs in the Wagnerian manner, which become associated with
the chief characters and ideas in the drama. The urge for unity led
him to end all three acts on the same chord. Differently arranged in
each case, this chord assumes the functions of a Tonic. The snatches
of popular song in the score create an attractive contrast to the atonal
idiom of the opera. Appearing in so special a context, they take on a
strange wistfulness.

The full orchestra is used mainly in the interludes. The scenes themselves are accompanied by smaller groups of instruments in the chamber-music style so dear to the Viennese school. In the Largo from Act II—the scene between Wozzeck and Marie—Berg divides the ensemble into a main group and a chamber orchestra modelled on the Chamber Symphony Opus 9 of Schoenberg. "I intended thereby to pay homage to my teacher and master at this pivotal point of the opera." During the dance at the inn we hear a band on the stage against the orchestra—violins tuned a tone higher than normally, clarinet in C, accordion, guitars, and bombardon (a kind of bass tuba).

One has but to hear the Captain's opening line—*Langsam, Wozzeck, langsam* ("Slow, Wozzeck, go slow!")—to realize how deeply this work, for all its originality, is rooted in German operatic tradition. The utterances of the hysterical Captain show a kinship to Herod's jagged vocal line in *Salome*. Wozzeck's music is more sustained in manner. His reply introduces the chief motive associated with him, on the words *Wir arme Leut* ("We poor folk!").

Wir ar - me Leut!   Sehn Sie, Herr Haupt-mann, Geld, Geld!   Wer kein Geld hat!

This motive in various guises underlines the key statement of the scene, beginning with *Ja, wenn ich ein Herr wär:* "Yes indeed, if I were a fine gentleman and had a silk hat and watch and an eyeglass, and could talk fancy, I would be virtuous too. But I'm a poor nobody. Our kind is unlucky in this or any other world! I really think that if we got to Heaven we'd be put to helping with the thunder."

Scene 2, in the fields, is one of several in which Berg conjures up an atmosphere of fear through his handling of the orchestra. Flickerings of sound on piccolos, oboes, and clarinets admirably prepare for Wozzeck's *Du, der Platz ist verflucht!* ("Say, this place is haunted!") In this scene we have the first of the songs, that of Andres. It is an example of Berg's evocative distortion of popular elements. In the following scene Berg, like Mahler, uses military music in a most poignant way. Marie's song *Soldaten sind schöne Burschen* ("Soldiers are handsome fellows!") is one of the tonal passages in the opera: in A-flat major. The lullaby that follows—*Mädel, was fangst Du jetzt an?* ("Girl, what song shall you sing? You've a little child but no husband!")—is a hauntingly lovely bit. When the child falls asleep, Marie remains lost in thought. The strings intone a motive of fifths closely associated with her. "Their harmonic immobility," Berg wrote, "expresses, as it were, her aimless waiting, which is only terminated with her death."

In the scene between Wozzeck and the Doctor we return to the atmosphere of obsession. The theme of the Passacaglia—the *idée fixe* —is a twelve-tone row, a most interesting circumstance in view of the

fact that the dodecaphonic technique had not yet been worked out when Berg wrote it. The final scene of Act I, bringing with it the climax of the action thus far, is the briefest.

The first scene of Act II involves another motive of fear, this time felt by the child, when Marie bursts out impatiently *Schlaf, Bub!* ("Go to sleep, boy!"): a minor second on the xylophone, which returns in various forms throughout the scene.

When Wozzeck's suspicions are aroused by the earrings, this motive reappears in slow tempo as a canon on the muted trombones:

The second scene, between the Captain, the Doctor, then Wozzeck, is the Invention and Fugue on three subjects. It culminates in Wozzeck's agonized outcry, *Himmel! Man könnte Lust bekommen sich aufzuhängen!* ("God in Heaven! A man might want to hang himself!") There follows the brooding Largo during which Wozzeck threatens Marie. When he raises his hand against her, Marie's words point to the tragic outcome—*Mensch! Rühr mich nicht an:* "Man, don't touch me. Better a knife in my flesh than a hand on me. My father didn't dare when I was ten." The scene at the inn—the Scherzo—begins as a slow Ländler in 3/4 and brings into prominence the popular elements of Berg's score. The song of the two young workingmen, the waltz, the chorus, the song of Andres, Wozzeck's jealousy, and the mock sermon of the drunken young fellow are welded into a vivid scene in which Berg skillfully exploits the clash between the band onstage and the orchestra. Equally memorable is the scene in the guard house, which opens with the uneasy sighs of the sleeping soldiers.

Marie's reading of the Bible—an Invention consisting of seven variations on a theme—is one of the most moving scenes in the opera. The fifth variation, her story about the poor little orphan, is in F minor. A fugue unfolds as she reads about Mary Magdalen and pleads that the Lord forgive her frailty. The murder scene—the Invention on one note—abounds in ominous sonorities, as at Marie's words *Wie der Mond rot aufgeht* ("How red the moon is!"), where the strings hold a B-natural spread out over five octaves against muted trombones and fluttertonguing on muted trumpets. Unforgettable is the repeated stroke on the timpani, going from a whisper to a spine-chilling fortissimo as Wozzeck cries *Ich nicht, Marie! und kein Andrer auch nicht!* ("If not me, Marie, then no other!") just before he kills her. The drum stroke returns to a pianissimo. In the interlude that follows, the note *B* is sustained by the orchestra for thirteen bars in a dramatic crescendo, punctuated by the brutal rhythm which symbolizes the catastrophe.

An out-of-tune piano accompanies the wild Polka with which the scene in the tavern opens. The haunted atmosphere returns as Wozzeck goes back to the pond. How poignant is his *Marie! Was hast du für eine rote Schnur um den Hals?* ("Marie, what is that red string around your neck?") His last words, *Ich wasche mich mit Blut . . .* ("I wash myself in blood—the water is blood . . . blood . . .") usher in ghostly chromatic scales that, starting in the strings, pass over to the woodwinds and brass.

The ensuing Invention on a key—D minor—is in the nature of a symphonic epilogue, a passionate lament for the life and death of Wozzeck. This inspired fantasy indicates how richly Berg's art was nourished by the romanticism of Mahler. One must also mention the final curtain—the little boy calling *Hopp, hopp* and riding off on his hobbyhorse to the sound of clarinet, drum, xylophone, and strings *ppp*. For sheer heartbreak this moment has few to equal it in the contemporary lyric theater.

What *Carmen* revealed to the nineteenth century—"the tragic irony that constitutes the kernel of love," to borrow Nietzsche's famous phrase—*Wozzeck* brought to the twentieth. Like *Carmen* and *Boris Godunov*, *Pelléas*, and *Salome*, *Wozzeck* creates an atmosphere all its own. It envelops the listener in a hallucinated world in which the hunters are as driven as the hunted. *Wozzeck* could have come only out of central Europe in the Twenties. But its characters reach out beyond time and place to become eternal symbols of the human condition.

CONCERTO FOR VIOLIN AND ORCHESTRA

Berg's last composition, the Violin Concerto (1935), was undertaken on a commission from the American violinist Louis Krasner. He put off writing it, as he was uncertain what form the work should take, until an external event provided the stimulus: the tragic death of Manon Gropius, the eighteen-year-old daughter of Alma Mahler, to whom he was deeply attached. His grief found a creative outlet in the Concerto, which became in his mind a "Requiem for Manon." He wrote the piece with a rapidity that was unusual for him, and dedicated it "to the memory of an Angel." Six months later Berg was dead; and the Concerto, which received its premiere in April of the following year, became a requiem for the composer himself.

The Violin Concerto underlines Berg's position as the intermediary between twelve-tone music and the tonal world; it reconciles dodecaphonic procedures with those of tonal harmony. Two traditional melodies are quoted in the Concerto and become formative elements— a Carinthian folk tune, and the chorale from Bach's Cantata No. 60, *O Ewigkeit, du Donnerwort* (Oh Eternity, thou word of thunder). The words of this melody, which Berg included in the score, breathe a gentle resignation: "It is enough! Lord, when it pleases you, free me from harness. My Jesus comes: Good night, oh world! I go to the heavenly house. . . ." (The chorale tune on which Bach based his

cantata was written by a seventeenth-century composer, Johann Ru-
dolph Ahle.)

But the strongest tonal determinant in the Concerto is the tone row
on which the work is based. This is a sequence of eight ascending
thirds followed by a whole-tone scale. The thirds, naturally, form traditional chords: two major and two minor triads. In other words, Berg
deliberately opened his basic series to the implications of triadic harmony.

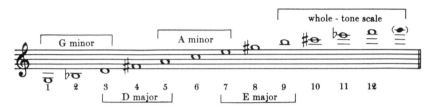

It will be noted that tones 1, 3, 5, and 7 of the row (the roots of
the four triads) correspond to the four strings of the violin: *G, D, A,*
and *E*. Berg obviously wanted to let the soloist make full use of the
open strings. The Concerto is notable for the fluency of the writing.
Within the twelve-tone method of Schoenberg an altogether different
personality reveals itself: gentler, more lyrical.

There are two movements, each subdivided into two sections. Berg's
intimates have interpreted the first movement as a musical portrait of
Manon, and the second as depicting the catastrophe of her death and
the search for consolation in religious belief. The work is scored for
an orchestra of the usual size, including an alto saxophone.

Ia. *Andante* (Preludium). The introduction presents arpeggios in
improvisatory fashion, the solo violin alternating with clarinets and
harp. The movement proper begins in 2/4 time, with a few measures
of accompaniment that establish a G-minor atmosphere. The violin
presents the tone row quoted above, then its inversion:

Notice the delicacy of the orchestral background and the idiomatic
writing for the violin. A tenderness pervades this music. The Andante
is in three-part form. Berg was partial to the A-B-A pattern, as lyric

composers have always been, even though Schoenberg's dynamic conception of form did not favor repetition. A triplet rhythm predominates in the middle part. The restatement is ushered in with an embellished variant of the row on the violin. The material is repeated in abbreviated form.

Ib. *Allegretto* (Scherzo), 6/8–3/8. This is a Scherzo with two Trios. The A-B-A pattern predominates not only in the form as a whole (Scherzo–Trio–Scherzo) but also within the middle part: Trio I–Trio II–Trio I. The music is permeated with the spirit of the Viennese *Ländler,* which asserts itself in the capricious charm of the opening motive.

This motive is an ingenious derivation of the basic row, as are the two that follow, which Berg labelled *wienerisch* and *rustico.* The Trios, more intense in character, serve to develop the thematic material and present exciting figuration on the solo instrument. The Scherzo is repeated with subtle variation, the material being curtailed. The Coda brings with it the Carinthian folk tune. This triadic melody is introduced by the horn, whence it passes to the trumpet; the violin plays a countersubject. Berg here, for the first time since the early days of his career, reverted to the use of a key signature. The movement ends quietly on the Tonic-seventh chord of G minor (G–Bb–D–F♯).

IIa. *Allegro* (Cadenza), 3/4. This section is written in a style of rhapsodic improvisation. Berg directed that it be played freely, "like a cadenza." The dramatic opening gesture indicates the theater composer; the mood is one of approaching catastrophe. A dotted rhythm dominates the music, similar to patterns which in Berg's operas are associated with fear and anxiety.

The A-B-A form prevails again. The first part of the cadenza, with its virtuoso figuration, is heard against an orchestral background. In the middle section the orchestration is reduced to a few lines, against which the violin disports itself. The opening section is repeated in varied form and leads to the agonizing climax (Berg marked it

Höhepunkt) based on the threatening rhythm. A three-note motive derived from the row comes to the fore against menacing sounds from the brass. The tension subsides. A transitional passage leads into the Adagio.

IIb. *Adagio* (Chorale Variations), 4/4. The chorale emerges in its majestic four-square rhythm to evoke the atmosphere of religious solace. Berg lets it be sung in alternate phrases by the violin and the woodwinds, which suggest the reed pipes of the organ. The opening phrase of the chorale is a whole-tone sequence which corresponds to

the last four tones of the row. Berg retains Bach's harmonization of the chorale melody.

Two variations, abounding in canonic imitation and kindred devices, display Berg's mastery of contrapuntal writing. The climax is achieved through rhythmic intensification: the movement proceeds from quarter notes to eighths, to triplets, finally to sixteenth notes. Berg again indicates the *Höhepunkt* or emotional peak of the section.

A wonderful calm descends upon the music. There follows a passage marked *wie aus der Ferne* (as from a distance), in which Berg's genius takes flight in sounds of transcendent beauty. The Carinthian tune returns in an idealized version, reconciled with the whole-tone atmosphere that surrounds the opening of the chorale. (Did this represent for Berg a symbolic reconciliation of life and death?) The violin bears aloft the tone row in a final transformation, ending on G. The movement loses itself in celestial heights, in the manner of Mahler's *Song of the Earth*, coming to rest—like that work—on an inconclusive chord which encompasses both the major and minor triad (Bb–D–F–G). The mood is one of resignation and serene farewell.

ᴥ§ 58 ᴥ
Anton Webern (1883-1945)

"With me, things never turn out as I wish, but only as is ordained for me—as I must."

Now THAT the third quarter of our century is under way, Anton Webern is beginning to come into his own. He is still unknown to the public at large. But his works are shaping the musical thinking of our time in an ever more decisive fashion.

AMP

Anton Webern

HIS LIFE

Anton von Webern (he dropped the prefix of nobility in later life) was born in Vienna. His musical gifts asserted themselves at an early age. In addition to his work in composition he studied musicology at the University of Vienna under Guido Adler, and received his doctorate in that field. He was twenty-one when he met Schoenberg and, with Alban Berg, formed the nucleus of the band of disciples who gathered around the master. Webern studied with Schoenberg from 1904 till around 1910. Although he worked independently thereafter, he maintained the closest contact with both Schoenberg and Berg, and participated directly in the shaping of the new atonal language.

After leaving the University in 1906, Webern conducted at various German provincial theaters and in Prague. But Vienna was the hub of his world. In 1918, when Schoenberg founded his "Society for Private Musical Performances," at whose concerts many important works were presented for the first time, Berg and Webern were his trusted aides in preparing the programs. Webern soon began to conduct the Vienna Workers' Symphony Concerts organized by the authorities of the then socialist city. But as the years passed he found public activity less and less congenial to his retiring disposition. After the First World War he settled in Mödling, a suburb of Vienna, where he lived quietly, devoting himself to composition and teaching.

Webern suffered great hardship after Austria became part of the Third Reich. The Nazis regarded his music as *Kulturbolshevismus*, forbade its performance, and burned his writings. He was permitted to teach only a few pupils, and had to give his lectures—in which he expounded the Schoenbergian point of view—in secret. In order to avoid forced labor during the war, he worked as proofreader for a Viennese publisher. To escape the Allied bombings of Vienna, Webern and his wife sought refuge at the home of their son-in-law in Mittersill, a small town near Salzburg. But fate awaited him there. On September 15, 1945, as he stepped out of his house in the evening to smoke a cigarette (the war had ended five months before, but Mittersill was still under a curfew), he failed to understand an order to halt and was shot by a trigger-happy sentry of the American occupying forces. "The day of Anton Webern's death," wrote his most celebrated admirer, Igor Stravinsky, "should be a day of mourning for any receptive musician. We must hail not only this great composer but also a real hero. Doomed to total failure in a deaf world of ignorance and indifference, he inexorably kept on cutting out his diamonds, his dazzling diamonds, of whose mines he had such a perfect knowledge."

HIS MUSIC

Webern responded to the radical portion of Schoenbergian doctrine, just as Berg exploited its more conservative elements. Of the three masters of the modern Viennese school, he was the one who cut himself off most completely from the tonal past. Indeed, he has been called the only real atonal composer, as he never accepted even the limited coexistence of tonal and atonal elements which is to be found in the works of Schoenberg and Berg. Webern developed an extremely novel and personal style, yet one that was neither capricious nor arbitrary, for it represented the most minute working out of the principles upon which he based his art.

This style evolved toward an ideal of the utmost purity and economy in the articulation of musical thought. Building upon the Schoenbergian doctrine of perpetual variation, Webern suppressed all repetition of material. "Once started, the theme expresses all it has to say," he wrote. "It must be followed by something fresh." This belief embodied his desire for continual renewal in the creative process, and his attempt to achieve ever fresh invention. The Schoenbergians, we saw, abandoned the spacious classical forms in favor of extreme compression. Webern carried this urge for brevity much farther than either of his comrades, as we shall see from his *Five Orchestral Pieces*, the longest of which lasts a minute.

Such conciseness seems to nullify the very notion of time as we have come to understand it in music. The composition is over almost before we are aware that it has begun. This economy of utterance, which carried to hitherto unimagined extremes the twentieth-century desire for the exclusion of nonessentials, answered a real need of Webern's temperament. The *Six Bagatelles for String Quartet*, Opus 9 have been well characterized as "melodies in one breath." Arnold Schoenberg wrote of them: "Think of the concision which expression in such brief forms demands! Every glance is a poem, every sigh a novel. But to achieve such concentration—to express a novel in a single gesture, a great joy in a single breath—every trace of sentimentality must be correspondingly banished."

Hardly less novel is the musical fabric in which Webern clothed his ideas. His inordinate sensitivity to sound went hand in hand with what Henry Cowell has called "an almost frighteningly concentrated interest in the possibilities of each individual tone." This caused him to place the utmost expressive value on each sonority. His scores call for the most unusual combinations of instruments. Each tone is assigned its specific function in the over-all scheme. The instruments, used in their extreme registers, frequently play one at a time, and very little. This technique results in an extreme attenuation—one might call it atomization—of the musical fabric, which confers upon the individual sonority an importance it never had before. A four-tone chord will be distributed among as many instruments playing in four different registers. Webern applied Schoenberg's principle of the nonrepetition of pitches to color. There are passages in his works where each tone in a melodic line is played by a different instrument. This procedure, of course, can be traced back to the Schoenbergian concept of *Klangfarbenmelodie* or "tone-color melody." (See page 357.) When no instrument is allowed to play more than one or two notes of a theme in succession, the changing timbre takes on almost a melodic value; indeed, in such passages the color is at least as important as the pitch.

This preoccupation with sound for sound's sake is, of course, one of the hallmarks of the contemporary approach to music. Webern's works abound in the most delicate effects, with much contrast between muted and unmuted instruments, the division and subdivision of strings, pianissimo trills and tremolos, and the most precise instructions as to how the individual tone is to be produced. His sensitivity to timbre is matched by the subtle dynamic level at which he pitches his discourse. There are passages that are no more than a whisper. A superabundance of rests serves to set off the individual tones. This is music in which silence is hardly less expressive than sound. The rhythmic designs through which the material is presented are of the most elusive. The single phrases have their special character and coherence; but the metrical scheme is not readily apparent. Webern's deliberate avoidance of strongly accentuated patterns, his way of placing the weightier sounds on the offbeat and of perpetually varying the rhythmic phrase imparts to his music its indefinable quality of "hovering suspension," of immobility. The effect of discontinuity is strengthened by the wide leaps in the melodic lines of both his vocal and instrumental music. A pointillisme so rarefied needed a strong structural sense to sustain it if it were not to degenerate into the flimsiest impressionism. From his earliest works Webern displayed a constructive sense whose logic and power grew with each successive composition. Underlying the disembodied sound is a firmly knit architecture based on interval proportion and projected in musical space by the most careful ordering of all its elements. The interval became the basic structural element in Webern's music, ultimately taking the place of the theme. Major sevenths and minor ninths, major and minor thirds and their derivatives are the most important intervals in his music. Beneath the evanescent sound is the hard core, the cutting edge. Hence the aptness of Stravinsky's comparison with diamonds.

The music of Webern's formative period shows the influence of Schoenberg; yet he took only what could nourish his personal style, and soon diverged from his master in order to enter a domain uniquely his own. The Passacaglia for Orchestra, Opus 1 was followed by a number of significant works: *Five Movements for String Quartet*, Opus 5 (1909); *Six Orchestral Pieces*, Opus 6 (1910); *Six Bagatelles for String Quartet*, Opus 9 (1913); and *Five Orchestral Pieces*, Opus

10 (1913). These were flanked by the poetic songs—some with piano, others with instrumental accompaniment—in which Webern's essentially lyric gift found a congenial outlet.

Once he had carried the art of aphorism to a limit beyond which there could be only total silence, Webern had to turn back in the direction of more extensive forms. He found the answer to his structural problem in the twelve-tone method. He adopted this in his Opus 17, the *Three Sacred Folk Songs* for voice, clarinet, bass clarinet, and violin (1924); and he remained faithful to it for the rest of his life. Within the framework of the dodecaphonic system he evolved a style of writing based upon the most intellectual disciplines of the art of counterpoint. The close-knit texture of his music represents the summit of musical economy. In this motivic fabric, concentration of thought and purity of style are carried to the farthest point. The devices of canonic writing are handled with true virtuosity. Double canons in contrary motion are common occurrences in Webern's music. His fondness for structural abstraction led him into intricacies which rival those of the medieval contrapuntists.

With his Symphony, Opus 21 (1928) Webern came into his fully matured style. In this and the works that followed, the twelve-tone technique is used with unprecedented strictness; the material is made to create its own forms. To this last period belong the Quartet for violin, clarinet, tenor saxophone, and piano, Opus 22 (1930); the songs of Opus 23 (1934) and Opus 25 (1935); the *Concerto for Nine Instruments*, Opus 24 (1934); and *Das Augenlicht* (The Light of Our Eyes), Opus 26 (1935), for mixed chorus and instrumental ensemble. From these years date also the Piano Variations, Opus 27 (1936); String Quartet, Opus 28 (1938); and Webern's last three works: two cantatas for solo voices, chorus, and orchestra, Opus 29 (1939) and Opus 31 (1943); and the Variations for Orchestra, Opus 30 (1940). These reveal a master who has vanquished the most complex problems of counterpoint, and who uses his mastery to achieve the Schoenbergian goal of deriving "an abundance of thematic forms from the least possible musical material in the smallest possible space, while at the same time holding these forms to a strict unity."

Schoenberg had contented himself with an organization based upon fixed series of pitches. Webern extended this concept to include timbre and rhythm. Therewith he moved toward complete control of the sonorous material—in other words, total serialization. His disciples, for instance Pierre Boulez and Karlheinz Stockhausen, have carried the implications of Webern's music to its farthest consequences by applying the serial technique to pitches and rhythms, timbres, dynamics, and densities. As a result, Webern has emerged as the dominant figure in the dodecaphonic thinking of the mid-century.

Webern's total output was thirty-one works, all recorded on four long-playing records. This is not much to show for a creative activity that extended over thirty-five years, but the music is so carefully calculated that it impresses one as having been written at the rate of a few notes a day. Many of the inner relationships that hold it together —the canons, retrograde forms, and inversions—are hardly discernible to the ear. They concern the twelve-tone initiate rather than the ordinary listener. However, one need not be aware of the technical complexities to savor the eerily beautiful sonorities that flow from this strange, lonely music. They evoke the remote region inhabited by Webern, a region that only a few will choose to enter. "They alone will understand these pieces," wrote Schoenberg, "who hold the faith that one expresses in tones what can be said only in tones. . . . Subtle, indeed, are the senses that can differentiate here. Fine is the mind capable of finding pleasure in things so recondite!"

⤳ 59 ⤶

Three Works by Webern

"Ecstasy was his natural state of mind. His compositions should be understood as musical visions."

Erwin Stein

FIVE PIECES FOR ORCHESTRA, OPUS 10

THE *Five Pieces for Orchestra* (1911–13) show, early in Webern's career, his concern for composing exclusively with the material of sound. Already he was striving for that rigorous control of the time-space continuum which became so compelling a preoccupation of his later years. These pieces bring to the fore what Webern called "the almost exclusively lyrical nature" of his music. The concentrated lyricism here makes for unprecedented brevity: the set of five numbers lasts no more than four and a half minutes. The fourth is the shortest piece in the entire orchestral literature; six and one-third bars that take nineteen seconds to play. Yet the *Five Pieces for Orchestra* cannot be regarded as miniature versions of larger forms. Constructed out of motivic cells, they carry their own structural logic and are complete within themselves. Clearly Webern was functioning in another dimension of time, one that bore no relation to the time sense of the post-romantic era.

The work is scored for a chamber orchestra in which each instrument is a soloist. Webern includes mandoline and guitar, instruments that have been favored by the Viennese composers because of their bright pointed sound. The pieces belong to the composer's atonal—that is to say, pre-twelve-tone—period, and come out of the expressionist atmosphere that prevailed in *Mitteleuropa* at that time. The conception, however, is wholly Webernian.

1. *Sehr ruhig und zart* (very calm and soft). For flute, clarinet; muted trumpet and trombone; celesta, harp, glockenspiel; muted violin, viola, and cello. In 2/4 time, with the triplet rhythms which figure so prominently in Webern's music. The piece opens with single tones on muted trumpet and harp followed by a chord on the viola and a single note fluttertongued on the flute. A sparse motivic texture is woven for twelve and a half bars, the dynamic level ranging from *ppp* to *pp*.

2. *Lebhaft und zart bewegt* (lively, moving softly). The second piece, the only rapid one of the set, is in triple meter, save for two brief reversions to 2/4 time. It is scored for piccolo, oboe, two clarinets; muted horn, trumpet, and trombone; harmonium, celesta, harp, glockenspiel, cymbals, triangle; muted violin, viola, cello, and double bass. Clarinet and violin state their respective motives in the opening measure. (See musical example, next page.) A delicate fabric of sound extends for fourteen bars, woven out of motivic cells and single-note sonorities moving from *p* to a fortissimo of menacing urgency.

3. *Sehr langsam und äusserst ruhig* (very slow and extremely calm). A true son of Austria, Webern loved the mountains of his native land and their bell sounds. The third piece is almost a study in bell sonorities, evoking as it does the clear open spaces of a mountain scene. It is eleven and a half measures in length, in 6/4 time. Harmonium, mandoline, guitar, celesta, harp, glockenspiel, and cowbells play trills and repeated notes, discreetly reinforced by the drums; while clarinet, muted horn and trombone, violin, muted viola, and cello trace their brief, tenuous motives.

4. *Fliessend, äusserst zart* (flowing, extremely soft) in 3/4 time. Clarinet, muted trumpet and trombone, mandoline, celesta, harp, snare drum, muted violin, and viola unfold their traceries for precisely six and one-third measures. A figure on the mandoline is followed by one

Webern, Opus 10, No. 2

on the muted trumpet. The violin finishes with five notes played *ppp*, *wie ein Hauch* (like a whisper).

5. *Sehr fliessend* (flowing). Allegretto, in 3/4 time, with an occasional measure in 2/4. The last number is the longest of the set— thirty-two bars. It is also the most elaborately scored, for flute, oboe, clarinet, bass clarinet; muted horn and trumpet; harmonium, mandoline, guitar, celesta, harp, glockenspiel, xylophone, bass and snare drum, cymbals; and the four stringed instruments, muted. The flickering motives work up to a climax with a fortissimo chord on the harmonium. There is a sudden subsiding; a second dynamic peak is reached with several percussive chords that run the gamut of the orchestra. The music trails off into silence.

SYMPHONY FOR SMALL ORCHESTRA, OPUS 21

The Symphony Opus 21—for clarinet, bass clarinet, two horns, two harps, violins, violas, and cellos—ushered in the most important phase of Webern's career, when his desire for absolute purity of language led him to his own completely original style. With this work Webern became the first of the modern Viennese school to undertake the grand form of the classical Viennese period. (As we saw, neither Schoenberg nor Berg cultivated the symphony.) It goes without saying that Webern's piece is as far removed from the expansion-and-development techniques traditionally associated with symphonic style as it is from the Tonic-Dominant polarity that made the symphony the embodiment of tonal thinking. Webern's Symphony takes just under ten minutes to play, and shows the same concentration of thought and sparseness of writing as do his other scores. The single-note texture, punctuated now and again with two-note chords, is of the utmost refinement. The lines are shaped in such a fashion as to place maximum emphasis upon the individual tone, its placement and color. This music, as René Leibowitz remarked, is "stripped to its barest essentials."

The Symphony is based on a tone row of strikingly symmetrical construction. The row divides into two halves, separated by a diminished fifth (the interval that divides the octave in half, as it contains six semitones). The last six notes of the row, when read backward,

Original

duplicate the order of intervals of the first six notes read forward. In other words, we are dealing with a series whose twelve constituents are related in the pattern 1–2–3–4–5–6: 6–5–4–3–2–1. If we use a + sign to indicate movement up, a — sign for movement down, and write the number of semitones that separates each of the twelve tones from the next, we obtain the following symmetrical pattern of movement within the two halves of the row: —3, +1, +1, —4, +1: —1, +4, —1, —1, +3. The series as a whole, read backward, is the same as the original row transposed up six semitones; as is evident if we compare

Retrograde

the original row with its retrograde form (R). By using a row that turns in upon itself, as it were, Webern achieves that sense of immobility, of movement beyond time, which was one of his preoccupations.

The twelve-tone technique, we found, is based on the use of four versions of the row—the original, inversion, retrograde, and retrograde of the inversion. Since in this case the row and its retrograde are identical, Webern limits the possibilities to only two forms of the row— the original and its inversion. (We saw, in Schoenberg's works, that the different row forms are derived from the basic set. The pre-eminence of the basic row is underlined by Schoenberg's handling of the technique and by his habit of indicating the principal voice in his scores. This hierarchy of values does not apply to Webern's music, which frequently unfolds several forms of the row simultaneously, and on equal terms. Hence, although it is convenient in analyzing his music to regard one row form as the basic set and the others as derivations, this view generally has no basis in the music itself.)

I. *Ruhig schreitend* (moving quietly). The first movement unfolds as a double canon for four voices—that is to say, two canons running simultaneously, each for two voices, with the answering voice imitating the leader in contrary motion. Notice, in the opening passage of the Symphony, how Webern departs from the usage of traditional counterpoint by continually crossing the voices. Notice too the wide leaps in each melodic line due to octave displacement. (The leading voice presents *O*, the imitating voice *I*.) Webern's extraordinarily delicate use of color serves to set off not only the several voices but also the different motives within the row. Taking the upper canon first, we see that the first motive (tones 1–2–3–4) is played by second horn and answered by first horn. The second motive (5–6–7–8) is played by clarinet and imitated by bass clarinet. The third motive (9–10–11–12) is stated by cellos and answered by violas. Thus the relationship between the leading voice and the answering voice is underlined by the use of homogeneous tone color—brass, woodwind, and string respectively. (See opposite page.)

In the second or lower canon the individualization of timbre is carried out in even more mobile fashion. The first tone of the row is played by the harp; tones 2–3–4 are presented by the cellos; 5 by second violins; 6–7 simultaneously, as a chord, by the harp, which continues with 8. (When the texture consists for the most part of one or two tones sounding at a time, an increase in density by the addition of a tone changes the quality of the sound.) Tones 9–10 are heard in the second horn, 11–12 in the harp. In the imitating voice, the first tone

of the row is played by the harp, tones 2–3–4 by violas, 5 by first violin, 6–7 as a chord by the harp, which continues with 8; 9–10 are heard in the first horn, 11–12 in the harp. The leading voice presents the inversion of the row beginning on F; the answering voice presents the row itself, beginning on C-sharp. In all four voices, the last two tones in the first statement of the row (tones 11–12) become the first two tones in the next statement.

In other words, Webern makes use of overlapping or interlocking rows in order to tighten the structure. Various forms of the row are unfolded simultaneously and seem to follow fairly simple patterns; but the simplicity is deceptive. Webern's way of beginning the row on different beats of the measure, his distinctive use of rests, and his subtle displacing of accent create the complex rhythmic structure which is an indispensable feature of his style.

The movement is divided into two parts, each of which is repeated (measures 1–24, and 25–66). The first ten measures of part two (25–34) are immediately repeated backwards (35–44). Throughout the first part the prevailing rhythmic values are whole notes, halves, and quarters. The second part brings a quickening of the movement: eighth notes appear. The first part ranges from low to medium-high register; the second climbs to high. The first part, except for one solitary *forte,* moves between *pianissimo* and *mezzo-piano;* the second builds to a *forte* passage. The first violins are almost completely silent in the first part, but emerge into prominence in the second. All these factors point to a steady intensification. The climax comes in the second part on the *forte* passage and consists of the simultaneous unfolding of the row by various instruments. The intensity of this passage is reinforced by the various members of the string group playing successively in unison, and by a high open D in the first horn—its highest note throughout the movement. There is a quick subsiding; the Coda unfolds a canon in contrary motion for two voices. A muted solo violin plays for three consecutive measures—a continuity of color not often found in Webern. The movement ends *pianissimo.*

II. *Variationen* (Theme and Variations). The second—and last—movement, consisting of a theme, seven brief variations, and a coda, injects into the symphony the element of perpetual variation so dear to the Schoenbergian school. The theme, marked *Sehr ruhig* (very quiet), is a musical sentence of eleven measures. Measure 6 is the turning point; after it the first half of the theme is repeated backward. The theme as a whole, read backward, is the same as the forward version transposed up an augmented fourth. (This interval, which cuts the

Theme

octave in half, plays a special role in the tone-row structures of dodecaphonic music. Indeed, certain theorists see in the imitation of the row
at the augmented fourth an analogy to the Tonic-Dominant relationship
in tonal music.)

Observe that the note values are identical whether read forward or
backward. This symmetry causes the rests to fall on different beats of
the measure in the second phrase (compare measures 2 and 10, 5 and
7), thus ever so slightly changing the pattern of accentuation. The
theme is an A-B-A form. It is based on an inversion of the basic series
beginning on F, and is harmonized by the retrograde form of the row
beginning on B. The A segment, measures 1 to 4, presents tones 1–2–3–4
in the melody, harmonized by tones 12–11–10–9 in the bass. The middle segment, measures 5–6–7, contains the middle four tones of the
series; the same tones, backward, are in the bass. The third segment—
measures 8–9–10–11—contains tones 9–10–11–12 in the melody, and
tones 4–3–2–1 in the bass. The theme is presented in a single color—
clarinet. The bass notes, as the example indicates, are divided between
harp and horns. The first and third segments consist entirely of quarter
notes. The middle part contains eighths and dotted quarters. What
emerges from all these details is the fact that the very shape of
Webern's idea is determined by the twelve-tone method. His art, in
other words, is marked by complete unity between the musical thought
and its expression.

Each variation, like the theme, is eleven measures long. The first, marked *lebhafter* (livelier), is a double canon for four voices in contrary motion, played by the muted strings. This continuity of a single color, a feature of this movement but otherwise unusual in Webern's music, is relieved by an alternation of pizzicato notes and those played with the bow. From the middle of the canon on, all the voices play the first half backward. Variation 2, *sehr lebhaft* (very lively), is a trio for clarinet, bass clarinet, and horn, with chords on the harp and occasional interjections by the strings. Clarinet and bass clarinet play a canon, while the horn plays a continuous line of eighth notes which unfold both forward and backward versions of the row, alternately sounding a note of each. Variation 3, *wieder mässiger* (again more moderately), is a kind of diminutive toccata movement in which Webern returns to his usual style of pointillist instrumentation. The symmetrical construction, in which the second half of the variation repeats the first half backward, is maintained in this and the following variations.

The fourth variation is the slowest. Marked *äusserst ruhig* (extremely quiet), it occupies the central position in the movement. The texture increases in density at this point. For the first time in the symphony five tones are sounded simultaneously. The complex canonic writing links this section to the first and last variations. The fifth variation, *sehr lebhaft* (very lively), corresponds to the toccata movement of Variation 3. Based on an ostinato in the strings, this variation develops the harmonic implications of the row. The first four tones of the row are projected vertically in a cluster-like chord in the violas and cellos; the last four tones are arranged in a similar chord played by first and second violins; while the four central tones give rise to augmented octaves that alternate with major sevenths, played by the harp. The variation proceeds in a steady crescendo from *ppp* to *pp, p, mp,* and *mf*. The rhythm is based on groups of sixteenth notes that form symmetrical patterns of their own. Despite the rapidity of movement, this variation strongly gives the impression of turning around itself—an impression which, because of the reversible structure of the row, is present in all the variations. There results that special effect of near-immobility which is so germane to Webern's style.

Variation 6, *marschmässig* (like a march), is a trio for clarinet, bass clarinet, and horn, like Variation 2, but without any string color. Clarinet and bass clarinet again play a canon; while the horn—this time in sustained notes—alternates tones drawn from two forms of the row. Variation 7, *etwas breiter* (somewhat broader), is a double canon in contrary motion. The over-all scheme of the variations is therefore revealed to be as symmetrical as the theme itself: Variations 1 and 7 are double canons, 2 and 6 are trios, 3 and 5 are toccata-like movements, and Variation 4 is the keystone. The Coda maintains the reversible form of the variations. It consists of twenty-four tones which spell out the theme and its retrograde, fragmented and distributed among clarinet, harp, first violin, and cello. The Symphony ends with two single notes on the harp.

CANTATA NO. I, OPUS 29

The Cantata Opus 29 (1939), for soprano, mixed chorus, and orchestra, transfers to another genre the problems that occupied Webern in the Symphony. As in all his vocal works, his lyricism has fuller play than in the purely instrumental works. The various possibilities—orchestra alone, chorus alone, both together, solo voice and orchestra, solo voice and chorus with orchestra—are employed to set off and illumine one another, with much thought given to the balance between the different bodies of sound. At the same time, the tightness of structure, strict logic, and concentration of thought present in the Symphony obtain also in the later work. The Cantata lasts just under seven minutes.

The orchestra, treated soloistically throughout, is of the kind we associate with Webern: flute, oboe, clarinet, bass clarinet; horn, trumpet, trombone; timpani, percussion, celesta, harp, mandoline; and strings (without double basses). The mystical nature poetry of Hildegarde Jone, which he set in several of his works, was obviously congenial to his temperament and imagination. It not only released the music in him but also stimulated him to occasional flights of word-painting. The Cantata is one of his most dramatic compositions.

The tone row on which the work is based is as symmetrically constructed as was the one used in the Symphony. There the row was equivalent to its transposed retrograde (O = R). Here the row, if read backward, gives its inversion transposed a fifth higher. In other words,

the retrograde is the same as the inversion (R = I). By the same token, the row read backward and inverted gives the original row a fifth higher (O = RI).

Notice that the row divides into two halves. The second half gives the same sequence of intervals—although in contrary motion—as the first half read backward. (Or, put differently, the second half read backward gives the same sequence of intervals—inverted—as the first half.) We can see this symmetrical pattern if we use a + to indicate ascending motion, and a — for descending motion, and write the number of semitones from one tone to the next: +4, —3, +1, —4, +1 : (—3): +1, —4, +1, —3, +4. The last five numbers in this series are the first five read backward. By making the original version of the row equal to its retrograde inversion, Webern once again—as he did in the Symphony—reduced the four possible versions of the row (O, I, R, RI) to two.

1. *Getragen—lebhaft* (solemn, lively). The first movement, for chorus and orchestra, alternates between these two tempos. In some instances each prevails for only a single measure.

Zündender Lichtblitz des Lebens schlug Lightning, that kindles life, hurled
ein aus der Wolke des Wortes.   Out of the cloud the Word.
Donner, der Herzschlag, folgt nach,   Thunder, the heart beat, follows after
bis er in Frieden verebbt.   Until in peace it dissolves.

The brief orchestral introduction opens with three pianissimo chords which inaugurate four forms of the row. The muted trumpet starts the original row-form on G. Muted violas begin the inverted (or backward) form of the row on C-sharp. The muted trombone introduces the inverted (or retrograde) form of the row on G-sharp. Muted cellos play the row starting on D. In the first six measures, which contain 48 notes, the four derivations of the row unfold simultaneously. Each row-form is fragmented and distributed among various instruments. Let us, for example, trace the original row. Tones 1–2–3, muted trumpet; 4–5, violin; 6, harp; 7–8–9, first violin; 10–11–12, muted trumpet. The second chord, consisting of a major ninth superposed on a major seventh, stands out from the other two because of a sudden crescendo. It has special significance and becomes a structural element. Webern returns to it in measure 7, after he has unfolded the four forms of the row. He uses it again on the last word of the chorus (*verebbt*), and as the final chord of the movement.

The introduction builds a sense of expectancy. The sonority changes constantly, as does the meter: 7/2, 5/4, 3/4, 4/4, 3/4, 6/2 and so on, resulting in the continual shifting of rhythmic patterns that is so much

a part of Webern's style. A fortissimo blow in the percussion, reinforced by trombone, prepares for the "lightning" on which the chorus
enters. Sopranos, altos, tenors, and basses simultaneously unfold four
forms of the row. The chorus is treated alternately in harmonic and
contrapuntal fashion. The chordal passages preponderate, but are set
off now and again by a few measures in canonic style. In the following
characteristic passage, in which the chorus is unaccompanied, the altos
move in contrary motion to the sopranos, while tenors and basses
duplicate the same pattern a major second below. (All four voices
sing the same text.)

The constant alternation between the two tempos ("solemn" and
"lively") makes for maximum dramatic contrast. At the same time it
enables the music to mirror the words with the utmost fidelity. In the
first two lines of the poem, for example, the slackening of tension on
the word *Lebens* (life) contrasts most vividly with the abrupt and
incisive rendering of the action words—*Lichtblitz* (lightning), *schlug*
(hurled), *des Wortes* (the Word). A roll on the kettledrums and two
fortissimo chords usher in the thunder. Webern, who at heart was a
poet of nature, indulges here in the kind of word-painting that was
so dear to the masters of the Baroque. In the last two lines the relaxation on the word *Herzschlag* (heartbeat) similarly contrasts with
the tension on the words *Donner* (thunder) and *folgt nach* (follows
after). The setting of the words *in Frieden verebbt* (in peace dissolves)
indicates the subtlety of differentiation possible in a style that is gen-

erally as nondifferentiated as Webern's. The preceding chord, on the second syllable of *Frieden,* consists of minor seconds, the most frictional of intervals (the chord reads C, C♯, D, D♯). This friction dissolves in the chord on the second syllable of *verebbt* (dissolves), the last chord sung by the chorus. The reader will recall that a dissonant chord may give a sense of completion at a cadence because it is less dissonant than what came before; this is what happens here. A striking orchestral postlude leads to the final cadence on the same chord.

II. *Leicht bewegt* (slightly agitated). The second movement, for soprano solo and orchestra, alternates between 3/16 and 2/8, with an occasional excursion to 5/16.

Kleiner Flügel, Ahornsamen, schwebst im Winde!	Little maple leaf, soaring in the wind!
Musst doch in der Erde Dunkel sinken.	You must sink to earth in darkness.
Aber du wirst aufersteln dem Tage,	But you will rise again with the day,
all den Düften und der Frühlingszeit;	With the fragrance of springtime.
wirst aus Wurzeln in das Helle steigen,	From your roots you will ascend to the light,
bald im Himmel auch verwurzelt sein.	Soon to strike roots in heaven.
Wieder wirst aus dir du kleine Flügel senden,	Once again you will put forth little leaves,
die in sich schon tragen deine ganze	That already bear your whole
schweigend Leben sagende Gestalt.	Silent, life-affirming image.

The row is presented in a single color—clarinet, starting on D—in a symmetrical rhythmic pattern that reads the same forward and backward. This extension of the serial concept to include rhythm as well as pitch led, we saw, to the idea of total serialization.

As in the Symphony, Webern achieves a tightly integrated structure through the use of interlocking rows, the last tones of one statement of the row becoming the first tones of the next.

The serial technique is handled with extraordinary refinement in the six measures of the instrumental introduction. The harp, for example, plays a three-tone chord in the first measure. The top note of this chord launches one row-form, the middle note another row-form, and the bottom note a third. The harp plays three chords in these six measures, in alternation with three in the strings. When the texture is as sparse as here, the vertical coincidence of three tones becomes an important expressive factor. Webern places the chords on different beats within the measure but never on the first. This rhythmic dislocation adds in most subtle fashion to the suspenseful character of the introduction. It is only in the sixth measure that the harp finally plays its chord on the first beat, thereby preparing for the entrance of the soprano solo on the second.

Webern for the most part sets the text with one syllable to a note. In this way he is able to highlight the key words by suddenly extending a single syllable for two or more notes. He also brings words into prominence through a wide leap in the melody line. For example, on the words *in der Erde Dunkel sinken* (sink in darkness to the earth) we hear two downward leaps of a diminished octave. Similarly, the word *auferstehn* (rise) is emphasized by an upward leap of a minor ninth. For this kind of word-painting Webern of course has ample precedent in the vocal music of Bach and Handel. Notice the striking expansion of the words *Frühlingszeit* (springtime), *Helle* (light), *steigen* (ascend), *Himmel* (heaven). The melodic line is marked by the wide leaps characteristic of the dodecaphonic style. This angularity of line results from octave displacement, as is evident if we rewrite Webern's melody so that the tones fall within the same octave. A

melody of this kind is still regarded as being almost impossible to sing; yet one has only to listen to the recording of this movement by Marni Nixon to realize that the time is approaching when all this will be considered to "lie within the voice."

III. *Ruhig* (quietly).

Tönen die seligen Saiten Apolls,
wer nennt sie Chariten?
Spielt er sein Lied durch den wachsen-
den Abend,
wer denket Apollon?
Sind doch im Klange die früheren
Namen

Resound the blessed strings of Apollo,
Who calls them Graces?
When he plays his song through the
gathering evening,
Who thinks of Apollo?
For in this sound the earlier names

alle verklungen;	Have all faded away;
Sind doch im Worte die schwächeren Worte	For in this word the feebler words
lange gestorben;	Have long since died;
und auch die blasseren Bilder	And even the fainter images
zum Siegel des Spektrums geschmolzen.	Have melted in the seal of the spectrum.
Charis, die Gabe des Höchsten:	Charis, the gift of the all-highest:
die Anmut der Gnade erglänzet!	The charm of her graciousness shines bright!
Schenkt sich im Dunkel dem werdenden Herzen	She offers in darkness her maturing heart
als Tau der Vollendung.	As dew of perfection.

The third movement, for soprano solo, chorus and orchestra, opens with a two-voice canon distributed among the four parts of the chorus. The imitating voice follows the leader at a distance of five quarter notes, at the interval of an augmented fourth (the tritone) which plays so prominent a part in Webern's canonic writing. The meter shifts continually from 2/4 to 2/2, 3/4 and 5/4, resulting in a most plastic rhythm.

The first four lines of the poem are followed by an orchestral interlude of eight measures. The importance of rests in Webern's music may be gauged from the fact that, of the twenty-two beats in these eight measures, eleven are silent. The orchestral texture is of the thinnest: either a single note is heard, or two together. Except at two points, the notes all fall on the offbeat. The emphasis on the low register prepares effectively for the entrance of the high voices of the chorus. There is a quickening of tempo as the sopranos and altos unfold a canon in contrary motion, the imitating voice following the sopranos at the distance of an eighth note, at the interval of a fifth. This is taken over by tenors and basses and continued by the full chorus as a four-part canon in contrary motion on the words *auch die blasseren Bilder* (and even the fainter images). The canon, continued in the orchestra, leads—with a broadening of the tempo—to the high point of the movement and of the Cantata as a whole—the entrance of the soprano voice on a high B-flat, fortissimo, leaping down almost an octave and a half on the word *Charis*. It makes a brilliantly effective climax. Canonic imitation is resumed on the words *Schenkt sich* (offers). From this point until the end there is an antiphonal exchange between chorus and soprano. Notice the effective setting of the words *Dunkel* (darkness), *Herzen* (heart), and the dying away on the final word, *Vollendung* (perfection).

The composer of this intensely lyric and concentrated work was content to go his way, an obscure figure in the musical circles of his time, overshadowed by those who made a bigger noise in the world. Selflessly dedicated to his austere vision of sonorous beauty, he was sustained only by an inner faith in the ultimate rightness of his intuitions. He had no way of knowing that, little over a decade after his death, avant-garde musicians in Europe and America would think of themselves as belonging to "the age of Webern."

⪻ 60 ⪼

Two Late Works by Stravinsky

"I hold that music is given to us to create order."

AGON

BALLET FOR TWELVE DANCERS

Agon occupies a special place in Stravinsky's output. The earliest parts of it date from December, 1953—from the period, that is, when Stravinsky was becoming increasingly interested in dodecaphonic music. Parts of the ballet were written in 1954, before *Canticum Sacrum;* the rest in 1956 and 1957. The first numbers of the ballet recapture the rhythmic dynamism of his earlier works, and contain stylistic references to *Petrushka, Le Sacre, L'Histoire du soldat,* and other compositions of his neo-classic period. The later parts of *Agon* show the master's more consistent use of serial technique and his growing preoccupation with the procedures of Webern. The opening and closing fanfares, like the interludes that set off the main divisions of the work, are not in the twelve-tone style. The harmonic language ranges from diatonic to bitonal, from polytonal and atonal to out-and-out dodecaphonic. Thus the score literally shows Stravinsky in the process of taking possession of his final style period. What welds the twelve-tone and nontwelve-tone elements in *Agon* into a stylistic unity is the unmistakable personality behind the music.

Agon consists of twelve short pieces (the work lasts just over twenty minutes) modeled on court-dance sequences of the time of Louis XIII and XIV, as set forth in a French dance manual of the mid-seventeenth century. The work consequently takes its place in the series of classical ballets which includes *Apollon Musagète* and *Orpheus.* Unlike those, it has no central theme, but consists instead of a series of abstract patterns belonging to no specific period, for four male and eight female dancers. Stravinsky uses the Greek word *agon* to signify a dance contest. The first performance took place in Los Angeles in June, 1957, in celebration of the composer's seventy-fifth birthday.

Although the score of *Agon* calls for a fairly large orchestra, the ensemble for the most part is not used in its entirety. This makes for a chamber-music texture of extraordinary refinement, each dance being conceived for a contrasting group of instruments used soloistically. The score is notable for unusual combinations—solo violin, xylophone, tenor and bass trombone in one number; trumpets, mandoline, harp, and cello solo in another. The intimate, pointed tone of the mandoline

A scene from the New York City Center Ballet production of *Agon*.

is pitted against the other instruments in most novel fashion. The individualization of timbre throughout, in combination with the highly concentrated idiom, makes this one of the most tightly wrought of Stravinsky's scores, in which careful calculation exists side by side with brilliancy of sound and vivacity of movement.

The work is divided into three parts. The first consists of a *Pas de quatre* for four male dancers, who advance from the rear with their backs to the audience; a double *Pas de quatre*; and a triple *Pas de quatre* for the entire company. The music for the third dance is a variation of the second. Part Two begins with a short orchestral prelude. The first *Pas de trois* begins with a Saraband-Step for solo male dancer, followed by a Galliard for two female dancers and a Coda for all three. A brief orchestral interlude leads into the second *Pas de trois*, consisting of a *Bransle Simple* for two male dancers, a *Bransle Gay* for solo female dancer, and a *Bransle de Poitou* for all three dancers. The third part begins, after a few measures of orchestral stretto, with four duos (quartet of four couples). There follow the last two numbers—a dance of three trios, each consisting of one male and two female dancers, and the Coda for three groups of four: that is, the entire group. Near the end, where the music returns to the fanfares of the opening, the female dancers leave the stage and the male dancers resume their positions with their backs to the audience, as at the beginning.

The pattern, then, is identical in all three parts: first a male dancer or dancers, then female, then both together, with the full ensemble appearing only near the beginning and at the end. The music subtly indicates the difference between male and female dances; those for the men are more dynamic in rhythm, bolder in contrapuntal line and instrumentation. Trumpets, xylophone, trombones underline the character of the male dances, as flutes, mandoline, and castanets do for the female numbers.

Three tone rows may be discerned in the work. The first alternates whole and half steps, and ends with an interval of a fourth followed by a diminished fifth.

This series divides into segments that can be manipulated so as to give a tonal sound. In the Coda to the first *Pas de trois*, harp and cello solo unfold the row while mandoline and two trumpets, sustaining the per-

fect fifth C–G, conjure up a C-major tonality. (Notice that Stravinsky repeats several tones of the row.) The predominance of small intervals in the row is characteristic of Stravinsky's handling of serial technique.

When these intervals are subjected to octave displacement, as in the above example, they produce the sevenths and ninths that give his contrapuntal lines a specific character. A few measures later the solo violin plays a sequence of chromatic sixths which reinforces the impression of C major. Stravinsky fashions a counterpoint for flutes and mandoline out of an inversion of the row, which appears at the end of the number in a canon between violin and cello.

The second row divides into two almost symmetrical halves, each ending with a perfect fifth—an interval that does not figure prominently in twelve-tone music because of its strong tonal implications.

This row furnishes the material for the three *Bransles*. The first half of the row, transposed up a tone, appears at the beginning of the *Bransle Simple* as a canon between two trumpets; while the second half serves as the foundation of the *Bransle Gay*. Here too, despite the use of serial technique, we encounter tonal implications: D major for the first *Bransle*, B-flat for the second. The vigorous *Bransle de Poitou* opens with a full statement of the row in the violins. The outer sections

of the piece exploit the melodic implications of the row, while in the middle section it is used vertically—that is, harmonically.

Row III alternates minor thirds and semitones. This row comes into its own in the final numbers, where the music comes closest to the

Webernian ideal. The texture grows increasingly sparse, the lines are more and more fragmented. A typical use of the row occurs in the strict twelve-tone passage in the Four Duos, where a three-voice fugato

for violas, cellos, and basses unfolds against a counterpoint of tenor and bass trombones.

The score abounds in "finds," such as the extraordinary passage in the Prelude to the first *Pas de trois* where a G-major triad is sounded in the treble by three basses playing harmonics; the single-note writing for the piano; the combination of violin solo, xylophone, tenor and bass trombones in the Saraband-Step; or of trumpets, mandoline, harp, and cello solo in the Coda of the first *Pas de trois*. Rhythm plays a formative role throughout. For, as the texture grows more and more attenuated, the darting specks of sound are firmly held together by the rhythmic impulsion. The interplay of lines shows that desire to penetrate the uttermost secrets of counterpoint which was the preoccupation of so many great composers in their ripest years. What emerges from almost every measure of the score is the fact that when a creative artist takes over a new system, he becomes its master, and not the other way around. In its enameled sonorities, its concision and rhythmic intensity, its vitality and wit, *Agon* is wholly Stravinsky's. It could have come from no one else's pen.

THRENI: ID EST LAMENTATIONES JEREMIAE PROPHETAE
(THRENODIES: BEING THE LAMENTATIONS OF THE PROPHET JEREMIAH) FOR SOLOISTS, CHORUS, AND ORCHESTRA

Threni, Stravinsky's longest work since *The Rake's Progress*—it lasts thirty-five minutes—is also his first to be conceived exclusively in the twelve-tone technique. It is therefore more unified stylistically than the partly twelve tone compositions that preceded it. Here Stravinsky has completely assimilated the serial technique into his personal style and turns it with utter freedom to his own use. When Stravinsky adopts—or, better, adapts—the twelve-tone technique, he continues to sound like himself. He does not wholly enter into the chromatic realm of the Viennese composers, for his music retains something of its tonal foundation and essentially diatonic flavor. What he takes over, chiefly, is the rigid control of the order of intervals and the formal logic of the compositional procedure. Stravinsky completed *Threni* in 1958.

Threni is a work of enormous dignity and restraint, deriving in equal measure from the liturgical music of the old polyphonists and the works of Webern. The piece is marked by an austere expressiveness of an almost hieratic impersonality. The lamentations of the Prophet are stylized into patterns of formal beauty that are lifted from the personal to the abstract through the most severe procedures of contrapuntal art. The use of Latin has the same effect in *Threni* as in *Oedipus Rex* and *Symphony of Psalms;* it interposes a sense of distance, of monumentality between the work and the listener. The anguish that men are heir to is viewed under the aspect of eternity.

Threni is scored for large orchestra. Bassoons and trumpets are not included; but the score adds an alto bugle (flügelhorn), alto clarinet, and sarrusophone (a double-reed instrument made of metal, related to the oboe family). The vocal forces consist of six soloists—soprano, alto, two tenors, and two basses—and mixed chorus. In line with the subject of the work, which is penitence and prayer, the orchestral coloring is on the dark side. Trombones and the bass instruments are emphasized. There are no massed effects of choral and orchestral sound. For the most part only a few instruments of the orchestra are used at any one time, and these are treated in the manner of chamber music. The instruments are subordinate to the voices, even as the chorus is subordinate to the soloists. The vocal lines, especially in the unaccompanied canons, make cruel demands on the singers. The instrumental writing is extremely sparse, with emphasis on single-note textures; yet the sonority is fresh and pungent.

The words are taken from the Latin (Vulgate) version of the *Lamentations of Jeremiah*, Psalms One, Three, and Five. Hence the subtitles: *De Elegia Prima, De Elegia Tertia, De Elegia Quinta.* The three Psalms, which Stravinsky slightly condensed for musical purposes, move from despair to hope, from hope to prayer. The middle section, longer than the other two combined, is again divided into three parts: *Querimonia* (Complaint), *Sensus spei* (Perceiving Hope), and *Solacium* (Solace). This three-part structure suggests Stravinsky's concern for the classical virtues of symmetry and balance; also it lends itself to a grand design. Other symmetries connect the first and third sections, such as the presence in both of the speaking chorus. In the original text, letters of the Hebrew alphabet are used to introduce the different verses of the Psalms (*Aleph, Beth, Gimmel, Daled, Eiyin*, and so on). These letters Stravinsky sets as choral interjections whose harmonic texture stands out against their contrapuntal surroundings. They mark the structural subdivisions of the work, almost in the manner of cadences (except that they precede rather than round off the musical phrase). They seem like the illumination of the initial letter of a chapter in medieval manuscripts, and are of singular beauty.

The work is based on a twelve-tone row and its derivative orders— inversion, retrograde, and retrograde inversion. From these forms

Stravinsky derives the thematic materials of *Threni* with great fertility of invention. The constitution of the row reveals an emphasis on consonances rather than on the dissonant intervals which prevail in the Schoenbergian domain. Since the row establishes an order of intervals as well as of pitches—what Stravinsky has well called "a music of intervals"—the preponderance of consonances in the basic set of *Threni* cannot but set it apart from the works of the Viennese school. Indeed, the prominence in the row of perfect fourths and fifths, intervals fraught with tonal implications (tones 2–3, 4–5, 6–7, 11–12), imparts a diatonic quality to many a passage in the work. This impression is strongly reinforced by the harmonic setting of the Hebrew letters.

Stravinsky takes many liberties with the series. He repeats various segments of the row so as to form new successions of intervals; links segments of different transpositions of the row to one another; and even combines segments of different forms of the row. In the *Solacium* he derives two auxiliary rows from the basic set.

Through these and kindred liberties Stravinsky shapes the dodecaphonic technique to his own expressive ends, even to the extent of occasionally restoring the harmonic functions that prevail in the tonal world.

In respect to rhythm, *Threni* continues the subtleties of *Agon*, although—in view of the austerely religious character of the piece—the propulsive force typical of Stravinsky's music is far less in evidence here. The lyricism that found an outlet in *Canticum Sacrum* is absent from *Threni*, in whose aloof grandeur Stravinsky comes as close as he ever has to the Apollonian universality of style he sought in his neoclassic period. The influence of Webern is manifest in the extremely wide leaps, often more than an octave; the angular contrapuntal lines;

the use of triplet rhythms; the atomization of texture; the prominence
of complex contrapuntal procedures, such as double canons; and the
way in which, in many a passage, each note is assigned to a different
instrument—a practice that can be traced back, through Webern, to
Schoenberg's *Klangfarbenmelodie* (tone-color melody).

I. *De Elegia Prima.*   The opening section is introduced by the line
Incipit lamentatio Jeremiae Prophetas (Thus begins the lamentation of
the Prophet Jeremiah). This part contains five little sections that follow
the pattern A-B-A-B-A, set off from each other by one or another of
the Hebrew letters, which the chorus repeats several times at the beginning of each section. (For the full Latin-English text of *Threni*,
see Appendix IV).

1. *ALEPH. Quomodo sedet sola civitas* (How does the city sit solitary). The whispering chorus presents the text in steady eighth-note
rhythm against a powerful orchestral ostinato that emphasizes the
lower register and creates an archaic atmosphere. The instrumental
background consists of clarinet, bass clarinet, violas, cellos, and basses;
then of horns, sarrusophone and piano. A vigorous tenor solo, supported by the female chorus, is pitted against the plangent sound of
the alto bugle in brilliant concertante style. Variable meters—3/8, 5/8,
4/8, 8/8, 7/8, and so on—create the supple rhythm one associates with
the Russian master. 2. *BETH. Plorans ploravit in nocte* (She weepeth
sore in the night). Subtitled *Diphona I,* this is a brief unaccompanied

duet between first and second tenors. The emotional sense of the text is vividly projected by the descending semitone at the beginning of the tone row. The first tenor sings the original row while the second unfolds an inversion of the retrograde. Notice Stravinsky's repetition of segments within the twelve-note series.

3. *HE. Facti sunt hostes ejus in capite* (Her adversaries are the chief). Whispering chorus, tenor solo, alto bugle, and female chorus repeat the music of the first section with new text. The material is subtly varied. 4. *CAPH. Vide, Domine, et considera* (See, O Lord, and consider). This is *Diphona II*, the second duet between the two tenors. 5. *RESH. Vide, Domine, quoniam tribulor* (Behold, O Lord, for I am in distress). The choral interjection on the letter *RESH* is accompanied by a brief double canon in contrary motion in the strings. The music of the first and third sections is repeated with new text, again with subtle variation, and completes the pattern A-B-A-B-A.

II. *De Elegia Tertia.* A. *Querimonia* (Complaint). The first section of the middle part consists of four unaccompanied numbers, each containing three verses. The Hebrew letter is sung at the beginning of each verse by female voices supported by three trombones, therewith marking off the divisions within the form.

1. *ALEPH. Ego vir videns paupertatem meam* (I am a man that hath seen affliction). A bass solo—*Monodia*, Stravinsky calls it—whose elaborate rhythmic structure approximates the plasticity of Gregorian chant. 2. *BETH. Vetustam fecit pellem meam et carnem meum* (My flesh and skin hath he made old). A canon for two voices—Tenor I and Bass II—which continues the complex rhythmic organization of the preceding number. 3. *VAU. Et fregit ad numerum dentes meos* (He hath also broken my teeth). A canon for three—Tenor I, Bass I, Bass II—in a somewhat simpler style. 4. *ZAIN. Recordare paupertatis* (Remembering mine affliction). A double canon for four: Tenor II imitates the melody of Bass II in a canon at the fifth, Tenor I follows Bass I in a canon at the minor sixth. The two themes are differentiated by use of contrasting rhythms.

Stravinsky's treatment of the row in this section shows interesting irregularities. In the first number, for example, he begins with the third tone of the row, bringing in the first two after the twelfth. He also uses overlapping segments of the row and, as we indicated, combines segments drawn from different forms of the row.

B. *Sensus spei* (Perceiving Hope). This section is a chain-form of eight numbers in the pattern A-B-B'-C-D-E-F-C'. In other words, the second and third numbers are linked textually and musically, as are the fourth and eighth. Here too each number contains three verses which are marked off by the Hebrew letters.

1. *HETH. Misericordiae Domini* (It is of the Lord's mercies). The chorus is used antiphonally, sopranos and basses pitted against altos and tenors. The four soloists sing the letter *Heth.* 2. *TETH. Bonus est Dominus* (The Lord is good). A dialogue between solo alto and solo tenor, with the chorus resuming the articulation of the Hebrew letters. 3. *LAMED. Ut conteret sub pedibus suis omnes vinctos terrae* (To crush under his feet all the prisoners of the earth). The mood of the preceding number is continued in this dialogue between Bass II, singing falsetto, and Tenor I, with sharp rhythmic differentiation between the two lines. 4. *NUN. Scrutemur vias nostras* (Let us search and try our ways). A four-part chorus marked *Lento,* the chordal texture of which contrasts with the contrapuntal nature of what has gone before. At this point the basses sing the Hebrew letter.

5. *SAMECH. Operuisti in furore et percussisti nos* (Thou hast covered with anger and persecuted us). Tenor I and female chorus engage in a dialogue, with Bass II taking over from the tenor. A brief recitative is divided between tenor and bass. 6. *EYIN. Oculus meus afflictus est* (Mine eye trickleth down). A freely contrapuntal texture for four soloists. Soprano and alto are set off against the tenor line which is doubled by the bass. 7. *TSADE. Venatione ceperunt me* (Mine enemies chased me sore). This is an unaccompanied rhythmic canon for four soloists, each voice imitating not the pitch line but the rhythmic pattern of the other voices. The six soloists unite on the chordal setting of the key word *Perii* (I am cut off). 8. *COPH. Invocavi nomen tuum, Domine* (I called upon thy name, O Lord). The music sung by the chorus in the fourth section is now assigned to solo soprano and alto. Stravinsky skillfully manipulates the row to create an atmosphere of supplication. His melody has something of the character of Gregorian chant.

In - vo - ca - vi   no - men tu - um Do -   mi -   ne

Bass II has a brief recitative-like passage. Then the six soloists, augmented by two voices from the chorus, unite in eight-part chords on the words *Ne timeas* (Fear not), bringing this part of the work to an end on a note of affirmation.

C. *Solacium* (Solace). This section contains three numbers. The arrangement of three verses to each number continues. 1. *RESH. Judicasti, Domine, causam animae meae* (O Lord, thou hast pleaded the causes of my soul). A duet for solo soprano and alto, each line with its own strongly integrated rhythm, is accompanied by chords on the woodwinds. 2. *SHIN. Audisti opprobrium eorum, Domine* (Thou hast heard their reproach, O Lord). The contrapuntal style of No. 1, with its decisive rhythmic inflection, is continued in this duet for Tenor I and Bass I, accompanied by four horns. 3. *THAU. Reddes eis vicem, Domine* (Render unto them a recompense, O Lord). An unaccompanied piece for four soloists and part of the choir. Soprano I and Tenor I sing one line, alto solo and the altos of the choir a second, Bass I and the basses of the choir the third. The soprano-tenor line dominates the others.

III. *De Elegia Quinta.* The Hebrew letters are discontinued in the final section. Each number contains three verses. The subtitle, *Oratio Jeremiae Prophetae* (The Prayer of the Prophet Jeremiah), set as a duet between Bass I and Bass II, serves as an introduction. *Recordare, Domine, quid acciderit nobis* (Remember, O Lord, what is come upon us), is whispered by the chorus in a fleeting reminiscence of the first part. The chorus, supported by pedal points in the orchestra, is answered by soloists. *Converte nos, Domine, ad te* (Turn Thou us unto thee, O Lord). Chorus and soloists unite in a passage in chordal style, accompanied by four horns. The rest of the orchestra has fallen silent. The music ends on a note of utter serenity.

Threni, like *Symphony of Psalms*, is a work imbued with religious faith. But the two are completely unlike in conception and execution. The difference between them, to paraphrase a remark of Stravinsky's in another context, is thirty years. In *Threni* his personal belief in man's need to submit to God works hand in hand with his equally strong belief in the artist's need to submit to order and discipline. Given this conception of art, it should have come as no surprise that Stravinsky ended by submitting to the most stringent musical discipline our age has yet devised.

～§ 61 ～

Luigi Dallapiccola (1904-)

*"I use any method I need to express myself. The important thing
is to have a vital idea."*

IN THE music of Luigi Dallapiccola the centuries-old tradition of Italian vocal lyricism has commingled with the stream of twelve-tone thinking emanating from Vienna. His music demonstrates how an ancient culture can assimilate elements alien to it and still retain its essential character.

HIS LIFE

Dallapiccola was born at Pisino, a small town on the Istrian peninsula which at that time was part of Austria. In the latter part of the First World War the Dallapiccolas, together with other Italian families, were moved away from the border and interned in the town of Graz. Here the future composer, who was then twelve, came into contact with the German classics in opera and symphony. He had played the piano since childhood, and now decided to devote himself to music. The war over, the family returned to Pisino. The youth pursued his studies first in Trieste, then at the Conservatory in Florence. After his graduation he was appointed to the faculty of the Conservatory as a teacher of piano, a post he holds to this day.

In 1930 Dallapiccola and the violinist Materassi formed a duo that specialized in the performance of modern music. He had already begun to compose and had turned out a number of works, mostly songs and choral pieces. It was with the performance of his *Partita* in 1933 that his reputation spread beyond Florence. Within a few years he was widely recognized in advanced musical circles as the outstanding composer among Italy's younger generation.

Dallapiccola is one of the contingent of European composers who have influenced musical life in the United States. In 1951 and 1952 he taught at the summer school of the Berkshire Music Center at Tanglewood. He was also professor of composition, for several years, at Queens College of the City of New York. The dynamic little man proved to be a forceful teacher with a capacity for taking infinite pains, and possessed of a mordant wit which blithely transcended the barriers of language.

HIS MUSIC

The turning point of Dallapiccola's career came with his study of the works of Alban Berg and Anton Webern. Although he later dedicated one of his compositions to Arnold Schoenberg, it was the two disciples who influenced his development. Himself an Italian born in an Austrian province, he was uniquely fitted to become the mediator between the main currents of Austro-German musical thought and the Italian tradition. Thus, Dallapiccola's position today is somewhat analogous to that occupied a generation ago by Ferruccio Busoni—a composer, incidentally, whom he very much admires.

The *expressionismus* out of which emerged the Viennese atonal school was altogether foreign to the Mediterranean view of life that was Dallapiccola's heritage. His solution was to temper the severity of twelve-note thinking with tonal and modal elements, thereby affirming his loyalty to the Italian past: to the inherited wealth of Gregorian chant, the music of the Renaissance, and the treasures of Italian choral polyphony. Dallapiccola set out from a world of sound rooted in seven-tone modal patterns. His harmonic language was more strongly infused with chromatic elements as he moved closer to the mature twelve-tone style of his maturity. In this development he consistently maintained the lineaments of his own personality. His melody line avoids the jagged intervals characteristic of the Viennese school, shaping itself instead to the natural curve of the voice. In his music, as in Alban Berg's, the basic row often carries tonal implications. When it suits his purpose he does not hesitate to depart from strict twelve-tone procedure. "The twelve-tone method," he writes, "must not be so tyrannical as to exclude a priori both expression and humanity. The only relevant problem is whether a work is a genuine work of art or not, irrespective of what technique may have been employed for its creation." His music is suffused with lyricism and bears a wholly personal stamp. Dallapiccola has encompassed a goal most difficult to achieve. Within the purlieus of Viennese dodecaphony he has managed to remain an Italian.

Dallapiccola belongs among those composers whose imagery is fundamentally vocal, whether they happen to be writing for instruments or the voice. His output shows a preponderance of vocal works. He has explored the possibilities of solo voice and chamber orchestra, which is one of the chief preoccupations of the Viennese school. His sensitivity to the unaccompanied choral style is part of his birthright as an Italian. The earlier choral works, such as the *Six Choruses on Texts of Michelangelo Buonarotti the Younger* (a nephew of the painter), dating from 1933–36, show his spiritual affinity with the Italian Renaissance. The style is thoroughly madrigalian, and is based on the continuous imitation of motives whose rhythmic transformation is carried out with the utmost invention. The writing is sparse and sinewy, the lines of the texture wide apart. The technique is influenced by Webern, although the results are different.

Dallapiccola's loyalty to the Italian past is further manifest in his fondness for forms that antedate the eighteenth-century sonata and symphony. The *Partita* for orchestra (1933) consists of a Passacaglia, Burlesca, Recitativo e fanfara, and Naenia (Lament). The *Tre Studi* (Three Studies, for soprano and chamber orchestra, 1932) are sub-titled Sarabanda, Giga (gigue), and Canzone. The *Divertimento in Quattro Esercizi* (Divertimento in Four Studies, for soprano and five instruments, 1934), contains an Arietta, a Bourrée and a Siciliana. In his addiction to these old song and dance types, Dallapiccola looks back to the seventeenth century when Italian instrumental music was pre-eminent for the rounded beauty of its forms. The twelve-tone technique frees his imagination from traditional restraints, setting up a frame within which he can deploy his virtuoso handling of contrapuntal processes such as canonic imitation. Yet the Latin in him prevents him from being drawn into abstraction or tempted by complexity for its own sake. He uses the devices of the twelve-tone style solely for the purpose of emotional expression. His works amply refute the charge that dodecaphonic writing is cerebral.

In his *Canti di prigionia* (Songs of Captivity, 1938–41), a set of choral songs on texts by three famous prisoners—Mary Stuart, Boethius, and Girolamo Savonarola—Dallapiccola recorded the reactions of a sensitive artist to the world about him; specifically, emotions aroused by the ominous events on the eve of the Second World War. Written at a time when Europe was becoming more and more like a prison, Dallapiccola's triptych became—within the context of those fateful years—an eloquent hymn to the freedom of the human spirit. The unusual percussion-and-bell sonorities of the instrumental ensemble combine with the plastic beauty of the vocal writing to form one of the remarkable works of our time. Its absence from our record catalogues is a grave omission.

Dallapiccola is best known for his opera *Il prigioniero* (The Prisoner,

1944–48). The libretto was adapted by the composer from *La Torture par l'espérance* (Torture through Hope) by Villiers de l'Isle-Adam, into which he interpolated a fragment from the Flemish classic *La Légende d'Ulenspiegel* by Charles de Coster. The action depicts in symbolic terms the fate of the individual trapped by forces he can neither control nor comprehend. The Prisoner is encouraged to hope for freedom by the Jailer who pretends to befriend him. Yet as he walks toward the liberty he thinks awaits him, he finds himself—at the shattering climax of the work—locked in the arms of the Jailer, who turns out to be none other than the Grand Inquisitor himself.

Il prigioniero is based on tone-rows that are used according to dodecaphonic procedure. The work admirably displays Dallapiccola's dramatic gift, his capacity for musical characterization and for building suspense; his ability to create a pervasive atmosphere—in this case, of an almost hallucinatory character—with the simplest means, as well as his luminous orchestral color and expressive vocal line. The same qualities are manifest in *Job*, a *sacra rappresentazione* which received its premiere in Rome in 1950. Of Dallapiccola's other works, mention should be made of the opera *Volo di notte* (Night Flight, on a libretto by the composer after a story by Antoine de Saint-Exupéry, 1940); *Marsyas*, ballet in one act (1948); three song cycles based on poems of Sappho, Alceus and Anacreon, for solo voice and instruments (1942–45); and *Tartiniana*, for violin and orchestra, on themes of Tartini (1952).

VARIAZIONI PER ORCHESTRA

Variazioni per Orchestra (1954) was written as a commission from the Louisville Orchestra. The piece is scored for a moderately large orchestra, including harp, celesta, xylophone, and vibraphone.

Variazioni per Orchestra, Dallapiccola explains, "are not at all variations in the traditional sense of the word. At the base of the whole composition there is the same twelve-tone row that I am using for my *Songs of Liberation*, a work for chorus and orchestra now in progress, and that I used for *Annalibera's Notebook* for piano. The *Variations* represent the orchestral interpretation of the latter. Annalibera is the name of my little daughter, and her name stems from the same root as liberation. In the notebook I have tried to explain the treatment of the twelve-tone row applied to the different elements of music.

"In the orchestral version I have eliminated the original titles of *Annalibera's Notebook* (shown here in parenthesis) and kept only the tempo indications. The twelve-tone row is varied in each piece in a different way and the indications of tempi are as follows: 1. *Quasi lento, misterioso* (Symbol)—where in spite of the difficulties of the twelve-tone system, I could base this on the name of *B-A-C-H*. 2. *Allegro con fuoco* (Accents). 3. *Mosso scorrevolo* (Contrapunctus primus). 4. *Tranquillamento mosso* (Lines). 5. *Poco allegretto, alla Serenata* (Contrapunctus secundus). 6. *Molto lento, con espressione parlante* (Friezes). 7. *Andantino amoroso* (Contrapunctus tertius). 8. *Allegro, con violenza* (Rhythms). 9. *Affettuoso, cullante* (Color). 10. *Grave* (Shadows). 11. *Molto lento, fantastico* (A quatrain constructed like a strophe of four verses)."

This work, then, stems out of the "character variations" of the nineteenth century, in which a theme projected a series of moods or images through changes in its constituent elements which altered its character. Dallapiccola's piece, from its mysterious opening—an ostinato set up by timpani, bass drum, tam-tam and double basses against sustained chords in the bassoons, horns, and trombones—is rich in atmosphere and drama. The eleven variations take fourteen minutes; the shortest lasts twenty-two seconds. They unfold before us as a series of moods and visions ranging from mystery to violent conflict. They contain wonderful sonorities, and a pervading lyricism that is the composer's very own.

"I am a man of the middle ages," Dallapiccola has said of himself. All the same, his music stands in the mainstream of contemporary thought and feeling. It is original, distinguished, and altogether Italian.

⤳§ 62 §⤵

Partly Twelve-Tone

> "Obedience to rules of style is only an elegance, a pleasure of the spirit, that does not constitute any proof of value."
>
> Frank Martin

A NUMBER of composers have been strongly influenced by the Schoenbergian doctrine, even when they do not adhere to it exclusively. Some have used the dodecaphonic technique in modified form, thereby adapting it to their own expressive aims. Others combine certain aspects of the twelve-tone style with tonal writing. In either case these composers testify to the widespread influence exerted by the modern Viennese school.

FRANK MARTIN (1890–)

Frank Martin is the most important figure among present-day Swiss composers. He was born in Geneva, where he pursued his musical studies, and lived for a time in Zürich, Rome, and Paris. Upon his return to his native city he taught at the Jaques-Dalcroze Institute and the Zürich Conservatory. He spent two years in Amsterdam; was professor of composition at the Cologne Conservatory for six years; then returned to Switzerland, where he now resides.

Martin's has been a slow but steady growth. He began as a traditionalist; his early works show the influence of Franck, Fauré, and the impressionists. There followed a transitional period (1925–32) during which he experimented with oriental and ancient meters, emulated Bartók in exploiting the unequal rhythms of Bulgarian song and dance, and enriched his style with elements drawn from folk music. An intensive study of Schoenberg's music impelled him, between 1932 and 1937, to compose in the strict twelve-tone style. To this period belong several important works: the Piano Concerto (1934), Trio for violin, viola, and cello (1936), String Quartet (1936), and Symphony (1937). Martin was one of the first musicians within the French orbit to adhere to Schoenbergian doctrine; yet, as he himself put it, "I may say that, while I came under Schoenberg's influence, I opposed him with all my musical sensibility." He embraced the technique but rejected the esthetic.

This conflict was resolved when he found his way to a personal language that combined twelve-tone and tonal elements. "Rules," he maintains, "have no other purpose than the enrichment of style." Where Schoenberg's teachings consistently elevate truth of expression above beauty, Martin believes that "in music, what succeeds is beauty." His ability to construct a long melodic line with true economy of material goes hand in hand with flowing contrapuntal textures which derive their inspiration from Bach. His chromatic idiom incorporates diatonic elements in a prevailingly atonal ambience. Martin uses twelve-tone rows in conjunction with major and minor triads, which take on a special coloring from the juxtaposition. More important, he uses the row in such a way as to restore traditional harmonic functions. For example, he places the row in the bass as a foundation for the harmony, a concept quite foreign to Schoenberg's system. This reconciliation of dodecaphonic with the older harmonic functions has been Martin's specific contribution to contemporary style.

Le Vin herbé (The Bleached Wine, 1938–41), a "dramatic oratorio" based on an excerpt from Joseph Bédier's version of the Tristram and Iseulte story, for twelve solo voices, seven string instruments and piano, is a full-length work in Martin's neo-romantic vein. *In terra pax* (Peace on Earth, 1944) is a short oratorio for five solo voices, double chorus, and orchestra. The massive *Golgotha*, on texts drawn from the New Testament and the writings of St. Augustine, for five solo voices, chorus, organ and orchestra (1945–48), revives the tradition of the Passion-Oratorio of Bach. Among Martin's instrumental compositions are *Petite Symphonie Concertante*, for harpsichord, harp, piano, and double string orchestra (1945), his most widely played work; Concerto for seven wind instruments, kettledrums, and strings (1949); the Violin Concerto of 1951, and the Concerto for harpsichord and small orchestra of 1952. The list includes also a set of six monologues from Hugo von Hofmannsthal's *Jedermann* (Everyman), for baritone and orchestra (1943); *The Tempest* (1955), after Shakespeare, an opera in which romantic and impressionist elements freely intermingle; and the oratorio *La Mystère de la nativité* (1960), in which the seventy-year-old composer returned to certain of the influences that dominated his youth.

GOFFREDO PETRASSI (1904–)

Goffredo Petrassi, the outstanding Italian composer of his generation, was born in Zagarolo, near Rome, and did not begin serious musical study until he was twenty-one. Despite the late start, he acquired a mastery of compositional technique. He came under the influence of Casella and was much impressed by Hindemith's music. From these two composers he took over the classical orientation which served as his point of departure.

The Partita of 1932, based on three old forms—*gagliarda, ciaconna,* and *giga*—revealed a musical personality of immense assurance. The bold thematic material and lithe contrapuntal writing, powered by driving rhythms, set forth the composer's kinship to the neo-classic esthetic, as did his penchant for a flexible diatonic idiom flavored with dissonance. The *Introduction and Allegro* for violin and eleven instruments (1933), Toccata for piano (1933) and Concerto No. 1 for Orchestra (1934) continued in the same direction.

There followed several large choral works in which Petrassi revealed his profoundly religious nature. *Psalm IX* for chorus, strings, brass, two pianos and percussion (1934–36) has its roots in the sumptuous architecture of the Roman Baroque. (Petrassi was a choir boy in his youth and at an impressionable age absorbed the choral polyphony of Palestrina and other Roman masters.) His finest achievement in this medium is *Coro di Morti* (Chorus of the Dead, 1941), a "dramatic madrigal" for four-part male chorus, three pianos, brass, double basses, and percussion, set to the poem of Leopardi. The glacial percussive sonorities of this work bear some relationship to Stravinsky's *Les Noces*, but the language is Petrassi's own. He expands his harmonic idiom to include modal, polytonal and atonal as well as tonal elements; yet these are fused into stylistic unity through the composer's command of large-scale structure. In his third large choral work, the cantata *Notte oscura* (Obscure Night, 1951), on a text of Giovanni Della Croce, Petrassi assimilates Schoenberg's twelve-tone technique, thereby welding the disparate elements of his musical language into the strictest unity.

In the works that follow, Petrassi incorporates the serial technique into his orchestral language. The Second Concerto for Orchestra (1951) is based on an "entirely unrestricted freedom of invention," as the composer calls it, which has little in common with the developmental procedures of the classical style. The Third Concerto for Orchestra, entitled *Recréation Concertante* (1953), continues Petrassi's amalgamation of the concertante instrumental style with twelve-tone devices. Petrassi's output includes the fourth and fifth Concertos for Orchestra (1954, 1955); piano and vocal music; two operas and two ballets, dating from the late Forties, that are the least impressive part of his output; and an engaging choral piece, *Nonsense* (1952), on poems of Edward Lear.

In seeking to adapt the methods of the modern Viennese school to his own feeling as an Italian, Petrassi has faced one of the crucial problems confronting the more advanced composers among his compatriots. His solution has not only shaped his own development but will play an important role in determining the impact of twelve-tone thinking upon the younger Italians.

ROLF LIEBERMANN (1910–)

Rolf Liebermann was born in Zürich. After studying law at the University there, he decided to follow his bent and devote himself to music. He subsequently joined the musical staff of Radio-Zürich.

Liebermann has developed an eclectic style that combines classic, romantic, and twelve-tone elements. His *Concerto for Jazzband and Symphony Orchestra* (1954) is an attempt to bridge the gap between the improvisational style of the jazz band and the formal style of the orchestra. Such attempts, of course, are nothing new. The novel thing about Liebermann's Concerto is that it is based on a twelve-tone row. The work testifies to the vitality of expression and sensuous quality of sound that are among the composer's strongest assets. Liebermann's opera *Penelope* (1954) had a great success in Germany and has entered the repertory of the chief opera houses of that country. *Leonore* (1940–45) and *The School for Wives*, a one-act opera after Molière (1955), made a less decisive impression. Mention should be made too of his Symphony No. 1 (1949) and Piano Sonata (1951); two orchestral works—*Furioso* (1953), and *Musique* for narrator and orchestra (1956); two cantatas—*Streitlied zwischen Leben und Tod* (Song of Struggle between Life and Death), and *Une des fins du monde* (One of the Ends of the World); and the *Capriccio for Soprano, Violin and Orchestra* (1959), a lively piece infused with the spirit of virtuosity.

HANS WERNER HENZE (1926–)

Hans Werner Henze at an early age established his reputation as one of the most talented among the new generation of German composers. His unorthodox handling of the twelve-tone idiom springs on the one hand from a penchant for romantic lyricism, on the other from a flair for opera that does not hesitate to employ diverse stylistic elements in the interest of dramatic expression.

Henze was born in Güttersloh, Westphalia. He began his musical studies in Braunschweig, was drafted into the army, and spent some time as a prisoner of war in England. After his repatriation he went to Heidelberg to study with the composer Wolfgang Fortner, and subsequently worked with René Leibowitz in Paris. He acquired a practical knowledge of the musical theater by working at various provincial opera houses, and for two years served as musical adviser for ballet at the Opera in Wiesbaden. In 1951, when he was twenty-six, his Piano Concerto won the Robert Schumann Prize at Düsseldorf. A year later he gave up his activities in the theater in order to devote himself entirely to composition. He settled on the island of Ischia, in Italy, and subsequently lived in Naples.

Henze has been influenced in equal degrees by Schoenberg and by

Stravinsky; by his teacher Wolfgang Fortner; by Boris Blacher, whose "variable meters" became an essential element of his style; and by Alban Berg and Webern. Out of these elements he has forged an original language marked by brilliance of instrumentation, rhythmic urgency, and lyric intensity. In works like Berg's Violin Concerto he found a model for his union of twelve-tone elements with traditional harmonic relationships. Therewith he achieved an individual approach to twelve-tone technique, within a framework that combines tonal, bitonal, polytonal, and atonal elements. Endowed with a strong rhythmic imagination, Henze has contributed much to the revival of ballet in Germany. Indeed, the spirit of ballet permeates several of his orchestral works, such as the *Ballet Variations* (1949) and *Ballet Scenes for Orchestra* (1950). He manages to inject emotional intensity into his handling of the serial technique, and departs from the Schoenbergian canon by subordinating contrapuntal devices to a style oriented toward clear harmonic relationships.

Henze's opera *Boulevard Solitude* (1951) transfers the Manon Lescaut story to present-day Paris. The work, which attracted attention because of the originality of both the musical and dramatic conception, was preceded by *Das Wundertheater* (The Theater of Wonders, 1948), a one-act opera after an intermezzo by Cervantes; and was followed by Henze's most substantial achievement in the lyric theater to date, *König Hirsch* (King Stag, 1952–55), a fantasy in which "men turn into animals and animals behave with human characteristics." Henze has written two radio operas—*Ein Landarzt* (A Country Doctor, 1951) and *Das Ende einer Welt* (The End of a World, 1953). *Prinz von Homburg*, a full-length opera, aroused much discussion at its premiere in Germany in 1959, and was repeated at the Spoleto Festival of 1960. Among Henze's ballets are *Anrufung Apolls* (Invocation to Apollo, 1949); *Jack Pudding*, the score of which incorporates jazz elements (1949); *Labyrinth*, a "choreographic fantasy on the Theseus theme" (1950); *Tancred und Canthylene* (1952); *Der Idiot*, after Dostoievsky (1952), and *Maratona di danza* (1956), a work depicting a dance marathon in a Roman suburb, in which the twelve-tone music heard in the orchestra is combined with the strains of a Cuban rhythm band and a jazz combo onstage. Henze won his biggest success as a ballet composer with *Undine* (1959), which not only was performed widely in Europe, but as a repertory piece of the Royal Ballet established his reputation in England and the United States. In this score Henze moves as far as he ever has from the twelve-tone outlook, returning to such traditional procedures as clearly defined tonalities and modulations, triads, ostinatos and sequences, regular phrase construction, and danceable meters.

Despite his preoccupation with opera and ballet, Henze has written an impressive amount of orchestral music. The list includes three symphonies (1947, 1949, 1951); *Chamber Concerto* for piano, flute, and strings (1947); Violin Concerto (1947); Symphonic Variations (1950); *Ode to the West Wind*, for cello and orchestra (1953); *Symphonic Etudes* (1955); *Quattro Poemi* (Four Poems, 1955), a symphonic suite; and *Concerto per il Marigny* (1956). Henze has also written a number of vocal and chamber works.

IAIN HAMILTON (1922–)

Iain Hamilton, born in Glasgow, Scotland, is among the best-known composers of his generation in Britain. He graduated with highest honors from the Royal Academy of Music in London and from London University. His early works show the influence of Berg and Bartók, occasionally of Stravinsky. However, in the mid-Fifties the impact of Webern proved to be a liberating force. Since then his work has developed along serial lines, with no affinity to any particular school. An increasing preoccupation with form and clarity of expression is evident in all his work; also a virtuoso handling of orchestration. He has written several light works, among which the *Scottish Dances* have been highly successful. They have been recorded twice.

Among his earlier works are the Symphony No. 2, which won a Koussevitzky Foundation Award in 1951; Concerto for Violin and Orchestra (1952); *The Bermudas*, for baritone, chorus, and orchestra; also sonatas for viola (1950), piano (1951), and clarinet (1954). Recent works include the Sinfonia for Two Orchestras (1959), which was commissioned by the Edinburgh Festival; Sonata for Cello and Piano (1959); Concerto for Piano and Orchestra (1960); Sextet (1961); *Pharsalia*, for baritone and instrumental ensemble (1961); *Arias for Chamber Orchestra* (1963); *Sonatas for Ten Winds* (1963); and *Cantos for Orchestra* (1964).

Hamilton lived in London from 1929 to 1961, when he accepted a professorship in composition at Duke University in Durham, North Carolina. His Piano Sonata has been recorded, as has the Sonata for Cello and Piano. These works offer a fine introduction to his distinctive style.

IX. EXPERIMENTALISTS

"It may well be—I take it upon myself to predict it—that the apotheosis of the machine age will demand a subtler tool than the tempered scale, capable of setting down arrangements of sounds hitherto neglected or unheard. . . ."

Le Corbusier

‹§ 63 §›

Electronic Music

"What we want is an instrument that will give us a continuous sound at any pitch. The composer and the electrician will have to labor together to get it."

Edgar Varèse (in 1922)

IT IS a truism that each stage of social evolution engenders its own artistic forms. Thus it was inevitable that the great scientific advances of the past half century, specifically in the field of electronics and acoustics, would have a profound effect upon the course of music.

Electronic music, generally speaking, is music based on techniques that generate, transform, and manipulate sounds electronically. This music frees the composer from his bondage to the seventy or eighty pitch levels that are produced by conventional instruments. It frees him as well from the traditional dynamic levels and time values. Electronic music makes available to him the entire range of frequencies audible to the human ear, from about fifty cycles per second to fifteen thousand. It places at his disposal innumerable precisely calculated dynamic levels, and an infinite number of rhythmic patterns based on durational values that are measured in centimeters on tape. In fine, electronic music opens up to the composer a new world of possibilities never before envisaged.

There were several milestones in the conquest of this world: the invention of the electronic tube in 1906; the building of electrophonic concert instruments in the years after the First World War; and the discovery some twenty years later of how to record sound on tape. Technical advances, however, have significance only when they answer human needs in the domain of the intellect and imagination. Even as these inventions were being developed, the signs were not wanting that new conceptions were taking shape whose ultimate implications led beyond the resources of traditional instruments. The "emancipation of the dissonance" effectuated by Debussy and his generation was one such sign. Busoni's desire for an "uninterrupted continuity" of the musical material was another. He spoke of the possible fissure of sounds, experimented with microtonal scales (based, that is, on intervals smaller than a semitone), and in *A New Aesthetic of Music* described an instrument that could transform electrical current into a controlled number of vibrations. A more immediate precursor was Edgar Varèse, who already in the Twenties was exploiting percussion and bell sonorities in unprecedented fashion. Varèse's assumptions formed one of the points of departure for the experimental composers who emerged a quarter century later.

Electronic music as we know it today came to the fore shortly after 1950. Three principal schools led the way—French, American, and German. The French composers developed *musique concrète*, using magnetic tape to record and recompose sounds gathered mainly from extramusical sources: from nature, from industry, from the noises of the city. These sounds were treated electronically and modified—that is to say, transformed into new sound forms—by superimposing one tape upon another, or playing several tapes simultaneously on multiple sound tracks; by cutting up and splicing the tapes; and by playing them forward or backward at various speeds. *Musique concrète*, then, applied electronic devices to sounds which were of nonelectronic origin. The Paris school developed at the research center of Radiodiffusion Française, under the direction of Pierre Scheaffer, and included, in addition to Scheaffer, the composers Olivier Messiaen and Pierre Boulez.

The American school is centered at Columbia University, where Otto Luening and Vladimir Ussachevsky began to experiment with music for tape recorder at about the same time that *musique concrète* was getting under way. The first public concert of compositions for tape recorder in the United States was given in New York at the Museum of Modern Art in October, 1952. The program included Ussachevsky's *Sonic Contours*, and Luening's *Low Speed*, *Invention*, and *Fantasy in Space*. There followed the *Rhapsodic Variations for Tape Recorder and Orchestra*, by Luening and Ussachevsky, which was presented by the Louisville Orchestra in the spring of 1954. Unlike the French group, Luening and Ussachevsky used, as their raw material, sounds derived from conventional musical instruments and the human voice. By treating these electronically they were able to transform piano sounds, flute sounds, and the like into sonic formations resembling deep-toned gongs and bells, harmonic clusters of an organ-like richness, or the percussion-and-bell sounds of the oriental gamelan. In 1959 the laboratory for electronic music at Columbia University received a Rockefeller grant—to be administered by Luening and Ussachevsky jointly with Roger Sessions and Milton Babbitt of Princeton University—which made it possible to expand the scope of their experimental work.

The German school centers about the experiments conducted in the studio of the West German Radio in Cologne under the direction of Herbert Eimert. The leading composer of this group is Karlheinz Stockhausen. The Cologne school uses sounds derived from an electric generator rather than from nonelectronic sources. Indeed, the Germans believe that the term "electronic music" applies properly only to compositions fashioned out of electronically produced sounds. They emphasize building up complex sound forms from what are known as *sinusoidal sounds*—pure sounds divested of their overtones. Esthetically, the Cologne school takes its point of departure from the music of Anton Webern. Stockhausen and his confreres have taken over Webern's ideal of an absolutely pure music controlled in every dimension. Standard composing devices—canon, imitation, augmentation, diminution, and retrograde motion—are to be found in the experimental music of the French and the Americans; but the Cologne school pursues Webern's idea to its farthest consequences. The concept of the tone row—that is to say, of a fixed series that determines the order of events in a composition, which Schoenberg applied to the single element of pitch—is extended by the Germans to include rhythm, dynamics, timbre, and density. The result is total control over the elements of composition—in other words, total serialization. As Paul Gredinger has put it, "Our aim is an art in which proportion is everything—a *Serial Art*." Total serialization, in the practice of Webern's followers, goes hand in hand with athematic writing, a style of composition which avoids definite themes that recur and are developed.

Technological developments and greater experience in handling the sonic material have impelled all three schools in recent years to concentrate more and more on electronically produced sounds. An important step forward was the development of the RCA Electronic Synthesizer. This costly electronic system can generate any imaginable musical tone or combination of tones, in a variety of pitch levels, timbres, and complex rhythmic patterns that go far beyond what is possible for conventional instruments. In 1960 the Synthesizer was installed at the Columbia-Princeton Center for Electronic Music, and provided an invaluable stimulus to further experimentation in this field.

Electronic music eliminates the performer. It enables the composer to reach his audience directly, even as the painter or sculptor does, without the intermediacy of the interpreter's personality. It has appeared in an age when science plays an ever more crucial part in our daily lives; when the emphasis of progressive musicians is on the sound

The RCA Electronic Synthesizer at the Columbia-Princeton Center for Electronic Music.

stuff itself rather than on the emotional meanings that have accrued to it; when many composers aspire to an objective, abstract music that can be controlled down to the minutest detail. This is the music of a machine age, the product of an urbanized culture which, significantly, has appeared at a time when the art of music is moving closer to the limits of what can be done with the twelve tones of the tempered scale. It is still too early to assess the outcome of this new art. We do not know whether it will root out forever the personal element that has been the most precious quality of music through the ages, or whether a way will be found to reconcile man and machine in a new synthesis of artistic expression. In any case, one has only to listen to a recording of an electronic composition to realize that he is hearing the music of the future.

ৰূ 64 ৯৬

Karlheinz Stockhausen (1928-)

"The elementary conditions necessary for composition with electronic means have been worked out. We have created prototypes in sound; we have grasped the essence of what is to be learned from these prototypes. . . ."

KARLHEINZ STOCKHAUSEN is one of the leaders of the avant-garde in Europe. His career shows a propitious coincidence of the forces that make for success in the musical world. He appeared on the scene at a time when, after the years of Nazi regression, the German public was receptive to the progressive spirit in art. This favorable climate was further strengthened by the political and economic resurgence of West Germany. Stockhausen is one of the editors of *Die Reihe* (The Row), the quarterly review of serial music published by Universal Edition of Vienna, whose powerful resources have been marshaled behind the propagating of his ideas and music. His works, which figure prominently in the European festivals of contemporary music, have been hailed with enthusiasm by some of the most influential critics of Germany.

Stockhausen was born in Modrath, near Cologne; he worked first with Frank Martin at the Musikhochschule in Cologne, then with Olivier Messiaen in Paris. His interest in physics and acoustics, which he studied at the University of Bonn, prepared him for his later activities. Stockhausen produced the first published score of electronic music in his *Electronic Studies* (1953–54).

At Cologne he works with three signal generators that produce respectively pure tones, impulses, and so-called "white noise" (which includes all the sounds and all their overtones, even as white light includes the entire spectrum of color). "He mixes the sounds from the three generators, a very complicated process," Harold C. Schonberg reported in the *New York Times* in the summer of 1956. "Some sounds last only a twentieth of a second, and it may take several hours of work to produce these sounds exactly as he wants them." Stockhausen's aims, the *Times* report went on to say, are those of any composer—to be master of his material, to employ the laws of musical form, and to create an emotional entity. "Naturally he had to work out a new system of musical notation, for each work demands indications of intensity, duration and other special markings."

Stockhausen feels that the new concepts in music can no longer be expressed through an orchestral apparatus inherited from the nineteenth century. The orchestra as we know it and the institution of the public concert that revolves around it are, he believes, things of the past. Just as the symphonies, operas, and oratorios of the classic-romantic period performed a significant social function in their time, so the new electronic music, he maintains, will find its place in the social fabric. The masterpieces of the past, from his point of view, no longer need communal listening, as they can be heard just as well at home through recordings or the radio. Electronic music, on the other hand, embodies new conceptions of time and space that can be projected properly only in concert halls specially designed for this purpose. He envisions a spherical auditorium with walls studded with loudspeakers, equipped with a platform in the center for the listeners, who will hear the music coming from all directions, stereophonically. "I want to be able to bring sounds from every surface area of the room," he says. There would be fixed programs that would be changed at intervals and that could be heard at all hours of the day, just as one sees a film in a motion picture theater. Under such conditions, he argues, it would make sense for people to leave their homes in order to hear a piece of music. Communal listening would thus regain its social function and its artistic significance.

Stockhausen began his career with works for conventional instruments: *Kreuzspiel* (Crossplay) for oboe, bass clarinet, piano, and percussion, written in 1951 when he was twenty-two; *Spiel* (Piece) for orchestra (1952); and a Percussion Quartet for piano and three timpanists (1952). *Kontra-Punkte* for ten instruments—flute, clarinet, bass clarinet, horn, trumpet, trombone, piano, harp, violin, and cello —takes its point of departure from Webern. The piece displays all the lineaments of Stockhausen's style—the meticulous craftsmanship, the flexible rhythms, the placement of each note so as to maximize its significance and its power to surprise, and the joy of weaving sound patterns for their own sake. The *Piano Pieces I-X* were written between 1952 and 1954. *Piano Piece XI* (1956) has aroused widespread interest. The work, as Stockhausen's publishers put it, is available in three forms. It comes in a roll packed in a cardboard carton; or with a wooden stand to put on the piano; or on a board. When the roll is unfurled it measures 37 x 21 inches. The piece consists of nineteen fragments which the pianist is permitted to play in whatever order his eye falls on them, with any of six different tempos, dynamics, and types of touch (staccato, legato, and the like). This offers the performer a vast number of possible versions. "When he has played one fragment three times, the piece must end." The work reflects Stockhausen's concern with the element of chance in composition, and his desire to grant the player a more creative role than he has had in recent times.

Gruppen (Groups) for three orchestras (1955–57) stems out of Stockhausen's preoccupation with the spatial dimension in music. With this work, he writes, "a new development of instrumental music in space has begun. Three self-sufficient orchestras surround the audience; they play—each under the direction of its own conductor—partially independently in different tempi; from time to time they meet in common rhythm; they call to each other and answer each other; one echoes the other; for a whole period of time one hears only music from the left, from in front, or from the right; the sound wanders from one orchestra to the other." This conception has its historical precedent in the music of the seventeenth-century Venetian composers, who wrote works for antiphonal double choir which exploited the sound space of St. Mark's Cathedral. "The spatial aspects of the music," Stockhausen points out, "are functional. One finds oneself listening in the midst of several temporal-spatial manifestations which together create a new musical *time space*."

As a disciple of Webern Stockhausen has continued the Viennese master's attempt to achieve minute control over all the elements of composition. He has expanded the concept of the series to include not only the pitch but also the rhythm, timbre, dynamics, and densities of a piece, in this way achieving total serialization. He handles the serial technique in virtuoso fashion. Stockhausen is careful to point out that electronic music should not imitate the sound of the traditional orchestra, just as orchestral music "has no need to deck itself out with pseudo-electronic effects." At the same time, one realizes that his sound image in his writing for conventional instruments has been significantly influenced by his experiments with electronic music.

This is certainly the case with his *Zeitmasse* (Tempo, 1956) for five woodwinds—oboe, flute, English horn, clarinet, and bassoon, which has been recorded. The design of this work is articulated with maximum clarity because of the way in which individual notes are emphasized within the texture. Pitch functions in the closest possible relationship to tone quality, register, density, and color; this is obvious from the appearance of the score, where practically every note (save in the rapid passages) has its own dynamic marking. The piece is based on a concept of relative rather than absolute rhythm. Stockhausen makes this clear in his instructions: "The tempo 'as fast as possible' applies to the shortest note-value of a group. Within this group the chosen mensural unit remains constant, while the effective speed varies with the note-values employed. The tempo 'as slow as possible' is determined by the breathing capacity of the woodwind player, who has to perform a particular series of groups in one breath. The greatest total duration for the series determines the constant mensural value." The music exploits the agility of the woodwinds, and has an admirable improvisational quality. It may sound a little too long to some listeners, as it did to the present writer, and somewhat repetitious. But there is no denying the freshness of the conception, the fascinating suppleness of rhythm and tempo, and the sheer delight in sonorous patterns projected by Stockhausen's score.

Of his electronic works, the most important is *Gesang der Jünglinge* (Song of the Youths, 1956), in which Stockhausen combines the sound of the human voice with pure electronic sound. The piece was presented at the international convention of musicologists in Cologne in 1958, but has not yet been made available on commercial recordings; nor, being written in graphs and geometrical figures, can it be read by those versed only in musical notation.

Stockhausen's writing on music are the counterpart of his experiments in composition. They reveal a vigorous mind, endowed with a plenitude of imagination, which is attempting to come to grips with some of the new problems confronting the art of music. He is unquestionably the most exciting figure to have emerged in German music since the Second World War.

∾§ 65 §∾

Pierre Boulez (1925-)

"Structure—one of the key words of our epoch. . . ."

PIERRE BOULEZ is the most important French composer of the younger generation. His art raises issues that are of crucial importance to our time, and is attracting much attention in advanced musical circles.

HIS LIFE

Boulez was born in Montbrison, near Clermont Ferrand. He attended the Paris Conservatoire, whose traditionally minded professors of composition he describes, with characteristic directness, as imbeciles. In Olivier Messiaen, whose harmony class he attended with enthusiasm, he found the master who formed his esthetic. He also studied counterpoint privately with Andrée Vaurabourg, the wife of Honegger. In 1946 René Leibowitz's book on Schoenberg and his school was published in Paris, causing a stir among the younger musicians. Boulez forthwith became a student of Leibowitz, who initiated him into the serial technique which became the foundation of his style. At the age of twenty-two Boulez was made musical director of the theater company of Jean-Louis Barrault and Madeleine Renaud, with whom he toured Europe, North and South America, and the Far East.

He attracted notice as a composer when his works began to be presented at the festivals of contemporary music at Darmstadt and Donaueschingen (the former in particular offers a hospitable platform to serial composers). His association with Barrault and Renaud was an extremely happy one, as both the actor and his wife had profound admiration for their musical director. In 1954 they made it possible for him to organize a series of concerts that have become famous—the *Domaine Musicale*. As the guiding spirit of this undertaking, Boulez has introduced many important avant-garde works to the Parisian public.

HIS MUSIC

"It is not deviltry but only the most ordinary common sense which makes me say that, since the discoveries made by the Viennese, all composition other than twelve-tone is useless." This sweeping statement marks Boulez's total commitment to the dodecaphonic point of view. He himself has indicated his musical ancestry. "Before the discovery of Webern, the scores of Debussy and of Stravinsky were my constant guides; and this has not changed since Webern opened paths for me—in the domain of dynamics and timbre—that Debussy and Stravinsky alone could not."

Boulez is one of a generation of composers who turned to twelve-tone music because it seemed to offer them greater freedom, in terms of the transformation and variation of musical material, than did tonal music. His goal is the total organization of the world of sound according to the laws of serial structure: the achievement of infinite variety within a form that is rigorously controlled down to the smallest detail. Taking his point of departure from Webern's later works, Boulez—like Stockhausen—has moved toward total serialization. He is a type of musician who belongs peculiarly to our time, in whom artistic sensibility goes hand in hand with mathematical speculation. He is fascinated by the problem of the artist's freedom of choice within the rules of his art. "There is no creation," he has stated, "save in the unforeseen as it becomes necessity." Hegel's doctrine of freedom as "the recognition of necessity"—in a twelve-tone setting! A man of passionate temperament, Boulez is keenly aware of the value of restraint and self-discipline. Hence he is impelled to pursue the unforeseen with rigorous logic to its farthest consequences. "At the present stage of history," he states in one of his ebullient manifestos, "the composer's situation demands that he should play the game with the most rational dice and according to the strictest rules he can imagine—yet never forget that, in Mallarmé's phrase, 'A throw of dice will never abolish chance.'"

Boulez became aware of a certain disequilibrium in the "classical" twelve-tone works, occasioned by the fact that the revolutionary advances in melody, harmony, and counterpoint of the modern Viennese school were not equalled by advances in rhythm. He attempted to overcome this disequilibrium, on the one hand by continuing along the path charted by Webern, on the other by taking over the plastic rhythms of his teacher Messiaen and putting them to his own use. He began to work with the basic rhythmic cells that are native to his style, opposing them each to the other as he extracted from them all the diversity and tension inherent in their nature. The method is apparent in so early a work as the Sonatine for Flute and Piano (1946). "It was in this Sonatine," he wrote, "that I tried for the first time to articulate independent rhythmic structures, of which Messiaen had revealed to me the possibilities, upon classical serial structures." Boulez frees his music from the traditional concept of meter as projected by the measure and the barline. In his music the barline loses its independent function. Rhythm ceases to be something that flows *through* the meter; it *becomes* the meter. In fine, there is only rhythm—infinitely free and supple, as in the music of the Oriental cultures Boulez profoundly admires.

The emotional content of Boulez's music extends from a gentle lyricism to a furious expressionism that ranges him with the "angry young men" of our time. Boulez himself has stated, in an essay on rhythm, "I think that music should be a collective magic and hysteria." His violent emotions find their necessary compensation in the mathematical rigor with which his structural schemes are worked out. His writing is marked by extreme concentration of thought, as by the great freedom with which he uses the serial technique. He tends to avoid sensuous charm for its own sake. Yet from Messiaen, and the latter's preoccupation with the music of the Far East, he has taken over a fondness for bell-and-percussion sounds that evoke the Oriental gamelan. He is partial to that great favorite of the contemporary French school, the vibraphone. His limpid orchestral texture is based on the clearest possible differentiation of timbres. In his orchestral piece *Doubles* (1958), although he used conventional forces, he directed that the players be seated in a new arrangement. "No one will contradict me," he explained, "if I state that when tone-colors follow each other rapidly they should not be laboriously delayed because of the obstacle of distance. The ear of our time demands stereophonic listening in its desire for clarity and movement."

The list of his instrumental works opens with *Three Psalmodies* for piano (1945). In his First Sonata for piano (1946) Boulez no longer uses the initial pitch-series required by classical twelve-tone procedure. He unfolds instead a succession of athematic intervals whose structural opposition, powered by the rhythmic cells of which we have spoken, provide the tensions for the form. (*Athematicism*—the absence of clearcut themes—has become a growing preoccupation of the twelve-tone school.) The Second Sonata for piano, one of Boulez's most impassioned works, dates from 1948. He describes it as representing "a total and deliberate break with the universe of classical twelve-tone writing . . . the decisive step towards an integrated serial work, that will be realized when serial structures of tone-colors and dynamics will join serial structures of pitch and rhythm."

The Third Piano Sonata (1957) gives the interpreter the same kind of creative participation as is offered by Stockhausen's *Piano Piece XI*. However, where Stockhausen directs the player to perform certain structures in the order that his eye falls upon them, thereby permitting the element of chance to enter into the finished product, Boulez gives the player certain fixed choices in the arrangement of the work. In effect, he allots a more limited role to chance than does Stockhausen. Among the other instrumental works are several movements for string quartet; *Polyphony* for eighteen solo instruments (1951, rewritten in 1957–58 for a larger ensemble); and *Structures* for two pianos (1952). These, like the Third Sonata and *Doubles* for orchestra, the composer considers to be unfinished. He intends to add more movements to each in the future.

Vocal works are among the most important items in Boulez's output. His favored poet is the surrealist René Char. *Le Soleil des eaux* (River in the Sun, 1948–50) is a cantata for soprano, tenor, men's chorus, and orchestra, on two poems of Char. *Le Visage nuptial,* for soprano, alto, women's chorus, and orchestra (1951), is based on five poems of Char. Boulez here responds to the passion with which the poet has depicted the transports of love. In both works he ingeniously adapts the *Sprechgesang* (song-speech) of Schoenberg's *Pierrot Lunaire* to his own expressive scheme. The third work based on Char's poetry is *Le Marteau sans maître,* which we will discuss. Among the vocal works are also two *Improvisations,* based on Mallarmé (1957), and *Poésie pour pouvoir* (Poetry for Power, 1958), on verses of Henry Michaux.

Given his scientific bent, Boulez was challenged by the possibilities of *musique concrète.* He regarded with the liveliest interest a music which at one stroke wiped out both the limitations of existing instruments and the intervention of undependable interpreters. In his *Two Studies* he attempted to apply total serialization to this highly mechanized music. He subsequently became interested in the electronic music of Stockhausen and the Cologne studio. It is more than likely that he will return to this field in years to come.

Boulez has shrewdly assessed the role of his type of composer. "I think that our generation will give itself to synthesizing as much as—if not more so than—discovering: the broadening of techniques, generalising of methods, rationalisation of the procedures of writing—in sum, a synthesis of the great creative currents that have manifested themselves principally since the end of the nineteenth century." To this synthesis he is making his own contribution.

LE MARTEAU SANS MAÎTRE
(THE HAMMER WITHOUT A MASTER)

Le Marteau sans maître (1953–54), Boulez's best-known work, presents the chief traits of his style within a compact frame. As it is available on records, it offers a good introduction to his music. *Le Marteau* is a suite of nine movements based on three short poems of René Char. It is written for contralto and a group of six instruments, of which the flute in G, viola, and guitar are most in evidence. These are supported by a xylorimba, an instrument whose tone combines the metallic sonority of the xylophone with the gentler wood-sound of the marimba; and a vibraphone, which lends a touch of magic to the ensemble. The sixth "instrument" is a varied group of percussion manipulated by a single player, consisting of a tambourine; two pairs of bongos (single-headed drums played by thumping with the fingers); maracas, claves (a pair of short round sticks of hard wood which are held so that the hollow of one hand acts as a resonating cavity when the sticks are struck together); bell, triangle, high and low tam-tam, gong, suspended cymbal, and two little cymbals. The full group never plays. Instead, each of the nine movements presents another selection of instruments from the ensemble.

The over-all sound is of the bell-and-percussion variety. It is limpid, brilliant, full of light, and evokes the atmosphere of Far Eastern music. The attenuation of texture, rarefied sound, dramatic use of silence, discontinuity, and occasional immobility of this music places it in the legitimate line of descent from the late works of Webern. Voice and instruments seem at times to be moving not only independently but even unaware of one another, attaining a new dimension of freedom.

The vocal line is characterized by the wide leaps and the stylized setting we have come to associate with twelve-tone music. As might be expected, Boulez does not hold that the musical setting should serve primarily to make clear the words of a poem. "If you wish to 'understand' the text," says he, "read it!" Music, he believes, should lift the words to another level of experience. It should bring to the text a heightening of expression rather than a realistic setting. This approach establishes a certain kinship between *Le Marteau sans Maître* and Schoenberg's *Pierrot Lunaire*. Certainly the later work would have been inconceivable without the earlier. Certainly, too, no singer should undertake this score unless she has absolute pitch.

Char's poetry is thoroughly surrealist in the violence of its images, which are superposed in a kind of hallucinatory montage. There is the closest affinity between Boulez's music and Char's verses. The reader may find the translation more than a little mystifying. So is the original.

I. L'Artisanat furieux	*I. Furious Artisans*
La roulotte rouge au bord du clou	The red caravan at the edge of the prison
Et cadavre dans le panier	And a corpse in the basket
Et chevaux de labours dans le fer à cheval	And work horses in the horseshoe
Je rêve la tête sur la pointe de mon couteau le Pérou	I dream with my head on the point of my Peruvian knife

II. *Bel édifice et les pressentiments*

J'écoute marcher dans mes jambes
La mer morte vagues par-dessus tête

Enfant la jetée-promenade sauvage
Homme l'illusion imitée

Des yeux purs dans les bois
Cherchent en pleurant la tête habitable

II. *Beautiful Building and Premonition*

I hear walking in my legs
The dead sea waves over my head

Child—the wild promenade-pier
Man—the imitated illusion

Pure eyes in the woods
Seek, weeping, a head to live in

III. *Bourreaux de solitude*

Le pas s'est éloigné le marcheur s'est tu
Sur le cadran de l'Imitation
Le Balancier lance sa charge de granit réflexe

III. *Hangmen of Solitude*

The step has receded the walker is silent
On the dial of Imitation
The Pendulum thrusts its load of reflex granite

The work is arranged in interlocking movements. The first, third, and seventh are related, both through intervallic structure and timbre. They consist of a prelude (No. 1), the setting of *L'Artisanat furieux* (No. 3), and a postlude (No. 7). A similar kinship exists between the fifth and ninth movements. The first of these contains the setting of *Bel édifice*, while No. 9 is its *double*—Boulez uses the word in the eighteenth-century sense of variation. In the same way the second, fourth, sixth, and eighth are allied. They include the setting of *Bourreaux de solitude* (No. 6) and three instrumental commentaries (Nos. 2, 4, and 8).

1. "Before *L'Artisanat furieux*." For flute in G, vibraphone, guitar and viola. This prelude introduces the pulverised sonority of the post-Webern world. The tempo marking is *rapide;* yet despite the speed of the movement, single notes stand out with extreme clarity. The tense, plucked-string guitar sound here is analogous to the sound of the mandoline in certain works of Schoenberg and Berg. Boulez's serial technique, with its emphasis upon intervals such as the augmented and diminished octave, makes for a highly integrated piece.

2. "First commentary on *Bourreaux de solitude*." For flute, xylorimba, tambourine, and muted viola. *Lent* (slow). The dynamic markings alternate between *piano, pianissimo,* and *mezzo piano,* with each note carrying its own dynamic shading. The drum sound provides a gently percussive background for the traceries of the flute. Bongos are introduced into a rapid middle passage, in which xylorimba and viola are clearly differentiated in regard to dynamics. Then the flute returns.

3. *L'Artisanat furieux.* The tempo is *moderé sans rigueur* (moderate, without strictness). In this duet between contralto and flute the ornate melismatic line of the voice has its counterpart in the roulades of the instrument. The meter changes practically with every measure. The

result is the free, improvisational line that twentieth-century composers have taken over from the music of the East. Notice particularly the fluttertonguing on the flute, an effect dear to Mahler, Schoenberg, and Berg.

4. "Second commentary on *Bourreaux de solitude.*" *Assez rapide* (quite fast). For xylorimba, vibraphone, small cymbals (cymbalettes), guitar, and viola. A continual accelerando and ritardando create what European writers call a "respiratory" rhythm. The fragmentation of the musical line goes hand in hand with the rests that punctuate the movement. These points of rest, Boulez directs, should be like brusque interruptions in the tempo. The texture is of a single-note variety, and calls for great agility on the part of the instruments.

5. *Bel édifice et les pressentiments,* first version: *Assez vif* (quite lively). For voice, flute, guitar, and viola. In this number the tempo and nuances are what Boulez calls "unstable." Almost every measure contains a change of tempo. The vocal line is punctuated by purely instrumental passages. The unusual intervals lift the text to a high level of expressivity, especially the final line of the poem, the last words of which are executed by the voice alone.

6. *Bourreaux de solitude. Assez lent* (quite slow). Strict tempo. For voice and flute, xylorimba, vibraphone, maracas, guitar, muted viola. Percussion sound—in this movement, maracas—unifies the texture, which reinforces the impression of immobility presented by some of the earlier numbers. The sustained notes on flute and viola contribute strongly to this effect, as does the slow tempo. The vocal line is languid and free. By contrast, vibraphone and viola unfold a canon.

7. "After *L'Artisanat furieux.*" *Rapide.* For flute, vibraphone, guitar. This extremely short number is related to the first, both in its intervallic structure and sound texture.

8. "Third commentary on *Bourreaux de solitude.*" *Assez lent* (quite slow). For flute, xylorimba, vibraphone, maracas, claves. As in the other two commentaries on *Bourreaux,* the percussion group—first claves, then bell, finally bongos and maracas—set up a unifying background for the tenuous contrapuntal web. This is one of the longest movements in the suite.

9. Variation on *Bel édifice et les pressentiments.* Free tempo. For xylorimba, vibraphone, percussion, guitar, voice, viola. The opening words, *J'écoute marcher,* are sung to the same major-seventh interval as *le marcheur* in the sixth movement. The variant resembles the first version (No. 5) not only in its "unstable" rhythm but also in regard to formal design and the disposition of the rhythmic-sonorous cells. An

effect introduced earlier in the work—the reverberation of the very deep tam-tam (gong)—brings the work to a close.

Boulez's is a very special music which, as *Grove's Dictionary* circumspectly observes, has "aroused general attention and, in some quarters, enthusiasm." Twelve-tone devotees regard *Le Marteau sans maître* as a work of genius. Other listeners may well be puzzled by sounds that depart so radically from the musical language to which they are accustomed. We know that Beethoven's final piano sonatas and string quartets completely bewildered his contemporaries, yet today these works appear on fairly popular programs. It is therefore entirely possible that, a century hence, a big public will be responding to *Le Marteau*. That is, if they are still listening to live music.

◄§ 66 §►

Other Avant-Garde Composers

Bruno Maderna (Venice, 1920–) is an outstanding figure among the most advanced group in Italy today. He was one of the founders of the Studio di Fonologia Musicale at the Milan Radio, which has become one of the centers of the new electronic music. His electronic compositions—for example, *Sequenze e strutture*, *Notturno*, and *Syntaxis*—have been widely performed. They bear witness to a well-thought-out attempt to explore the possibilities for artistic expression inherent in a purely electronic idiom.

Maderna's compositions for conventional instruments show his preference for limited combinations rather than large orchestral or choral forces. Within this domain his Italian sensibility, which is of a predominantly lyric nature, accommodates itself to his desires to achieve an integral ordering of the musical material. Maderna's constructivism is based on complex serial calculations that predetermine each detail of the structure. Having inherited the innovations of the modern Viennese school in respect to the melodic, harmonic, contrapuntal, and instrumental elements of music, he has sought to develop new principles of rhythm and form to go with them. From his earlier works, such as the *Introduzione e passacaglia* for orchestra (1947), Concerto for Two Pianos (1948), and the expressionistic *Studi per "Il Processo" di Kafka* (Studies for *The Trial* of Kafka, 1950), for recitation, soprano, and small orchestra, Maderna has moved steadily toward the totally integrated serialism of his later compositions. Among these are the *Serenata No. 2 for 11 Instruments* (1955), one of Maderna's most accessible pieces, in which the mandoline plays as prominent a part as in Schoenberg's *Serenade*. The String Quartet of 1956, the second movement of which is a retrograde of the first, has an extremely complex rhythmic structure, and shows how thoroughly the Italians have assimilated the most advanced procedures of present-day instrumental writing. This line of thought is continued in the Piano Concerto of 1959, in which a post-Webern idiom is united with unconventional handling of the solo instrument.

Luciano Berio (Oneglia, 1925–) was associated with Maderna in establishing the Studio di Fonologia Musicale at Milan. He studied with Giorgio Ghedini at the Conservatory of Milan and with Luigi Dallapiccola at the Berkshire Music Center in Tanglewood. He adheres to a technique whereby every note in a score, together with its duration, intensity, and timbre, is predetermined according to the permutations of a series. Despite this desire for an absolutely controlled music whose logic is proof against the vagaries of human emotion, Berio's tone structures bear the imprint of an intense musical personality.

Berio's computational methods are embodied in a number of chamber works, such as the Quartet for wind instruments (1949); *Two Pieces for Violin and Piano* (1951); *Chamber Music*, for voice and three instruments, on the poems of James Joyce (1952); *El mar, la mar* for voice and five instruments (1953); the String Quartet of 1956; and the *Serenade No. 1* for flute and fourteen instruments (1958). The orchestral works include the *Magnificat* of 1950; *Two Pieces for Orchestra* (1952); *Variations for String Orchestra* (1953); *Nones* (The Ninth Hour), inspired by the poem of W. H. Auden (1954); the *Alleluia* of 1956; and the rigorously constructed *Composition for Orchestra* of 1959. *Mutazioni* (Mutations, 1956) is an electronic work. In

Différences (1958), Berio combines five conventional instruments— flute, clarinet, viola, cello, harp—with magnetic tape. The players record part of the score before the concert. At certain points in the performance this recording is broadcast in the hall by four loudspeakers. In other words, the musicians stop playing but one continues to hear them in another dimension. In *Hommage à Joyce* (1959) Berio uses as his starting point—in the manner of *musique concrète*—a female voice reading a fragment from *Ulysses,* which is then reconstructed electronically to serve as raw material for the composition.

Luigi Nono (Venice, 1924–) is one of the most gifted among the radicals of the post-Webern generation in Italy. He studied with Bruno Maderna and Hermann Scherchen; and adhered to the twelve-tone system from the beginning of his career. Both in his electronic music and his works for conventional instruments Nono has striven for a strict constructivism based on total serialization. At the same time Nono's imagination is stimulated by the presence of a text; hence the large amount of vocal music in his output. Among his works are *Variazioni canoniche* (1950) for orchestra, based on the tone row of Schoenberg's *Ode to Napoleon;* the cycle *Polifonica—Monodia—Ritmica,* for flute, clarinet, bass clarinet, alto saxophone, horn, piano xylophone, and percussion (1951); *Due espressioni* for orchestra (1953); and *Music for violin solo, strings and woodwinds* (1957). The sparse texture of these early pieces gives way, in the choral compositions and the later works for orchestra, to an intense idiom that abounds in violent contrasts in sound. Nono thus moves toward a dramatic lyricism, transforming the twelve-tone technique into a vehicle for powerful expressionism. This trend is to be noticed in the *Epitaph for Federico García Lorca* (1952–54), for chorus and orchestra, and several compositions written in the late Fifties: the cantata *Il Canto sospeso* (The Suspended Song); *La Victoire de Guernica,* for chorus and orchestra, based on the poem of Éluard, which in turn was inspired by Picasso's famous painting; *Diario polacco* (Polish Diary), for orchestra; and *Composizione No. 1,* for orchestra. *Il Canto sospeso* has as its text excerpts from letters actually written by nine resistance fighters just before their execution: a Bulgarian teacher, an Italian printer, a Greek student, a Polish peasant, a young Russian girl, and others. The settings affirm, in a thoroughly contemporaneous way, the unbreakable courage of the human spirit. Nono's *Cori di Didone* (1958) is an extremely difficult work for chorus and percussion based on texts from Giuseppe Ungaretti's *La terra promessa,* in which the text is broken up not only into separate syllables but also into consonant and vowel sounds passing continually from one part to another. This fragmentation of the sonorous material derives, of course, from Webern.

Giselher Klebe (Mannheim, 1925–) is one of the most active composers among the new German school. He studied with Josef Rufer and Boris Blacher. "With the work on my String Quartet, Opus 9," he writes, "I realized that the serial technique offers the opportunity I had sought to achieve the optimum union of invention, expression, and continuity." Klebe stands about midway between Stockhausen and Henze. Although an innovator by nature, he is not as radical as the former; yet he is more deeply committed to the twelve-tone system than is the latter. "I am occupied with mathematical problems that excite my imagination." These problems pertain chiefly to the permutations of a twelve-tone row with a rhythmic series. Klebe's style represents a well-sustained attempt to combine various elements—his own natural lyricism, the dramatic expressionism of Berg, the "perpetual variation" technique and condensation of form advocated by Schoenberg, the computational methods of Webern's late works. He argues eloquently for such stylistic synthesis. "There are in music endless possibilities of statement that do not necessarily have to exist apart from each other. On the contrary, only through a many-sided interpenetration and blending of the most disparate elements can the musical experience remain vital."

Klebe's opera *Die Räuber* (The Robbers, after Schiller, 1956) was followed by *Die tödlichen Wünsche* (The Fatal Wish, adapted from Balzac's famous story *Le Peau de chagrin*, 1957). The latter work, like *Wozzeck*, is in fifteen "lyric scenes." It does not approach its model in dramatic intensity; but Klebe's opera shows a capacity for creating mood and atmosphere within the twelve-tone framework which augurs well for his future development as a dramatic composer. Klebe's works give the impression of having been composed with great ease. The list includes *Geschichte vom lustigen Musikanten* (Story of the Jolly Musician, 1946–47), for tenor, chorus, and five instruments; the Wind Quintet of 1948; *Con Moto*, for orchestra (1948); *Divertissement joyeux* for chamber orchestra (1949); *Der Zwittermaschine* (The Twitter-Machine, an orchestral piece inspired by a painting of Paul Klee, 1950); *Two Nocturnes* for orchestra, and the ballet *Pas de Trois*, both of 1952; *Symphony for 42 String Instruments* (1953); Concerto for violin, cello, and orchestra (1954); *Moments musicaux* for orchestra (1956); Concerto for cello and orchestra (1958); and the ballet

Menagerie, based on the same story material as Berg's opera *Lulu* (1958). Klebe has also written a quantity of chamber music, including the String Quartet of 1951.

The Swedish composer Bo Nilsson belongs to the younger generation of avant-garde musicians; he was born in 1937. "My most important stimuli," he states, "have come from Webern, Messiaen, and the musical mathematics of the fifteenth and sixteenth centuries." Nilsson's work exemplifies the post-Webern constructivism that combines total serialism with an interest in electronic music. Among Nilsson's works in this category are *Audiogramme* (1955) and Electronic Composition No. 2, *Würfelspiel* (Play of Dice, 1958). Several of Nilsson's works have attracted notice in advanced musical circles. *Two Pieces for Flute, Bass Clarinet, Piano and Percussion; Zeitpunkte* (Points in Time) for ten woodwinds; and *Doppelspiel* (Double-play) for thirty-six percussion, date from the years 1956–58, as does *Das Spektrum* for fourteen percussion, strings, and woodwinds. *Frequenzen* (Frequencies, 1959), for piccolo, flute, percussion, guitar, xylophone, vibraphone, and double bass, extends the serial principle to include intensities, tempos, rhythms and time values, tone colors, and frequencies (high or low pitch). Some of Nilsson's works are so designed as to give the interpreter a creative participation in the music; as in his *Piece for Alto Voice, Alto Flute and 18 Instruments* (1960), which allows the conductor utter freedom of choice in regard to the tempos.

The Dutch composer Henk Badings may be included with the experimentalists even though his music for instruments and voices is traditional in character; he was a pioneer in the development of electronic music. Badings was born in Bandoeng, Indonesia, in 1907, but was brought up in Holland. He studied to be a mining engineer. This scientific background prepared him for his later experiments. Electronic aids play a major part in Badings's radiophonic opera *Orestes*, and in the oratorio *Job*, both written in the mid-fifties. His electronic ballet *Cain and Abel* employs seven magnetic tape recorders, sometimes five at a time. Eight symphonies form the core of Badings's considerable output, which includes operas, ballets, concertos, a variety of orchestral pieces, and chamber works. In 1941 Badings became director of the Royal Conservatory at The Hague.

We have mentioned only a few of the composers who exemplify the advanced tendencies on the contemporary musical scene. Enough has been said, however, to indicate clearly that these tendencies, far from being confined to any one place, are international in their scope and character.

Part Three

THE AMERICAN SCENE

"The way to write American music is simple. All you have to do is to be an American and then write any kind of music you wish."

Virgil Thomson

⁓§ 67 §⁓
Music in America

"A true musical culture never has been and never can be solely based upon the importation of foreign artists and foreign music, and the art of music in America will always be essentially a museum art until we are able to develop a school of composers who can speak directly to the American public in a musical language which expresses fully the deepest reactions of the American consciousness to the American scene."

Aaron Copland

THE BACKGROUND

IT IS our nation's great achievement to have created, out of elements inherited from Europe, something completely new and fresh; something specifically un-European. We all recognize what is American in music, although we should be hard put to it to define exactly what that quality is. Having been shaped by a wide variety of factors, the American quality is not any one thing.

American artists became increasingly aware of a wealth of native material that was waiting to be used. Grant Wood, *American Gothic*. (Chicago Art Institute)

447

Conditions in a pioneer country did not foster the emergence of music as a native art. Consequently, throughout the nineteenth century we imported Italian opera and German symphony. The great American composer of the pre-Civil War period issued neither from the tradition of Haydn and Mozart nor from that of Rossini and Bellini. He came out of the humbler realm of the minstrel show, and his name was Stephen Foster.

In the second half of the nineteenth century, a native school of serious composers emerged. First to achieve more than ephemeral fame was John Knowles Paine (1839–1906), who for thirty years was professor of music at Harvard. Paine was the mentor of the so-called Boston or New England group that included the leading American composers at the turn of the century. Among them were George W. Chadwick (1854–1931), Edgar Stillman Kelley (1857–1944), Horatio Parker (1863–1919), and Mrs. H. H. A. Beach (1867–1944). Arthur Foote (1853–1937) and Henry F. Gilbert (1868–1928) also belonged to this generation. These composers, musically speaking, were German colonists. They studied in Leipzig, Weimar, Munich, or Berlin, and worked in the tradition of Schumann and Mendelssohn or Liszt and Wagner. It was their historic mission to raise the technical level of American music to the standards of Europe. But their music, weakened by their genteel outlook on art and life, bore no vital relationship to their milieu. It has not survived.

A more striking profile was that of Edward MacDowell (1861–1908), the first American composer to achieve a reputation abroad. His four piano sonatas and two concertos for piano and orchestra show him to have been at home in the large forms. MacDowell was at his best, however, in the small lyric pieces which are still favorites with young pianists. The *Woodland Sketches*, whence the perennial *To a Wild Rose;* the *Fireside Tales* and *New England Idyls* are the work of a miniaturist of charm and poetic sensibility.

The composers just mentioned, although they lived in the postromantic era, were really romanticists who had come too late. In the world arena they have been overshadowed by their European contemporaries, compared to whom they unquestionably take second place. Yet comparisons are hardly in order. The European postromantics were the heirs of a rich past. The Americans were building for a rich future. They were pioneers dedicated to a lofty vision. We have every reason to remember them with pride.

THREE GENERATIONS OF AMERICAN COMPOSERS

The composers born in the 1870s and 80s faced a difficult task. They had to effect the transition from the postromantic era to the modern. And they had to discover what an American music would be like. Some of them continued more or less in the path of their predecessors. Frederick Shepherd Converse (1871–1940), Henry Hadley (1871–1937), Daniel Gregory Mason (1873–1953) and David Stanley Smith (1877–1949) carried on the genteel tradition of the earlier New England group. Although they and their fellows had an occasional success, the fact remains that during the first quarter of our century the serious American composer was something of a stepchild in his own country. His music faced a twofold handicap: it was contemporary, and it lacked the made-in-Europe label that carries such weight with our public. He had no powerful publishers to champion his cause, no system of grants and fellowships to give him the leisure to compose, no famous conductors to bring him the performances he needed. On the rare occasions when a work of his was played, as like as not it was sandwiched between two masterpieces of the ages, almost as if to point up the fact that we had no Bach or Beethoven in our midst. As we follow the careers of the older generation of modern American composers—those, that is, who were born between 1870 and 1890—we cannot help feeling that they appeared upon a scene which was not quite ready for them.

The middle generation—composers born between 1890 and 1910—had an easier time. The gradual victory of contemporary music in Europe could not but have repercussions here. Besides, the emergence of a strong native school became a matter of national pride and found support in various quarters. The era of prosperity in the Twenties encouraged private patronage in the form of grants and fellowships. Of enormous value to the members of this generation were the Guggenheim fellowships, the Prix de Rome (which gives the recipient three years at the American Academy in Rome), the Pulitzer Prize, and the grants of the National Academy of Arts and Letters. Equally helpful were the commissions for new works offered by the League of Composers, the Alice M. Ditson Fund of Columbia University, the Elizabeth Sprague Coolidge Foundation and, somewhat later, the Koussevitzky Foundation. Increased opportunities were offered the composer to see his work in print, through the publication awards of the Eastman School of Music, the Juilliard School, the Society for the

Publication of American Music, and similar organizations. For a time the radio networks, such as the National Broadcasting Company and the Columbia Broadcasting System, adopted the imaginative policy—now unhappily discontinued—of commissioning new works. Hand in hand with these advances went a variety of prizes that could not but encourage the creative musician in his labors.

Confronted by a public that listened eagerly to the older music but steadfastly ignored their own, American composers began to band together in associations expressly designed to foster the new music. In 1921 was founded the International Composers' Guild. There followed the League of Composers, the United States section of the International Society for Contemporary Music (I.S.C.M.), the American Composers' Alliance, and the National Association of American Composers and Conductors (N.A.A.C.C.). Towards the end of this period the powerful organizations of the writers of popular music—ASCAP (American Society of Composers, Authors and Publishers) and B.M.I. (Broadcast Music, Incorporated)—began to take increasing interest in the composer of serious music.

Of great help was the forward-looking policy of conductors like Serge Koussevitzky, Leopold Stokowski, and Dimitri Mitropoulos, who made a point of giving the American composer a hearing. The conservatories too, which had hitherto concentrated on the training of instrumentalists and singers, began to turn their attention to the needs of young composers. This was accompanied by a significant change in the administration of our music schools. It had been the custom to appoint celebrated performers as the directors of conservatories; Josef Hoffman, Efrem Zimbalist, Ossip Gabrilowitch, and Ernest Hutcheson were among those who served in this capacity. Now it began to be recognized that a composer was perhaps a more appropriate figure to supervise the training of musicians. The appointment of Howard Hanson as the director of the Eastman School of Music in Rochester set an important precedent. The trend gathered strength as the younger generation of American composers came to the fore. William Schuman was selected to direct the Juilliard School in New York; the Peabody Institute in Baltimore came under the guidance of Peter Mennin. Mention should be made too of the remarkable summer school of the Berkshire Music Center at Tanglewood, Massachusetts, founded by Serge Koussevitzky in 1940, where a whole generation of young American composers received their start.

During the time of the middle generation, the music departments in our colleges and universities took on new importance as centers of progressive musical activity. The widespread policy of hiring composers to teach composition opened up a much wider sphere of influence to our creative musicians. It also provided them with a means of livelihood that did not entirely interfere with their creative work. (One wishes that the last statement were a little truer than it is. In many colleges the teaching and administrative load is so heavy as to reduce the composer to weekend and summer writing.) The fact that American composers began to occupy chairs at our leading universities further underlined the growing prestige of the modern American school.

During this time our composers were actively experimenting with the techniques of contemporary musical speech. In craftsmanship, their scores began to bear comparison with the best of Europe's. They mastered the symphony, chamber music, and choral music; they made progress in conquering what has always been the last stronghold to resist a native art—the opera. And they created an environment in which a young American who wished to compose could receive the finest possible training without having to go abroad. The decade before the Second World War saw this country emerge as the musical center of the world. The presence in our midst of Stravinsky, Schoenberg, Bartók, Hindemith, Milhaud, Krenek, Martinu, and their confreres had a tremendous impact on our musical life. Many of our younger musicians studied with these masters and came directly under their influence.

In the years after the Second World War our native music made important strides forward. Publishing houses and recording companies assumed an ever more receptive attitude toward contemporary American works. Another significant trend was the emergence of the opera workshop, which has offered a strong incentive to the writing of American operas. The government came to the assistance of deserving musicians through the Fulbright grants; during the Fifties the large foundations began to contribute to our musical life in ways that helped composers. As a result of these and kindred developments, especially the emergence of a public interested in hearing American works, the third generation of the contemporary American school—composers, that is, born since 1910—have found an incomparably more favorable climate for their work than did their forebears.

TOWARD AN AMERICAN MUSIC

As American composers became more sure of themselves, they aspired in ever greater measure to give expression to the life about them.

At first they concentrated on those features of the home scene that were not to be found in Europe: the lore of the Indian, the Negro, and the cowboy. They became increasingly aware of a wealth of native material that was waiting to be used: the songs of the southern mountaineers, which preserved intact the melodies brought over from England three hundred years ago; the hymns and religious tunes that had such vivid associations for Americans everywhere; the patriotic songs

As our artists became more sure of themselves, they aspired in ever greater measure to give expression to the life about them. Edward Hopper, *New York Movie*. (Collection Museum of Modern Art)

of the Revolutionary period and the Civil War, many of which had become folk songs; the tunes of the minstrel shows which had reached their high point in the songs of Foster. There were, in addition, the work songs from various parts of the country—songs of sharecroppers, lumberjacks, miners, river men; songs of prairie and railroad, chain gang and frontier. Then there was the folklore of the city dwellers—commercialized ballads, musical-comedy songs, and jazz: a world of melody, rhythm, and mood.

Certain composers, on the other hand, resisted this kind of local color. They preferred the international idioms of twentieth-century music which had been stripped of folk elements: impressionism, neo-classicism, atonality, and twelve-tone music. Others managed to reconcile the two attitudes. They revealed themselves as internationally minded in certain of their works, but employed folklore elements in others. It was gradually realized that Americanism in music was a much broader concept than had at first been supposed: American music could not but be as many-faceted as America itself. A work did not have to quote a Negro spiritual, an Indian harvest song, or a dirge of the prairie in order to qualify for citizenship.

The music of the contemporary American school follows no single formula. Rather, it reflects the contradictory tendencies in our national character: our jaunty humor, and our sentimentality; our idealism, and our worship of material success; our rugged individualism, and our wish to look and think like everybody else; our visionary daring, and our practicality; our ready emotionalism, and our capacity for intellectual pursuits. All of these and more are abundantly present in a music that has bigness of gesture, vitality, and all the exuberance of youth.

⤳ 68 ⤶

Impressionists

"It is only logical that when I began to write I wrote in the vein of Debussy and Stravinsky; those particular wide-intervaled dissonances are the natural medium of the composer who writes today's music."

Charles T. Griffes

CHARLES MARTIN LOEFFLER (1861–1935)

THE DEVICES of impressionist music figure prominently in the works of the Alsatian-born Charles Martin Loeffler, who came to this country when he was twenty. He is remembered chiefly for *A Pagan Poem* (1905–06), an evocative work for thirteen instruments which he subsequently rewrote for piano and orchestra. Loeffler was a recluse and a mystic. His was a music of shadowy visions; it showed his affinity for Gregorian chant, medieval modes, and impressionist harmonies. His works bear some resemblance to the style that came to be associated with Debussy; yet he found his way to it in the 1890s, before he could have heard much of the Frenchman's music.

Loeffler anticipated one of the most significant developments in American musical life—the turning from German to French influence. The enormous popularity of impressionism in this country during the first quarter of our century broke the grip of the German conservatory. The new generation of American musicians went to Paris, even as their predecessors had gone to Leipzig or Weimar. This trend, strengthened by the boycott of all things German during the First World War, engendered a significant new orientation during the Twenties.

Among the composers receptive to French influence were John Alden Carpenter (1876–1951), Edward Burlingame Hill (1872–1960), Arthur Shepherd (1880–1958), and Deems Taylor (1885–). Carpenter achieved a vogue in the Twenties with two ballets that sought to incorporate the rhythm and tempo of American life: *Krazy Kat* (1922) and *Skyscrapers* (1926). Taylor's two operas, *The King's Henchman* (1926) and *Peter Ibbetson* (1930), were produced at the Metropolitan Opera House with great fanfare, but soon dropped out of sight. Many other Americans took to impressionism. Indeed, a young American beginning to compose in the Twenties turned as naturally to Debussy's idiom as his successors twenty years later turned to Stravinsky's, or forty years later to Webern's.

CHARLES TOMLINSON GRIFFES (1884–1920)

The most gifted among the American impressionists was Charles Tomlinson Griffes (Elmira, New York, 1884–1920, New York City). At nineteen he went to study in Germany. His four years in Berlin brought him into contact with a rich musical culture. Upon his return he accepted a teaching job at a boys' preparatory school in Tarrytown, New York. His chores at the Hackley School interfered seriously with his composing, but he was never able to escape; he remained there until his death.

Recognition finally came to Griffes in the last year of his life, when his works were accepted for performance by the Boston, New York, and Philadelphia orchestras. *The Pleasure Dome of Kubla Khan*, presented by the Boston Symphony in its home city and in New York, scored a triumph. A few days later, the accumulated strain of years took its toll; Griffes collapsed. The doctors diagnosed his illness as pleurisy and pneumonia; the deeper cause was physical and nervous exhaustion. He failed to rally after an operation on his lungs, and died in New York Hospital at the age of thirty-six.

Griffes represents the current in American music most strongly oriented to foreign influence. His dream-like art could not be nurtured by indigenous folk song. A nostalgic yearning, a gently elegiac quality informs his music. Stimulated by far-off places and remote times, his imagination turned to moods and fancies rooted in romantic longing. He admired the composers who at that time were attracting the attention of progressive musicians—Debussy, Ravel, Musorgsky and Scriabin, Busoni, Stravinsky, Schoenberg. Another liberating influence was his preoccupation with the music of the Far East.

Griffes's fame rests on a comparatively small output. He favored the short lyric forms. Songs like *By a Lonely Forest Pathway* and *The Lament of Ian the Proud* reveal a lyricist of exquisite sensibility. He was no less successful with the short piano piece, and brought to American piano music a subtlety of nuance that had hitherto been found only among the French composers. Characteristic are the *Three Tone Pictures—The Lake at Evening, The Night Winds*, and *The Vale of Dreams* (1910–12); and the *Four Roman Sketches—The White Peacock, Nightfall, The Fountain of Acqua Paola*, and *Clouds* (1915–16). Of the orchestral works, the most important are *The Pleasure Dome of Kubla Khan* (1912), the *Poem* for flute and orchestra (1918), and *The White Peacock*, which Griffes transcribed for orchestra.

Inspired by the poem of Coleridge, *The Pleasure Dome of Kubla Khan* is an atmospheric piece whose shadowy beginning suggests the sacred river of Xanadu that ran "through caverns measureless to man, down to a sunless sea. . . ." A *Lento misterioso* in 6/4 time sets forth a B-major tonality overlaid with chromatic harmonies. Parallel chords on the piano, in the bass register, are used impressionistically for their clang rather than for any harmonic function. Out of the mist emerge delicate traceries of oboe and flute. The orchestral texture takes on light and movement as the music evokes Kubla Khan's famous pleasure dome, from the recesses of which come sounds of revelry and dancing. A modulation to B modal-minor ushers in the *Più mosso* with a sensuous theme on the oboe.

p lontano

The material is repeated; there is a striking modulation to the flat keys. One recognizes at once the genuinely musical impulse behind the surge of melody. The climax comes with the return to the home key of B. The dance section, a *Vivace* in 2/4 time, contains effects that were altogether novel in the second decade of our century. The *Tempo I* returns to the mood of the opening; the final measures are silvered with the tone of the celesta.

The composer of this haunting music did not live to fulfill the rich promise of his gifts. But the vision of beauty which formed the substance of his art, and the fastidious craftsmanship he attained in the projection of that vision, were of prime importance to the evolution of our native school.

X. NATIONALISTS

"Before a people can find a musical writer to echo its genius it must first possess men who truly represent it—that is to say, men who, being part of the people, love the country for itself: men who put into their music what the nation has put into its life. What we must arrive at is the youthful optimistic vitality and the undaunted tenacity of spirit that characterize the American man. That is what I hope to see echoed in American music."

Edward MacDowell

∻ 69 ∾

Charles Ives (1874-1954)

"Beauty in music is too often confused with something that lets the ears lie back in an easy chair. Many sounds that we are used to do not bother us, and for that reason we are inclined to call them beautiful. Frequently, when a new or unfamiliar work is accepted as beautiful on its first hearing, its fundamental quality is one that tends to put the mind to sleep."

CHARLES EDWARD IVES waited many years for recognition. Today he stands revealed as the first truly American composer of the twentieth century, and one of the most original spirits of his time.

HIS LIFE

Ives was born in Danbury, Connecticut. His father had been a bandmaster in the Civil War, and continued his calling in civilian life. George Ives was the ideal father for anyone who was to become an experimental composer. He was a singularly progressive musician with endless curiosity about the nature of sound. He listened carefully to church bells; and when he found that he could not duplicate their pitch on the piano, he built an instrument that would play the tones "in the cracks between the keys"—that is, quarter tones. Or he made his family sing *Swanee River* in the key of E-flat while he played the accompaniment in the key of C, "in order," his son later wrote, "to stretch our ears and strengthen our musical minds."

Charles at thirteen held a job as church organist and already was arranging music for the various ensembles conducted by his father. At twenty he entered Yale, where he studied composition with Horatio Parker. Ives's talent for music asserted itself throughout his four years at Yale; yet when he had to choose a career he decided against a professional life in music. "Assuming a man lives by himself and with no dependents, he might write music that no one would play prettily, listen to or buy. But—but if he has a nice wife and some nice children, how can he let the children starve on his dissonances? So he has to

Charles Ives

weaken (and if he is a man he *should* weaken for his children) but his music more than weakens—it goes 'ta-ta' for money! Bad for him, bad for music!" Ives thus began by assuming that society would not pay him for the kind of music he wanted to write. He was not mistaken.

He therefore entered the business world. Two decades later he was head of the largest insurance agency in the country. The years it took him to achieve this success—roughly from the time he was twenty-two to forty-two—were the years when he wrote his music. He composed at night, on weekends, and during vacations, working in isolation, concerned only to set down the sounds he heard in his head.

The few conductors and performers whom he tried to interest in his works pronounced them unplayable. Some smiled, persuaded that such writing could come only from one who was ignorant of the rudiments. Others, accustomed to the suavities of the postromantic period, concluded that the man was cracked. After a number of these rebuffs Ives gave up showing his manuscripts. When he felt the need to hear how his music sounded, he hired a few musicians to run through a work. Save for these rare and quite inadequate performances, Ives heard his music only in his imagination. He pursued his way undeflected and alone, piling up one score after another in his barn in Connecticut. When well-meaning friends suggested that he try to write music that people would like, he could only retort, "I can't do it—I hear something else!"

Ives's double life as a business executive by day and composer by night finally took its toll. In 1918, when he was forty-four, he suffered a physical breakdown that left his heart damaged. The years of unrewarded effort had taken more out of him emotionally than he had suspected. Although he lived almost forty years longer, he produced nothing further of importance.

When he recovered he faced the realization that the world of professional musicians was irrevocably closed to his ideas. He felt that he owed it to his music to make it available to those who might be less hidebound. He therefore had the *Concord Sonata* for piano privately printed, also the *Essays Before a Sonata*—a kind of elaborate program note that presented the essence of his views on life and art. These were followed by the *114 Songs*. The three volumes, which were distributed free of charge to libraries, music critics, and whoever else asked for them, caused not a ripple as far as the public was concerned. But they gained Ives the support of other experimental composers who were struggling to make their way in an unheeding world. Henry Cowell, Wallingford Riegger, and Nicholas Slonimsky espoused his cause, as did the critic Paul Rosenfeld. Significantly, Ives's music first won attention in Europe. Slonimsky conducted three movements from *Holidays* in Paris, Budapest, and Berlin. Anton Webern presented his work in Vienna. The tide finally turned in this country when the American pianist John Kirkpatrick, at a recital in Town Hall in January, 1939, played the *Concord Sonata*. Ives was then sixty-five. The piece was repeated several weeks later by Kirkpatrick and scored a triumph. The next morning Lawrence Gilman hailed the *Concord Sonata* as "the greatest music composed by an American."

Ives had already begun to exert a salutary influence upon the younger generation of composers, who found in his art a realization of their own ideals. Now he was "discovered" by the general public and hailed as the grand old man of American music. In 1947 his Third Symphony achieved performance, and won a Pulitzer Prize. This story of belated recognition was an item to capture the imagination, and was carried by newspapers throughout the nation. Ives awoke at seventy-three to find himself famous. Four years later the Second Symphony was presented to the public by the New York Philharmonic, exactly half a century after it had been composed. The prospect of finally hearing the work agitated the old man; he attended neither the rehearsals nor the performances. He was, however, one of millions who listened to the radio broadcast.

He died in New York City three years later, at the age of eighty.

HIS MUSIC

Charles Ives, both as man and artist, was rooted in the New England heritage, in the tradition of plain living and high thinking that came to flower in the idealism of Hawthorne and the Alcotts, Emerson and Thoreau. The sources of his tone imagery are to be found in the living music of his childhood: hymn tunes and popular songs, the town band at holiday parades, the fiddlers at Saturday night dances, patriotic songs and sentimental parlor ballads, the melodies of Stephen Foster, and the medleys heard at country fairs and in small theaters.

This wealth of American music had attracted other musicians besides Ives. But they, subservient to European canons of taste, had proceeded to smoothe out and "correct" these popular tunes according to the rules they had absorbed in Leipzig or Munich. Ives was as free from subservience to the European tradition as Walt Whitman. His keen ear caught the sound of untutored voices singing a hymn together, some in their eagerness straining and sharping the pitch, others just missing it and flatting; so that in place of the single tone there was a cluster of tones that made a deliciously dissonant chord. Some were a trifle ahead of the beat, others lagged behind; consequently the rhythm sagged and turned into a welter of polyrhythms. He heard the pungent clash of dissonance when two bands in a parade, each playing a different tune in a different key, came close enough together to overlap; he heard the effect of quarter tones when fiddlers at a country dance brought excitement into their playing by going a mite off pitch. He remembered the wheezy harmonium at church accompanying the hymns a shade out of tune. All these, he realized, were not departures from the norm. They *were* the norm of popular American musical speech. Thus he found his way to such conceptions as polytonality, atonality, polyharmony, cluster chords based on intervals of a second, and polyrhythms. All this in the last years of the nineteenth century, when Schoenberg was still writing in a post-Wagner idiom, when neither Stravinsky nor Bartók had yet begun their careers, when Hindemith had just been born. All the more honor, then, to this singular musician who, isolated alike from the public and his fellow composers, was so advanced in his conceptions and so accurate in his forecast of the paths that twentieth-century music would follow.

Ive's melodies represent the least revolutionary part of his canon. He is fond of quoting hymn tunes or popular songs, relying upon such allusions to establish the emotional tone. He is partial to procedures that later came to be associated with the Schoenbergian school—inversion, retrograde, rhythmic augmentation, and diminution. Although he was addicted to greater dissonance than almost any composer of his time, his harmonic progressions give an impression of unity because of the strong feeling of key behind them. His use of polychords is most original. He will set two streams of harmony going, treating them like single lines in counterpoint. There is imaginative polytonal writing in his music, and an occasional atonal passage. Ives was no less inventive in the domain of polyrhythms. Patterns of three, four, five, or six notes to the measure are pitted against units of seven, eleven, thirteen, or seventeen notes. (See the musical example on page 46.) He went from one meter to another with the flexibility that was later to be associated with Stravinsky and Bartók; and he anticipated Stravinsky in his use of dissonant chords repeated as a percussive-rhythm effect. He also created jazzlike rhythms long before jazz had emerged in its familiar form. Ives was one of the first musicians to write without regular barlines or time signatures, simply placing the barline wherever he desired an accented beat. He rebelled against the nineteenth-century habit of writing within the capacities of each instrument. He sought rather to transcend those capacities. The sound, for him, had to serve the musical idea. He moved away from symmetrical repetition to an off-balance freshness in the arrangement of the material, achieving a plasticity of form that was very much of the twentieth century.

The central position in his orchestral music is held by the four symphonies. The First (1896–98) dates from the period when he was evolving his style. The Second (1897–1902) is a romantic work in five movements. The Third (1901–04) quotes the old hymn *Take It to the Lord*, as well as the Welsh battle song known as *All Through the Night*, and is the most fully realized of Ives's symphonies. Fourth is the Symphony for orchestra and two pianos (1910–16), in which the composer introduces the hymn tune *Watchman, Tell Us of the Night*. Of similar dimension is *A Symphony: Holidays* (1904–13), based upon the "recollections of a boy's holidays in a Connecticut country town." The four movements are *Washington's Birthday, Decoration Day, Fourth of July*, and *Thanksgiving Day*.

Among his orchestral works are *Three Places in New England*, which we will discuss; and *Three Outdoor Scenes* (1898–1911), consisting of *Hallowe'en, The Pond*, and *Central Park in the Dark*, the last-named for chamber orchestra; also *The Unanswered Question* (1908). The Sonata No. 2 for piano—"Concord, Mass., 1840–1860"—which occupied him from 1910 to 1915, reflects four aspects of the flowering of New England. *Emerson* is an apocalyptic evocation of Ives's beloved philosopher. Second is the scherzo, *Hawthorne*, which conjures up some of that writer's "wilder, fantastical adventures into the half-childlike, half-fairylike phantasmal realms." Third is *The Alcotts*, a gentle slow movement that evokes "the memory of that home under the elms—the Scotch songs and the family hymns that were sung at the end of each day . . . a conviction in the power of the common soul which, when all is said and done, may be as typical as any theme of Concord and its transcendentalists." Fourth is *Thoreau*. The *114 Songs* (1884–1921) range from works in folk style to those which express passion, anger, and poetic feeling. Ives chose texts from Keats, Stevenson, Browning and Landor, as well as from modern poets. Some of the texts he wrote himself; others are by his wife. The songs are as unequal in quality as they are diverse in character. But the collection as a whole, which includes such striking things as the rugged cowboy ballad *Charlie Rutlage* and the evocative *Serenity, Evening*, and *Ann Street*, vividly reflects the personality behind it. Ives also wrote a variety of chamber, choral, and piano compositions.

There are crudities and rough spots in Ives's style, as there are in the prose of Theodore Dreiser, in the verse of Whitman. These are traceable on the one hand to Ives's temperament, on the other to the fact that since he never heard his music, he was not impelled to limit himself to what an audience could readily assimilate. His desire to express all the facets of life precluded his developing a homogeneous style. Nor did he ever acquire that solidity of technique which marks the professional composer. Aaron Copland, in a perceptive essay on Ives, has well summed up his predicament: "He lacked neither the talent nor the ability nor the metier nor the integrity of the true artist—but what he most shamefully and tragically lacked was an audience. 'Why do you write so much—which no one ever sees?' his friends asked. And we can only echo, 'Why, indeed?' and admire the courage and perseverance of the man and the artist."

THREE PLACES IN NEW ENGLAND

In this work (1903–1911) Ives evokes three place-names rich in associations for a New Englander. The score specifies the instruments but not the number of each, leaving it to the conductor to decide: piccolo, flute, oboe and English horn, clarinet, bassoon; horns, trumpets, trombones, tuba; percussion, piano, organ (optional), and strings.

I. *The "St. Gaudens" in Boston Common: Col. Shaw and his Colored Regiment. Very slowly.* It will suffice to quote the opening lines of the poem that Ives wrote into the score:

> Moving,—Marching—Faces of Souls!
> Marked with generations of pain,
> Part-freers of a Destiny,
> Slowly, restlessly—swaying us on with you
> Towards other Freedom! . . .

An atmosphere of solemn dedication envelops the opening measures. No familiar tunes are actually quoted in this movement, yet the melodic line unmistakably suggests the world of the Stephen Foster songs and the range of emotions attached to the Civil War. The ostinato patterns in the bass, the urgency of the brass, the complex chord structures on the piano used for their color value, the fluid polyrhythms, and the polytonal effects are all characteristic of the composer; as are the wide-apart instrumental lines and the effect of distance that Ives achieves at the emotional climax by pitting high woodwinds against low brass. The texture is predominantly homophonic. The form is free, in the manner of a prelude or fantasy. Ives's keen sense of rhythm shows itself in an observation in the score: "Any holding-back should be of a cursory kind. Often when a mass of men march up-hill there is an unconscious slowing up. The drum seems to follow the feet, rather than the feet the drum." The piece ends, as it begins, *ppp*.

II. *Putnam's Camp, Redding, Connecticut. Allegro* (Quick-Step Time). "Near Redding Center," Ives wrote, "is a small park preserved as a Revolutionary Memorial; for here General Israel Putnam's soldiers had their winter quarters in 1778–9. Long rows of stone camp fire-places still remain to stir a child's imagination." The scene is a "4th of July" picnic held under the auspices of the First Church and the Village Cornet Band. The child wanders into the woods and dreams of the old soldiers, of the hardships they endured, their desire to break

camp and abandon their cause, and of how they returned when Putnam came over the hills to lead them. "The little boy awakes, he
hears the children's songs and runs down past the monument to 'listen
to the band' and join in the games and dances."

In this genre painting Ives conjures up the frenetic business of having a good time on a holiday picnic in a small American town: the
genial hubbub, the sweating faces, the parade with its two bands that
clashingly overlap. The ardent nationalism that breathes from this
music is due not so much to the actual quotation of popular tunes—
although one or two do appear—as to the deep love of all things American that lies at the heart of this movement. There is an exciting poly-
metric passage where two march rhythms clash, four measures of the
one equalling three of the other. The intricate polyrhythms in the
final measures lead to a daringly dissonant ending, *ffff*. This is one of
those works that spring from the soil and soul of a particular place,
and could have been conceived nowhere else.

III. *The Housatonic at Stockbridge. Adagio molto* (Very slowly).
Ives quotes the poem of that name by Robert Underwood Johnson:

> Contented river! in thy dreamy realm—
> The cloudy willow and the plumy elm . . .
> Thou hast grown human laboring with men
> At wheel and spindle; sorrow thou dost ken. . . .
>
> . . . . Wouldst thou away!
> I also of much resting have a fear;
> Let me thy companion be
> By fall and shallow to the adventurous sea!

The strings set up a rippling current of sound that serves as background for the melody which presently emerges, divided between the

horn and English horn. It is a serene, hymnic tune that evokes the
prayer meetings of Ives's boyhood. The fluid rhythms of this contemplative nature piece impart to it an engaging plasticity. The music
flows calmly and steadily to the *fff* climax, then subsides to a pianissimo ending.

Ives holds a unique place in our musical life. Certainly no other
composer has so vividly captured the transcendental quality of the

New England heritage. Charles Ives is our great primitive. Like the writers he admired most, he has become an American classic.

⋖§ 70 §⋗

Douglas Moore (1893-)

"The particular ideal which I have been striving to attain is to write music which will not be self-conscious with regard to idiom, and will reflect the exciting quality of life, traditions, and country which I feel all about me."

HIS LIFE

DOUGLAS MOORE has been a consistent advocate of a wholesome Americanism in music. He was born in Cutchogue, on Long Island, and is a descendant of both Miles Standish and John Alden. He attended Yale University, where he studied with David Stanley Smith and Horatio Parker. One of his songs, *Good Night, Harvard*, became Yale's favorite football-rally song. Moore served in the First World War as a lieutenant in the navy. Out of this experience came a collection of songs, in collaboration with the ballad singer John Jacob Niles, under the provocative title *Songs My Mother Never Taught Me*. The war over, Moore went to Paris where he studied with Vincent d'Indy at the Schola Cantorum. He subsequently was appointed curator of music at the Cleveland Museum of Art.

His four years in Cleveland gave him his first experience as an educator and organizer of musical events. More important, he came in contact with a group of young American composers who were students of Ernest Bloch—Roger Sessions, Bernard Rogers, Quincy Porter, and Theodore Chanler. He too studied with Bloch and considers him the most inspiring teacher he ever had. A Pulitzer Traveling Fellowship enabled Moore to return to Paris and work with Nadia Boulanger. In 1926 he joined the faculty of Columbia University, and in time succeeded Daniel Gregory Mason as Edward MacDowell Professor and head of the music department. At Columbia, in addition to his more specialized duties, Moore developed a flair for making music understandable to the layman. Out of his very popular courses came two books—*Listening to Music* (1937) and *From Madrigal to Modern Music* (1942).

Moore's career moved forward steadily through the years. He had his greatest success when he was in his sixties, with the production of his opera *The Ballad of Baby Doe*. This work, along with those that preceded it, placed him in the forefront of our present-day nationalists.

HIS MUSIC

Moore had to shake off the French influence before he could find his true bent. This he was able to do only by going back to his roots. "I cannot believe," he wrote in the Twenties, "that the fashions decreed by such elegant couturiers as the Parisian Stravinsky or Ravel, successful as they are in permitting a post-war Europe to express herself in music, are likely to be appropriate or becoming for us."

Moore is a romantic at heart. He regards romanticism as a characteristic American trait. "We are incorrigibly sentimental as a race, and our realism in the drama and literature usually turns out to be meltingly romantic in execution. The best of what we accomplish is usually achieved by dint of high spirits, soft-heartedness, and a great deal of superfluous energy." He defends his conservatism on national grounds. "If we like a good tune now and then, if we still have a childish love for atmosphere, is it not well for us to admit the fact and try to produce something which we like ourselves?" His music is honest, unpretentious and clear. When he sets the verses of our poets—among his favorites are Stephen Vincent Benét, Vachel Lindsay, and Archibald MacLeish—his melodic line projects the rhythms and inflections of American speech. The national quality is implicit too in his orchestral pieces. *The Pageant of P. T. Barnum* (1924), a suite that ends with the roistering *Circus Parade; Moby Dick* (1928), after Melville's masterpiece; and the *Overture on an American Tune* (1931), which conjures up the boisterous optimism of Sinclair Lewis's *Babbitt*, exemplify Moore's sympathetic handling of Americana. In the same vein is *Village Music* (1942), and an engaging suite for chamber orchestra called *Farm Journal* (1947). Even his absolute music, such as the *Symphony in A* (1945), the jaunty *String Quartet* (1933), or the *Quintet* for clarinet and strings (1946), echoes the native scene, although of course in more stylized form.

"I've always liked setting words better than any other form of composition," Moore declared fairly early in his career, "and I've always had a passion for the theatre." This double affinity leads a composer in one direction—opera. Moore states his predilection with gusto. "I love to write operas. To me it is the most spontaneous form of expression. The music writes itself if the book is good." This is a big "if." Moore's first opera, *White Wings* (1934), after Philip Barry's play, did not get off the ground. *The Devil and Daniel Webster* (1938), with a libretto by Stephen Vincent Benét, based on his celebrated short story, did. This exuberant one-acter, which shows Daniel Webster matching his wits and eloquence against the Devil's, has established itself as an American classic. *Giants in the Earth* (1950), on a libretto by Arnold Sundgaard after the novel by O. E. Rölvaag, brought Moore a Pulitzer Prize; but his music was not able to surmount the handicap of a cumbersome book. The experience he gained, however, prepared him for his most ambitious effort in the theater—the opera about Baby Doe.

THE BALLAD OF BABY DOE

OPERA IN TWO ACTS

The Ballad of Baby Doe (1956) is based on an American legend that really happened: the rise and fall of Horace Tabor, who struck silver in Leadville, Colorado, became one of the wealthiest men of his time, and was ruined when the United States abandoned the silver

A scene from the New York City Center production of *The Ballad of Baby Doe.*

standard for gold. The action unfolds in a turbulent period of American history against the background of a Colorado mining town. The eternal triangle involves Horace; Augusta, his domineering and straitlaced wife, who accompanied him from his humble beginnings to wealth and power; and Baby Doe, as she was known among the miners —a twenty-year-old beauty with an uncertain past, for whose sake the middle-aged magnate divorced Augusta. John LaTouche provided a beautiful libretto—dramatically compelling, with characters who are three-dimensional and true. The story line is one that has been infallible in the drama ever since the Greeks—the destruction of the hero through the fatal flaw he carries within him. The intertwining of personal destiny with vaster issues is as imaginative as it is deft.

There are eleven scenes. The first takes place in 1880, on the night of the opening of the Tabor Opera House—Horace's gift to Leadville and culture. It is also the night of Baby Doe's arrival in Leadville. Moore's music, noisy and brash, projects the atmosphere of the Colorado mining town.

Scene II. Outside the Clarendon Hotel, later that evening. Baby Doe's song, "Willow, where we met together," establishes the sweet-

Wil-low, where we met to-geth-er.___   Wil-low when our love was new.___

Wil-low, if he once should be re-turn-ing, Pray tell him I am weep-ing too.

ness of the girl. It enraptures Horace and impels him to a lyric outburst: "Warm as the autumn light, soft as a pool at night, the sound of your singing, Baby Doe. . . ." In both arias Moore's melodic line, sensitively attuned to LaTouche's text, is unmistakably American.

Scene III. The Tabor apartment several months later. Augusta confronts Horace with proof of his infidelity. Both characters are clearly limned, musically and dramatically. Altogether admirable is Moore's handling of what has always been the thorniest problem of opera in English—the recitative.

Scene IV. The lobby of the Clarendon Hotel, shortly thereafter. Baby Doe has decided to leave Tabor and writes her mother to explain why. This adaptation of the "letter scene" of European opera comes to a dramatic climax when Augusta enters to confront her rival. Baby Doe pleads with her to understand Horace and not to judge so great a man by the usual standards. Augusta mocks this naive idealization of her husband and leaves haughtily. Baby Doe realizes that Augusta's domination must ultimately destroy everything in Horace that is clamoring for fulfillment, and decides to stay. In a tender duet she and Horace affirm their love.

Scene V. Augusta's parlor in Denver, a year later. Four of Augusta's friends inform her of Horace's intention to divorce her. Moore makes effective use of the women's voices in this scene, which reaches its peak with Augusta's declaration that Horace will rue the day if he should ever attempt to humiliate her in this fashion.

Scene VI. The Willard Hotel, Washington, D. C., 1883. Tabor, serving a thirty-day interim term as United States senator, marries Baby Doe. It transpires at the reception that both Baby Doe and Tabor have been divorced. The Catholic priest who has just performed the ceremony, realizing that he was not told the truth, leaves in horror. The reception is about to break up when the footman announces the President of the United States, Chester A. Arthur. This *deus ex machina* brings the first act to a theatrically effective close.

Act II, Scene 1. The Windsor Hotel in Denver, 1893, on the night of the Governor's Ball. A diatonic waltz nostalgically conjures up the Nineties. Baby Doe is startled by the arrival of Augusta, who has swallowed her pride in order to warn her that the country is about to abandon the silver standard. She pleads with Baby Doe to persuade Horace to sell his mines. Horace enters, misunderstands Augusta's motives, and orders her to leave. He makes Baby Doe promise that she will never sell the Matchless Mine.

Scene 2. A Club Room in Denver, 1895. Horace appeals to his wealthy cronies for financial help and informs them of his decision to support William Jennings Bryan, who is campaigning for the presidency on a free silver platform. They turn a deaf ear to his appeal. He gives vent to his sense of betrayal in an impassioned aria.

Scene 3. The Matchless Mine, summer, 1896. A campaign rally for Bryan. The atmosphere of brass-band festivity is evoked with a wealth of picturesque detail. Bryan's famous "Cross of Gold" speech is transformed into a big aria for bass-baritone. The great orator, hailed by the crowd, christens Horace's little daughter Silver Dollar.

Scene 4. Augusta's home in California. She hears the newsboys shouting the news of Bryan's defeat—which means Tabor's ruin—and is visibly moved. Baby Doe's mother arrives to ask her to help Horace; but Augusta has been too deeply hurt to be able to forgive him.

Scene 5. The stage of the Tabor Opera House, 1899. Tabor, a crushed old man, returns to the scene of his former glory. He relives the chief moments of his life in a strange kaleidoscope of past and future. The grimly accusing figure of Augusta fills him with a sense of failure. Baby Doe arrives to help the dying man. She sings of the one real thing among the shadows—their love. "Always through the changing of sun and shadow, time and space, I will walk beside my love in a green and quiet place. . . ." As the aria unfolds, we see her as a white-haired old woman by the Matchless Mine, keeping her promise to Horace. (The real Baby Doe guarded the mine, a solitary eccentric wearing castoff men's clothing, with gunnysacks wrapped around her feet, until she was found frozen to death on the floor of her shack in March, 1935.)

The Ballad of Baby Doe—"The Girl of the Silver West," as it was called by the critic Jay Harrison—unites lyric and dramatic elements in a fine theater piece. The music is rich in atmosphere. The characterization is vivid, the scoring adroit, the melodic line simple and relaxed. Here is an American opera that recreates our past in a literate way, that belongs to us in every word and note.

⋞ 71 ⋟

Roy Harris (1898-)

> "I am trying to write a music which expresses our time and period in America, and which is serviceable to our musical life. What I am trying to say in music is related principally to the region of the West where I was born and where I understand life best."

Roy Harris came out of the west almost as if he had been sent to answer the need for an American composer. He exploded on our scene as a kind of Carl Sandburg in music, a homespun and outspoken young man who boldly upheld his heritage. With his spare frame, soft drawl, and inexhaustible energy, looking "like a mid-western farmer in city clothes," Harris captured the imagination of his countrymen as no twentieth-century composer had done. During the Thirties he was the most frequently performed and most widely admired of contemporary American musicians. Then his star went into an eclipse from which it never emerged. By the time the mid-century arrived, Harris—who only fifteen years before had been hailed as the white hope of American music—was outside the mainstream of significant advance. And this at a time of life when he should have been doing his most important work.

Despite this premature exhaustion of his talent Harris, in his freshest and most meaningful work, made a genuine contribution to our music.

HIS LIFE

Roy Harris was born in Lincoln County, Oklahoma. His parents were of Scotch-Irish stock. They traveled by ox-cart to stake their claim to a homestead, and moved after a few years to less rigorous surroundings near Los Angeles. During his youth the future composer witnessed, as he put it, "the end of the pioneer days and the beginning of commercial, standardized America." His nascent impulse toward art drew him in his teens to a group of sensitive souls who met, like exiles from the town, to discuss literature and philosophy. The First World War interrupted his youthful attempts at farming. At eighteen he enlisted in the heavy artillery and spent an unhappy year trying to adjust to army life. With that behind him, he enrolled in the University of California. Some years later, driven by a vague restlessness, he drifted from place to place, doing odd jobs to keep body and soul together, seeking for something that had not yet taken shape in his mind. And ever the musical impulse within him gathered strength, until it would no longer be denied. His first attempts at composition were crude and halting. What he lacked in training he made up for in enthusiasm. At twenty-four he decided to devote himself to composition, and began to study with Arthur Farwell in Los Angeles. The young man made a deep impression on the teacher. Farwell, remembering the words with which Schumann hailed the genius of Chopin—"Hats off, gentlemen—a genius!"—began his own essay on his astonishing pupil with a witty variant: "Gentlemen, a genius—but keep your hats on!"

Harris's rise to fame was as spectacular as his start had been slow. Hoogstraten, conductor of the Hollywood Bowl concerts, played his *Andante for Orchestra* in the summer of 1926, and later repeated it at a Stadium concert in New York. In the meantime the piece had come to the notice of Howard Hanson, who accepted it for performance by the Rochester Symphony. The attention of the musical world was suddenly focused on this new voice from the west. Harris was given the opportunity to continue his studies in Paris where, at Aaron Copland's suggestion, he worked with Nadia Boulanger. He was one of the first American musicians to benefit from the Guggenheim fellowships, which enabled him to extend his stay abroad for two years.

He returned home to find himself *the* American composer. The time was uniquely ripe for him. Performances, broadcasts, commissions, and awards came in exciting profusion. Harris's vogue was based partly on the fact that he was the first native composer to forge a link between a broad segment of the American public and the hitherto esoteric music of the twentieth century. His colleagues addressed themselves to the most advanced minority of music lovers; Harris was able to discuss his aims in the down-to-earth language of the man in the street. "If nobody bought corn and wheat it meant that the corn and wheat were bad. Music wasn't much different. To buy music people had to like it. To like it it had to be good. If it weren't good no one would buy it. . . ." It reassured his countrymen no end to know that, despite an international success, Harris was still "the Oklahoma farm boy who gave up chickens for music." He was both willing and able to give them that assurance.

Yet, symptomatic of the fascinating contradictions within the man, Harris could also write of his metier with mystical exaltation. "The creative impulse is a desire to capture and communicate feeling. Call that feeling what you will. Call it romantic fervor—call it a longing for Truth—call it the atavistic burgeoning from the depth of the race soul. Always it is a lonesome hunger that gnaws within the human heart, forcing us to search for an understandable race-expression. The successful translation of creative impulses uncovers, objectifies and records our gamut of potentialities. It is small wonder then that humanity regards the creative impulse as sacred."

HIS MUSIC

Roy Harris represents a spontaneous type of artist both whose strength and weakness lie in yielding unreservedly to the creative impulse within. Such artists are apt to do their most compelling work early in their career, their art being nourished by the heart rather than the mind. In the Thirties the imperfections of Harris's style were dismissed because of the promise of greater things to come. Now the selfsame critics insist that his later works lack the vitality of the earlier ones. As a matter of fact, Harris has not changed very much in the past twenty-five years. The world has.

The American quality in his work goes deeper than the quotation of popular material—whether cowboy ditty, Civil War song, or hymn tune—that often serves him as a point of departure. His music is American in its buoyancy and momentum, its expansiveness and manly strength. He has identified himself so closely with the American dream that he expresses its temper best when he is most himself. "One would think, to read his prefaces," quips Virgil Thomson, "that he had been awarded by God, or at least by popular vote, a monopolistic privilege of expressing our nation's deepest ideals and highest aspirations."

Some have found in Harris's music the high epic quality and brooding loneliness of the prairie. Others—they are closer to the mark—hear in it the longing and frustration of American smalltown life. In either case there is no denying its high emotive content. Harris's melodies are long and flowing. They move along out of an inner momentum that gives the effect of fecund invention. His harmonic idiom is basically diatonic and depends on the triad, but is invigorated by dissonant polytonal combinations. He uses blocklike chords in parallel motion and is partial to the austerely archaic effect of modal harmonies. Although he avoids the use of key signatures, his music has a strong sense of tonality. The nervous tension of Harris's music derives in large measure from his fluctuating, irregular rhythms with their continual shifting of accent. The texture is predominantly contrapuntal. His works abound in canons, passacaglias, double and triple fugues. As often as not, what starts out bravely as a triple fugue soon lapses into a less ambitious stride. As all pronounced musical personalities do, Harris possesses an individual style of orchestration. His writing is lean and muscular, marked by an effective handling of the strings in their low register and the brass in their high.

Harris's epic-dramatic gift is at its best with the large forms of abstract instrumental music; symphonies form the central core of his output. The First was written in 1933, the others in the ensuing decade and a half. The Third is his finest work. The Fourth, the *Folk-song Symphony* (1939), is not a symphony at all, but a fantasia for chorus and orchestra on American popular tunes. In his *Fifth Symphony* (1942) Harris continues his role as a national poet, striving to portray the "qualities of heroic strength—determination—will to struggle—faith in our destiny" which he sees as the quintessence of the American character. This is the last of his symphonies to have made an impression on the public. Neither the Sixth (1944), based on Lincoln's Gettysburg Address and dedicated to "the Armed Forces of Our Nation," nor the Seventh (1951) have added to his reputation.

Of his pieces for orchestra, the best-known are the *Chorale for String*

Orchestra (1932); the overture *When Johnny Comes Marching Home* (1934); and the *Time Suite* (1936). Chamber music occupies an important place in Harris's work. The Quintet for Piano and Strings (1936) and the Third String Quartet (1937) are among his strongest compositions. The piano works include the early *Sonata*, written in Paris in 1928, and the suite *Children at Play* (1942), both of which have been recorded by the composer's wife, the pianist Johana Harris. His two major choral works—the *Song for Occupations* (1934) and *Symphony for Voices* (1935)—are on texts by Walt Whitman. The former was performed by the Westminster Choir on a European tour, and did much to establish Harris's reputation abroad.

THIRD SYMPHONY

Harris's most frequently performed work (1938) is in one movement made up of contrasting sections. The composer's description indicates the emotional content of the piece. "Section I: *Tragic*—low string sonorities. Section II: *Lyric*—strings, horns, woodwinds. Section III: *Pastoral*—emphasizing woodwind color. Section IV: *Fugue*—dramatic. *A.* Brass, percussion predominating. *B.* Canonic development of Section II material, constituting background for further development of fugue. *C.* Brass climax. Rhythmic motif derived from fugue subject. Section V: *Dramatic-Tragic*. Restatement of violin theme of Section I."

The opening motive expands into a long-breathed line on the cello that accords with Harris's goal of a self-generating melody. The even quarter-note movement is spaced at the end of the phrase by a longer

note or a rest—a rhythm derived, of course, from the imagery of the congregational hymn. (This is one of several American symphonies—Ives's Third, Copland's Third, and Virgil Thomson's *Symphony on a Hymn Tune* are other examples—whose opening theme is derived from our heritage of psalmody.) The full orchestra then presents a kind of chorale. In the section identified by Harris as lyric, his songful counterpoint asserts itself in the fluent, overlapping lines and in his antiphonal treatment of strings and winds. The word "section" is used loosely here. For the symmetrical, sectional structure of the classical symphony

Harris substitutes a seamless, continuously evolving texture. His contemplative lyricism has an affinity with the music of such symphonists as Brahms and Sibelius. The dark resonance is also related to the orchestral sound of those two masters.

The pastoral section evokes the "nature sound" of the romantic era in a twentieth-century environment. The warbling of the strings and the mounting animation of the brass conjure up a lovely landscape. The music abounds in free flexible rhythm. The harmonic idiom, for all its tensions, is diatonic.

The fugue subject is a commanding idea, with a sharp melodic profile and rhythmic urgency.

The elaborate fugal development builds up into what Harris calls the "brass climax." The restatement of the chorale-like theme broadens into a spacious coda based upon the steady beat of the drum. Although Harris thinks of the mood as "dramatic-tragic," this processional strikes the epic tone, and justifies those of Harris's admirers who find in his Third Symphony echoes of "the dark fastness of the American soul, of its despair and its courage, its defeat and its triumph."

Roy Harris was a vital force in our musical coming of age. His Third is still one of the finest symphonies yet produced by an American.

⊸§ 72 §⊷

Randall Thompson (1899-)

"A composer's first responsibility is, and always will be, to write music that will reach and move the hearts of his listeners in his own day."

RANDALL THOMPSON is a moderate by nature and conviction. His goal is the creation of an art grounded in the needs of the American scene, expressing "our own genuine musical heritage in its every manifestation, every inflection, every living example."

HIS LIFE AND MUSIC

Thompson was born in New York City. He received his musical training at Harvard, from which he graduated in 1920; he took his master's degree there two years later. He also studied with Ernest Bloch in New York. A fellowship at the American Academy in Rome gave him three years of freedom to compose. In the next two decades he held a variety of teaching positions—at Wellesley, Harvard, the Juilliard School, the University of California, University of Virginia, and Princeton. For two years he was director of the Curtis Institute of Music in Philadelphia. In 1948 he returned to Harvard, where he holds the Walter Rosen professorship.

Thompson is a widely performed composer. He owes this circumstance to a variety of qualities, chief among which is his ability to use melodic materials rooted in the inflections and rhythms of American popular song. These he molds into tasteful, craftsmanlike forms that are clear and direct. Thompson's most successful orchestral piece, the Second Symphony (1931), shows his characteristic traits. This work, the composer tells us, "like the symphonies of the eighteenth century, is primarily melodious and objective." The music is based on no program, "either literary or spiritual. I wanted to write four contrasting movements, separate and distinct, which together should convey a sense of balance and completeness." The jazzy rhythms, the blues of the slow movement, and the broad melody of the finale exemplify the essentially American quality of his music.

Thompson's flair for choral writing is manifest in his smooth counterpoint, broad over-all effects, and exemplary setting of English text. His choral pieces are enlivened by flashes of humor and whimsy. Among Thompson's most impressive achievements in this medium are *The Testament of Freedom,* which we will discuss, and *The Peaceable Kingdom,* inspired by one of the paintings of Edward Hicks (1780–1849), an early American folk artist called "the preaching Quaker of Pennsylvania."

Mention should be made too of the String Quartet No. 1 (1941), which Virgil Thomson called "one of the lovely pieces our country has produced, that any country has produced in our century." Of Thompson's later works, the most substantial is the Third Symphony (1949).

THE TESTAMENT OF FREEDOM

This work for chorus and orchestra (1943) was written to commemorate the two-hundredth anniversary of the birth of Thomas Jefferson. The four excerpts from Jefferson's writings that Thompson selected had particular relevance to the critical times through which our nation was then passing. In this work Thompson is a national poet, who addresses his countrymen through the massive columns of sound that frame the majestic cadences of Jefferson's prose.

I. *Largo.* "The God who gave us life gave us liberty at the same time; the hand of force may destroy but cannot disjoin them." Thompson's forthright diatonic harmonies are eminently suited to the emo-

tional content of the text. The virile sound of men's voices unites with a sturdy orchestral background and brave flourishes of the brass in a fresco painted with sweeping strokes of the brush. II. *Lento sostenuto.* "Our cause is just. Our union is perfect. Our internal resources are great." The dark orchestral sonority and ominous beat of the drum create an atmosphere of grave import. The music mirrors the oratorical style of Jefferson's writing, and builds up to a climax of ringing determination on the words, ". . . being with one mind resolved to die freemen rather than to live slaves."

III. *Alla marcia.* This movement, in quick double-time, unfolds over the steady tread of the bass. The text at this tempo is something of a mouthful—Jefferson's is not always a singable prose—but it is set adroitly. To facilitate the flow of the music Thompson wisely reduces the number of parts. IV. *Lento tranquillo.* The text of the final movement is drawn from one of Jefferson's letters to Adams, written almost half a century after the great revolutionary period of their youth. "I shall not die without a hope that light and liberty are on steady advance. . . ." This pronouncement of ripe old age impels Thompson to a flowing canon that is maintained for the greater part of the piece.

The climax is built on a reprise of the opening text, which at the end eloquently identifies liberty with life. It is all very grand, and very American.

⋞ 73 ⋟
Aaron Copland (1900-)

"I am hopelessly a musician."

IT HAS been Aaron Copland's preoccupation, for the better part of four decades, to express "the deepest reactions of the American consciousness to the American scene." Composer, teacher, writer on musical topics, and organizer of musical events, he is one of the most important figures of the contemporary American school.

HIS LIFE

"I was born on a street in Brooklyn that can only be described as drab. Music was the last thing anyone would have connected with it." Thus begins the autobiographical sketch in Copland's book, *Our New Music*. His father was a Russian-Jewish immigrant who, like many of his generation, found his opportunity in the new world. An older sister taught Aaron the piano. When he was fifteen he decided to become a composer. As the first step toward this goal he tried to learn harmony through a correspondence course. After a few lessons he realized the need for more substantial instruction and became a pupil of Rubin Goldmark. The latter, a thoroughgoing conservative, warned his pupil against having any traffic with the "moderns"; which only whetted the young man's curiosity. "By the time I was eighteen I already had something of the reputation of a musical rebel—in Goldmark's eyes, at any rate."

In the summer of 1921 Copland attended the newly founded school for Americans at Fontainebleau. On the faculty was Nadia Boulanger, a brilliant proponent of the Stravinskyan esthetic. He decided to stay on in Paris, and became Boulanger's first full-time American student in composition. The influence of this remarkable woman on Copland's generation can hardly be overestimated. In later years the

"Boulangerie" (a pun on the French word for bakery) included some of our leading composers, among them Roy Harris, Walter Piston, Douglas Moore, Virgil Thomson, Quincy Porter, and Marc Blitzstein.

Copland spent three years in Paris. He came in contact with the most significant developments in the modern movement, and took delight in following frankly experimental paths. He returned to New York in 1924, with an impressive commission: Nadia Boulanger had

Group of American composers. From left to right, sitting: Virgil Thomson, Gian Carlo Menotti, William Schuman. Standing: Samuel Barber, Aaron Copland.

asked him to write a concerto for organ for her American appearances. Copland composed the piece while working as the pianist of a hotel trio at a summer resort in Pennsylvania. The *Symphony for Organ and Orchestra* was given that season by the New York Symphony under the baton of Walter Damrosch. The genial conductor sensed that his audience would be shocked by the acerbity of the piece. When it was over, he turned round and said, "If a young man at the age of twenty-three can write a symphony like that, in five years he will be ready to commit murder."

It was Copland's good fortune that his gifts unfolded in an environment ready for them. He was helped by private patronage, fellowships, commissions, and by prizes such as the five thousand dollar award he received in 1929 from the RCA Victor Company for his *Dance Symphony*. At the same time he played a leading role in making his environment receptive to the music of the modern American school. With Roger Sessions he organized the Copland-Sessions Concerts, which functioned from 1928 to 1931 and featured the works of American composers. He was active in inaugurating the festivals of American music at Yaddo, in Saratoga Springs, New York. He was a moving spirit in the League of Composers throughout its existence. His concern for the composer's economic plight led to activity in that sphere, too: he was one of the founders of the American Composers' Alliance, and served as president of that organization for seven years. This unremitting activity went hand in hand with his writing and teaching. In numerous magazine articles he lucidly advocated the cause of modern music. The courses he presented at the New School for Social Research in New York City brought him an awareness of what the layman should be told about music. His books—*What to Listen for in Music* (1939) and *Our New Music* (1941)—found a wide public both here and abroad. He taught at Harvard University in 1935 and 1944, and returned to give the six Charles Eliot Norton lectures in 1951–52, which were published in his book *Music and Imagination*. He taught at Tanglewood from the time the Berkshire Music Center was founded, and took an active part there in training the younger generation of American musicians.

Copland's interest in Mexico, originally that of a tourist, deepened to a genuine appreciation of Latin-American culture. During the decade of the Second World War, when it was impossible to travel in Europe, he found congenial sources of inspiration below the Rio Grande. This predilection took a somewhat official turn when the Office of Inter-American Relations sent him, in 1941, on a goodwill tour of nine Latin-American countries. The State Department subsidized a similar journey in 1947.

These activities are the exterior landmarks of Copland's steady inner growth as an artist. Both together have made him a major force in American music for the past thirty years.

HIS MUSIC

Copland belongs to a generation of Americans who were nurtured by the Parisian view of life and art. As a pupil of Nadia Boulanger he found his point of departure in the neo-classicism of Stravinsky. He passed through a number of phases as he responded to one or another of the dominant forces in his milieu. After he completed his *Symphony for Organ and Orchestra* (in 1928 he reworked it, without organ, into his *First Symphony*), he became eager to write a work that would above all be American. "I had experimented a little with the rhythms of popular music in several earlier compositions, but now I wanted frankly to adopt the jazz idiom and see what I could do with it in a symphonic way." He encompassed this aim in *Music for the Theater* (1925), in which jazz was assimilated to the polytonal language of neo-classicism. Copland continued this line of thought in the Concerto for Piano and Orchestra, which he played with the Boston Symphony in 1927. "This proved to be the last of my 'experiments' with symphonic jazz. With the *Concerto* I felt I had done all I could with the idiom, considering its limited emotional scope. True, it was an easy way to be American in musical terms, but all American music could not possibly be confined to two dominant jazz moods: the 'blues' and the snappy number."

The first phase of Copland's development culminated in the *Symphonic Ode* of 1929. This important score brought into focus the chief elements of his early style: the rhetorical bigness of gesture—what Paul Rosenfeld called his "grandiosity"; the stylization of jazz polyrhythms; and the polytonal language he had learned in Paris. The works that followed the *Ode* were no longer so grand or, to use Copland's adjective, so fulsome. The *Piano Variations* (1930), the *Short Symphony* (1933), and the *Statements* for orchestra (1935) are more spare in sonority, more lean in texture. To the same period belong *Vitebsk* (Study on a Jewish Theme, 1928) for violin, cello and piano, the one piece in which Copland made use of Jewish material; and the *Sextet*, a reduced version of the *Short Symphony* for string quartet, clarinet, and piano. During this austere and frankly esoteric period Copland was much influenced by Stravinsky as well as by the "objectivism" that was in the air in those years.

At this time he became increasingly aware of a curious contradiction in his thinking. He was writing for the orchestra—a medium that by its very nature has to address itself to the big public. Yet he was turning out pieces couched in an idiom that could not possibly reach the average listener. He had to ask himself for whom he was writing. "During these years I began to feel an increasing dissatisfaction with the relations of the music-loving public and the living composer. The old 'special' public of the modern music concerts had fallen away, and the conventional concert public continued apathetic or indifferent to anything but the established classics. It seemed to me that we composers were in danger of working in a vacuum. Moreover, an entirely new public for music had grown up around the radio and phonograph. It made no sense to ignore them and to continue writing as if they did not exist. I felt that it was worth the effort to see if I couldn't say what I had to say in the simplest possible terms."

Copland's third style period was notable for his imaginative use of folklore elements—cowboy songs, New England and Quaker hymns, Latin-American rhythms; and for his preoccupation with media that communicate with a large public. Works such as *The Second Hurricane* (1936), a "play-opera" for high school children, and the *Outdoor Overture* (1941), written for the orchestra of the High School of Music and Art in New York City, subserve the goal of functional music. From his Latin-American travels came two of his most popular works, *El Salón México* (1936) and *Danzón Cubano*, a two-piano piece based on Cuban dance rhythms. In this category of *Gebrauchsmusik* are also pieces like *Music for Radio* and the five film scores that brought him to the attention of broad segments of the American public: for John Steinbeck's *Of Mice and Men* (1939), Thornton Wilder's *Our Town* (1940), Lillian Hellman's *The North Star* (1943), Steinbeck's *The Red Pony* (1948), and Henry James's *The Heiress* (1948). The score for *The Heiress* won an Academy award.

The three ballet scores of this period combined vivid rhythms and brilliant orchestral textures with a tender feeling for the rural American scene. *Billy the Kid* (1938) evokes the prairie with that suggestion of nostalgic longing, vastness and loneliness that Copland has made his own. The work centers about the desperado whose brief but eventful career became one of the legends of the Southwest. *Rodeo* (1942) continues the use of Americana in a somewhat lighter vein, based as it is on the efforts of an overly energetic cowgirl to get her man. The third work in this group, *Appalachian Spring*, which we will discuss, is unquestionably one of Copland's most distinguished scores. Related to these in intent are several patriotic works that reflect the travail of the war years, such as *A Lincoln Portrait* (1942) for speaker and chorus, on a text drawn from the Great Emancipator's speeches, and *Letter from Home* (1944), which was commissioned by the American

Broadcasting Company. At the same time Copland continued to cultivate the more serious aspects of his art. The Piano Sonata (1941),
Sonata for Violin and Piano (1943), Concerto for Clarinet and String
Orchestra that was commissioned by Benny Goodman (1948), and
Quartet for Piano and Strings (1950) are more mellow works than his
earlier essays in the large instrumental forms. The intervening years of
experience with the mass media had humanized Copland's art. The most
important composition of these years is the Third Symphony. Mention should be made too of the *Twelve Poems of Emily Dickinson* for
voice and piano (1948–50), in the composer's characteristic vein of
contemplative lyricism.

To these years belong Copland's single foray into the realm of
opera. *The Tender Land*, on a libretto by Horace Everett (1954), was
commissioned by Richard Rodgers and Oscar Hammerstein 2nd for
the thirtieth anniversary of the League of Composers. The work is
tender, and it is about land; but it lacks the dynamic conflict of personalities, the projection of human motives in musico-dramatic terms
which is of the essence in opera. There is little likelihood that Copland will make his mark in the lyric theater. Opera, like love, is best
discovered before one is fifty.

Copland's treatment inclines him to lucidity, order, and control. He
was setting forth his own esthetic when he wrote, "The typical contemporary composer prefers an objective, impersonal approach; a
complex, contrapuntal texture; a concentration on perfection of line
and beauty of proportion." This classicist creed does not rule out
either emotional expression or a direct relationship between music
and life. "What, after all, do I put down when I put down notes?
I put down a reflection of emotional states: feelings, perceptions, imag-
inings, intuitions. An emotional state, as I use the term, is compounded
of everything we are: our background, our environment, our convictions."

Copland's harmonic language is essentially diatonic. He needs the
key center if only because of his assiduous exploration of polytonal
relationships. The triad is basic to his thinking. Characteristic is his
wavering between major and minor (or his simultaneous use of both)
which lends an attractive ambiguity to many a passage. An archaic
modal flavor ofttimes pervades his music, imparting to it the inner
quietude which emerges from the slow movements of his larger works.

Copland has the temperament of the lyricist, a fact that was somewhat obscured during the earlier phases of his development. His melodies are simple and direct, relying on stepwise movement along the

scale and basic intervals such as thirds, fourths and fifths. He builds up his melodic forms through the use of motivic fragments which are repeated over and over, each time with accretions, in a process of cumulative growth. There results the long line which he regards as the prime requisite for musical architecture. His preoccupation with folk material greatly benefitted his melodic sense. The use of folk melodies, he points out, ought never to be a mechanical process. "They can be successfully handled only by a composer who is able to identify himself with, and re-express in his own terms, the underlying emotional connotations of the material."

Copland's music has a strong rhythmic impulse. In fast movements it thrusts forward with a motoric, toccata-like propulsion that generates excitement. He is much given to the use of ostinato and percussive rhythm, especially in his earlier works. The frequent changes of meter make for supple and vivacious movement. The accents are distributed with artful asymmetry, resulting in syncopations that possess the charm of the unforeseen. His meticulous workmanship is evident in his orchestral texture. Like Stravinsky, he uses as few notes as possible. The careful spacing of the chords is a delight to those who examine his scores. His spare instrumental writing emphasizes the high registers, particularly of the trumpets and violins. This helps him achieve the clean, transparent sound that is one of the hallmarks of his style.

In his later works, such as the *Fantasia for Piano* (1958), Copland shows himself receptive to the serial techniques of the twelve-tone school. Yet his adoption of Schoenbergian procedures by no means implies abandonment of the key principle. Rather, he assimilates the serial technique to his own harmonic language. In Copland's hands, as in Stravinsky's, the serial technique becomes a means for attaining maximum abstraction of thought and refinement of texture. Like the Russian master, when Copland writes twelve-tone music, he still sounds like himself.

Copland's music has the big-city restlessness and drive. True, it suggests the imagery of pastoral quietude and the memory of a simpler mode of life. But it does this by an act of imagination, by evoking that lost shadowy land which every artist carries in his heart. It projects a lonely feeling, and does so with infinite tenderness. This, really, is the romantic element in Copland's serenely classical art.

It is an art which stands in the mainstream of contemporary music. For many listeners Aaron Copland is the representative American composer of the mid-twentieth century.

Two Works by Aaron Copland

"I no longer feel the need of seeking out conscious Americanism. Because we live here and work here, we can be certain that when our music is mature it will also be American in quality."

APPALACHIAN SPRING

CONCERT SUITE

Appalachian Spring was composed in 1943–44 as a ballet for Martha Graham, on a commission from the Elizabeth Sprague Coolidge Foundation; it brought Copland a Pulitzer Prize. A year later (1945) the composer arranged a concert suite from the ballet, using a fuller orchestra than the original score. The action revolves about a pioneer celebration of spring in a newly built hill farmhouse in Pennsylvania in the early 1800s. The subject offered Copland an opportunity to use the bright clean sonorities so native to his style. Characteristic are the widely spaced triadic harmonies and resilient rhythms, the bold stride of the melody line, and the tender emotion that pervades the score.

The strong sense of tonality underlying this music becomes a structural element, for the eight sections contained in the work are set off by striking modulations. Copland quotes only one Shaker tune, "Simple Gifts"; but he has so fully assimilated the atmosphere of Shaker hymnody that the entire piece is steeped in the spirit of early American devotional song. *Appalachian Spring* thus follows his injunction that the composer who uses folk melodies must "re-express in his own terms the underlying emotional connotations of the material."

Copland's synopsis of his score identifies the opening section, marked *Very slowly,* as "Introduction of the characters, one by one, in a suffused light." The bride enters, then her young farmer husband, a neighbor, a revivalist, and his flock. This section consists of an expansion of the basic harmony—an A-major triad. Its structural function as an introduction is underlined through the sense of expectancy and wonder that envelops the music. A hymn-like melody emerges, combining the A-major arpeggio with fundamental intervals—perfect fifths and fourths—to create an atmosphere of calm and simplicity:

mf cantabile

"2. *Fast.* A sudden burst of unison strings in A-major arpeggios starts the action. A sentiment both elated and religious gives the key-note to this scene. 3. Duo for the bride and her intended—scene of tenderness and passion." This section brings back the material of the opening, but with fuller harmonies in the orchestra. The rise in emotional intensity is underscored by a modulation from B-flat to B major. "4. *Quite fast.* The Revivalist and his flock. Folksy feeling—suggestions of square dances and country fiddlers."

mf playfully

"5. *Still faster.* Solo dance of the bride—presentiment of motherhood. Extremes of joy and fear and wonder. 6. *Very slowly* (as at first). Transition scene to music reminiscent of the introduction." This section presents material derived from the music of Section 2. "7. *Calm and flowing.* Scenes of daily activity for the bride and her farmer husband. There are five variations on a Shaker theme." The theme is presented as a clarinet solo.

Simply expressive

p

Copland here adopts the favorite variation procedures used in the chorale preludes of the Baroque—rhythmic augmentation, canonic imitation, combination with new contrapuntal lines. These lead to changes in the character of the theme which are highlighted by its varied orchestral treatment. The theme finally appears as a majestic chorale that brings the variations to a stirring close. There follows the eighth and last section, a Coda that balances the Introduction. "The bride takes her place among her neighbors." They depart, and the couple remain "quiet and strong in their new house." A serene passage for muted strings, marked "like a prayer," returns to the mood of the opening and leads to the quiet ending.

SYMPHONY NO. 3

The Third Symphony (1944–46) is an expansive outdoor piece that evokes the landscape and the singing strength of Copland's American works. Certain of the themes suggest the New England and Shaker hymn tunes of *Appalachian Spring*, the cowboy motives of *Billy the Kid*, or the Latin-American dance rhythms of *El Salón México*. But these are not used for their anecdotal value. They are presented in stylized form as integral elements of the symphonic tissue. Thus Copland is justified in stating that the work "contains no folk or popular material. Any reference to jazz or folk material was purely unconscious."

I. *Molto moderato—with simple expression.* The opening movement is pervaded by the spirit of New England hymnody. Free in form, this movement—by turns lyrical and declamatory—begins and ends in the key of E major. The first theme is given out by the strings at the very start. The prominence of the primary intervals—fourths and fifths—and the constant return to the pivotal tone, E, imparts strength to this diatonic melody.

The second theme, presented by the violas, complements the first, its ascending fifths balancing the descending fourths of the other. The even stride of the melody, interrupted by longer notes at the cadences, as in the old chorales, reflects the hymn-tune influence.

The third theme—"of a bolder nature," as Copland describes it—is given out by two trombones, whence it passes to the horns. This theme, like the first, is referred to in subsequent movements of the symphony.

The orchestral sound is clean and bright; the wide-apart lines of the texture create a sense of space. The counterpoint mounts in rhythmic drive to a climax of great power. The movement, as the composer has pointed out, is in the shape of an arch. After the animation of the central portion the final section—an extended coda—presents the opening material in a broadened version. A sense of mystery accompanies the return to the mood of the opening, and a profound gentleness.

II. *Allegro molto.* The second movement is a scherzo in the usual A-B-A form (scherzo-trio-scherzo). It opens with the horns sounding a fanfare-like motive, out of which grows a vivacious melody which unfolds against a continuous eighth-note rhythm.

After a brilliant climax the movement subsides into the trio, with a modulation from F to B major and a change from quadruple to triple meter. A solo oboe ushers in a pastoral tune whose gentle melancholy recalls cowboy songs.

This melody, sung by the woodwinds in canonical imitation, is presently enveloped in glowing string tone. The scherzo theme returns, somewhat disguised, with a series of piano chords in high register, in the continuous eighth-note rhythm of the original statement. The first section is not repeated literally. After a full-throated pronouncement of the scherzo theme, the lyrical idea of the trio is heard in a new version, sung *fortissimo*—in canon—by the entire orchestra.

III. *Andantino quasi allegretto.* The slow movement opens in D major with a lyric meditation based on the expressive power of string tone. With the exception of a single horn and trumpet, no brass is used. Each section flows into the next "somewhat in the manner of a close-knit series of variations," as Copland puts it.

The quiet introduction is based on the third (trombone) theme of the first movement, which sounds remote and spiritualized in the high register of the unaccompanied violins. The idea is developed in a brief contrapuntal dialogue between first and second violins. A cadence in E—the key in which the symphony began—leads into the movement proper.

A solo flute introduces the main theme, a graceful idea marked by gently contracting intervals.

This melody serves as the basis for the variations—"sectional metamorphoses," Copland calls them—that follow. Each section is in another key: F major, A, G, then back to A. The variations unfold, to quote the composer, "at first with quiet singing nostalgia; then faster and heavier—almost dance-like; then more childlike and naive, finally vigorous and forthright." The buildup of the phrase through the repetition of the initial figure, adding a little to it with each recurrence, is characteristic of Copland, as is the rhythmic foreshortening at the end:

The opening mood of the movement returns. The music drifts off into the remote higher regions of the strings, out of which, Copland wrote, "floats the single line of the beginning, sung by a solo violin and piccolo, accompanied by harps and celesta." A modal transition leads into the final movement.

IV. *Molto deliberato—Allegro risoluto.* The final movement is the longest of the four and the closest in structure to traditional sonata form. The flourish with which it opens is based on the "Fanfare for the Common Man" that Copland composed during the war. After being outlined by flutes and clarinets *pianissimo*—the fanfare, of course, is not only a melody, but also a rhythm—it is given out in full force by brass and kettledrums. (There is a slight resemblance between this brave summons and the rhetorical motto theme that runs through Tchaikovsky's Fourth Symphony.) The chorale-like harmonization of the fanfare harks back to the hymn-tune atmosphere of the first movement.

The Allegro proper opens with an idea in animated sixteenth-note motion which at its first appearance is shared by oboe and clarinet. Because of the recurrence of the same fragment on different beats of the measure, this theme seems to be chasing its own tail:

The second theme, broader and more songlike in character, returns to the hymn-tune style, especially when it is presented antiphonally by alternating strings and woodwinds. The form shows an ingenious departure from the traditional sonata scheme: the second theme is embedded in the Development section instead of being in its customary place. A Latin-American dance rhythm, which appeared earlier in the movement, emerges briefly into prominence. The dance mood grows in abandon until it is cut short by the threatening chord of flutter-tongued brass and flutes, repeated against a single G-sharp on the piccolo—a memorable sonority, this—with which the Development comes to a close. The Recapitulation is much varied and curtailed. The Coda constitutes a grand summing up, with the second theme of the finale passing before us in even stride, transformed into a majestic anthem, followed by a final statement of the phrase with which the work began. It is a serenely beautiful peroration.

Despite its rhapsodic looseness of structure, the Third Symphony brings into an embracing synthesis all the earlier accretions of the Copland style. It is American in tone, yet intensely personal. This work is one of the notable achievements of our native school.

❧ 75 ☙

Other Nationalists

AMONG the Americanists of the older generation we should mention Arthur Farwell (St. Paul, Minnesota, 1872–1952, New York), who used Indian melodies in a number of his works; John Powell (Richmond, Virginia, 1882–) who achieved a success with his *Negro Rhapsody;* and Louis Gruenberg, who was born in Russia in 1884 but grew up in this country. Gruenberg is best known for his opera *Emperor Jones,* based on Eugene O'Neill's play, which was given at the Metropolitan Opera House in 1933.

Leo Sowerby (Grand Rapids, Michigan, 1895–) was the first American composer to hold the Prix de Rome. His best-known works are *Prairie* (1929), an impressionistic orchestral piece inspired by Carl Sandburg's poem; and *Canticle of the Sun,* for chorus and orchestra (1945), which won him a Pulitzer Prize. William Grant Still (Woodville, Mississippi, 1895–) is a dedicated proponent of Negro nationalism. He bases his music on the folk songs of his people, expressing their sorrows and aspirations. His most fully realized works are the *Afro-American Symphony* (1931); the cantata *And They Lynched Him on a Tree* (1940); and *In Memoriam: The Colored Soldiers Who Died for Democracy* (1943).

Ernst Bacon (Chicago, 1898–) describes himself as "an ardent believer in indigenous American music." He is a regionalist with a keen ear for musical dialect and an affinity for the Anglo-Celtic heritage manifest in our southern mountain tunes. His songs, of which he has written more than two hundred, show his sensitivity to the inflections of American speech. His works include two symphonies (1932, 1937); two orchestral suites—*Ford's Theater* (1943) and *From these States* (1943); and two operas in folk style—*A Tree on the Plains* (1942) and *A Drumlin Legend* (1949).

Elie Siegmeister (New York City, 1909–) is one of our outspoken Americanists. His preoccupation with folklore is reflected in several musical plays: *Doodle Dandy of the USA* (1942); *Sing Out, Sweet Land* (1944); and *Darling Corie* (1952). His orchestral works include *A Walt Whitman Overture* (1939), *Lonesome Hollow* (1946), and *Sunday in Brooklyn* (1946). Among his vocal works are *Strange Funeral in Braddock*, for solo voice and orchestra (1933) and *Abraham Lincoln Walks at Midnight*, for chorus. Siegmeister has written three symphonies, as well as chamber and piano music. He teaches at Hofstra College.

Morton Gould (New York City, 1913–) has fused the elements of popular American music with the form and structure of "classical." The jazz idiom is exploited in *Chorale and Fugue in Jazz* (1933); *Boogie-Woogie Etude* for piano (1943); *Four American Symphonettes* (1945), and *Big City Blues* (1950). Folklore influences abound in such pieces as *A Foster Gallery* (1940), *Cowboy Rhapsody* (1944), and *Minstrel Show* (1946). The American past is recreated in *A Lincoln Portrait* (1942) and *Fall River Legend* (1948), a ballet based on the famous Lizzie Borden murders. The Broadway musical comedy idiom is captured in the score for *Billion Dollar Baby* (1945). The most substantial work in this group is the *Spirituals for Orchestra* (1941), in five movements—*Proclamation*, *Sermon*, *A Little Bit of Sin*, *Protest*, and *Jubilee*. In his later works Gould has moved away from the facile popularity of his earlier style and has reached out toward deeper levels in both technique and expression. Among his more serious works are *Serenade of Carols* for small orchestra (1949); *Dance Variations for Two Pianos and Orchestra* (1953); *Jekyll and Hyde Variations* for orchestra (1957); and *Dialogues for Piano and String Orchestra* (1958), in which he adapts the serial procedures of twelve-tone music to his essentially diatonic idiom.

Carlos Surinach (Barcelona, 1915–) came to the United States in his thirties. He has combined the melorhythms of Spanish popular music with the classical procedures of thematic development; he has been influenced by the rhapsodic quality of flamenco music. Among Surinach's works are *Ritmo jondo* for clarinet, trumpet, xylophone, and percussion (1952), which won popularity as the ballet *Deep Rhythm;* the *Sinfonietta flamenca* of 1954, and the overture *Feria magica* (Magic Fair) of 1956.

⋖ 76 ⋗

Latin America

"A truly creative musician is capable of producing, from his own imagination, melodies that are more authentic than folklore itself."

Heitor Villa-Lobos

THE TWENTY republics of South and Central America boast a flourishing musical life. Their governments adhere to the European notion that art should be fostered by the state. Each of them has a ministry of fine arts or a music section within the ministry of education that supports conservatories, grants subsidies to orchestras and radio stations, organizes music festivals, and encourages native composers with prizes, fellowships and performances.

In eighteen of the twenty republics the language and culture are Spanish: Argentina, Bolivia, Chile, Colombia, Costa Rica, Cuba, Dominican Republic, Ecuador, Guatemala, Honduras, Mexico, Nicaragua, Panama, Paraguay, Peru, El Salvador, Uruguay, and Venezuela. In Brazil the language is Portuguese; in Haiti it is French. The European influence in all these countries has been superimposed upon native Indian and Negro elements. Thus, Latin-American civilization amalgamates the racial and cultural strains of three continents: Europe, South America, and Africa. The mixture of the elements varies according to the population of each republic. The Indian influence is strong in Mexico, Peru, Bolivia, Ecuador, and Central America. The Negro element, more pronounced in the West Indies, makes itself felt in the Latin-African character of Haiti's art, as well as in Afro-Cuban melodies and rhythms. The music of Brazil, on the other hand, is an admixture of all three strains. This fascinating diversity is being consolidated in each of the countries with the emergence of native schools of music with a strongly nationalist point of view.

493

❧ 77 ❧
Heitor Villa-Lobos (1887-1959)

"I compose in the folk style. I utilize the themes and idioms in my own way and subject to my own development. An artist must do this. He must select and transmit the material given him by his people."

THE FOREMOST composer of Latin America was a figure of international reputation. He left his imprint on every facet of Brazilian music, and in the process added a number of picturesque works to the twentieth-century repertory.

AMP

Heitor Villa-Lobos

HIS LIFE

Heitor Villa-Lobos was born in Rio de Janeiro. He learned to play the cello from his father, and made a living playing in the cafés and movie houses of Rio. At eighteen he undertook the first of several journeys to the remote villages of Brazil to gather folk songs and Indian lore. He also studied for a time at the Instituto Nacionál de Música in his native city.

494

In 1915 Villa-Lobos presented a program of his works in Rio de Janeiro. His bold exploitation of Brazilian idioms created a sensation. A stipend from the Brazilian government enabled the young composer to go to Paris. There, as well as in London, Vienna, and Berlin, he came in contact with the modern movement in music. Upon his return he quickly assumed the leading role in the musical life of Brazil. In 1932 President Vargas, who was most receptive to the composer's progressive plans, appointed him Director of Music Education of Rio de Janeiro. Villa-Lobos inaugurated a far-reaching program of teacher training that changed the entire system of public-school music in Brazil. He devised an ingenious method of indicating the degrees of the scale on the fingers of the hand, which made it possible for a chorus to sing without notes by following the conductor's indications. He established a conservatory where his pedagogic ideas were given practical application; published choral arrangements of Brazilian popular songs; encouraged school and community music through the founding of choruses and orchestras; and organized festivals throughout the country.

From 1935 on Villa-Lobos travelled widely outside his homeland, conducting and supervising the production of his works. His visits to Europe and the United States in the Forties did much to establish his music on the international scene. For a time his works were much played abroad. His compositions are less in evidence now; yet a number of them, particularly songs and piano pieces, have become favorites with the public.

HIS MUSIC

Villa-Lobos was an incredibly prolific composer. The complete list of his works runs to over two thousand items. This mass of music stemmed from an uninhibited creative energy that has been aptly compared to the luxuriant tropical vegetation of his homeland. It is, as one may imagine, a highly uneven output, since Villa-Lobos was incapable of self-criticism and retained everything he wrote. His freedom from convention led him to approach the popular music of Brazil with a sympathetic ear. Instead of "correcting" the tunes and rhythms according to Western canons of taste, he absorbed the native material—as Bartók, Vaughan Williams, and Falla did in their respective countries—in all its pungent freshness, adding to it the impressionist strain that he absorbed during his stay in Paris, as well as an exuberant romanticism.

Villa-Lobos wrote over a dozen symphonic poems, several of which evoke the atmosphere of the jungle, Afro-Brazilian rhythms, and tribal rites. The best-known is *Amazonas* (1917), which depicts the adventures of an Indian maid alone in the tropical jungle. Among his eighteen ballets are *Uirapuru* (the name of a legendary Indian chieftain whose playing of the flute put young girls under a spell)—the work dates from 1935—and *Dança da terra* (Dance of the Earth, 1943). Programmatic elements are prominent also in his twelve symphonies.

Villa-Lobos's lyricism favored improvisational forms rather than the carefully planned architectonics of the symphony. He did some of his best writing in the *chôros*, which was his original contribution to twentieth-century music. The chôros, as Villa-Lobos defined it, "represents a new form of musical composition in which a synthesis is made of different types of Brazilian music, Indian and popular, reflecting in its fundamental elements the rhythm and characteristic melodies of the people." His fourteen essays in this form are for various combinations of instruments. The first (1920) is for guitar, the second (1921) for flute and clarinet, the third (1925) for male chorus and seven wind instruments. The later chôros employ larger forces. Villa-Lobos was much preoccupied with what he called *sincretismo*—the fusion of native with outside influences. In his *Bachianas Brasileiras* he created a form intended to forge a link between the art of his homeland and the Western tradition. There is very little true counterpoint in these nine suites that were written "in homage to the great genius of J. S. Bach." But their easy tunefulness has recommended them to a wide public.

Villa-Lobos was at his best in short lyric forms like the song and piano piece. Outstanding among his piano music are the three suites of pieces called *Prole do Bébé* (Baby's Family), which depict a child's toys and dolls. The first of these sets contains his most popular piano piece, *Polichinello*. His most ambitious choral work is the oratorio *Vidapura* (The Pure Life, 1918). His copious output of chamber music centers around fifteen string quartets (1915–58).

Villa-Lobos was a tonal composer, although his music is marked by great flexibility of key. He was partial to polytonality, with emphasis upon the combination of C major and F-sharp major that Stravinsky used so memorably in *Petrushka*. His music stems out of a basically harmonic conception and is bolstered with powerful pedal points. Excitement is achieved through ostinato rhythms and an exploitation of percussive dissonance, the effectiveness of which he seems to have realized before he heard any of Stravinsky's music. His rhythm is vigorous, primitive, alive. His love of massive sonorities and novel color combinations went hand in hand with an original way of handling the instruments. He reinforced the traditional percussion group of the orchestra with all kinds of native instruments that imparted a special flavor to his works. The orchestration is too thick, due to his fondness for letting all the instruments assert themselves within the symphonic web. But the over-all effect is one of brilliance and vitality.

BACHIANAS BRASILEIRAS NO. 5

FOR SOPRANO AND EIGHT CELLOS

The fifth of the *Bachianas Brasileiras*, the most popular of the series, consists of two parts—*Aria* (1938) and *Dansa* (1945).

I. *Aria* (Cantilena). *Adagio.* In Brazilian usage an aria, Villa-Lobos explained, "is a kind of lyric song." The pizzicato of the cellos suggests the guitar sound, thereby evoking the atmosphere of the serenade so frequently met with in Latin-American music. Over a string background there unfolds one of those self-generating melodies for which the model was provided for all time by the famous Air from the *Suite No. 3* of Bach. The vocal line recaptures the flowing cantilena of

the Baroque. Yet this "return to Bach" has nothing in common with Stravinskyan neo-classicism, for it derives almost wholly from an orientation based upon nineteenth-century romanticism. The soprano intones the first section as a vocalise on the syllable "*ah*," with frequent changes of meter, the dark cello tone serving as a foil for the voice.

The nostalgic middle section is a setting of a poem by Ruth Correa. The text evokes the quiet hour when the sky is covered by pink transparent clouds. "Out of infinite space the moon rises, flooding the evening with gentle light. . . . To those who pass by she calls out her plaintive cry. . . . O cruel longing of the heart that laughs and weeps. . . ." The vocal line, marked by repeated notes, becomes a species of rhapsodic declamation heard over descending chromatic harmonies in the strings. The first part of the melody returns, and is now hummed.

II. *Dansa. Allegretto.* The strong accents of this dance-song in 2/4 time are suggested in the subtitle, *Martelo* (hammered). This movement, Villa-Lobos writes, "represents a persistent and characteristic

rhythm much like the *emboladas*, those strange melodies of the Brazilian hinterland. The melody suggests the birds of Brazil."

The text, by the Brazilian poet Manuel Bandeira, apostrophizes the
love-bird of the forest. "Irere, my little bird from the wilds of Cariri;
Irere, my companion, where are you going? Where, my dear? . . .
Ah, sad is the fate of the bird who flies singing but cannot fly to the
one who would sing of his love. . . . Ah, your song pours forth from
the depths of the forest like a breeze that softens the heart. . . ." At
times the lively melody line approaches patter song. Rapid repeated-
note figures and stepwise movement give way to upward leaps and
staccato motives that require agility on the part of the singer. As often
happens with Villa-Lobos, the ecstatic mood is projected in an atmosphere of unbridled primitivism. Music such as this bespeaks a national poet for whom art was synonymous with the expression of
spontaneous emotion.

Villa-Lobos's music possesses both the virtues and the faults of a
young culture. His collected works, whenever that project is put
through by a grateful nation, will cover a wall in the library at Rio de
Janeiro. Out of that mass of notes enough should survive to keep his
memory green.

◄§ 78 §►

Carlos Chávez (1899-)

"We have had to work for fifteen years in Mexico to free ourselves from the stuffy conservatory tradition, the worst kind of
academic stagnation. We have found ourselves by going back
to the cultural traditions of the Indian racial stock that still accounts for four-fifths of the people of Mexico."

HIS LIFE

CARLOS CHÁVEZ has played the same decisive part in the musical life of
Mexico as Villa-Lobos in that of Brazil. He was born in Mexico City
of Spanish-Indian ancestry. Chávez began to compose while in his
teens. He found himself as an artist in the early Twenties, the period
when the Mexican Revolution was entering upon its final phase. Pro-

foundly affected by the social upheaval about him, Chávez—along
with his friend Diego Rivera—became a leading figure among the
dedicated band of musicians, painters, and poets who captured the
spirit of the revolution in their work. They directed Mexican art away
from a pallid imitation of foreign models to a vigorous nationalism
rooted in the native soil.

The Mexican musicians, painters, and poets captured the spirit of the Mexican Revolution in their work. Diego Rivera, *Agrarian Leader Zapata*. (Collection Museum of Modern Art)

His journeys to the outlying mountain regions of his homeland revealed to him the power and richness of the music of the Mexican Indians. There followed several years of travel in Europe, during which he came in contact with the modern movement in Berlin, Paris, and other centers. During his twenties he also lived in New York City, where a number of his works were introduced at the concerts of the International Composers Guild. Chávez was in his late twenties when he assumed leadership of the musical upsurge in Mexico. In 1928 he became the conductor of the orchestra of the musicians' union, which he developed into the Orquesta Sinfónica de México, one of the finest ensembles of the Western hemisphere; he retained his connection with this organization for almost a quarter century. In 1928, he was appointed director of the Conservatorio Nacionál in Mexico City. During his six years in this post he inaugurated sweeping changes in the curriculum.

In 1933 Chávez became chief of the department of fine arts of the Secretariat of Public Education. Although he did not retain his post long, due to political changes within the government, he was able to orient the teaching in the schools toward the use of native Mexican-Indian materials. He founded an ensemble that used the ancient instruments, and stimulated a revival of interest in Aztec and Mayan music. He inspired a whole new generation of nationalist composers and gave them active encouragement by performing their works with his orchestra. It was against this varied activity that Chávez carried on his career as a composer. From the Fifties on he was somewhat less involved in the musical affairs of his native land, and correspondingly more active in the United States. His Third Symphony (1951) was commissioned by Clare Boothe Luce in memory of her daughter. The Fourth (1952) was written on a commission from the Louisville Orchestra. Chávez's Fifth—the *Symphony for Strings*—received its world premiere at Los Angeles in 1953, the composer conducting. Chávez subsequently taught at the Berkshire Music Center in Tanglewood. In 1959 he delivered the Charles Eliot Norton lectures at Harvard University. He has appeared as guest conductor with the New York Philharmonic, Boston, Philadelphia, Los Angeles and other orchestras throughout the country.

HIS MUSIC

Chávez's music bears the mark of a strongly independent mind irresistibly drawn to new paths. "Music," he writes, "cannot follow established theories, systems or procedures without the danger of eventually becoming sterile. It should always be new." And to the same point: "Creation involves progress. My works do not resemble each other. They are all different. I experiment."

In 1921—he was then twenty-two—Chávez was commissioned to write a ballet by José Vasconcelos, the fiery Secretary of Education who gave every encouragement to Mexican art. The young composer found inspiration in native Indian sources and produced *El fuego nuevo* (The New Fire, 1921). With this score, written for a large orchestra that included native percussion instruments, his career as a national composer began. He soon became interested in a constructivist music attuned to the imagery of the machine age. This phase of Chávez's development culminated in the ballet-symphony *HP* (that is, Horsepower, 1927), which the composer described as "a symphony of the sounds around us, a revue of our times." The folklore strain, in the meantime, was continued in the Indian ballet *Los cuatro soles* (The Four Suns, 1926), in which Chávez amalgamated both Indian and *mestizo* (Spanish-Indian) elements. He succeeded in writing music which, as Aaron Copland expressed it, "caught the spirit of Mexico— its native, stolid, *mestizo* soul." His works, as Copland aptly describes them, "are stoic, stark, and sombre like an Orozco drawing."

Chávez adheres to the neo-classic point of view. His writing is lean, virile, hard, like the tribal tunes from which he has drawn inspiration. In this connection one may quote the composer's perceptive remark: " 'Primitive' music is really not so primitive. It is ancient and therefore sophisticated." The music of Chávez is devoid of sentimentality. His style is austere and severely controlled; yet it is informed with energy. The writing has a clean bright sound. As in the scores of Stravinsky, emotion is converted into motion. The rhythms are complex, the dissonance content is high. The forms are concentrated, stripped to the bone, devoid of development in the traditional sense, often depending for their power on the reiteration of motivic fragments. The texture generally is contrapuntal. The astringent harmonies resulting from the interplay of the melodic lines suddenly give way to contrasting passages where all the voices move in rugged unison or in blocklike chords.

Chávez is a master of the orchestra. He favors a color that is hard and bright, like the flat surfaces of Diego Rivera's murals. Certain effects, such as the contrasting of high woodwinds with low strings, impart freshness to the scheme and show his personal sense of sound. Chávez avoids lushness of sonority as carefully as he does introspection, the result being a certain dryness of expression that endears his music to listeners of the classic persuasion.

During the Thirties Chávez composed the two pieces by which he is best known. The *Sinfonía de Antígona* (1933) had its origins in the incidental music he wrote for Jean Cocteau's version of the *Antigone* of Sophocles which was produced in Mexico City in 1932. Chávez here captured the hieratic quality of antique tragedy in a music that is grandly impersonal and austere. The *Sinfonía India* we will discuss in detail. Of his later works mention should be made of *Cuatro Nocturnos* (Four Nocturnes, 1939) for voice and orchestra; *Xochipilli Macuilxochitl* (the name of the Aztec god of music), a piece for Mexican orchestra—that is, for an ensemble of traditional Indian instruments (1940); the Piano Concerto of 1940, with its emphasis upon the capacity of the instrument for percussive dissonance; and the ballet, *Hija de Colquide* (Daughter of Colchis, 1944), which was presented by Martha Graham under the title *Dark Meadow*. In his Fourth Symphony, subtitled *Sinfonía romantica* (1952), Chávez moves towards a more relaxed and accessible style. The opera *Pamfilio and Lauretta* (1957) was burdened with such an impossible libretto that one could gain no clear picture of the composer's capacities in that medium.

SINFONÍA INDIA

The *Sinfonía India* (1936) was composed during one of Chávez's visits to New York. The work, in one movement, adapts the classical sonata form to the requirements of the indigenous material on which the symphony is based. This is the only one of Chávez's major compositions in which Indian melodies are quoted. The percussion section includes Indian drums, a water gourd, various rasps (such as the guiro), rattles and cymbals.

The thematic material has a primitive strength that admirably fits Chávez's rather severe style. The Indian melodies move within a comparatively narrow range; they stress single notes and repeat fragments. All this goes well with the hard bright colors, persistent rhythms, clear outlines, and deliberate matter-of-factness of Chávez's music. The harmonic language is diatonic-modal, and occasionally evokes a pentatonic atmosphere.

The opening section, marked *Vivo*, is in 5/8 time with brief excursions to 2/4 and 3/4. After a short introduction, oboes and violins present a strongly rhythmic melody of the Huichole Indians of Nayarit:

This idea is expanded with vigor. Then, in an *Allegretto cantabile,* the clarinet sings a melody of the Yaqui Indians of Sonora:

This tune is repeated with subtle variations, then combined with an attractive countermelody against an intriguing background of syncopated rhythms; this builds into an orchestral climax. Another Sonora Indian melody forms the basis of the adagio section. It is presented by flutes and horn, whence it passes to the strings.

The Recapitulation of the allegro themes follows in the usual manner. The finale introduces a dance theme of the Seri Indians in 6/8 time, with interesting cross-rhythms. The melody unfolds against a *perpetuum mobile* background, in an exciting coda marked by steadily mounting tension.

This music is wiry and lithe. Its quality has been admirably summed up by the composer's friend Aaron Copland: "Chávez's music is extraordinarily healthy. It is music created not as a substitute for living but as a manifestation of life. It is clear and clean-sounding, without shadows or softness. Here is contemporary music if there ever was any."

⤳ 79 ⟿

Other Latin-American Composers

FRANCISCO MIGNONE, one of Brazil's most distinguished composers, was born in São Paulo in 1897. He studied at the local Conservatory, then in Italy. Mignone has assimilated the harmonic practices of the contemporary Italian school to a style based on native song and dance elements. He inclines to the romantic ideal in art; his music is intense, emotional, expressive. Most of his major works are on Brazilian subjects, such as the opera *O Contractador dos diamantes* (The Diamond Merchant, 1924); the *Fantasias Brasileiras* for piano and orchestra, of which he wrote four (1931–37); *Suite Brasileira* for orchestra (1933); and the ballet *Quadros Amazonicos* (Amazonian Pictures, 1949).

Camargo Guarnieri was born in Tiété in the state of São Paulo in 1907, and received his training first at the Conservatory of São Paulo, then in France. Guarnieri avoids direct quotation of folk melodies, preferring to capture the Brazilian flavor in melodies of his own devising. These are projected in a music that is neo-classic in style and contrapuntal in texture. Guarnieri is a prolific composer. Among his works are two piano concertos; the Symphony No. 1, which was given its premiere by the Boston Symphony Orchestra in 1946, the composer conducting; the orchestral suite *Brasiliana* (1951); and Chôros for piano and orchestra, which shared the first prize at the Caracas Music Festival of 1957.

The gifted Mexican composer Silvestre Revueltas was born in Santiago Papasquiaro on the last day of 1899 and died in Mexico City on October 5, 1940. It was Chávez who encouraged him to devote himself seriously to composition. In 1937 Revueltas went to Spain, where he worked in the music section of the Loyalist government. After his return to Mexico he continued his career as composer and conductor. His health undermined by years of poverty, heavy drinking, and an irregular life, he succumbed to pneumonia in his forty-first year.

Revueltas' warmly romantic temperament found its best expression in short flexible forms. His melodic imagery is steeped in Mexican folklore, although he never quoted existing melodies. As he himself said, "Why should I put on boots and climb mountains for Mexican folklore if I have the spirit of Mexico deep within me?" The power of his music derives from compact melodic ideas of an almost primitive directness, which are woven into a vibrant texture of dissonant counterpoint and free polyrhythms. Among his orchestral works are *Cuauhnahuac*—this is the Indian name for Cuernavaca—(1932); *Esquinas* (Corners, 1930); *Ventanas* (Windows, 1931); *Caminos* (Roads, 1934) and *Planos* (Planes, 1934). Revueltas also wrote chamber music, songs, and several film scores. His premature death robbed Mexican music of one of its finest talents.

Alberto Ginastera (Buenos Aires, 1916–) is an outstanding figure among the younger generation of Argentinian composers. His music draws inspiration from folklore; it is compact in form and cast in an advanced harmonic idiom. Among his works are the ballets *Panambí* (1940) and *Estancia* (1941); the *Concierto Argentino* for orchestra (1941); *Sinfonia Porteña* (named after the port of Buenos Aires, 1942); and an Overture to Goethe's *Faust* (1944).

We should mention the leading composers of Chile, Humberto Allende (Santiago, 1885–) and Domingo Santa Cruz (La Cruz, 1899–), as well as the Cubans Joaquín Nin (Havana, 1879–), Alejandro Caturla (Remedios, 1906–1940) and Amadeo Roldán (Paris, 1900–1939, Havana). The last-named, a mulatto, had a vivid feeling for Afro-Cuban rhythms. From among the younger composers one may single out the "Group of Four" who form the vanguard of Mexican music today: Salvador Contreras (1912–), a pupil of Revueltas; Blas Galindo (San Gabriel, Jalisco, 1910–), a pupil of Chávez who has also studied with Aaron Copland at the Berkshire Music Center; Daniel Ayala (Abalá, Yucatán, 1908–), another pupil of Revueltas who, like Galindo, is of Indian blood; and Pablo Moncayo (Guadalajara, 1912–1958, Mexico City), another disciple of Chávez. They and their confreres throughout Latin America are continuing the efforts of the older men to create an art that unites national elements with contemporary modes of thought.

XI. CLASSICISTS

"Is the Dust Bowl more American than, say, a corner in the Boston Athenaeum?"

Walter Piston

⤳ 80 ⤳

Walter Piston (1894-)

"If a composer desires to serve the cause of American music he will best do it by remaining true to himself as an individual and not by trying to discover musical formulas for Americanism."

WALTER PISTON represents the international point of view in our music. His neo-classic esthetic transcends the local and reaches out toward universal values of craftsmanship and formal beauty.

Walter Piston

HIS LIFE

Piston was born in Rockland, Maine. His grandfather was a sailor who emigrated from Italy, married a New England girl, and Americanized the family name by dropping the final *e*. The future composer's family moved to Boston when he was ten. He studied the violin, taught himself the piano, and worked his way through art school by playing in dance halls and restaurants. During the First World War he enlisted in the Navy, where he played the saxophone as a "second-class musician." The technical rating, he feels, accurately described his handling of the instrument.

It was not until 1919, when he was twenty-five, that Piston began his formal training as a composer. He entered Harvard and received a thorough grounding in the rudiments of his art. Upon his graduation he won a fellowship that enabled him to go to Paris where, like Copland, he studied with Nadia Boulanger. Under her guidance he achieved the mastery of compositional technique that has won him the admiration of his fellow musicians.

Upon his return from Paris in 1926 Piston joined the music faculty of Harvard University. He was head of the music department for several years; and in 1951 was appointed to the newly endowed Naumburg professorship, which left him more time for composing. He retired in 1960. Piston's teaching aimed to reconcile modern concepts with tradition. Out of it came four books—*Principles of Harmonic Analysis* (1933), *Harmony* (1941), *Counterpoint* (1947), and *Orchestration* (1955)—which are used as college texts throughout the country.

HIS MUSIC

Piston displays a natural affinity for the large forms of absolute music: symphonies, concertos, sonatas, string quartets, and the like. His is the classical aim of conveying purely musical thoughts within beautifully rounded forms. Such an attitude precludes programmatic or descriptive intent. It also precludes a national style based on literary or anecdotal elements. "If the composers," he writes, "will increasingly strive to perfect themselves in the art of music and will follow only those paths of expression which seem to take them the true way, the matter of a national school will take care of itself. The composer cannot afford the wild-goose chase of trying to be more American than he is." Piston accordingly advocates the broadest possible interpretation of what is American. "The use of folk tunes and other Americana, instead of using one's own melodic ideas, is based, I think, on a naively mistaken conception of the nature of musical expression. Granting that to create a recognizable American musical idiom is perhaps a worthy objective, the plain fact is that American music is music written by Americans."

This is not to say that Piston's music bears no relationship to his environment. He has assimilated elements of the American popular idiom, especially of the jazz which figured so prominently in his youthful experiences as a musician. But he subjects these elements to a process of stylization, so that they become organic parts of a total expression whose chief goal lies elsewhere. Piston speaks the international language of neo-classicism, which is understood with equal readiness in Paris,

Classicism in contemporary American painting: Andrew Wyeth, *Christina's World*. (Museum of Modern Art)

London, Berlin, or New York. His style is admired no less for the distinction of its ideas than for the perfection of its workmanship. His art is based on linear counterpoint. Although he adheres to the principle of tonality, Piston has been intrigued by certain aspects of Schoenbergian thinking. He favors the intricate devices of fugal and canonic writing which to many contemporary musicians represent the ultimate refinement of thought. His is the consolidating type of mind that assimilates the most significant trends in the art of an epoch, welds them into a personal language, and sets upon them the seal of stylistic unity. His works are elegant, mature, architecturally clear, and self-contained. They constitute so many stations in a continuous journey towards self-realization. "Each new work is for me the start of a new problem, a new adventure the outcome of which I am never able to predict. It is in a sense another study towards the perfect balance between expression and form."

This balance was at first weighted on the side of form. Typical of his earlier period is the brilliant *Concerto for Orchestra* (1933), the witty *Concertino* for piano and chamber orchestra (1937), and the First Symphony of the same year, with its dissonant counterpoint and elaborate fugal devices. Piston thenceforth moved toward directness of utterance, simpler textures, more melodious phraseology, and, above all, a more personal lyricism. This development is manifest in the Second Symphony (1943); it comes fully into its own with the new expansiveness of the Third (1947), which received a Pulitzer Prize. The Fourth (1949) we will consider in detail. The Fifth (1954), a thoughtful, sensitive work, was followed in 1955 by the relaxed and songful Sixth and in 1961 by the deftly wrought Seventh.

Notable for their constructional logic, breadth of conception, and purity of speech, the symphonies form the center of Piston's output. His list includes three string quartets, two orchestral suites; the Violin Concerto of 1939, and a Quintet for piano and strings (1949) which is a distinguished addition to the limited contemporary literature for that combination. In 1938 Piston wrote a ballet called *The Incredible Flutist*, from which he extracted a tuneful orchestral suite that became his most popular work.

SYMPHONY NO. 4

The Fourth Symphony (1950) was commissioned by the University of Minnesota on the occasion of its centennial celebration in 1951. "This symphony," Piston wrote, "is melodic and expressive and perhaps nearer than my other works to the solution of the problem of balance between expression and formal design."

I. *Piacevole* (Agreeably). The composer has described this as "an easy-going moderately fast movement in large two-part form." The tonality is G. The principal theme is stated at the outset by the first violins—a flowing melody possessing the quality of inwardness that distinguishes Piston's lyricism. Leaps of a fourth and an octave impart amplitude to this theme, which unfolds in a long line.

mp dolce espressivo

The second theme serves as an effective foil. Introduced by the clarinet against a background of woodwind sound, it moves within a narrow range—either along the scale or with small leaps.

Characteristic of Piston is the subdued coloring achieved by using strings and brass in their lower register, as is also the quietly intro-spective mood of the music. The movement builds to a climax of quiet power. A short coda presents a variant of the first theme and leads to a serene close.

II. *Ballando* (Dancing). The tonality is A. Brimming over with rhythmic energy, the second movement is a genuinely symphonic Scherzo cast in rondo form. The main theme alternates with two subsidiary themes in the sequence A-B-A-C-A-B-A. The rugged or-chestral sound and emphasis on the high register make an effective con-trast with the first movement. The principal idea is characterized by irregular meters: 3/4 time alternates with 7/8, a procedure that en-genders plasticity of rhythm and lively syncopation. The B theme is

a graceful waltz. The C theme—that is to say, the central section—evokes the atmosphere of country fiddling. A fairly rare example, this, of Piston's use of outspokenly American elements. The movement is vigorous, terse, and drives to a rousing conclusion.

III. *Contemplativo.* In 12/8 time; the tonality is F. The slow movement is dark in sonority. Its seamless structure derives from the method of continuous expansion encountered in the music of the Baroque. The long florid line of the melody is admirably sustained, and looks back to the arabesque of Bach. The theme is played at the be-ginning by the clarinet alone, then in varied form by violas and Eng-lish horn. The movement explores further aspects of this melody. At the impassioned climax the brass gives out the theme in massive chordal blocks. The relaxed contrapuntal writing is typical of the composer.

IV. *Energico.* In 6/8 time; the tonality is B-flat. The finale shows off Piston's neat, concise handling of the classical sonata movement. The form is based on the tension between the sturdily rhythmic idea

introduced at the outset by strings, lower woodwinds, and horns, and the expansively lyric theme that is presently sung by a solo oboe. The Development is brief and eventful. In the Recapitulation the second theme is invested with glowing string tone. A stirring climax brings the symphony to a satisfying conclusion.

"It is not one of my aims to write music that will be called modern, nor do I set out to compose according to any particular style or system. I believe my music is music of today in both manner and expression, since I am inescapably influenced by the art, thought, and daily life of the present." Piston has achieved his aim of reconciling traditional values with twentieth-century modes of thought and feeling. He is in the fullest sense a modern classicist.

⋘ 81 ⋙

Quincy Porter (1897-)

IN A musical scene dominated by powerful influences, Quincy Porter has managed to retain his own individuality. His music sounds like no one else's. It draws its sustenance from the realm of chamber music, where subtlety of nuance goes hand in hand with delicacy of thought and feeling. It borrows nothing from poetry or drama, but exists for the sheer joy of its sound.

HIS LIFE AND MUSIC

Quincy Porter was born in New Haven, Connecticut. He is a direct descendant of Jonathan Edwards. His father and grandfather were professors at Yale, where he received his musical training under Horatio

Parker. After his graduation he went to Paris and worked with Vincent d'Indy, who freed him from the German influence that had dominated his student years. Upon his return to this country he lived for a time in New York City and played the violin in the Capitol Theater orchestra. Along with Roger Sessions, who had been a classmate of his at Yale, he studied privately with Ernest Bloch. When Bloch was appointed head of the Institute of Music in Cleveland, Porter followed him there for further study and, like Sessions, began his teaching career under Bloch's guidance at the Institute.

In 1928 Porter won a Guggenheim fellowship and returned to Paris, where he remained for three years. Already cognizant of the direction he wanted his music to take, he turned out a number of works—the String Quartet No. 3, Piano Sonata, Suite for Viola Alone, and Quintet for Clarinet and Strings—that display the lineaments of his mature style. In 1932 Porter joined the faculty of Vassar College, where he taught for six years. He turned his attention to the orchestra and produced several works in that medium: the *Poem and Dance* (1932), First Symphony (1934), *Dance in Three Time* (1937), and *Two Dances for Radio* (1938). He accepted an appointment as dean of the New England Conservatory in 1938, and became director of the school three years later. In 1946 he returned to Yale as professor of music.

Porter is given to serenely flowing melodies of a personal cast. His harmonic language leans toward the diatonic or modal. His neat, finely spun textures draw inspiration from the masters of sixteenth-century polyphony. The carefully molded lines are animated by a counterpoint of diversified rhythms which impart momentum to the musical fabric.

The central place in Porter's output is occupied by his eight string quartets (1923–50). The Viola Concerto (1948), with its meditative first movement and whimsical second, is an important contemporary addition to the literature for that instrument. *The Desolate City* (1950), an atmospheric *scena* for baritone and orchestra, represents one of Porter's rare departures from the field of absolute instrumental music. The *Concerto Concertante* for two pianos and orchestra won him a Pulitzer Prize in 1954.

STRING QUARTET NO. 8

Porter has been a string quartet performer—on the viola—all his life. Hence his particular sensitivity to the medium. The String Quartet No. 8 (1950) is a carefully wrought piece, consisting of an Allegro in the center flanked by two meditative slow movements. These follow one another without a break, giving the effect of a single-movement work in several sections marked by contrasts of pace and mood. This impression is reinforced by the flow of the piece, one idea leading into the next by the process of continuous expansion that we associate with the music of the Baroque. The result is a homogeneous texture of self-generating lines in which themes and motives exfoliate into fanciful patterns. This deftly molded counterpoint is borne forward by propulsive rhythms and diatonic-modal harmonies spiced with dissonance. The thematic material is well divided among the interweaving voices.

The opening Lento, which alternates between 5/8, 2/4, 3/4, and 4/4, has the quality of introspective lyricism—faintly tinged with nostalgia —that is so characteristic of Porter. The Allegro takes its point of departure from a theme of distinctive profile which contains several usable motives.

The concluding Adagio, which is marked *molto espressivo*, balances the opening *lento*. The Quartet is compact and hews to the point. Porter's constructive skill shows itself in the way he sustains the arch of the whole; the chiseled line of the work never falters. Shortly before the end he calls for a quarter-tone on the cello, between C-sharp and C. The final chord makes a striking sound; it unites the triads on A and on B. (One might more accurately describe it as a thirteenth chord on A with the seventh—G-sharp—omitted.)

Quincy Porter's music speaks the international neo-classic language of our time, yet in a way that is the composer's own. He has achieved a distinctive place in our music through a craftsmanship that is as impeccable as the musicality behind it is sincere.

◅§ 82 ?►

Other Classicists—I

RICHARD DONOVAN (New Haven, Connecticut, 1891–) is professor of music theory at Yale University. His style is precise and pithy. Characteristic are the *Symphony for Chamber Orchestra* (1936); *Design for Radio*, for orchestra (1945); and the lively *Suite for String Orchestra and Oboe* (1955). Bernard Wagenaar (1894–) was born in Holland. He settled in the United States in 1920, and has taught composition at the Juilliard School since 1927. Wagenaar's four symphonies are carefully constructed works. His output includes a variety of orchestral and chamber works, a violin concerto, and the *Triple Concerto* for flute, cello, and harp (1935).

Harrison Kerr (Cleveland, 1897–) is dean of the College of Fine Arts at the University of Oklahoma. His four symphonies (1945, 1948, 1951, 1954) are the central items in a varied list of orchestral, chamber, and choral works. Kerr has also written a number of sonatas for various instruments. Mark Brunswick (New York City, 1902–) is head of the music department of the College of the City of New York. Brunswick's most important work is the Symphony in B-flat (1947), in which his somewhat dissonant harmonic idiom is set forth within the clearcut tonal relationships that are basic to his style.

In an age that too often identifies quality with size, Theodore Chanler (Newport, Rhode Island, 1902–1961, Boston) made a special place for himself as a master of the miniature. He adapted the art song to twentieth-century needs, making of it a sophisticated epigrammatic form in which technical adroitness accompanies carefully wrought detail. Typical of his style are the settings of the verses of Walter de la Mare, such as the *Eight Epitaphs* (1937), *Three Epitaphs* (1940), and *Four Rhymes from Peacock Pie* (1940). His music is marked by pungent harmony and an abundance of dissonantal tension. His affinity for the large instrumental forms is manifest in a variety of works, among them the Concerto for Violin and Orchestra (1941), Variations and Epilogue for cello and piano (1946), and the Concerto for Two Pianos (1950). Chanler taught at the Longy School of Music in Cambridge, Massachusetts.

Nikolai Lopatnikov (Reval, Estonia, 1903–) came to this country in 1939. He is at his best in the large instrumental forms. He has written many works, among which are the Concerto for Violin and Orchestra (1941); the idiomatic Variations and Epilogue for cello and piano (1946); the Concerto for Two Pianos (1950), with its suggestion of jazz rhythms in the last movement; and the Third Symphony (1954). In recent years Lopatnikov has been affected by the trend toward simplification and has allowed freer rein to his melodic invention. He is professor of composition at the Carnegie Institute of Technology in Pittsburgh. Robert Sanders (Chicago, 1906–), professor of composition at Brooklyn College, has produced a diversified list of works, among them the Concerto in A minor for violin and orchestra (1935); two *Little Symphonies* (1939, 1954); Symphony in A (1955); and *A Celebration of Life*, a cantata for soprano solo, chorus, and chamber orchestra (1956). He has also written a quantity of chamber music.

Louise Talma (New York City, 1906–) is professor of music at Hunter College. Her earlier works—the piano duet *Four-Handed Fun* (1939), Piano Sonata (1943), and *Toccata for Orchestra* (1944) are in the neo-classic style. In her opera *Alcestis* (1956–59), on a libretto by Thornton Wilder, she adopted the twelve-tone technique. Miss Talma has written several vocal works, among them a number of effective songs. Burrill Phillips (Omaha, Nebraska, 1907–) began his career with the conviction that good American music must have a definitely American flavor. As he proceeded he moved closer to the neo-classic point of view. Phillips is best known for his *Selections from McGuffey's Reader* (1934), a programmatic orchestral work that includes such items as *The One-Hoss Shay, John Alden and Priscilla*, and *The Midnight Ride of Paul Revere*. In the neo-classic manner are the Concerto for Piano and Orchestra (1943); *Declaratives*, for women's voices and small orchestra (1943); and *Scherzo for Orchestra* (1944).

Halsey Stevens (Scott, New York, 1908–) taught in several schools before he joined the faculty of the University of Southern California (1946), where he now is chairman of the department of composition. His works include two symphonies (1941–45, 1945); *Green Mountain Overture* (1948); *Triskelion*, for orchestra (1953); chamber music, piano compositions, and songs. Stevens's book *The Life and Music of Béla Bartók* was the first definitive study of the Hungarian master.

Edwin Gerschefski (Meriden, Connecticut, 1909–) is dean of the School of Music of Converse College. His works include the *Classic Symphony*, a violin concerto, a piano concerto, Toccata and Fugue for orchestra, and the cantata *Half Moon Mountain*. Gerschefski has also written a number of chamber works.

Howard Swanson (Atlanta, Georgia, 1909–) is one of the outstanding Negro composers of his generation. He is best known for his *Short Symphony*. His list of works also includes the Symphony No. 1 (1945); *Night Music,* for chamber orchestra (1950); and *Music for Strings* (1951). Charles Jones (Ontario, Canada, 1910–) teaches at the Juilliard School and at the summer school in Aspen, Colorado. His style amalgamates the structural aspect of neo-classicism with a harmonic idiom that leans toward the atonal. Among his works are *Five Melodies for Orchestra* (1945) and the *Little Symphony* (1953).

◄§ 83 §►

William Schuman (1910-)

"A composer must create on his own terms, not simply write what the public thinks it wants at the moment. If his music has worth, the world will subsequently come to understand it."

HIS LIFE

WILLIAM SCHUMAN was born in New York City. Whatever music his boyhood contained belonged to the sphere of jazz. In time he formed a dance band in which he played the violin and banjo and sang. Together with a childhood friend, Frank Loesser, he turned out about forty songs, of which one—a ditty called *In Love with a Memory of You*—was published. (Loesser subsequently achieved success on Broadway with such musicals as *Where's Charley?* and *Guys and Dolls.*) Schuman worked for a time as a song plugger for a music publishing house. At the same time he enrolled in a business course at the New York University School of Commerce. He was almost twenty when he heard his first symphony concert. It opened up a new world for him. The next day he left the School of Commerce and quit the job he had taken with an advertising agency. Having heard that composers began with the study of harmony, he forthwith enrolled in a course in that subject.

At the age of twenty-three he entered Teachers College, and two years later received his degree. Schuman had unconventional ideas about how music should be taught and found a congenial outlet for them at Sarah Lawrence College, where he went in 1935. He soon established himself as an exciting teacher. Under his forceful direction the college chorus achieved a reputation. From this time dates his affinity for choral music, a medium in which he has produced some of his most characteristic works. No less important was the influence of Roy Harris, with whom he studied for two years. "Harris helped me to formulate my point of view," Schuman has stated. "Basically our esthetic springs from the same direction."

Despite his late start, Schuman forged ahead rapidly. His First Symphony was performed at a Composer's Forum Laboratory concert in the fall of 1936. Two years later the Second was played by Serge Koussevitzky and the Boston Symphony Orchestra. The Third Symphony, conducted by Koussevitzky in 1941, achieved an extraordinary success. The works that followed established Schuman in the forefront of the composers of his generation. He was performed by major orchestras in this country and abroad, and received his share of prizes and honors. Recognition came in another sphere when, in 1945, the board of directors of the Juilliard School of Music invited him to become president of the institution. At the age of thirty-five Schuman was the head of one of the most important music schools in the country. He introduced sweeping reforms into the curriculum, and transformed the school into a center for the propagation of contemporary music.

HIS MUSIC

The music of William Schuman stems from a temperament that is optimistic, assertive, and thoroughly at home in the world. It has vigor and energy, and is planned on a large scale. His earlier works betrayed a reticence bordering on shyness when it came to the revelation of private emotion. With maturity came a deeper perception of the expressive aspects of his art. There is an undercurrent of somber intensity beneath the bright surface of Schuman's music. This duality adds dimension to his later works and constitutes one of the interesting features of his style.

Schuman takes his point of departure from a melodic-rhythmic (rather than harmonic) conception. "My music," he has said, "is completely melodic. I write by singing, not by sitting at the piano." His tunes have an attractive boldness and sweep. The melodic line is long of breath—the sure sign of a large-scale composer. His music adheres to tonality, even though he dispenses with key signatures. The harmonic language is fresh and direct. At one time he was much taken with chords built on intervals of the fourth. Under the influence of Harris he rediscovered the triad, which he employs with great resourcefulness, embellishing the traditional harmonies with added tones to produce kaleidoscopically shifting dissonances. Schuman's music rests on a rhythmic foundation. His furious rhythms generate forms and ideas, propelling the melody line with irresistible momentum. His rhythms are American to the core, as is to be expected from one who found his way to music through jazz. This is particularly noticeable in the way he superimposes shifting cross-rhythms upon the steady pulse of the underlying meter.

Schuman has a natural affinity for the symphony, concerto, and string quartet; their architectonic structure is thoroughly congenial to his orderly mind. He handles the classical forms freely and in a contemporary spirit. He follows the present-day tendency of avoiding literal repetition, embellishing the material—when it is recapitulated —with a personal kind of melodic-rhythmic ornamentation. The neoclassic influence is apparent in Schuman's fondness for such forms as the passacaglia, fugue, toccata, and variation. These accord with the essentially polyphonic character of his music. The part writing is spare, sinewy, and deploys all the devices of dissonant counterpoint.

Schuman's scores are notable for their bright sonority. He pushes the instruments to the limit of their capacities, achieving unique effects. He shares the contemporary fondness for solid blocks of color and exploits the vivid contrasts of unmixed timbres. His massive style, marked by a predilection for the brass, supplies a solid underpinning for his conceptions. His addiction to sharp contrasts of soft and loud animates the orchestral texture.

Schuman's seven symphonies form the central item in his output. The Third (1941) is the most widely played of the series. The Fourth (1941) is neo-classical in spirit, contrapuntal in texture, objective in approach. The case is different with the *Symphony for Strings*, which dates from 1943. The austere character of the first movement and the somber coloring of the second are balanced by the jazzy rhythms of the finale. The Sixth Symphony (1948) achieves a synthesis of formal and expressive elements that bespeaks the mature artist. The Seventh was presented in 1960 and at once established itself as one of Schuman's strongest works.

To the category of large-scale works belong the Concerto for Piano and Small Orchestra (1942); the Concerto for Violin and Orchestra (1947); and the Fourth String Quartet which, from the arresting measures of the opening, shows a fine feeling for this purest of musical genres. The *American Festival Overture* (1939) is a bright, festive piece. In the *New England Triptych* (1956) Schuman pays homage to the American "primitive" who has aroused such interest among our present-day composers. The piece draws upon three anthems of Billings—*Be Glad Then, America; When Jesus Wept;* and *Chester,* one of the battle songs of the Revolution. Schuman's penchant for sturdy sonorities and sweeping lines found a natural outlet in choral music. He is at his best with the kind of poetry—for example, Walt Whitman's—which enables him to communicate manly, exuberant emotions. Whitman's verse inspired *Pioneers,* for eight-part unaccompanied chorus (1937), as well as the "secular cantata" *A Free Song* (1942). Another favored poet is Genevieve Taggard, whose poems Schuman set in *Prologue for Chorus* (1939); *This Is Our Time* (1941); and *Holiday Song* (1942).

Schuman has written several ballets. *Undertow* received its premiere at the Metropolitan Opera House in 1945. Antony Tudor's ballet depicts "the emotional development of a transgressor"—a sex-obsessed adolescent whose twisted fantasy comes to identify lust with murder. Schuman supplied a powerful score, rich in mood and color, which evokes the big-city milieu. Also vivid in atmosphere are the two ballets he wrote for Martha Graham—*Night Journey* (1947), and *Judith* (1948), a dramatic treatment of the Biblical story. His one-act opera *The Mighty Casey* (1953), after Ernest L. Thayer's immortal *Casey at the Bat,* did not quite come off. It was more difficult to transfer Thayer's classic to the opera house than either the composer or his librettist, Jeremy Gury, supposed.

CREDENDUM
(ARTICLE OF FAITH)

Credendum (1955) was written at the request of the United States National Commission for UNESCO through the Department of State—the first symphonic composition to be commissioned directly by a department of our government. Its vaulting melodies, athletic rhythms, orchestral brightness, and general exuberance are characteristic of Schuman's style. In accordance with the circumstances that brought it forth, the piece is weighty of discourse, expansive in its expression, and marked by a gravity of rhetoric appropriate for an affirmation of faith.

I. *Declaration. Moderato con fuoco.* The brass-and-percussion sound of the first movement has a vigorous quality eminently suitable for a movement which the composer has described as "oratorical." The opening flourish leads into a subject whose ample curves lend it power.

The music sweeps forward, deriving impetus from the metallic sound of the xylophone and a syncopated figure of repeated notes on the horns. The lofty rhetoric of the opening is set off by contrasting passages marked by rhythmic vivacity. The movement is short, concentrated, and comes to an end on a serene D-flat major chord sustained by trombones and tubas, while kettledrums tap out a rhythmic figure that is basic to the design.

II. *Chorale. Lento.* Introduced by the strings, the chorale is spun out in a broadly winding melodic line against a background that grows in complexity, and passes to the brass against a melodious countersubject in the strings, with animated figuration in the woodwinds. The mood is grave. The music builds up to a genuinely symphonic climax. This movement, like the first, is admirably terse. Toward the end, the chorale tune is carried by the horns. The violins refer fleetingly to the countersubject. The music comes to rest, *ppp,* on an E-major chord. A brief transition follows, in the course of which the timpani refer to the motive that was heard at the end of the first movement.

III. *Finale. Presto.* The scherzo-like opening depends for its effect on staccato figures given out by divided strings, bassoons, and bass clarinet. This material is expanded, giving way to bouncy figures distributed among the various string and woodwind instruments in a manner typical of Schuman's orchestral style. Out of the vivacious instrumental interplay emerges a long-breathed melody on the cellos. The first violins join in with a countermelody of their own. The scherzo mood returns, with ever mounting urgency. A theme derived from the cello melody comes to the fore, and is developed contrapuntally. Material from the earlier part of the movement is touched upon briefly, as is the chorale. The relationship to the first movement is underlined by the orchestral layout, which emphasizes the percussion, and the return of the basic motive on the timpani. The music of the Declaration is paraphrased in an exciting orchestral climax. The final measures take on a metallic brilliance from the sonority of chimes, cymbals, steel plate, gong, and xylophone. The repeated-note figure of the opening passage returns, and leads to an ending on a note of triumphant affirmation.

❦ 84 ❧
Lukas Foss (1922-)

"Composing music once meant to me writing the music I like. Now it means to me: writing out of a deep concern for new music and for the cause of new music."

HIS LIFE

FOR SHEER natural talent Lukas Foss is one of the most richly endowed among his generation. He was born in Berlin. His father was a professor of philosophy, his mother a painter. Foss's parents read the portents and left Germany immediately after Hitler's accession to power. They reached Paris in 1933, where Lukas continued his musical training. The family came to the United States in 1937, when the future composer was fifteen. He enrolled at the Curtis Institute in Philadelphia, where he studied composition with Rosario Scalero, orchestration with Randall Thompson, piano with Isabelle Vengerova, and conducting with Fritz Reiner. He graduated from the Curtis with honors at the age of eighteen. That year the Berkshire Music Center at Tanglewood opened its doors. Foss applied for the auditions to Koussevitzky's class in conducting. This was the beginning of an association that was most beneficial to Foss's career.

During his young years Foss was discovering America. His identification with his new homeland made him receptive to Carl Sandburg's poem *The Prairie*, which he read when he was nineteen. The sentiment, the imagery, the words seemed to be waiting for music. He set to work on a full-length cantata for four soloists, large chorus, and orchestra. *The Prairie* received its premiere in 1944. The breadth of the conception and the vividness of its execution established the twenty-two-year-old composer as a rising luminary on our musical scene. Foss served as pianist of the Boston Symphony Orchestra for several years. He relinquished this post in 1950 when he won the Prix de Rome. After his return from Italy he made a number of appearances as pianist and conductor, his virtuosity in the former role never failing to dazzle audiences, especially in his performances of contemporary music. Foss succeeded Schoenberg as professor of composition at the University of California in Los Angeles. In the summertime he teaches at the

Berkshire Music Center at Tanglewood, where his own activity as composer-pianist so auspiciously began.

HIS MUSIC

Foss's main problem has been to achieve an integrated style. This
was particularly difficult for him because of the variety of influences
to which he was subject. His heritage was the German romantic tradition. In adolescence he fell under the spell of Hindemith and the new
classicism. His stay in Paris made him sympathetic to the French taste
for incisive rhythm, clarity of thought, and precision of speech. He
came to maturity in the years when Stravinsky's influence was inescapable for any musician. At the same time the promptings of his
own romantic nature inclined him toward grandiloquent expression of
a somewhat Mahlerian cast. After he reached this country, an understandable desire to strike roots in his adopted land directed him toward
a poetic Americanism influenced by Copland.

Foss's work after *The Prairie* showed uncertainty of style and direction, because of his difficulty in finding a consistent esthetic orientation amid the conflicting ideas that attracted him. As a result, he took
longer than most of his contemporaries to find himself. He faced in
addition the problem of having to impose the discipline of the large
forms upon an essentially lyric temperament. However, in his most
recent works Foss's ability to harness his exuberant fancy and to shape
his melodic inspiration into a spacious symphonic architecture has
brought him to the stylistic synthesis his admirers have so long awaited.

Like many a pianist-composer before him, Foss had a tendency to
orchestrate "with his fingers"—that is to say, to think pianistically
when writing for the orchestra. In recent years he has found his way
to a genuinely orchestral style based on an animated interplay among
the different instrumental groups. His music is notable for its brightness
of sound, vivacious rhythm, freshness of invention, and tunefulness.
He is given to tender lyricism, to the powerful clash of massed harmonies, and to impetuous dance rhythms which indicate his vivid
response to jazz. His harmonic language is fundamentally diatonic,
with a rich overlay of chromatic elements. In his later work Foss has
moved toward a more tonal idiom marked by a sensitive use of dissonance. He develops his ideas by means of a shapely counterpoint that
draws its inspiration from the masters of the Baroque. The Copland
influence has waned; his texture is denser than Copland's, nor do his
rich harmonies display any of the older man's ascetic style. He is

Lukas Foss

Lukas Foss

given to the use of ostinatos, and builds effective climaxes through repetition and sequence. The over-all effect of his music is one of communicative lyricism and dramatic verve.

The Prairie has a youthful élan; the solo songs and massive choruses capture the mystical symbolism of Sandburg's lines. This is an astonishing work for a youth of twenty-one. The romantic aspect of Foss's style is manifest in two Biblical cantatas—the *Song of Anguish*, from the Book of Isaiah, for baritone and orchestra (1945); and the *Song of Songs*, for soprano and orchestra (1946). The sensuous love poem of the Old Testament inspired the composer to a score luxuriant with emotion. Foss made two more essays along similar lines: *A Parable of Death*, which we will discuss, and the *Psalms*, for chorus and reduced orchestra (1956).

The *Symphony in G*, written in 1944 when Foss was twenty-two, is a joyous work. The Second Piano Concerto, composed in 1951, shows Foss's susceptibility to Stravinskyan influence. The revised version (1953) is a twentieth-century evocation of the grand virtuoso concerto of the past, and has served as a brilliant vehicle for the composer's pianism. Foss has written a number of chamber-music works. The most substantial is the *String Quartet in G* (1947), the formal arrangement of which is highly ingenious. Songs and piano pieces are also included in his output.

His feeling for word and gesture make him an effective composer for the stage. His ballet *Gift of the Magi*, a vivacious score (1945), was followed in 1950 by *The Jumping Frog of Calaveras County*, a one-act opera on a libretto by Jean Karsavina based on Mark Twain's celebrated tale. A work replete with racy humor and vivid characterization, *The Jumping Frog* has made a place for itself among opera workshops throughout the country. Foss's second opera, *Griffelkin*, commissioned by the NBC Opera Theater and presented on television in November, 1955, is a whimsical fantasy.

With the *Symphony of Chorales* (1958), Foss entered upon a new phase of his development. The work, commissioned by the Koussevitzky Music Foundation, is a gesture of homage to Albert Schweitzer. It was given its premiere by the Pittsburgh Symphony Orchestra under William Steinberg, and was repeated shortly after by the Boston Symphony and the New York Philharmonic. The four movements are based on tunes which the composer selected from the chorales of Bach. Thus the symphony might be described as a cycle of chorale preludes. The spiritual ambience is one most congenial to Foss's mystical leanings. Characteristic of the composer are the repeated-note figures in the first movement; the full-throated pathos of the second; the fugue based on the *B-A-C-H* motive that has served so many admirers of the Cantor of St. Thomas's (H in German terminology is B-flat); the childlike innocence of the intermezzo; and the virtuoso writing of the finale. This music, which shows the increasing complexity of Foss's thought in recent years, has breadth and power. Its drama is projected with the craftsmanship of a mature artist. In the *Symphony of Chorales* the bright promise of *The Prairie* comes to fulfillment.

In *Time Cycle* (1960), for soprano and orchestra, Foss moves in new directions. The tonality, while clearly defined in some places, is wholly destroyed in others. Each song develops its own serial devices, of which the twelve-tone row is used the least. The work is based on four poems which "refer to time, clocks, or bells." The first two poems, by W. H. Auden and A. E. Housman, are followed by an excerpt from Franz Kafka's *Diaries* and a passage from Nietzsche's *Thus Spake Zarathustra*. The unifying element is the chord C-sharp, A, B, D-sharp, which is varied continually as it moves from one movement to the next. In *Time Cycle* Foss's lyric line is more simple and direct than in some of his earlier works. The orchestral and vocal writing is imaginative and moving.

In recent years Foss has developed an interest in ensemble improvisation. He has formed a chamber ensemble consisting of four musicians beside himself—percussion, flute, clarinet, and cello; he officiates at the piano. This group plays without written or memorized music, creating harmony, melody, and counterpoint on the spur of the moment—within a system of controlled chance. This new form of music-making transfers to the concert hall the excitement of the "jam session," and is one of a number of attempts by composers both here and abroad to recapture for art music the random, spontaneous elements of improvisation.

A PARABLE OF DEATH

A Parable of Death (1953) confronted the composer with an interesting technical problem. The commission of the Louisville Symphony specified that the work was to be written for a solo narrator. Foss consequently not only had to combine the spoken voice with music—a hazardous undertaking at best—but had to use a text that would justify the use of the spoken word. He found it in *Geschichten vom lieben Gott* (Stories of the Dear Lord) by the German poet Rainer

Maria Rilke. The Narrator, Foss points out, "tells quietly and intimately what appears to be an old legend about a man, a woman and Death. Chorus and solo tenor comment on the story. Their lines are taken from poems by the same author." In the *Passions* of Bach Foss found his model for a simple narrative upon which the chorus reflects. "It was my task to put story and poems together so that the whole would make the kind of text I needed." He succeeded in remarkable fashion in fusing the disparate elements of his tale into an artistic whole.

Foss's attitude toward the setting of text reflects the thinking of the true vocal composer. "The composer in love with the task of setting words to music will not be satisfied with merely assigning notes to the syllables. He will want the music, the melodies, the vocal phrases to grow out of the word." He understands that the music superimposes its own dimension upon the words, robbing them forever of their independence. "Each composer kills the poem he loves by setting it, by 'using' it. We always destroy when we 'use.' Whenever I set poetry I seem to say to the author, 'Forgive me for murdering the subtlety of your work. Take my musical setting as my apology, my homage and offering instead." The text of *A Parable of Death* is sung in a literate English translation by Anthony Hecht.

I. *Prologue.* Archaic harmonies in the orchestra establish the quality of remoteness essential to the tale, leading into a spacious chorus marked *Molto sostenuto* in 3/2 time. "O God, give unto every man his Death. . . ." Foss's smooth counterpoint is knit together by the motive of a descending minor third in the opening phrase, which is effectively balanced by the major third that follows soon after:

The chorus moves to an eloquent close.

II. "There once were two people, a man and a woman, and they loved one another. . . ." The tenor solo, an Allegretto in 3/4 time, introduces the rhapsodic lyricism that is so much a part of Foss's style. The supple arabesque of Bach is here recreated in twentieth-century terms, even to the repetition of text and the melismatic extension of key words over several notes.

IIIa. *Con moto*, 3/4. "Who built this house where the heart has led?" This chorus is presented in chorale style, its phrases set off by the brief interpolations of the orchestra. IIIb. The Narrator—first alone, then against an orchestral background—tells of the house that the man and woman built. "One morning at the door there waited the tall and immaculate figure of Death." The chorus takes up the word *Death*, the orchestra vividly suggesting the terror of his presence.

IVa. *Agitato ma sostenuto*, 4/4. "Listen! This might have been your heart's epiphany." In this chorus Foss achieves dramatic and rhythmic tension with the simplest means. IVb. *Maestoso*, 3/4. "Immense is Death. We are his pleasure." The commentary of the chorus is again presented as a moving chorale, with brief interjections on the part of the orchestra.

V. "Tears, tears rising to drown me. . . ." In this tenor solo Foss again harks back to the contemplative lyricism of the solos in the *St. Matthew Passion*. Chromaticism is used here, as in the music of Bach, for heightened expressivity rather than for sensuous allure. Highly dramatic is the entrance of the chorus with its burden, "Immense is Death. . . ."

VI. "We know him not, this lordly caller." Moderato, 4/4. An imperious downward gesture opens this chorus, a fine example of Foss's command of polyphonic style.

VII. Narrator and chorus bring the parable to its culmination. Death came not to harm but to offer the man and woman a seed, which subsequently blossomed into a shrub. "As they came into the sunlit garden, then they knew: Out of the sharp black leaves of the strange bush . . . a pale blue flower." Thus what Rilke calls the sprout of Death turns out to be the pale-blue flower of romanticism, blossoming in a twentieth-century soil. There is a passage for high trumpet followed by solo violin, which makes a lovely sound. The music flows to a serene cadence on a C-major chord.

Neo-classic, neo-Baroque, and Americanist elements abound in the music of Lukas Foss. But in a work such as this we encounter the romantic lyricism that is at the heart of his music.

⋍§ 85 ξ⋍

Peter Mennin (1923-)

"I cannot see how the musical language of the young American composer can fail to have both American rhythm and folk material, unless he leads a hermetic life or the past is too much with him."

HIS LIFE

PETER MENNIN was born in Erie, Pennsylvania. At nineteen, when he was a student at Oberlin Conservatory, he had finished his First Symphony, a string quartet, and a variety of songs. His musical career was interrupted by the Second World War; he served in the Air Force. After his discharge he attended the Eastman School of Music, where he worked with Howard Hanson and Bernard Rogers. He completed his studies in 1945.

That year the Allegro from his Second Symphony won the George Gershwin Memorial Award and a performance by the New York Philharmonic. He also wrote the *Folk Overture*, which was played by a number of orchestras and brought his name before the public. In 1947 Mennin joined the faculty of the Juilliard School, where he taught for eleven years. In 1958 he was appointed director of the Peabody Institute in Baltimore. During the intervening years, new works of his were heard each season and established his reputation as one of the vigorous talents of his generation. His appointment in Baltimore brought still another American composer into a position where he could shape the course of music education in this country.

HIS MUSIC

Mennin's forceful personality is attuned to his environment. His music reflects his time and place. He belongs to a generation that arrived on the scene after the battle for an American music had been won. Nationalism, for these composers, is no longer the burning issue it was for their predecessors. As the quotation at the head of this chapter makes clear, Mennin views Americanism in music not as a goal the composer has to strive for, but as something that is inevitably part of his thinking.

527

Mennin's is a young man's music, characterized by high spirits and a relentless forward drive. His works have established themselves because of his assured handling of the large forms, and the sense of bustling energy that flows from his writings. The impression of bigness in Mennin's music springs from his adroitness in shaping long singing melodies that flow easily and confidently. These are fundamentally diatonic in character, even though they draw freely upon the twelve tones of the scale. The physical exuberance of his music depends on his propulsive rhythms. Mennin's harmonic idiom relies on an effective —but on the whole, circumspect—use of dissonance. He has been strongly influenced by the medieval modes, which he handles flexibly, changing frequently from one to another. This of course underlines his orientation away from chromaticism. Mennin is a natural contrapuntist. In his music the harmonies are determined by the interweaving of the melodic lines, rather than the other way around. His orchestral writing is clear and economical; he favors primary colors rather than mixtures. The form and the color scheme unfold in broad outlines, without fussy emphasis on detail.

Mennin's seven symphonies (1942–55) show his steady growth in the manipulation of his ideas. They vary in scope and character, but all display solid workmanship illumined by a strong musical mind. They are flanked by a variety of pieces, among them the *Fantasia for Strings*, the Violin Concerto, and the *Sinfonia* for chamber orchestra, all three dating from 1947; and the *Partita for Piano* (1950), an effective addition to the contemporary literature for that instrument.

The Christmas Story (1951) is a cantata in nine parts based on the Gospel according to St. Luke and verses from the Book of Isaiah. Among Mennin's later works the weightiest items are the String Quartet No. 2 (1952); *Concertato for Orchestra* (1954); Cello Concerto (1956), commissioned for the fiftieth anniversary of the founding of the Juilliard School; *Sonata Concertante for Violin* (1958), which shows Mennin moving toward a simplification of style; and the dashing Piano Concerto (1958).

SYMPHONY NO. 3

Mennin's Third Symphony (1946) displays an integration of style one would hardly expect from a composer in his twenty-third year. The work unfolds in a texture of self-generating counterpoint that derives from the fantasia-like forms of the Renaissance and Baroque rather than from the ordered symmetries of the classical era. Mennin prefers the continual variation of ideas to the classical technique of thematic-motivic development. The music tends to avoid traditional major-minor relationships, moving from one pitch-center to the next along modal paths. Chromatic inflection gives the melodic lines their suppleness. An F-natural will reappear, a beat or two later, as F-sharp; on its next appearance it has returned to F-natural. Notable too is the plastic rhythm, modeled on the usage of Renaissance—that is to say, pre-metrical—music. The melodies disport themselves within the measure independently of the barline, propelled by the rhythmic impulsion to which we have alluded. A source of clarity is the brightness of the sound, which results from Mennin's vivid way of contrasting the woodwinds, brass, and strings.

I. *Allegro robusto.* The opening theme is stated in dramatic unison by strings and bassoon, with energetic support from horns, tuba, and percussion. This idea, in very free rhythm, dominates the movement.

A related idea is introduced almost at once by horns and woodwinds over the steady tread of the bass, in half notes, in the lower strings. We encounter here the chromatic inflection characteristic of Mennin's melodies—in this case the interchange between E-flat and E-natural:

The third idea is a long-limbed melody derived from the initial idea, which is sung by the violins over a canonic background in the violas and cellos. The forthright presentation of the material makes for consistency of texture and terse expression.

After a full statement of the second subject, the material is elaborated. "A gradual linear intensification of ideas," the composer writes, "takes place before the orchestra breaks out in full song." After a fervid climax the movement comes to an end on a C–G–C chord.

II. *Andante moderato.* The second movement opens, as the composer puts it, "with material stated without harmonic background, and continues with statements of two related subjects of considerable

length." These flow out of one another in sustained lines, marked by a contemplative songfulness. Solo oboe and flute respectively present the themes, supported by chorale-like harmonies in the lower woodwinds and strings. A striking pianissimo passage in the high strings ushers in an elaboration of the material. The music builds to a moment of impassioned lyricism, after which it subsides to a pianissimo ending.

III. *Allegro assai.* The finale opens with a restless rhythmic figure in the violas, which the lower strings continue for most of the movement. The two main themes are related to melodic formations in the earlier movements. The first idea is presented by the woodwinds and becomes a structural element in the building of an orchestral climax.

The repetition of this melody leads to the ample second subject. Both ideas are subjected to continuous variation, the mood ranging from dramatic intensity to lyricism. A fugato is followed by a broadly fashioned section in which the second theme is stated in augmentation against vigorous comments by the brass. The final section generates excitement and flows to a majestic cadence on an E-major chord. The breadth of this work and the confidence with which it is handled add up to convincing symphonism. Among the composers of his generation Peter Mennin must be accounted one of the most successful practitioners of the grand form.

◄§ 86 §►

Other Classicists—II

THE MUSIC of Arthur Berger (New York City, 1912–) exemplifies one of the most significant trends in the present-day American scene—the interpenetration of stylistic elements drawn from Stravinskyan neo-classicism with those of the Schoenbergian school. Berger studied with Walter Piston at Harvard, Darius Milhaud and Nadia Boulanger in Paris. After his return from Europe in 1939 he quickly established himself as one of the most thoughtful among the younger music critics. His reviews in the *New York Herald Tribune* (1946–53), his book on Aaron Copland and other writings revealed a mind that thought trenchantly on the problems of twentieth-century music, and a wholehearted dedication to the esthetic that exalts music as an autonomous art. In 1953 Berger resigned his post and shortly thereafter joined the faculty of Brandeis University.

Berger belongs to the intellectual type of musician in whom the creative process is severely controlled by the critical faculty. He writes slowly, subjecting everything he puts down to the sternest scrutiny. His most widely played work, the Quartet in C major for woodwinds, dates from the earlier part of his career (1941). This sunny piece, which has been recorded, is witty and elegant, and well displays the spontaneous aspect of Berger's talent. His later works are more complex. Wide leaps in the melodic line, syncopated staccato rhythms and mordant dissonances impart nervosity and tension to Berger's writing. His harmonic language is predominantly diatonic, although chromatic elements occasionally come to the fore. The fragmented, gapped thematic lines show his responsiveness to the influence of Webern. His instrumental writing is extremely refined, and derives both delicacy and power from the wide spacing of the chords, which often range over several octaves. Berger is not a prolific composer, nor does he work on a large scale. His weightiest work is *Ideas of Order*, which was commissioned by Dmitri Mitropoulos for the New York Philharmonic (1953). Another important work is the *Serenade Concertante* (1946, revised 1951) in which the technique of the Baroque concerto grosso is assimilated to the social spirit of the classical divertimento. Among Berger's chamber works are *Three Pieces for String Quartet*

(1945) and a series of carefully wrought Duos—two for violin and piano (1948, 1950), one for cello and piano (1951), one for oboe and clarinet (1952). His list also includes Three Pieces for String Orchestra (1945); piano compositions, and vocal music.

Ingolf Dahl (Hamburg, Germany, 1912–) came to the United States in 1935. He teaches at the University of Southern California. Dahl's works show the composer's orientation toward free dissonant counterpoint of the neo-classic kind. Among them are *Divertimento*, for viola and piano (1948); a concerto for saxophone and wind orchestra (1949); *Symphony Concertante* for two clarinets and orchestra (1953); and a symphonic legend, *The Tower of Saint Barbara*, (1955). Dahl also made a two-piano arrangement of Stravinsky's *Danses Concertantes*. Everett Helm (Minneapolis, 1913–) has written a *Concerto for String Orchestra* (1950); a Concerto for five instruments, percussion, and strings (1953); two piano concertos (1954, 1956); an opera, a ballet, chamber works, piano and choral pieces, and songs. As the officer in charge of music under the Military Government in Germany (1948–50), Helm played an important part in establishing the summer school at Darmstadt, which has since become a center of avant-garde music.

Gardner Read (Evanston, Illinois, 1913–) is a prolific composer whose list of works runs to over one hundred opus numbers. His four symphonies (1936, 1942, 1948, 1955) constitute the central item in a varied output that includes orchestral and choral works, chamber music, piano and organ pieces, songs, and several large compositions for voice and orchestra. Among them are the Passacaglia and Fugue for orchestra (1938); First Overture (1943); *Temptation of St. Anthony*, a dance-symphony (1953) and *Toccata Giocosa* (1954).

Charles Mills (Asheville, North Carolina, 1914–) combines a graceful classicism with the strain of mysticism that is ingrained in his nature. Among the items on his list are three symphonies (1940, 1942, 1946); Concerto for Piano and Orchestra (1948); and *Prologue and Dithyramb* for string orchestra (1955). John Lessard (San Francisco, 1920–) composes in the tradition of Parisian neo-classicism: he is a pupil of Nadia Boulanger and a disciple of Stravinsky. His works include a Violin Concerto (1941); Quintet for violin, viola, cello, flute, and clarinet (1943); *Box Hill Overture* and *Cantilena for oboe and strings*, both of 1946; *Mother Goose*, a cycle of six songs (1953); Octet for winds (1954); and the Concerto for harpsichord and chamber orchestra (1959).

Roger Goeb (Cherokee, Iowa, 1914–) is best known for his Third

Symphony (1951), which has been recorded by Leopold Stokowski. Also available on records are his *Prairie Song*, for woodwind quintet (1947); the *Quintet for Trombone and Strings* (1950); and the *Quintet for Woodwinds* (1949). Goeb has an affinity for the abstract instrumental forms—chamber music, suite, symphony, and *concertant* (a term he uses for a twentieth-century type of concerto grosso). These show his command of dissonant texture of the neo-classic variety. A list of about fifty works has established Goeb's reputation as one of the substantial figures of his generation.

Gail Kubik (South Coffeyville, Oklahoma, 1914–) is best known to the public through his score for the animated cartoon *Gerald McBoing Boing* (1950). His imaginative orchestral style abounds in bright sonorities and gay rhythms. Among his large works are three symphonies and the *Symphonie-Concertante* for piano, viola, trumpet, and chamber orchestra (1952). For this example of contemporary concerto-grosso style Kubik was awarded a Pulitzer Prize. His list includes the *Thunderbolt Overture* (1944); an opera in folk style, *Mirror for the Sky*, on the life of Audubon (1947); and choral arrangements of American folk songs that have been widely performed.

Alexei Haieff (Blagovestchensk, Siberia, 1914–) is one of the more elegant composers to have come out of the orbit of Stravinskyan neo-classicism. His music possesses the rhythmic vitality, orchestral brightness, and distinguished workmanship of that school. His easy handling of the textures of dissonant counterpoint goes hand in hand with fastidious taste, clarity of thought, and logical design. Haieff's output includes a symphony (1942); *Serenade*, for oboe, clarinet, bassoon, and piano (1942); *Divertimento*, for small orchestra (1944); a sonata for two pianos (1945); the Violin Concerto of 1948, the Piano Concerto of 1952—a virtuoso piece in the grand line—and the rather austere Piano Sonata of 1955. He has also written ballets, piano pieces, and songs. His is not a large list; but the items on it are of high caliber and represent an attractive aspect of the French-international style.

Irving Fine (Boston, 1914–1962) belongs to the group that received its impetus from Stravinskyan neo-classicism. He was a composer of sensibility and charm, whose music is none the less eloquent for making its point through understatement. Fine attracted attention in 1944 with *The Choral New Yorker*, a cantata based on poems from *The New Yorker* magazine. His compositions include the Violin Sonata of 1946; *Toccata Concertante* and *Partita for Wind Quintet* (1948); *The Hour Glass*, a choral cycle (1949); the String Quartet of 1950; *Serious Song*, "a lament for string orchestra" (1959); also piano pieces and songs.

Fine taught at Brandeis University, where he organized the music division.

David Diamond (Rochester, New York, 1915–) emerged in the Forties as one of the fresh lyric voices of his generation. The four symphonies he wrote between 1940 and 1945 won much acclaim, as did several of his large-scale works: the *Concerto for Chamber Orchestra* (1940); *Concerto for Two Pianos* (1941); three string quartets; *Rounds for String Orchestra* (1944), his most widely played work; the Piano Sonata of 1947; *Music for Romeo and Juliet*, a concert suite for chamber orchestra (1947); and the "symphonic portrait" *Timon of Athens* (1949). In these Diamond blended his innate romanticism with neo-classic elements, the result being a style marked by melodic grace, a crisply dissonant texture, and tightly knit forms. Diamond in recent years has been living in Italy, which partly explains why he has not maintained his pre-eminence on the American scene. His later style is foreshadowed in the Concerto for Piano and Orchestra of 1950, and the highly individual Quintet for clarinet, two violas, and two cellos of the same year. The Fifth Symphony (1950–57), Sixth Symphony (1954), *Sinfonia Concertante* (1955), and Fourth String Quartet (1957) are difficult works, uncompromising, violent, problematical. They show this gifted musician going through a transition period whose ultimate direction has not yet been defined.

Robert Palmer (Syracuse, New York, 1915–) is one of the major exponents of the classical point of view. He owes his eminence to his adroit handling of spaciously designed movements which serve as vehicles for lyric emotion of an introspective cast. Palmer is primarily concerned with the development of purely musical ideas; hence he finds his natural expression in the large forms of instrumental music. His thematic material, which in a number of his works is based on a scale of alternating whole tones and semitones, is pronouncedly melodious. The prominence in his music of asymmetrical rhythmic patterns—five, seven, and other odd-numbered formations—indicates his affinity for the supple rhythms of sixteenth-century polyphony. He is given to fugal and canonic procedures. His forms unfold through a process of motivic expansion and development based on varied repetition. His relationship to the masters of the Renaissance—especially the Tudor and Elizabethan composers—is manifest in his fondness for modal harmony, which he uses in effective contrast with passages of a markedly chromatic cast. Palmer has been interested in writing what he describes as "a totally organic music with purity and sensitiveness of texture." Among his important works are the Concerto for Orchestra (1943); *Symphonic Elegy for Thomas Wolfe* (1945); *Variations, Chorale and Fugue* for orchestra (1954); *Chamber Concerto No. 1*, for violin, oboe, and strings (1949), in which he adapts the Baroque concerto grosso to his own expressive ends; and the First Symphony (1953). His list also includes chamber, choral, and piano music. Since 1943 Palmer has taught at Cornell University.

Vincent Persichetti (Philadelphia, 1915–) is one of those composers who assimilate the diverse influences of their time and synthesize them into a personal style. Persichetti's impressive compositional technique is at its best in the large forms of instrumental music. His harmonic language is strongly tonal. The texture of his music is homophonic, being based on the vertical progression of harmonies rather than on the contrapuntal interplay of lines. His instrumental writing is notable for its warmth and brilliance, and shows an imaginative adaptation of traditional figures to the demands of contemporary style. Persichetti tends to avoid the rhythmic complexities that attract so many of his colleagues. This, together with the underlying simplicity of his color scheme, gives his music its sturdy construction and sweeping line. Persichetti's output centers about his six symphonies. Nine piano sonatas, six piano sonatinas, eight serenades (suite-like compositions in free style for various combinations of instruments), and the *Concerto for Piano Four Hands* (1952) are flanked by a number of substantial works, such as the Concertino for piano and orchestra (1941); *Pastoral Quintet for Winds* (1943); *Fables*, for narrator and orchestra, on texts drawn from Aesop (1943); String Quartet No. 2 (1944); *The Hollow Men* (1944), for trumpet and string orchestra, after the poem by T. S. Eliot; and the Piano Quintet No. 2 (1955). Persichetti teaches at the Philadelphia Conservatory and the Juilliard School of Music.

Ellis B. Kohs (Chicago, 1916–) teaches at the University of Southern California. He has assimilated certain twelve-tone devices to his basically neo-classical style. His music is marked by striking asymmetrical rhythms. He is much given to variation procedures, which he handles with adroitness. Among his works are the *Concerto for Orchestra* (1942), a cello concerto (1947), and two symphonies, the second with chorus (1950, 1956). Kohs has also written a variety of chamber, choral, and piano pieces.

Labels cannot be easily attached to Ulysses Kay (Tucson, Arizona, 1917–), whose music contains a mixture of both neo-classic and romantic elements. One may, however, classify this gifted Negro composer as a strong creative personality whose early promise has fulfilled itself in a vigorous flowering. Kay has evolved a polyphonic style that utilizes the procedures of imitative counterpoint with great freedom and freshness. His melodic line is amply proportioned; his harmony, which can be acridly dissonant when it suits his purpose, is expressive and purposeful. The rhythmic impulse behind his music is clearcut and full of drive. His orchestration "sounds," and he uses it to serve his ideas without indulging in sonority for its own sake. The bulk of Kay's substantial output is cast in the absolute instrumental forms, which he handles tersely and with confidence. His list includes such sturdily designed works as the *Suite for Orchestra* (1945); *Suite for Strings* (1947); *Concerto for Orchestra* (1948); and String Quartet No. 2 (1956). Among the vocal pieces there stand out the cantata *Song of Jeremiah* (1945); *Song of Ahab*, for baritone voice and ten instruments (1950); and *Three Pieces after Blake*, for dramatic soprano and orchestra. Kay, since 1953, has served as editorial adviser on the staff of Broadcast Music, Inc.

Frank Wigglesworth (Boston, 1918–) teaches at the New School in New York City. His works include *Telesis*, for chamber orchestra and percussion (1949); *Serenade* for flute, viola, and guitar (1952); *Quintet for Brass* (1957); and two symphonies (1957, 1958).

Harold Shapero (Lynn, Massachusetts, 1920–) has been much concerned with finding a relationship to the great tradition. His search for a "usable past" has centered about Beethoven—especially the Beethoven of the late piano sonatas and string quartets. Hence his position as a "radical conservative" who attempts to strike a balance between the present and the past. Shapero writes with authority and sincerity; he works slowly. His music has won a wide degree of acceptance with the public. Among his compositions are the *Serenade in D* for string orchestra (1945); *Symphony for Classical Orchestra* (1947); *The Travelers*, an overture (1948); *Credo for Orchestra*, one of the series of Louisville commissions (1955); and *Concerto for Orchestra* (1958). His chamber-music works include a Trumpet Sonata (1939), String Quartet (1940), and Violin Sonata (1942). Shapero's *Piano Sonata for Four Hands* (1941) was followed by the *Three Amateur Sonatas* of 1944, striking pieces filled with youthful spirit. The Beethoven influence is manifest in his affinity for piano variations. One set in C minor dates from 1948, another—the *Arioso Variations*—from 1949. Since 1952 Shapero has taught at Brandeis University.

Robert Kurka (Chicago, 1921–1957, New York City) was a natural musician, worthy heir to the spontaneous lyric tradition of his Czech forebears. In the course of his brief career he taught at various schools, among them the College of the City of New York, Queens College, and Dartmouth. He died of leukemia shortly before his thirty-sixth birthday. Some months earlier he had won the Creative Arts Award of Brandeis University, the citation of which read: "To Robert Kurka, a composer on the threshold of a career of real distinction." Kurka's major work is the opera *The Good Soldier Schweik*, after the novel by Jaroslav Hašek. As his librettist Lewis Allen put it, Kurka saw in Schweik "the long-tried, abused, victimized, patient common man who somehow always manages to survive the brutal stupidities of his rulers, rebuild his world and laugh." Kurka used an orchestra of winds and percussion—no strings—to give the lean brittle sound he wanted for his satire. Kurka, who knew he was dying, raced against time to finish the opera. He wrote most of the orchestration; and his friend Hershy Kay finished the score from his sketches. This gifted musician left behind a variety of compositions, among them two symphonies, five string quartets, four sonatas for violin and piano, the *Serenade for Small Orchestra, Concertino for Two Pianos and String Orchestra*, and the *Julius Caesar Overture*. His death was a great loss for American music.

Andrew Imbrie (New York, 1921–), one of the talented composers of the younger generation, is a neo-classicist whose style is based on a contrapuntal texture notable for its lucidity. His formal organization is compact and elegant, his melody line salient and individual. Imbrie is fond of combining the piano with other instruments—a not too frequent procedure in contemporary music—as in *Shaggy Dog*, for flute, clarinet, trumpet, trombone, two saxophones, and piano (1947); *Divertimento for Six Instruments*—flute, bassoon, trumpet, violin, cello and piano (1948); and the *Serenade* for flute, viola, and piano (1952). Among his other works are the String Quartet of 1944; Trio for violin, cello, and piano of 1946; *Ballad for Orchestra* and Piano Sonata (1947); *On the Beach at Night* for mixed chorus and string orchestra (1948); and String Quartet No. 2 (1953).

Leo Kraft (New York City, 1922–) writes in a neo-classic idiom tempered with romantic elements. Among his works are the *Variations for Orchestra* (1958); a one-act opera, *The Bell-Witch* (1959); and the String Quartet of 1959. Kraft teaches at Queens College.

The music of Daniel Pinkham (Lynn, Massachusetts, 1923–) exemplifies the neo-classic emphasis on formal elegance, contrapuntal texture, and motoric rhythm. Among his works are the Piano Concertino of 1950; Concertante No. 1, for violin and harpsichord soli, strings, and celesta (1954); *Wedding Cantata* (1956); *Christmas Cantata* (*Sinfonia Sacra*, 1957); and Concertante No. 2, for violin and strings (1958). Lester Trimble (Bangor, Wisconsin, 1923–) favors the pandiatonic harmony and dissonant counterpoint native to the neo-classic style. His most important orchestral works are the *Concerto for Winds and Strings* (1956) and the *Symphony in Two Movements* (1959). Trimble has written two string quartets (1950, 1957), works for solo voice and for chorus, and the opera *The Plane Tree*, after a tale in Boccaccio's *Decameron*.

Benjamin Lees (Harbin, China, 1924–) grew up in the United States. His works include the *Sonata for Two Pianos* (1951); *The Veil is Narrowed*, a choral piece (1951); *Profile for Orchestra* (1952); String Quartet No. 2 (1955); Piano Concerto No. 1 (1955); and a one-act opera, *The Oracle* (1956).

Russell Smith (Tuscaloosa, Alabama, 1927–) is one of the younger men who, instead of affirming their loyalty to any single esthetic, attempt rather to synthesize the varied resources of contemporary musical speech into a personal idiom. Among his works are the one-act comic opera *The Unicorn in the Garden* (1949), *Concert Piece for Piano and Orchestra* (1950), and the Anglican Mass of 1954. Smith's *Tetrameron* (1957) has been recorded (the title refers to a four-part formal structure). The piece shows elegance of style and an individual sense of sound.

The composers born in the Thirties are beginning to make themselves heard. None has begun his career more auspiciously than Easley Blackwood (Indianapolis, 1933–), a pupil of Messiaen, Hindemith, and Nadia Boulanger. His First Symphony was written when he was twenty-three. It is a work of surprising assurance for one so young, couched in an austerely dissonant idiom of the diatonic variety, and shows a gift for thematic development that marks the composer a symphonist. Blackwood's String Quartet of 1958, commissioned by the Fromm Foundation, displays the same vigorous expressivity.

XII. ROMANTICISTS

"The new romanticism strives neither to unify mass audiences nor to impress the specialists of intellectual objectivity. Its guiding motive is the wish to express sincere personal sentiments with a maximum of directness and of spontaneity. It tends consequently to avoid impersonal oratory; and it is wary about the conventionalistic tendencies bound up with consistent and obligatory dissonance."

Virgil Thomson

⋖§ 87 §⋗

Virgil Thomson (1896-)

"I wrote in Paris music that was always, in one way or another, about Kansas City. I wanted Paris to know Kansas City, to understand the ways we like to think and feel on the banks of the Kaw and the Missouri."

VIRGIL THOMSON's music reflects a special personality and point of view. It has its own physiognomy and points up a significant trend in the art of our time.

HIS LIFE

Thomson was born and raised in Kansas City, Missouri, in an atmosphere conducive to the sturdy nationalism that plays so important a part in his make-up. Baptist hymns, folk songs, and the popular tunes of the post-Civil War period formed the substratum of his tone imagery. The Missouri period ended with the First World War; after two years in the Army Thomson resumed his musical studies and went to Harvard.

A fellowship made possible a year's residence in Paris. Like Copland and Harris, he studied with Nadia Boulanger and was initiated into the esthetic of Stravinsky. There followed three years of musical activity in Harvard and New York, during which his first articles appeared in *Vanity Fair* and the *American Mercury*. In the summer of 1925 Thomson abandoned his teaching and literary endeavors, and returned to Paris. Arriving there with five hundred dollars in his pocket, he sat down to compose. If he must starve, he reasoned, he would at least do it where the food was good.

The French capital was in the forefront of the artistic ferment of the postwar period. This was the Paris of Picasso, of Cocteau and *Les Six*, of Gertrude Stein and the expatriates. Thomson's eager mind was vastly stimulated by the atmosphere of experimentation that surrounded him. Endowed with a gift for friendship, he formed close associations with the leaders of the contemporary movement in painting, poetry, and music. He came to feel at home among the arts in a way that is unusual for professional musicians, and laid the foundation for the embracing culture that gave his subsequent writings on music their unique frame of reference. His friendship with Gertrude Stein led to an eventful decision: an opera. This was *Four Saints in Three Acts*, with a cryptic libretto worthy of the "Mother Goose of Montparnasse." The work reached New York early in 1934. It aroused no end of discussion, fascinated some theatergoers and puzzled others, and received over fifty performances—an unprecedented run for a serious American opera. Thomson came home to find himself famous.

In the next years he divided his time between New York and Paris. His activities led him from the somewhat precious estheticism of the Parisian scene to vigorous contact with the American public. He was associated with Orson Welles on the Federal Theater Project during the early Thirties and composed incidental music for *Injunction Granted*, the Negro *Macbeth*, and for several Broadway plays. There followed a memorable series of scores for documentary films—Pare Lorenz's *The Plough that Broke the Plains* (1936) and *The River* (1937); *The Spanish Earth*, produced by Hemingway and Joris Ivans in 1937, the music for which Thomson wrote in collaboration with Marc Blitzstein; and Robert Flaherty's *Louisiana Story* (1948). These established him as an outstanding figure among serious American film composers.

When he returned from Paris in 1940—he remained there until the Germans marched in—there opened up to him a wider sphere of action. He succeeded Lawrence Gilman as music critic of the *New York Herald Tribune*. For a decade and a half his trenchant reviews were an enlivening feature of American musical reportage, and were read as assiduously by those who did not agree with his views as by those who did. In 1955 he withdrew from this post in order to devote himself to composition. The decision obviously came out of a deep inner need, but it had the unhappy result of depriving us of the wittiest chronicler of our musical scene.

HIS MUSIC

Thomson belongs to that group of American artists who found themselves through their contact with French civilization. Paris revealed to them the fine reserve of the Gallic spirit, its worship of clear and lucid expression, its impeccable taste and urbane wit. Residence abroad served to make them more aware of their native inheritance. At

Romanticism in contemporary American painting: John Koch, *Still Life with Stringed Instruments*. (Collection of Mr. William F. Carr)

the same time it purged them of all remnants of provincialism and forced them to measure themselves against the craftsmanship and esprit of a great tradition.

Thomson in his early writing followed the neo-classic style that prevailed in Paris during the Twenties. His *Sonata da chiesa* for five instruments (1926) marks the high point of his attempts in this direction. After a time, however, dissonant counterpoint and the striving for intellectual detachment became less and less congenial to a temperament that was essentially warm and lyrical. He found his true path through contact with Erik Satie and *Les Six*. Indeed, he became the link between Satie's esthetic and the contemporary American school, preaching a return to a simple idiom that would be free alike from the grandiloquent rhetoric of the postromantic era and from what he has called "our own century's rigidly modernist neo-classicism." Like Satie, Thomson sought a musical language that would be elegant, precise, and not above spoofing itself. Music had been taking itself too seriously, he maintained. Now it must learn to relax. Behind this attitude was Thomson's conviction that modern music had become too complex, too intellectual. He became one of the most articulate proponents of the new romanticism, and sought to recapture the lyric tradition in twentieth-century terms.

Thomson's melodies, based on hymns and folk tunes, are supported by forthright diatonic harmonies. Characteristic is his predilection for organ-like masses of brass and woodwind sonority wreathed in the resonance of the familiar major keys. He uses dissonance sparingly, but with effect. Heightening of tension is secured through abrupt changes of key, sometimes superimposed on one another in a kind of bitonal montage. The chords are widely spaced, the texture limpid. His orchestral palette, handled with delicacy and precision, shows the influence of French impressionism. He has not been unresponsive to modes of thought emanating from the twelve-tone school. These strands are woven together in an idiom characterized by economy of means and a studious avoidance of everything that smacks of the pretentious. A gentleness pervades Thomson's music. Beneath its veneer is a liberal dose of sentiment, a nostalgia for the scenes of his childhood, and a deep-lying need to communicate with his fellows.

The *Symphony on a Hymn Tune* (1928) was followed by a *Second Symphony* (1931), both based on folk material. *The Seine at Night* (1947), a symphonic sketch, has for its companion pieces an American landscape composed a year later, *Wheatfield at Noon*, and *Sea Piece with Birds* (1952). A melodious *Concerto for Cello and Orchestra* (1949) has been widely played. Thomson has produced much vocal music to French and English texts, and a number of choral works. A Mass of 1959 is his major achievement in this area. His ear is remarkably sensitive to the inflections of American speech, a gift which enables him to set our language with great effectiveness. He lets the words float on the music without ever submerging them.

His works for the piano include four sonatas. Among the chamber works are two string quartets (1931–32). Thomson's four sets of *Variations and Fugues on Gospel Hymns*, for the organ, are a worthy contribution to the literature of that neglected instrument. The concert suites he fashioned from his film scores, such as *The Plough that Broke the Plains* and *Louisiana Story*, reveal him in a genre in which he has always been at his best.

The work that catapulted Thomson to fame, *Four Saints in Three Acts* (1928), was an exciting experience in the theater of the Thirties. The brilliant acting and singing of the Negro cast imposed upon the free-association prose of Gertrude Stein an illusion of continuity and sustained movement that was ably seconded by imaginative decor, costuming, dancing, and staging. Miss Stein's libretto offered Thomson a vehicle excellently suited to his temperament. The score reveals his homespun traits. Unmistakable is the preacher-like style of delivery in the recitatives, the sensitive setting of the words, the unabashed return to the three basic triads. Harmonium and brass choir create the atmosphere of a revivalist meeting. In *Four Saints in Three Acts* a variety of elements are skillfully fused into a choral folk drama of religious experience that is tender, rhapsodic, and nostalgic by turn.

The collaboration with Miss Stein produced a second work, *The Mother of Us All* (1947), dealing with the life and career of the feminist leader Susan B. Anthony. An odd assortment of characters from different periods of American history are fancifully juxtaposed in the various scenes. General Grant, expressing himself in excellent Steinese, declares bravely, "As long as I sit I am sitting." Miss Anthony sings persuasively, "You're entirely right but I disagree with you," and is informed that "a Cause is a Cause because." *The Mother of Us All* is a vivid bit of Americana that proved to possess ample vitality when it was revived in New York in 1959. It is clear from these two operas that Thomson needs very special material to be able to function in the lyric theater. The collaboration with Miss Stein came to an end with her death. One wonders what their next would have been like.

LOUISIANA STORY

Robert Flaherty's documentary film *Louisiana Story* (1948) dealt with the impact of the oil industry upon the bayou country as seen through the eyes of a boy. The concert suite consists of four pieces.

I. *Pastoral* (The Bayou and the Marsh Buggy) is an impressionistic tone painting. In the film this music accompanies the boy's paddling through his beloved bayou. The piece evokes a lonely landscape of sky, water, and giant trees. The mood is embodied in the modal folk tune which is first heard on the English horn.

The music gathers momentum as the boy's canoe approaches the marsh buggy—an amphibious tractor used in prospecting—and is almost overturned.

II. *Chorale* (The Derrick Arrives).   A vivacious folk song alternates with the chorale which is associated in the score with the derrick. The chorale, based on a twelve-tone row, depicts the boy's wonder as he gazes at the lofty mesh of steel that thrusts against the sky.

III. *Passacaglia* (Robbing the Alligator's Nest).   A ground bass in 5/4 time is repeated over and over, now with a countertheme, now without. The music creates an atmosphere of suspense as the boy, in the act of stealing the alligator's eggs, is confronted by the enraged beast.

IV. *Fugue* (Boy Fights Animal).   The fourth piece, which accompanies the dramatic struggle at the climax of the film, is in the form of a fugue. The subject is announced by bassoons, trombones, and tuba. The chromatic idiom employed here, descended from the harmonic language of Liszt and Franck, is manifest in the use of chords traditionally associated with suspense and excitement. It is to be noted that Thomson, in so descriptive a score, employs three of the forms of the Baroque—chorale, passacaglia, and fugue. This underlines the tendency of twentieth-century composers, like those of the eighteenth, to impose musical forms on the drama rather than to allow the drama to shape musical form.

Longing, we have seen, is the essence of romantic art. A great longing pervades Thomson's music and motivates its glances to the past. Is this the nostalgia of the sophisticate for a simplicity forever lost? Be that as it may, Virgil Thomson is a profoundly American romantic.

⊸§ 88 ৡ⊷

Howard Hanson (1896-)

"I recognize of course that romanticism is at the present time
the poor stepchild without the social standing of her elder
sister, neoclassicism. Nevertheless I embrace her all the more
fervently, believing as I do that romanticism will find in this
country rich soil for a new, young, and vigorous growth."

HIS LIFE AND MUSIC

HOWARD HANSON's achievement extends beyond his activities as a composer. It may safely be said that in the second quarter of the twentieth century no individual in the United States did more for the cause of American music than he.

Hanson was born in Wahoo, Nebraska, of Swedish parents. His interest in music manifested itself at an early age. After the local schools he attended the Institute of Musical Art in New York; and was graduated from Northwestern University at nineteen. He taught until 1921, when the American Academy in Rome offered its first competition in music. Hanson won the Prix de Rome and spent three years in the Italian capital. During a visit home he went to Rochester to conduct his *Nordic* Symphony. There he came to the attention of George Eastman, the Kodak tycoon who had recently endowed a music school at the University of Rochester. The dynamic young composer, possessed of a strong personality and obvious administrative gifts, seemed just the man to head the new venture. Hanson at twenty-eight found himself head of the Eastman School of Music.

As director of the school and teacher of composition, Hanson influenced a generation of young American musicians. But this, he knew, was not enough. A public had to be created for American music. In 1925 he inaugurated the American Composers' Orchestral Concerts, under the auspices of the Eastman School. These were supplemented by annual festivals of American music given by Hanson with the Rochester Symphony Orchestra, at which some of the most important works of the past quarter century received their first performance.

In his own music Hanson is traditional and eclectic. He has cultivated the symphonic poem as perfected by Liszt and the "poematic" symphony as practiced by Franck and Sibelius. Of his five symphonies the most important are the First, the *Nordic* (1922), and the Second,

545

the *Romantic* (1930). His aim in the *Romantic* Symphony, he wrote, was to create a work "young in spirit, romantic in temperament, and simple and direct in expression." The composition, in three movements, opens with a motto theme of Franckian vintage that recurs in various guises. The music abounds in sweet violin tone in high register, proclamatory trumpets and horns, and shattering climaxes. In an age opposed to sentiment and rhetoric, this symphony is unashamedly sentimental and rhetoric. Hanson's symphonic poems include *Lux Aeterna* (1923) and *Pan and the Priest* (1926). We should mention too his chief choral work, *The Lament for Beowulf* (1925), and his opera *Merry Mount* (1934). In addition to a varied list of orchestral and choral works, Hanson produced a substantial amount of chamber, piano, and organ music, and songs.

   Hanson's music spoke persuasively to a generation of music lovers brought up on Franck, Brahms, and Sibelius, assuring them that twentieth-century music had something to say that they could understand. This needed doing in the Twenties and Thirties, and Hanson filled the need. But his most important contribution to American music was his championing of our native composers at a time when they needed someone to plead their cause.

⤙ 89 ⤚

Other Romanticists— I

A NUMBER of American composers have followed the romantic tradition. Among the older generation, mention should be made of Lazare Saminsky (Odessa, Russia, 1882–1959, New York City), who wrote five symphonies, four operas, and much other music; also several books, among them *Music of the Ghetto and the Bible* (1934) and *Living Music of the Americas* (1949). Philip James (Jersey City, New Jersey, 1890–) was for many years chairman of the music department of New York University. He is best known for his satirical suite for orchestra, *Station WGZBX* (1932) and the Symphony No. 1 (1943). James wrote a variety of orchestral and chamber works. His choral compositions are widely performed.

   Frederick Jacobi (San Francisco, 1891–1953, New York City) produced a number of works in which the Hebraic influence was paramount. Most important of these is the *Sabbath Evening Service* of 1952. Certain of his compositions were inspired by the songs and ritual dances of the Pueblo Indians of New Mexico and Arizona: the *String Quartet on Indian Themes* (1924) and *Indian Dances* for orchestra (1928). Jacobi taught composition at the Juilliard School. Bernard Rogers (New York City, 1893–) is head of the composition department of the Eastman School of Music in Rochester, in which post he has influenced many of our younger composers. His four symphonies follow the ideal of intense personal expression. Rogers has also written a variety of shorter pieces of a programmatic nature. His most important work is *The Passion*, for solo voices, mixed chorus, and organ (1942), an impressive, deeply felt version of the last hours and death of Christ.

Leroy Robertson (Fountain Green, Utah, 1896–) is head of the music department at the University of Utah. His works include the String Quartet of 1840, *Rhapsody* for piano and orchestra (1944), and the symphonic piece *Trilogy* (1947). Herbert Elwell (Minneapolis, Minnesota, 1898–) is best known for his ballet *The Happy Hypocrite*, after Max Beerbohm, from which he fashioned a successful concert suite (1927). He has written orchestral, vocal, chamber and piano music. Elwell is head of the composition course at the Cleveland Institute, and is music critic of the *Cleveland Plain Dealer*. Joseph Wagner (Springfield, Massachusetts, 1900–) has written orchestral, chamber, choral, and piano music. Among his works are three symphonies (1943, 1943, 1951); three ballets, the best known of which is *Hudson River Legend* (1941); and the Violin Concerto (1952–54). John Vincent (Birmingham, Alabama, 1902–) is professor of music at the University of California in Los Angeles. He has written chamber, vocal, and piano music; a book on contemporary musical theory, *The Diatonic Modes in Modern Music* (1951); and a Symphony in D (1954).

Paul Creston (New York City, 1906–) combines a romantic orientation with elements derived from impressionism and a predilection for modal harmony. "I make no especial effort to be American," he states. "I conscientiously work to be my true self, which is Italian by parentage, American by birth, and cosmopolitan by choice." Creston is at his best in generously fashioned works of solid facture and sober hue, marked by earnestness of approach and careful construction. Of his five symphonies the most successful are the Second (1944), consisting of an *Introduction and Song, Interlude and Dance;* and the Third (1950), which depicts the "three Mysteries" of the Nativity, Crucifixion, and Resurrection. Several of Creston's shorter works have been widely played: the *Second Choric Dance* of 1938, the orchestral fantasy *Walt Whitman* (1951), *Invocation and Dance*, for orchestra (1953), and the *Lydian Ode* (1956). Creston has also written a quantity of choral, chamber, and piano music.

Hunter Johnson (Benson, North Carolina, 1906–) is best known for the score of Martha Graham's ballet, *Letter to the World* (1940). He has also written a symphony (1931), *Elegy* for clarinet and strings (1936), and chamber music. Normand Lockwood (New York City, 1906–) is a prolific composer who has been especially active in the field of choral music. His oratorio *Children of God*, for five soloists, chorus, and orchestra (1957) is his major achievement in this category. Lockwood has also written a symphony (1941); an opera, *The Scarecrow* (1945); a quantity of chamber music, including six string quartets; and piano music. Josef Alexander (Boston, 1910–) teaches at Brooklyn College. Among his compositions are two symphonies, a piano concerto, *Epitaphs* for orchestra, also choral and chamber works.

◄§ 90 §►
Samuel Barber (1910–)

"I began composing at seven and have never stopped."

SAMUEL BARBER is a composer of great charm and refinement. He owes his eminence, first, to the songful character of his music; second, to the fact that he has worked along traditional lines and in an accessible idiom.

HIS LIFE

Barber was born in West Chester, Pennsylvania, a quiet town not far from Philadelphia. He grew up in a solidly middle-class environment where art and culture were much admired. When the Curtis Institute of Music was established in Philadelphia in 1924, Barber was among the first group of students to enter. He was then fourteen, and remained associated with the school for the next nine years, toward the end as a student-teacher. He studied the piano with Isabelle Vengerova, voice with Emilio de Gogorza, and composition with Rosario

Scalero, who gave him a thorough grounding in his craft. Barber is one of the very few composers who is a trained singer. The circumstance helps to explain the essentially lyrical nature of his music.

Barber was twenty-three when Alexander Smallens and the Philadelphia Orchestra played his Overture to *The School for Scandal*. In 1935 the New York Philharmonic, under Werner Janssen, performed his *Music for a Scene from Shelley*. Both works gave evidence that a fresh voice had arrived in our midst. While he was abroad on a Prix de Rome Barber met Toscanini, who played a decisive part in establishing his fame. In 1938 the maestro presented two works by the young composer—the *Adagio for Strings* and the *Essay for Orchestra*, both of which were soon known throughout the musical world.

In 1943 Barber was inducted into the Army. As the result of an unusually enlightened policy, he was commissioned to write a symphony for the Air Force. The work was performed by the Boston Symphony Orchestra under Koussevitzky in March, 1944. The event brought Barber the most memorable piece of fan mail he ever received. "Dear Corporal," the note ran, "I came to hear your symphony. I thought it was terrible, but I applauded vociferously because I think all corporals should be encouraged."

HIS MUSIC

Barber's natural inclination toward lyricism of a somewhat elegiac cast drew him inevitably into the romantic camp. He belongs to the internationalist wing among the contemporary American school. Both in his personal viewpoint and in his esthetic he is a citizen of the world. This orientation was bound to attract conductors such as Arturo Toscanini and Bruno Walter, who were the arbiters of musical taste in the second quarter of the century. They were instrumental in bringing Barber's works to a public that could not fail to be impressed by his assured handling of the large forms, his elegant craftsmanship, and his refined taste. Barber's music patently issued from a genuine creative impulse. It was deeply felt, it had a distinctive profile, it bore the mark of a poetic imagination. As a result, Barber for a number of years was one of the most frequently performed composers of the contemporary American school, especially in Europe.

He is among the musicians who have adhered to the principle of tonality. Like many of his contemporaries, he has extracted much expressive variety from the continual shifting between major and minor. His contrapuntal writing has vitality, his rhythms are varied and resilient. They abound in unexpected turns and, in his songs, are delicately attuned to the inflections of the text. He never found it necessary to rebel against the traditional forms he absorbed in his student years, but he handles sonata and symphony in a personal way. His vivid sense of sound is evident in his orchestration, which exploits the singing capacity of the instruments and finely animates the vision behind the music.

Barber's qualities are manifest in the light-hearted Overture to *The School for Scandal*, Opus 5 (1932), a work of youthful exuberance, which was followed in 1933 by *Music for a Scene from Shelley*. Inspired by lines from the second act of *Prometheus Unbound*, this poetic piece aptly evokes Shelley's flamelike incorporeality. *The Adagio for Strings* (1936) is one of Barber's best-known works; another is the first *Essay for Orchestra*, which we will discuss. The Symphony No. 1, Opus 9, was written in 1936 and revised by the composer six years later. The four movements of the traditional symphonic form are synthesized into a single movement (the piece is occasionally referred to as the *Symphony in One Movement*). The last three sections are derived from ideas presented in the first; the final section is a Passacaglia. To this period belong *Dover Beach*, Opus 3 (1931), a setting of Matthew Arnold's poem for solo voice and string quartet; the *Three Songs*, Opus 10 set to poems from James Joyce's *Chamber Music* (1936); and the Concerto for Violin and Orchestra, Opus 14 (1939).

In the second decade of Barber's career a significant change took place in his style. The romanticism of the first years was enriched by elements that betokened a deepening awareness of contemporary procedures. He absorbed the rhythmic and polytonal innovations of Stravinsky and experimented with the serial techniques of the twelve-tone school. His harmonic texture became more dissonant; the vocal line grew more expressive and assumed chromatic inflection. The *Symphony Dedicated to the Air Forces*, Opus 19 (1944) bears the marks of this turbulent period in its dissonant harmonies and the wide leaps in its melodic lines. This development in Barber's style is already to be observed in several works that preceded the Symphony. *A Stopwatch and an Ordnance Map*, Opus 15 (1940), for men's voices and three kettledrums (with optional accompaniment for brass instruments) is a deeply felt setting of Stephen Spender's poem about the death of a soldier in the Spanish Civil War. The *Second Essay for Orchestra*, Opus 17 (1942) retains the epigrammatic character of the First, but is broader in scope. The *Capricorn Concerto* for flute, oboe, trumpet, and strings, Opus 21 (1944) is a witty concerto grosso—the composer's bow to Stravinskyan neo-classicism. The Cello Concerto, Opus 22 (1945) is an important addition to the literature of that neglected instrument.

We will discuss the ballet *Medea* as an example of Barber's mature style. *Knoxville: Summer of 1915* for soprano and orchestra, Opus 24 (1947), is a setting of a prose poem by James Agee which appeared first in *Partisan Revue*. (This is also the opening chapter of Agee's book *A Death in the Family*.) Barber invested this Proustian evocation of childhood in an American town with a remarkably sensitive vocal line. In the Sonata for Piano, Opus 26 (1949), Barber achieved a notable synthesis of his earlier and later manner. The opening Allegro shows a bigness of conception that stamps it as a mature work. The work ends with a fugue of fantastic difficulty. *Prayers of Kierkegaard* for mixed chorus, soprano solo, and orchestra, Opus 30 (1954), a cantata surcharged with mystical feeling, is one of Barber's strongest works. Unfortunately, it has not yet been recorded.

Barber for many years was eager to write an opera, but could not find a suitable libretto. The problem was solved by Gian Carlo Menotti, who wrote the libretto of *Vanessa* for him. The opera received its premiere at the Metropolitan Opera House in 1958. The heroine has waited for years for her lover, who has never come back; she is prepared to accept his son Anatol in his stead because she wants love: but love associated with such mundane symbols as a house in Paris and parties to which Everybody will come. Anatol's goal is very simple: a woman who will keep him. The real heroine is Vanessa's niece Erika, the only one in the play who is touched by nobility: she sacrifices her own chance of happiness when she realizes that she can never give Anatol the things he wants. Out of this artificial story Barber fashioned a surprisingly substantial opera. He was somewhat tentative in the first act, as though he had to find his bearings. Thereafter he was carried along by his ability to spin a long melodic line.

ESSAY FOR ORCHESTRA, NO. 1

Lyric composers come into their basic style almost from the beginning of their career, as is apparent from the *Essay for Orchestra*, which was written in 1938 when Barber was twenty-eight. The use of the word *essay* as a title conjures up the literary form in which ideas are developed concisely within an intimate framework.

The introductory section, *Andante sostenuto*, opens with the main theme on the violas and cellos. This contains a three-note motive which

becomes a germinating force within the work. The music mounts in urgency through an effective passage for the brass that culminates in a flourish. There follows the *Allegro molto, leggiero* that constitutes the main body of the piece. This section captures the elfin lightness of the Mendelssohnian scherzo, but infused with the satanism that descended through the romantic era from Liszt and Berlioz to Mahler, whence it passed into the mainstream of twentieth-century music. The germinal motive appears in augmentation beneath the warblings of woodwinds and strings. A brilliant climax leads into the *Largamente sostenuto* which presents the initial theme in a mood of affirmation. The music subsides. At the very end the first violins present the basic motive in inverted form.

MEDEA'S MEDITATION AND DANCE OF VENGEANCE

The score of *Medea* (1955) was commissioned by the Ditson Fund of Columbia University for Martha Graham, and was first danced by her and her company in New York in 1946, under the title *Cave of the Heart*. Neither Miss Graham nor Barber, he points out, "wished to use the Medea-Jason legend literally in the ballet. These mythical figures served rather to project psychological states of jealousy and vengeance which are timeless. The choreography and music were conceived, as it were, on two time levels, the ancient-mythical and the contemporary. Medea and Jason first appear as godlike, superhuman figures of the Greek tragedy. As the tension and conflict between them increase, they step out of their legendary roles from time to time and become the modern man and woman, caught in the nets of jealousy and destructive love. In both the dancing and music, archaic and contemporary idioms are used."

Barber subsequently extracted from the score an orchestral suite in seven movements. In 1955 he rescored the work for large orchestra as a kind of tone poem in one movement based on material from the ballet which is directly related to the central character. "Tracing her emotions," Barber writes, "from her tender feelings towards her children, through her mounting suspicions and anguish at her husband's betrayal and her decision to avenge herself, the piece increases in intensity to close in the frenzied Dance of Vengeance of Medea, the Sorceress descended from the Sun God."

The music evokes the moods that carry Medea from her dark brooding to her decision to murder the two children she bore Jason. The heroine's states of mind are reflected in the indications that supplement the usual tempo markings in the score: "Broadly, from the distance . . . mysterious . . . anguished . . . somber, with dignity . . . with gradually increasing intensity . . . with mounting frenzy." These indicate the highly emotional character of the music. The opening sonority creates an atmosphere of strangeness and foreboding: xylophone solo and a pianissimo roll on the bass drum, against a sustained chord on harp, piano and strings, with harmonics in the first violins and cellos. A solo flute presents a characteristic melody against archaic harmonies.

Barber's soloistic writing for woodwinds and strings creates a texture of great delicacy. Certain passages that present an effect of discontinuity show how well he has amalgamated newer modes of thought with his own lyric style. It is apparent that his conception was influenced by the expressionist content and the angular movements of Martha Graham's style of dancing. The music is tense, abrupt, flexible in rhythm, vivid in movement and gesture. The sound has an indefinably oriental quality which is achieved by none of the usual means. Medea exults over her vengeance in a dance of wild abandon, ushered in by a syncopated ostinato on the piano which is reiterated over and over with hypnotic effect. Muted trumpets and trombones are handled in free style and with great imagination. Fiercely dissonant harmonies, used in percussive-rhythm fashion, build up to a violent climax, at which point there emerges a broad impassioned melody sung by woodwinds and strings. From that point, tension is maintained until the frenetic end.

Couched in a tense, richly chromatic idiom, this music shows Barber to have come a long way from his mellifluous earlier works. But like those, *Medea* bears the imprint of a fastidious and poetic sensibility.

◄§ 91 §►

Norman Dello Joio (1913-)

"What I strive for most of all is the complete confidence, the lyric quality, the feeling for line that we find in Verdi."

HIS LIFE

NORMAN DELLO JOIO represents a phenomenon uniquely characteristic of our cultural life—a first-generation American who assimilates the heritage of his fathers to the thought and feeling of the land of his birth. Dello Joio was raised in New York City, descended from a line of Italian musicians. His father, a church organist who had emigrated from a small town near Naples, gave him a thorough grounding in piano, organ, and the rudiments of theory. At twelve the boy held his first church job. Organ, choir loft, and the Catholic liturgy were influences of prime importance in the shaping of his musical consciousness. Hardly less potent was the literature of Italian opera gleaned from the singers who frequented the Dello Joio home.

To these were added more indigenous influences. The young musician conceived a passion for jazz, and for a number of years led his own dance band. At nineteen he entered the Institute of Musical Art, and later studied at the Juilliard School. In 1940, at the Berkshire Music School in Tanglewood, he encountered the single most powerful influence on his artistic development—Paul Hindemith. The German master's constant endeavor to dig down to the ethical core of esthetic experience left an indelible mark on his pupil.

A voracious worker, Dello Joio moved from one score to the next with such momentum that, despite his late start, he soon achieved a conspicuous place among the composers of his age group. He joined the faculty of Sarah Lawrence College in 1945, and taught there for six years. In 1947 he was invited by the Polish government, along with Aaron Copland and Samuel Barber, to appear in a series of concerts in that country. He has taught composition at the David Mannes School, and has appeared as commentator on the Saturday afternoon broadcasts from the Metropolitan Opera House. These have been no more than passing distractions in an existence devoted chiefly to the business of composing.

HIS MUSIC

We have indicated the principal elements in the molding of Dello Joio's style: Gregorian chant, jazz, Italian opera, and—through Hindemith—German neo-classicism. He combines a romantic need to project emotion with a classical sense of design. His music is elegant of facture, simple, and clear. Dello Joio is not the intellectual type of composer who loves to theorize about art. He represents rather the intuitive, natural musician who is concerned primarily with the doing. He takes as his models the prolific masters of the past who realized themselves through a prodigal exercise of their gift. He writes in a rush of enthusiasm and is inclined to look askance at the composer who, weighing each note, puts together one piece a year.

Dello Joio's writing is marked by an ease that springs from his command of the metier. His harmony is freely dissonant, based as it is on unrestricted use of the twelve tones around a center. It leans toward the diatonic; but when his aim warrants it, he will marshall the expressive resources of chromaticism. His frequent use of the medieval modes imparts to his idiom an archaic flavor that blends well with the contemporary elements of his style. His kinetic rhythms are rooted in the ballet. They give his music lightness and thrust. He shows great invention in the subdivision of the measure, as befits a former jazz player; yet this vivacity unfolds above the regular beat of a few simple patterns. Although his texture is often contrapuntal, the interweaving voices are directed by the clearcut movement of the harmony. Dello Joio's orchestral coloring is neat and precise, and points up the lucidity of the thought. The discipline of the classicist is apparent in his handling of form. He fashions self-contained structures marked by clarity of contour and directness of statement. The focal point of Dello Joio's music is the melody. His melodies are supple and expressive. They range in mood from gentle nostalgia to a robust joviality; but they are unmistakably his.

In *Concert Music* (1944), a kind of symphonic rondo in three sections, we find the composer's fully formed style. The middle section contains some striking antiphonal writing for the brass. *To a Lone Sentry* (1943) is a mood piece dating from the war years, and shows

Dello Joio's penchant for lyricism of a meditative cast. His ability to make the orchestra sing is well exemplified by the *Serenade* (1948); *Epigraph* (1951), the opening section of which is a long-breathed cantilena for the strings; and *Meditations on Ecclesiastes*, which brought him a Pulitzer Prize in 1957. *New York Profiles* (1949) is a characteristic suite in four movements evoking scenes dear to all lovers of the city. The work is based on a Gregorian theme that is ingeniously varied as the mood demands. Dello Joio's most ambitious orchestral work to date is the *Variations, Chaconne and Finale*, which we will discuss.

Dello Joio has written a number of concertos. The weightiest item in this category is the *Three Ricercare for Piano and Orchestra* (1946), in which the composer himself has appeared as soloist. Of his chamber music, mention should be made of the *Trio for Flute, Cello and Piano* (1943) and the *Variations and Capriccio for Violin and Piano* (1948), an attractive piece in the neo-classic manner. The Second Piano Sonata (1943) and the Third (1947) display the composer's idiomatic writing for his own instrument. Dello Joio's rhythmic invention makes him a natural ballet composer. His best-known work in this area is *On Stage* (1945), which became one of the hits of the Ballet Theater.

Dello Joio has written a number of songs. *The Lamentation of Saul* (1954) is a "dramatic cantata" for solo baritone accompanied by flute, oboe, clarinet, viola, cello, and piano, on a text by D. H. Lawrence. (There is also a version for orchestra.) The choral works include three on texts by Walt Whitman—*Vigil Strange, Mystic Trumpeter,* and *Jubilant Song. Western Star,* a "symphony for voices" on the poem by Stephen Vincent Benét (1944), is an amply designed piece that celebrates the American pioneering spirit. In another vein is *A Psalm of David* (1950), a searching work on a Latin text, by turn meditative and dramatic, in which the composer pays obeisance to the sixteenth-century polyphonists, notably Josquin.

Given his lyric gift and dramatic temperament, it was to be expected that Dello Joio would be caught up in the operatic ferment of recent years. He has written three operas to date. *The Trial at Rouen* (1955) is an adaptation of an earlier full-length opera on the life of Joan of Arc, which had been produced by Sarah Lawrence College as *The Triumph of Joan,* in 1950. For the shorter version the composer wrote his own libretto. Dello Joio's second opera, *The Ruby* (1955), is a one-acter on a libretto by William Maas based on Lord Dunsany's once popular shocker *A Night at an Inn.* The two works stem out of a dramatic impulse and have moments of theatrical urgency. However, one missed in both a moving love story to release the composer's lyricism. This lack was obviated in *Blood Moon* (1961), a three-act romantic opera on a powerful theme, in which Dello Joio reached his stride as a dramatist.

VARIATIONS, CHACONNE AND FINALE

Scored for an orchestra of the usual size, the *Variations, Chaconne and Finale* (1947) displays the limpidity of texture, freshness of communication, and polished craftsmanship that are Dello Joio's outstanding traits. His point of departure is a Gregorian melody—the Kyrie of the *Mass of Angels*—which is introduced at the outset by the oboe. This graceful melody serves as basis for six variations that make up the first movement. As it appears also in the chaconne and the finale, the three movements may be regarded as an extended variation procedure.

Dello Joio adheres to the tradition of the character variation, in which the theme—through changes in rhythm, meter and tempo, harmony, color, register, dynamics, key, and mode—assumes a different personality with each presentation. The goal throughout is to explore the possibilities of the theme for emotional expression rather than to treat it as an objective manipulation of sonorous material. In other words, the character variation is a romantic form and is eminently suited to Dello Joio's natural bent.

The theme, in 4/4 time, is wreathed in a modal atmosphere of archaic

stamp. The first variation, *Semplice e grazioso* in 6/8 time, presents a slight intensification because of the triplet rhythm; yet it remains within the realm of songful lyricism. There follows an *Andante religioso* in the character of a meditation, with an inner intensity that links this variation to the spirit of the chorale prelude. Third is a *Vivacissimo*, a scherzo of elfin lightness that brings a mischievous gaiety into the orchestra. With the *Allegro pesante* Dello Joio explores the dramatic potential of his theme. The music takes on a sense of mounting tension that erupts into an imperious climax in the brass. The fifth variation, in contrast, is a flowing pastorale in 6/8 time, the relaxed lyricism of which sets off the tragic character of the sixth. Marked *Funèbre*, this is in the nature of a lament. A brief envoi returns the theme to its original guise and rounds off the form.

The Chaconne is built on a chromatic outline of the first four notes of the Gregorian theme. Dello Joio manifestly understands the chaconne not only as a procedure based on the repetition of a harmonic progression but also as a mood and a style; he recaptures here the lofty spirit of the Baroque form. He is aided in his design by the rich chromaticism of the language he uses in this section. The Chaconne unfolds in a continuous texture, moving broadly to a climax of compelling intensity. The peroration, with its inexorable drumbeat, aspires to the quality of lyric tragedy. Toward the end of the movement the lower strings play pizzicato—a device much favored by this composer. The finale, marked *Allegro vivo, giocoso e ritmico*, overflows with an exuberance born of relentless dynamic impulsion. Yet this is no jazzed-up version of the basic idea. The dance element is refined and stylized, so that there is no incongruity between the religious origin of the theme and its manifestation in the third movement as an ecstatic dance. The lyric spirit prevails here side by side with the balletic. Both elements are united when the Gregorian theme is presented as a majestic chorale in the woodwinds against the vivacious countertheme of the strings.

Behind this music stands an imaginative musician for whom the communication of feeling is the prime purpose of composing. It is this circumstance that makes Norman Dello Joio one of the leading figures in the romantic camp.

⊷ 92 ⊶

Other Romanticists—II

PAUL NORDOFF (Philadelphia, 1909–) won a Pulitzer Prize in 1940 with his Piano Quintet. His works include the *Secular Mass* for chorus and orchestra (1934); the Piano Concerto of 1935; and the score for Martha Graham's ballet *Every Soul is a Circus* (1937).

Alan Hovhaness (Somerville, Massachusetts, 1911–) grew up in New England, but his identification with the heritage of his Armenian ancestors led him to modes of expression rooted in the music of the Orient. His is a tranquil, contemplative music that often takes on the character of mystic incantation. His melody is a species of rhapsodic

cantillation, abounding in repeated-note patterns and fanciful arabesques that capture the improvisational quality of the songs of the
Near East. Hovhaness's works bear titles that suggest their spiritual
provenance: *Lousadzak* (The Coming of Light, 1945) and *Sosi* (Forest
of Prophetic Sounds, 1945) are instrumental works; *Arekaval* (Season
of the Sun, the name for Lent in the Armenian Church) is an orchestral suite (1952). *Haroutiun* (Resurrection) is a piece for trumpet and
string orchestra (1954). Hovhaness has written symphonies, concertos,
cantatas, dramatic music, two *Armenian Rhapsodies* for orchestra;
chamber, piano, and violin music; songs, and religious works.

Wayne Barlow (Elyria, Ohio, 1912–) teaches at the Eastman School.
Among his works are *Three Moods for Dancing*, for orchestra (1940);
Madrigal for a Bright Morning, for unaccompanied chorus (1942);
and *Sinfonia in C* (1950).

Peggy Glanville-Hicks (Melbourne, Australia, 1912–) has found
her way to a sophisticated romanticism that is akin, in its clarity and
simplicity, to the tradition of Satie. At the same time, her preoccupation with the music of the Far East has led her to unusual combinations
of instruments, to exotic scales, and an unconventional treatment of
the percussion. Among her works are *Letters from Morocco*, a cycle
of six songs for tenor and orchestra on texts drawn from letters to the
composer by Paul Bowles (1952); *Sinfonia da Pacifica* (1953); and
Etruscan Concerto, for piano and chamber orchestra (1955). Also two
operas—*The Transposed Heads* (1953), on a novella by Thomas Mann,
and *The Glittering Gate* (1959), after a one-acter by Lord Dunsany.

Tom Scott (Campbellsburg, Kentucky, 1912–) has injected romantic elements into his originally Americanist style. Romanticism is in
the ascendant in his weightiest work to date, *The Fisherman* (1956),
an opera in two acts based on a fairy tale by Oscar Wilde. Scott's
orchestral works include the Symphony No. 1 (1945) and *Binorie
Variations* (1953). He has written chamber and vocal music, and folk
song arrangements that have been widely performed.

Jan Meyerowitz (Breslau, Germany, 1913–), who came to the
United States in 1946, is a prolific composer in the postromantic Central European tradition. Among his operas are *The Barrier* (1950), on
Langston Hughes's drama *Mulatto;* and *Eastward in Eden* (1951), on
Dorothy Gardner's play about Emily Dickinson. His list of works includes *The Glory Around His Head*, "a cantata of the Resurrection"
on a poem of Langston Hughes (1953); *Missa Rachel Plorans* (Mass
of Rachel Weeping, 1955); and the symphony *Midrash Esther*, on the
Biblical story of Esther and Haman (1957).

Gordon Binkerd (Lincoln, Nebraska, 1916–) has produced a varied list of works, the central item being four symphonies (1955, 1957, 1959, 1960). Among his chamber compositions are the Sonata for cello and piano (1952) and the Trio for clarinet, viola, and cello (1955). He has also written much chamber music.

Robert Ward (Cleveland, Ohio, 1917–) has written three symphonies (1941, 1947, 1950) that exemplify the approach of his generation of composers to the romantic tradition. His list of works includes a variety of orchestral pieces: *Jubilation Overture* (1946), *Concert Music* (1948), *Fantasia* for brass choir and timpani (1953), and *Euphony for Orchestra* (1954). His weightiest work to date is the three-act opera *He Who Gets Slapped*, on a libretto by Bernard Stamler after the symbolist play of Leonid Andreyev (originally produced as *Pantaloon*, 1956). This work leaves no doubt of Ward's affinity for the lyric theater.

John LaMontaine (Oak Park, Illinois, 1920–) combines a postromantic idiom with influences emanating from the French school. His seven *Songs of the Rose of Sharon*, for soprano and orchestra (1957), set to Biblical texts, is one of several vocal works that show off his agreeable lyricism. The amply designed Piano Concerto brought him a Pulitzer Prize in 1958. LaMontaine's overture *From Sea to Sunlit Sea* (1960) was played at the inaugural concert of President Kennedy, presumably as an earnest of the new administration's desire to show an interest in present-day American music.

William Bergsma (Oakland, California, 1921–) teaches at the Juilliard School of Music. An outstanding exponent of the romantic point of view, he has distinguished himself in both vocal and instrumental music. His works include the *Symphony for Chamber Orchestra* (1943); *Music on a Quiet Theme*, for orchestra (1943); Symphony No. 1 (1946–49); *A Carol on Twelfth Night*, for chorus and orchestra (1953); and the three-act opera *The Wife of Martin Guerre* (1956), which has been recorded. Bergsma has written a number of chamber works, including two string quartets (1942, 1944); pieces for various instruments; and a variety of choral works, among them *In a Glass of Water* (1945) and *On the Beach at Night* (1946).

Jack Beeson (Muncie, Indiana, 1921–) teaches at Columbia University. Among his works are *Hymns and Dances for Orchestra* (1958), *Transformations*, for large orchestra (1959), and a symphony (1959); also songs, choral works, and a variety of piano pieces, including five sonatas. He has written several operas, among them *Hello Out There*, a stark chamber opera on the one-act play by William Saroyan (1954), and *The Sweet Bye and Bye,* on a libretto by Kenward Elmslie (1957), centering about the amorous misadventures of a lady evangelist in the hectic Twenties.

Ned Rorem (Richmond, Indiana, 1923–) is one of the gifted song writers of his generation. The five years that he spent in France oriented him to the Gallic view of life and art, more especially to the tradition of Satie and Poulenc. Such songs as *The Lordly Hudson, What If Some Little Pain, Alleluia,* and *Lullaby of the Mountain Woman* are in the line of descent from the great French art song of the postromantic period. Rorem has written three symphonies (1951, 1956, 1958), two piano concertos (1950, 1951), *Design for Orchestra* (1955), *Sinfonia* for woodwind and percussion (1957), two string quartets, two piano sonatas, and *The Poet's Requiem* (1955), for chorus, soprano solo, and orchestra, on texts drawn from Kafka, Rilke, Cocteau, Gide, and others.

William Flanagan (Detroit, Michigan, 1926–) shows a special affinity for vocal music. His songs are notable for their sensitive lyricism; among them are *My Long Strayed Eyes, Go and Catch a Falling Star,* and *Goodby, My Fancy. The Weeping Pleiades* (1953), on poems by A. E. Housman, is one of several song-cycles by Flanagan. He has written *The Lady of Tearful Regret* (1959), a cantata on a text by Edward Albee, and several choral works. The orchestral pieces include *A Concert Overture* (1948), *Concert Ode* (1951), and *Notations for Large Orchestra* (1960).

From among the younger men one may single out Marvin David Levy (Passaic, New Jersey, 1932–), whose full-length Christmas oratorio *For the Time Being,* on a poem by W. H. Auden, for narrator, six soloists, large chorus and orchestra (1960), showed an impressive ability to sustain a large canvas. Levy has produced several operas, among them *The Tower,* a one-act comic opera on a libretto by Townsend Brewster (1958), and *Escorial,* after the play by the Belgian dramatist Michel de Ghelderode, a one-act lyric drama in the romantic tradition that concerns itself with the love and revenge of a Spanish king. Levy has also written orchestral, choral, and chamber works.

XIII. OF THE THEATER

"First, last, and always, the appeal of any stage piece must be
to the heart."

Gian Carlo Menotti

᪣ 93 ᪣

George Gershwin (1898-1937)

"Jazz I regard as an American folk music; not the only one
but a very powerful one which is probably in the blood and
feeling of the American people more than any other style of
folk music. I believe that it can be made the basis of serious
symphonic works of lasting value."

GEORGE GERSHWIN'S career, cut short at its peak by his premature
death, has become something of a legend among us. In terms of native
endowment he unquestionably was one of the most gifted musicians
this country has produced.

HIS LIFE

Gershwin was born in Brooklyn of Russian-Jewish parents who had
immigrated some years before. He grew up on the teeming East Side
of New York City. The dynamic, extrovert youngster was about ten
when he began to study the piano. Given his intensity and his eagerness to learn, he might have gone on to a conservatory, but his future
direction already was clear to him. The sixteen-year-old boy, discussing jazz with his teacher, said, "This is American music. This is the
kind of music I want to write."

He took the first step towards his ultimate goal when he became a
song plugger for Remick's, a well-known publisher of popular music.
His first published song, *When You Want 'Em You Can't Get 'Em*
(1916), netted him five dollars. From these modest beginnings Gershwin's career moved rapidly forward. In 1919 he wrote his first musical
comedy score, *La La Lucille*, and his first hit, *Swanee*, which was
brought to fame by Al Jolson. In the ensuing decade he produced a

562

substantial number of the memorable songs associated with his name, among them *Somebody Loves Me* from the *Scandals of 1924; Oh Lady Be Good* and *Fascinating Rhythm* from *Lady Be Good* (1924); *The Man I Love* from *Tip Toes* (1925); and '*S Wonderful* from *Funny Face* (1927).

In these show tunes we encounter the distinctive profile of the Gershwin song: fresh lyricism; the subtle rhythms, now caressing, now driving; the chromatic harmony; and the sudden modulations. Gershwin's imagination impelled him to transcend the limitations of what was a stereotyped commercial form. He found his lyricist in his brother Ira, whose unconventional word patterns perfectly suited his notes. Together they helped to bring into being a sophisticated type of popular song which caught the pulse of the Twenties.

In the meantime Gershwin established himself in the field of orchestral music. His first major effort in this direction was the *Rhapsody in Blue*, which Paul Whiteman presented at an eventful concert at Town Hall on February 12, 1924. The piece was the high point of Whiteman's attempt to make jazz respectable. The *Rhapsody* was a fantastic success, and carried Gershwin's name round the globe. The *Concerto in F* received its premiere at Carnegie Hall in 1925, with the composer playing the solo part and Walter Damrosch conducting the New York Symphony Orchestra. In this work Gershwin continued his efforts to "make a lady out of jazz," to the satisfaction of all concerned. During his last trip abroad in 1928 he heard the European premiere of the Concerto at the Paris Opera, where it scored a resounding success.

To the final group of musicals belong *Strike Up the Band* and *Girl Crazy* (1930), and *Of Thee I Sing* (1931). Meanwhile he had made several additions to his list of orchestral works, chief of these being *An American in Paris*. In 1933 Gershwin was ready for the crowning task of his life—the opera *Porgy and Bess*, based on the novel and play by Dorothy and DuBose Heyward, with lyrics by his brother Ira. Presented in 1935 by the Theatre Guild, *Porgy and Bess* was only a moderate success. Like *Carmen* some sixty years before, it did not achieve its triumph until after its composer was dead.

Physically attractive and endowed with a magnetic personality, George Gershwin was the center of an adoring circle of friends. He played his own music with enormous flair, and thoroughly enjoyed doing so. He fell in love frequently, but never married. In his early thirties he became interested in painting and turned out a number of canvases that show talent. The last year and a half of his life was spent in Hollywood, where he wrote the music for two Fred Astaire movies

—*Shall We Dance?* and *A Damsel in Distress*. He was not happy working in pictures, for the conventions of Hollywood were even less tractable than those of Broadway; besides, he missed the excitement of New York. But he never returned. After a brief illness, he was found to have a brain tumor. He did not survive the operation.

HIS MUSIC

Gershwin took the three ingredients that went into the folk song of the streets of New York—jazz, ragtime, and the blues (to which, in *Porgy and Bess*, he added the Negro spiritual)—and out of these wove a characteristic popular art. He was able to do so because of his spontaneous lyric gift. As he himself said, he had more tunes in his head than he could put down on paper in a hundred years.

His aim was to reconcile jazz and "classical"; or, as it used to be put in those days, to bring Tin Pan Alley to Carnegie Hall. Composers before him had seen the possibilities of jazz as a basis for serious works. Witness Stravinsky's *Ragtime for Eleven Instruments* and Milhaud's *La Création du monde*, both of which antedated the *Rhapsody in Blue;* also the experiments of Debussy and Satie. But for these men jazz was an exotic dish which they served up more or less self-consciously. For Gershwin, on the other hand, jazz was a natural mode of expression. Thus he was able to reveal to the world the charm and verve of our popular music.

In his forays from Times Square to 57th Street Gershwin encountered serious technical problems, which he solved within the limits of his time and place. For his forms he turned to the nineteenth century, using them in rather artless fashion. The rhapsody, the concerto, and the symphonic poem of Liszt were his models. The rhapsody, being the freest of romantic forms, lent itself best to his purpose. The *Rhapsody in Blue* is a dashing work in which is consummated the union of Lisztian pianism and jazz. The composer fared less well with the concerto, since his equipment as a serious composer was insufficient to sustain a composition in the grand form. So too *An American in Paris* betrays the limitations of Gershwin's technique in its naive structure and the absence of a truly symphonic conception.

The case is different with *Porgy and Bess*. As time goes on, Gershwin's masterpiece more and more takes on the character of a unique work. True, he failed to solve the problem of operatic recitative; nor was he able to fuse arias into a flexible musico-dramatic structure such as the *scena*. No matter. He had tenderness and compassion, and the instinct of the musical dramatist. He had the lyrics of his brother Ira, and the wonderful tunes to go with them. And so he captured, as Lawrence Gilman put it, "the wildness and the pathos and tragic fervor that can so strangely agitate the souls of men." A dozen operas launched at the Metropolitan with recitative and arias in the most approved German or French manner have fallen into oblivion, while this "folk opera"—as Gershwin called it—goes on to new triumphs with the years, and has been hailed the world over as an American classic.

AN AMERICAN IN PARIS

Gershwin was thirty when he visited the French capital. In this symphonic poem (1928) he sought, as he put it, "to portray the impressions of an American visitor in Paris as he strolls about the city, listens to the various street noises, and absorbs the French atmosphere." The work is cast in the loose form in which Gershwin felt most at home. "This new piece," he wrote, "really a rhapsodic ballet, is written very freely and is the most modern music I've yet attempted. The rhapsody is programmatic only in a general impressionistic way, so that the individual listener can read into the music such episodes as his imagination pictures for him."

An American in Paris lacks the organic development of themes and motives which was at the heart of the symphonic poem as created by Liszt. But it is brash and gay and restless, and its tone of hectic animation—about midway between jazz and the cancan—is set off against a succulent blues, one of those warm-hearted sweeping melodies of which Gershwin held the secret. This tune symbolized for the composer an access of homesickness; or was it perhaps that teasing nostalgia which even in Paris may make one long to be somewhere else?

George Gershwin, like Bizet after *Carmen*, died as he stood on the threshold of important advances in his art. Because he was so close to us we are prone to view him within the framework of the Broadway musical theater. It is well to remember that so severe a judge as Arnold Schoenberg said at the time of his death, "I grieve over the deplorable loss to music, for there is no doubt that he was a great composer."

⋖§ 94 ⋗⋗
Kurt Weill (1900-1950)

"I write only to express human emotions."

KURT WEILL was one of the most original figures to emerge in Germany in the period after the First World War. A native of Dessau, he studied at the Berlin Hochschule with Humperdinck. At twenty he was acquiring practical experience as a coach and conductor in provincial opera houses. He returned to Berlin at twenty-one and spent three years studying with Busoni, whose classical teachings bore fruit in Weill's lifelong devotion to economy of means, directness of statement, and clarity of texture.

It was in the theater that Weill found his personal style. Borrowing elements from the political cabaret and the satiric review, he fused those into the new genre of topical opera that pungently hit off the temper of the time. *Aufstieg und Fall der Stadt Mahagonny* (Rise and Fall of the City of Mahagonny, 1927), a satire on modern life, on a libretto by the poet Bert Brecht, ministered to the vogue of jazz that then prevailed in Europe. In *Der Jasager* (The One Who Says Yes, 1930), based on an old Japanese legend, Weill showed his sympathy with the ideals of *Gebrauchsmusik*. The piece was written in a simple idiom so that it could be performed by school children. The supreme achievement of his Berlin days was, of course, *Die Dreigroschenoper* (The Three-Penny Opera, 1928), on Brecht's libretto, which transformed *The Beggar's Opera* of John Gay, written in 1728, into a biting satire of the Berlin underworld of exactly two hundred years later.

Already in 1929 Hitlerite students were creating disturbances when Weill's music was played, both because of the political content of his operas and because he was Jewish. He left Germany in 1933, and after spending two years in Paris and London came to the United States. He adapted himself to his new environment with amazing flexibility, his unerring sense of theater making inevitable his conquest of Broadway. He struck a new note in American musical comedy with his scores for Paul Green's *Johnny Johnson* (1935), Franz Werfel's *The Eternal Road* (1937), Maxwell Anderson's *Knickerbocker Holiday* (1938), Moss Hart's *Lady in the Dark* (1941), Elmer Rice's *Street Scene* (1947), and Anderson's *Lost in the Stars* (1949), after Alan Paton's novel *Cry the Beloved Country*. He also did the music for *One Touch of Venus* (1943); the book was by S. J. Perelman and Ogden Nash. Weill transplanted the *Gebrauchsmusik* ideal to the American scene in *Down in the Valley*, an opera for young people based on a Kentucky mountain song; it has been widely performed by college workshops. He had just completed plans to collaborate with Maxwell Anderson on an opera based on Mark Twain's *Huckleberry Finn* when, at the age of fifty, he died of a heart attack.

As far as the international public is concerned, Kurt Weill is the composer of *The Three-Penny Opera*. Upon the lusty plot of John Gay's comedy Weill and Brecht superimposed the despair of Germany in the aftermath of the First World War. This starkly sardonic theater piece, instinct with social protest, caught the mood of a nation on the threshold of spiritual breakdown. Launched in 1928, the work became a fabulous success. It achieved more than two thousand performances in Germany, was translated into eleven languages and presented all over Europe. Revived in New York City in 1954, in a beautiful English version by Marc Blitzstein, with Weill's widow Lotte Lenya singing the role she had created twenty-six years before, the piece proved to be an extraordinary experience in the theater. Six years after it opened, it was still running strong.

The action unfolds in set numbers—arias, duets, trios, quartets, choruses. The supporting chamber ensemble—piano, two clarinets, two trumpets, trombone, percussion, and banjo—makes a sound that conjures up all the flavor of the Twenties. The "Ballad of Mack the Knife" is one of the indestructible tunes of our century, and even survived a season of being ground out by every juke box in the country. And Jenny's pirate song, "The Ballad of the Black Freighter," with its terrible mingling of loneliness, hate, and poetry, is as gripping a moment as the contemporary lyric theater has to offer.

It is sometimes given to an artist to capture a moment in time, and by an act of imagination to endow it with meaning for all who come after. Kurt Weill did precisely this in *The Three-Penny Opera*. The moment he was fated to illumine—when butter cost a hundred thousand marks a pound and the brown shirts were beginning to march—can never cease to have meaning for our generation.

~§ 95 §~
Marc Blitzstein (1905-1964)

"I am a musician addicted to the theater, not a playwright. If I write plays, it is in order to put music to them."

MARC BLITZSTEIN is one of the most interesting figures among the group of artists who came out of the Thirties. His librettos capture in remarkable fashion the rhythms of hard-boiled American speech.

Blitzstein was born in Philadelphia. He was graduated from the University of Pennsylvania, studied with Rosario Scalero at the Curtis Institute in Philadelphia, and subsequently worked with Nadia Boulanger in Paris and Arnold Schoenberg in Berlin. Blitzstein began his career with abstract instrumental works in a severely dissonant style. He found his true bent by acclimating on our stage the socially conscious musical play that was cultivated in Germany in the Twenties by Kurt Weill, Ernst Krenek, and others. He won fame with *The Cradle Will Rock* (1936) which, with its mixture of violence, satire, and tenderness, was one of the memorable documents of the Depression era. (Its revival almost a quarter century later proved that the work was strictly of its time.) *No for an Answer* (1941), lacking the sardonic wit of its predecessor, made a less decisive impression. During the Second World War the composer, while serving with the Air Force in England, produced *The Airborne*, a symphony for soloists, chorus, and orchestra, commissioned by and dedicated to the 8th Army Air Force.

Blitzstein's most ambitious opera is *Regina*, based on Lillian Hellman's play *The Little Foxes* (1949). His instinct as musical dramatist shows itself in the sure hand with which, from the rise of the curtain, each of the Hubbards is drawn. In Blitzstein's libretto, simple familiar words take on a hiss and a crackle one would never have suspected they possess. We sorrow for the characters of the operatic stage who suffer and die for love. But the Hubbards do their nasty deeds for money; and when they sing about money, money becomes something to sing about. There are set pieces: a love song in the Broadway manner; a memorable quartet about rain by the "good people" in the play who are ringed about by the little foxes; the waltz in which Regina sets forth her creed of greed and power; the chorus at her party that functions in the manner of the courtiers and ladies at royal balls in traditional opera—but with a difference! Notable are the scenes that develop in large dramatic units through the use of arioso, as when Regina curses her husband while the dance of her guests serves as background—a curtain that Meyerbeer himself would have approved—or Birdie's pathetic confession that she drinks. Inevitably the shadings of Miss Hellman's play are obscured; opera has room only for black and white. Regina is beauty and evil incarnate. She descends from the great Mephistophelian breed of black cloak and pointed beard. She is an electrifying presence on the stage; and, despite the hellishly difficult part the composer has written for her, a musical presence. She will live for the same reason that other operatic personages live: because there is a truth at the hard core of her.

In *Regina* Marc Blitzstein brought our lyric theater a long step forward. He well merits Virgil Thomson's description of him as one who "can draw laughter and tears as few living composers can."

⤐ 96 ⤏

Gian Carlo Menotti (1911-)

> "As far back as I can remember, I wanted to be on the stage. And now, of course, I can't sing well enough to appear in my own pieces. All that's left for me is to write them."

GIAN CARLO MENOTTI's inclusion in the American school stretches a point, since he has never renounced his Italian citizenship. But he has spent the greater part of his life in this country; he writes his librettos in English; and—perhaps the best reason for considering him one of our own—although his operas are much played in Europe, it is in the United States that he has won his greatest success.

HIS LIFE

Menotti was born in Cadegliano, near Lake Lugano, the sixth in a family of ten children. His father was a wealthy exporter. The future composer grew up in a musical home. His mother gave him his first lessons. He wrote a song when he was four, and at six decided that he would be a composer. When he was eleven he wrote an opera in which, he recalls, "everyone sings and plays all the time and dies in the last act."

He attended the Verdi Conservatory in Milan. At seventeen he came to Philadelphia to study composition with Rosario Scalero at the Curtis Institute. Innumerable Americans had gone to Europe to study. For a young Italian to come here was something new. In the next years Menotti gave ample promise of future achievement. *Amelia Goes to the Ball* was an astonishingly deft work for a composer in his twenties. Given its premiere at the Curtis Institute in 1937, it was presented the following year at the Metropolitan Opera House and established Menotti's reputation. This was the first in a series of lyric dramas that brought him worldwide fame.

In recent years Menotti has extended his activities to include his native land. He has organized an ambitious "Festival of Two Worlds" at Spoleto, the aim of which is "to bring young artists from the New World into contact with those of the old." Spoleto probably heralds the composer's intention to return to Italy. "I'm getting old. I'm sick of telephones and taxis. I want to go back to a quiet, uncomfortable place." One hopes the quiet place will be uncomfortable enough that he will continue to divide his time between the two worlds he has brought so much closer together through his art.

HIS MUSIC

Menotti's intensely personal vision of life finds its natural habitat in the opera house. He has the theater in his blood. He springs out of the tradition of Italian opera and handles its conventions, even its clichés, with spontaneity and freshness. His immediate forebears are Puccini and Mascagni. He was nourished too by the Verdi of *Falstaff* and the stylized comedy of *opera buffa*. To these have been added other influences indigenous to his time and place: the tension of the expressionistic theater, the suspense and horror of Grand Guignol, the powerful harmonies of Musorgsky, the grotesquerie of Mahler and Prokofiev.

Menotti writes his own librettos, and by so doing insures his having the kind of story that will release the music in him. In Menotti's theater the words and the music are inseparable halves of a single dramatic conception. He handles our language imaginatively. Having learned English when he was grown, he never takes it for granted. Ordinary words sound fresh and rich to him. "The phrase 'a pane of glass' which I use in *The Consul* has a special tang to me. The word *paper* is somehow different to me. These words set me to thinking in terms of music." Unlike those benighted souls who maintain that English is difficult to sing, Menotti considers it to be the ideal language of opera. He achieves an expressive declamation that brings out the inflections of English speech, but in so individual a manner as to be immediately recognizable as his. He is a master of the impossible art of libretto writing. His librettos are rich in atmosphere and taut in action. They are impregnated with an infallible theater sense, behind which stands a compassionate nature endlessly fascinated by the unexpected twists of man's destiny. Menotti has broken down the wall that separated the American theater public from the opera house. *The Consul* ran for almost seven months on Broadway, attaining a total of two hundred and sixty-nine performances. In divesting the operatic form of the grand rhetoric of the past, Menotti—like Britten—has moved toward the chamber-opera style. His are intimate works marked by nuance of feeling and subtlety of characterization. His musical impulse is so closely wedded to the dramatic that the music seems hardly to exist apart from the action. Significantly, the composer calls his works not operas but "plays with music" or "musical dramas."

Menotti's first important piece, *Amelia Goes to the Ball* (1934), adapts the Italian *opera buffa* tradition to the modern theater. In this work the composer with amiable satire evokes the glittering salons of his youth in Milan. *The Old Maid and the Thief*, a "radio opera," written in 1938 on a commission from the National Broadcasting Company, deftly combines lyricism and romantic comedy. There followed in 1942 Menotti's one failure, *The Island God*, which was written for the Metropolitan Opera House. The grand-opera frame defeated his dramatic intuitions, as did the mystical subject. "My error," he observed later, "was in trying to write an opera around a philosophic theme."

The Medium, commissioned by the Alice M. Ditson Fund, was introduced in 1946 by the opera theater of Columbia University. This two-act opera for five singers, one dance mime, and an orchestra of fourteen is a melodrama that gives the composer ample opportunity to indulge his love of Grand Guignol terror and suspense. The work has achieved close to two thousand performances since its premiere— impressive proof of the need it fills in the contemporary lyric theater. *The Medium* is generally presented on a double bill with *The Telephone*, an airy bit of persiflage.

In *The Consul*, which brought him a Pulitzer Prize for 1950, Menotti

evoked the human condition in our troubled time. The hopelessness of
millions who were trapped by history is embodied in the tragedy of
Magda Sorel. Her big aria in the second act, "To this we've come—
that men withhold the world from men!"; the scene with the magician,
who is able to conjure anything out of his sleeve save the precious
visa; and the duet between the sad little woman who sings of her woes
in Italian and the sad little man who translates her words into English
are among the high spots of a profoundly compassionate drama.

From a purely musical standpoint *The Saint of Bleecker Street* (1954)
represents Menotti's most important achievement thus far. In two extended arias of the second act he trusted his musical intuitions in far
greater degree than ever before: he did not hesitate to stop the action
and let music take over. Unfortunately the theme, which moves somewhere between religious mysticism and hysteria, repelled a great many
theater goers (including the present writer). Despite some excellent
things in the score—especially the scene of the wedding in the second
act—it is unlikely that *The Saint of Bleecker Street* will achieve a lasting place in the theater.

Maria Golovin, which was commissioned by the National Broadcasting Company, received its premiere at the Brussels World Fair in
the summer of 1958. As in *The Consul,* the action is laid against a
turbulent background. Young Donato, blinded in the war, falls madly
in love with Mme. Golovin, whose husband is a prisoner in another
country. His love, because of his helplessness, takes on an obsessional
intensity. Their relationship is limned with an almost Proustian subtlety, although both the script and the music show signs of the haste
in which the piece was completed. Menotti has also written a "madrigal
ballet," *The Unicorn, the Gorgon and the Manticore* (1956), and
several instrumental works.

AMAHL AND THE NIGHT VISITORS
OPERA IN ONE ACT

Amahl (1951) is the first opera to have been commissioned expressly
for television. In his introduction to the recording the composer relates how, with Christmas as his deadline, he found himself without a
single idea in his head. Walking rather gloomily through the rooms of
the Metropolitan Museum, he chanced to stop in front of the *Adoration of the Kings* by Hieronymus Bosch. (The Three Kings play the
same role for Italian children as Santa Claus does for ours). "I then
realized they had come back to me," Menotti remarks, "and had

brought me a gift." It took Menotti's kind of imagination to proceed from this starting point to the conception of the crippled boy and his mother. The work was presented by the NBC Opera Theater on Christmas Eve, 1951.

Amahl unfolds within the frame of the chamber opera. The arias are short, the episodes move along a tight story line; the characterization, both dramatic and musical, is clear and vivid. The scoring is economical: flute, two oboes, clarinet, bassoon, horn, trumpet, harp, piano, percussion, and strings. Menotti exploits the contrast between the twelve-year-old boy's soprano and the mature voices of the grown-ups about him. The music is drenched in emotion, and the characters are such that we at once take them to our hearts.

The fairy-tale atmosphere is established in a short orchestral prelude, out of which emerges the naive little tune played by Amahl on his

pipe. The relationship between mother and son is set forth most vividly. Amahl, forever telling tall tales, has the artist's imagination; she is the realist. She fears for the next day, when they will have nothing to eat; Amahl describes how they will go begging from door to door, and the king himself will reward them. The scene ends with a tender goodnight.

There is a change of key to A-flat. Mysterious chords in the bass herald the arrival of the three Kings. The march that accompanies their entrance is properly fantastic, with a touch of Prokofiev-like grotesquerie. Kaspar's aria about his magic box is followed by one of the most moving passages in the opera—the duet of Melchior and the mother, in which he describes the Child whom they seek while she sings of her own poor child. The entrance of the shepherds, who have been summoned by Amahl, is the occasion for some effective choral song. Their dance in honor of the Kings combines, as Menotti puts it, "the qualities of primitive folk dancing and folk ritual." Shy and fearful at first, the shepherds end with a joyous Tarantella. When they have taken their leave, the Kings, Amahl and his mother go to sleep.

A few atmospheric measures brings us to the heart of the play. Dawn comes. The mother sings her moving aria: "All that gold! I wonder if rich people know what to do with their gold! Do they know how a child could be fed?" She tries to steal the treasure and is caught by the page. Amahl tearfully defends his mother, the Kings are awakened. In a passage of great nobility Melchior sings: "Woman, you may keep the gold. The Child we seek doesn't need our gold. On love, on love alone He will build His Kingdom . . . and the keys of His city belong to the poor."

A scene from the NBC Television production of *Amahl and the Night Visitors:* Amahl surrenders his crutch. (NBC)

The drama builds so naturally that the climactic moment when Amahl is miraculously healed needs no underlining. It is done very simply, on a sustained B-flat tremolo in the orchestra, *pianissimo,* as each of the Kings and the mother repeat in an incredulous whisper, "He walks. . . ." Superb theater, this. Hardly less compelling is the ending. The Kings set forth on their journey. Amahl goes with them, to bring his crutch as an offering to the Child. He plays his pipe, waves to his mother just before he disappears at the bend in the road. The snow begins to fall.

Amahl is replete with the wonder and fantasy that are at the core of romantic art. For the children of a television era it has come to play the same role as did Dickens's *A Christmas Carol* in a simpler age. Its

creator occupies a unique place in the artistic life of our time. He has
created a popular musical theater all his own.

⋙ 97 ⋘

Leonard Bernstein (1918-)

"I have the feeling that the musical is growing in such a vital
way that it may wind up—and I hope it does—in some kind of
American musical-theatrical form which I hesitate to call opera
—but that's the only word I can find for it at the moment, which
would treat the English or rather American language in a natural way, so that you could do serious things through music
and say serious things about music in the theater without sounding like a translation from *Aida*."

LEONARD BERNSTEIN owes his great fame to a variety of musical activities which have not left him the time to devote himself consistently
to serious composition. He was born in Lawrence, Massachusetts, the
son of Russian-Jewish immigrants. At thirteen he was playing with a
jazz band. He entered Harvard when he was seventeen and studied
composition with Walter Piston. He attended the Curtis Institute in
Philadelphia, then became one of the band of disciples whom Serge
Koussevitzky gathered about him at Tanglewood. In 1943, when he
was twenty-five, he was appointed Artur Rodzinski's assistant at the
New York Philharmonic. A few weeks later Bruno Walter, the guest
conductor, was suddenly taken ill; Rodzinski was out of town. Bernstein, at a few hours' notice, took over the Sunday afternoon concert
and coast-to-coast broadcast, and gave a spectacular performance.
Overnight he was famous. Thereafter his career proceeded apace until,
in 1958, at the age of forty, he succeeded Dimitri Mitropoulos as director of the New York Philharmonic, the first American-born conductor to occupy the post.

Bernstein speaks the language of contemporary music with great
ease. He is not an innovator; rather he absorbs what others have in-
vented and sets upon it his own stamp. He has been influenced on the
one hand by Stravinsky and Copland, on the other by Mahler and
Richard Strauss. His style therefore is a blend of neo-classic and postromantic elements. He has a real flair for orchestration. The spacing

and balance of sonorities, the use of the brass in high register, the idiomatic writing that displays each instrument to its best advantage—all these show his deftness. His harmonic idiom is spicily dissonant, his jazzy rhythms have vitality. The formal structure tends to be diffuse, as is natural with a temperament that is lyrical and prone to improvise.

Bernstein's *Jeremiah Symphony* (1942) was an impressive achievement for a composer in his middle twenties. The work is in three movements—*Prophecy, Profanation,* and *Lamentation.* In the third movement, which is sung in Hebrew by a mezzo-soprano, Bernstein with astonishing fidelity captures the accents of Biblical cantillation.

His Second Symphony, *The Age of Anxiety,* for piano and orchestra (1949), takes its point of departure from the poem of that name by W. H. Auden. The piece contains some unusual jazz writing for the solo instrument and captures the restlessness of Auden's four characters and the atmosphere of their disjointed time. Bernstein's list of works includes the ballet *Facsimile* (1946); the song cycle *La Belle Cuisine,* an amusing setting of four French recipes (1947); the *Serenade for Violin Solo, Strings and Percussion* (1954), after Plato's *Symposium;* and *Trouble in Tahiti,* a one-act opera satirizing suburban life, on his own libretto (1952).

Bernstein's feeling for the urban scene—specifically the New York scene—is vividly projected in his theater music. He brings to the popular Broadway show a compositional technique and a knowledge of music that few of its practitioners have possessed. In *On the Town,* a full-length version of his ballet *Fancy Free* (1944), *Wonderful Town* (1953), and *West Side Story* (1957) he achieves a sophisticated kind of musical theater that explodes with movement, energy, and sentiment. These works capture "the hectic quality, the lonely quality and the athletic quality" which the composer regards as constituting the special character of American music.

Although it is hazardous to prognosticate the course of any artist, the chances are that Bernstein will make his contribution to our music in the field of the Broadway theater. In any case, he will go down in the annals of his art as one of the extraordinary musical personalities of our time.

✑ 98 ✐

Other Opera Composers

VITTORIO GIANNINI (Philadelphia, 1903–) inherited the tradition of Verdi and Puccini, to which he has added an admixture of the rhythmic vigor and sumptuous orchestral panoply of Richard Strauss. *The Scarlet Letter* (1938), after Hawthorne's masterpiece, and *Blenerhasset*, a radio opera based on Aaron Burr's traitorous attempt to carve an empire for himself in the southwest, suffered from the combining of American story material with an essentially European style. In *The Taming of the Shrew* (1953), on the other hand, Giannini found a capital vehicle for his gifts. Shakespeare's lusty tale, with its picturesque Italian setting, makes a perfect *opera buffa;* and the composer adroitly utilizes all the possibilities offered by the plot. Giannini has tried his hand at orchestral, choral, and chamber music; but his natural habitat, unquestionably, is the opera house.

Carlisle Floyd (Latta, South Carolina, 1926–), who teaches at the Florida State University in Tallahassee, won success with *Susannah* (1955). In this opera, for which he wrote the libretto, Floyd united two dependable themes—the Biblical tale of Susannah and the Elders, and the Sadie Thompson–Reverend Davidson involvement immortalized by Somerset Maugham in *Rain*. Floyd's technique was not yet sufficiently advanced to support the dramatic conception; but there was no mistaking the robust creative impulse behind the work. In 1958 Floyd wrote *Wuthering Heights*, again on his own text. It took courage for a composer to measure himself against the blazing genius of Emily Brontë's novel; and real skill to fashion so smooth a libretto out of her fateful tale. Heathcliff and Cathy are among the great romantic conceptions of English literature. One may forgive Floyd if at this stage of his career he did not rise to the full ecstasy of the love scene on the heath, or to the full evil that life implanted in Heathcliff. The fact remains that, in moving beyond the folklore orbit of *Susannah*, Floyd took a great stride forward. American opera in the coming years has every reason to expect much of him.

Stanley Hollingsworth (Berkeley, California, 1924–) studied with Gian Carlo Menotti. His opera *La Grande Bretèche*, after Balzac's celebrated story, was presented by the NBC Opera Company in 1957, but failed to make an impression. It was apparent that the composer was not quite ready for his task. On the other hand, an earlier work, *The Mother* (1954) after Hans Christian Andersen, is a moving one-acter that captures the poetry of the fairy tale on which it is based. Hollingsworth has written choral and instrumental music, but his real affinity seems to be for the theater.

Lee Hoiby (Madison, Wisconsin, 1926–) was also a pupil of Menotti. *The Scarf*, his second opera, was introduced at the Festival of Two Worlds in Spoleto, Italy, in the summer of 1958. The work stems out of the romantic tradition and has the indefinable theater quality which is of the essence in lyric drama. The music suggests the heroine's hunger for love, her dreams and her frustrations; and builds to the tragic climax. The libretto by Harry Duncan, on a story by Chekhov, is literate and viable theater. Hoiby has written several orchestral works, also chamber and choral music; but it is more than likely that, like his teacher, he will make his contribution as an opera composer.

XIV. TOWARD A NEW
EXPRESSIONISM

"I am not trying to write 'modern,' 'American' or 'neo-classic' music. I am seeking always and only the coherent and living expression of my musical ideas."

Roger Sessions

❧ 99 ❧
Carl Ruggles (1876-)

"Music which does not *surge* is not great music."

CARL RUGGLES, like Charles Ives, came into an environment that was not prepared to receive him. The circumstance affected him no less profoundly that it did his fellow New Englander. Although he has had a long life, he produced only a handful of works. There was no public to stimulate him, to demand that he write. After the Thirties he fell silent.

"The Cape Cod composer" was born in the town of Marion, Massachusetts, near Buzzard's Bay. When the time came for him to prepare for a profession, he went to Boston intending to study the art of ship design. He ended up at Harvard, studying composition with John Knowles Paine. After eleven years of conducting an orchestra in Winona, Minnesota, Ruggles went to New York and became active in the affairs of the International Composers' Guild, which at that time represented the most advanced tendencies in American music. From these exciting years date the four works on which his reputation rests —*Men and Angels* (1920), *Men and Mountains* (1924), *Portals* (1926), and *The Sun Treader* (1933).

"In all works," Ruggles maintains, "there should be the quality we call mysticism. All the great composers have it." Music for him has a symbolic meaning, in terms of poetic suggestion and emotion, over and above the notes. This is apparent both from the titles of his works and the literary mottoes he associated with them. *Men and Mountains*

579

derives its title from a line of Blake: "Great things are done when men and mountains meet." *Portals* bears on its score a quotation from Walt Whitman: "What are those of the known but to ascend and enter the Unknown?" Similar titles are *Men and Angels*, *The Sun Treader*, and *Vox clamans in deserto* ("A Voice Crying in the Wilderness," for solo voice, chorus and orchestra). There is a visionary quality in Ruggles's music, a burning intensity. He has well been called an apostle of ecstasy.

His need to communicate emotion finds its natural outlet in a harmonic language based on chromatic dissonance, which he regards as the element of expressive tension. Hence we find that, as in the case of the Schoenbergians, his music draws its forward impulsion from varying levels of dissonance rather than from the contrast of dissonance and consonance. The chromatic element in Ruggles's writing derives from his desire to exploit to the full the capacities of the twelve tones of the scale. As a result, he never repeats a tone, or any octave of it, before nine or ten others have intervened. His reluctance to emphasize a central tone led Ruggles away from traditional tonality. Like the composers of Schoenberg's school he is fond of the devices of sixteenth-century counterpoint—canonic imitation, inversion, and retrograde. He writes a bold melodic line, full of thrust and rhythmic vigor, and capable of sustained flight. His melodies are marked by sweeping outlines, chromatic inflection, and wide leaps. He is essentially an orchestral composer. Characteristic is the monumental effect he achieves by making the instruments play in unison, especially the brass.

Ruggles's music may be characterized as atonal; it bears a certain relationship to that of the modern Viennese school. Nonetheless, he issued from an environment totally different from that of Schoenberg and his disciples. He found his way to certain principles that resembled theirs, because these principles were in the air. But his music moves in another world of feeling and has its own expressive goal.

Lilacs, the middle movement of *Men and Mountains*, has been recorded. It is a rhapsodic adagio for string orchestra, cast in a free form that accords with its emotional content. *Portals* too is available on records. Originally written for thirteen strings, it was subsequently rescored for full string orchestra. The piece is dramatic in mood, urgent in tone. Like Schoenberg, the composer indicates the principal voice in his score. The emotion is of an unflagging intensity that rises in a relentless line to the *fff* climax. There follows a postlude of six measures marked *slow and serene*, leading to a transcendental cadence. This five-minute piece shows the concentration of thought that is one of

Ruggles's prime traits, and is strangely prophetic of much that came after.

The composer of these poetic measures was a natural-born musician; yet untoward circumstances cheated him of the full flowering of his gifts. His admirer Charles Seeger suggested this in an apt passage: "Here is a man who has an unusual number of the attributes of genius: might it not be that if he had been born at another time or in a different place he would have been able to make his grandiose dreams more palpable, turn out a bulk of work that would compel the acceptance of his notions of beauty as the standard of his day, and fix him in the honored position of the first great musician of an epoch?" We shall never know.

⊰ 100 ⊱
Roger Sessions (1896-)

"I have sometimes been told that my music is 'difficult' for the listener. There are those who consider this as praise, those who consider it a reproach. For my part I cannot regard it as, in itself, either the one or the other. But so far as it is so, it is the way the music comes—the way it has to come."

ROGER SESSIONS stands high in the regard of the musical fraternity. He concerns himself with problems fundamental to contemporary musical thought, and does so on the highest level of artistic responsibility.

HIS LIFE

Sessions was born in Brooklyn, New York, of an old New England family. His parents returned to Massachusetts shortly after the future composer was born. He gave early evidence of his talent, and wrote an opera, *Launcelot and Elaine*, at the age of twelve; he entered Harvard when he was fourteen. After graduating from Harvard, Sessions continued his musical studies with Horatio Parker at Yale. In 1917, when he was twenty-one, he was appointed to the faculty of Smith College and taught there for four years. He had already begun to compose, but was dissatisfied with the results. At this point he found an inspiring teacher in Ernest Bloch, under whose guidance he discovered his own creative path. "It would be impossible," he has said of Bloch, "to exaggerate what I owe to him."

When Bloch became head of the Cleveland Institute of Music he brought his pupil there as his assistant. Sessions remained in Cleveland for four years. From this period dates the music for Leonid Andreyev's symbolic drama *The Black Maskers;* the score is dedicated to Bloch. In 1925, when Bloch was dismissed from his post by the directors of the Institute, Sessions resigned in protest. He spent the next eight years in Europe: three in Florence, three in Rome, and two in Berlin. He returned to the United States in 1933; taught for a time at various

Edward B. Marks Music Corporation

Roger Sessions

schools in the Boston area and at the New School in New York; and in 1935 joined the music faculty of Princeton University, where he remained for a decade. He then became head of the music department at the University of California in Berkeley. In 1953 he returned to Princeton.

Sessions has taken an active part in the propagation of the new music. With Aaron Copland he organized the Copland-Sessions concerts, one of the first sustained attempts to bring contemporary music to the New York public. He was on the board of directors of the League of Composers; and for eight years was president of the United States section of the International Society for Contemporary Music. His writings include "The Composer and his Message," in a collection of essays assembled by Augusto Centero under the title *The Intent of* the *Artist* (1941); *The Listening Experience of Composer, Performer, Listener* (1950); and a textbook, *Harmonic Practice* (1951).

HIS MUSIC

Sessions, like Piston, is one of our internationally minded composers. The deliberate search for a nationalist music implies, for him, a limiting of the artist's freedom of choice. Americanism in music, he maintains, "is bound to come only from within, a quality to be discovered in *any* genuine and mature music written by an American." The classical approach is fundamental to his view of art and life. In an earlier chapter we quoted a paragraph of his that became the prime formulation of the neo-classic creed (pp. 163–164). Sessions upholds the classical primacy of pure musical form and ideas. "For me, and I believe for nearly all composers, musical ideas have infinitely more substance, more specific meaning, and a more vital connection with experience than any words by which they can be described." All the same, there is a romantic strain in his thinking that sets him apart from the Stravinskyan esthetic. The German romantic tradition—the heritage of Wagner, Bruckner, Richard Strauss—played a seminal part in his development. If he was influenced by the neo-classic esthetic of Stravinsky, he responded in no less degree to the visionary romanticism of Bloch. As his pupil Mark Schubart has pointed out, his thinking "follows the German conception of music as a grandly expressive art, rather than the French conception of it as a sensuous or coloristic one." We may therefore expect to find that Sessions's music contains powerful chromatic elements. Nor need it surprise us that in his maturity he reaffirmed his affinity with the German tradition by becoming one of the outspoken admirers of Arnold Schoenberg.

This amalgam of elements places Sessions among a group of composers who cannot be easily assigned to either the classic or romantic camp. (Not that it is essential to attach a label to every creative artist.) If we have considered him among the neo-expressionists it is because he has gravitated both toward an atonal chromaticism and toward a preoccupation with the expressive capacity of his art. "My music," he writes, "is always expressive in intent, and often has very concrete associations for me. In composing, however, I follow not the associations but the impulsion of the musical ideas themselves." Music reaches down "to the energies which animate our psychic life. It reproduces for us the most intimate essence, the tempo and the energy of our spiritual being. It reproduces these far more directly and more specifically than is possible through any other medium of human communication."

Sessions has been profoundly influenced by Schoenbergian thought. His music lies in the area between atonal chromaticism and the twelve-tone system; he prefers to remain on the periphery of the dodecaphonic school. The complexity of his music is inseparable from the complexity of his thinking. His is a subtle, allusive mind that sees all the ramifications of an idea and delights in tracing them to their ultimate consequences. Sessions is not one to try to make things easy for the listener. Yet his music, he feels, is not unduly difficult for those who take the trouble to familiarize themselves with it. "Experience has shown me over and over again that the 'difficulty' of my music is anything but insuperable. This is, of course, true of all new music if it is genuine, if it really has something to say. I have had ample occasion to observe that a work which was 'difficult,' say, ten or twelve years ago is no longer so. Both for performer and listener these difficulties have meanwhile cleared up, with results that have been surprising to all concerned. What the listener needs is familiarity with the language —sufficient familiarity to be able to respond to the tones, melodies, harmonies and rhythms it contains."

The simplest introduction to Sessions's music is through *The Black Maskers* (1923). Written when he was twenty-seven years old, the incidental music to Andreyev's symbolist play dates from the period when he was most susceptible to romantic influences. The sumptuous orchestral writing (quite Straussian in spots) foreshadows Sessions's later mastery in this domain. His mature output centers about the large forms of instrumental music. The Piano Sonata of 1930 is a deeply felt piece that shows his ability to discipline his emotions, as does also the String Quartet in E minor (1936). A milestone in Sessions's development is the Violin Concerto (1935), whose close-grained texture and concentrated thought make it an exceptionally difficult work for performer and listener alike. The Second Piano Sonata (1947) combines the dissonant texture of neo-classicism with a chromatic idiom and violent contrasts of moods.

The central place in Sessions's output is held by his four symphonies (1927, 1946, 1957, 1958). These bear the imprint of profound thought and concentrated emotion so characteristic of the composer. The Third belongs to a group of works marked by a more personal lyricism and a more accessible style than his earlier compositions. This group includes the Second String Quartet (1951), the brilliant Concerto for Piano and Orchestra (1956), the *Idyll of Theocritus* for soprano and or-

chestra, which we will discuss, and the Mass (1958). In the Third
Symphony Sessions adapts the serial techniques of twelve-tone music
to his own ends. As he points out, he is not among the composers who
commit themselves to the twelve-tone system as a value in itself, preferring to regard it "as a tool to be used in the forging of music valid
on quite different and perennially vital grounds."

Sessions has written a one-act opera, *The Trial of Lucullus;* the
libretto is based on a play by Bertolt Brecht in which the celebrated
Roman general stands trial after his death, his jury consisting of the
little people whose lives were shattered by his triumphs. The opera was
presented at the University of California in 1947, and a decade later at
Princeton. Despite the seriousness with which Sessions approached his
task, the piece revealed no genuine gift for the theater.

SYMPHONY NO. 1

The First Symphony (1927) is a sunny, unproblematic piece that
sums up the characteristics of Sessions's neo-classic period. It is scored
for an orchestra of usual size, including piano.

I. *Giusto,* 2/4, E minor. The imperious flourish with which the
movement opens leads into a closely woven texture of imitative counterpoint with propulsive force and vigor. This Allegro takes its point
of departure from a compact idea that lends itself admirably to motivic
treatment.

The emphasis on winds rather than strings makes for the bright "objective" sonority that was in vogue in the Twenties. The frequent dislocation of accent engenders a foreshortening of the measure which
adds to the rhythmic tension. A contrasting motive emerges in the
brass. But a movement such as this depends upon the principle of continuous expansion as practiced by the Baroque rather than on the
sectional contrasts of the Haydn-Mozart period. In the Recapitulation
Sessions adroitly varies the musical fabric, especially in regard to the
distribution of the thematic material among the voices.

II. *Largo,* 2/4, C major. This slow movement in A-B-A form is
steeped in manly lyricism. The florid singing line draws inspiration
from the arabesque of Bach. The emphasis is on the vibrant expressive-

ness of the strings. The soloistic treatment of the instruments results in a chamber-music texture. In the middle part, clarinet and piano set up a diaphanous background of triplets for the traceries of oboe and flute. The A section is repeated in curtailed form.

III. *Allegro vivace*, 2/4, E major. The finale captures the dancelike impulsion of the classical rondo. Here lighthearted rhythm is released into the pure joy of pattern making. The strong tonal feeling in this movement, as in the rest of the symphony, nourishes the energy of the music and the clarity of its drive. The rondo theme is properly vivacious, the texture is limpid, the color bright. A rhythmic intensification leads to a forthright coda and vigorous cadence in E.

IDYLL OF THEOCRITUS

The *Idyll of Theocritus* was written in 1954. Theocritus's poem, Sessions tells us, captured his imagination as far back as 1912. He did not really feel its impact until forty years later when he read the translation of the English poet Robert Trevelyan. "The idea of a musical setting did not immediately occur to me, however; even after certain of the lines began to take musical shape in my mind, I dismissed the idea, which presented formidable difficulties to both singer and composer. First of all I found it unthinkable to set merely portions of this poem, which its translator calls 'perhaps the greatest love-poem in the whole of ancient and modern literature.' It is, however, very long, and not only demands a very large design on the part of the composer, but I foresaw that it would make the most exacting demands on any singer: forty-odd minutes of uninterrupted singing, with the utmost intensity, resourcefulness of expression, and keenness of ear and musicianship." All the same, when the Louisville Orchestra offered Sessions a commission to write a large work, he decided to execute his long-cherished plan. The piece is dedicated to Luigi Dallapiccola.

The poem is in the form of a monologue by a girl, Simaitha, who has not seen her lover for twelve days and fears he is unfaithful to her. "Invoking the moon-goddess in the various guises of Artemis, Selene, and 'the infernal Hecate,' she brews magic spells, hoping to conjure him back to her, and sends her servant to apply them. Left alone, she tells the goddess how she saw the young athlete Delphis at a religious pageant, and was stricken ill with love from him; how, unable to bear it, she sent her servant to fetch him from the wrestling school; how she took him into her arms, and how subsequently their love was flawless, until now, after twelve days without seeing him, she hears from a neighbor that he is unfaithful. So, if her spells prove futile, she will take deadly vengeance on him. She takes leave of the goddess, the stars, and the night, resigned to her misery." (Complete text in App. IV.)

The piece is a long aria, intensely dramatic in character. "The whole is dominated by the singer," Sessions writes, "and the expression is concentrated above all in the melody which she sings. This melody is far-flung, free in rhythm, and extremely flexible; the design is of the largest." Two refrains punctuate the musical discourse at regular intervals. The first is heard on the words "O magic wheel, draw hither to my house the man I love," against mysterious flickerings of sound compounded of glissandos on the harp and tremolos in the strings. This chromatically inflected melody, which dominates the first third of the

O ma - gic wheel, ___   draw hith-er to my house the man I   love. __

piece, is slightly varied when it reappears. Musical fragments derived from it are heard throughout the work. The second refrain, on the words "Bethink thee of my love and whence it came, O holy Moon," unfolds a melodic line of remarkable amplitude that undergoes much greater variation than the first since it changes with the emotional and musical context. It begins with a rising six-tone pattern which develops somewhat differently with each recurrence.

Be - think thee of my love___   and whence it came, O ho -   ly Moon.__

There are five main sections in the work which, Sessions points out, are similar in large design but not in inner structure to the contrasting movements of a symphony. 1. *Allegro appassionato* (the spells), followed by a short interlude. 2. *Allegretto semplice* (the pageant). 3. *Adagio—Deciso e con fuoco—ritenuto* (Simaitha's anguish, her summons, and Delphis's arrival). 4. *Un poco allegro e con fuoco* (Delphis's speech to Simaitha, and the love scene between them). 5. *Adagio tranquillo* (Delphis's faithlessness, Simaitha's resolution, and her farewell).

The work is expressionist in its chromatic-atonal idiom, which strives for maximum intensity throughout, and in the vocal line, which abounds in wide leaps and difficult intervals such as major sevenths, major ninths, and diminished octaves. The consistently full orchestral texture does not permit sufficient contrast between sections, although the change of pace and mood at certain points is most striking. There are felicitous examples of word painting: the bell sounds on the line *Quick, beat the brazen gong;* or the sense of distant horizons conveyed by the music when Samaitha sings, "Behold, the sea is silent." Extremely effective is the climax of the piece, when the maiden recalls the fulfillment of her love: "The greatest deeds of love were done, and we both reached our desire." However, Sessions is considerably handicapped by the length of the poem, and by the fact that it had to be set continuously. A shorter monologue with choral interjections would have been more compelling from a dramatic point of view. Furthermore, Trevelyan's lines resist musical setting; for, despite his faithfulness to Theocritus, he failed to capture the sensuous beauty, the passion and fire of the original.

This music, both subtle and strong, displays the rather special cast of Roger Sessions's mind. It underlines his position as one of the most distinguished representatives of the contemporary American school.

⤳ 101 ⤶
Elliott Carter (1908-)

"I like music to be beautiful, ordered, and expressive of the more important aspects of life."

OF THE composers who came into prominence in the mid-Forties, none is more widely admired by musicians than Elliott Carter. His works are not of the kind that achieve easy popularity. But their sureness of line, profundity of thought and maturity of workmanship bespeak a musical intellect of the first order.

HIS LIFE

Elliott Cook Carter is a native of New York City. When he entered Harvard he majored in English literature. It was not until his last year there that he decided to be a musician. He stayed on as a graduate student and studied with Walter Piston.

In 1932 Carter went to Paris, where for three years he worked with Nadia Boulanger. From this period dates the first of his works to be heard in public, incidental music for a performance of the *Philoctetes* of Sophocles by the Harvard Classical Club. For the same group he wrote, after his return to the United States in 1935, the music for Plautus's *Mostellaria*. One number from this score, the *Tarantella*, was widely performed by the Harvard Glee Club. Carter settled in New York City in 1936. His articles on modern music published in various periodicals won him a reputation as a thoughtful critic. In 1940 he accepted an appointment to the faculty of St. John's College in Annapolis, Maryland, where the philosopher Scott Buchanan had inaugurated a "great books" program. Given Carter's broad intellectual interests, he could not but be sympathetic to a curriculum in which music was taught not only as an esthetic experience but also as a branch of physics and mathematics. The idealist philosophy that underlay the teaching at St. John's was congenial to his own outlook, which he has described as being "in the direction of Platonism, as seen by Whitehead." He not only planned a music program closely integrated with the general course of study at the college, but also conducted a freshman seminar in the great books of Greek philosophy. Carter's experience at St. John's gave him a fine insight into the role that the musical disciplines can play in a liberal arts education.

His duties at St. John's interfered with his composing, however; so Carter relinquished his post and went to Santa Fé, New Mexico, where, in the winter of 1942, he completed his First Symphony. He served during the war as music consultant at the Office of War Information, and taught for a time at the Peabody Conservatory in Baltimore. But his chief activity in the past decade and a half has been composing.

HIS MUSIC

Carter's chief concern has been with the expressive and imaginative elements of his art. His music has grown more intricate as he has found his own voice and cut away those things that are not essential to his vision. His concern is never with technique as an end in itself;

he uses it only to focus what he wishes to say. His is an elaborate kind of music that exists on many levels and reflects an original and subtle mind. It requires careful listening, for it is as concentrated in thought as it is complicated in facture. To those who make the effort,

American abstract expressionism: Robert Motherwell, *The Voyage*.
(Collection of Museum of Modern Art)

it reveals a sensibility that, although quite special, is as germane to the American scene as anything being written in this country today.

Carter started out with a musical idiom rooted in diatonic-modal harmony. His gradual assimilation of a dissonant chromaticism went hand in hand with his response to the many influences that directed his development. He absorbed dodecaphonic no less than Stravinskyan elements; but he uses both in an independent fashion. His contrapuntal writing shows secure workmanship and constructive logic. His language is abstract, his style is one of extreme control. Withal, he achieves a personal tone.

Carter inherited the rhythmic suppleness that was the legacy to his generation of both Stravinsky and Bartók. He has listened carefully to the madrigals of the Renaissance, whose elastic cross-rhythms follow the natural accentuation of the language rather than a fixed meter. From jazz he took over the concept of a strict rhythmic bass with free improvisation above it, a device he uses both in his String Quartet No. 1 and the Sonata for Cello. He made a novel attempt to use fluctuations in tempo and meter as form-building elements. Through the use of shifting accents and irregular scansion of phrases he achieved the polyrhythmic counterpoint that gives his music its plasticity. From this point he arrived at the concept he calls "metrical modulation," a technique whereby he passes from one metronomic speed to another by lengthening or shortening the value of the basic unit. In the past such changes involved changes in speed based on simple metrical proportions: for example, a quarter-note unit in one passage equalled a half-note unit in another. Carter has carried such "modulations" to the utmost refinement and exactitude in terms of metronomic timing. In the Adagio of his Cello Sonata, to cite one case, he begins with the eighth note at 70 and, through a subtle "modulation," emerges with the eighth note at 60. This lengthening of the unit note in the irregular proportion of 7:6 is carried out within a frame of strict meter, and with such fine gradation that the effect is utterly smooth.

Carter is a slow worker; his reputation rests on a comparatively small number of works. Of the earlier ones, the ballet *Pocahontas* (1939) may be singled out as a vigorous score in which are abundantly manifest his command of technique and rhythmic invention. *The Defense of Corinth* (1941), for speaker, men's chorus, and piano four-hands, on a text drawn from Rabelais, is an exuberant piece that reveals the lighter side of a composer who is generally serious. In the First Symphony (1942), written for an orchestra of classical size, Carter moves toward a simplification of style. The lyricism of this work gains in power from the sobriety, both of color and mood, that the composer has imposed upon his material.

The first period of Carter's development is summed up in two admirable works. The *Holiday Overture* of 1944 is a joyous, extroverted piece whose high spirits recall *The Defense of Corinth*. *The Harmony of Morning*, also of 1944, is a setting of Mark Van Doren's poem *Another Music* for four-part women's chorus and chamber orchestra. The Piano Sonata, composed in 1946, is a broadly conceived work noteworthy for careful detail, imaginative use of piano figuration, and the irregular scansion of the metrical patterns. In his ballet *The Minotaur* (1947) and in *Emblems*, a setting for men's chorus and piano of three poems of Allen Tate (1947), Carter projects somber moods with an intensity of feeling that is new to his music. The Woodwind Quintet of 1948—for flute, oboe, clarinet, horn, and bassoon—is a charming tribute to his teacher Nadia Boulanger and to the neo-classic point of view of which she has been so eloquent a proponent. The Sonata for Cello and Piano (1948) is a darkly expressive piece that sets forth the principle of "metrical modulation" as well as Carter's subtle insight into the problem of sonority and balance.

Eight Etudes and a Fantasy (1950) for woodwind quartet—flute, oboe, clarinet, and bassoon—are studies in sonority that reveal the more fanciful side of the composer's style. The exploration of sheer sound undertaken here is continued in the *Pieces for Four Kettledrums* of the same year. The *Sonata for Flute, Oboe, Cello, and Harpsichord* (1952) has some vivid contrasts in color, and is a fine example of the current revival of interest in the grand keyboard instrument of the Baroque. Carter's two string quartets (1951, 1960)—bold, uncompromising works—constitute the most significant contribution to the genre since Bartók. The Second brought the composer a Pulitzer Prize.

VARIATIONS FOR ORCHESTRA

The *Variations for Orchestra* (1955), one of Carter's finest achievements, introduces the listener to a very special world of sonority. This work exploits the resources of the orchestra in virtuoso fashion. The conception is thoroughly symphonic; at the same time the orchestral texture is of an almost chamber-music delicacy and refinement.

We have noted the tendency of the twentieth-century sonata to introduce developmental elements into the movement as a whole instead of confining them to the development section. Carter similarly applies the variation procedure continuously instead of in self-contained units, as was done in the variation forms of the eighteenth and nineteenth centuries. The piece is based on a theme that undergoes many transformations, and on two ritornels which are repeated literally except for transpositions of pitch and speed. The first of these is stated rapidly near the outset and becomes progressively slower with each restatement. The second, contrariwise, is played in slow notes by the solo violin as a counterpoint to the theme and accelerates with each reappearance. The ritornels emphasize the unity of the conception even as the variations themselves—each with its own method of development—nourish the diversity of the work.

The introduction, marked *Allegro*, which takes on urgency from a leaping figure in the strings and a repeated-note motive in the brass, serves as a kind of summary of the melodic and harmonic configura-

tions to be heard throughout the piece. The theme, an *Andante*, is a serene idea that unfolds in a series of lyric phrases interspersed with flickering figures on instruments of contrasting color. Variation 1, *Vivace leggero,* is a rapid dialogue of motives drawn from various parts

of the theme, presented in contrasting rhythms. Variation 2, *Pesante,* unfolds a more dramatic aspect of the basic idea. The theme, introduced by the brass in an almost literal quotation, is pitted against its own variants derived from it by intervallic expansion and diminution. This juxtaposition results in striking contrasts of character and mood. Variation 3, *Moderato,* opens with a singing melodic line on the violins and builds up tension to a climax that surges through the whole orchestra.

The fourth, fifth, and sixth variations are more uniform in character. Variation 4 is a study in controlled ritardando based on changing metronomic units—a matter which, as we saw, is one of Carter's preoccupations. The procedure used here involves groups of four measures, each of which begins at ♩ = 200 and slows down to half that speed. Variation 5, *Allegro misterioso,* has an almost Webernian immobility and transparency of texture, in which the changing orchestral combinations stand out with remarkable clarity. The sixth variation balances the fourth, being a study in controlled accelerando. Thenceforth the process of development moves beyond the single variation: the seventh, eighth, and ninth variations are interlocked in a continuous process on a single plane of rhythm established mostly by the woodwinds. Variation 7 is an *Andante*. One of its ideas is carried over into Variation 8 within the changed emotional context of an *Allegro giocoso*. Variation 9, also an *Andante*, develops the three ideas of Variation 7 in a contrapuntal texture, thereby exemplifying the twentieth-century fondness for presenting simultaneously elements that were first heard in succession.

The finale, *Allegro molto,* juxtaposes a variety of elements in animated interplay, thus intensifying the contrasts between them. The rapid motion is interrupted, first, by an expressive section for strings that leads to a quotation of the two ritornels; then by a recitative for trombones, based on the notes of the first half of the theme, while muted strings play those of the other half. The work ends as the first ritornel slowly ascends through a quiet string background while the winds rush downward with the second. The *Variations for Orchestra*, the composer points out, is not a twelve-tone piece. "Its quality of harmony is derived from the theme and is arrived at by ear and not by a system." At the same time the *Variations for Orchestra* shows Carter's involvement with the issues that have concerned advanced musicians since the mid-century.

STRING QUARTET NO. 2

"I regard my scores as scenarios, auditory scenarios, for performers to act out with their instruments, dramatizing the players as individuals and as participants in the ensemble. To me the special teamwork of ensemble playing is very wonderful and moving, and this feeling is always an important consideration in my chamber music." In the String Quartet No. 2 (1959) Carter carries out this dramatic approach to the instrumental ensemble with extraordinary sureness and control. The four lines of this tightly knit "auditory scenario" function at maximum tension throughout. The bold curves of the melodic lines, with their wide leaps, is matched by the utmost freedom of movement from low to high register. This unrestricted range nourishes the abrupt, imperious gestures of Carter's instrumental writing. His is an impassioned style that demands the highest virtuosity from the player; it is a style whose "metrical modulation" and rhythmic flexibility impart a subtly improvisational quality to the music. Here is florid counterpoint—a term widely applied to the polyphony of the Baroque masters —in a new guise.

The work consists of four movements: 1. *Allegro fantastico;* Cadenza for Viola. 2. *Presto scherzando;* Cadenza for Cello. 3. *Andante espressivo;* Cadenza for Violin. 4. *Allegro.* These, set within the frame of an Introduction and Conclusion, are played without interruption. Each of the four instrumental parts has its own character which is embodied, Carter explains, "in a special set of melodic and harmonic intervals and of rhythms that result in four different patterns of slow and fast tempi with associated types of expression." Maximum individualization prevails in the first two movements. Co-operation and exchange of ideas come to the fore in the last two, even though the cadenzas turn more and more to a *concertante* idea—opposition between the solo and accompanying instruments. "The Conclusion," as Carter puts it, "returns to the state of individualisation of the first part of the work."

The composer directs that the first violin should play with insistent rigidity where indicated, but more often in a bravura style. He describes the first violin part as "fantastic, ornate, and mercurial." These qualities are revealed in the opening measures of the first movement.

The second violin "has a laconic, orderly character which is sometimes humorous." The viola part is predominantly expressive. The cello part is on the impetuous side. The four parts are further differentiated in their intervallic structure. The first violin plays primarily minor thirds, perfect fifths, major ninths, and major tenths (aside from the seconds, major and minor, which all the instruments share). The second violin part features major thirds, major sixths, and major sevenths. The viola makes wide use of augmented fourths, minor sevenths, and minor ninths; the cello of perfect fourths, minor sixths, and minor tenths. The first violin dominates the opening movement, the second violin the *Presto scherzando;* the viola comes to the fore in the third movement, the cello in the fourth.

Further individualization is achieved by means of the rhythmic structure. The first violin part is marked by contrasting note values. The second violin part is much more regular in its rhythm. When its note values change, they do so in a simple one-to-two relation: that is, an eighth note followed by a quarter, or a quarter by a half. Also, the second violin moves at a much more consistent metronomic speed than do the other parts. The more mobile character of the viola part is indicated not only through rhythmic changes, but also by the glissandos and portamentos in its music. The cello part is rich in rubato; groups of accelerating and retarding notes underline the fantasy-like character of its music. On the next page is a characteristic passage from the cello cadenza: Carter uses the dotted line and arrow to indicate the various *gruppetti* whose intervening notes are to be played as a continuous accelerando (or, where the notation indicates it, a ritardando).

In order to make the listener aware of the differences in the four lines, Carter suggests that the performers sit farther apart on the stage than is usual. However, the instruments are so clearly individualized within the structure of the music that this spatial differentiation, as the composer points out, is not essential. The form "does not follow traditional patterns but is developed directly from the relationships and interactions of the four instruments, that result in varying activities, tempi, moods, and feelings."

A work of the utmost invention and brilliance of execution, the Quartet received extraordinary critical acclaim when it was first heard in New York in 1960. It confirms the position of Elliott Carter as one of the most important composers in America today.

◄§ 102 ৯►
Hugo Weisgall (1912-)

"I can sing anything I write. If I can't sing it I don't write it."

HUGO WEISGALL was born in Czechoslovakia and came to the United States when he was eight. He grew up in Baltimore, attended the Peabody Conservatory, graduated from Johns Hopkins University, and went on to a Ph. D. in German literature. He studied composition with Roger Sessions, and conducting under Fritz Reiner at the Curtis Institute. During the Second World War Weisgall served as assistant military attaché to the Allied Governments in Exile in London and later in Prague. In 1946 he became cultural attaché at the American Embassy in Prague. He was active as a conductor both during his stay abroad and after his return to Baltimore. He taught at Johns Hopkins University, the Jewish Theological Seminary of New York, and the Juilliard School of Music. In 1960 he accepted an appointment to teach composition at Queens College of the City of New York.

Essentially an opera composer, Weisgall writes in a contemporary idiom that ranges from atonal chromaticism to the twelve-tone style: an area he describes as "pretty much the place where Schoenberg was before his final decisive leap into serialism, and where Berg was in *Wozzeck*." His surcharged harmonic language lends itself to the tensions of the expressionist theater. Hence his affinity for European dramatists like Strindberg, Wedekind, and Pirandello.

Weisgall's music shows a high degree of dissonance tension; the sound is dominated by major and minor seconds, sevenths, and ninths. He writes long plastic melodies, sometimes diatonic, oftener chromatic, that contain wide leaps. His vocal line sensitively mirrors the natural inflections of English—better, American—speech, and at the same time incisively delineates character, situation, and the psychological nuances of the action. Weisgall's sophisticated kind of theater does not favor lyrical expansion as an end in itself; yet his operas require the singers really to sing.

His is a free, supple rhythm that follows the motoric impulses of our language. He belongs to the generation that learned from Stravinsky's *L'Histoire du soldat* to make do with modest instrumental resources. He favors a Mozartian orchestra, to which he generally adds a piano and percussion. In this matter he is guided not only by his own predilection but by the economic considerations that govern the production of new operas. He orchestrates sparsely but vividly, mixes his colors carefully, and leans toward chamber-music textures. The inner voices move sturdily within the contrapuntal web. The age-old problem of operatic structure—how to reconcile the exigencies of the drama with those of the music—Weisgall approaches in a personal way. He organizes the material in large sections (sometimes in a sustained musical form such as a scherzo or fugue), and in the continuous type of setting that keeps the action steadily moving forward.

The Tenor (1950), on a libretto by Karl Shapiro and Ernst Lert derived from Frank Wedekind's drama Der Kammersänger, calls for a chamber orchestra, including piano and percussion. The action centers on the operatic tenor Gerardo, famous for his interpretation of Tristan, who is as irresistible to women as he is susceptible to them. He reaches a crisis in his personal life when, faced by the choice between the reality of love and the make-believe of his career as a heroic tenor, he chooses—inevitably—the latter. Despite an occasional attempt on the part of the librettists to place the work in the United States, the atmosphere of the drama is unmistakably European. The Stronger (1952), on a libretto by Richard Hart based on August Strindberg's one-act play, is a much shorter work; it takes less than half an hour. The action is laid in the cocktail lounge of an American hotel; the atmosphere is subtly underlined by the inclusion of an alto and tenor saxophone in the group of eight players called for by the score. Estelle, a silly, chattering, possessive wife, exults in her triumph over her husband's former mistress, Lisa, who never utters a word throughout the opera. Here too the psychological overtones of the situation lend themselves well to Weisgall's music. Both The Tenor and The Stronger have been recorded, and afford a good introduction to his style.

Weisgall's most impressive achievement to date is Six Characters in Search of an Author (1953–56), based on Pirandello's celebrated parable on the nature of illusion and reality. A recent revival of the play left some theatergoers, including the present writer, with the impression that Six Characters had aged heavily, and that its style and symbols belonged to the Twenties. Weisgall's music seemed to release all the turmoil locked in the six characters and their companions. Dennis Johnston's literate libretto retains the flavor of the original. The music, by turns sardonic, witty, compassionate, tender, creates a pervasive atmosphere for the bizarre doings on stage. The orchestral investiture is elegant, the vocal line uninhibited. Supported by mature craftsmanship and a sure instinct for the stage, *Six Characters* is a strikingly original work that makes a real contribution to our burgeoning American opera.

Weisgall's list of compositions includes also *Soldier Songs* for baritone and orchestra (1946), a setting of nine poems which communicate the horror and futility of war; *A Garden Eastward* (1952), cantata for high voice and orchestra on a Hebrew text of Moses Ibn Ezra; and *Purgatory* (1958), based on the last play of W. B. Yeats, in which a twelve-tone row is used almost throughout.

◦§ 103 §◦

Leon Kirchner (1919-)

"An artist must create a personal cosmos, a verdant world in continuity with tradition, further fulfilling man's 'awareness,' his 'degree of consciousness,' and bringing new subtilization, vision, and beauty to the elements of experience."

IN THE years since the Second World War, Leon Kirchner has emerged as one of the distinctive personalities of his generation. His music bears the imprint of a powerful creative imagination. It is personal, serious, uncompromising, and profoundly moving.

HIS LIFE

Kirchner was born in Brooklyn, New York, of Russian-Jewish parentage. His family moved to the West Coast when he was a boy. Los Angeles during the middle Thirties, the composer recalls, "had become a vortex of musical activity. A concert was an *event:* the balconies served as the meeting place for the young and ambitious talents of the city."

Kirchner studied the piano when he was a child, and made his first attempts at composition while he was in his teens. However, deferring to his parents' wishes, he undertook to prepare himself to study medicine; but his musical bent was too strong to be denied. When Schoenberg came to the University of Los Angeles, Kirchner abandoned his premedical course and went to study with him. He subsequently transferred to the University of California in Berkeley, where he did graduate work in composition, and came under the influence of Ernest Bloch. In 1942 he won the George Ladd prize, which enabled him to go to New York and study with Roger Sessions.

After a three-year stint in the Army Kirchner returned to Berkeley, completed his graduate work, and in 1947 was appointed to the faculty as a lecturer. A Guggenheim fellowship made possible another stay in New York, during which his name began to be heard in musical circles. In 1950 he returned to his post at the University of Southern California. Four years later he accepted an appointment as professor of music at Mills College in Oakland, California.

Kirchner's talent has been recognized by a number of important commissions and prizes, among them an award in 1951 from the National Institute of Arts and Letters.

HIS MUSIC

The most arresting characteristic of Kirchner's music is its powerful expressivity. As Aaron Copland put it, Kirchner's best pages "are charged with an emotional impact and explosive power that is almost frightening in intensity." The quotation at the head of this chapter makes it clear that Kirchner takes his stand with those who regard music as an expression of thought and emotion. "It is my feeling," he writes, "that many of us, dominated by the fear of self-expression, seek the superficial security of current style and fad worship and make a fetish of complexity, or with puerile grace denude simplicity. Idea, the precious ore of art, is lost in the jungle of graphs, prepared tapes, feedbacks, and cold *minutiae*." Kirchner maintains that only when the artist projects his personal world will "idea, powered by conviction and necessity, create its own style and the singular, momentous structure capable of realizing its intent."

Kirchner regards Schoenberg and Sessions as the two composers who most strongly influenced his development. In his early years he came under the spell of Mahler, and later, of Bartók. His emotional intensity relates him to Alban Berg. Kirchner's roots, therefore, are to be found in the tradition of central European expressionism. At the same time he belongs to a generation for whom Stravinsky was a seminal influence. Like all artists of decisive personality, Kirchner assimilated from these sources only what accorded with his inner needs. His music exemplifies the significant process of acculturation whereby even those who are not strictly twelve-tone composers are carrying the Schoenbergian influence into the mainstream of contemporary American music.

Kirchner's remarkably expressive melody line abounds in patterns of free ornamentation that are closely allied to the spirit of rapturous improvisation. He writes in an advanced, freely chromatic idiom whose highly charged dissonances can be characterized as post-tonal; they may follow tonal drives, yet as frequently lean toward the atonal. Significant are the fluctuations of tempo. Underlined by changes in dynamics, these become a form-building element in his style. Kirchner's music is propelled by powerful rhythms that suggest the turbulent world of emotion out of which they sprang. His intensity derives from an inner state of exaltation verging on ecstasy; yet this exaltation goes hand in hand with an impressive command of large-scale structure. Kirchner's sense of form depends upon his power to generate and sustain tension over large areas. In his later works he moves toward stable forms which follow ample classical patterns, using passages of tonal harmony to round out and define the structure. The method of construction most congenial to his taste is additive, as he himself has indicated: "A few measures, an idea, constitute a gesture; the purpose of the work as a whole is to extend this in time. A phrase sets up the need for balance and extension which is satisfied by what follows. This then constitutes a larger complex which sets up still more implications. The entire piece is built up and forms an entity with infinite implications." His forms combine the continuous-expansion principle of the Baroque with the thematic-motivic processes of the classic-romantic era. They follow a line of inner growth that is organic, therefore convincing.

Most important of Kirchner's earlier compositions are the Piano Sonata of 1948, a work of unmistakable creative afflatus, and the String Quartet No. 1 (1949), which he dedicated to Roger Sessions. This searching piece, marked by inwardness of spirit, is in the tradition of the Bartók quartets. The *Little Suite for Solo Piano* (1949) in five short movements—Prelude, Song, Toccata, Fantasy, and Epilogue— is a fine example of contemporary music accessible to the amateur. Two works for soprano and piano, both on texts of Walt Whitman— *Of Obedience* and *The Runner*—date from 1950. Kirchner's mature orchestral writing stands fully revealed in the *Sinfonia* of 1950. The piece was comissioned by Rodgers and Hammerstein for the League of Composers, and received the Naumburg Foundation Award. "Most great music," Kirchner wrote at this time, "is highly technically oriented. In order to produce a powerful musical vision and revelation, a composer must have extraordinary technical equipment. Composers of any period must create their own technical equipment; that, in fact, is what we call style." The evolution of his highly individual style may be traced in the five major works that followed: *Sonata Concertante* for violin and piano (1952); the Piano Concerto, which we will discuss; a Trio for violin, cello, and piano (1954), which was commissioned by the Elizabeth Sprague Coolidge Foundation; a Toccata for strings, solo winds, and percussion (1955); and the String Quartet No. 2 (1957), which was written for the Fromm Foundation.

CONCERTO FOR PIANO AND ORCHESTRA

Kirchner is best known for his Piano Concerto (1953), a large-scale, visionary work cast in a tensely expressive idiom that marshals all the resources of chromaticism. In this piece he revives the grand style of the concerto in which piano, pitted dramatically against orchestra, dominates the scene. An excellent pianist himself, Kirchner treats the solo instrument with great originality. His writing, by turns brilliant, introspective, impassioned, and lyrical—one passage is marked *tenderly*—harks back to the romantic piano style, although the moods of tension and suspense that dominate much of this work could have issued only out of twentieth-century expressionism. The piano part is fantastically difficult. As with the nineteenth-century masters who were Kirchner's models, he never treats virtuosity as an end in itself but makes it subservient throughout to the expression of thought and feeling.

I. *Allegro.* The introductory passage on the piano establishes B-flat as the point of departure for the movement. It also presents the dotted rhythm and the interval of a diminished fifth (tritone) which become form-building elements in the work. (The diminished fifth is indicated by brackets.)

With these is associated the interval of a semitone, brought into prominence by the piano accompaniment and then presented as a triplet
figure by the bassoon. In a work as chromatic as this, the half-tone
inevitably is prominent, both melodically and harmonically. Kirchner's
materials are of the simplest. It is only in the course of the piece that
the themes and motives reveal their capacity for growth and development. In this structural approach he is the classicist. The expansion of
the basic material into melodic and rhythmic forms is carried out most
imaginatively, and with sovereign command of developmental technique.

The solo part ranges unrestrainedly across the keyboard, deriving
from this freedom of movement some of its urgency. Characteristic is
the way Kirchner uses xylophone and celesta to offset the piano tone.
The cadenzas abound in *fioriture*, a revival of the Baroque ideal of
improvised embellishment. An extraordinary sonority—muted violas
and cellos, harmonics on three solo violins, tremolo on the celesta, and
fluttertonguing on flute and piccolo—ushers in an Andante whose
soaring contrapuntal lines center about C minor. This culminates in an
appassionato that shows Kirchner's far-flung melodic imagery:

The ensuing cadenza unfolds in a memorable display of pianistic
fantasy. The minor-second motive is prominent both here and in the
whirlwind section that serves as a shortened Recapitulation and Coda.
At the very end trombones, cellos, and double basses present the basic
motive of semitone and diminished fifth. The final harmony is an
eleventh chord on B-flat. The effect is that of a polychord:

II. The profoundly introspective slow movement is the legitimate progeny of the brooding "night-piece" of Bartók. Flickering sounds on piano, celesta, and flutes evoke a hidden landscape of the soul. A solo bassoon traces a melodic line whose intervals are related to what has gone before.

Passages of lyric meditation on the piano alternate with dramatic recitatives in the orchestra, in an impassioned dialogue whose model obviously is the Adagio of Beethoven's G-major Concerto. Dotted rhythms impart tension to a florid cantilena in the lower strings. The movement culminates in another fantasy-like cadenza which, within its twentieth-century setting, has an indefinably Chopinesque ring. Presently the first violins burst into a melody whose roulades capture the spirit of rapturous song.

The movement ends pianissimo on a serene polychord that combines the B and G major triads.

III. Dotted rhythm comes into its own in the impetuous finale. Piano and orchestra thrust against one another in dissonant masses of sound that conjure up an atmosphere of violence, through which resound the stentorian pronouncements of the orchestra. The changes of tempo that Kirchner is so fond of not only clarify the formal scheme but also, through effective contrast, set off the dominant mood. An interlude that recalls the slow movement serves to slacken the tension. The headlong pace is resumed in a battle between piano and orchestra, with powerful reiterated chords falling like hammer blows on the crest of the movement. Powerful tensions are generated from the interaction of the two sound-masses, which propel the finale to a cadence of explosive energy.

"A great piece of music," Kirchner has stated, "sets up a kind of anxiety as it unfolds: what will happen next? What follows then produces a kind of catharsis. In this way, music that has real quality stirs something in the human consciousness; if one listens intently, one cannot help but be a changed human being." This ideal view of music is rooted in the humanism of a past age. Leon Kirchner has reinterpreted the great tradition in terms that are profoundly relevant to our own time.

✑ 104 ✎

Other Expressionist Composers

MIRIAM GIDEON (Greeley, Colorado, 1906–) has adopted the atonal idiom to her own expressive purposes. She writes well for the voice, as in *Three Sonnets by Edna St. Vincent Millay*, for high voice and string trio (1952). Her instrumental works include *Lyric Pieces* for string orchestra (1941), a string quartet (1946), and *Three Masks* for violin and piano (1958).

Ezra Laderman (New York City, 1924–) is one of the consistently productive composers of his generation. Laderman's works divide into two groups. The most personal line in his music is manifest in a series of chamber compositions which use the thematic idea as the basis for a continuous process of development. These are ample sonata forms couched in an atonal-chromatic idiom. In this category are the Sonata for Violin and Cello (1955); the String Quartet of 1958; and *Stanzas* for twenty-one solo instruments (1959). In his theater works Laderman writes in a tonal style marked by lyricism and simplicity. From this line of thought stem such works as the one-act opera *Sarah* (1958); *The Hunting of the Snark*, after Lewis Carroll (1960); the dance-drama *Esther* (1960); and *The Eagles Stirred*, an oratorio (1961).

Billy Jim Layton (Corsicana, Texas, 1924–) is one of the talented composers among the younger men. His works include *Five Studies for Violin and Piano*, a string quartet and a piano sonata, all dating from 1952; the choral work *Twenty-four Years* (1955); and the "symphonic overture" *An American Portrait* (1959). Robert Starer (Vienna, 1924–) came to the United States in 1947. Among his works are two symphonies (1950, 1953); the Piano Concerto No. 2 (1955);

The Intruders, a one-act opera (1957); the Viola Concerto (1959); and a full-length ballet, *The Dybbuk* (1960). Starer teaches at the Juilliard School of Music.

Gunther Schuller (New York, 1925–) is one of the best known among the new crop of American composers. His writing displays the influences to which the younger generation has been responsive. On the one hand, he has been affected by the rhythmic freedom and instrumental innovations of experimental jazz. On the other, he has absorbed the serial techniques of the twelve-tone method, which he handles in an unorthodox and quite personal manner. He leans toward an expressively chromatic atonal idiom, which he uses with poetic imagination and a flair for vivid timbres. His output is devoted to abstract instrumental works. Among them are a Cello Concerto and a Suite for woodwind quintet (1945); a Cello Sonata (1946); *Fantasia Concertante*, for three oboes and piano (1947); a Trio for oboe, horn, and viola (1948); and a Quintet for four horns and bassoon (1949). In the *Symphony for Brass and Percussion* (1950) Schuller explores the expressive capacities of the brass choir in a novel fashion. *Contours* for chamber orchestra (1956) exemplifies his capacity for evoking poetic sounds. The list also includes *Dramatic Overture* (1951); *Five Pieces for Five Horns* (1952); *Recitative and Rondo*, for violin and piano (1953); *12 by 11*, for chamber orchestra and jazz improvisation (1955); *Sonata for Oboe and Piano* (1958); and String Quartet (1958). *Modern Jazz: Variants* (1961), music for a ballet with choreography by George Balanchine, abounds in exciting sonorities and rhythms.

Seymour Schifrin (Brooklyn, New York, 1926–) is assistant professor of music at the University of California at Berkeley. He is represented on records by the *Serenade for Five Instruments* (oboe, clarinet, French horn, viola and piano), which was commissioned by the Juilliard School of Music as part of its fiftieth anniversary festival in 1956. The title, Schifrin points out, "derives primarily from the character of the slow middle movement and the relative directness and simplicity of the formal procedures used throughout." The piece shows how deeply the composer has been affected by twelve-tone thinking. It illustrates Schifrin's highly selective method of writing, and the rather rarefied texture that he achieves thereby.

Yehudi Wyner (Calgary, Canada, 1929–) evolved from Hindemith's kind of neo-classicism to Stravinsky's. He then moved toward a greater involvement with more chromatic materials, and has been most profoundly influenced by Schoenbergian music, although he has never used serial techniques. His affinity is for ample instrumental works that display sustained lyricism of an introspective cast. His compositions include *Dance Variations* for wind septet and cello (1953); a striking Piano Sonata (1954); *Concert Duo* for violin and piano (1959); and *Serenade for Seven Instruments* (1958). Wyner has also written choral and organ music, piano pieces, and songs.

XV. TWELVE-TONE COMPOSERS

> "The abandonment of keys does not necessarily mean the complete negation of 'music,' as some excellent but conservative musicians seem to think, but rather its potential enrichment in the discovery of new tonalities, with new possibilities of texture, both harmonic and polyphonic, of melody (albeit in a new guise) and of form—all of which I felt to be not only in the line of historical development, but above all truly expressive of the age in which we live, while losing nothing of the universally human."
>
> Wallingford Riegger

❧ 105 ❧
Wallingford Riegger (1885-1961)

> "When I undertook to create, it was in spite of my environment."

WALLINGFORD RIEGGER'S music made its way slowly, for its qualities were not such as impress the crowd. It was not until he reached his sixties that he was recognized as one of the truly substantial figures of his generation.

HIS LIFE

Riegger was born in Albany, Georgia. His parents, who came from Indianapolis, moved to New York when the future composer was fourteen. He first played the violin, then changed to the cello. A scholarship sent him to Cornell for a year, after which he returned to New York and entered the newly founded Institute of Musical Art. Upon his graduation two years later he went to Berlin, where he attended the Hochschule and concentrated on the cello, also studying composition with Max Bruch and Edgar Stillman Kelley. "I blushingly admit to having upheld at that time good old academic tradition, so much so that at the first Berlin performance of Scriabin's *Poème de l'Extase* I hissed in exactly the same manner as did the Philadelphia boxholders twenty years later when Stokowski gave my own *Study in Sonority*."

Riegger taught at Drake University, at the Institute of Musical Art and at the Conservatory in Ithaca. During these years he made his first attempts at composing, and gradually freed himself from subservience to the German tradition. Upon his return to New York he became friendly with the pioneers of the modern movement in America —Charles Ives, Carl Ruggles, Edgar Varèse, and Henry Cowell. "We had rejected the neo-classicism of a war-weary Paris and had struck out for ourselves, each in his own way. We formed the Pan-American

AMP

Wallingford Riegger

Association of Composers and gave, at a tremendous expense of time and energy, numerous concerts both here and abroad."

In the meantime Riegger persisted doggedly at what he has called "the expensive luxury of composing." His works accumulated slowly, separated by periods of unproductiveness. "To turn an honest penny I made several hundred choral arrangements"—the list ranges from Palestrina to *Tea for Two*—"wrote a couple of violin methods, and did editing, proofreading and even copying." Nevertheless he managed to sustain the psychic tension that enables a man to go on creating. The opus numbers mounted up, year after year. Recognition came gradually, first among discerning musicians—particularly the younger men, who responded to the special quality of Riegger's music—then among the critics and public. In 1947 his Third Symphony was commissioned by the Alice M. Ditson fund of Columbia University. A sum of five hundred dollars was added for copying the parts, which prompted the composer to remark, "It is my first composition which has not cost me money." The symphony brought Riegger's music to the attention of a wider audience than had ever known it before. After a lifetime of dedicated effort he found himself occupying the position to which his gifts entitled him.

HIS MUSIC

Riegger found his style through the Schoenbergian technique, which freed him from dependence on the classic-romantic heritage. He uses the twelve-tone language in a highly personal way. Despite his commitment to atonality, he will revert to tonal writing when it suits his needs. So too he feels free to depart from orthodox tone-row procedure when necessary. "The idiom to me is secondary, depending on the nature of the musical idea. A man who writes dry music in the twelve-tone technique will do so in any style."

Given this independent approach, Riegger has most ingeniously combined dodecaphonic techniques with elements drawn from the classical tradition. While using a twelve-note series he will derive motives which he proceeds to develop in the traditional manner; and he creates focal points in the harmonic texture that take over the function of tonic and dominant. Riegger's mature period opens with the *Study in Sonority* for ten violins (or any multiple of ten, 1927), which sets forth his approach to the problems of texture, harmony, rhythm, and form; as do also the witty *Canons for Woodwinds* (1931) and the *Fantasy and Fugue* for orchestra and organ (1931). *Dichotomy*, for chamber orchestra (1932), is based on two opposing tone rows; hence the title. It is one of Riegger's strongest works. In the First String Quartet (1938), which displays his strict use of twelve-tone technique, discipline and logic serve to strengthen the emotion. The Second String Quartet, completed a decade later, is in a modified twelve-tone style. The *Canon and Fugue* for strings (1941) is one of Riegger's best known works; as is the *New Dance* (1942), which has won popularity not only as an orchestral piece but also in its two-piano version. (The composer arranged it for other combinations as well.) *Music for Brass Choir* (1949), scored for ten trumpets, four (or eight) horns, ten trombones, two tubas, and timpani, comes out of a bold instrumental imagination. Symphony No. 4, one of Riegger's most important works, was first heard in 1957. The foregoing are the principal items in a varied list that centers about orchestral, chamber, and choral pieces.

SYMPHONY NO. 3, OPUS 24

The Third Symphony (1948; revised in 1957 as Opus 42) was written when the composer was sixty-three. It displays Riegger's mastery of twelve-tone devices, and shows as well the distinction of his thought, the resiliency of his rhythms, the compactness of his forms. Lyric simplicity and dramatic urgency mark this work, which ranks high among the American symphonies of our time.

I. *Moderato—Allegro.* The tone row on which the movement is based is presented, after a three-measure introduction, as a lyric theme on the oboe:

The basic series is immediately transformed by the first violins into a continuous pattern of sixteenth notes, which serves as a background for the other lines:

"After the brass," Riegger wrote, "has asserted itself rather positively and at some length, there is a simmering down to prepare for the subordinate theme, consisting of soaring blocks in the upper register of the violins." In accordance with the classical conception of the symphony, the second theme does not rival the first in importance, but represents only a momentary slackening in the forward thrust of the movement. Riegger follows the contemporary practice of shortening the Recapitulation. Indeed, the second theme does not appear in it at all. "Its place is taken," he explains, "by fugue-like treatment of the first seven notes of the series, which serves as a coda."

II. *Andante affettuoso.* The meditative lyricism of the opening passage is typical of the composer. The theme, presented by the wood-

winds, is taken from *With My Red Fire,* a dance that Riegger composed in 1936 for Doris Humphrey. "Nothing has been changed," Riegger points out, "for sixteen measures; then, instead of drum beats, the strings intercede to continue the mood." Wide leaps give the melody line its sweeping contours. The movement builds up to a fortissimo statement of the chorale-like, sinuously chromatic theme. There follows a fugato in which a rhythmically vital subject, announced by English horn and clarinets, is imitated first by the bassoon, then by the flute. Excitement dies down. The opening sixteen bars are repeated with fuller instrumentation, leading to a pianissimo ending.

III. *Moderato.* The third movement is a Scherzo, marked by a sharpness of gesture and rhythmic vibrancy that stem from the ballet. This almost pantomimic quality, infused with humor, rests on a physical vitality that is underlined by the angular melody line. An extended fugal passage in the center of the movement has a striking subject, in which intervals of a major seventh and augmented octave play a de-

cisive role. Just before the end of the movement the mood of the opening returns.

IV. *Beginning rather slowly—Allegro.* The finale is cast in the form of a passacaglia and fugue. The theme of the passacaglia is a phrase of five measures presented by the double basses, in which the interval of a major seventh is prominent.

The theme, Riegger states, "is eventually taken up by other instruments, culminating in excited pizzicato passages (compressed statements of the theme) leading into a lively and energetic fugue." Marked *Allegro feroce,* the fugue abounds in intervals native to the twelve-

tone style—minor seconds, major sevenths, augmented fourths. "Finally the passacaglia theme reappears, this time in the violins, answered in the basses and leading into a sustained climax, with which the movement ends." Notice that the fugue is a variant of the passacaglia.

With its fertility of invention and integrity of style, this music bespeaks a mind that thinks spontaneously in terms of symphonic and contrapuntal procedures. It reveals Wallingford Riegger to be one of our most distinguished and independent composers.

◄§ 106 §►

Ernst Krenek (1900-)

"Twelve-tone technique, like any other technical means, is sensible in so far as it increases the mastery of the human mind over natural resources."

ERNST KRENEK grew up in Vienna, where he studied with Franz Schreker. In his development as a composer he passed through several phases. Starting out from the post-Mahler romanticism that prevailed in the Vienna of his youth, he was drawn into the extreme experimentation of the early Twenties, as is apparent from his first two symphonies (1921–22). At the same time he responded to the neo-classic impulse toward stabilization of the modern idiom. This influence shaped such works as the two *Concerti grossi* (1921, 1924); the first four string quartets (1921–24); and the Symphony for wind instruments and percussion (1925). Krenek then found his way to what he described as "the aggressive idiom of atonality, whose main organizing agency was elemental rhythmic force." Combining this with elements of jazz, he produced the opera *Jonny spielt auf!* (Johnny plays!, 1927), on his own libretto. The work was translated into eighteen languages, was heard in more than a hundred opera houses, and gave Krenek an international reputation.

The neo-classic, atonal, and jazz phases in Krenek's career were followed, significantly, by a return to romanticism of an almost Schubertian kind. Thenceforward the road led to the dodecaphonic technique, in which he finally found what he had been seeking—"a very high degree of logical coherence and intelligible significance." His first important work in the twelve-tone idiom was the grandiose

Karl V (Charles V), which was completed in 1933. The opera was caught in the gathering political storms of the Thirties. Krenek was one of a number of contemporary composers whose work was banned from the Third Reich because they were guilty of *Kulturbolshevismus*. Although *Karl V* had been commissioned by the Vienna Opera, Nazi pressure succeeded in preventing the production. In 1938, the year of Hitler's annexation of Austria, Krenek joined the contingent of European musicians who found a haven in the United States.

He was professor of composition at Vassar College from 1939 till 1942, when he became head of the music department at Hamline University in Minnesota. He became an American citizen in 1945, and two years later moved to California. In recent years he has avoided a permanent teaching post, although he has given courses at various universities—Michigan, Wisconsin, New Mexico. He makes his home in Los Angeles.

Krenek is one of the most prolific composers of our time. He gave up using opus numbers after his ninety-sixth work. His "irrepressible fecundity," as someone called it, has by now produced a list of over a hundred and twenty works. Among them are eleven operas, three ballets, incidental music for seven plays; about thirty choral pieces, including the *Lamentations of the Prophet Jeremiah*, for unaccompanied chorus (1942), and *The Santa Fé Time Table* (1947), in which a chorus intones the names of stations on the Santa Fé Railroad from Albuquerque to Los Angeles; a diversified collection of songs and piano pieces, including six piano sonatas; five symphonies; four piano concertos; and eight string quartets. He has also written several books, the best-known of which has been translated into English as *Music Here and Now* (1939). Krenek is a severely intellectual composer who has relinquished the desire to reach the big public. His music bristles with complexities, makes no concessions, and is an authoritative expression of certain advanced tendencies in twentieth-century musical thought.

◈ 107 ◈
Erich Itor Kahn (1905-1956)

To THE structural logic and concentrated thought of twelve-tone writing, Erich Itor Kahn brought the warmth of a lyric temperament. His was a highly personal music in which refined craftsmanship was joined to subtlety of feeling and expression: a music suffused with the composer's total dedication to his vision of artistic truth.

Kahn was born in Germany, at Rimbach-im-Odenwald. He grew up in Koenigstein, in a musical home, and showed his talent at an early age. His discovery of Schoenberg's music—at a time when the master was practically unknown outside a small circle—was a turning point in Kahn's development. He studied at the Frankfurt Conservatory and in 1928, at the age of twenty-three, joined the staff of the radio station in Frankfurt, where he worked in an atmosphere sympathetic to the cause of contemporary music. This period in his life was brought to an end by Hitler. Kahn and his wife settled in Paris, where he was active as pianist, teacher, and composer until the outbreak of the Second World War brought another dislocation. The composer was interned in a succession of French military camps. In 1941 the Kahns made their way to the United States. (Frida Kahn's *Story of a Generation* vividly evokes the wanderings that were shared by so many thousands during those disjointed years.) Kahn continued his career in New York, where he founded the Albeneri Trio with Alexander Schneider as violinist and Benar Heifetz as cellist. He appeared in piano recitals, wrote his most important compositions, and was active in the musical community until his premature death.

The turbulent circumstances that attended so much of Kahn's life were not conducive to sustained creative effort. Also, a good deal of his time and energy went into his duties as a professional pianist. Hence he left behind a comparatively small number of completed works. But these show a striking creative gift and a sovereign command of the composer's craft. Kahn is best known for the *Ciaccona dei tempi di guerra* (Chaconne in Time of War, 1943), a monumental work for piano in which he handles the variation procedure with Baroque richness of invention and mastery of contrapuntal device. Based on a twelve-tone ground bass, the *Chaconne* is cast in a freely dissonant idiom which incorporates tonal elements. Both Beveridge Webster and the composer gave memorable performances of this powerful piece.

Of equal importance is the *Actus Tragicus* (Tragic Deed, 1947) for ten instruments, in which the lyric elements native to Kahn's style exist side by side with declamatory passages of a more dramatic kind. (Kahn borrowed the title from one of the cantatas of Bach.) This is a twelve-tone work in the form of a rondo, with the instruments treated in a soloistic manner. *Music for Ten Instruments and Soprano* was begun in 1927 but was not given its final form until 1953. The years in France (1933–40) saw the production of several pieces in a popular vein: Three Madrigals for mixed a cappella choir; *Hassidic Rhapsody* for unaccompanied men's voices; *Symphonies bretonnes* and *Petite Suite bretonne* for orchestra; and *Trois chansons populaires* for voice and piano. His later works include *Two Psalms for Mezzo Soprano and Piano* (1942); *Nenia Judaeis qui hoc aetate perierunt* (Lament for the Jews who Perished in this Age, 1943) for cello and piano; the String Quartet of 1953, one of Kahn's profoundest works; and *Four Nocturnes* (1954), among them a strikingly romantic setting of Victor Hugo's *Les Djinns*. Kahn also wrote a number of piano pieces, among them the *Eight Inventions* of 1937 and the *Six Bagatelles* of 1939.

Kahn found his point of departure in the serial technique as established by Schoenberg. But his flexible approach to this technique enabled him to strike a personal tone, and to realize the opportunities for lyric expression offered by the new idiom.

⤳ 108 ⤆
Twelve-Tone and Partly Twelve-Tone Composers

AMONG contemporary composers Stefan Wolpe (Berlin, 1902–), professor of composition at Post College, is a thorough-going original. He has been influenced by the rhythmic innovations of Stravinsky, as well as by the melodic and harmonic procedures of Bartók. At the same time he responded to the jazz influence that was so powerful in Germany in the Twenties; and during a four-year stay in Jerusalem assimilated elements of Hebrew, Yemenite, and Arab folk music. In his handling of dodecaphonic technique Wolpe aspires to total serialization. He has especially explored the harmonic implications of the twelve-tone system. He conceives of his music as moving from one harmonic region to the next, and considers the basic row to be not so much a succession of pitches as what he calls a "generic series." Each transposition of this series has its own structural and expressive function. Thus, one may be associated with canonic imitation, another with asymmetrical formations, a third with spatial proportions, and so on.

Wolpe came to the United States in 1939. Since then he has produced a number of works that bear the imprint of a personal style. Among them are the *Toccata in Three Movements*, for piano (1941); *The Man*

Twelve-tone, Partly Twelve-tone Composers 617

from Midian, a ballet on the life of Moses (1942); Sonata for Violin and Piano (1949); and the Quartet for Trumpet, Saxophone, Piano, and Drums (1950) which reflects the composer's interest in jazz. The later works include Enactments for Three Pianos (1951–53); Quartet for Oboe, Cello, Percussion, and Piano (1955); Quintet with Voice (1957); and *Form for Piano* (1959). Cast in an uncompromising idiom, these works bespeak the composer's severely intellectual preoccupations. They embody an intensely personal vision which Stefan Wolpe has pursued with a single-mindedness born of relentless dedication to his ideals.

Ross Lee Finney (Wells, Minnesota, 1906–) is composer-in-residence at the University of Michigan. His earlier works found their point of departure in the American heritage. His cantata *Pilgrim Psalms* (1945) is based on a selection of tunes from the Ainsworth Psalter. Folksong elements figure in the Piano Concerto of 1934, the *Barber Shop Ballad* for orchestra of 1937 and the Violin Concerto of 1944. In recent years Finney has joined the growing number of American composers who are finding a solution for their structural and stylistic problems in the tone-row procedures of twelve-tone music. The serial technique suits both the chromatic texture of his music and his desire for compactly integrated forms. At the same time his music retains its allegiance to tonality and the functional character of tonal harmony. Among Finney's important works are seven string quartets (it is in the Sixth, dating from 1950, that the new orientation is manifest); a number of sonatas—four for piano, and one each for viola and cello; a song cycle on poems of Archibald MacLeish (1937); and the *Communiqué* for orchestra (1943).

George Perle (Bayonne, New Jersey, 1915–) teaches at Queens College of the City University of New York. His earliest twelve-tone works date from 1939. From the beginning of his creative career, however, he has tried to expand the Schoenbergian concept to include the possibilities for harmonic tension and direction inherent in the major-minor system. Thus, in a language based on the twelve-tone scale, he has retained the concept of tonal centers and the traditional differentiation between the vertical and horizontal dimensions of music. In order to achieve a systematic organization of the harmonic material, he has modified the Schoenbergian canon by providing what he calls "harmonic modes" for twelve-tone music. These modes are generated by certain symmetrical tone-rows, as in his *Two Rilke Songs* (1941); Six Preludes for Piano (1946); Piano Sonata (1950); and the Rhapsody for Orchestra of 1953, which was commissioned by the Louisville

Orchestra and has been recorded. In the same stream of thought are Perle's *Three Movements for Orchestra* (1960), which received its premiere at the 1963 ISCM Festival in Amsterdam, and the Fifth String Quartet (1963).

Perle's preoccupation with the problem of making harmonic sense in non-diatonic music has led him also to compose a large number of monophonic works, in which the problem is resolved by the *absence* of harmony. Among the compositions that exemplify this trend are the Sonata for Solo Viola of 1942, *Monody I for Solo Flute* of 1960, and a number of works for unaccompanied clarinet, bassoon, violin, double bass, and other instruments. These works do not employ a tone row, but are freely conceived in a twelve-tone idiom that combines various serial details with melodically generated tone-centers, intervallic cells, symmetrical formations, and similar devices. Perle is among the composers who have been experimenting with a rhythmic concept based on a beat that is variable in duration but at the same time susceptible of coherent organization. The techniques he developed in the writing of his monophonic works were eventually incorporated in a number of polyphonic compositions, such as the Quintet for Strings (1958), one of his strongest works, which has been recorded; and the two Wind Quintets of 1959 and 1960. Perle is one of the leading theoreticians of contemporary music. His book, *Serial Composition and Atonality* (1962), is a milestone in its field. Of particular importance are his studies on Alban Berg, which he plans to incorporate in a book on Berg's operas.

Milton Babbitt (Philadelphia, 1916–) studied with Roger Sessions privately and at Princeton University, where he is now professor of music. A trained mathematician (he taught mathematics at Princeton during the war), Babbitt prizes the structural logic of the twelve-tone method. It is his conviction that "the twelve-tone set must absolutely determine *every* aspect of the piece." In other words, he applies serial procedures not only to pitch, but also to rhythm, dynamics, timbre, and register. He stands with those who believe in a strict application of dodecaphonic principles. Thus, he believes in maintaining the fixed order of the twelve tones in the vertical (harmonic) as well as horizontal (melodic) succession. One need hardly add that Babbitt is a severely intellectual composer. "I believe in cerebral music," he has stated, "and I never choose a note unless I know why I want it there." And to the same point: "The structural idea is the idea from which I begin." The result is a music concentrated in thought, complex in facture, and marked by the utmost degree of organic unity, which embodies the composer's ideal of "a really autonomous music that does not depend upon analogies with tonal music."

Babbitt feels that one should no more expect the layman to understand advanced present-day music than one would expect him to understand advanced physics or mathematics. The serious composer today should therefore accept his isolation from the public as a necessary condition of his functioning, and should proceed to develop the resources of his art in works neither suitable nor intended for the average listener. Only in this way, he believes, can music continue to evolve along its own path, unhampered by the prejudices of the uninitiated. Babbitt's list includes *Three Compositions for Piano* (1947); *Composition for Twelve Instruments* (1948), which has been widely played in Europe; *Composition for Viola and Piano* (1950); *Du*, a song cycle (1951); Woodwind Quartet (1953); String Quartet No. 2 (1954); *All Set*, for seven jazz instrumentalists (1957); and *Composition for Tenor and Six Instruments* (1960). Babbitt has taught at the Salzburg Seminar in American Studies (1952), at the Berkshire Music Center in Tanglewood (1957, 1958), and at the Princeton Seminar in Advanced Musical Studies (1959, 1960).

With his scientific turn of mind, it is only natural that Babbitt is very much preoccupied with electronic media. As far back as 1939 he became interested in the handwritten sound track, and in 1947 began to apply the operations of the twelve-tone system to non-pitch elements. He is one of the directors of the Electronic Music Center operated jointly by Columbia and Princeton Universities, and has given much thought to the possibilities for musical expression offered by the newly developed RCA Synthesizer. (Ernst Krenek describes him as "the only man thus far who both speaks our language and can also communicate with the machine.") Babbitt has received a Guggenheim Fellowship for the purposes of research in electronic music, and a commission from the Fromm Foundation for a composition in this field.

Ben Weber (St. Louis, Missouri, 1916–), one of the most musical among the younger Schoenbergians, shows a poetic sensibility. His works lie in the region between atonal chromaticism and the twelve-tone system. He is not committed to that system the way some of his dodecaphonic colleagues are, for he will use whatever technique at any given moment serves his expressive goal. His piano compositions take their point of departure from the short pieces of Schoenberg. The Five Bagatelles, Opus 2 (1939) display his sensitivity to the instrument, as do the two Suites—especially the Second, Opus 27 (1948)—and the impressive Fantasia, Opus 25 (1946). Weber's lyricism finds outlet in a number of distinguished songs, several of them on texts of Rilke. Like Schoenberg and Alban Berg he favors the solo song with orchestral or chamber-music accompaniment. This predilection is manifest in his setting of Rilke's *Lied des Idioten*, Opus 10, for soprano and orchestra; the *Concert Aria after Solomon*, Opus 29 (1949), for soprano and wind quintet, violin, cello, and piano; and the *Symphony in Four Movements on Poems of William Blake*, for baritone and chamber orchestra, Opus 33 (1950). Weber has a natural affinity for chamber music, as is evident from his two string quartets and two sonatas for violin and piano; *Serenade* for harpsichord, flute, oboe, and cello, Opus 39 (1954); and a number of compositions in intimate chamber style. Yet in both his Violin Concerto, Opus 41 (1954) and the *Prelude and Passacaglia for Orchestra*, Opus 42 (1955) he displays an impressive capacity for lyricism on a larger scale.

George Rochberg (Paterson, New Jersey, 1918–) stands in the forefront of those who find that the twelve-tone method stimulates their imagination and strengthens the flow of their ideas. "Perhaps the greatest danger of the serial method," he writes, "lies in its tendency to induce a sterile and mechanical academicism, especially if it is treated as both means and end. To balance this push in the direction of technique with the pull of expressive needs—this seems to me to constitute the core of the composer's concern with his art." Rochberg feels that the twelve-tone technique opens to the composer a new dimension of human feeling and thought. "For me, the vocabulary of the twelve tones and the potentialities of serial devices correspond with the need to speak in terms which are synonymous with a new way of hearing and imagining sound. As these terms are better understood and mastered, the greater are the possibilities for projecting them in works which realize more and more fully the unique and personal expressive needs of the composer."

Rochberg's list of works includes the orchestral piece *Night Music* (1952); two symphonies (1949, 1956); *Songs of Innocence and Experience* for voice and chamber ensemble (1957); and a number of chamber works, such as the String Quartet No. 1 (1952), *Dialogues for Clarinet and Piano* (1957), Duo for oboe and piano (1959), and the *Cheltenham Concerto* for chamber orchestra, which won first prize at the Rome Festival of Contemporary Music in 1959. The Second Symphony shows how effectively Rochberg has adapted the dodecaphonic technique to his expressive needs. The basic row from which the symphony derives is divided into groups of six tones—hexachords, the composer calls them—that are used with great imagination and constructive skill. There results a work that, within the serial procedure, achieves the sense of inner logic and dynamic development basic to large-scale form.

⤳ 109 ⤲
Mel Powell (1923-)

HIS LIFE AND MUSIC

MEL POWELL, who teaches at Yale University, was born in New York City. He became a jazz pianist while still in his teens, and made his reputation playing in Benny Goodman's band. After three years in the Army Air Force he found himself in Hollywood on the threshold of a promising career in popular music. He had already studied composition with Bernard Wagenaar and with the mathematico-musical theorist Joseph Schillinger; he now continued with Ernst Toch. His early works show his preoccupation with the twelve-tone method. At this juncture Powell and his wife, the actress Martha Scott, came east; Powell became a pupil of Hindemith at Yale.

From Hindemith Powell acquired a neo-classic orientation later buttressed by his study of Stravinsky's scores; ultimately he passed into a form of post-Webernism. Within this frame Powell evolved a language of his own marked by a fastidious musicality. His is an art of the utmost economy, in which predominate the classical virtues of moderation, proportion, and carefully wrought form. His intellectual preoccupations are warmed by grace and humor; his polished craftsmanship delights in spinning pure patterns of sound.

Powell's natural affinity for intimate expression finds an ideal outlet in chamber music. His Trio for piano, violin, and cello, which received its premiere in New York in 1957, is a fine contribution to the contemporary literature. The piece has been recorded, as has his Divertimento for violin and harp (1955) and the Divertimento for Five Winds (1955). A special work is the *Recitative and Toccata Percossa for Harpsichord* (1954), in which the brilliance of the Scarlatti style is evoked in twentieth-century terms.

In recent years Powell has returned to the serial procedures that formerly interested him. His bright sonorities tend to avoid the intensely emotional atmosphere that sometimes goes with total chromaticism. In the Piano Quintet (1957), commissioned by the Koussevitzky Foundation and first performed in 1959 at the Library of Congress, he bases serial manipulation on intervals rather than on pitches. A similar design is found in *Eight Miniatures for Baroque Ensemble* (1958), which was played in Europe in the summer and fall of 1959 and heard in New York the following spring. These works, Powell points out, "reflect my innate distrust of the *Sehnsucht* and central European self-pity that has colored so much recent music."

Powell's new direction is manifest in *Stanzas* for chamber orchestra (1959), a piece which shows the fascination that Webern's music exercises upon our younger composers. In an article on Webern in the *New York Times* Powell described the nature of this attraction: "The beauty and precision of the miniature, the intense expressivity of a purged art, the essential directness and simplicity of statement, once its strange surface has been penetrated—these already symbolize an affirmation which, true to its own nature, will not be shouted."

FILIGREE SETTING FOR STRING QUARTET

Filigree Setting for String Quartet (1960) exemplifies the preoccupations of the post-Webern school of composers, especially the new ways of handling total serialization. In this piece serial controls are applied not only to pitch, rhythm, and timbre, but also to register, rate of speed, direction of melodic intervals, and density of texture. The basic series itself—whether of pitches, rhythms, or timbres—is subject to permutation, which makes possible an extremely flexible approach to the twelve-tone method. Not only does pitch lose its favored position as the ultimate determinant of musical structure, but the emphasis lies on the relations between the components of the series rather than upon the components themselves. Nor is it difficult to see why this should be so. As music becomes more complex, the number and the kind of things happening simultaneously are increased so that it is ever more difficult to grasp details; hence greater stress must be put on the relations which determine those details and reveal them in their true perspective.

In *Filigree Setting* Powell, within his own style, pursues a goal similar to Stockhausen's—that is, he seeks to reconcile the freedom of improvisation with the rigor of a predetermined score, to unite seemingly random elements within the frame of a controlled form. He goes even further than Stockhausen by exploiting the contrast between definite pitches and indeterminate ("non-pitched"), purely percussive sounds: for instance, drumming with the fingers on different parts of the instrument, or producing "random" pitches by stopping the strings with the wood of the bow instead of with the fingers. It becomes apparent that the distinction between musical sound and what used to be regarded as noise is not quite as rigid as was hitherto supposed. As in Stockhausen's *Zeitmasse,* passages are marked "as quickly as possible,"

the exact tempo depending on the player's dexterity. These indeterminate speeds, functioning as free rhythm, alternate with fixed tempos
common to all four players, and are strictly co-ordinated within the
over-all rhythmic structure. By combining new tone colors and new
ways of handling the string instruments with four distinctly different
rates of speed, Powell achieves effects unlike anything in the previous
quartet literature.

From the structural point of view, the serialization of all the elements
of music forces the composer to limit his possibilities; for, as the number of ways of varying material is increased, the actual number of
items he is working with will tend to be reduced. In *Filigree Setting*
Powell works with a three-note nucleus rather than with a twelve-
tone row. The three notes can be presented in three different arrangements, each of which has its retrograde. These six forms can be inverted, which gives twelve permutations of the three basic notes (O =
original, R = retrograde).

The three-note cell is similar to the one which opens and closes the
basic set of Webern's Opus 29 (see page 397); but Powell draws entirely different implications from the material. His thematic use of the
nuclei is apparent from the following melody in the first violin part.

The four lines intermingle in a filigree of striking sonorities and fanciful arabesques. The esthetic goal is the same as in traditional music: a
maximum of diversity within a maximum of unity. It is the means for
attaining this goal that have changed. The emphasis on single notes is
characteristic of present-day writing, as is the interest in pure sonority
and pure rhythm. The music has a high emotive content, which is projected in alternations of dramatic tension and lyric relaxation. Most
important of all, the interpenetration of musical sounds and "noise" approaches the limits of what can be done using the instruments of the
past. In effect, *Filigree Setting* points to the electronic future.

XVI. EXPERIMENTALISTS

"Our musical alphabet must be enriched. Speed and synthesis are characteristic of our epoch. We need twentieth-century instruments to help us realize those in music."

Edgar Varèse

⋙ 110 ⋘
Edgar Varèse (1885-)

"I refuse to submit myself only to sounds that have already been heard."

EDGAR VARÈSE is one of the truly original spirits in the music of our time. The innovations of Stravinsky, Schoenberg, and Bartók unfolded within the frame of the traditional elements of their art, but Varèse went a step farther: he rejected certain of those elements altogether.

HIS LIFE

Varèse was born in Paris of Italian-French parentage. He studied mathematics and science at school, since his father intended him for an engineering career. But at eighteen he entered the Schola Cantorum, where he worked with Vincent d'Indy and Roussel, and later was admitted to the master class of Charles-Marie Widor at the Paris Conservatoire. In 1909 he went to Berlin, where he founded a chorus devoted to the performance of old music. During this time he became a close friend of Busoni, who strongly influenced his thinking.

With the outbreak of war in 1914 Varèse was mobilized into the French army, but was discharged the following year after a serious illness. He came to the United States in December, 1915, when he was thirty, and lost no time in making a place for himself in the musical life of his adopted land. He organized an orchestra in New York City that devoted itself to contemporary works, but became increasingly aware that there was no audience for new music in this country. Accordingly, in 1921 he and Carlos Salzedo founded the International Composers' Guild, for the express purpose of presenting the music of living composers. In the six years of its existence the Guild presented works by fifty-six composers of fourteen nationalities, including the first performances in this country of Schoenberg's *Pierrot Lunaire* and Stravinsky's *Les Noces,* and introduced to America such composers as Webern, Berg, Chávez and Ruggles.

The greater part of Varèse's music was written during the Twenties and early Thirties. He found a champion in Leopold Stokowski, who performed his scores despite the violent opposition they aroused in conventionally minded concert goers. Then, like his colleagues Ives and Ruggles, Varèse fell silent when he should have been at the height of his powers. During the next twenty years he followed the new scientific developments in the field of electronic instruments, and resumed composing in 1952, when he began to work on *Deserts.*

By that time the scene had changed; there existed a public receptive to experimental music. When an enterprising record company made available four of his works, Varèse was enabled to reach an audience that had never before heard his music. He was invited by the State Department to conduct master classes in composition in Darmstadt, Germany. The younger generation of European composers who were experimenting with tape-recorded music suddenly discovered him as one whose work had been prophetic of theirs. The long-neglected master finally came into his own.

HIS MUSIC

Several important currents within the mainstream of contemporary music came together in Varèse's works; the desire to root out private feelings from art and to achieve a completely objective style; the spirit of urbanism, and the attempt to evoke the imagery of a machine civilization; the rejection of tonal harmony; the interest in primitivism, with its revitalization of rhythm and its attendant emphasis on the percussive instruments; the attempt to return music to its pristine sources, and to mold it into architectural forms as pure sound. Given Varèse's early training in science and his mathematical turn of mind, it was almost inevitable that he would be sensitive to these trends. He adopted a frankly experimental attitude toward his art that placed him among the extreme radicals of our time.

The abstract images that brood over Varèse's music are derived from the life of the big city: the rumble of motors, the clang of hammers, the shriek and hiss and shrilling of factory whistles, turbines, steam drills. His stabbing, pounding rhythms conjure up the throb and hum of the metropolis. There is a steely hardness, a cutting edge to Varèse's music. Its tensions result from the collision of sound masses. Its sense of distance comes from the superposition of sonorous planes. Understandably, Varèse's expressive goal led him away from melody and harmony, the principal elements of the classic-romantic style. The ingredients of his music are pure sonority and pure rhythm. The harmonic texture as such is strongly dissonant, consisting mainly of minor seconds or ninths and major sevenths. Hence the glitter and tension of this music, which is animated by his intricate counterpoint of rhythms. In this area Varèse is one of the prime innovators of our time. His powerfully kinetic rhythms recall the complex percussive patterns of African and Far Eastern music. It follows that his attention is focused on that group in the orchestra which stands closest to sheer sonority and rhythm, the percussion, which he handles with inexhaustible invention.

It goes without saying that his music does not lend itself to the conventional procedures of thematic-motivic development. Varèse works with rhythmic-sonorous cells that continue to be transformed as long as the music lasts. His sound pieces have a surprising unity. They are precisely calculated, written in a stripped, laconic style that makes for economy and refinement of means. He rejects the romantic interest in timbre for its own sake. "I do not use sounds impressionistically as the impressionist painters used colors. In my music they are an intrinsic part of the structure." This lapidary music unfolds in geometrical patterns based on the opposition of sonorous planes and volumes— patterns which, in their abstraction, are the counterpart in sound of the designs of cubist painting. Varèse's music was utterly revolutionary in its day. It sounded like nothing that had ever been heard before.

The fanciful names Varèse gave his works indicate the connection in the composer's mind between his music and scientific processes. *Amériques* (1922), a symphonic poem making use of a large orchestra, is "a symbol of discovery: new worlds on earth, in the stars and in the minds of men." *Hyperprism* (1923) is for a chamber orchestra of two woodwinds, seven brass, and sixteen percussion instruments. The title, Varèse stated, "has a geometrical connotation and implies a fourth-dimensional significance." It is a neatly organized piece that communicates even to those who, like the present writer, know nothing about the fourth dimension. *Arcana* (1927), for orchestra, is one of the few works by Varèse that follow a traditional formal procedure. The piece develops a basic idea through melodic, rhythmic and instrumental variation, somewhat in the manner of a passacaglia.

Octandre (1924) is a chamber work for eight instruments—flute, clarinet, oboe, bassoon, horn, trumpet, trombone, and double bass—whose lines interweave in a polyphonic texture of freshness and brilliancy. *Intégrales* (1925) combines melodic writing for flutes, clarinets, trumpets, trombones, oboe and horn with the intricate percussive-

Varèse's music unfolds in geometric patterns which, in their abstraction, are the counterpart in sound of the designs of cubist painting. Georges Braque, *Oval Still Life*. (Collection Museum of Modern Art)

rhythm textures of a variegated battery handled by four players. *Ionisation* we will discuss in detail. Of Varèse's other works we should mention *Equatorial* (1934), for bass baritone, trumpets, trombones, organ, percussion, and thereminovox; and *Density 21.5*, written in 1935 for the inauguration of the platinum flute of Georges Barrère (21.5 is the specific gravity of platinum). Varèse's handling of unaccompanied melody in this work is notable for the illusion of depth achieved through his skillful exploitation of the different registers of the instrument.

Varèse's expressive needs impelled him to take an increasing interest in electrical instruments such as the theremin and the *ondes Martenot*. The advent of electronic media, he saw, opened a new era for composers. "I have been waiting a long time for electronics to free music from the tempered scale and the limitations of musical instruments. Electronic instruments are the portentous first step toward the liberation of music."

The principal work of Varèse's later years, *Deserts* (1954), was conceived for two different media: instrumental sounds played by four woodwinds, ten brasses, a variety of percussion instruments, and a piano; and real sounds recorded on magnetic tape and interpolated in the score at three different points. The tapes of "organized sound"—a term Varèse likes to apply to his music—are based on industrial sounds "of friction, percussion, hissing, grinding, puffing." These were processed —that is, filtered, transposed, and mixed by means of electronic devices, and then, Varèse points out, "composed to fit the pre-established plan of the work." With this piece Varèse, on the threshold of seventy, entered the new world of electronic music.

IONISATION

Varèse's most celebrated work is scored for thirty-five different instruments of percussion and friction, played by thirteen performers. The work constitutes a daring exploration of percussion and bell sounds freed from their traditional subservience to melody and harmony. *Ionisation* (1931) is an imaginative study in pure sonority and rhythm.

The instruments used fall into three groups. Those of definite pitch include tubular chimes, celesta, and piano. Among those of indefinite pitch are drums of various kinds, cymbals, tam-tam (gong), triangle, slapstick, Chinese blocks, sleighbells, castanets, tambourine, and two anvils. Also a number of exotic instruments, such as bongos (West Indian twin drums with parchment heads, played either with small wooden sticks or with the fingers); a guiro (a Cuban dried gourd, serrated on the surface and scratched with a wooden stick); maracas (Cuban rattles); claves (Cuban sticks of hardwood); and a cencerro (a cowbell struck with a drumstick). The instruments of continuous pitch include two sirens and a lion's-roar (a medium-sized wooden barrel with a parchment head through which a rosined string is drawn, the sound being produced by rubbing the string with a piece of cloth or leather). Varèse directed that a theremin—one of the first electrophonic instruments—might be substituted for the sirens.

The score displays the characteristic traits of Varèse's style, especially his uncanny ability to project masses of tensile sound that generate a sense of space. The ear is teased by complex rhythmic patterns whose subtle texture recalls the rhythms of African and Asian music. Varèse deploys his array of noisemakers on interlocking planes, analogous to the soprano, alto, tenor, and bass levels of the orchestra and choir. Used in this fashion, the percussion instruments create a harmony and counterpoint all their own. The sirens set up a continuous pitch. Their protracted wail, with its mounting sense of urgency, takes shape as a vast shadowy image of our Age of Anxiety. Most adroitly managed is the relaxation that comes toward the end with the entrance of the chimes and the tone clusters in the low register of the piano. The energies stored up in these sonorous "ions" has been released; the machine comes gently to rest.

Varèse's imagery is poetic; but the poetry derives from turbines, generators, the paraphernalia of the laboratory. His metallic music is about force and energy. His emphasis on sheer sonority presaged one of the most important trends of our era. In this respect Varèse pointed the way for the composers of electronic music. In the light of what is happening today *Ionisation* stands revealed as one of the prophetic scores of the twentieth century.

POÈME ÉLECTRONIQUE

In 1958 Philips, a Dutch electrical company, commissioned Le Corbusier to design a pavilion at the Brussels Fair that would be "a poem of the electronic age." The French-Swiss architect invited Varèse to write the music for an eight-minute fantasy of light, color, rhythm, and tone designed to put its audience "in the presence of the genesis of the world." The sounds were to be distributed over four hundred loudspeakers, so arranged as to create a sense of spatial dimension. No matter when the spectator arrived, he heard the piece in its entirety as he passed through the pavilion. The *Poème électronique* has been made available on records.

Varèse wrote most of the music directly on tape. Some of the drum sounds were created by a pulse generator. The human element is represented by a girl's voice, but one that has been treated electronically. Drum sounds, bell sounds, sirens, and persistent rhythmic patterns unfold in a continuum whose curiously depersonalized quality grips the imagination and conjures up visions of a strange new world. There is something almost terrifying about the accumulation of energy in this music; yet its inner tensions are unfolded within the bonds of a form that has a rigorous logic all its own.

Thus, at seventy-three, the intrepid explorer was still pursuing new paths, bringing back to his less venturesome fellows the shapes and sounds of the music of the future.

~§ 111 §~

Other Experimental Composers

OTTO LUENING (Milwaukee, 1900–) was a pioneer in the development of electronic music in America. He has carried on his experiments in collaboration with his younger colleague at Columbia University, Vladimir Ussachevsky (Hailar, Manchuria, of Russian parentage, 1911–). Their *Rhapsodic Variations for Tape Recorder and Orchestra* (1954) and *A Poem of Cycles and Bells*—both works have been recorded—show their imaginative use of the new medium, as does the *King Lear Suite* for tape recorder alone (1956). "Through numerous manipulations with tape slicing," Luening explains, "and tape speed-variations, a breadth of range and of rhythmic complexity is achieved which is impossible to obtain within the limits of any single instrumental group. The piano may acquire an additional range of two octaves below the lowest A, and the timpani can play in the upper flute range." Luening has also written three tape-recorded pieces for flute: *Fantasy in Space, Low Speed*, and *Invention* (1952). He is one of the directors of the Electronic Music Center operated jointly by Columbia and Princeton Universities.

In his music for conventional instruments Luening makes wide use of polytonal writing, juxtaposition of unrelated tonalities, and the tensions born of dissonance. The lyric element is prominent in his music. Among his orchestral works are *Two Symphonic Fantasias* (1924, 1939), *Two Symphonic Interludes* (1935), *Prelude on a Hymn Tune by William Billings* (1937), and *Louisville Concerto* (1951). Luening has also written a variety of chamber works, including three string quartets; the opera *Evangeline* (1930–48); choral music; pieces for string and wind instruments; organ and harpsichord music; about fifty songs; and numerous piano pieces. As professor of composition at Columbia, he has exerted an influence on the younger generation of American composers.

Henry Cowell (Menlo Park, California, 1897–) attracted attention during the Twenties with his "tone-clusters" on the piano. By pressing down a number of keys with his palm or forearm he was able to wreathe his melody in the sonorous halo of which the instrument is uniquely capable. Such an aggregate of tones exploited the percussive possibilities of the piano in a way that had not been envisaged before, and was in line with the experiments in dissonant harmony that were in the air at that time. Cowell subsequently composed an enormous amount of music, the chief item on his list being thirteen symphonies of a romantic cast abounding in folklore elements.

George Antheil (Trenton, New Jersey, 1900–1959, New York City) began his career as a composer by embracing what he called "an anti-expressive, anti-romantic, coldly mechanistic esthetic." This culminated in the sensational *Ballet mécanique,* which created a furore in Paris in 1927. "I scored the ballet for eight pianos, a pianola and an airplane propeller." When the piece was presented in New York the number of pianos was doubled; anvils, bells, automobile horns, and buzzsaws were added. The audience responded with cheers and hisses; Antheil leaped into international fame as "the Bad Boy of music," a role he thoroughly enjoyed. In 1929 Antheil had another success with his opera *Transatlantic,* on his own libretto, a work of an almost tabloid realism, whose action unfolds in an ocean liner, in a Child's restaurant, in a nightclub that is raided. The heroine sings an extended aria while in her bathtub. Antheil in later years settled down to writing Hollywood film scores and amply designed instrumental music. His last symphonies—he wrote six—are grandiose works in a postromantic style.

Harry Partch (Oakland, California, 1901–) has singlemindedly pursued the goal of a microtonal music—a music, that is, based on intervals smaller than the semitone of our chromatic scale. In his early twenties Partch evolved a scale of forty-three microtones to the octave. He devised special instruments to play his music, and a special notation for writing it down. Partch's most important work to date is his setting of Yeats's version of the *Oedipus Rex* of Sophocles, in which the music follows the inflections of the spoken lines and the actors intone on pitch in the microtonal scale. Partch has recorded *King Oedipus* and the *Plectra and Percussion Dances.* The music is whimsical and imaginative, although surprisingly conventional in rhythm. Partch's experiments had relevance in the Thirties. As things look now, the main line of advance in this direction will be through electronic music.

John Cage (Los Angeles, 1912–) belongs to the ultramodern wing among his generation. His music on the one hand moves along the line of experimentation inaugurated by composers such as Varèse and Cowell. On the other it has assimilated certain techniques of the twelve-tone school. Cage attracted wide attention with his music for "prepared piano." The preparation consists of muffling and altering the piano tone by inserting sundry objects of rubber, felt, or wood, as well as screws, nuts, and bolts between the strings; the result is to transform the instrument into an ensemble of softly percussive timbres which conjure up the gongs and drums of the Balinese gamelan. By freeing himself from the exigencies of melodic line and harmonic progression, Cage has evolved a subtle vocabulary that seems quite oriental in the luminosity of its timbres. He developed rhythm, as Virgil Thomson wrote, "to a point of sophistication unmatched in the technique of any other living composer."

Cage's music rejects the development of ideas, the arousal of emotion, and the buildup of architectural forms, all of which constitute the great tradition in Western music. The fragmentation of phrase structure, punctuated by dramatic points of silence, he derives from the dodeca-phonic composers, especially Webern. Of his stage works, the ballets *Four Dances* (1944) and *The Seasons* (1947) are characteristic. The music for percussion orchestra includes the *Third Construction* of 1940; *Imaginary Landscape* No. 3 (1941), which uses electrical instruments; *Construction in Metal* (1944) for seven percussionists who play bowls, pots, bells, metal bars, tin sheets, and an assortment of gongs; and *Quartet for Tom-toms*. In the category of music for prepared piano Cage made his most significant contribution with the Sixteen Sonatas and Four Interludes (1946–48). Cage's experiments will most likely be superseded, in the next years, by the advances made possible through electronic media. However, during the Forties he pointed new directions for contemporary music, and exerted an influence on a number of avant-garde composers both here and abroad.

Henry Brant (Montreal, Canada, 1913–) is one of the foremost experimenters in the field of directional—or antiphonal—music, in which separate groups of performers are placed at some distance from one another so that the sounds reach the listener from different directions. This, of course, is the concept embodied in stereophonic recordings. Brant's efforts in this direction antedate those of Stockhausen and other

European composers by a number of years. His works tend to underline the "separateness" of the various instrumental choirs rather than their togetherness. Not only does he direct that various groups of performers are to be situated in different parts of the hall, but he causes them to play in different keys, rhythms, tempos, and meters. Brant has written more than ten large compositions based on this principle. The best known of these are *Antiphony One*, which was first heard in New York City in 1953, and *Grand Universal Circus* (1956), in which the possibilities of "space music" are exploited with technical adroitness and imagination. Brant's earlier works include two symphonies (1931, 1937); *Music for an Imaginary Ballet* (1947); a cantata, *Spanish Underground* (1947); *Millennium No. 22*, for ten trumpets, ten trombones, eight horns, two tubas, and four percussion instruments (1954); and a number of works for unusual combinations of instruments.

Lou Harrison (Portland, Oregon, 1917–), like Henry Cowell and John Cage, undertook to create a music for pure percussion. (It is worthy of note that all three come from the Pacific Coast.) He has been influenced variously by neo-classicism, by Schoenberg, by sixteenth-century counterpoint, and by the exotic sounds of Hindu and Balinese music. His works include fourteen "sinfonias" for percussion orchestra; two Suites for string orchestra (1948); Symphony in G (1949); *Seven Pastorales for String Orchestra* (1951); and the *Mass for Male and Female Voices, Trumpet, Harp and Strings* (1954). Harrison has written three operas—*Rapunzel*, which is based on a twelve-tone row and mingles serial procedures with devices borrowed from tonal composition; *The Only Jealousy of Emer;* and *The Marriage at the Eiffel Tower*. He has also composed two ballets; songs; piano pieces; and incidental music.

Morton Feldman (New York City, 1926–) stands out among the avant-garde composers whose music has come to the fore in recent years. Among his teachers were Wallingford Riegger and Stefan Wolpe. Feldman acknowledges a deep esthetic kinship with such abstract expressionist painters as Willem de Kooning, Jackson Pollock, Franz Kline, and Philip Guston. "The new painting," he states, "made me desirous of a sound world more direct, more immediate, more physical than anything that had existed before. To me my score is my canvas, my space. What I do is try to sensitize this area—this time-space. The reality of clock-time comes later in performance, but not in the making of the composition. In the making of a composition the time is frozen. The time structure is more or less in vision before I begin. I know

I need eight or ten minutes as an artist needs five yards of canvas."

This approach has led Feldman to experiment with music in which certain elements are predetermined, while others are left to chance or to the performer's choice: what is known as aleatoric or random music. He devised a notation on graph paper for his works, each box being equal to a clock-time duration. *In Projection #2* for flute, trumpet, violin, and cello (1951), the register, time values, and dynamics are clearly designated but the actual pitches within the given registers are freely chosen by the performers. Two orchestral works dating from the same year—*Intersection #1* and *Marginal Intersection*—use still larger masses of sound. Here not only the actual pitches within the registers are freely chosen by the performer, but also dynamics and entrances within the given time structure.

Feldman developed his esthetic in a number of later works such as *The Swallows of Salangan* (1960), for chorus, five flutes, five trumpets, two tubas, two vibraphones, two pianos, and seven cellos. The pitch indications are given, but no rhythmic indications, the performer determining for himself the precise duration of the notes. On the other hand, in *The Straits of Magellan* (1961), for flute, French horn, trumpet, guitar, harp, piano, and double bass, the durations are specified but not the notes. The player, writes Feldman, "enters on or within the duration of each box (unless a box is empty, in which case he is silent). The number of sounds to be played within each box is given. Register and choice of notes are for the most part free, with occasional indications that high or low register be used within a specific box. The color (flutter-tongue, harmonics, and the like) is given, as well as the dynamics, which are very low throughout."

Feldman is a prolific composer, especially of chamber and piano works. A number of his compositions have been recorded, among them *Durations,* a series of five pieces composed in 1960–61, and *Out of "Last Pieces"* (1961), performed by Leonard Bernstein and the New York Philharmonic. These afford the listener an excellent introduction to Feldman's highly personal and subtle style. His music vividly reflects an exciting new trend on the contemporary scene.

We leave off without having mentioned many talented members of the contemporary American school. To give anywhere near a full account of their work would carry us far beyond the limits of this book. Enough has been said, however, to indicate the diversity of our composers and the tendencies they represent. Their manifold activity proves that we have established in this country all the preconditions for a mature musical culture. Our conservatories and colleges turn out musicians whose technical equipment is second to none anywhere. We have literally hundreds of composers functioning throughout the land, writing, teaching, organizing musical activities in their schools and communities. It would be unrealistic to suppose that all their works are of first rank; but that is hardly the point. History shows that a Bach, a Beethoven, or a Stravinsky emerges only out of a tradition that is flourishing and a climate that is ready. There can be no question that our efforts in the past half century have given us such a tradition and climate.

➳ 112 ☙

Postscript

WE HAVE traced the course of contemporary music through the first six decades of the twentieth century. We have chronicled the flux and reflux of musical forces that began with the revolt against the romantic heritage. It is clear that the changes which took place in the past sixty years are as momentous as any that the history of music has witnessed, and as dislocating to those who lived through them as any revolution is apt to be.

A survey of music in the early eighteenth century would have revealed a homogeneous picture of musical practice, in spite of the individual differences between Bach and Handel, Vivaldi and Scarlatti. The same would have been true a century later, even though one might have discovered much greater divergence between Chopin and Mendelssohn, Wagner and Verdi. This book presents an infinitely greater variety of esthetic goals and harmonic idioms. What common denominator can be applied to a scene that contains Schoenberg and Prokofiev, Webern and Poulenc, Menotti and Stockhausen? The absence of a common practice among composers, of a universal tradition and homogeneous language, makes for a diversity that is fascinating, but that is also apt to be more than a little bewildering. All the more important, then, to pause and take stock of what our century has achieved thus far.

What emerges from such stocktaking is that twentieth-century music does not represent so drastic a break with the past as listeners of forty years ago supposed. The leaders of the modern movement, as we have seen, disclaimed revolutionary intent. They viewed the upheaval that they inaugurated as part of the dynamic process of evolution to which all human endeavor is subject. Their innovations have become part of the vocabulary of music. The areas of thought and expression that they opened up are being further explored by their disciples and heirs. The turbulent half century against which their lives unfolded is taking its place in history as the latest—and, because closest to us, the most exciting—chapter in that eternal process of change which attends the growth of a living art. The works of Stravinsky, Schoenberg, Berg, Webern, and their compeers issued out of the great tradition of Western music and eloquently affirm the continuity of that tradition. At the same time they represent the next step forward, one made inevitable by what came before.

The reader who has perused these pages has glimpsed the vast musical panorama of our time. One can but hope that he will pursue his investigations farther. He will find in the appendices a list of books that will assuredly expand his understanding and enjoyment of the heady musical art of the twentieth century. Yet he must remember that there is only so much that can be written or read about sounds. The magic, the true meaning, lies in the sounds themselves. Let him therefore use the books as an introduction to what is, finally, the one valid thing we can do about music—to listen to it! Let him listen carefully, perceptively, over and over again: with curiosity, with eagerness, with joy.

Basic Concepts

I-a. MELODY (Background Material for Chapter 4)

MELODY DURING the classic-romantic era tended toward symmetrical structure. Melodies consisted of phrases that were generally four measures long, with a cadence at the end of each. For example:

Way   down u - pon the Swa- nee Riv-er,   far,   far   a - way,

That's where my heart is turn- ing   e- ver, that's where the Old   Folks   stay.

All   the world   is   sad   and drear-y, eve- ry - where   I   roam,

Oh   dark-ies, how my heart grows wear-y, far   from the Old   Folks at   home.

The incomplete cadence, like the comma in punctuation, indicates that more is to come. The complete cadence, like the period in punctuation, gives a sense of finality. In the above example, the first and third phrases end in incomplete cadences. The final cadence is the point where the melody line reaches its destination and comes to rest.

I-b. HARMONY (Background Material for Chapter 5)

Intervals. By an interval we mean the distance—that is, the difference in pitch—between two tones; also the relationship between them. If two tones are sounded in succession they outline a melodic interval; if simultaneously, they establish a harmonic interval. The combination of the two tones creates a sonorous entity with a quality of its own quite distinct from either of its constituents.

Intervals are named according to the distance between the tones.

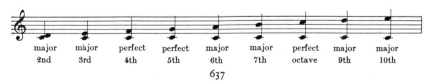

major	major	perfect	perfect	major	major	perfect	major	major
2nd	3rd	4th	5th	6th	7th	octave	9th	10th

A minor interval is a half-tone smaller than a major interval. A diminished interval is a half-tone smaller than a perfect or minor interval. An augmented interval is a half-tone larger than a perfect or major interval.

| minor | minor | minor | dim. | dim. | dim. | aug. | aug. | aug. |
| 3rd | 6th | 7th | 4th | 5th | 3rd | 2nd | 4th | 5th |

Chords. Harmony pertains to the movement and relationship of chords. A chord may be defined as a combination of tones that occur simultaneously and are conceived as an entity. (In broken chords—arpeggios—the tones of the chord are heard in succession.) The melody unfolds above the harmony, and together constitute a single entity.

The triad is a three-tone chord formed by combining every other degree of the scale; that is, steps 1–3–5 (*do-mi-sol*); 2–4–6 (*re-fa-la*); 3–5–7 (*mi-sol-ti*); 4–6–8 (*fa-la-do*), and so on. In other words, the triad consists of two intervals of a third superimposed upon each other. Following are triads based on the scale of C major.

The Tonic or I chord is the chord of rest. The other triads, representing a greater or lesser degree of activity, seek to be resolved to the Tonic. The Dominant or V chord represents a greater degree of activity than the Subdominant or IV chord. The Tonic, Dominant, and Subdominant triads suffice to harmonize many a famous tune, as in the following example:

Way down upon the   Swanee River   Far, far, a-way,
I——————————— IV————— I———— V————
There's where my heart is turning ever, There's where the Old Folks stay.
I——————————— IV————— I————————— V—— I——
All the world is   sad and dreary,   Everywhere I   roam,
V————— I————————— IV————— I—— (V) ——
Oh darkies, how my heart grows weary, Far from the Old Folks at home.
I——————————— IV————— I———— V———— I——

When the process of chord-building is carried one step farther, we obtain a seventh chord (steps 1–3–5–7 of the scale, or 2–4–6–8, 3–5–7–9, and so on).

Continuing the process of superimposing thirds, we obtain ninth chords (steps 1–3–5–7–9, 2–4–6–8–3, 3–5–7–9–4, and so on).

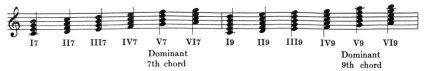

| I7 | II7 | III7 | IV7 | V7 | VI7 | I9 | II9 | III9 | IV9 | V9 | VI9 |

Dominant 7th chord   Dominant 9th chord

The Dominant-seventh chord resolving to the Tonic is the standard final cadence of the classic-romantic period. It is especially prominent in works dating from 1775–1825, the era of Haydn, Mozart, Beethoven, and Schubert.

I-c. TONALITY (Background Material for Chapter 6)

If we look at the piano keyboard we observe that from one tone to its octave—for example, from C to the C above it—there are twelve keys, seven white and five black. These are a half-tone or semitone apart. From C to C-sharp is a half tone; from C-sharp to D the same. From C to D is a whole tone. The seven white and five black keys thus represent the twelve semitones into which the octave is divided in our system of music.

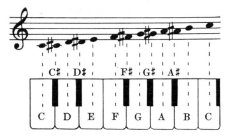

A scale is an arrangement of a series of tones in consecutive order, ascending or descending. (The word is derived from the Latin *scala*, "ladder.") The twelve semitones of the octave pictured above comprise the chromatic scale. *Chromatic* implies movement by semitones.

A key is a group of related tones with a common center or Tonic. This "loyalty to the Tonic" is inculcated in us by most of the music we hear. It is the unifying force in the *do-re-mi-fa-sol-la-ti-do* scale. You can test for yourself how strong is the pull to the Tonic by singing the first seven tones of this pattern, stopping on *ti*. You will experience an almost physical compulsion to resolve the *ti* up to *do*. This sense of relatedness to a central tone is what we mean by *tonality*. When we listen to a composition in the key of A we hear a piece based in large part upon the family of tones that revolve around and gravitate to the common center A.

A scale presents the tones of the key in consecutive order. It is, really, a statement of movement. The music of the eighteenth and nineteenth centuries was based on two contrasting scales, the *major* and the *minor*. These consisted of seven tones—eight, if you prefer, as the *do* is duplicated at the end of the series. The major scale is the familiar *do-re-mi-fa-sol-la-ti-do* pattern. Its seven tones were chosen out of the possible twelve in order to form a centralized family or key out of which musical compositions could be fashioned. The relationship of the major scale to the chromatic scale is manifest in the piano keyboard. The chromatic scale, we saw, included the seven white and five black keys. The major scale is sounded by the seven white keys from C to C. In other words, the major scale represents the "seven-out-of-twelve" way of listening that prevailed in the period from Bach and Handel to Tchaikovsky and Brahms.

The Major-Minor System. If you look at the diagram of the keyboard given above, you will notice that the seven white keys from C to C are not equally distant from one another. Where the white keys have a black between, they are a whole tone (two half tones) apart. This is the rule, with two important exceptions: there is no black key between the third and fourth steps, E-F, and between the seventh and eighth steps, B-C. These tones, therefore, are a semitone apart. When we sing the *do-re-mi-fa-sol-la-ti-do* sequence we are measuring off a pattern of eight tones that are a whole tone apart except steps 3–4 (*mi-fa*) and 7–8 (*ti-do*). Sing this scale and try to distinguish between the whole- and half-tone distances.

The major scale implies certain relationships based on tension and resolution. We have already indicated the most important of these—the thrust of the seventh step to the eighth (*ti* seeking to be resolved to *do*). There are others. If we sing *do-re* we are left with a sense of incompleteness which is resolved when *re* moves down to *do*. *Fa* gravitates to *mi; la* descends to *sol*. Most important of all, the major scale defines the two poles of classical harmony—the *do* or Tonic, the point of ultimate rest; and the *sol* or Dominant, representing the active harmony. Tonic going to Dominant and returning to Tonic became the basic progression of classical harmony, as well as the basic principle of classical form.

The major scale, we saw, is a "ladder" of whole and half tones. A ladder may be placed on high ground or low, but the distance between its steps remains the same. So too the major scale may be measured off from one starting point or another without affecting the sequence of whole and half steps within the pattern.

Any one of the twelve tones of our octave may serve as starting point for the scale. Whichever it is, that tone at once assumes the function of the tonic or key center. The other tones are chosen according to the pattern of the ladder. They immediately assume the functions of activity and rest implicit in the major scale. Most important, they all take on the impulse of gravitating more or less directly to the tonic.

With each different tonic we get another group of seven out of the possible twelve. In other words, every major scale has a different number of sharps or flats. The scale of C major is the only group that has no sharps or flats. If we build the major scale from G we must include an F-sharp in order to conform to the pattern of whole and half steps. (Try building the pattern whole step, whole step, half step, whole step, whole step, whole step, half step, from G. You will find that there is no F in this group.) If we build the major scale pattern from D, we get a group of seven that includes two sharps. If F is our starting point the scale includes B-flat. (See page 642 for table of major and minor scales.)

Whether the major scale begins on C, D, E, or any other tone, it follows the same model in the arrangement of the whole and half steps. This model is known as a *mode*. All the major scales exemplify the major mode of arranging whole and half steps. There is also a minor mode, which complements and serves as a foil to the major. This differs from the major primarily in that its third degree is flatted; that is, the scale of C minor has E-flat instead of E. In the harmonic minor the sixth step is also flatted: C-D-E♭-F-G-A♭-B-C. (The minor scale exists in two other versions, the melodic minor and natural minor.) The minor is pronouncedly different from the major in mood and coloring. *Minor*, the Latin word for "smaller," refers to the fact that the distinguishing interval C-E♭ is smaller than the corresponding interval C-E in the major ("larger") scale.

Like the major, the pattern of the minor mode may be duplicated from each of the twelve tones of the octave. In each case there will be another group of seven out of twelve—that is, the scale will have another number of sharps and flats. It becomes clear that every tone in the octave may serve as starting point or keynote for a major and minor scale. This gives us twelve major keys and twelve minor keys.

Just as we are able to build a scale from any one of twelve tones, we are able to sing or play the same melody beginning on C, C-sharp, D, and so on. In each case the tune will be in another key. The pitch and the keynote will be different, as will the number of sharps or flats. But the melody line will remain unchanged because the pattern of whole and half steps is retained in the new key as in the old. This is why the same song can be published in various keys for soprano, alto, tenor, or bass. When we shift a piece of music from one key to another we *transpose* it. Transposition should be carefully distinguished from *modulation*, the act of going from one key to another. Modulation is a highly emotional factor in music, for it opens up the circle of the key and shifts the listener into a new key area. Modulation consequently is a prime factor for variety in music. Transposition, on the other hand, is simply the shifting of the melody and its harmonies to a higher or lower key.

I-d. RHYTHM AND METER (Background Material for Chapter 7)

Rhythm denotes the controlled movement of music in time. Meter denotes the organization of time within which that movement takes place. In other words, meter connotes the fixed time units—the measures—within which musical events unfold. Within these units the rhythm flows freely, now more, now less eventfully. Meter involves the arrangement of beats into measures, while rhythm pertains to the arrangement of time values within the measure. Every waltz has the same meter: ONE-two-three ONE-two-three. Within that meter, each waltz follows its own rhythm. In the jazz band, the drum, double bass, and the pianist's left hand establish the pattern of the meter. The melody instruments and the pianist's right hand articulate the rhythm that flows above that pattern.

In classic-romantic music meter depends upon the organization of time in equal measures marked by the regular recurrence of accent. There are two basic metrical patterns—duple and triple meter. Duple meter, generally

encountered as two-four time (2/4), consists of a succession of beats in which a strong alternates with a weak: ONE-two ONE-two; or in marching, LEFT-right LEFT-right. That is to say, there are two beats in the measure, the accent on the first. The pattern is familiar from many nursery rhymes and marching songs.

Twín - kle	twín - kle	lít - tle	stár - - - -,
ONE - two	ONE - two	ONE - two	ONE - two

Hów I--	wón - der	whát you	áre - - - -.
ONE - two	ONE - two	ONE - two	ONE - two

The other basic metrical pattern is that of an accented beat followed by two unaccented: three beats to the measure, or triple meter. This is the pattern of three-four time (3/4) traditionally associated with the waltz and minuet.

A celebrated example of triple meter is *The Star-Spangled Banner*.

Oh	sáy can you	sée _____ by the
three	ONE - two - three	ONE - two - three

	dáwn's ear - ly	líght ____
	ONE - two - three	ONE - two

Duple and triple are the primary meters; all others are compound. By combining two measures of duple we obtain a measure of four beats, or quadruple meter. The primary accent falls on the first beat of the measure, with a subsidiary accent on the third: ÓNE-two-Thrée-four. Quadruple meter, generally encountered as four-four time (4/4), is found in some of our most widely sung melodies:

Wáy ____ dówn u - pon the	Swá - nee Ríver ____
ONE two Three four	ONE two Three four

Fár, ____ fár a -	wáy _____
ONE - two - Three - four	ONE - two - Three - four

Two measures of triple time may be combined to make sextuple meter: six-four or six-eight time. This is often marked by a gently flowing effect.

Drínk to me ón - - ly	wí - ith thine éy - es and
ONE - two - three - Four - five - six	ONE - two - three - Four - five - six

Í _____ will plé - edge with	míne _____
ONE - two - three - Four - five - six	ONE - two - three - Four - five - six

Other compound meters are based on five, seven, nine, eleven, or twelve beats to the measure. However, the four patterns just discussed are the ones most frequent in the music of the nineteenth century.

I-e. TEMPO

Meter tells us how many beats there are in the measure, but it does not tell us whether these beats occur slowly or rapidly. The *tempo*, by which we mean the rate of speed, the pace of the music, provides the clue to this vital matter. Consequently the rhythmic organization of music involves three things: meter, which organizes musical time into measures; rhythm, which organizes time values within the measure; and tempo, which determines the speed of the measures, their duration in actual time.

Because of the close connection between tempo and mood, tempo markings have come to indicate not only the pace of the music but its character as well. The tempo terms are generally given in Italian, a survival from the time when the opera of that nation dominated the European scene. Most frequently encountered are the following.

Very slow: *Largo* (literally, "broad")
Grave (literally, "heavy")

Slow: *Lento*
Adagio (literally, "at ease")

Moderate: *Andante* (literally, "going")—at a walking pace
Andantino—somewhat faster than andante, "sauntering"
Moderato

Fairly fast: *Allegretto* (literally, "a little lively")—not as fast as allegro

Fast: *Allegro* (literally, "cheerful," "happy," "lively")

Very fast: *Vivo*—lively
Vivace—vivacious
Allegro molto—very lively
Presto—quick
Prestissimo—as quick as possible

As important as the tempo terms are those indicating a change of pace. The principal ones are *accelerando* (getting faster) and *ritardando* (holding back, getting slower); *a tempo* (in time) indicates a return to the original tempo.

I-f. DYNAMICS

Dynamics denotes the degree of loudness or softness at which the music is played. Modern instruments place a wide gamut of dynamic effects at the composer's disposal. The principal dynamic indications are:

Very soft: *pianissimo* (*pp*)
Soft: *piano* (*p*)
Moderately soft: *mezzo piano* (*mp*)

Moderately loud: *mezzo forte* (*mf*)
Loud: *forte* (*f*)
Very loud: *fortissimo* (*ff*)

As the modern orchestra increased in size and precision, composers extended the range of dynamic shadings in both directions, so that we find *ppp* and *fff*. In late nineteenth-century scores, four and even five *p*'s or *f*'s were used.

Of special importance are the changes in dynamics. The commonest are:

Growing louder: *crescendo* (◁══════)
Growing softer: *decrescendo* or *diminuendo* (══════▷)
Sudden stress: *sforzando* (*sf*), (literally, "forced")—accent on a single note or chord

I-g. DEVICES OF COUNTERPOINT (Background Material for Chapter 8)

When several independent lines are combined, composers try to give unity and shape to the texture. A basic procedure for achieving this end is *imitation*, in which a subject or motive is presented in one voice and then duplicated in another. While the imitating voice restates the theme, the first voice goes on to a countersubject. This duplication of an idea—at different times and pitches—by all the voice parts is of the essence in contrapuntal thinking.

How long is the statement that is to be imitated? This varies considerably. It may be the entire length of a voice part that runs from the beginning to end of a piece. Or the imitation may occur intermittently. When the whole length of a voice part is imitated, we have a strict type of composition known as a *canon*. The name comes from the Greek word for "law" or "order." Each phrase heard in the leading voice is repeated almost immediately in an imitating voice throughout the length of the work. The most popular form of canon is the round, in which each voice enters in succession with the same melody. Composers do not often cast an entire piece or movement in the shape of a canon. What they do is to use canonic imitation as an effect in all sorts of pieces.

Contrapuntal writing is marked by a number of devices that have flourished for centuries. *Inversion* is a species of imitation in which the melody is turned upside down; that is, it follows the same intervals but in the opposite direction. Where the melody originally moved up by a third, the inversion moves down a third. Where it descended by a fourth, it now ascends a fourth. Thus, D-E-F inverted becomes D-C-B. *Augmentation* consists of imitating a theme in longer time values. A quarter note may become a half, a half note a whole, and so on. In consequence, the theme in its new version sounds slower. *Diminution* consists of imitating a theme in shorter time values. A whole note may become a half, a half note a quarter; which makes the theme in its new version sound faster. *Retrograde*, also known as *cancrizans* or *crab motion*, means to imitate the melody backwards. If the original sequence of notes reads B-D-G-F, the imitation reads F-G-D-B. Retrograde-and-inversion imitates the theme by turning it upside down and backwards. These devices of sixteenth-century counterpoint have been revived in contemporary music, especially by Arnold Schoenberg and his school.

The Fugue. From the art and science of counterpoint issued one of the most exciting types of Baroque music, the *fugue*. The name is derived from *fuga*, the Latin for "flight," implying a flight of fancy (possibly the flight of the theme from one voice to the other). In a fugue, several independent voices—generally three or four—take turns in presenting a striking theme or subject. A fugue may be written for a group of instruments; for a solo instrument such as organ, harpsichord, or even violin; for several solo voices or for full chorus. Whether the fugue is vocal or instrumental, the several lines are called voices, which indicates the origin of the type. In vocal and orchestral fugues each line is articulated by another performer or group of performers. In fugues for keyboard instruments the ten fingers—on the organ, the feet as well—manage the complex interweaving of the voices.

The subject is stated at the outset in one of the voices (soprano, alto, tenor, or bass) without accompaniment. It is then imitated in another voice —this is the answer—while the first continues with a countertheme or countersubject. It will then appear in a third voice and be answered in the fourth, if there are four, while the first two weave a free contrapuntal texture against these. When the theme has appeared in each voice once, the first section of the fugue—the exposition—is at an end. The exposition may be repeated, in which case the voices will enter in a different order. From there on the fugue alternates between exposition sections that feature the entrance of the subject, and less weighty interludes known as episodes. The latter serve as areas of relaxation.

Each recurrence of the theme reveals new facets of its nature. It may be presented in longer or shorter note values, turned upside down, presented backwards, or upside down and backwards. It may be combined with new subjects or with some other version of itself. It may be presented softly or vigorously. The composer manipulates the subject as pure musical material in the same way that the sculptor molds his clay. Especially effective is the *stretto* (from the Italian for "close") in which the theme is imitated in close succession, with the subject entering in one voice before it has been completed in another. The effect is one of voices crowding upon each other, creating a heightening of tension that brings the fugue to its climax. There follows the final statement of the subject, generally in triumphal mood. The mission has been accomplished, the tension released.

Another important form of contrapuntal music is the *concerto grosso*, a composition based on the opposition between two dissimilar masses of sound. (The verb *concertare* means "to fight side by side," "to vie with one another as brothers in arms.") A small group of instruments known as the *concertino* is pitted against the large group, the concerto grosso or tutti. The contrast is one of color and dynamics. The concerto grosso was extensively cultivated during the Baroque era, and has been revived in the twentieth century.

I-h. INSTRUMENTS OF THE ORCHESTRA
(Background Material for Chapter 9)

The same tone will sound different when produced by a trumpet or a violin. The difference lies in the characteristic color, or *timbre*, of each instrument. (The word retains its French pronunciation, *tam'br*.) Timbre focuses our musical impressions. By the way in which the composer chooses his timbres, blending and contrasting them, he creates the particular sound-world that a given piece inhabits.

The orchestra is organized in four sections or choirs—string, woodwind, brass, and percussion. Known as "the heart of the orchestra," the string section played a most important part—both for lyric and dramatic effects—in the scores of the classic-romantic era. The string section includes four instruments—violin, viola, cello, and double bass—which correspond roughly to soprano, alto, tenor, and bass. In these instruments the strings are set vibrating by the action of the bow. The player *stops* the string by pressing down a finger of his left hand at a particular point, thereby changing the length of that portion of the string which is free to vibrate, and with it the rate of vibration and the pitch.

The string instruments are pre-eminent in playing *legato* (smooth and connected), though they are capable too of the opposite quality of tone, *staccato* (short and detached). A special effect, *pizzicato* ("plucked"), is executed by the performer's plucking the string with his finger instead of playing with the bow, thereby producing a guitarlike tone. *Vibrato* refers to the throbbing tone which the violinist achieves by moving his finger slightly away from and back to the required spot, thus enriching the resonance. In *glissando* the player moves his hand rapidly along the string, sounding all the pitches of the scale. *Tremolo*, the rapid repetition of a tone through a quick up-and-down movement of the bow, is associated in the popular mind with suspense and excitement. No less important is the *trill*, a rapid alternation between a tone and its neighbor, giving a birdlike effect. *Double-stopping* involves playing on two strings simultaneously. It is possible too to sound three or four notes together. Thereby the violin, essentially a melody instrument, becomes capable of harmony. The *mute* is a three-pronged clamp which is slipped onto the bridge of the instrument to muffle the tone. *Harmonics* are flutelike crystalline tones in the very high register, produced by lightly touching the string at certain points instead of stopping it in the usual way.

The woodwind section of the orchestra consists of four principal instruments—flute, oboe, clarinet, and bassoon. Each of these is supplemented by at least one instrument of the same family: the flute by the piccolo, the oboe by the English horn, the clarinet by the bass clarinet, and the bassoon by the contrabassoon. Saxophones too are included in this group. The woodwinds are not as homogeneous a group as the strings. They are not necessarily made of wood; and they represent several methods of setting in vibration the column of air within the tube. The clarinet and saxophone are single-reed instruments; the oboe and bassoon are double-reed instruments; while in the flute the player blows directly across a mouth hole cut in the side of the pipe (the *embouchure*). The woodwinds do, however, have two features in common: first, the holes in the side of the pipe; and second, their timbres, which are such that composers think of them and write for them as a group. Because they are more vivid and distinctive in color than the more neutral strings, they must be used somewhat more sparingly.

The brass section is the "heavy artillery" of the orchestra. Its four members—trumpet, horn, trombone, and tuba—are indispensable for melody, for sustaining harmony, for rhythmic accent, for the weight of their massed tone, and for the flamelike sonority they contribute to climaxes. These instruments have a cup-shaped mouthpiece. The column of air within the tube is set vibrating by the tightly stretched lips of the player, which act as a kind of double reed. To go from one pitch to another requires not only mechanical means, such as a slide or valves, but also variation in the pressure of the lips and breath, which demands great muscular control. Fatigue of the lip muscles will cause even an expert player to go off pitch.

The percussion section, sometimes referred to as "the battery," comprises a variety of instruments that are made to sound by striking or shaking. Certain ones consist of an elastic material such as metal or wood. In others, such as the drums, vibration is set up by striking a stretched skin. The percussion instruments fall into two categories, those of definite and those of indefinite pitch. In the former class are the kettledrums or timpani, which are used in sets of two or three. Also of definite pitch are the glockenspiel, celesta, xylophone, marimba, and chimes. Among the percussion instruments of indefinite pitch are the bass drum, the side drum (also known as snare drum); tambourine and castanets; the triangle, cymbals, and gong. We have mentioned in the text, in connection with particular works, such exotic percussion instruments as the guiro, claves, and bongo drums.

The harp, a plucked-string instrument, is a charter member of the orchestra. Modern orchestral scores frequently call for a piano. The orchestra as a whole is constituted with a view to securing the best balance of tone. Approximately two-thirds of the ensemble are string players, one-third are wind players. The following distribution is typical of our larger orchestras.

Strings, about 65:	18 first violins 16 second violins 12 violas 10 violoncellos 10 double basses
Woodwinds, about 15:	3 flutes, 1 piccolo 3 oboes, 1 English horn 3 clarinets, 1 bass clarinet 3 bassoons, 1 double bassoon
Brass, 11:	4 horns 3 trumpets 3 trombones 1 tuba
Percussion, 5:	2 kettledrum players 3 men for bass and side drum, glockenspiel, celesta, xylophone, triangle, cymbals, tambourine, etc

The conductor has before him the score of the work. This consists of from a few to as many as twenty-five or more lines, each representing an instrumental part. All the staves together comprise a single composite line. What is going on at any moment in the orchestra is indicated at any given point straight down the page. (See music examples on pages 46, 58, and 59.) The term *tutti* ("all") refers to the orchestra as a whole. The term *concertante*, on the other hand, refers to an orchestral style in which single instruments or groups are pitted against each other in a soloistic manner.

The following table illustrates the comparative range of the various instruments.

THE HUMAN VOICE

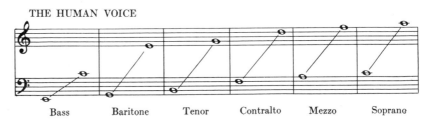

Bass   Baritone   Tenor   Contralto   Mezzo   Soprano

STRINGED INSTRUMENTS

Violin   Viola   Cello   Double - bass

WOODWIND INSTRUMENTS

Piccolo   Flute   Oboe   English Horn   Clarinet in A

Bass Clarinet in B♭   Bassoon   Double - bassoon   Tenor Saxophone in B♭

BRASS INSTRUMENTS

Trumpet in C   Horn   Trombone   Tuba

PERCUSSION INSTRUMENTS

Kettle - drums   Bells   Glockenspiel   Celesta   Xylophone

OTHER INSTRUMENTS

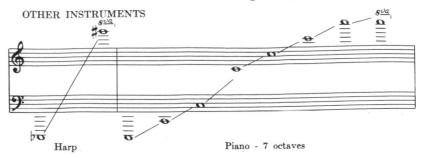

Harp   Piano - 7 octaves

I-i. THE LARGE MUSICAL FORMS (Background Material for Chapter 10)

The Sonata-Symphony. The grand form in music, the sonata-symphony, is based on the exposition, development, and restatement of themes. The theme becomes the first in a chain of musical situations, all of which grow out of the basic idea as naturally as does the plant from the seed. Hence the term *germ theme*, which indicates the capacity of the initial idea to flower, to expand, and to develop in such a way as to create an effect of organic unity. The most tightly knit kind of expansion in our music is known as *thematic development*. To develop a theme means to unfold its latent energies, to search out its capacities for growth and bring them to fruition.

In the process of development, certain procedures have proved to be particularly effective. The simplest is repetition, which may occur either at the same pitch or at another. A basic technique is the breaking up of the theme into its constituent fragments, the *motives*. A motive is the smallest segment of a theme that forms a melodic-rhythmic unit. The motives are the germ cells of musical growth. Through fragmentation of themes, through repeating and varying the motives and combining them in ever fresh patterns, the composer imparts to the musical organism the quality of dynamic evolution and growth. Development may also proceed by imitation—that is, the theme is presented in one voice and forthwith imitated in another. Or the theme may be combined with other melody lines or fragments in an intricate texture. Through these and kindred devices the theme takes on fresh forms and displays unsuspected facets of its personality.

The name sonata comes from the Italian *suonare*, "to sound," indicating a piece to be sounded on instruments, as distinct from cantata, a piece to be sung. A sonata is an instrumental work consisting of a cycle of contrasting movements, generally three or four in number. The name sonata is used when the music is intended for one or two instruments. If more than two are involved the work is called, as the case may be, a trio, quartet, quintet, sextet, septet, octet, or nonet. A sonata for solo instrument and orchestra is called a concerto; for full orchestra—a symphony. The sonata cycle, clearly, accounts for a large part of the instrumental music we hear.

The First Movement. The most highly organized and characteristic member of the several movements that make up the cycle is the opening allegro.

Basic Concepts

This is in *sonata form*. The terms *first-movement form* and *sonata-allegro form* are also used to describe this movement. *First-movement form* is somewhat misleading, as this type of structure is also used for the last movement. *Sonata-allegro form* correctly suggests that this type of structure is at its most characteristic in a lively or allegro movement, but fails to take into account that slow movements, especially in the eighteenth-century symphony, were also cast in this form.

Sonata form is summed up in the following somewhat simplified outline:

Exposition	Development	Recapitulation (or Restatement)
(Slow introduction) First theme or theme group in home key Bridge—modulates Second theme or thematic group in contrasting key Codetta. Cadence in contrasting key	Frequent modulation (away from home key) Fragmentation and manipulation of themes Building up of tension against return to home key Retransition to home key	First theme or thematic group in home key Bridge Second theme or thematic group transposed to home key (or close to it) Coda. Cadence in home key

Even as the dramatist creates opposing personalities as the chief characters of his work, so the composer achieves a vivid contrast between the musical ideas that form the basis of the movement. The opposition between two themes may be underlined in a number of ways. Through a contrast in dynamics—loud against soft; in register—low against high; timbre—strings against winds, one instrumental combination against another; rhythm and tempo—an animated pattern against one that is sustained; tone quality—legato against staccato; type of melody—an active melody line with wide range and leaps against one that is quieter; type of harmony—consonance against dissonance, diatonic harmony against chromatic; type of accompaniment—quietly moving chords against extended arpeggios. One contrast is required, being the basis of the form: the contrast of key. And the opposition may be further intensified by putting one theme in the major and the other in minor.

The conventional description of sonata form, by its emphasis upon the two or three themes that serve as building blocks for an instrumental movement, seems to imply that everything between these themes is in the nature of transitional material. On the contrary: the sonata movement is an organic unity in which the growth, the development, the destiny of the idea is no less important than the idea itself (just as in a human action whose consequences are no less important than the deed proper). From the symphonic point of view the theme includes not only the germinal idea *but also its expansion and development;* not only the few notes given in the musical examples in the text but also the "*etc.*"—that is, the passage or section into which the initial idea flowers. It is only when we take this larger view of the theme that we come to understand the symphonic movement for what it is: a continuous expansion and growth of musical ideas from first note to last, from which not a measure may be omitted without disturbing the equilibrium and the organic oneness of the whole.

The Other Movements. The second movement of the symphonic cycle is generally the slow movement. This may be a simple A-B-A form, in which the middle section contrasts with the outer two. Or it may be a theme and variations. Or, as we already have indicated, it could be—and in the eighteenth-century symphony frequently was—a sonata form. The third movement in the classical cycle was the minuet and trio, an A-B-A form in which the minuet was repeated after the middle part (the trio). The minuet was displaced, in the nineteenth-century symphony, by the scherzo, which differs from the minuet in its headlong pace, vigorous rhythm, and more varied character.

The final movement in the classical cycle was often a rondo. This is a movement consisting of symmetrical sections and based on the recurrence of a central idea—the rondo theme—in alternation with one or more subsidiary themes; as in the pattern A-B-A-B-A, in which there is only one other theme; or A-B-A-C-A, where there are two; or some variation, as in the pattern A-B-A-C-A-B-A. The rondo furnished a happy ending for the classical symphony. The final movement might also be a rondo-sonata, a type that joined the lightness of the rondo with the developmental procedures of sonata form; or a theme and variations; or a sonata form. Nineteenth-century composers favored a large sonata form that would balance the first movement and bring the symphony to a rousing conclusion.

Following is an outline of the cycle of movements in the sonata-symphony of the classic-romantic era:

MOVE-MENT	FORM	CHARACTER	TEMPO	
			Mozart: Symphony No. 40	*Beethoven: Symphony No. 5*
First	Sonata form	Epic-dramatic	Allegro molto	Allegro con brio
Second	A-B-A Sonata form Theme and variations	Slow lyrical movement. May range, however, from the whimsical to the tragic	Andante	Andante con moto
Third	A-B-A	Dance movement: Minuet (18th century) Scherzo (19th century) Both in ¾ time	Allegretto	Allegro
Fourth	Rondo Sonata form Rondo-sonata Theme and variations	Lively finale (18th century Triumphal ending: the romantic "apotheosis" (19th century)	Allegro molto	Allegro

I-j. THE "CHORD OF NATURE": THE HARMONIC SERIES

Musical tones are produced by vibrations. The pitch of a tone—by which we mean its location in the musical scale in relation to high or low—is determined by the rate of vibration. This in turn depends on the length of the vibrating body. The shorter a string or column of air, the more rapidly it vibrates and the higher the pitch. The longer a string or column of air, the fewer the vibrations per second and the lower the pitch. The width, thickness, density, and tension of the vibrating body also affect the outcome.

When a string or a column of air vibrates, it does so not only as a whole but also in segments—halves, thirds, fourths, fifths, sixths, sevenths, and so on. These segments produce the *overtones,* which are also known as *partials* or *harmonics.* What we hear as the single tone is really the combination of the fundamental tone and its overtones, just as what we see as white light is the combination of all the colors of the spectrum. Although we may not be conscious of the partials, they play a decisive part in our listening; for the presence or absence of overtones in the sound wave determines the timbre, the color of the tone. Following is the table of the Chord of Nature: the fundamental and its overtones or harmonics. Those marked with an asterisk are not in tune with our tempered scale.

The fundamental tone and its overtones comprise the harmonic series, the "Chord of Nature" that resounds when any string or column of air is set vibrating. Half the string gives the second member of the series, the octave above the fundamental. This interval is represented by the ratio 1:2; that is to say, the two tones of this interval are produced when one string is half as long as the other and is vibrating twice as fast. The one-third segment of the string produces the third member of the harmonic series, the fifth above the octave. This interval is represented by the ratio 2:3. We hear it when one string is two-thirds as long as the other and is vibrating one and a half times (3/2) as fast. The one fourth segment of the string produces the fourth member of the series, the fourth above. This interval is represented by the ratio 3:4, for its two tones are produced when one string is three-fourths as long as the other and vibrates one and a third times (4/3) as fast. One fifth of the string produces the fifth member of the harmonic series, the major third, an interval represented by the ratio 4:5. Its two tones are produced when one string is four-fifths as long as the other and vibrates one and a fourth (5/4) times as fast. One sixth of the string produces the sixth member of the series, the minor third, represented by the ratio 5:6; and so on. As the segments grow shorter, the intervals they produce grow correspondingly smaller. From the seventh to the eleventh partials we find whole tones; this interval is represented by the ratio 7:8.

Between the eleventh harmonic and its octave, 22, the semitone appears. This interval is represented by the ratio 11:12. After partial 22 we enter the realm of microtones—third tones, quarter tones, sixth and eighth tones, and so on.

The triad is given by the first six tones of the series, specifically by tones 4–5–6. The chord of the dominant seventh is represented by tones 4–5–6–7; the dominant ninth chord by tones 4–5–6–7–9; an eleventh chord by tones 4–5–6–7–9–11; and a thirteenth chord by tones 4–5–6–7–9–11–13.

The evolution of man's harmonic sense seems to have followed the harmonic series. Music began as monophonic—that is, single-line melody. In other words, the early musicians were aware only of the fundamental. The Greeks appear to have developed a style of singing in which men and women, or men and boys, sang the same melody an octave and/or a fifth apart. In other words, the ancients discovered the perfect consonances—octave, fifth, fourth—formed by the first four tones of the harmonic series. This covers the period of ancient and primitive music, up to the period of organum about a thousand years ago. (For an example of medieval organum see page 116.) Toward the end of the middle ages the major third and the minor third were accepted, first as dissonances, ultimately as imperfect consonances. This made possible the introduction of the triad (tones 4–5–6 of the series), and prepared the way for the supplanting of the medieval modes by triadic harmony—a development that carried music well into the Renaissance. The Dominant seventh chord (tones 4, 5, 6, 7 of the series) was a governing force in harmony throughout the Baroque and classical eras. With the addition of the ninth overtone, which introduces the chord of the Dominant-ninth (tones 4, 5, 6, 7, 9 of the series), we are in the period of Wagner, Liszt, and César Franck. Thus, by the end of the nineteenth century Western harmony had pretty thoroughly explored the possibilities of the first nine tones of the Chord of Nature.

Debussy's experiments, which ushered in the twentieth century, centered about the whole-tone scale: tones 7, 8, 9, 10, 11, 13 of the series. At the same time composers moved forward to the eleventh and thirteenth chords formed by those harmonics. The next step was taken with the turning from triadic to quartal harmony: from chords based on the third to those based on the fourth. A leader in this development was Scriabin, whose "mystic chord" consisted of tones 8, 11, 14, 10, 13, and 9 of the harmonic series. (For this chord and other examples of quartal harmony, see page 27.) In other words, twentieth-century harmony moved with astonishing rapidity to explore the higher overtones of the harmonic series. This development was given enormous impetus by Schoenberg, who based his harmonic language on the chromatic—better, the twelve-tone—scale found in the harmonic series between tones 11 and 22. Indeed, theorists used to explain the difference between Stravinsky and Schoenberg by saying that Schoenberg's harmony explored higher overtones than did Stravinsky's. (This, of course, was in the days before Stravinsky turned to twelve-tone music.)

If the historical analogy holds, then the next century will be spent in exploring still higher reaches of the Chord of Nature—that is to say, the realm of microtones now being opened up by the development of electronic music.

The harmonic series shows why the octave is the basic interval in all music. The octave is the first overtone, and is so close to the fundamental that when both tones are struck together they sound practically like one.

∙§ APPENDIX II §∙
A List of Recordings

IN THE following list the basic works discussed in the text are marked with an asterisk (*). A supplementary list of recorded works is included for those readers interested in further study. The situation in regard to recordings of contemporary music is extremely fluid. New titles are continually being added and old ones are being dropped. Up-to-date information will be found in the monthly issues of the *Schwann Long Playing Record Catalog*.

Chapter 2: THE TWILIGHT OF ROMANTICISM

WAGNER, Tristan and Isolde, Prelude and Love-Death
FRANCK, Symphony in D minor
TCHAIKOVSKY, Symphony No. 6 (Pathétique)
BRUCKNER, Symphony No. 4 (Romantic)
BRAHMS, Symphony No. 1

Chapter 3: THE CLASSICAL HERITAGE

HAYDN, Symphony No. 104 in D (London)
MOZART, Symphony No. 39 in E-flat
BEETHOVEN, Symphony No. 1

Chapter 4: MELODY IN CONTEMPORARY MUSIC

MOZART, Symphony No. 40 in G minor, first movement
TCHAIKOVSKY, Symphony No. 6 (Pathétique), first movement
BARBER, School for Scandal Overture
SHOSTAKOVICH, Symphony No. 1, first movement

Chapter 5: THE NEW HARMONY

MOZART, Piano Sonata in A, Turkish Rondo, last movement
WAGNER, Tristan and Isolde, Act II, Love Duet
IVES, Concord Piano Sonata, first movement

Chapter 6: NEW CONCEPTIONS OF TONALITY

PROKOFIEV, Peter and the Wolf (displacement of tonality)
HINDEMITH, Mathis der Maler Symphony, 2nd movement (expansion of tonality)
VAUGHAN WILLIAMS, Pastoral Symphony, first movement (modal harmony)

STRAVINSKY, Petrushka (bitonality)
MILHAUD, Les Choéphores (polytonality)
PROKOFIEV, Sarcasms for Piano (bitonality)

Chapter 7: RHYTHM IN CONTEMPORARY MUSIC

Gregorian chant: Kyrie from Mass Lux et Origo (free rhythm)
HAYDN, Symphony No. 94 in G major (Surprise), third movement (metrical rhythm)
BARTÓK, Allegro barbaro for piano (modern percussive rhythm)
BARTÓK, Romanian Dances (nonsymmetrical rhythm)
STRAVINSKY, Rite of Spring, "Sacrificial Dance of the Chosen Virgin" (multi-rhythm)
IVES, Three Places in New England, third movement (polyrhythm)

Chapter 8: TEXTURE IN CONTEMPORARY MUSIC

Gregorian chant: Alleluia, Assumpta est Maria (monophonic texture)
BACH, Little Fugue in G minor (polyphonic texture)
CHOPIN, Waltz in B minor (homophonic texture)
HINDEMITH, Concert Music for Strings & Brass (dissonant counterpoint)

Chapter 9: NEW CONCEPTS IN ORCHESTRATION

BACH, Brandenburg Concerto No. 5 (early 18th-century orchestration)
HAYDN, Symphony No. 94 in G (late 18th-century orchestration)
MENDELSSOHN, Italian Symphony (early 19th-century orchestration)
STRAUSS, The Merry Pranks of Till Eulenspiegel (late 19th-century orchestration)
DEBUSSY, La Mer (early 20th-century orchestration)
STRAVINSKY, Orpheus (20th-century orchestration)

Chapter 10: NEW CONCEPTIONS OF FORM

MOZART, Eine kleine Nachtmusik (classical form)
BEETHOVEN, Symphony No. 7
PROKOFIEV, Classical Symphony ⎫ 20th-century
SHOSTAKOVICH, Symphony No. 1 ⎬ adaptation of classical
STRAVINSKY, Symphony in C ⎭ form
BLOCH, Concerto Grosso No. 1 (20th-century adaptation of Baroque form)

Chapter 11: THE POSTROMANTIC GENERATION

FAURÉ, Ballade for Piano and Orchestra; Requiem; Sonata No. 1 for Violin; Songs; Quartet No. 2
ELGAR, Dream of Gerontius; Enigma Variations; Falstaff—Symphonic Study; Introduction & Allegro for Strings; Symphony No. 2

Chapter 12: GUSTAV MAHLER

*Das Lied von der Erde (The Song of the Earth)
Kindertotenlieder; Songs of a Wayfarer; Symphonies Nos. 1–10; Youth's Magic Horn

Chapter 13: RICHARD STRAUSS

*Salome
Ariadne auf Naxos; Death and Transfiguration; Don Juan; Don Quixote; Elektra; Ein Heldenleben; Rosenkavalier; Songs; Thus Spake Zarathustra; Till Eulenspiegel

Chapter 14: JEAN SIBELIUS

*Symphony No. 2 in D
Concerto in D minor for Violin; En Saga; Symphonies Nos. 1, 4, 7; Swan of Tuonela

Chapter 15: ALEXANDER SCRIABIN

*Poem of Ecstasy
Concerto for Piano and Orchestra; Prometheus (Poem of Fire); Preludes; Sonatas for Piano Nos. 3, 5, 9.

Chapter 16: OTHER LATE ROMANTICS

JANÁČEK, Diary of One Who Vanished; From the House of the Dead; Slavonic Mass
WOLF, Italian Serenade; Songs
REGER, Variations & Fugue on a Merry Theme by Hiller; Variations & Fugue on a Theme by Mozart
PFITZNER, Lieder
PUCCINI, Turandot
ALBENIZ, Iberia; Navarra; Spanish Dances
GRANADOS, Goyescas, Spanish Dances
LIADOV, Baba Yaga; Enchanted Lake; Kikimora
ARENSKY, Variations on a Theme by Tchaikovsky
GLAZUNOV, Violin Concerto; The Seasons; Stenka Razin (symphonic poem)
RACHMANINOV, Piano Concerto No. 2; Symphony No. 2; Rhapsody on a Theme of Paganini; Songs
D'INDY, Istar—Symphonic Variations; Symphony on a French Mountain Air
DUPARC, Songs
CHAUSSON, Poème de l'Amour et de la Mer; Poème for violin and orchestra; Symphony in B-flat
DUKAS, La Péri; The Sorcerer's Apprentice; Symphony in C

Chapter 17: IMPRESSIONISM
Chapter 18: IMPRESSIONIST METHODS

DEBUSSY, La Cathédrale engloutie (modal harmony); Preludes for Piano, Book I—Voiles (whole-tone scale); Preludes for Piano, Book I—La Fille aux cheveux de lin (pentatonic scale); Estampes for piano, No. 1—Pagodes (pentatonic scale); Estampes for piano, No. 2—Soirée dans Grenade (gliding chords); Chansons de Bilitis, No. 1 (parallel fifths); Preludes for Piano, Book I—Ce qu'a vu le vent d'Ouest (unresolved final cadence); Preludes for Piano, Book II—General Lavine, Eccentric (escaped chords)

Chapter 19: CLAUDE DEBUSSY

*Ibéria
*La Cathédrale engloutie
*La Chevelure
   Arabesques; Children's Corner Suite; La Damoiselle élue; Danse; Estampes
for piano; Le Martyre de St. Sébastien; La Mer; Nocturnes for orchestra—
Nuages, Fêtes, Sirènes; Pelléas et Mélisande; Petite Suite; Prélude à l'après
midi d'un faune; Preludes for piano; Quartet in G minor; Sonata for violin
and piano; Songs; Suite bergamasque

Chapter 20: MAURICE RAVEL

*Daphnis and Chloé, Suite No. 2
*Jeux d'eau
   Alborada del Gracioso; Boléro; Concerto in D minor for the Left Hand;
Concerto in G for piano and orchestra; L'Enfant et les sortilèges;
Gaspard de la nuit; L'Heure espagnole; Introduction and Allegro; Ma
Mere l'Oye; Pavane pour une Infante défunte; Quartet in F; La Valse;
Valses nobles et sentimentales; Shéhérazade; Trio in A minor

Chapter 21: FREDERICK DELIUS

*Sea Drift
   Appalachia; Brigg Fair; On Hearing the First Cuckoo in Spring; Walk
to the Paradise Garden; Song of Summer; Mass of Life; Paris

Chapter 22: OTHER IMPRESSIONISTS

RESPIGHI, Ancient Airs and Dances; Fountains of Rome; Pines of Rome
SZYMANOWSKI, Violin Concerto; La Fontaine d'Aréthuse; Quartet in C

Chapter 23: NEW TRENDS—THE FLIGHT FROM ROMANTICISM

BARTÓK, Allegro barbaro (primitivism)
HONEGGER, Pacific 231 (machine music)
HONEGGER, Rugby (influence of sports)
HONEGGER, Concertino for Piano and Orchestra, last movement (jazz influence)
HINDEMITH, 1922 Suite for Piano (jazz influence)
STRAVINSKY, Ragtime for Eleven Instruments (jazz influence)

Chapter 25: IGOR STRAVINSKY
Chapter 26: THREE WORKS BY STRAVINSKY

*Le Sacre du printemps
*L'Histoire du soldat
*Symphony of Psalms
   Apollon Musagète; Le Baiser de la Fée; Capriccio for piano and orchestra;
Danses Concertantes; Suite from The Firebird; Les Noces; Octet; Oedipus

Rex; Orpheus; Petrushka; The Rake's Progress; Symphony in C; Symphony in Three Movements (For Stravinsky's late works, see entries for Chapter 60.)

Chapter 27: BÉLA BARTÓK
Chapter 28: THREE WORKS BY BARTÓK

*Concerto for Orchestra
*Music for String Instruments, Percussion and Celesta
*Fourth String Quartet
  Allegro barbaro; Bagatelles; Romanian Dances; Piano Concertos Nos. 1, 2, 3; Violin Concerto; Divertimento for String Orchestra; Mikrokosmos; Suite from The Miraculous Mandarin; Quartets Nos. 1–6; Sonata for Two Pianos and Percussion; Two Portraits for Orchestra; The Wooden Prince

Chapter 29: PAUL HINDEMITH

*Symphony: Mathis der Maler
  Concert Music for Piano, Brass and Two Harps; Concerto for Orchestra; Kleine Kammermusik, Opus 24, No. 2; Nobilissima Visione; Schwanendreher, for viola and orchestra; Sonata No. 3 for Piano; Symphonia Serena; Symphonic Metamorphosis on Themes by Weber; Symphony Harmonie der Welt; Symphony in E-flat; Theme and 4 Variations, The Four Temperaments

Chapter 30: ERIK SATIE

*Parade
  Mass for the Poor; Piano Music; Socrate; Three Pieces in the Shape of a Pear; Trois Gymnopédies

Chapter 31: LES SIX. See entries for Chapters 32, 33, 34
Chapter 32: DARIUS MILHAUD

*La Création du monde
*Scaramouche
  Le Boeuf sur le toit; Carnaval d'Aix, for piano and orchestra; La Cheminée du Roi René; Les Choéphores; Kentuckiana; Les Malheurs d'Orphée; Pastorale; Le Pauvre Matelot; Protée—Symphonic Suite No. 2; Saudades do Brasil; Serenade for Orchestra; Suite Française; Symphony No. 2

Chapter 33: ARTHUR HONEGGER

*Symphony No. 5
  Concertino for piano and orchestra; Jeanne d'Arc au Bûcher; Pacific 231; Pastorale d'Été

Chapter 34: FRANCIS POULENC

*La Voix humaine
  Le Bal masqué; Piano Concerto; Dialogues des Carmélites; Litanies à la Vierge Noire de Rocomadour; Mouvements perpetuels; Songs; Stabat Mater

GLIÈRE, The Red Poppy, Ballet Suite; Symphony No. 3, Ilya Murometz
MIASKOVSKY, Symphony No. 19 in E-flat

Chapter 43: SERGEI PROKOFIEV

*Piano Concerto No. 3
Alexander Nevsky; Suite No. 1 from The Buffoon; Cinderella—Suites Nos. 1 and 2; Classical Symphony; Piano Concertos Nos. 1, 2, and 5; Violin Concertos Nos. 1 and 2; Lieutenant Kije Suite; Suite from The Love for Three Oranges; Peter and the Wolf; Piano music; Romeo and Juliet; Piano Sonatas Nos. 1–9; Sonatas for violin and piano, in F minor and in D; The Stone Flower; Symphonies Nos. 4, 5, 6, 7; Visions Fugitives

Chapter 44: DMITRI SHOSTAKOVICH

*Symphony No. 5
The Age of Gold; Ballets Suites Nos. 1, 2, 3; Piano Concerto No. 2; Violin Concerto; Quartets Nos. 1, 2, 4, 5; Song of the Forest; Symphonies Nos. 1, 6, 7, 9, 10, 11; Trio in E minor for piano, violin, cello

Chapter 45: OTHER SOVIET COMPOSERS

KHATCHATURIAN, Cello Concerto; Piano Concerto; Violin Concerto; Gayane —Ballet Suites Nos. 1 and 2; Spartacus—Ballet Suite; Symphony No. 2
KABALEVSKY, Children's Pieces; Colas Breugnon Suite; The Comedians; Cello Concerto; Piano Concerto No. 3; Violin Concerto; Symphony No. 4
KHRENNIKOV, Much Ado about Nothing—Suite; Symphony No. 1

Chapter 46: RALPH VAUGHAN WILLIAMS

*A London Symphony
English Folk Song Suite; Fantasia on a Theme by Tallis; Greensleeves; Mass in G minor; Norfolk Rhapsody; On Wenlock Edge; Serenade to Music; Symphonies Nos. 1, 3, 4, 5, 6, 7, 8, 9; The Wasps

Chapter 47: BENJAMIN BRITTEN

*Peter Grimes
A Ceremony of Carols; Les Illuminations; The Little Sweep; The Prince of the Pagodas; Serenade for tenor, horn, strings; The Turn of the Screw; Variations on a Theme of Frank Bridge; Young Person's Guide to the Orchestra

Chapter 48: TOWARD A NEW ROMANTICISM

DOHNÁNYI, Piano Concerto No. 2; Serenade in C; Variations on a Nursery Theme
PIZZETTI, Concerto dell'Estate; La Pisanella—Suite
CASTELNUOVO-TEDESCO, Violin Concerto No. 2; Overture, Much Ado about Nothing
IRELAND, Piano Concerto in E-flat
BAX, Coronation March; Garden of Fand; Tintagel

Lulu; Quartet, Opus 3; Sonata for Piano, Opus 1; Three Pieces for Orchestra, Opus 6

Chapter 58: ANTON WEBERN
Chapter 59: THREE WORKS BY WEBERN

*Five Pieces for Orchestra, Opus 10
*Symphony for Small Orchestra, Opus 21
*Cantata No. 1, Opus 29
  The complete works of Anton Webern

Chapter 60: TWO LATE WORKS BY STRAVINSKY

*Agon
*Threni: Id est Lamentationes Jeremiae Prophetae
  Cantata; Canticum Sacrum; In Memoriam Dylan Thomas; Mass; Two Motets; Septet; Three Shakespeare Songs

Chapter 61: LUIGI DALLAPICCOLA

*Variazioni per Orchestra
  Tartiniana for violin and orchestra

Chapter 62: PARTLY TWELVE-TONE

MARTIN, Ballade for flute and orchestra; Petite Symphonie Concertante
PETRASSI, Concerto for Orchestra; Coro di Morti; Don Quixote—ballet suite
LIEBERMANN, Concerto for Jazz Band and Orchestra; Furioso for orchestra; School for Wives

Chapter 64: KARLHEINZ STOCKHAUSEN

*Zeitmasse

Chapter 65: PIERRE BOULEZ

*Le Marteau sans maître

Chapter 66: OTHER AVANT-GARDE COMPOSERS

The European composers of this group are not yet represented on American commercial recordings. But their music is certain to become available on records as time goes on.

Chapter 67: MUSIC IN AMERICA

CHADWICK, Symphonic Sketches
FOOTE, Suite in E for Strings
MACDOWELL, Piano Concertos Nos. 1 and 2; Piano Sonata No. 4, Keltic; Indian Suite; Woodland Sketches

Chapter 68: IMPRESSIONISTS

LOEFFLER, Memories of My Childhood; Poem—La Bonne Chanson
CARPENTER, Adventures in a Perambulator; Gitanjali Songs

HILL, Prelude for Orchestra; Sextet for piano and winds
TAYLOR, Through the Looking Glass
GRIFFES, The Pleasure-Dome of Kubla Khan; Poem for Flute and Orchestra;
  Sonata for Piano; The White Peacock

Chapter 69: CHARLES IVES

*Three Places in New England
  Set of Pieces; Sixty-Seventh Psalm; Sonatas for violin and piano, Nos. 1–4;
  Songs; Symphonies Nos. 2, 3, and 4

Chapter 70: DOUGLAS MOORE

*The Ballad of Baby Doe
  The Devil and Daniel Webster; Farm Journal; In Memoriam; Pageant
  of P. T. Barnum; Symphony No. 2

Chapter 71: ROY HARRIS

*Third Symphony
  Kentucky Spring; Sonata for Violin and Piano; Symphony 1933; Symphony No. 7; Trio

Chapter 72: RANDALL THOMPSON

*The Testament of Freedom
  Alleluia; Mass of the Holy Spirit; The Peaceable Kingdom

Chapter 73: AARON COPLAND
Chapter 74: TWO WORKS BY COPLAND

*Appalachian Spring
*Symphony No. 3
  Billy the Kid; Concerto for clarinet and orchestra; Dance Symphony;
  Danzón Cubano; A Lincoln Portrait; Piano Variations; Quartet for
  Piano and Strings; Quiet City; The Red Pony; Rodeo; El Salón México;
  Sonata for piano; Statements for Orchestra; Twelve Poems of Emily
  Dickinson; Variations for orchestra; Variations for piano; Vitebsk, Study
  on a Jewish Theme

Chapter 75: OTHER NATIONALISTS

GRUENBERG, Concerto for Violin and Orchestra
SOWERBY, All on a Summer's Day; Classic Concerto for Organ and Or-
  chestra; Toccata for organ
STILL, Afro-American Symphony
BACON, Enchanted Island; Five Hymns; From Emily's Diary
SIEGMEISTER, Sunday in Brooklyn
GOULD, Ballad for Band, Declaration Suite; Fall River Legend; Interplay for
  Piano and Orchestra; Jekyll and Hyde Variations; Latin-American Sym-
  phonette; Spirituals for Orchestra
SURINACH, Concerto for piano, strings and cymbals; Overture, Feria Magica;
  Ritmo Jondo; Sinfonietta Flamenca; Symphony No. 2; Tientos

A List of Recordings

665

Chapter 76: LATIN AMERICA. See entries under
Chapters 77–79
Chapter 77: HEITOR VILLA-LOBOS

*Bachianas Brasileiras No. 5
Alvorada na Floresta Tropical; Bachianas Brasileiras Nos. 1, 2, 4, 6–9;
Chôros Nos. 1, 7; Fantasia Concertante for orchestra of cellos; Forest of
the Amazon; Little Train of the Caipira; Momoprecoce; Piano music;
Songs; Uirapurú

Chapter 78: CARLOS CHÁVEZ

*Sinfonía India
Sinfonía Antígona; Sinfonía Romántica; Toccata for percussion; Tree
of Sorrow

79: OTHER LATIN-AMERICAN COMPOSERS

GUARNIERI, Dansa Brasileira; Sonatina for flute and piano; Suite IV Cente-
nario
REVUELTAS, Cuauhnahuac; Homenaje a Federico García Lorca; Ocho por
Radio; Songs
GINASTERA, *Estancia* (ballet suite); Lamentations of Jeremiah; Pampeana No.
3; Panambí (ballet suite); Quartet No. 1; Variaciones Concertantes
NIN, Vilancicos
CATURLA, Cuban Suite No. 1 for piano and winds
ROLDÁN, Ritmica No. 1 for piano and winds
GALINDO, Sones Mariachi
AYALA, Tribú
MONCAYO, Cumbres; Huapango

Chapter 80: WALTER PISTON

*Symphony No. 4
The Incredible Flutist (ballet suite); Quintet for wind instruments; Sere-
nata; Sonata for violin and piano; Symphonies Nos. 3 and 6; Tunbridge
Fair

Chapter 81: QUINCY PORTER

*String Quartet No. 8
Concerto Concertante for two pianos; Poem and Dance; Quartet No. 6;
Symphony No. 1

Chapter 82: OTHER CLASSICISTS—I

DONOVAN, New England Chronicle; Suite for oboe and string orchestra
WAGENAAR, Concert Overture
KERR, Trio for violin, cello and piano
LOPATNIKOV, Concertino for orchestra; Music for orchestra; Variations and
Epilogue for Cello and Piano
PHILLIPS, Selections from McGuffey's Reader.

STEVENS, Like as the Culver; Sinfonia Breve; Symphony No. 1; Triskelion
GERCHEFSKI, Saugatuck Suite
SWANSON, Night Music; Suite for cello and piano

Chapter 83: WILLIAM SCHUMAN

*Credendum
  Chester (overture for band); George Washington Bridge; New England
  Triptych; Symphony No. 6; Undertow; Voyage

Chapter 84: LUKAS FOSS

*A Parable of Death
  Capriccio for cello and piano; The Jumping Frog of Calaveras County;
  Psalms; Behold! I Build a House; Quartet No. 1

Chapter 85: PETER MENNIN

*Symphony No. 3
  Canzona for band; Quartet No. 2; Symphony No. 6

Chapter 86: OTHER CLASSICISTS—II

BERGER, Duo for cello and piano; Polyphony for Orchestra
READ, Three Preludes on Old Southern Hymns; Toccata Giocosa
DAHL, Allegro and Arioso; Music for brass instruments; Tower of St. Bar-
  bara—Symphonic Legend
HELM, Concerto No. 2 for Piano and Orchestra
MILLS, Prelude and Dithyramb; The True Beauty
LESSARD, Concerto for winds and strings
GOEB, Concertino II for Orchestra; Quintet for woodwinds; Symphony No. 3
KUBIK, Sonata for piano; Celebrations and Epilogue; Symphonie-Concer-
  tante; Symphony No. 2
HAIEFF, Ballet in E; Quartet No. 1; Symphony No. 2
FINE, Music for Piano; Quartet; Serious Song—Lament for String Orchestra
DIAMOND, Rounds for String Orchestra; Symphony No. 4
PALMER, Quartet for piano and strings
PERSICHETTI, Concerto for piano, four hands; Divertimento for band; Sym-
  phonies Nos. 4, 5, 6
KOHS, Chamber Concerto for viola and strings; Symphony No. 1
KAY, How Stands the Glass Around?; Round Dance and Polka; Serenade for
  orchestra
WIGGLESWORTH, Symphony No. 1
SHAPERO, Credo for Orchestra; Symphony for Classical Orchestra; Three
  Sonatas for piano
IMBRIE, Quartets Nos. 1, 2, and 3; Sonata for piano
LEES, Quartet No. 1; Symphony No. 2
PINKHAM, Cantilena for Violin and Harpsichord; Concerto for Celesta and
  Harpsichord; Madrigal
SMITH, Songs of Innocence; Tetrameron
BLACKWOOD, Symphony No. 1

A List of Recordings

Chapter 87: VIRGIL THOMSON

*Louisiana Story
   Cello Concerto; Filling Station; Psalms 123 and 126; Quartet No. 2; A
   Solemn Music; Variations on Sunday School Tunes

Chapter 88: HOWARD HANSON

Chorale and Alleluia; Elegy; Fantasy Variations on a Theme of Youth;
   Lament for Beowulf; Merry Mount Suite; Serenade for flute, harp, strings;
   Songs from Drum Taps; Symphonies Nos. 2, 4, 5

Chapter 89: OTHER ROMANTICISTS—I

JAMES, Symphony No. 1
JACOBI, Concerto for violin; Concertino for piano; Music Hall Overture
ROGERS, Five Fairy Tales; Soliloquy for flute and strings; Three Japanese
   Dances
ELWELL, Concert Suite for violin and orchestra
VINCENT, Symphony In D
CRESTON, Celebration Overture; Choric Dances; Dance Overture; Invoca-
   tion and Dance; Lydian Ode; Symphonies Nos. 2 and 3
JOHNSON, Trio for flute, oboe and piano

Chapter 90: SAMUEL BARBER

*Essay for Orchestra, No. 1
*Medea's Meditation and Dance of Vengeance
   Adagio for strings; Capricorn Concerto; Hermit Songs; Music for a scene
   from Shelley; Overture to "The School for Scandal"; Quartet No. 1;
   Sonata for cello and piano; Symphonies Nos. 1 and 2; Vanessa

Chapter 91: NORMAN DELLO JOIO

*Variations, Chaconne and Finale
   Meditations on Ecclesiastes; Piano Sonata No. 3; Symphonic suite, Air
   Power; Triumph of St. Joan Symphony; Variations and Capriccio for
   violin

Chapter 92: OTHER ROMANTICISTS—II

NORDOFF, Winter Symphony
BARLOW, Rhapsody for oboe, The Winter's Past
GLANVILLE-HICKS, Sonata for harp; Sonata for piano and percussion; The
   Transposed Heads
BOWLES, Music for a Farce; Picnic Cantata
SCOTT, Binorie Variations
HOVHANESS, Concertos for orchestra Nos. 1 and 7; Meditation on Orpheus;
   Mysterious Mountain; Prelude and Quadruple Fugue; Suite for violin,
   piano and percussion
WARD, Euphony for Orchestra; Symphony No. 2

BERGSMA, Carol on Twelfth Night; The Fortunate Islands; Music on a Quiet Theme; Quartet No. 3; The Wife of Martin Guerre
BEESON, Hello Out There
ROREM, Design for Orchestra
LEVY, For the Time Being

Chapter 93: GEORGE GERSHWIN

*An American in Paris
Concerto in F for piano; Cuban Overture; Porgy and Bess; Preludes for piano; Rhapsody in Blue; Songs

Chapter 94: KURT WEILL

Berlin theater songs; Rise and Fall of the City of Mahagonny; Seven Deadly Sins; Songs; The Three-Penny Opera

Chapter 95: MARC BLITZSTEIN

Regina

Chapter 96: GIAN CARLO MENOTTI

*Amahl and the Night Visitors
The Consul; Maria Golovin; The Medium; The Saint of Bleecker Street; The Unicorn, the Gorgon, and the Manticore

Chapter 97: LEONARD BERNSTEIN

The Age of Anxiety; Fancy Free; Serenade for violin, strings and percussion; Trouble in Tahiti; West Side Story

Chapter 98: OTHER OPERA COMPOSERS

Giannini, The Taming of the Shrew

Chapter 99: CARL RUGGLES

*Lilacs
Evocations; Portals; Organum for orchestra

Chapter 100: ROGER SESSIONS

*Symphony No. 1
*Idyll of Theocritus
The Black Maskers; Chorale No. 1 for organ; From My Diary; Quartet No. 2; Sonata No. 2 for Piano; Symphony No. 2

Chapter 101: ELLIOTT CARTER

*Variations for Orchestra.
*String Quartet No. 2.
Eight Etudes and a Fantasy; The Minotaur; Quartet No. 1; Woodwind Quintet

Chapter 102: HUGO WEISGALL

The Stronger; The Tenor

Chapter 103: LEON KIRCHNER

*Piano Concerto.
  Quartet No. 1; Sonata Concertante for violin and piano; Trio for violin, cello, and piano

Chapter 104: OTHER EXPRESSIONIST COMPOSERS

GIDEON, How Goodly Are Thy Tents; Symphonia Brevis
LADERMAN, Quartet; Theme, Variations and Finale
LAYTON, Quartet in Two Movements
STARER, Five Miniatures for Brass
SCHIFRIN, Serenade for Five Instruments

Chapter 105: WALLINGFORD RIEGGER

*Symphony No. 3.
  Concerto for piano and woodwind quintet; Dance Rhythms; New Dance; Quintet; Variations for Piano and Orchestra; Variations for Violin and Orchestra

Chapter 106: ERNST KRENEK

Eleven Transparencies; Lamentations of Jeremiah; Sonatas for organ, Nos. 1, 3, 4; Sonatas for piano, Nos. 3, 4, and 5

Chapter 108: TWELVE-TONE AND PARTLY TWELVE-TONE COMPOSERS

WOLPE, Sonata for violin; Passacaglia; Percussion Quartet; Ten Songs from the Hebrew
FINNEY, Piano Quintet; Quartet No. 6
PERLE, Rhapsody for Orchestra
BABBITT, Woodwind Quartet; All Set
WEBER, Concertino for flute, oboe, clarinet and string quartet; Prelude and Passacaglia; Symphony on Poems of William Blake

Chapter 109: MEL POWELL

*Filigree Setting for String Quartet
  Divertimento for Five Winds; Divertimento for Violin and Harp; Trio for violin, cello and piano

Chapter 110: EDGAR VARÈSE

*Ionisation
*Poème électronique
  Density 21.5; Hyperprism; Intégrales; Octandre

Chapter 111: OTHER EXPERIMENTAL COMPOSERS

LUENING AND USSACHEVSKY, Poem in Cycles and Bells for Tape Recorder and
   Orchestra; Rhapsodic Variations for Tape Recorder and Orchestra
COWELL, Music 1957; Ongaku for orchestra; Piano music
ANTHEIL, Ballet mécanique
PARTCH, King Oedipus; Plectra and Percussion Dances
CAGE, Indeterminacy
BRANT, Angels and Devils—Concerto for Flute; Signs and Alarms; Galaxy 2
HARRISON, Four Strict Songs; Mass for Mixed Chorus, Trumpet, Harp,
   Strings; Song of Quetzalcoatl; Suite for violin, piano and small orchestra

❧ APPENDIX III ☙

A List of Books

(a) GENERAL

Abraham, Gerald. *Eight Soviet Composers.* London: Oxford U. Press, 1944.
———. *This Modern Music.* N.Y.: Norton, 1952.
Bacharach, A. L., ed. "The Twentieth Century," Vol. 4 of *The Music
   Masters.* Baltimore: Penguin Books, 1957.
Bauer, Marion. *Twentieth Century Music.* N.Y.: Putnam, 1947.
Boelza, Ign F. *Handbook of Soviet Musicians.* London: Pilot Press, Ltd.,
   1943.
Brook, Donald. *Composers' Gallery.* London: Rockliff, 1946.
———. *Five Great French Composers.* London: Rockliff, 1946.
———. *Six Great Russian Composers.* London: Rockliff, 1946.
Cardus, Neville. *Ten Composers.* London: Jonathan Cape, 1945.
Calvocoressi, M., and G. Abraham. *Masters of Russian Music.* N.Y.: Knopf,
   1936.
Chase, Gilbert. *America's Music, from the Pilgrims to the Present.* N.Y.:
   McGraw-Hill, 1955.
Demuth, Norman. *Musical Trends in the Twentieth Century.* London:
   Rockliff, 1952.
Dyson, George. *The New Music.* N.Y.: Oxford U. Press, 1924.
Ewen, David, ed. *The Book of Modern Composers.* N.Y.: Knopf, 1950.
Frank, Alan. *Modern British Composers.* London: Dobson, 1953.
Goss, Madeleine. *Modern Music Makers.* N.Y.: Dutton, 1952.
Graf, Max. *Modern Music.* N.Y.: Philosophical Library, 1946.
Gray, Cecil. *A Survey of Contemporary Music.* N.Y.: Oxford, 1924.
Hartog, Howard, ed. *European Music in the Twentieth Century.* New
   York: Frederick A. Praeger, 1957.
Hill, Edward. *Modern French Music.* N.Y.: Houghton Mifflin, 1924.

Howard, John Tasker, and James Lyons. *Modern Music*. N.Y.: Crowell, 1957.

Howard, John Tasker. *Our Contemporary Composers*. N.Y.: Crowell, 1941.

Lambert, Constant. *Music Ho!* London: Faber & Faber, 1941.

Mellers, Wilfrid. *Romanticism and the Twentieth Century*. Fairlawn, N.J.: Essential Books, 1957.

————. *Studies in Contemporary Music*. London: Dobson, 1947.

Myers, Rollo H. *Music in the Modern World*. London: Arnold, 1948.

Pannain, Guido. *Modern Composers*. London: Dent, 1932.

Pleasants, Henry. *The Agony of Modern Music*. N.Y.: Simon and Schuster, 1955.

Reihe, Die, No. 1. *Electronic Music*. Bryn Mawr: Presser, 1957.

Reis, Claire. *Composers in America*. N.Y.: Macmillan, 1938.

Rosenfeld, Paul. *An Hour With American Music*. Philadelphia: Lippincott, 1929.

Rostand, Claude. *French Music Today*. N.Y.: Merlin Press.

Sabaneyev, L. *Modern Russian Composers*. N.Y.: International, 1927.

Salazar, Adolfo. *Music in Our Time*. N.Y.: Norton, 1946.

Saminsky, Lazare. *Living Music of the Americas*. N.Y.: Crown, 1949.

————. *Music of Our Day*. N.Y.: Crowell, 1932.

Slonimsky, Nicolas. *Music of Latin America*. N.Y.: Crowell, 1945.

————. *Music Since 1900*. N.Y.: Coleman-Ross, 1949.

Swan, Alfred J. *Music, 1900–1930*. N.Y.: Norton, 1929.

Thompson, Oscar. *Great Modern Composers*. N.Y.: Dodd, Mead, 1941.

(b) BOOKS ON MUSICAL THEORY

Carner, Mosco. *A Study of Twentieth-Century Harmony*. N.Y.: Mills Music, Inc.

Dallin, Leon. *Techniques of Twentieth-Century Composition*. Dubuque: Wm. C. Brown Co., 1957.

Eschman, Karl H. *Changing Forms in Modern Music*. Boston: E. C. Schermer, 1945.

Forte, Allen. *Contemporary Tone-Structures*. N.Y.: Columbia U. Press, 1955.

Hanson, Howard. *The Harmonic Materials of Modern Music*. N.Y.: Appleton, 1960.

Hindemith, Paul. *The Craft of Musical Composition*. N.Y.: Associated Music Publishers, 1945.

Katz, Adele T. *Challenge to Musical Tradition*. N.Y.: Knopf, 1945.

Krenek, Ernst. *Studies in Counterpoint*. N.Y.: G. Schirmer, 1940.

Messiaen, Olivier. *The Technique of My Musical Language*. Paris, A. Leduc, 1956.

Leibowitz, René, and Jan Maguire. *Thinking for Orchestra*. N.Y.: G. Schirmer, 1960.

Lenormand, René. *A Study of Twentieth-Century Harmony*. Transl. Herbert Antcliffe. N.Y.: Mills Music, 1915.

Miller, Horace. *New Harmonic Devices*. Philadelphia: Oliver Ditson, 1930.

Piston, Walter. *Counterpoint*. N.Y.: Norton, 1947.

————. *Harmony*. N.Y.: Norton, 1948.

————. *Orchestration*. N.Y.: Norton, 1955.

Reti, Rudolf. *Tonality—Atonality—Pantonality*. N.Y.: Macmillan, 1958.

Rochberg, George. *The Hexachord and its Relation to the Twelve-Tone Row*. Bryn Mawr: Presser, 1955.

Rufer, Josef. *Composition with Twelve Notes Related to One Another*. London: Rockliff, 1954.

Schoenberg, Arnold. *Models for Beginners in Composition*. N.Y.: G. Schirmer, 1943.

———. *Theory of Harmony*. N.Y.: Philosophical Library, 1948.

———. *Structural Functions of Harmony*. N.Y.: Norton, 1954.

Searle, Humphrey. *Twentieth Century Counterpoint*. N.Y.: De Graff, 1954.

Vincent, John N. *The Diatonic Modes in Modern Music*. N.Y.: Mills, 1951.

Yasser, Joseph. *A Theory of Evolving Tonality*. N.Y.: American Library of Musicology, 1932.

(c) BOOKS BY COMPOSERS ON MUSICAL ESTHETICS

Chávez, Carlos. *Toward a New Music*. N.Y.: Norton, 1937.

Copland, Aaron. *Music and Imagination*. Cambridge: Harvard Univ. Press, 1952.

———. *Our New Music*. N.Y.: Whittlesey House, 1941.

Cowell, Henry Dixon. *American Composers on American Music*. Stanford: Stanford Univ. Press, 1933.

Debussy, Claude. *Monsieur Croche*. N.Y.: Vilny, 1928.

Hindemith, Paul. *A Composer's World*. Cambridge: Harvard Univ. Press, 1952.

Krenek, Ernst. *Music Here and Now*. N.Y.: Norton, 1939.

Schoenberg, Arnold. *Style and Idea*. N.Y.: Philosophical Library, 1950.

Sessions, Roger. *The Musical Experience of Composer, Performer, Listener*. Princeton: Princeton Univ. Press, 1950.

Stravinsky, Igor. *Poetics of Music*. Cambridge: Harvard Univ. Press, 1947.

Stravinsky, Igor, and Robert Craft. *Conversations with Igor Stravinsky*. N.Y.: Doubleday, 1959.

———. *Memoirs and Commentaries*. N.Y.: Doubleday, 1960.

Vaughan Williams, Ralph. *The Making of Music*. Ithaca: Cornell Univ. Press, 1955.

———. *National Music*. London, 1934.

(d) BOOKS ON INDIVIDUAL COMPOSERS

Armitage, Merle, ed. *Schoenberg*. N.Y.: G. Schirmer, 1937.

———. *George Gershwin*. N.Y.: Longmans, 1938.

Armitage, Merle. *George Gershwin, Man and Legend*. N.Y.: Duell, Sloan, 1958.

Barricelli, Jean Pierre and Leo Weinstein, *Ernest Chausson*. Norman, Okla.: Univ. of Oklahoma Press, 1955.

Berger, Arthur. *Aaron Copland*. N.Y.: Oxford Univ. Press, 1953.

Broder, Nathan. *Samuel Barber*. N.Y.: G. Schirmer, 1954.

Busoni, Ferruccio. *Letters To His Wife*. Tr. by Rosamond Ley. London: E. Arnold, 1938.

Cowell, Henry, and Sidney Cowell. *Charles Ives and His Music*. N.Y.: Oxford Univ. Press, 1955.

Demuth, Norman. *Albert Roussel, A Study*. London. United Music Publishers, 1947.

———. *Vincent D'Indy*. London: Rockliff, 1951.

———. *Ravel*. London: Dent, 1947.

Dent, Edward J. *Ferruccio Busoni*. London: Oxford Univ. Press, 1933.

Ekman, Karl. *Jean Sibelius*. Tr. Edward Birse. N.Y.: Knopf, 1938.

Fassett, Agatha. *The Naked Face of Genius: Béla Bartók's American Years*. Boston: Houghton Mifflin, 1958.

Foss, Hubert J. *Ralph Vaughan Williams. A Study*. London: Harrap, 1950.

Gatti, Guido M. *Ildebrando Pizzetti*. London: Dobson, 1951.

Goldberg, Isaac. *George Gershwin, A Study in American Music*. N.Y.: Ungar, 1958.

Goossens, Eugene. *Overture and Beginners*. London: Methuen, 1951.

Haraszti, Emil. *Béla Bartók: His Life and Works*. Paris: Lyrebird, 1938.

Hell, Henri. *Francis Poulenc*. N.Y.: Grove Press, 1959.

Heseltine, Philip. *Frederick Delius*. London: John Lane, 1923.

Hoover, Kathleen, *Virgil Thomson*. N.Y.: Yoseloff, 1959.

Howes, Frank. *The Music of Ralph Vaughan Williams*. N.Y.: Oxford Univ. Press, 1954.

———. *The Music of William Walton*. London: Oxford Univ. Press, 1942.

Hull, Arthur E. *A Great Russian Tone-Poet, Scriabin*. London: K. Paul, Trench, Trubner & Co. Ltd., 1916.

Hutchings, Arthur. *Delius*. N.Y.: Macmillan, 1948.

Jablonski, Edward. *The Gershwin Years*. N.Y.: Doubleday, 1958.

Johnson, Harold. *Jean Sibelius*. N.Y.: Knopf, 1959.

Koechlin, Charles. *Gabriel Fauré*. Tr. L. Orrey. London: Dobson, 1945.

Lederman, Minna, ed. *Stravinsky in the Theatre*. N.Y.: Pellegrini & Cudahy, 1949.

Leibowitz, René. *Schoenberg and His School*. Tr. by Dika Newlin. N.Y.: Philosophical Library, 1949.

Lockspeiser, Edward. *Debussy*. N.Y.: Pellegrini and Cudahy, 1951.

Mahler, Alma. *Gustav Mahler*. N.Y.: Viking, 1946.

Maine, Basil. *Elgar, His Life and Works*. London: W. Bell & Sons Ltd., 1933.

Maisel, Edward M. *Charles T. Griffes: The Life of an American Composer*. N.Y.: Knopf, 1943.

Manuel, Roland. *Maurice Ravel*. Tr. Cynthia Jolly. London: Dobson, 1947.

Martynov, Ivan. *Dmitri Schostakovich, The Man and his Works*. N.Y.: Philosophical Library, 1947.

Milhaud, Darius. *Notes Without Music*. N.Y.: Knopf, 1953.

Mitchell, D. and Keller, Hans, editors. *Benjamin Britten: A Commentary on his Works from a Group of Specialists*. London: Rockliff, 1952.

Mitchell, Donald. *Gustav Mahler: The Early Years*. London: Rockliff, 1958.

Myers, Rollo. *Erik Satie*. London: Dobson, 1948.

———. *Introduction to the Music of Stravinsky*. London: Dobson, 1950.

Nestyev, Israel. *Sergei Prokofiev*. Stanford, Calif. Stanford Univ. Press, 1946.

Newlin, Dika. *Bruckner, Mahler, Schoenberg.* N.Y.: Columbia Univ. Press, 1947.

Newman, Ernst. *Richard Strauss.* London: John Lane, 1908.

Pahissa, Jaime. *Manuel de Falla.* London: Museum Press, 1954.

Pakenham, Simona. *Ralph Vaughan Williams: A Discovery of his Music.* London: Macmillan, 1957.

Redlich, Hans. *Alban Berg.* N.Y.: Abelard-Schuman, 1957.

———. *Bruckner and Mahler.* London: Dent, 1955.

Reich, Willi. *Alban Berg.* Vienna: H. Reichner, 1937.

———. *A Guide to Alban Berg's Opera, Wozzeck.* N.Y.: League of Composers, 1931.

Reihe, Die. No. 2. *Anton Webern.* Bryn Mawr: Presser, 1957.

———. No. 4. *Young Composers.* Bryn Mawr: Presser, 1960.

Schreiber, Flora R. and V. Persichetti. *William Schuman.* N.Y.: Schirmer, 1954.

Seroff, Victor. *Debussy, Musician of France.* N.Y.: Putnam, 1956.

———. *Dmitri Schostakovich: The Life and Background of a Soviet Composer.* N.Y.: Knopf, 1943.

———. *Maurice Ravel.* N.Y.: Holt, 1953.

Shera, Frank Henry. *Debussy and Ravel.* London: Oxford Univ. Press, 1925.

Smith, Julia. *Aaron Copland.* N.Y.: Dutton, 1955.

Sofránek, Miloš. *Bohuslav Martinu, The Man and his Music.* N.Y.: Knopf, 1944.

Stevens, Halsey. *The Life and Music of Béla Bartók.* N.Y.: Oxford Univ. Press, 1953.

Stravinsky, Igor. *Igor Stravinsky: An Autobiography.* N.Y.: Steuer, 1958.

Strobel, H. *Stravinsky: Classic Humanist.* N.Y.: Merlin Press, 1955.

Stuckenschmidt, Hans H. *Arnold Schoenberg.* N.Y.: Grove Press, 1960.

Tansman, Alexandre. *Igor Stravinsky: The Man and his Music.* Tr. Therese and Charles Blufield. N.Y.: Putnam, 1949.

Thompson, Oscar. *Debussy, Man and Artist.* N.Y.: Dodd, Mead, 1937.

Trend, John B. *Manuel de Falla and Spanish Music.* New ed. N.Y.: Knopf, 1934.

Walker, Frank. *Hugo Wolf, A Biography.* N.Y.: Knopf, 1952.

Walter, Bruno. *Gustav Mahler.* N.Y.: Knopf, 1958.

Weissman, John S. *Goffredo Petrassi.* Milan: Suvini-Zerboni, 1957.

Wellesz, Egon. *Arnold Schoenberg.* N.Y.: Dutton, 1925.

White, Eric Walter. *Benjamin Britten: A Sketch of his Life and Work.* New ed. rev. and enl. London: Boosey & Hawkes, 1954.

———. *Stravinsky: A Critical Survey.* N.Y.: Philosophical Library, 1948.

Vallas, Léon. *The Theories of Claude Debussy.* London: Oxford Univ. Press, 1929.

Vlad, Roman. *Luigi Dallapiccola.* Milan, Suvini Zerboni, 1957.

Young, Percy M. *Elgar, O.M.* London: Collins, 1955.

Young, Percy. *Vaughan Williams.* London: Dobson, 1953.

APPENDIX IV

Texts and Translations of Vocal Works

Das Lied von der Erde, Sea Drift, Threni, Idyll of Theocritus

(The text of Carmina Burana has not been included in this appendix since it is available in libretto form from Associated Music Publishers.)

DAS LIED VON DER ERDE

Aus dem Chinesischen übertragen von Hans Bethge.

I. DAS TRINKLIED VOM JAMMER DER ERDE

Schon winkt der Wein im gold'nen Pokale,
Doch trinkt noch nicht, erst sing' ich euch ein Lied!
Das Lied vom Kummer
Soll auflachend in die Seele euch klingen.
Wenn der Kummer naht,
Liegen wüst die Gärten der Seele,
Welkt hin und stirbt die Freude, der Gesang.
Dunkel ist das Leben, ist der Tod.

Herr dieses Hauses!
Dein Keller birgt die Fülle des goldenen Weins!
Hier, diese Laute nenn' ich mein!
Die Laute schlagen und die Gläser leeren,
Das sind die Dinge, die zusammen passen.
Ein voller Becher Weins zur rechten Zeit
Ist mehr wert, als alle Reiche dieser Erde!
Dunkel ist das Leben, ist der Tod.

Das Firmament blaut ewig und die Erde
Wird lange fest steh'n und aufblühn im Lenz.
Du aber, Mensch, wie lang lebst denn du?

THE SONG OF THE EARTH

Adapted from the Chinese by Hans Bethge

I. THE DRINKING SONG OF THE EARTH'S LAMENT

The wine gleams in the golden goblet,
But do not drink yet—first I'll sing you a song!
Let the song of sorrow
Resound with laughter in your souls.

When sorrow approaches,
The gardens of the soul lie waste,
Joy and song wither away and die.

Dark is life, dark is death.

Master of this house!
Your cellar hides a wealth of golden wine.
But I can call this lute my own!
The lutes resound and the wine glasses are emptied.
These are the things that go well together.
A full cup of wine at the right time

Is worth more than all the treasures of this earth.
Dark is life, dark is death.

The firmament is forever blue, and the earth
Will stand firm and blossom in the spring.
But you, o mortal, how long is your span?

675

Nicht hundert Jahre darfst du dich ergötzen	You have no hundred years to delight
An all dem morschen Tande dieser Erde!	In all the fleeting pleasures of this earth!
Seht dort hinab! Im Mondschein auf den Gräbern	Look over there! In the moonlight on the graves
Hockt eine wild-gespenstische Gestalt—	A ghostly apparition crouches.
Ein Aff' ist's! Hört ihr, wie sein Heulen	It is an ape! Listen, how his howling
Hinausgellt in den süssen Duft des Lebens!	Cuts across the sweet scent of life!
Jetzt nehmt den Wein! Jetzt ist es Zeit, Genossen!	Now drink the wine. Now it is time, my friends!
Leert eure gold'nen Becher zu Grund!	Drain your golden cups to the bottom.
Dunkel ist das Leben, ist der Tod!	Dark is life, dark is death!

II. DER EINSAME IM HERBST	II. THE LONELY ONE IN AUTUMN
Herbstnebel wallen bläulich überm See;	Bluish autumn mists drift over the sea;
Vom Reif bezogen stehen alle Gräser;	The grass is covered with frost.
Man meint, ein Künstler habe Staub von Jade	One would think an artist had scattered
Über die feinen Blüten ausgestreut.	Dust of jade over the delicate leaves.
Der süsse Duft der Blumen ist verflogen;	The sweet scent of flowers has vanished;
Ein kalter Wind beugt ihre Stengel nieder.	A cold wind bends the stems.
Bald werden die verwelkten, gold'nen Blätter	Soon the faded golden leaves of the lotus blossoms
Der Lotosblüten auf dem Wasser zieh'n.	Will float on the water.
Mein Herz ist müde. Meine kleine Lampe	My heart is weary. My little lamp
Erlosch mit Knistern, es gemahnt mich an den Schlaf.	Goes out sputtering, I long for sleep.
Ich komm' zu dir, traute Ruhestätte!	I come to you, trusty house of rest!
Ja, gib mir Ruh', ich hab' Erquickung not!	Yes, give me rest, for I have need of refreshment!
Ich weine viel in meinen Einsamkeiten.	I weep often in my loneliness.
Der Herbst in meinem Herzen währt zu lange.	The autumn in my heart lasts too long.
Sonne der Liebe, willst du nie mehr scheinen,	O bright sun of love, will you shine no more
Um meine bittern Tränen mild aufzutrocknen?	And gently dry my bitter tears?

III. VON DER JUGEND

Mitten in dem kleinen Teiche
Steht ein Pavillon aus grünem
Und aus weissem Porzellan.

Wie der Rücken eines Tigers
Wölbt die Brücke sich aus Jade
Zu dem Pavillon hinüber.

In dem Häuschen sitzen Freunde,
Schön gekleidet, trinken, plaudern,
Manche schreiben Verse nieder.

Ihre seidnen Ärmel gleiten
Rückwärts, ihre seidnen Mützen
Hocken lustig tief im Nacken.

Auf des kleinen Teiches stiller
Wasserfläche zeigt sich alles
Wunderlich im Spiegelbilde.

Alles auf dem Kopfe stehend
In dem Pavillon aus grünem
Und aus weissem Porzellan;

Wie ein Halbmond steht die Brücke,
Umgekehrt der Bogen. Freunde,
Schön gekleidet, trinken, plaudern.

IV. VON DER SCHÖNHEIT

Junge Mädchen pflücken Blumen,
Pflücken Lotosblumen an dem Ufer-
rande.
Zwischen Büschen und Blättern sitzen
sie,
Sammeln Blüten in den Schoss und
rufen
Sich einander Neckereien zu.

Gold'ne Sonne webt um die Gestalten,
Spiegelt sie im blanken Wasser wider.

Sonne spiegelt ihre schlanken Glieder,

Ihre süssen Augen wider,
Und der Zephir hebt mit Schmeichel-
kosen
Das Gewebe ihrer Ärmel auf,
Führt den Zauber
Ihrer Wohlgerüche durch die Luft.

O sieh, was tummeln sich für schöne
Knaben

III. OF YOUTH

In the middle of the little pond
There stands a pavilion
Of green and white porcelain.

Like a tiger's back
A bridge of jade
Arches to the pavilion beyond.

In the little house friends sit,
Well-dressed, drinking, chatting;
Some are writing little verses.

Their silken sleeves slip
Backward, their silken caps
Perch merrily on the back of their
heads.

In the quiet surface of the little pond
Everything is reflected
Wonderfully, as in a mirror.

Everything standing on its head
In the pavilion
Of green and white porcelain;

Like a half-moon stands the bridge,
With its arch upside down. Friends,
Well dressed, drink and chat. . . .

IV. OF BEAUTY

Young maidens pick flowers,
Pick lotus flowers on the river bank.

They sit among the bushes and leaves,

Gathering blossoms in their lap and
calling
Each other all kinds of teasing names.

The golden sunlight envelops them,
Throwing their reflection in the glis-
tening water.
The sunshine mirrors their slender
limbs
And their sweet eyes,
And the gentle breeze with a caress

Lifts the fabric of their sleeves,
Wafting the magic
Of their fragrance through the air.

O see, where a group of handsome lads

IV. VON DER SCHÖNHEIT

Dort an dem Uferrand auf mut'gen
   Rossen,
Weithin glänzend wie die Sonnen-
   strahlen;
Schon zwischen dem Geäst der grünen
   Weiden
Trabt das jungfrische Volk einher!

Das Ross des einen wiehert fröhlich auf

Und scheut und saust dahin,
Über Blumen, Gräser wanken hin die
   Hufe,
Sie zerstampfen jäh im Sturm die hinge-
   sunk'nen Blüten.
Hei! Wie flattern im Taumel seine
   Mähnen,
Dampfen heiss die Nüstern!

Gold'ne Sonne webt um die Gestalten,

Spiegelt sie im blanken Wasser wider.
Und die schönste von den Jungfrau'n
   sendet
Lange Blicke ihm der Sehnsucht nach.
Ihre stolze Haltung ist nur Verstellung.
In dem Funkeln ihrer grossen Augen,
In dem Dunkel ihres heissen Blicks
Schwingt klagend noch die Erregung
   ihres Herzens nach.

IV. OF BEAUTY

Rides noisily along the bank on bold
   steeds,
Glistening far-off like the rays of the
   sun;
Already through the branches of the
   green willows
The youthful company advances, trot-
   ting gaily!

The horse of one of the youths neighs
   delightedly,
Shies and dashes forward,
His hoofs poised over flowers and
   grass,
Trampling like a storm the hidden
   blossoms.
Hei! His mane waves in a frenzy,

His nostrils steaming.

Golden sunlight envelops the young
   figures,
Mirrors them in the shining water.
And the loveliest of the maidens

Sends him a parting glance of longing.
Her proud bearing is only a pretense.
In the sparkle of her wide eyes,
In the darkness of her hot glance
There reveals itself sadly the excite-
   ment of her heart.

V. DER TRUNKENE IM FRUHLING

Wenn nur ein Traum das Leben ist,
Warum denn Müh und Plag'!?
Ich trinke, bis ich nicht mehr kann,
Den ganzen, lieben Tag!
Und wenn ich nicht mehr trinken kann,
Weil Kehl' und Seele voll,
So tauml' ich bis zu meiner Tür
Und schlafe wundervoll!
Was hör ich beim Erwachen? Horch!

Ein Vogel singt im Baum.
Ich frag' ihn ob schon Frühling sei,
Mir ist als wie im Traum.
Der Vogel zwitschert: Ja!
Der Lenz ist da, sei kommen über
   Nacht!
Aus tiefstem Schauen lauscht' ich auf,

V. THE DRUNKEN ONE IN SPRING

Since life is but a dream,
Why then toil and trouble?
I drink till I can hold no more,
So pleasantly the livelong day!
And when I can drink no more
Because gullet and soul are full,
I stagger home to my door
And sleep marvelously well.
What is this sound when I awake?
   Listen!
A bird is singing in the tree.
I ask him if spring has come,
I seem to be in a dream.
The bird chirps: Yes!
Spring is here, spring came overnight!

I look up and gaze intently,

V. DER TRUNKENE IM FRUHLING

Der Vogel singt und lacht!
Ich fülle mir den Becher neu
Und leer' ihn bis zum Grund
Und singe, bis der Mond erglänzt
Am schwarzen Firmament!
Und wenn ich nicht mehr singen kann,
So schlaf' ich wieder ein,
Was geht mich denn der Frühling an!?
Lasst mich betrunken sein!

V. THE DRUNKEN ONE IN SPRING

The bird sings and laughs!
I fill my cup anew
And empty it to the bottom,
And sing until the moon lights up
The darkening firmament.
And when I can no longer sing,
I fall asleep again.
What matters spring to me?
Let me get drunk again!

VI. DER ABSCHIED

Die Sonne scheidet hinter dem Gebirge.
In alle Täler steigt der Abend nieder
Mit seinen Schatten, die voll Kühlung
sind.
O sieh! Wie eine Silberbarke schwebt
Der Mond am blauen Himmelssee he-
rauf.
Ich spüre eines feinen Windes Weh'n
Hinter den dunklen Fichten!

Der Bach singt voller Wohllaut durch
das Dunkel.
Die Blumen blassen im Dämmerschein.
Die Erde atmet voll von Ruh' und
Schaf,
Alle Sehnsucht will nun träumen.
Die müden Menschen geh'n heimwärts,
Um im Schlaf vergess'nes Glück
Und Jugend neu zu lernen!
Die Vögel hocken still in ihren
Zweigen.
Die Welt schläft ein!

Es wehet kühl im Schatten meiner
Fichten.
Ich stehe hier und harre meines
Freundes;
Ich harre sein zum letzten Lebewohl.
Ich sehne mich, o Freund, an deiner
Seite
Die Schönheit dieses Abends zu ge-
niessen.
Wo bleibst du! Du lässt mich lang
allein!
Ich wandle auf und nieder mit meiner
Laute
Auf Wegen, die vom weichen Grase
schwellen.
O Schönheit! O ewigen Liebens—
Lebens—trunk'ne Welt!

VI. THE FAREWELL

The sun sets behind the hills.
Evening descends upon all the valleys
With its shadows, bringing coolness.

O see how the moon, like a silver boat,
Floats up on the blue sea of heaven.

I feel a soft wind stirring
Behind the dark pine trees.

The brook sings sweetly in the dark.

The flowers grow pale in the twilight.
The earth breathes gently, full of rest
and sleep.
All longing flows into a dream.
Weary men go homewards,
So that in sleep they may recapture
Forgotten joy and youth!
The birds crouch in the branches.

The world goes to sleep.

It is cool in the shadows of my pine
trees.
I stand here and await my friend;

I await his last farewell.
I long, o my friend, to enjoy

The beauty of this evening by your
side.
Where do you tarry? You leave me too
long alone.
I wander up and down with my lute

Along paths billowing with soft grass.

O beauty! O world drunk with eternal
love and life!

VI. DER ABSCHIED	VI. THE FAREWELL
Er stieg vom Pferd und reichte ihm den Trunk Des Abschieds dar.	He alighted from his horse and offered him The cup of farewell.
Er fragte ihn, wohin er führe	He asked him where he was journeying
Und auch warum es müsste sein.	And why it must be so.
Er sprach, seine Stimme war umflort: Du, mein Freund,	He spoke, his voice was veiled: O my friend,
Mir war auf dieser Welt das Glück nicht hold!	My lot was hard in this world.
Wohin ich geh'? Ich geh', ich wand're in die Berge.	Where do I go? I go wandering in the mountains.
Ich suche Ruhe für mein einsam Herz.	I seek rest for my lonely heart.
Ich wandle nach der Heimat, meiner Stätte.	I journey to my homeland, my abode.
Ich werde niemals in die Ferne schweifen.	I will nevermore roam afar.
Still ist mein Herz und harret seiner Stunde!	My heart is still and awaits its hour!
Die liebe Erde allüberall Blüht auf im Lenz und grünt aufs neu!	The lovely earth everywhere Blossoms in the spring and becomes green again.
Allüberall und ewig blauen licht die Fernen!	The distant sky shines blue everywhere, ever . . .
Ewig . . . ewig . . .	Ever . . . ever. . . .

(English translation by Joseph Machlis)

SEA DRIFT

Out of the Cradle Endlessly Rocking
(Walt Whitman)

Chorus: Once Paumanok
When the lilac scent was in the air and Fifth month grass was growing,
Up this seashore in some briers
Two feather'd guests from Alabama, two together,
And their nest, and four light green eggs spotted with brown.
Solo: And every day I, a curious boy, never too close, never disturbing them,
Cautiously peering, absorbing, translating.
Chorus: Shine! shine! shine!
Pour down your warmth, great Sun!
While we bask, we two together, two together!
Winds blow south, or winds blow north,
Day come white, or night come black.
Solo: Home, or rivers or mountains from home,
Chorus: Singing all the time, minding no time,
While we two keep together.

Solo: Till of a sudden,
May-be kill'd, unknown to her mate,
One forenoon the she-bird crouch'd not on the nest,
Nor return'd that afternoon, nor the next,
Nor ever appear'd again.
And thenceforward all summer in the sound of the sea,
And at night under the full moon in calmer weather,
Over the hoarse surging of the sea,
Or flitting from brier to brier by day,
I saw, I heard at intervals the remaining one, the he-bird,
The solitary guest from Alabama.
Chorus: Blow! blow! blow!
Blow up sea-winds along Paumanok's shore;
I wait and I wait till you blow my mate to me.
Solo: Yes, when the stars glisten'd,
All night long on the prong of a moss-scallop'd stake,
Down almost amid the slapping waves,
Sat the lone singer, wonderful, causing tears.
He call'd on his mate,
He pour'd forth the meanings which I of all men know.

Yes, my brother, I know,
The rest might not, but I have treasur'd every note,
For more than once dimly down to the beach gliding,
Silent, avoiding the moonbeams, blending myself with the shadows,
Recalling now the obscure shapes, the echoes, the sounds and sights after
    their sorts,
The white arms out in the breakers tirelessly tossing,
I, with bare feet, a child, the wind wafting my hair,
Listen'd long and long.
Listen'd to keep, to sing, now translating the notes,
Following you, my brother.
Chorus: Soothe! soothe! soothe!
Close on its wave soothes the wave behind,
And again another behind embracing and lapping, every one close,
But my love soothes not me, not me.
Low hangs the moon, it rose late,
It is lagging—Oh, I think it is heavy with love, with love.
Solo: O madly the sea pushes upon the land,
With love, with love.
O night! do I not see my love fluttering out among the breakers?
What is that little black thing I see there in the white?
Loud! loud! loud!
Loud I call to you, my love!
High and clear I shoot my voice over the waves,
Surely you must know who is here, is here.
Chorus: Surely you must know who is here, is here,
You must know who I am, my love.
O rising stars!

Perhaps the one I want so much will rise, will rise with some of you.
O throat! O trembling throat!
Sound clearer through the atmosphere!
Pierce the woods, the earth,
Somewhere listening to catch you must be the one I want.
Solo: Shake out carols!
Solitary here, the night's carols!
Carols of lonesome love! Death's carols!
Carols under that lagging, yellow, waning moon!
O under that moon where she droops almost down into the sea!
O reckless despairing carols.

But soft! sink low!
Soft! Let me just murmur
And do you wait a moment, you husky-nois'd sea,
For somewhere I believe I heard my mate responding to me,
So faint I must be still, be still to listen,
But not altogether still, for then she might not come immediately to me.

Hither, my love! Here I am! here!
With this just-sustain'd note I announce myself to you,
This gentle call is for you, my love, for you.
Chorus: Do not be decoy'd elsewhere,
That is the whistle of the wind, it is not my voice,
That is the fluttering, the fluttering of the spray,
Those are the shadows of leaves.
O darkness! O in vain!

Solo: O, I am very sick and sorrowful,
O brown halo in the sky near the moon, drooping upon the sea!
O troubled reflection in the sea!
O throat! O throbbing heart!
And I sing uselessly, uselessly all the night.

O past! O happy life! O songs of joy!
In the air, in the woods, over the fields,
Loved! Loved! Loved! Loved! Loved!
But my mate no more, no more with me!
We two together no more.
Chorus: No more, no more.

THRENI: id est Lamentationes Jeremiae Prophetae

(Threnodies: being the Lamentations of the Prophet Jeremiah)

De Elegia Prima	*Chapter One*
ALEPH. Quomodo sedet solo civitas plena populo! Facta est quasi vidua domina gentium:	ALEPH. How doth the city sit solitary, that was full of people! How is she become as a widow! she that was great among the nations,

princeps provinciarum facta est
sub tributo.
BETH. Plorans ploravit in nocte,
et lacrymae ejus in maxillis ejus.
HE. Facti sunt hostes ejus in capite,
inimici ejus locupletati sunt.
Quia Dominus locutus est super eam
propter multitudinem iniquitatum
ejus.
CAPH. Vide, Domine, et considera,
quoniam facta sum vilis.
RES. Vide, Domine, quoniam tribulor,

conturbatus est venter meus,
subversum est cor meum in neme-
tipsa
quoniam amaritudine plena sum.
Foris interficit gladius,
et domi mors similis est.

De Elegia Tertia

I. QUERIMONIA

ALEPH. Ego vir videns paupertatem
meam
in virga indignationis ejus.
Me menavit, et adduxit in tenebras,

et non in lucem.
Tantum in me vertit,
et convertit manum suam tota die.

BETII. Vctustam fecit pellem meam

et carnem meum, contrivit ossa mea.
Aedificavit in gyro meo,
et circumdedit me felle et labore.

In tcncbrosis collocavit me,
quasi mortuos sempiternos.
VAU. Et fregit ad numerum dentes
meos,
cibavit me cinere.
Et repulsa est a pace anima mea,
oblitus sum bonorum.
Et dixi: Periit finis meus,
et spes mea a Domine.

and princess among the provinces,
how is she become tributary!
BETH. She weepeth sore in the night,
and her tears are on her cheeks.
Her adversaries are the chief,
her enemies prosper;
for the Lord hath afflicted her
for the multitude of her transgres-
sions.
CAPH. See, O Lord, and consider;
for I am become vile.
RES. Behold, O Lord, for I am in dis-
stress:
my bowels are troubled;
mine heart is turned within me;

for I have grievously rebelled:
abroad the sword bereaveth,
at home there is as death.

Chapter Three

I. COMPLAINT

ALEPH. I am the man that hath seen
affliction
by the rod of his wrath.
He hath led me, and brought me into
darkness,
but not into light.
Surely against me is he turned;
he turneth his hand against me all
the day.
BETH. My flesh and skin hath he
made old;
he hath broken my bones.
He hath builded against me
and compassed me with gall and
travail.
He hath set me in dark places,
as they that be dead of old.
VAU. He hath also broken my teeth
with gravel;
he hath covered me with ashes.
And my soul is removed from peace.
I forgat prosperity.
And I said, My strength
and my hope is perished from the
Lord.

ZAIN. Recordare paupertatis, et trans-
gressionis
meae, absinthii et fellis.
Memoria memor ero,

et tabescet in me anima mea.
Haec recolens in corde meo,
ideo sperabo.

II. SENSU SPEI

HETH. Misericordiae Domini,
quia non sumus consumpti;
quia non defecerunt mierationis ejus.
Novi diluculo,
multa est fides tua.
Pars mea Dominus, dixit anima mea;

propterea exspectabo eum.
TETH. Bonus est Dominus sperantibus
in eum,
animae quaerenti illum.
Bonum est praestolari

com silentio salutare Dei.

Bonum est viro, cum portaverit
jugum ab adolescentia sua.
LAMED. Ut conteret sub pedibus suis
omnes vinctos terrae;
Ut declinaret judicium viri
in conspectu vultus Altissimi;
Ut perverteret hominem in judicio
suo,
Dominus ignoravit.
NUN. Scrutemur vias nostras,
et quaeremus, et revertamur ad Dominum.
Levemus corda nostra cum manibus

ad Dominum in coelis.
Nos inique egimus, et ad iracundiam
provocavimus;
incirco tu inexorabilis es.

SAMECH. Operuisti in furore,
et percussisti nos;

II. PERCEIVING HOPE

ZAIN. Remembering mine affliction
and my misery,
the wormwood and the gall.
My soul hath them still in remembrance,
and is humbled in me.
This I recall to my mind,
therefore have I hope.

HETH. It is of the Lord's mercies
that we are not consumed,
because his compassions fail not.
They are new every morning:
great is thy faithfulness.
The Lord is my portion, saith my
soul;
therefore will I hope in him.
TETH. The Lord is good unto them
that wait for him,
to the soul that seeketh him.
It is good that a man should both
hope
and quietly wait for the Lord's salvation.
It is good for a man
that he bear the yoke in his youth.
LAMED. To crush under his feet
all the prisoners of the earth;
To turn aside the right of a man
before the face of the most High;
To subvert a man in his cause,

the Lord approveth not.
NUN. Let us search and try our ways,
and turn again to the Lord.

Let us lift up our hearts with our
hands
unto God in the heavens.
We have transgressed and have rebelled;
thou hast not pardoned.
SAMECH. Thou hast covered with
anger
and persecuted us;

occidist, nec pepercisti.
Opposuisti nubem tibi,

ne transeat oratio.

Eradicationem et abjectionem posuisti me
in medio populorum.
AIN. Oculos meus afflictus est, nec tacuit,
eo quod non esset requies.
Donec respiceret et videret Dominus de coelis.
Oculus meus depraedatus est animam meam
in cunctis filiabus urbis meae.

TSADE. Venatione ceperunt me
quasi avem inimici mei gratis.
Lapsa est in lacum vita mea,

et posuerunt lapidem super me.
Inundaverunt aquae super caput meum;
dixi: Perii.
COPH. Invocavi nomen tuum, Domine,

de lacu novissimo.
Vocem meam audisti; ne avertas aurem tuam
a singultu meo et clamoribus.

Appropinquasti in die quando invocavi te;
dixisti: Ne timeas.

thou hast slain, thou has not pitied.
Thou hast covered thyself with a cloud,
that our prayer should not pass through.
Thou hast made us as the offscouring and refuse
in the midst of the people.
AIN. Mine eye trickleth down and ceaseth not,
without any intermission.
Till the Lord look down and behold from heaven.
Mine eye affecteth mine heart

because of all the daughters of my city.
TSADE. Mine enemies chased me sore, like a bird, without cause.
They have cut off my life in the dungeon,
and cast a stone upon me.
Waters flowed over mine head;

then I said, I am cut off.
COPH. I called upon thy name, O Lord,
out of the low dungeon.
Thou hast heard my voice:

hide not thine ear at my breathing, at my cry.
Thou drewest near in the day that I called upon thee;
thou saidst, Fear not.

III. SOLACIUM

RES. Judicasti, Domine, causam animae meae,
redemtor vitae meae.
Vidisti, Domine, iniquitatem illorum adversum me.
Vidisti omnem furorem,
universas cogitationes
eorum adversum me.
SIN. Audisti opprobrium eorum, Domine,

III. COMPENSATION

RES. O Lord, thou hast pleaded the causes of my soul;
thou hast redeemed my life.
O Lord, thou hast seen my wrong.

Thou hast seen all their vengeance
and all their imaginations
against me.
SIN. Thou hast heard their reproach, O Lord,

omnes cogitationes eorum adversum me:

Labia insurgentium mihi, et meditationes eorum

adversum me tota die.

Sessionem eorum, et resurrectionem eorum vide,

ego sum psalmus eorum.

THAU. Reddes eis vicem Domine,

juxta opera manuum suarum.

Dabis eis scutum cordis, laborem tuum.

Persequeris in furore, et conteres eos

sub coelis, Domine.

and all their imaginations against me.

The lips of those that rose up against me,

and their device against me all the day.

Behold their sitting down and their rising up;

I am their music.

THAU. Render unto them a recompense, O Lord,

according to the work of their hands.

Give them sorrow of heart, thy curse unto them.

Persecute and destroy them in anger

from under the heavens of the Lord.

De Elegia Quinta

Oratio Jeremiae Prophetae

Recordare, Domine, quid acciderit nobis;

intuere et respice opprobrium nostrum.

Tu autem, Domine, in aeternum permanebis,

solium tuum in generationem et generationem.

Converte nos, Domine, ad te, et convertemur;

innova dies nostros, sicut a principio.

Chapter Five

The Prayer of the Prophet Jeremiah

Remember, O Lord, what is come upon us;

consider, and behold our reproach.

Thou, O Lord, remainest for ever;

thy throne from generation to generation.

Turn thou us unto thee, O Lord, and we shall be turned;

renew our days as of old.

IDYLL OF THEOCRITUS

WHERE are those laurels? Bring them, Thestylis, and the love charms too. Wreath the cauldron with a crimson fillet of fine wool; that I may cast a fire-spell on the unkind man I love, who now for twelve whole days, the wretch, has never come this way, nor even knows whether I be alive or dead, nor once has he knocked at my doors, ah cruel! Can it be that Love and Aphrodite have borne off his roving heart elsewhither? To Timagetos' wrestling school tomorrow will I go, and find him and reproach him with the wrong he is doing me. But now by fire-magic will I bind him. Thou, O moon, shine fair; for to thee softly, dread Goddess, will I chant, and to infernal Hekate, at whom the very whelps shudder, as she goes between the dead men's tombs and the dark blood. Hail, awful Hekate! and be thou my helper to the end, making these spells prove no less potent than the charms of Circe, or of Medea, or the gold-haired sorceress Perimede. O magic wheel, draw hither to my house the man I love. First in the fire barley grains must burn. Come, throw them on, Thestylis. Miserable girl, whither now are flown thy wits? Even to thee am I, vile wretch, become a thing to scorn? Cast them on, and say thus: "The bones of Delphis I am casting."

Delphis has wrought me anguish, so against Delphis do I burn this laurel shoot; and as it catches fire and crackles loud, and is burnt up so suddenly we see not even the ash, so may the flesh of Delphis be wasted in the flames. O magic wheel, draw hither to my house the man I love. Even as now I melt this wax by the aid of Hekate, so speedily may Myndian Delphis melt away through love. And even as turns this brazen wheel by Aphrodite's power, so restlessly may he too turn and turn around my doors. O magic wheel, draw hither to my house the man I love. Now will I burn the bran. Yea thou, Artemis, thou hast power to move Hell's adamantine gates, and all else that is stubborn. Thestylis, hark, the dogs are baying throughout the town: at the crossroads is the Goddess. Quick, beat the brazen gong. O magic wheel, draw hither to my house the man I love.

Behold, the sea is silent, and silent are the winds; but never silent is the anguish here within my breast, since I am all on fire for him who has made me, unhappy me, not a wife but a worthless woman, a maiden now no more. O magic wheel, draw hither to my house the man I love. Thrice do I pour libation, Goddess, and thrice speak this prayer: Whether it be a woman lies beside him, or a man, let such oblivion seize him as on Dia once, they tell, seized Theseus, when he quite forgot the fair-tressed Ariadne. O magic wheel, draw hither to my house the man I love.

Horse-madness is a herb that grows in Arcady and maddens all the colts that range the hills, and the fleet-footed mares. Even so frenzied may I now see Delphis: to this house may he speed like a madman from the oily wrestling school. O magic wheel, draw hither to my house the man I love. This fringe from his mantle did Delphis lose which now I pluck to shreds and cast it into the ravenous fire. Woe's me, remorseless Love. Why, clinging like a fen-born leech, hast thou sucked from my body the dark blood, every drop? O magic wheel, draw hither to my house the man I love. A lizard will I bray, and bring him a deadly draught tomorrow. But now, Thestylis, take these magic herbs, and secretly smear them upon his upper lintel while it is night still. Then spit, and say: "It is the bones of Delphis that I smear." O magic wheel, draw hither to my house the man I love.

Now that I am alone, whence am I to bewail my love? Wherefrom begin my tale? Who was it brought this upon me? Anaxo, daughter of Euboulos, bearing the mystic basket, passed this way in procession to the grove of Artemis, many a wild beast thronging round her, among them a lioness. Bethink thee of my love and whence it came, o holy Moon. So Theucharidas' Thracian nurse, who since has gone to bliss, but then was living at our doors, besought and entreated me to come and see the pageant; and I, poor luckless fool, went with her in a linen gown, a lovely trailing robe, over which I had thrown a cloak that Klearista lent me. Bethink thee of my love and whence it came, o holy Moon. And now, half-way along the road as we passed Lykon's house, I saw Delphis and Eudamippos walking side by side. Their beards were more golden than flower of helichryse, and far more brightly shone their breasts than thou thyself, o Moon; for from the wrestling school they came, fresh from their noble toil. Bethink thee of my love and whence it came, o holy Moon. O then I saw, and fell mad straight, and my whole heart was fired (woe is me!) and my comely cheeks grew pale, nor did I heed that pageant any longer. And how I came back home I know not; but a parching fever seized me and consumed me, so that I lay pining in bed for ten days and ten nights. Bethink thee of my love and whence it came, o holy Moon.

And often pale as boxwood grew the color of my flesh, and the hairs kept falling from my head, till what was left of me was naught but skin and bones. To whom did I not now resort? What old crone's house did I not visit, who was skilled in spells? But that way remedy was none, and time fled swiftly by. Bethink thee of my love and whence it came, o holy Moon. So at last I told the whole truth to my serving maid and said: "Go, Thestylis, find me a cure for my sore malady. Wholly am I become (woe's me!) the Myndian's slave. But go, go now and lie in wait for him at the school of Timagetos; for there it is he most resorts, there that he loves to lounge." Bethink thee of my love and whence it came, o holy Moon. "And when you are sure no one is near, nod to him silently and say, 'Simaitha calls you,' and bring him hither straight."

So did I speak; and she went hence, and brought back to my house Delphis, the sleek-limbed youth. But I, no sooner was I ware of his light footfall, as he crossed the threshold of my door—bethink thee of my love and whence it came, o holy Moon—in every limb I froze more cold than snow, and from my brow the sweat came streaming forth and trickling down like drops of dew. Nor had I strength to speak one word, not so much as a child's whimpering murmur, when it calls to its mother dear in sleep; but all my lovely body turned as stiff as any doll. Bethink thee of my love and whence it came, o holy Moon. Then, seeing me, that heartless man, with eyes fixed on the ground, seated himself upon my bed, and sitting there spoke thus: "Truly, Simaitha, your command by just so much outstripped my coming, when you called me hither to your house, as I outstripped charming Phinos not long since in the race." Bethink thee of my love and whence it came, o holy Moon. "For of myself I should have come, yes, by sweet Love, I should, with comrades two or three besides, as soon as it was night, carrying in my tunic folds apples of Dionysus, a wreath of poplar garlanding my brows, the holy tree of Herakles, with twining purple ribbons all enlaced." Bethink thee of my love and whence it came, o holy Moon. "And had you welcomed me, why then, it had been joy; for famed am I among my comrades for beauty and speed of foot. Had I but kissed your lovely mouth, I would have slept content. But if you had repulsed me, and bolted fast the door, with axes and with torches you would then have been besieged." Bethink thee of my love and whence it came, o holy Moon. "And now to the Cyprian, in truth, first do I owe my thanks; but after Cypris, it is you, Lady, who from the flames have rescued me when first you sent to invite me to your house, half consumed as I am. Yes, Love oft enkindles a blaze more fiery than Hephaistos' self, the god of Lipatra." Bethink thee of my love and whence it came, o holy Moon. "And he drives with evil frenzy the maiden from her bower and the bride from her lord's embrace leaving the bed yet warm."

So did he speak; and I that was so easy to be won, took him by the hand and drew him down to the soft couch. And soon limbs at the touch of limbs grew love-ripe, and our faces glowed warmer still, and yet more warm, and we whispered sweet words. So not to lengthen out my tale and weary thee, dear Moon, the greatest deeds of love were done, and we both reached our desire. Since then so long as yesterday no fault had he to find in me, nor I in him. But now today there came to me the mother of our flute-player Philista and of Melixo, just when the horses of the sun were climbing up the sky, bearing forth from the Ocean the Dawn with rosy arms. After much other gossip she said Delphis was in love; but what desire has mastered him, for a woman or a man, she was not sure, but knew this only, that he was ever pledging his love in cups of unmixed wine, and at last rushed away swearing he'd crown with garlands the threshold of his dear. Such is the tale the woman told me, and it is the truth. For he was wont to visit me three or four times each day, and often would he leave his Dorian oil-flask with me here. But now 'tis twelve whole days since I so much as looked upon him. Can he have found some other solace, and forgotten me?

Now with these philtres will I strive to enchant him, but if still he should grieve me, at Hell's gate soon, by the Fates, he shall knock: Such evil drugs to work his bane here in a chest I store, whose use, dear Mistress, an Assyrian stranger taught me once. But thou, Goddess, farewell, and turn thy steeds to the Ocean stream, and I will endure my misery still, even as I have borne it. Farewell, bright-faced Selene; and farewell too, ye stars, that follow the slow-moving chariot of the tranquil Night.

(English translation by R. F. Trevelyan,
used with permission of Cambridge University Press)

⊷§ APPENDIX V §⊶

A Chronological List of Modern Composers, World Events, and Principal Figures in Literature and the Arts

(The list of composers does not presume to be complete. It includes those mentioned in the text and some additional names.)

THE POST-ROMANTIC ERA

Emmanuel Chabrier 1841–94	1900. Boxer Rebellion in China. Count Zeppelin tests dirigible balloon. Dr. Walter Reed organizes campaign against yel-	Pierre Auguste Renoir 1841–1919 W. H. Hudson 1841–1922

Gabriel Fauré 1845–1924

Sir Charles Hubert Parry 1848–1918

Henri Duparc 1848–1933

Vincent d'Indy 1851–1931

Sir Charles Villiers Stanford 1852–1924

Arthur Foote 1853–1937

Alfredo Catalani 1854–1893

Engelbert Humperdinck 1854–1921

Leoš Janáček 1854–1928

George W. Chadwick 1854–1931

Ernest Chausson 1855–1899

Anatole Liadov 1855–1914

Sir Edward Elgar 1857–1934

Edgar Stillman Kelley 1857–1944

Ruggiero Leoncavallo 1858–1919

Giacomo Puccini 1858–1924

Hugo Wolf 1860–1903

Gustav Mahler 1860–1911

Isaac Albéniz 1860–1919

Gustave Charpentier 1860–1956

Anton Arensky 1861–1906

Edward MacDowell 1861–1908

Charles Martin Loeffler 1861–1935

low fever. Philadelphia Symphony founded.

1901. President McKinley assassinated. Queen Victoria dies, succeeded by Edward VII. Marconi sends first signal across Atlantic. De Vries's mutation theory.

1902. Boer War ends in British victory. Cuba becomes a republic. First International Arbitration Court at The Hague. 145,000 miners strike in Pennsylvania.

1903. Wright Brothers' first successful flight. Ford organizes motor company. Panama declares its independence of Colombia, encourages U.S. to build canal. Massacre of Jews in Kishinev, Russia. First transcontinental automobile trip.

1904. Russo-Japanese War. London Symphony founded. New York subway opened.

1905. Fort Arthur surrendered to Japan. Opening of Duma, first Russian parliament. Norway separates from Sweden. Freud establishes psychoanalysis. Einstein's theories, 1905–1910

1906. San Francisco earthquake and fire. Harry K. Thaw shoots famous architect Stanford White.

1907. Financial panic in U.S. Second Hague Conference. Triple Entente. First round-the-world cruise of U.S. fleet. William James's *Pragmatism.*

1908. Model T Ford produced. Fire destroys Chelsea, Mass.

Stéphane Mallarmé 1842–98

George Brandes 1842–1927

Henry James 1843–1916

Paul Verlaine 1844–96

Gerard Manley Hopkins 1844–99

Friedrich Nietzsche 1844–1900

Henri Rousseau 1844–1910

Anatole France 1844–1924

Robert Bridges 1844–1930

Max Liebermann 1847–1935

Paul Gauguin 1848–1903

Augustus Saint-Gaudens 1848–1907

Joris-Karl Huysmans 1848–1907

August Strindberg 1849–1912

Guy de Maupassant 1850–93

Robert Louis Stevenson 1850–94

George Moore 1852–1933

Vincent van Gogh 1853–90

Arthur Rimbaud 1854–91

Oscar Wilde 1856–1900

Louis H. Sullivan 1856–1924

John Singer Sargent 1856–1925

Sigmund Freud 1856–1939

George Bernard Shaw 1856–1950

Joseph Conrad 1857–1924

Hermann Sudermann 1857–1928

Claude Debussy 1862–1918
Frederick Delius 1862–1934

Horatio Parker 1863–1919
Pietro Mascagni 1863–1945

Richard Strauss 1864–1949
Alexander Grechaninov 1864–1956

Paul Dukas 1865–1935
Alexander Glazunov 1865–1936
Jean Sibelius 1865–1957

Ferruccio Busoni 1866–1924
Erik Satie 1866–1925
Francesco Cilèa 1866–1950

Enrique Granados 1867–1916
Mrs. H. H. A. Beach 1867–1944
Umberto Giordano 1867–1948

Henry F. Gilbert 1868–1928

Albert Roussel 1869–1937
Hans Pfitzner 1869–1949

Henry Hadley 1871–1937
Frederick Shepherd Converse 1871–1940

Alexander Scriabin 1872–1915
Alexander von Zemlinsky 1872–1942
Arthur Farwell 1872–1952

1909. Peary reaches North Pole. First flight across English Channel.

1910. Discovery of protons and electrons. Edward VII dies, succeeded by George V. Glenn H. Curtiss wins $10,000 prize for first continuous flight, Albany to New York. J. B. McNamara and brother tried for dynamite explosion at Los Angeles *Times;* defended by Clarence Darrow. Pathé Newsreel appears in Paris.

1911. Mexican Revolution. Amundsen reaches South Pole. *Mona Lisa* stolen from Louvre. Supreme Court antitrust decisions against Standard Oil and American Tobacco Co.

1912. Capt. Robert F. Scott reaches South Pole; dies on return journey. China becomes a republic. Balkan Wars: Montenegro, Bulgaria, Serbia, and Greece defeat Turkey. T. Roosevelt founds Bull Moose Party; Wilson elected. *Titanic* sunk.

1913. Peace Palace dedicated at The Hague. Federal income tax in U. S.

1914. Archduke Francis Ferdinand of Austria assassinated at Sarajevo. Outbreak of World War I. German army invades Belgium. U. S. intercedes in Mexico; Marines land at Vera Cruz. Socialist (Second) International meets at Brussels. Presidium includes five future heads of governments: Lenin, Ebert, Ramsay MacDonald, Stauning (Denmark), and Branting (Sweden). First ship through Panama Canal.

Selma Lagerlöf 1858–1940
Georges Seurat 1859–1891
Childe Hassam 1859–1935
A. E. Housman 1859–1936
Henri Bergson 1859–1941
Knut Hamsun 1859–1952

Anton Chekhov 1860–1904
Sir James Barrie 1860–1937
Rabindranath Tagore 1861–1941
Aristide Maillol 1861–1945
O. Henry 1862–1910
Arthur Schnitzler 1862–1931
Edith Wharton 1862–1937
Gerhart Hauptmann 1862–1946
Maurice Maeterlinck 1862–1949
Konstantin Stanislavski 1863–1938
Edward Munch 1863–1944
George Santayana 1863–1952

Henri de Toulouse-Lautrec 1864–1910
Frank Wedekind 1864–1918
Gabriele D'Annunzio 1864–1938
George Grey Barnard 1864–1938
Louis Eilshemius 1864–1941
Irving Babbitt 1865–1933
Rudyard Kipling 1865–1936
William Butler Yeats 1865–1939

Ralph Vaughan Williams 1872–1958

Edward Burlingame Hill 1872–1960

Max Reger 1873–1916

Sergei Rachmaninov 1873–1943

Daniel Gregory Mason 1873–1953

Josef Suk 1874–1935

Arnold Schoenberg 1874–1951

Charles Ives 1874–1954

Samuel Coleridge-Taylor 1875–1912

Maurice Ravel 1875–1937

Italo Montemezzi 1875–1952

Reinhold Glière 1875–1956

Julián Carrillo 1875–

Manuel de Falla 1876–1936

Ernest H. Schelling 1876–1939

Ermanno Wolf-Ferrari 1876–1948

John Alden Carpenter 1876–1951

Carl Ruggles 1876–

David Stanley Smith 1877–1946

Ernö (Ernst von) Dohnányi 1877–1960

Franz Schreker 1878–1934

Mabel Daniels 1878–

Ottorino Respighi 1879–1937

John Ireland 1879–1962

Joaquín Nin 1879–

Arthur Shepherd 1880–1958

Béla Bartók 1881–1945

1915. German submarines blockade England. *Lusitania* sunk. Poison gas used at Ypres. Nurse Edith Cavell shot. First transcontinental telephone, New York to San Francisco.

1916. Battle of Verdun. German submarine *Deutschland* visits New York. Rasputin killed. Easter Rebellion in Dublin; Sir Roger Casement hanged. Tom Mooney sentenced for bomb explosion at Preparedness Day parade in San Francisco.

1917. Balfour Declaration on Palestine. Germany begins unrestricted submarine warfare. United States enters war. Mata Hari shot. Russian Revolution. Bolsheviks seize power. Prohibition Amendment.

1918. Bolsheviks execute Czar and family. Wilson's Fourteen Points. Russia makes separate peace. Paris bombarded. Battles of Somme, Aisne, Argonne. Germany surrenders. Kaiser abdicates.

1919. Treaty of Versailles. Third International formed. Anti-British demonstrations in India. First nonstop flight New York to San Francisco.

1920. League of Nations convenes at Geneva. Women's suffrage. Sacco and Vanzetti accused of murder in payroll holdup. First transcontinental air-mail route.

1921. Peace treaty signed with Germany. Limitation of Armaments Conference meets in Washington.

1922. Mussolini marches on Rome. Violence in coal strike at Herrin, Ill. Discovery of

Bernard Berenson 1865–1959

Lincoln Steffens 1866–1936

Romain Rolland 1866–1943

Wassily Kandinsky 1866–1944

Benedetto Croce 1866–1952

Arnold Bennett 1867–1931

John Galsworthy 1867–1933

Luigi Pirandello 1867–1936

Käthe Kollwitz 1867–1945

Edmond Rostand 1868–1918

Stefan George 1868–1933

Edgar Lee Masters 1868–1950

Edwin Arlington Robinson 1869–1935

André Gide 1869–1951

Norman Douglas 1869–1952

Henri Matisse 1869–1954

Frank Lloyd Wright 1869–1959

Stephen Crane 1870–1900

Ernst Barlach 1870–1938

John M. Synge 1871–1909

Leonid Andreyev 1871–1919

Marcel Proust 1871–1922

Theodore Dreiser 1871–1945

Paul Valéry 1871–1945

Georges Rouault 1871–1958

Aubrey Beardsley 1872–1898

Serge Diaghilev 1872–1929

Piet Mondriaan 1872–1946

John Marin 1872–1953

Nikolai Miaskovsky 1881–1950

Georges Enesco 1881–1955

Ernest Bloch 1881–1959

Ildebrando Pizzetti 1881–

Karol Szymanowski 1882–1937

Joaquín Turina 1882–1949

Arthur Schnabel 1882–1951

Lazare Saminsky 1882–1959

Igor Stravinsky 1882–

Gian Francesco Malipiero 1882–

Zoltán Kodály 1882–

John Powell 1882–1963

Mary Howe 1882–

Riccardo Zandonai 1883–1944

Anton Webern 1883–1945

Alfredo Casella 1883–1947

Lord Berners (Gerald Tyrwhitt) 1883–1950

Sir Arnold Bax 1883–

Charles Tomlinson Griffes 1884–1920

Bernard van Dieren 1884–1936

Emerson Whithorne 1884–1958

Louis Gruenberg 1884–

Alban Berg 1885–1935

Wallingford Riegger 1885–1961

Edgar Varèse 1885–

Deems Taylor 1885–

Humberto Allende 1885–

John J. Becker 1886–

Marion Bauer 1887–1955

insulin. John Dewey's *Human Nature and Conduct.*

1923. French and Belgian troops occupy Ruhr. Adolf Hitler attempts Beer Putsch in Munich; imprisoned in Landsberg, writes *Mein Kampf.* Pancho Villa killed in ambush.

1924. Lenin dies at 54. Dawes Reparations Plan. Mrs. Nellie Tayloe Ross first woman governor (Wyoming). Leopold-Loeb case.

1925. Locarno Conference. Rhineland demilitarized. John T. Scopes, defended by Clarence Darrow, found guilty of teaching evolution in Dayton, Tenn.

1926. General strike in Britain. Germany admitted to League of Nations.

1927. Lindbergh flies across Atlantic. Sacco-Vanzetti executed despite worldwide protest. Snyder-Gray case. Trotsky expelled from Communist Party.

1928. First all-talking film. *Graf Zeppelin* crosses Atlantic. First radio broadcast of New York Philharmonic Orchestra.

1929. Teapot Dome scandal. Stock market crash. Papal State reconstituted as State of Vatican City.

1930. London Naval Reduction Treaty. Penicillin discovered. Judge Crater vanishes.

1931. Japan invades Manchuria. Spain becomes a republic. Depression in U. S. Empire State Building completed.

1932. Japan establishes puppet

Bertrand Russell 1872–

Pío Baroja 1872–

Jakob Wassermann 1873–1934

Max Reinhardt 1873–1943

Willa Cather 1873–1947

Colette 1873–1953

Max Beerbohm 1873–1956

Amy Lowell 1874–1925

Hugo von Hofmannsthal 1874–1929

Henri Barbusse 1874–1935

G. K. Chesterton 1874–1936

Gertrude Stein 1874–1946

W. Somerset Maugham 1874–

Rainer Maria Rilke 1875–1926

Thomas Mann 1875–1955

Albert Schweitzer 1875–

Jack London 1876–1916

Sherwood Anderson 1876–1941

José Maria Sert 1876–1945

Constantin Brancusi 1876–1957

Maurice Vlaminck 1876–1958

Marsden Hartley 1877–1943

Mikhail Artzybashev 1878–1927

Isadora Duncan 1878–1927

Ferenc Molnar 1878–1952

Carl Sandburg 1878–

John Masefield 1878–

Upton Sinclair 1878–

Vachel Lindsay 1879–1931

Paul Klee 1879–1940

E. M. Forster 1879–

Heitor Villa-Lobos
1887–1959
Ernst Toch 1887–

Bohuslav Martinu
1890–1959
Jacques Ibert 1890–

Sergei Prokofiev 1891–
1953
Frederick Jacobi
1891–1953
Frank Martin 1891–
Sir Arthur Bliss 1891–
Richard Donovan
1891–

Arthur Honegger
1892–1955
Darius Milhaud 1892–

Eugene Goossens
1893–1962
Arthur Benjamin
1893–
Paul Pisk 1893–
Federico Mompou
1893–
Douglas Moore 1893–
Bernard Rogers 1893–
Alois Hába 1893–

Willem Pijper 1894–
1947
Walter Piston 1894–
Bernard Wagenaar
1894–
Karol Rathaus 1895–
1954
Paul Hindemith 1895–
1963
Carl Orff 1895–
Mario Castelnuovo-
Tedesco 1895–
William Grant Still
1895–
Leo Sowerby 1895–

Virgil Thomson 1896–
Roger Sessions 1896–
Howard Hanson
1896–
Ernesto Lecuona
1896–

state in Manchukuo. Franklin
D. Roosevelt elected. James
J. Walker, under investigation,
resigns as Mayor of New
York.

1933. Hitler becomes German
Chancellor. Van der Lubbe
accused of setting fire to
Reichstag. Germany quits
League of Nations. Roosevelt
proclaims bank holiday, signs
National Recovery Act, recognizes Soviet Union. Federal dole. Prohibition re-
pealed. TVA established.

1934. Chancellor Dollfuss of
Austria assassinated by Nazis.
Hindenburg dies; Hitler be-
comes Fuehrer.

1935. Hitler reintroduces universal military training. Nuremberg Laws deprive Ger-
man Jews of citizenship and
ban intermarriage. Italy invades Ethiopia. John L. Lewis
founds CIO. Social Security
Act signed. Will Rogers dies
in plane crash.

1936. Civil War in Spain. Hitler
reoccupies Rhineland, breaking Locarno Pact. Italy annexes Ethiopia. First socialist
government in France, under
Léon Blum. German-Japanese
anti-Comintern Pact, later
joined by Italy. George V of
England dies, succeeded by
Edward VIII, who renounces
throne for Mrs. Wallis Simp-
son. Sulfa drugs introduced
in U. S. First sitdown strike.

1937. Loyalist government
moves to Barcelona. Japan
seizes Peiping. Hitler repudiates Treaty of Versailles. Italy
withdraws from League of
Nations. Marshall Tukha-
chevsky and other Soviet
generals executed for treason.

Wallace Stevens 1879–
Raoul Dufy 1879–
Guillaume Apolli-
naire 1880–1918
Ernst Kirchner 1880–
1938
André Derain 1880–
1954
Scholem Asch 1880–
1957
Henry L. Mencken
1880–1959
Sir Jacob Epstein
1880–1959
Emil Ludwig 1881–
1948
Pablo Picasso 1881–
Sean O'Casey 1881–
Fernand Léger 1881–
Max Weber 1881–
James Joyce 1882–
1941
Virginia Woolf 1882–
1945
Sigrid Undset 1882–
1949
Georges Braque 1882–
Jacques Maritain 1882–
Franz Kafka 1883–
1924
Kahlil Gibran 1883–
1931
José Ortega y Gasset
1883–1955
William Carlos Wil-
liams 1883–1959
José Clemente Orozco
1883–1949
Walter Gropius 1883–
Max Eastman 1883–
Amadeo Modigliani
1884–1920
Maurice Utrillo 1884–
1955

Lion Feuchtwanger
1884–
D. H. Lawrence 1885–
1930
Sinclair Lewis 1885–
1951
Sascha Guitry 1885–
1957
André Maurois 1885–

Alexander Tansman
1897–
Henry Cowell 1897–
Quincy Porter 1897–
Francisco Mignone
1897–

George Gershwin
1898–1937
Vittorio Rieti 1898–
Marcel Mihalovici
1898–
Roy Harris 1898–
Ernst Bacon 1898–
Silvestre Revueltas
1899–1940
Francis Poulenc 1899–
1963
Georges Auric 1899–
Alexander Tcherepnin
1899–
Randall Thompson
1899–
Carlos Chávez 1899–
Domingo Santa Cruz
1899–

Amadeo Roldán 1900–
1939
Kurt Weill 1900–50
George Antheil 1900–
59
Henry Barraud 1900–
Aaron Copland 1900–
Otto Luening 1900–

Henri Sauguet 1901–
Edmund Rubbra
1901–
Werner Egk 1901–
Marcel Poot 1901–
Harry Partch 1901–

Sir William Walton
1902–
Stefan Wolpe 1902–
Theodore Chanler
1902–1961
Mark Brunswick
1902–
John Vincent 1902–

Aram Khatchaturian
1903–

Nylon introduced. Amelia
Earhart lost in Pacific.

1938. Insurgent planes bomb
Barcelona. Hitler annexes
Austria. Betrayal at Munich:
Britain and France agree to
dismemberment of Czecho-
slovakia. Chamberlain promises "peace in our time."
1939. Spanish Civil War ends in
victory for Franco. Hitler enters Prague. Germany and
Italy form Axis. German-
Russian Pact. Russia invades
Finland. Nazi invasion of Poland precipitates World War
II.

1940. Nazis overrun Nether-
lands, Belgium, Luxembourg.
Churchill becomes Prime
Minister. Evacuation of Dun-
kirk. Germans enter Paris;
France capitulates. Japan in-
vades French Indo-China.
Nazi air raids against Britain.
R.A.F. halts invasion threat.
Roosevelt elected to third
term. Leon Trotsky assassi-
nated in Mexico. First radio
broadcast of Metropolitan
Opera.

1941. Hitler attacks Russia. Japan attacks Pearl Harbor.
U.S. enters the war. Yugoslavia surrenders; Tito leads
guerrilla war. Nazis enter
Athens. FDR and Churchill
agree on war aims, announce
Atlantic Charter.

1942. British stop Rommel at El
Alamein. U.S. forces land in
North Africa; army under
Patton lands in Sicily. Bataan
Death March. Corregidor sur-
rendered. Six million Jews die
in Nazi extermination camps.
First nuclear chain reaction
achieved by Enrico Fermi,
among a group of scientists.

1943. Germans defeated at Stal-

François Mauriac
1885–
Ezra Pound 1885–
William Rose Benét
1886–1950
Diego Rivera 1886–
1957
Pearl S. Buck 1886–
Oskar Kokoschka
1886–
Thornton Wilder
1887–
Robinson Jeffers
1887–1962
William Zorach 1887–
Alexander Archi-
penko 1887–
Marc Chagall 1887–
Le Corbusier 1887–
Arnold Zweig 1887–
Georgia O'Keeffe
1887–
Eugene O'Neill 1888–
1953
Maxwell Anderson
1888–1959
Giorgio di Chirico
1888–
T. S. Eliot 1888–
John Crowe Ransom
1888–
Thomas Hart Benton
1889–
Arnold J. Toynbee
1889–
Karel Čapek 1890–
1938
Franz Werfel 1890–
1945

Christopher Morley
1890 1957
Mark Tobey 1890–
Henry Miller 1891–
Jean Cocteau 1891–
1963
Grant Wood 1892–
1944
Jean Giraudoux 1892–
1944
Edna St. Vincent Mil-
lay 1892–1950
Rebecca West 1892–
Sir Osbert Sitwell
1892–

Introduction to Contemporary Music

Boris Blacher 1903–
Vittorio Giannini
1903–
Nikolai Lopatnikov
1903–

Manuel Rosenthal
1904–
Dmitri Kabalevsky
1904–
Luigi Dallapiccola
1904–
Goffredo Petrassi
1904–

Constant Lambert
1905–51
Erich Itor Kahn
1905–56
André Jolivet 1905–
Michael Tippett 1905–
Alan Rawsthorne
1905–
Marc Blitzstein 1905–
1964
Alejandro Caturla
1906–40
Dmitri Shostakovich
1906–
Paul Creston 1906–
Ross Lee Finney
1906–
Louise Talma 1906–
Normand Lockwood
1906–
Robert Sanders 1906–
Miriam Gideon 1906–

Henk Badings 1907–
Burrill Phillips 1907–

Olivier Messiaen
1908–
Elliott Carter 1908–
Daniel Ayala 1908–

Elie Siegmeister 1909–
Howard Swanson
1909–
Paul Nordoff 1909–

Rolf Liebermann
1910–
Samuel Barber 1910–
Charles Jones 1910–

ingrad and in North Africa. Mussolini deposed. Italy surrenders. Teheran Conference: Roosevelt, Churchill, and Stalin decide on invasion of France. Roosevelt approves withholding income tax. Race riots in Detroit.

1944. Hitler wounded in bomb plot. Gen. MacArthur returns to Philippines. Invasion of France. Battle of the Bulge. Roosevelt elected to fourth term.

1945. Yalta Agreement. Roosevelt dies at 63, succeeded by Truman. United Nations Conference opens at San Francisco. U.S. troops cross Rhine, invade Iwo Jima and Okinawa. Hitler, Goebbels commit suicide. Germany surrenders. Atom bomb dropped on Hiroshima. Japan surrenders.

1946. Philippines become independent. First meeting of U.N. General Assembly. Victor Emmanuel III abdicates. Nuremberg trials. Goering's suicide; Hans Frank, Streicher, von Ribbentrop hanged as war criminals.

1947. Truman Doctrine. Marshall Plan. India wins independence. Moscow forms Cominform. Communists take power in Hungary and Romania. Henry Ford dies. Taft-Hartley Act.

1948. Gandhi assassinated. Communists take over Czechoslovakia. Israel proclaimed a nation, attacked by Arabs. Soviet blockade of Berlin; airlift begun. Tojo and other Japanese leaders hanged as war criminals. Organization of 21 American states. Alger Hiss case.

1949. Truman's Point Four Pro-

Elmer Rice 1892–
Pearl S. Buck 1892–
Ernst Toller 1893–
1939
George Grosz 1893–
1959
John P. Marquand
1893–1960
Herbert Read 1893–
S. N. Behrman 1893–
Joan Miró 1893–
Carlos Mérida 1893–
Dorothy Parker 1893–
E. E. Cummings 1894–
1962
Katherine Anne
Porter 1894–
James Thurber 1894–
1961
Aldous Huxley 1894–
1963
Ben Hecht 1894–1964
David Siqueiros 1894–
László Moholy-Nagy
1895–1946
Paul Eluard 1895–
Lin Yutang 1895–
Edmund Wilson
1895–
Abraham Rattner
1895–
F. Scott Fitzgerald
1896–1940
Robert Sherwood
1896–1955
John Dos Passos 1896–
William Faulkner
1897–1962
Louis Aragon 1897–
Liam O'Flaherty
1897–
Kenneth Burke 1897–
Sergei Eisenstein
1898–1948
Bertolt Brecht 1898–
1956
Ludwig Bemelmans
1898–
Erich Maria Remarque 1898–
Alexander Calder
1898–
René Clair 1898–
Ernest Hemingway
1898–1961

Paul Bowles 1910–
William Schuman
1910–
Josef Alexander 1910–
Blas Galindo 1910–

Gian Carlo Menotti
1911–
Alan Hovhaness 1911–

Igor Markevitch 1912–
Jean Françaix 1912–
Arthur Berger 1912–
John Cage 1912–
Hugo Weisgall 1912–
Peggy Glanville-
Hicks 1912–
Wayne Barlow 1912–
Tom Scott 1912–
Salvador Contreras
1912–
Pablo Moncayo 1912–

Benjamin Britten
1913–
Tikhon Khrennikov
1913–
Norman Dello Joio
1913
Morton Gould 1913–
Jan Meyerowitz 1913–
Gardner Read 1913–
Henry Brant 1913–

Roger Goeb 1914–
Alexei Haieff 1914–
Gail Kubik 1914–
Charles Mills 1914–

David Diamond 1915–
Irving Fine 1915–1962
Robert Palmer 1915–
Vincent Persichetti
1915–
George Perle 1915–
Carlos Surinach 1915–

Ben Weber 1916–
Milton Babbitt 1916–
Alberto Ginastera
1916–

Ulysses Kay 1917–
Robert Ward 1917–
Lou Harrison 1917–

gram to aid backward areas.
Communists defeat Chiang
Kai-shek in China. USSR explodes atomic bomb. North
Atlantic Defense Pact. Trial
and conviction of U.S. Communist leaders.

1950. North Koreans invade
South Korea. U.S. Marines
land at Inchon. U.S. plans
hydrogen bomb.

1951. Ilse Koch sentenced for
atrocities at Buchenwald.
Schuman Plan pools coal
and steel markets of six European nations. Truce talks
in Korea.

1952. George VI dies; succeeded
by Elizabeth II. King Farouk
of Egypt abdicates. Owen
Lattimore indicted for per-
jury; charges subsequently
dismissed. Eisenhower
elected President.

1953. Stalin dies. Armistice in
Korea. Mau-Mau attacks in
Kenya. Mount Everest scaled.
Uprising in East Berlin.
Beria executed in USSR.

1954. First atomic-powered submarine, *Nautilus*, launched.
War in Indo-China. Supreme
Court rules segregation in
public schools illegal. Arbenz
overthrown in Guatemala.
Communist Party outlawed
in U.S.

1955. Churchill, at 80, succeeded
by Anthony Eden. First Summit Conference. Peron ousted
in Argentina. AFL and CIO
merge. Salk serum for in-
fantile paralysis.

1956. Soviet leaders disavow
Stalinism and "cult of personality." Egypt seizes Suez
Canal. Russia launches Sput-
nik, first man-made satellite.

Hart Crane 1899–
1932
Federico García Lorca
1899–1936
Stephen Vincent Benét
1899–1943

Noel Coward 1899–
Elizabeth Bowen 1899–
C. S. Forester 1899–
Rufino Tamayo 1899–
Léonie Adams 1899–
Vincent Sheean 1899–
Eugène Berman 1899–
Allen Tate 1899–
Thomas Wolfe 1900–
1938
Antoine de Saint-
Exupéry 1900–44
Ignazio Silone 1900–
Julian Green 1900–

John van Druten
1901–1957
Vittorio de Sica 1901–
André Malraux 1901–
John Steinbeck 1902–
Langston Hughes
1902–
Kenneth Fearing 1902–
Carlo Levi 1902–
George Orwell 1903–
1950
Kay Boyle 1903–
Ogden Nash 1903–
Erskine Caldwell
1903–
James Gould Cozzens
1903–
Mark Rothko 1903–
Salvador Dali 1904–
Paul Cadmus 1904–
Graham Greene 1904–
George Balanchine
1904–
Christopher Isher-
wood 1904–
James T. Farrell 1904–
Isamu Noguchi 1904–
Willem de Kooning
1904–
Lillian Hellman 1905–

Jean-Paul Sartre 1905–

Gottfried von Einem
1918–
Leonard Bernstein
1918–
George Rochberg
1918–
Frank Wigglesworth
1918–

Leon Kirchner 1919–

Bruno Maderna 1920–
Harold Shapero 1920–
John Lessard 1920–

Robert Kurka 1921–
57
Jack Beeson 1921–
Andrew Imbrie 1921–

Lukas Foss 1922–

Peter Mennin 1923–
Mel Powell 1923–
Ned Rorem 1923–
Leo Kraft 1923–
Raffaello de Banfield
1924–

Billy Jim Layton
1924–

Pierre Boulez 1925–
Gunther Schuller
1925–

Luigi Nono 1926–
Hans Werner Henze
1926–
Carlisle Floyd 1926–
Lee Hoiby 1926–
William Flanagan
1926–
Seymour Schifrin
1926–

Russel Smith 1927–

Karlheinz Stockhausen 1928–

Yehudi Wyner 1929–

Uprising in Hungary. Eisenhower re-elected. First transcontinental helicopter flight and transatlantic telephone cable.

1957. Eisenhower Doctrine for aid to Middle East. Russia launches satellite carrying dog. Eisenhower orders U.S. troops to enforce school integration. First underground atomic explosion. USSR announces successful intercontinental missile.

1958. Egypt and Syria form United Arab Republic under Nasser. Alaska becomes 49th state. Fifth Republic in France under De Gaulle. Pope Pius XIII dies, succeeded by John XXIII. Boris Pasternak refuses Nobel Prize for *Doctor Zhivago.*

1959. Castro victorious over Batista. Soviet launches first man-made planet. Intercontinental missile tested. Hawaii becomes 50th state. Dulles dies. Khrushchev visits U.S. Congressional committee investigates television quiz shows.

1960. Eisenhower visits Europe, Asia, Africa. Desire for nuclear disarmament throughout the world. South African natives revolt against *apartheid.* Chou En-lai visits India. Syngman Rhee forced out by popular discontent in South Korea. Turkish student demonstrations against Menderes regime. Caryl Chessman executed. Princess Margaret of England weds commoner. American U-2 plane shot down in Russia. Kennedy elected President.

Arthur Koestler 1905–
John O'Hara 1905–
Mikhail Sholokhov
1905–
Roberto Rossellini
1906–
Clifford Odets 1906–
1963
W. H. Auden 1907–
Christopher Fry 1907–
Alberto Moravia 1907–
Theodore Roethke
1908–
William Saroyan
1908–
Stephen Spender
1909–
Eudora Welty 1909–
Jean Anouilh 1910–
Nicholas Montserrat
1910–
Alfred Hayes 1911–
Terence Rattigan
1911–
Lawrence Durrell
1912–
William Baziotes
1912–
Jackson Pollock 1912–
56
Albert Camus 1913–
60
Irwin Shaw 1913–
William Inge 1913–
Dylan Thomas 1914–
1953
Tennessee Williams
1914–
John Hersey 1914–
Thomas Merton 1915–
Arthur Miller 1915–
Robert Motherwell
1915–
Robert Lowell 1917–
Carson McCullers
1917–
Jerome Robbins 1918–
J. D. Salinger 1919–
Howard Nemerov
1920–
James Jones 1921–
Norman Mailer
1923–

Marvin David Levy
1932–
Easley Blackwood
1933–

Paddy Chayefsky
1923–
Truman Capote 1924–

INDEX

Index